Modern Brazil

Herbert Klein and Francisco Luna present a sweeping narrative of social change in Brazil that documents its transition from a predominantly rural and illiterate society in 1950, to an overwhelmingly urban, modern, and literate society in the twenty-first century. Tracing this radical evolution reveals how industrialization created a new labor force, how demographic shifts reorganized the family and social attitudes, and how urban life emerged in what is now one of the most important industrial economies in the world. A model for modern social histories, the book also examines changes in social stratification and mobility, the decline of regional disparities, education, social welfare, race, and gender. By analyzing Brazil's unprecedented Brazilian political, economic, and social changes in the late twentieth and twenty-first centuries, the authors address an under-explored area in current scholarship and offer an invaluable resource for scholars of Latin American and Brazil.

Herbert S. Klein is Gouverneur Morris Professor Emeritus of History at Columbia University and Research Fellow and Latin American Curator at the Hoover Institution at Stanford University, California.

Francisco Vidal Luna is Professor of Economics in the Faculty of Economics and Administration (FEA) at the Universidade de São Paulo.

Modern Brazil

A Social History

HERBERT S. KLEIN
Columbia University, Columbia University and Stanford University

FRANCISCO VIDAL LUNA
Universidade de São Paulo

CAMBRIDGE
UNIVERSITY PRESS

CAMBRIDGE
UNIVERSITY PRESS

University Printing House, Cambridge CB2 8BS, United Kingdom

One Liberty Plaza, 20th Floor, New York, NY 10006, USA

477 Williamstown Road, Port Melbourne, VIC 3207, Australia

314–321, 3rd Floor, Plot 3, Splendor Forum, Jasola District Centre, New Delhi – 110025, India

79 Anson Road, #06–04/06, Singapore 079906

Cambridge University Press is part of the University of Cambridge.

It furthers the University's mission by disseminating knowledge in the pursuit of education, learning, and research at the highest international levels of excellence.

www.cambridge.org
Information on this title: www.cambridge.org/9781108489027
DOI: 10.1017/9781108773683

First published 2020

Printed in the United Kingdom by TJ International Ltd, Padstow Cornwall

A catalogue record for this publication is available from the British Library.

ISBN 978-1-108-48902-7 Hardback
ISBN 978-1-108-73329-8 Paperback

Cambridge University Press has no responsibility for the persistence or accuracy of URLs for external or third-party internet websites referred to in this publication and does not guarantee that any content on such websites is, or will remain, accurate or appropriate.

Contents

Maps

Graphs

Tables

Introduction

Brazil in 1950 was a very different country from the country it is today. In the space of one person's lifetime, Brazil has gone from being a traditional underdeveloped rural-dominated economy with a pre-modern demographic structure to a modern urban society. In 1950, it was only one-third urbanized and almost three-quarters of its labor force was involved in an agriculture which only partially fulfilled the nation's food needs. Poverty and hunger affected a significant share of the population. Life expectancy was reduced, and mortality and fertility were quite high by world standards. Given this demographic pattern, Brazil was a nation dominated by youth, who made up almost half of the population. It was also a predominantly illiterate society, with women less educated than men.

Today Brazil is over 80% urban, only a tenth of its labor force work in agriculture and hunger no longer significantly affects the population. It has become a more complex society with a large middle class and an organized working class now incorporated into a modern social welfare system. In the second decade of the twenty-first century it educates all of its children of primary school age, women are now better educated than men, and the birth and death rates along with life expectancy are close to first world standards.

The question we ask in this book is how and why this radical change occurred. In previous work we have looked at the economic changes which occurred in this period, first within the most dynamic of its regions, that of São Paulo, and then of the nation as a whole. Most recently we have examined in great detail the modernization of Brazilian agriculture in this period. But in our previous work the social changes have been only summarily treated and for this reason we have undertaken here a more systematic review of this subject.

There is no set standard of what a social history of a country should entail. Such a history could involve a study of labor relations, or the family or popular culture, or any number of alternative themes. Thus, each historian has approached this subject from their own perspective and each social history tends to be *sui generis*. In this work we have selected a series of different themes and institutions which we feel broadly defined Brazilian society from the mid-twentieth century until today. It is obvious that other scholars would stress different themes or take alternative approaches to examine the social changes which have occurred. What is evident to us is that Brazil experienced extraordinarily rapid change in just these 75 or so years, and this change has created a fundamentally different society from the one that existed in 1950.

Our concern is to try to understand the contours of this change and offer possible explanations for how and why they occurred. It is essentially a macrohistory rather than the microhistory which is now more common in certain historical traditions. But few before us have attempted such a macro analysis, and we thus see our work as a first attempt to define the fundamental changes which have taken place, a necessary first step in providing the context in which detailed microhistories can be produced.

We begin this study with an analysis of what Brazil looked like in 1950 in terms of economic and social conditions that existed before massive change had occurred. We then examine in a summary fashion the political and economic changes after 1950 that would shape Brazilian society in this period. One of the most import developments in this society was the profound change in demographic structure and patterns of behavior which occurred in the decade of the 1960s. It was then that Brazil began its demographic transition period, when fertility dropped dramatically, finally matching its slow mortality decline which had preceded this shift. In turn, a very rapid decline in mortality would now ultimately add twenty years to the life expectancy of the national population for women and sixteen years for men in this period of half a century. Just as significant as industrialization, agricultural modernization, and the demographic transition, has been the role of the national government in influencing Brazilian societal change in this period. It was in the post-1950 period that a modern welfare state program was finally implanted in Brazil, the creation of which profoundly altered the lives and income of the entire national population. All of these changes have occurred as millions of Brazilians have migrated to the rapidly expanding cities as the majority of the population has shifted from rural to urban residence. The rise of the metropolis and its impact on Brazilian society is the theme we treat in the first chapter.

Having outlined the basic structural changes, we then move on to specific groups and themes. Clearly, the changing role of woman in society is the one gender issue which has experienced the most change. In the post-1950 period women have massively increased their participation in the workplace and have now come to be better educated than the men in Brazilian society, in a reversal of pre-1950 patterns. Changes in fertility have also had their impact on family size, and the introduction of civil divorce and the decline of the Roman Catholic Church have also impacted on women and the family.

All this change in the economy and society has led to quite different patterns of social mobility and class structure. As Brazil began massively to industrialize, there was initially a relatively open period of mobility when large numbers of previously poor persons achieved ever higher status and income than their parents. But soon this same system slowly closed down again as Brazil becomes a modern industrial society; class mobility has become more circular and mobility into the top groups has slowed. One of the ongoing historical issues still facing Brazil, as in all American societies with histories of African slave labor, is the question of race. This is an issue in constant debate and discussion in Brazil and we try to present all the conflicting issues on this theme.

The creation of a modern welfare state has been of crucial importance in bringing the Brazilian population a new level of health and welfare that is far more universal than ever before. Finally codified in almost all its aspects in the Constitution of 1988, the Brazilian welfare state for all its inefficiencies and financial constraints has had a major impact in reducing regional inequality – a theme we stress in all the chapters. There have been shifts in the economic importance and per capita GDP of some regions, and here the rise of the Center-West to co-equal economic status with the traditionally richer South and Southeastern states is fundamental. But other regions, above all the Northeast, have not kept pace and are clearly economically well below the norm of the three richest regions. But, in terms of health, demographic characteristics, welfare, and life expectancy, there is now a national standard that is the norm in all regions, and this is largely due to government action, both in creating a modern welfare system and in the adoption of cash transfers to the poor and unincorporated part of the population.

Finally, we examine an unusual and quite new feature of Brazilian society which mostly developed in the post-1950 period, which is the rise of voluntary organizations. Since the foundation of the Republic in 1899, religious groups have been essentially voluntary associations with no state aid. But, since the massive civil opposition to military rule in the 1970s and 1980s, Brazil has developed a vast array of non-state voluntary non-religious (social) organizations which play an increasingly important role in society. They exist in areas of environmental protection, education, health, and organized labor. There has also been a major shift in religious associations with the recent rapid expansion of evangelical churches, of massive size, with profound political power. Although traditionally it has been assumed that civil society in Brazil was weak to non-existent, we find that this thesis does not hold for the nation today.

In this text we have converted standard Brazilian color terms into the English words white (*branco*), brown (*pardo* or *mulato*), and black (*preto*). These are usually self-defined categories in all censuses and surveys and so often shift with changing national beliefs on race and identity. Sometimes government data list results for a combined Afro-Brazilian population which we define as browns and blacks (*pardos* and *pretos* combined). Throughout the book we reproduce finding on race based on these criteria.

In writing this book we have been aided by many persons and would like to thank Matiko Kume Vidal, Renato Augusto Rosa Vidal, Sonia Rocha, Donald J. Treiman, Simon Schwartzman, and William Summerhill for their generous assistance.

I

Brazil at Mid-Century

In 1950, Brazil was still in many ways a traditional society. The majority of the population lived in rural areas and just over a third lived in towns. Agriculture absorbed almost three-quarters of the male labor force and manufacturing accounted for only 13% of employed workers.[1] Over half of the population 15 years of age and older could neither read nor write,[2] with women being more illiterate than men.[3] It was also a traditional society in demographic terms, with very high fertility and mortality making it a classic pre-modern society. Women had on average over 6 children (total fertility rate for women in their fertile years), making Brazil's crude birth rate of 44 per 1,000 resident population one of the highest in the world. Its crude mortality rate of 20 was high even by Latin American standards.[4] The country was also split between a poor Northeast region whose standard of living was that of India and a Southeastern region whose living standard was close to that of Belgium.[5] But it also had tremendous potential. Its 52 million persons in 1950 made Brazil the eighth largest country in the world in terms

---

[1] These percentages exclude inactive males and males who were students or in unpaid domestic labor. IBGE, *Recenseamento geral de 1950*, Série Nacional, Censo demográfico, vol. 1 (Rio de Janeiro, 1956), pp. 26–29, Table 22.

[2] IBGE, *Estatísticas do Século XX* (2003), Table pop_S2T02.

[3] Some 60% of the women were literate compared to 54% of the men. More than half of white men and Asian men and women and 49% of white women were literate. Among browns and blacks, the literacy rate was less than 30% for both men and women. IBGE, *Recenseamento geral de 1950*, Série Nacional, vol. 1, p. 20, Table 17.

[4] For the crude birth and death rates in 1950, see IBGE, "Séries históricas e estatísticas," Tables POP 201 and POP 261. Accessed at: https://seriesestatisticas.ibge.gov.br/series.aspx?t=taxa-mortalidade-infantil&vcodigo=CD100.

[5] Edmar Bacha and Herbert S. Klein, eds., *Social Change in Brazil, 1945–1985: The Incomplete Transformation* (Albuquerque: University of New Mexico Press, 1989), p. 3.

of population and it was ranked fifth in land mass. The per capita GDP in 1950 was US$ 952 (in 1995 dollars) and the national GDP stood at US$ 463 billion.[6] At 6.1 persons per square kilometer it was one of the less-densely populated of nations and still had an open frontier with great potential.[7]

But the population was still living below advanced world standards in a host of indices. Its high levels of poverty and lack of infrastructure in health and sanitation meant that the average life expectancy at birth had only reached the lower 50s by mid-century. Brazilians were then averaging 10 to 15 years less of life expectancy than Argentines, Uruguayans, or even Paraguayans, all neighbors in this year of 1950. This difference existed for both sexes. Brazilian men averaged 49.1 years of life in 1950, 14 years less than Uruguayan men, and Brazilian women averaged 52.8 years of life, some 15 years less then Uruguayan women.[8]

But these indices of birth, death, and life expectancy were slowly changing. In the first national census of 1872, life expectancy was only in the upper twenties for both men and women.[9] Life expectancy in 1910 reached 34.6 years for both sexes and slowly increased to 37.3 years by 1930, representing an increase of 0.4% per annum. Change was faster in the next two decades, with life expectancy now increasing at 1.7% per annum and reaching 52.3 years for both sexes combined by the early 1950s.[10] By 1950, Brazilian life expectancy was finally reaching the middle ranks of the Latin American Republics and was just below the regional average life expectancy (see Graph 1.1).

The primary reason life expectancy was so low compared to its neighboring countries was the fact that Brazil still had a very high infant

---

[6] Carlos Roberto Azzoni, "Concentração regional e dispersão das rendas per capita estaduais: analise a partir de séries históricas estaduais de PIB, 1939–1995." *Estudos Economics* 27.3 (1997), Tables A2 and A3.

[7] Density is taken from Giorgio Mortara, "The Development and Structure of Brazil's Population," *Population Studies* 8.2 (1954), p. 134. Population ranking is taken from www.un.org/esa/population/pubsarchive/india/20most.htm#1950. Size as of 1961 is taken from https://data.worldbank.org/indicator/ag.lnd.totl.k2.

[8] CELADE, *Observatorio demográfico* 3 (2007), pp. 33–37, Table 5.

[9] Eduardo E. Arriaga, *New Life Tables for Latin American Populations in the Nineteenth and Twentieth Centuries* (Berkeley: Institute of International Studies, University of California, 1968), pp. 29–35, Tables III-3–III-6.

[10] IBGE, "Séries históricas e estatísticas," Table POP 209. Accessed at: https://seriesestatisticas.ibge.gov.br/series.aspx?no=10&op=0&vcodigo=POP209&t=esperanca-vida. CELADE current estimate for 1950–1955 is only 51 years for both sexes for Brazil, a year lower than the IBGE estimate. CELADE, *Observatorio demográfico* 3 "Population projection," p. 33, Table 5.

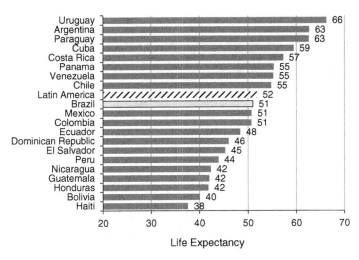

GRAPH 1.1 Life Expectancy (Both Sexes) by Country, Latin America, 1950–1955
Source: CELADE, *Observatorio Demográfico* 3 (1977), p. 35, Table 5.

mortality rate at mid-century. Its infant mortality rate was 135 deaths per 1,000 live births, a rate that was double or more than its Southern neighbors and even above the 128 deaths average rate for Latin America.[11] The same occurred with the child death rates (that is, children under the age of 5 dying per 1,000 live births). In 1950, it was 190 deaths of children under the age of 5 per 1,000 live births, which was close to the Latin American average but much higher than its southern neighbors, including even Paraguay (which was just 102 deaths).[12] Given these still very high child and infant mortality rates in the pre-modern period, a significant number of children died before their fifth birthday because of compromised socio-economic and disease conditions. In fact, almost a quarter of deaths reported in 1950 were to people under 15 years of age. This compares to only 9% of persons dying by that age in 1950 in the United States.[13]

[11] CELADE, *Observatorio demográfico* 9 (2010), p. 48, Table 6. For a general discussion of pre-1950 patterns of fertility and mortality, see Mortara, "The Development and Structure of Brazil's Population," pp. 121–139, and Elza Berquó, "Demographic Evolution of the Brazilian Population in the Twentieth Century," in Daniel Joseph Hogan, ed., *Population Change in Brazil: Contemporary Perspectives* (Campinas: NEPO/UNICAMP, 2001).
[12] CEPALSTAT. Accessed at: http://interwp.cepal.org/sisgen/ConsultaIntegrada.asp?idIndicador=37&idioma=e.
[13] CELADE, "Brasil: Tablas Abreviadas de Mortalidad, 1950–55," *Boletín demográfico. América Latina: Tablas de Mortalidad, 1950–2025*, 34.74 (2004), p. 62, Table 14, and Felicitie C. Bell and Michael L. Miller, *Life Tables for the United States Social Security*

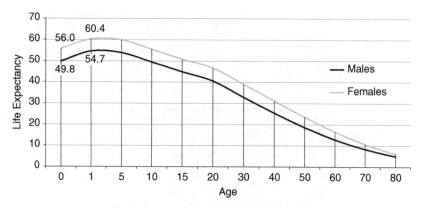

GRAPH 1.2 Average Life Expectancy for Brazil by Sex, 1949/1951
Source: IBGE, *Estatísticas do Século XX*, Table Saúde1952AEB-02.

Life expectancy at this stage of demographic development was mostly determined by changes in infant mortality. The impact of these high rates of infant mortality can be seen in 1950 in the differences in life expectancy for both men and women at birth and after one year of life. If one survived the first year of life, then 4 to 5 years were added to life expectancy (see Graph 1.2).

But despite its relatively higher mortality rates compared to its immediate neighbors to the south, Brazil in this period was finally beginning to experience a more rapid rate of decline in mortality, especially among newborns. This slow decline in mortality began earlier, with systematic vaccination and sanitation movements in the period from the 1890s to the 1910s, which were particularly important in lowering mortality levels in the expanding urban areas. It was a pattern common to all Latin America countries, though the richer ones declined much faster than the poorer ones prior to 1930.[14] The introduction of antibiotics after World War II was the next major factor to reduce mortality along with the earlier efforts to provide potable water, sanitation, and the pasteurization of milk. Finally, there was the steady growth of national agriculture after mid-century which also led to the slow but steady decline in food prices and increased availability of food to both rural and urban populations. All these factors can be seen in their impact on Brazil's crude death rate, which went from an average decline of just −0.3%

Area 1900–2100, Actuarial Study No. 120 (Washington, DC: Social Security Administration Office of the Chief Actuary, 2005), p. 41, Table 6.

[14] Eduardo E. Arriaga and Kingsley Davis, "The Pattern of Mortality Change in Latin America." *Demography* 6.3 (1969), p. 226.

per annum between 1910 and 1930 to more than double that rate (or –1.0%) between 1930 and 1950. In the next twenty years, the crude death rate would decline at 3.1% per annum (see Graph 1.3).

This decline in the crude death rate was first driven by the decline in infant mortality – from 162 deaths of infants under 1 year of age per 1,000 live births in 1930 to 135 deaths per 1,000 live births in 1950 – a decline of 0.9% per annum. Unlike the crude death rate, however, this decline did not accelerate in the next twenty years, dropping only at 0.8% per annum from 1950 to 1970 (see Graph 1.4). But in the twenty-year period from 1970 to 1990 the decline would be explosive,

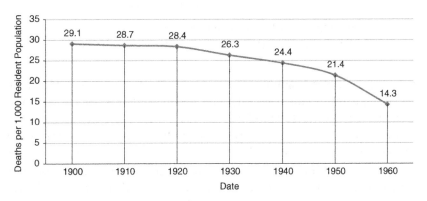

GRAPH 1.3 Crude Death Rates for Brazil, 1900–1960
Source: Berquó, "Demographic Evolution of the Brazilian Population in the Twentieth Century" (2001), Table 3.

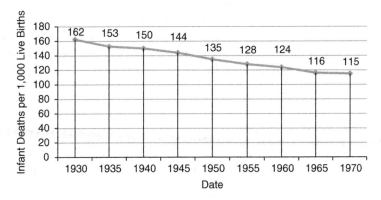

GRAPH 1.4 Infant Mortality Rate in Brazil, 1930–1970
Source: IBGE, *Séries históricas*, Table CD100.

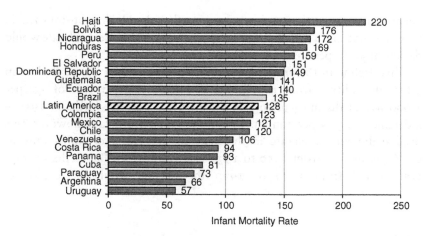

GRAPH 1.5 Infant Mortality Rate by Latin American Countries, 1950–1955
Source: CELADE, *Boletín demográfico* 34.74 (2004), p. 24, Table 6.

increasing to a very significant rate of –4.2% per annum.[15] However, even though the infant mortality rate declined, it was still a very high mortality rate by world standards in 1950, with most of the advanced countries then experiencing a rate in the range of 20 to 50 infant deaths per 1,000 live births, with only the most underdeveloped nations having rates over 100 infant deaths.[16] It was also high compared to its southern neighbors, being twice the rate of Argentina in this period and even above the average rate for all of Latin America (see Graph 1.5).

If mortality was on an ever-increasing downward slope in 1950, fertility changed only moderately from 1900. It has been estimated that from 1900 to 1905 the average number of children being born to women in the age cohort of 14 to 49 years was 7.[17] This meant that the crude birth rate was something like 46 to 47 births per 1,000 resident population. By 1950, it was still at around 44 births per 1,000 residents and the total fertility rate was 6 children.[18] Thus the total fertility rate in the twenty-year period from the 1930s to the 1950s had declined by only 0.4% per annum (see Graph 1.6).

---

[15] IBGE, "Séries históricas e estatísticas," Table CD100. Accessed at: https://seriesestatisticas .ibge.gov.br/series.aspx?t=taxa-mortalidade-infantil&vcodigo=CD100.

[16] IBGE, *Anuário Estatístico do Brasil*, 1953, p. 562, Table IV.

[17] Cláudia Júlia Guimarães Horta, José Alberto Magno de Carvalho, and Luís Armando de Medeiros Frias, "Recomposição da fecundidade por geração para Brasil e regiões: atualização e revisão," Paper presented at the XII Encontro Nacional de Estudos Populacionais, ABEP, 2016, Table 6.

[18] Mortara, "The Development and Structure of Brazil's Population," p. 22.

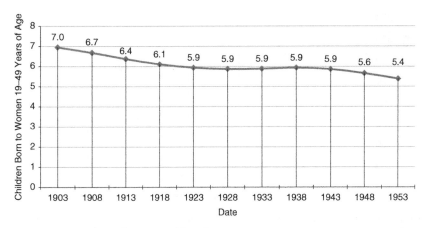

GRAPH 1.6 Total Fertility Rate of Brazil, 1903–1953
Source: Horta, Carvalho, and Frias, "Recomposição da fecundidade por geração
para Brasil e regiões," Table 6

Not only did fertility remain high in the first half of the twentieth century
and in fact it increased slightly in the 1960s, but the average age for women
giving birth also remained quite high, with the peak period for having
children being 25 to 29 years, and with a very significant 24% of births
occurring to women 35 years of age and older in 1950. All of which suggests
a low use of contraception, since when contraception becomes common
women avoid giving birth when they are older. One consequence of this is
a reduction in family size. By comparison, in the United States in 1950, which
had a total fertility rate of only 3 children, births peaked in the 20 to 24 age
group and only 11% of the total births in that year occurred to women 35
years of age and older. This explains why the median age of mothers giving
birth in Brazil was a very high 30 years of age as opposed to the United States,
where the median age was 26 years (see Graph 1.7).[19]

Between the slowly declining death rate and the high fertility rate, the
population was now growing at a very impressive rate in the last quarter of
the nineteenth century and the first twenty years of the twentieth century. In
fact, few countries in the world in the nineteenth century grew as rapidly as
Brazil. On average, Brazil was growing at 2.3% per annum for the century
after 1870, which meant that the population was doubling every thirty

[19] Horta, Carvalho, and Frias, "Recomposição da fecundidade por geração para Brasil
e regiões," Table 3, and calculated from United States Department of Health, Education,
and Welfare, *Vital Statistics of the United States, 1950* (Washington, DC, 1954), vol. 1, p. 85,
Table 6.13.

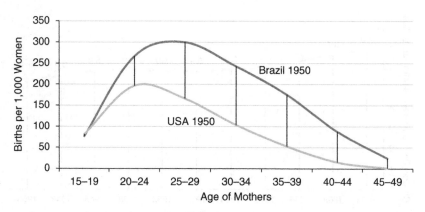

GRAPH 1.7 Birth Rate by Age of Mother, Brazil, 1950–1955
   (live births per 1,000 women in specified age group)
Source: Horta, Carvalho, and Frias, "Recomposição da fecundidade por geração
para Brasil e regiões," Table 3; USA Vital Stat 1950, Table 6.08

years.[20] It reached its all-time high in the decade of the 1950s when it peaked
at 2.99% per annum between the census of 1950 and that of 1960.[21] At this
rate the Brazilian population of 52 million of that year would have doubled
to over 100 million by 1972. That this did not happen would be due to the
very sudden and rapid decline in fertility after 1960, which we will examine
in more detail in later chapters.

   Between 1850 and 1950, the Brazilian population added an estimated
44.8 million persons, of which 41.4 million were due to the natural increase
of births over deaths and only 3.4 million were due to net immigration.[22] The
continued economic dynamism of Brazil from the sugar and gold cycles of
the colonial period through the coffee boom in the nineteenth century led to
the massive introduction of African slaves and free European and Asian
immigrants. Given this combination of high natural increase and of immigration, the Brazilian population grew so rapidly in the nineteenth century
that by 1900 it had replaced Mexico as the largest nation in Latin America.[23]

[20] Thomas W. Merrick and Douglas H. Graham, *Population and Economic Development in Brazil, 1800 to the Present* (Baltimore, Md.: Johns Hopkins University Press, 1979), pp. 30–31.
[21] It would decline to 1.1% per annum between the census of 2000 and the census of 2010. IBGE, "Séries históricas e estatísticas," Table CD106. Accessed at: https://seriesestatisticas.ibge.gov.br/series.aspx?no=10&op=0&vcodigo=CD106&t=taxa-media-geometrica-crescimento-anual-populacao.
[22] Mortara, "The Development and Structure of Brazil's Population," p. 122.
[23] Nicolás Sánchez-Albornoz, *La población de América latina: desde los tiempos precolombinos al año 2025* (Madrid: Alianza, 1994), p. 143.

Eventually, Brazil obtained over 10 million foreign-born immigrants – some 4.8 million of them Africans who arrived as slaves up to 1850 and 5.6 million European and Asian free workers who primarily arrived after the abolition of slavery.[24] It thus absorbed more African slaves than any other single colony or nation in the Americas and was able to attract a comparable number of free European immigrants. Along with Argentina it was the only Latin American state able to compete with the United States and Canada in taking a significant share of the great European transatlantic migration of the late nineteenth and early twentieth centuries.

But because of the high natural growth rates of the native-born population, European immigration had only a moderate impact on national population growth compared to its impact in Canada and Argentina in the same period. It was estimated that immigrants accounted for 14% of total growth of the national population between 1872 and 1890, some 30% in the peak decade of 1890–1900, and just 7% to 8% in the following four decades.[25] Brazil was more like the United States in this respect, since immigration accounted for less than 10% of the total growth in both countries in the century from 1841 to 1940.[26]

Although international immigration brought in primarily adults of working age both in the era of the slave trade and after 1888, Brazil still had an extremely young population due to the very high levels of natural growth and very high fertility. Thus in the census of 1890 those under 19 years of age represented 51% of the total population, and this share rose to 55% of the national population in 1900 and 57% by the census of 1920.[27] Even as late as 1950, some 52% of the resident population was under the age of 19, and 42% under the age of 15, with both rates quite high by world standards.[28] With its high mortality rate and low life expectancy, only 3% of the population was over the age of 65. This meant that the median age of the national population in 1950 was 19 years of age. Because of this high ratio of children

---

[24] The number of Africans is the estimated rate taken from the Trans-Atlantic and Intra-American slave trade databases at Emory University. Accessed at: www.slavevoyages.org/assessment/estimates; European and Asian immigration figureas are taken from Maria Stella Ferreira Levy, "O Papel da Migração Internacional na evolução da população brasileira (1872 a 1972)," *Revista de Saúde Pública* 8 (Supl.) (1974), pp. 71–73, Table 1, and for 1820 to 1871 from Directoria Geral de Estatística, *Boletim commemorativo da exposição nacional de 1908* (Rio de Janeiro: Directoria Geral de Estatística, 1908), pp. 82–85.

[25] Merrick and Graham, *Population and Economic Development*, p. 37.

[26] Merrick and Graham, *Population and Economic Development*, pp. 38–39.

[27] Calculated from IBGE, *Estatísticas históricas do Brasil*, vol. 3, *Séries econômicas, demográficas e sociais de 1550 a 1988* (2nd edn), p. 31, Table 1.6: "População presente. segundo o sexo e os grupos de idade – 1872–1920." All figures are only for the population whose age is known.

[28] Mortara, "The Development and Structure of Brazil's Population," p. 125

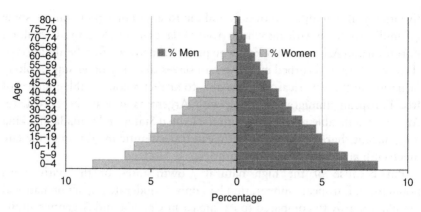

GRAPH 1.8 Age Pyramid of the Population of Brazil in 1950
Source: CELADE, Population Projections, Revision 2013.

and low median age of the population, Brazil had a relatively high dependency ratio, that is the ratio of active workers aged 15–64 to dependent children and the elderly. The ratio was of 80 non-working dependents for every 100 working-age (15–64) adults.[29] The dependency rate reached its peak in 1960, at 83.2 non-workers to 100 workers. Because of their lower ratio of children to total population, the United States, United Kingdom, and France in 1950 had dependency rates of between the mid-50s to the mid-60s dependents per 100 workers.[30] But this was the peak year for Brazil and the very rapid decline of fertility in the following decades led to a steady decline in the dependency ratio which by 2016 was just half of the 1960 rate.[31]

Brazil in 1950 thus had all the characteristics of a pre-modern population experiencing both high fertility and high mortality, with a large base in infants and a low ratio of elderly resulting in a perfect pyramid of ages by sex (see Graph 1.8).

Brazilians at mid-century still predominantly defined themselves as white. This was due to the post-emancipation impact of European immigration and a continued level of racism which defined white as higher-status norm. Before the abolition of slavery in 1888, it seemed that Brazil would be

[29] Brazilian Age data, "Long-Term Population Estimates and Projections, 1950–2100." Revision 2013. Accessed at: www.cepal.org/celade/proyecciones/basedatos_bd.htm.

[30] World Bank data for 1960 and 2016. See https://data.worldbank.org/indicator/SP .POP.DPND.

[31] For dependency rates after 1950, see IBGE, "Séries históricas e estatísticas," Table POP 220. Accessed at: https://seriesestatisticas.ibge.gov.br/series.aspx?no=10&op=0&vcodigo=PO P220&t=razao-dependencia. According to the World Bank, the ratio was 44 in 2016. See https://data.worldbank.org/indicator/SP.POP.DPND.

a predominantly African American-based population. Brazil was the largest recipient of African slaves of any country in the Americas, with an estimated 4.8 million arriving to its shores between the early 1500s and 1850.[32] Thus it is no surprise that in the census of 1872 some 58% of the population of some 10 million persons were blacks and browns. At the same time, the end of the slave trade in 1850 and the lack of significant free migration meant that by the time of the first national census of 1872 just 3% of the imperial population were foreign-born.[33] This would change dramatically after 1889 with the massive arrival of free European and Asian immigrants coming to replace the former slaves on the coffee plantations of the center southern region. Between 1880 and 1930 alone some 4.1 million European, Middle Eastern, and Asian immigrants arrived in Brazil.[34] These immigrants had an impact in slowly but steadily changing the color composition of the national population. But since color was always self-defined in the censuses, it is evident that color prejudice increased in this period among the native-born as well.[35] Thus the percentage of the population listing themselves as white went from 38% to 44% of the national population between the censuses of 1872 and 1890, peaked at 64% in 1940, and was still at 62% by the census of 1950. Since color and class were initially highly correlated due to the original poverty of the emancipated slaves and ongoing racial prejudice, and since European immigrants shunned the more traditional sugar areas for the more dynamic coffee centers, the color composition varied by wealth of the region, with the South and Southeast being far less non-white than the Northeast. But from the peak of 1940 whites have been steadily declining as a share of the population, and by the census of 2010 they were once again a minority of the Brazilians.[36] Since there has been no massive

---

[32] Herbert S. Klein, *The Atlantic Slave Trade* (2nd edn; Cambridge: Cambridge University Press, 2010), Appendix, Table A2.

[33] NEPO, CENSO 1872: Quadros do Império, Table 2, população presente em relação à idade (sexo, condição, cor, idades), as reproduced and recalculated by NEPO/UNICAMP – Universidade Estadual de Campinas.

[34] Maria Stella Ferreira Levy, "O Papel da Migração Internacional na evolução da população brasileira (1872 a 1972)," *Revista de Saúde Pública* 8 (Supl.) (1974), [São Paulo], pp. 71–73, Table 1.

[35] IBGE, *Tendências demográficas, uma análise dos resultados da amostra do Censo demográfico 2000* (Estudos e Pesquisas no. 13; Rio de Janeiro, 2004), p. 17, Graph 2; and Ricardo Henriques, ed., *Desigualidade e pobreza no Brasil* (Rio de Janeiro: Ipea, 2000), p. 5, Table 1.

[36] IBGE, POP106, "População presente e residente, por cor ou raça (dados do universo e dados da amostra), Decenal 1872–2000," and IBGE, PD336, "População residente, por cor ou raça, Anual 2001–2009." Accessed at: http://seriesestatisticas.ibge.gov.br/lista_tema.aspx?op=o&n o=10. But color definitions are notoriously fluid in Brazil, especially when the usual manner of counting is by self-definition. It is interesting to note that by 2005 whites had fallen to less than half the total Brazilian population and have steadily declined through the census of 2010 where they were only 47% of the national population, though still being the largest majority in Brazil.

immigration of non-whites to Brazil since 1940, the origin of this shift is due to two possible explanations, both of which we will examine in later chapters. The first is declining negative associations related to color, above all of browns, who seem to be becoming associated with the national identity of all Brazilians. Secondly is the possibility of a steady increase of browns due to increased marriages and relationships crossing color lines. Thus, mid-century Brazilians still defined themselves in the majority as white, just as they overwhelmingly identified themselves as Roman Catholics. But, just as the birth and death rates were changing, so too was the sense of identity and religion in these subsequent decades.

Brazil, despite significant educational advances, was still overwhelmingly illiterate in this period. Although the majority of immigrants were literate, overall the literacy rate in the late nineteenth-century and early twentieth-century Brazilian censuses was very low. This was because Brazil for most of its imperial and early republican history was a relatively backward nation in terms of providing public education for its population even by Latin American standards. In the census of 1890, only 15% of persons could read and write,[37] which was almost identical to the figure in the first imperial census of 1872. This level put it among the poorest nations of the hemisphere. But the shift of education to state responsibility after 1899 meant that there was a major investment in schools in the more advanced regions. In fact, Brazil experienced the most rapid change in its literacy rates between 1899 and 1933 of any Latin American country.[38] By the census of 1920, the national literacy rate had doubled to 29%.[39] As late as 1871, there were only 134,000 youths who were students for a population of over 10.1 million, which represented barely 13 children matriculated in schools for every 1,000 inhabitations.[40] Of these students only 7% were in secondary schools, and overall only 28% of all students were women. By 1889, the ratio was 18 children per 1,000 residents; by 1907, it was 29; and by

---

[37] Directoria Geral de Estatística, *Sexo, raça e estado civil, nacionalidade, filiação culto e analfabetismo da população recenseada em 31 em Dezembro de 1890* (Rio de Janeiro: Officina da Estatística, 1898), p. 373, Table: "População recenseada na República dos Estados Unidos do Brasil quanto ao analfabetismo."

[38] Aldo Musacchio, André Martínez Fritscher, and Martina Viareng, "Colonial Institutions, Trade Shocks, and the Diffusion of Elementary Education in Brazil, 1889–1930." Working Paper 10-075, Harvard Business School, 2010. Accessed at: www.hbs.edu/research/pdf/10-075.pdf.

[39] Alceu Ravanello Ferraro, "Analfabetismo e níveis de letramento no Brasil: o que dizem os censos?" *Revista Educação & Sociedade* 23.81 (2002), p. 34, Table 1.

[40] Data from *Relatório do Ministério dos Negócios do Império 1871, Apresentado em Maio de 1872*, pp. 27–36.

1920, it was 41 children per 1,000 resident population.[41] Clearly, while total enrollments of primary school children was increasing, there still was a deficit of children at the primary grades, and secondary education, both public and private, was still available only for the elite. By 1950, there were 6 million students registered at a rate of 115 students per 1,000 population, but there was little growth in secondary and tertiary education. Of the 6 million enrolled students, 85% were in primary school, only 7% in secondary school, and 4% in tertiary education, with the other 4% in a diversity of commercial, agricultural, and pedagogical institutes.[42] But even with this growth the net matriculation rate only reached 73% of the population of 5- to 9-year-olds in 1950, and only 8% of children in the age cohort of 10 to 19 years of age were enrolled in school.[43] Moreover, Brazil was unusual by South American standards in having one of the lowest rates of school attendance for children 6–19 years of age even a decade later, comparable only to the poorest Central American countries and Bolivia (see Graph 1.9).

This lack of education in general and the traditional discrimination against women receiving an education can be seen in the rates of illiteracy by sex and age in the census of 1950. In that year, 54% of all men and 60% of all women were illiterate. When these figures are broken down by age, the long-term discrimination against women in education is clearly evident. However, by mid-century female literacy was finally ahead of men's in the 10–14 age group and equal to them in the 14–19 age cohort, indicating that education was now becoming available to women. For women over 20 years of age, illiteracy rates were consistently higher than men. Even for those born as recently as 1925 to 1929, over half of women were illiterate and this rate of illiteracy only increased the older the age cohort. For men, illiteracy rates were over 50% for those born in the 1890s and before (see Graph 1.10).

The backwardness of Brazil in educating its population can be seen in the comparisons with all other Latin American countries in 1950. In this case Brazil had a higher illiteracy rate than all of the other nations of South

[41] All this was due to the increase in state investment in education, which went from an average of R$ 0.7 m. per student in 1900 to R$ 1.2 m. (both in R$ 1913 m.) in 1925. In the period 1899 to 1933, the number of primary schools went from 8,157 to 28,707 and total primary school enrollments from 258,804 to 2,218,569. André Martínez-Fritscher, Aldo Musacchio, and Martina Viarengo, "The Great Leap Forward: The Political Economy of Education in Brazil, 1889–1930," Working Papers 03-2010, Universidade de São Paulo, Faculdade de Economia, Administração e Contabilidade de Ribeirão Preto, 2010, pp. 48, 52, Tables 2 and 8.

[42] IBGE, *Estatísticas do Século XX (2003)*, Table "EducacaoM1954aeb-048."

[43] These data are taken from FGV-CPDOC, "A educação no segundo governo Vargas" (2017). Accessed at: http://cpdoc.fgv.br/producao/dossies/AEraVargas2/artigos/EleVoltou/Educacao.

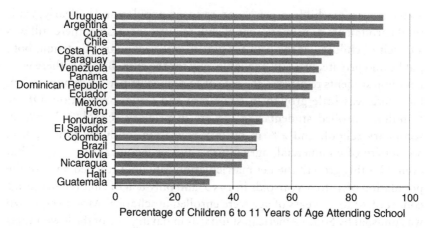

GRAPH 1.9 Ratio of Children 6 to 11 Years of Age Attending School by Country, 1960
Source: CEPAL, *Anuario Estadística de América Latina y el Caribe* (1980), p. 102, Table 35.

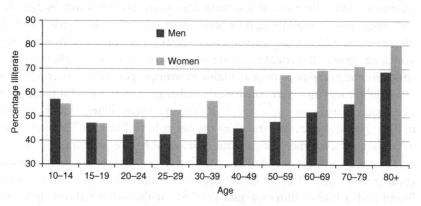

GRAPH 1.10 Percentage of Illiterates by Age and Sex, Census 1950
Source: *Recenseamento geral de 1950*, Série Nacional, Censo demográfico, vol. 1, pp. 20–21, Table 17.

America, except for Bolivia, and was closer to the poorest nations of Central America (see Graph 1.11).

Although still predominantly rural and a relatively traditional and stable society, Brazilians had begun to experience ever increasing geographic mobility. There was always a steady migration of poor farmers to the western frontier from the colonial period onward. But by the mid-twentieth century

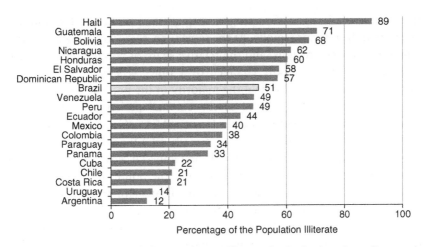

GRAPH 1.11 Percentage of the Population Illiterate by Latin American Country in 1950
Source: CEPAL, *Anuario Estadística de América Latina y el Caribe* (1980), p. 97, Table 33.

a new and massive inter-regional and rural to urban migration was added to this traditional agricultural worker migration. With the end of major international migration in the 1920s, internal migrants became the new source of rural and urban labor for the dynamic regions of the Southeast and South. Native-born Brazilians from the Northeastern region now migrated to the Southeastern region in search of work. Much of this shift in population was due to the replacement of sugar by coffee as Brazil's major export in the nineteenth and early twentieth centuries. In the colonial period, sugar was concentrated in the Northeast and only slowly moved to the Southeast. But the coffee plantation economy was totally concentrated in the Southeast region from the beginning and drew both slave and free workers into the region. By the 1880s, coffee dominated Brazilian exports, while the traditional Northeastern sugar industry was primarily supplying the internal market. It was the Southeast and its thriving international economy which concentrated ever more slave workers from other regions before 1888, just as it attracted most European and Asian migrants after the 1880s and Northeastern native-born Brazilians after 1920.

This post-1920 migration involved rural to rural migration, inter-regional migration, and rural to urban movements. A vast internal frontier existed to the west and most of the provinces/states had many regions which were only sparsely settled until the end of the twentieth century. This meant that there was a constant stream of farmers and workers moving toward the open frontiers as the Indians were progressively pushed back, and the railroads penetrated the interior regions. At the same time, there was a major internal migration between regions, and the relative share of population residing in given regions systematically changed over time. Whereas the traditional provinces of the Northeast held the majority of the population in the early eighteenth century, by the end of the colonial period the south-central provinces of Espírito Santo, Rio de Janeiro, Minas Gerais, and São Paulo began to challenge that dominance, especially after the move of the imperial capital to Rio de Janeiro in 1763. By the first imperial census of 1872, each of these two largest zones (the Northeast and the Southeast) between them contained 87% of the national population. That share dropped to 78% by 1950, and there was a major shift in dominance. Whereas the old Northeastern states were dominant to 1890, by the 1950 census their share had declined to 35% of the national population, and the Southeast share had risen to 43% of that population (Maps 1.1 and 1.2).

Despite some western and northern frontier movement, most of this internal migration to 1950 was along the coast. Thus, the relative weight

MAP 1.1 Regional Distribution of the Brazilian Population in 1872 (n = 9.9 million)

MAP 1.2 Regional Distribution of the Brazilian Population in 1950
(n = 51.9 million)

of the population of the interior regions of the North and Center-West changed little between the censuses of 1872 and 1950 (increasing their share by only 1% in this 78-year period). On the other hand, the South doubled its share, going from 7.3% to 15.1%, and the dynamic Southeast became the leading region of the country as early as the census of 1890. This dynamism was due to the fastest growing state of this region, São Paulo. By 1900, it had replaced Bahia as the largest state in the republic. In the period from 1872 to 1950 São Paulo grew at 3.2% per annum. The big states of the Northeast, Bahia and Pernambuco, both grew at under 2% in this period which explains their relative decline by 1950 (see Table 1.1).

This regional migration also included some rural to urban migration in its early stages, a pattern which would soon become dominant in the last half of the twentieth century. Brazil was surprisingly late in the proliferation of major cities. Even by 1950 it had only two urban centers greater than 1 million persons. Rio de Janeiro with its port and federal government was still the predominant city, but the city of São Paulo was rapidly catching up to this

Table 1.1 Population of Brazil by State and Region from the Censuses of 1872 to 1950 Using Current Regional Definitions

Region/State	1872	1890	1900	1920	1940	1950
North	332,847	476,370	695,112	1,439,052	1,627,608	2,048,696
Rondônia	–	–	–	–	–	36,935
Acre	–	–	–	92,379	79,768	114,755
Amazonas	57,610	147,915	249,756	363,166	438,008	514,099
Roraima	–	–	–	–	–	18,116
Pará	275,237	328,455	445,356	983,507	944,644	1,123,273
Amapá	–	–	–	–	–	37,477
Tocatins	–	–	–	–	165,188	204,041
Northeast	4,638,560	6,002,047	6,749,507	11,245,921	14,434,080	17,973,413
Maranhão	359,040	430,854	499,308	874,337	1,235,169	1,583,248
Piauí	202,222	267,609	334,328	609,003	817,601	1,045,696
Ceará	721,686	805,687	849,127	1,319,228	2,091,032	2,695,450
Rio Grande do Norte	233,979	268,273	274,317	537,135	768,018	967,921
Paraíba	376,226	457,232	490,784	961,106	1,422,282	1,713,259
Pernambuco	841,539	1,030,224	1,178,150	2,154,835	2,688,240	3,395,766
Alagoas	348,009	511,440	649,273	978,748	951,300	1,093,137
Sergipe	176,243	310,926	356,264	477,064	542,326	644,361
Bahia	1,379,616	1,919,802	2,117,956	3,334,465	3,918,112	4,834,575
Southeast	4,016,922	6,104,384	7,824,011	13,654,934	18,345,831	22,548,494
Minas Gerais	2,039,735	3,184,099	3,594,471	5,888,174	6,763,368	7,782,188
Espírito Santo	82,137	135,997	209,783	457,328	790,149	957,238
Rio de Janeiro	1,057,696	1,399,535	1,737,478	2,717,244	3,611,998	4,674,645

(continued)

22

São Paulo	837,354	1,384,753	2,282,279	4,592,188	7,180,316	9,134,423
South	721,337	1,430,715	1,796,495	3,537,167	5,735,305	7,840,870
Paraná	126,722	249,491	327,136	685,711	1,236,276	2,115,547
Santa Catarina	159,802	283,769	320,289	668,743	1,178,340	1,560,502
Rio Grande do Sul	434,813	897,455	1,149,070	2,182,713	3,320,689	4,164,821
Center-West	220,812	320,399	373,309	758,531	1,093,491	1,532,924
Mato Grosso do Sul	–	–	–	–	238,640	309,395
Mato Grosso	60,417	92,827	118,025	246,612	193,625	212,649
Goiás	160,395	227,572	255,284	511,919	661,226	1,010,880
Brazil	9,930,478	14,333,915	17,438,434	30,635,605	41,236,315	51,944,397

Source: IBGE, Sidra, Table 1286.

23

leading center. A town of 80,000 in 1872, São Paulo reached 2.2 million persons by 1950 and was competitive to the federal capital in Rio de Janeiro with its 2.4 million inhabitants. The next largest urban center was Recife in Pernambuco, with just 788,000 persons.[44] Only 36% of the population resided in towns and cities in the census of that year, despite the urban definition being quite liberal. Even the most urbanized Southeastern region listed just 48% of the population as urban, while the next largest region, the Northeast, had only 26% urban. By the standards of other Latin American nations Brazil was still only moderately urbanized and was more like Mexico, Peru, Colombia, and Venezuela than its southern neighbors.[45] But future change seemed evident as by the 1950s the urban population of Brazil was growing at twice the rate of the rural population.[46]

If agriculture was Brazil's predominant occupation in 1950, it was still a very backward agriculture. Only coffee was directed toward the international market and most crops were produced with neither fertilizers nor insecticides and were planted and harvested with hand tools. It was the constant expansion into virgin land which kept coffee productivity from declining over time. In the 1950s, when some 10.6 million hectares were brought into production and 4.5 million farm workers were added to rural labor, there finally began to appear machines on Brazilian farms in significant numbers. As was to be expected, most of these tractors and plows were concentrated in the South and Southeast regions. In the Northeast there was now 1 plow for every 310 hectares while there was 1 plow for every 5 hectares in the South and every 11 hectares in the Southeast. As for tractors, there was one for every 3,114 hectares in the Northeast and just 1 per 292 hectares in the Southeast, with São Paulo as usual being the leading state, with a ratio of 1 tractor for every 177 hectares (see Table 1.2).

Despite the relative backwardness of the Brazilian agriculture, the sector does not seem to have represented an obstacle to the development of industry since it was able to supply the basic food needs of an expanding urban and industrial population by increasing output through traditional means. Significant growth occurred in agriculture during the 1940s and 1950s, although it maintained the structure inherited from the colonial period, except in areas influenced by coffee, and did not show any gains in productivity from earlier periods. This growth in

---

[44] IBGE, *Estatísticas do Século XX* (2003), Table pop_S2T04.

[45] Merrick and Graham, *Population and Economic Development*, p. 186, Table VIII-1.

[46] The urban growth rate was 3.9% per annum, though at a much lower base than the rural population which was growing at just 1.6% per annum. IBGE, "Séries históricas e estatísticas," Table CD93. Accessed at: https://seriesestatisticas.ibge.gov.br/series.aspx?n o=10&op=o&vcodigo=CD93&t=taxa-crescimento-anual-populacao-situacao-domicilio.

Table 1.2 *Crop Areas, Personnel, Tractors, and Plows Employed by State, 1950–1960*

	Crop Areas		Personnel Employed		Tractors		Plows	
	1950	1960	1950	1960	1950	1960	1950	1960
North	234,512	458,490	326,502	536,619	61	266	381	306
Northeast	5,283,804	9,306,681	4,334,936	6,566,035	451	2,989	14,489	21,171
Southeast	8,447,903	10,297,939	3,999,860	4,465,344	5,155	35,215	318,863	394,696
Minas Gerais	2,937,126	3,673,466	1,868,657	2,076,829	763	5,024	79,968	93,040
São Paulo	4,257,633	4,973,300	1,531,664	1,683,038	3,819	28,101	224,947	286,580
South	4,530,566	8,279,870	1,949,923	3,174,233	2,566	22,720	383,435	604,050
Paraná	1,358,222	3,471,131	507,607	1,276,854	280	4,996	30,405	82,324
Rio Grande do Sul	2,502,691	3,795,840	1,071,404	1,277,390	2,245	16,675	312,001	449,467
Center-West	608,272	1,416,805	385,613	678,623	139	2,303	3,091	11,797
Total	19,095,057	29,759,785	10,996,834	15,521,701	8,372	63,493	714,259	1,031,930

Source: IBGE, *Séries históricas retrospectivas.*

Table 1.3 *GINI Index of Land Ownership in Brazil and Principal Agricultural States, 1920–1950*

	1920	1940	1950
Brazil	0.832	0.833	0.844
São Paulo	0.764	0.773	0.773
Minas Gerais	0.724	0.753	0.764
Paraná	0.810	0.749	0.734
Santa Catarina	0.768	0.693	0.674
Rio Grande do Sul	0.802	0.767	0.761
Pernambuco	0.623	0.782	0.837
Bahia	0.797	0.793	0.802

Source: Szmrecsányi, "O Desenvolvimento da Produção Agropecuária (1930–1970)" (1995), p. 193.

production came from the employment of new land and more workers. This demand for food was driven by the post-war growth in population, which both permitted agriculture to release more workers into the urban area at no cost to its own needs and created an increased demand for agricultural products in the expanding cities. This so-called "labor reserve army" permitted farmers and plantation owners to continue obtaining cheap laborers given the increasing number of workers entering the market due to declining mortality and steady and high fertility. This cheap labor supply thus reduced farm-owner interest in creating more efficient means of production. At the same time, the availability of new agricultural land was also a disincentive to the more intensive use of capital in the form of plows, tractors, fertilizers, and pesticides. Only in some economically denser regions, especially in São Paulo and the Southern states, the increasing scarcity of land stimulated the timid introduction of more efficient inputs and equipment.

The beginnings of modernization in agriculture only occurred in the 1960s when agriculture became a significant area of government investment, but land ownership still remained highly concentrated even after modernization began. This can be shown by the concentrated structure of ownership of land, which remained virtually unchanged between 1920 and 1950 and until today. During this period, the GINI index for the distribution of land ownership among agricultural establishments remained virtually unchanged in the nation as a whole, rising from 0.83 to 0.84 (see Table 1.3), and increased somewhat in most regions except the three Southern states known for the importance of their commercial small farms. But, given their relatively modest size, these Southern states had little impact on the very high national indices of inequality.[47]

Given the low level of urbanization, the high concentration of land ownership, and the dominant role of landless rural workers in the labor force, it is not surprising that Brazil in 1950 was one of the most highly stratified and unequal societies in the world. It was divided between richer and poorer regions, between a small upper class, a very modest middle class, and a massive class of poor and indigent population, the majority concentrated in the rural area. Like all ex-slave societies in the Americas it was also divided by race, with blacks at the bottom along with browns, and with whites at the top of the economic and social pyramid.

The regions reflected these divisions, with strong disparities in both total and per capita GDP. The national GDP was US$ 17 billion, with a per capita income of US$ 244. The Southeast accounted for the majority of the gross domestic income but for only 43% of the population. The Northeast was the only region which had a smaller ratio of GDP than its share of population. The state of São Paulo alone generated 32% of the domestic income of the country. In terms of income per capita, the Northeast population only obtained a little over a quarter of what the richest Southeastern residents earned and yet had 35% of the population in 1950 (see Table 1.4).

Table 1.4 *Percentage of GDP by Region, Index of per Capita Income US$ by Region (1950)*

	% of GDP	% of Population (1950)	Per Capita Income (Southeast = 100)
North	2%	4%	32
Northeast	16%	35%	28
Southeast	61%	43%	100
South	18%	15%	70
Center-West	2%	3%	34

Source: IBGE, *Anuário Estatístico do Brasil*, 1963; Carlos Roberto Azzoni, "Concentração regional e dispersão das rendas per capita estaduais: analise a partir de séries históricas estaduais de PIB, 1939–1995," *Estudos Economics* 27.3 (1997), Table A3.

[47] Although the overall mean remained stable, it decreased significantly in some states, such as Santa Catarina, Paraná, Acre, and Amazonas. In other states such as Maranhão, Pernambuco, and Mato Grosso, concentrations increased. The index in São Paulo remained stable, at around 0.77.

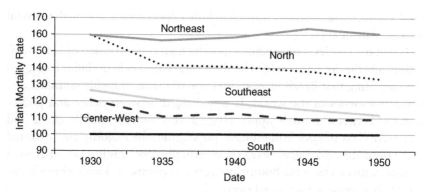

GRAPH 1.12 Index of Infant Mortality Rate by Region, 1930–1950 (South=100)
Source: https://seriesestatisticas.ibge.gov.br/series.aspx?t=taxa-mortalidade-
infantil&vcodigo=CD100.

The same disparities by region could be found in other indices. Thus, infant mortality, for example, while slowly declining everywhere from 1930 to 1950, declined the slowest in the Northeast (see Graph 1.12), which still had not closed its difference with the healthiest South region despite the fact that all other regions changed more rapidly than the South and therefore were approaching the Southern region norm by 1950.

So profound were these differences, that despite the common language and culture, Brazil could really be considered several different nations. The Northeast had among the world's worst levels of education and health and a modern advanced Southeastern and Southern region had levels approaching southern European norms.

There were also profound class differences everywhere. Recent calculations of the distribution of income show that the richest top 1% of persons in Brazil owned 24% of the wealth of Brazil (defined as both income and capital gains), consistently, from the 1930s through the 1970s. This is compared to the United States, which, by the 1970s, had the top 1% owning 9% of the total national wealth, and Sweden, where top-income people held just 6% of the total wealth in the 1970s. But, even as these rates have risen in recent years for other countries, Brazil has remained, even in the second decade of the twenty-first century, at 23%, which is above the average of 20% for most Latin American countries and the United States, and far above the 10% average for most of the advanced industrial societies in the world.[48] In terms of salaried workers, the

---

[48] Pedro Herculano Guimarães Ferreira de Souza, "A desigualdade vista do topo: a concentração de renda entre os ricos no Brasil, 1926–2013," PhD thesis, Universidade de Brasília, 2016, p. 249, discussion and Table 5.

poorest 50% of workers in 1960 received just 14% of the total salaried income whereas the top 10% received almost half of the total income (48%).[49]

Brazil was also a country highly stratified by race. The color of one's skin had a powerful influence on one's education, income, occupation, health, and even longevity. Of the 52 million Brazilian residents in the country in 1950, 19.5 million were self-defined as black or brown. These non-white persons were dominant in the poorest states and far less representative in the richest ones. They were on average less educated than whites, considerably poorer than them, had higher mortality rates, and lower life expectancy. In 1950, it was estimated that the average life expectancy of whites was 47.1 years and of Afro-Brazilians (browns and blacks) 40.5 years.[50] Unfortunately, the best data on race and social and economic conditions come only with the national household surveys (*Pesquisa Nacional por Amostra de Domicílios* – PNAD), which began in the late 1970s. But the numerous analyses of these surveys and the national censuses show that little had changed in Brazil in terms of racial differences in all these basic indices. Thus, in 1976, non-whites had only 23% of total income even though they represented 49% of the population.[51] In the 1980s, young blacks and browns were still twice as likely not to be in school as whites.[52] This was a long-term phenomenon, as can be seen in the data on literacy going back to the census of 1950. Then, both white men and women were far less illiterate than both blacks and browns of both sexes (see Graph 1.13).

These differences also help explain the findings from the 1999 PNAD survey which shows that blacks and browns had double the poverty rate of whites.[53] In surveys of maternal mortality in the rich Southern states of Brazil in the early twenty-first century, black mothers had eight times and brown mothers four times the maternal mortality rate of white mothers. The difference was also evident in terms of infant mortality, although less extreme. A survey in 1986 showed that 40 infant deaths

[49] Rodolfo Hoffmann and João Carlos Duarte, "A distribuição da renda no Brasil," *Revista de Administração de Empresas* 12.2 (1972), p. 58, Table 9.

[50] Charles H. Wood, José Alberto Magno de Carvalho, and Cláudia Júlia Guimarães Horta, "The Color of Child Mortality in Brazil, 1950–2000: Social Progress and Persistent Racial Inequality," *Latin American Research Review* 45.2 (2010), p. 126, Table 2.

[51] Rafael Guerreiro Osorio, "A desigualdade racial de renda no Brasil: 1976–2006," PhD thesis, Universidade de Brasília, 2009, p. 85, Graph 2 and p. 164, Graph 4.2.

[52] Carlos A. Hasenbalg and Nelson do Valle Silva, "Raça e oportunidades educacionais no Brasil," *Cadernos de pesquisa* 73 (2013), p. 6, Table 2.

[53] Ricardo Henriques, "Desigualdade racial no Brasil: evolução das condições de vida na década de 90," Texto para discussão 807, Rio de Janeiro, Ipea, 2001, p. 11, Table 6.

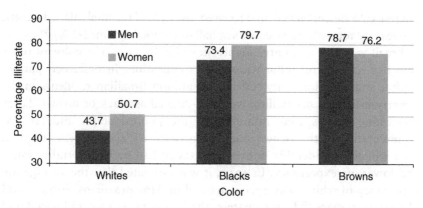

GRAPH 1.13 Percentage Illiterate by Sex and Color, Census 1950
Source: *Recenseamento geral de 1950*, Série Nacional, Censo demográfico, vol. 1, pp. 20–21, Table 17.

per 1,000 live births was the national norm for whites, 67 deaths for browns, and 69 deaths for blacks.[54]

Finally, Brazil was still a highly unequal society in terms of gender. Until the mid-century, women traditionally received less education than men, made less money than men when they worked, and were by the standards of the day quite restricted in their participation in the labor force. It was estimated that in 1960 the female labor force participation rate for Brazil was only 18.5% compared to 88.7% for men. This female participation rate was at this time below the Latin American average and below even that of Mexico.[55] Although the rate grew over the next two decades, it still reached only 27.8% in 1976.[56] Salaries for women who did work in Brazil, as in most countries, were well below those of men for the same jobs and with the same skill set. While this slowly improved, salaries were still a third lower for women than for men in 1981,[57] and a quarter less than male salaries for the same work with the same input of skills until the late 1990s.[58] Women were less educated and more illiterate than men at this

---

[54] Estela Maria Garcia de Pinto da Cunha, "Mortalidade infantil segundo cor: os resultados da PNAD 84 para o Nordeste," Paper presented at the IX Encontro Nacional de Estudos Populacionais, ABEP, 2006, p. 203, Table 1.

[55] World Bank data. Accessed at: https://data.worldbank.org/indicator/SL.TLF.CACT.FE.ZS.

[56] Lauro R. A. Ramos and Ana Lúcia Soares, "Participação da mulher na força de trabalho e pobreza no Brasil," Texto para discussão 350, Rio de Janeiro, Ipea, 1994, p. 2, Table 1.

[57] Jaime Tenjo, Rocío Ribero, and Bernat D. Luisa Fernanda, *Evolución de las diferencias salariales por sexo en seis países de América Latina: un intento de interpretación* (Bogotá: Centro de Estudios sobre Desarrollo Económico, Facultad de Economía, Universidad de los Andes, 2005), p. 23, Table 3.5.

[58] Carlos Salas and Marcia Leite, "Segregación sectorial por género: una comparación Brasil-México," *Cadernos PROLAM/USP* 7.2 (2007), p. 248.

point in Brazilian development. Until mid-century, Brazil spent more on educating men than women. This was seen in the national literacy rates, which in 1950 showed that women were more illiterate than men and the older the woman the greater was the difference from men.[59] But the fact that in 1950 boys and girls 5 to 9 years of age were finally equally enrolled as primary grade students[60] meant that this difference would eventually disappear in subsequent census years.

Thus, in terms of region, class, race, and gender, Brazil was far from being a united and uniform society. Cities were wealthier than rural areas, the South and Southeast states were far richer than the other regions, and the non-white population had the worst income and health indices in the country. Moreover, the upper class took a greater share of national income than in almost all other major countries in the world. As the economist Edmar Bacha noted, Brazil at mid-century had two societies and two economies – one at the level of Belgium and the other at the level of India, to which he gave the name Belíndia.

Yet even in the decade of the 1950s there were indications of developments which would change this profoundly traditional society. Probably the most important factor was the growth of industry which would begin to shift workers out of agriculture and promote the growth of cities. In 1940, there were only 669,000 workers (operários) in industry, but by 1950 this had risen to 1 million. This was still dominated by clothing, food, and civil construction, but change was occurring at a far more rapid pace. By the census of 1960, there existed 111,000 industrial establishments in Brazil, employing 1.5 million workers, of which almost 41% were employed in the areas of textiles, clothing, food, and drinks – down from 55% in 1940 and 51% in 1950. This sector of light industry thus still accounted for over half the industrial workers and represented half the value of industrial production in 1950. In the next decade, however, metallurgy, equipment manufacturers, the transport material industry, and the chemical industry would increase their relative share of workers and of capital, reaching about a third of the value of industrial production. Alone, the metallurgical industries went from accounting for just 11% of the workers in industry to 17% in 1960.[61]

The growing industrial sector was mostly located in the principal cities but expanded due to the increasing integration of a national market following the construction of a major railroad and port facilities from the 1870s to the 1910s and the development of modern roads after that date. This industry was initially dominated by textiles using nationally grown cotton and by food processing

[59] IBGE, *Censo demográfico 1950*, Série Nacional, vol. 1, p. 18, Table 5.
[60] IBGE, *Censo demográfico 1950*, Série Nacional, vol. 1, p. 22, Table 19.
[61] IBGE, *Censo industrial, 1950*, Série Nacional, vol. 3.1, p. 1, and IBGE, *VII Recenseamento geral do Brasil*, Série Nacional, vol. 3, *Censo industrial de 1960*, Table 2a.

companies using national crops. The impact of the closing of the world markets in World War I and World War II also helped develop a modest capital goods industry. But, as a late industrializing country, Brazil needed massive government support to generate the capital required to create a modern industrial sector.

The idea of the government as a major participant in the national economy goes back to the 1930s and the Vargas era, but came to full fruition in the post-1945 period under the government of Juscelino Kubitschek (1956–1961). During this period the government developed an industrialization plan which included the generation of a new automotive industry and a push to expand industry beyond its traditional light industry and into capital goods production. The construction of Brasília, completed in 1960, was considered the major synthesis of all the developmental plans of the government, and also had a major influence on both the Brazilian society and economy.[62] On the one hand, the size of investments and the location of the new capital changed the spatial occupation of Brazil, stimulating its shift from the coast, where population and economic activities had been concentrated, toward the interior of the country. This shift also required constructing a major highway infrastructure in the Center-West, where Brasília was located, opening up this region for agricultural development.

The second part of the transformation promoted by the central government in the 1950s was the opening up of Brazil to foreign capital. The first phase of Brazilian industrialization, based on traditional sectors such as textiles, food, and drink, had developed largely with national capital. After World War II it was foreign capital which became an important factor in the maturation of this sector. This new industrial expansion also permitted Brazilian involvement in the international market. An aggressive entrepreneurial state which invested heavily in infrastructure and basic or heavy industries became attractive to multinational companies. The government manipulated a set of instruments in the form of subsidies, credit, foreign exchange, tariff protection, and direct investments in infrastructure or sectors where the private sector, domestic or foreign, would find it attractive to invest. Brazil's

[62] The relocation of the capital to the center of the country appeared as a wish of the republican government as early as the first republican constitution in 1891. But it was only with the government of Juscelino Kubitschek (1956–1961) that the decision was made to build Brasília. Construction began in 1956, and in 1960 came the formal change of the national capital from Rio de Janeiro to Brasília, although the transfer of the central administration was not completed until 1970.

development bank, the BNDE, had a key role in defining the priority projects that would count on its essential support.[63]

From the beginning of the 1950s, the public sector systematically expanded its participation in economic activity, with significant participation not only in infrastructural investments, particularly in transportation, but also in the production of basic inputs. The government dominated the steel industry through the *Companhia Siderúrgica Nacional* and oil production, refining, and the petrochemical industry through *Petrobras* and private capital. The extraction and exportation of iron ore was dominated by the state-owned *Companhia Vale do Rio Doce* and it became a major owner and producer of hydroelectric power companies. It was the public sector which now performed a fundamental industrial and economic role directly or through investment in public enterprises, or by manipulating a set of instruments – taxes, foreign exchange, and financial instruments – which gave it an overall control over the process of ongoing development. The public sector now accounted for between 17% and 18% of GDP, and that did not count its activities through participation in public enterprises.

The changes which were occurring in the economy between 1930 and 1960 had an impact on the economically active population (EAP). Employment in the agricultural sector grew less than employment in industry and services, thus reducing the relative importance of agriculture. A large increase in employment occurred in the services sector, which now employed a third of the population economically active in 1960 compared to 13% in industry and 54% in agriculture. Although these changing indicators show the result of a process of rural exodus in search of opportunities in cities in the period 1930 to 1960, the agricultural population was still growing in this period at an annual rate of 1.6% (see Graph 1.14).

All these government and private investments in the 1950s led to significant expansion of industrial production, which showed a mean annual growth of 11% in the period, of commerce, which also showed outstanding performance (an average 8% annual growth), and even of agriculture, which, though less supported, still showed almost a 6% annual growth in this period.

Thus, on the eve of a major industrial and agricultural transformation, Brazil still had most of the characteristics of an underdeveloped society: high fertility and mortality, high levels of illiteracy, and an economy which absorbed a majority of the labor force in agriculture. It was also a society

---

[63] Rosane de Almeida Maia, "Estado e Industrialização no Brasil: Estudo dos Incentivos ao setor privado, nos quadros do Programa de Metas do Governo Kubitschek" (MA thesis, São Paulo, FEA-USP, 1986).

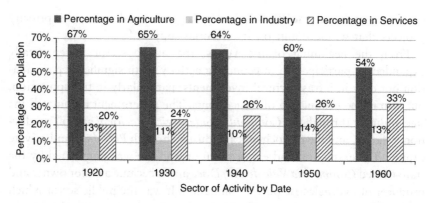

GRAPH 1.14 Composition of the Economically Active Population by Sector of Activity, 1920–1960
Source: Thomas W. Merrick and Douglas H. Graham, *Population and Economic Development in Brazil, 1800 to the Present* (Baltimore, Md.: Johns Hopkins University Press, 1979), pp. 64–65.

deeply divided by class, race, gender, and region. It contained within its borders two quite different regions with distinct economies and societies which had little in common with each other, save language. There was an impoverished Northern area and a more modern and advanced Southern one. It was also one of the most unequal societies in the world, with divisions along class, race, and gender lines, and with one of the world's most unequal distributions of land. Yet it was this profoundly divided nation that would industrialize, urbanize, and create a modern economy in the next sixty-nine years. It was industrialization, agricultural modernization, and urbanization backed by major government programs of social and economic investment which would finally lead to the decline of differences between regions as the nation became a more cohesive and uniform society in the past quarter century.

2

Political and Economic Evolution of Brazil

Brazil went from being a colony to an empire in 1822 with relatively less conflict than occurred for most of the countries of Latin America in the nineteenth century. From 1822 to 1889, a constitutional monarchy governed the country and brought an unusual level of political stability to the country. But the transition from empire to republic was not an easy one and from 1889 to the present Brazil passed through several periods of centralizing and decentralizing regimes and slowly and hesitatingly moved from an oligarchic and limited democratic republic to a full representative democracy. But that long process from 1889 to the present was broken by military interventions and a political party system which was fragmented and incapable of sustaining and developing a coherent national political elite. Between 1930 and 1985, only four presidents were elected through direct voting and only two concluded their mandate: one of them, Juscelino Kubitschek, under constant threat of a military coup. During this period, two long authoritarian periods occurred; the longest one, from 1964 to 1985, was a government totally controlled by the military. It was the shock of a long and ruthless military dictatorship which finally created a climate of political compromise and democratic commitment which has enabled Brazil to emerge as a well-structured democratic state in the post 1985 period.

In 1930, as a response to the world economic crisis which seriously affected Brazil, the power of the regional republican oligarchies was broken. Getúlio Vargas, former Finance Minister, and the defeated candidate in the 1929 presidential elections, took power by carrying out a coup. Although he initially maintained the democratic process, Vargas moved toward an ever more authoritarian position, which culminated with the establishment of the *Estado Novo* (New State) in 1937. Vargas then established a right-wing dictatorship similar to the European Fascist models, abolishing the existing parties and abandoning parliamentary government. There was political repression, with imprisonment, torture, and the deportation of political leaders. But this was also a government which incorporated workers and new urban classes into the governing structure. The Vargas era, which thus lasted from 1930 to 1945, also deeply marked the whole second half of the twentieth century with its economic policies through its initiation of an active state intervention in the economy, both in terms of regulation and in terms of direct investment in the productive sector. Industrialization now became a national state objective.

This period was also outstanding in the establishment of public regulatory agencies to control vital sectors of the economy such as coffee, sugar and alcohol, steel, water, and energy. This robust and centralizing state, investing both in infrastructure and in several productive sectors of the economy, was the legacy of the Vargas Era and became a basic feature of the interventionist style Brazilian state; and remained the norm until the beginning of the 1990s.[1] Vargas himself returned to power as a legally elected president in 1951, and, while continuing his economic policies, was no longer able to control the political opposition. Under threat of impeachment, he committed suicide in 1954.

After a complicated transition and under the permanent risk of a military coup, Juscelino Kubitschek, a political leader from Minas Gerais, was elected president in 1955 with the support of the same Vargas coalition of forces. During his government, the most coherent industrialization program ever implemented was established and the new capital city of Brasília was built. Not only did Kubitschek create numerous autonomous government agencies to oversee and invest in the economy, but he promoted the entry of foreign capital into the productive sector. But his ambitious program led the government to spend beyond its means, generating inflationary pressure.[2] A series of unstable democratic regimes followed with the military increasing pressure to prevent a more radical regime from emerging. The last civilian president in this period was João Goulart, the former vice president, who emerged after

---

[1] For the Vargas period see Boris Fausto, *A revolução de 1930* (São Paulo: Editora Brasiliense, 1972); Sonia Draibe, *Rumos e metamorfoses: estado e industrialização no Brasil, 1930/1960* (Rio de Janeiro: Paz e Terra, 1985); Maria do Carmo Campello de Souza, *Estado e partidos políticos no Brasil 1930 a 1964* (São Paulo: Alfa-Omega, 1990); Thomas E. Skidmore, *Brasil: de Getúlio a Castelo* (Rio de Janeiro: Paz e Terra, 2003). For a survey of the economy and politics of the republican period, see Francisco Vidal Luna and Herbert S. Klein, *The Economic and Social History of Brazil since 1889* (Cambridge: Cambridge University Press, 2014).

[2] On the government of Kubitschek, see Maria Victoria de Mesquita Benevides, *O governo Kubitschek* (Rio de Janeiro: Paz e Terra, 1976).

the resignation of the president. But the continued hostility of the military and the US government led to a military coup in April 1964. This time the generals decided to rule in their own name and thus began twenty-one years of military government, following the wave of such regimes emerging in other Latin American countries.

On April 9, the new military regime decreed the first of a long list of institutional acts which moved the country away from a democratic position toward an authoritarian one. It granted Congress the power to elect the new president of the Republic and Congress. Repression became the norm and thousands of people were arrested, including dissident officers, union leaders, and left-of-center political figures. The northeastern peasant leagues were disbanded, and their leaders were imprisoned. During the military government, censorship, repression, imprisonment, and torture became generalized practices. But the military regime which governed Brazil in this period showed odd characteristics. On the one hand, it was repressive and ferociously anti-communist and committed to the Cold War as a staunch US ally. It was also committed to a powerful centralized state with the dominance of the federal executive branch. At the same time, it tried to maintain elections and kept a much-controlled Congress functioning. Fearing the emergence of a powerful personalistic regime under a caudillo, the military establishment committed itself to fixed presidential terms and formal "elections." During the entire military period, a form of presidential election was carried out by Congress which confirmed the prior selection of the military establishment. Internal conflicts in the choice of new presidents were kept under military control. Different groups alternated in power, but always required a consensus in the military to maintain themselves in power.[3]

The late 1960s to the mid-1970s would be the years of major euphoria in the economy, with high growth rates as the government devoted large sums to promoting industry and modernizing agriculture. Although it was also

---

[3] There is a large literature on the military period which is summarized in a general survey of this period found in Herbert S. Klein and Francisco Vidal Luna, *Brazil, 1964–1985: The Military Regimes of Latin America in the Cold War* (New Haven, Conn.: Yale University Press, 2017). This is also surveyed in the classic works of Thomas Skidmore and Elio Gaspari. See Thomas E. Skidmore, *The Politics of Military Rule in Brazil, 1964–85* (New York: Oxford University Press, 1988) and the several volumes of Elio Gaspari, *A ditadura envergonhada* (São Paulo: Companhia das Letras, 2002); *A ditadura escancarada* (São Paulo: Companhia das Letras, 2002); *A ditadura derrotada* (São Paulo: Companhia das Letras, 2003); and *A ditadura encurralada* (São Paulo: Companhia das Letras, 2004). Of the many books that have appeared recently, especially useful are Rodrigo Patto Sá Motta, *As universidades e o regime militar* (Rio de Janeiro: Zahar, 2014) and the essays in Daniel Aarão, Marcelo Ridenti, and Rodrigo Patto Sá Motta, eds., *A ditadura que mudou o Brasil: 50 anos do golpe de 1964* (Rio de Janeiro: Zahar Editora, 2014).

a period of increasing income concentration, high growth created a better standard of living for the middle class, and the creation of new industries incorporated vast new contingents of the population into the formal labor market. This meant that workers now had formal work permits, paid into a social security scheme, and had access to health care and other benefits. These results gave the government a relatively popular acceptance despite its ferocious censorship, repression, and constant violation of individual rights. Finally, the transition to democratic government started in 1974 with president General Geisel's inauguration, but did not end until 1985. The frequent setbacks that occurred put in doubt the viability of the process under way. But at the end of the Geisel administration there were also more positive developments. The Institutional Act no. 5,[4] the key legislation underlying the authoritarian regime, was abolished, habeas corpus was re-established, prior censorship terminated, the Judiciary recovered its independence, and banishment was revoked for many traditional democratic leaders.

Despite all the violence and political instability of the military era, it was in this period that a major industrial structure was created. In 1959, for example, there were just 1.4 million workers in manufacturing, but by 1985 there were over 4 million. Even with all the subsequent crises and neoliberal reforms, manufacturing jobs kept increasing.[5] By 2016, there were 7.5 million workers in manufacturing (see Graph 2.1). Along with the

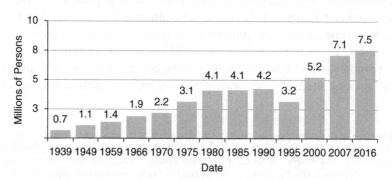

GRAPH 2.1 Growth of Industrial Labor Force in Manufacturing, 1939–2016
IBGE, *Séries históricas*, Table IND04006 and Sidra, Tables 1964, 2221.

---

[4] Institutional Act no. 5, the most authoritarian legal measure of the military dictatorship, was promulgated on 13 December 1968 and went into force on 31 December 1978.
[5] Using the definition of "industrias de transformação" to 1985 and "produção de bens e serviços industriais" for 2000 and 2010.

growth of manufacturing has developed an important services industry, which by 2000 had 19.4 million workers which increased to 22.7 million by 2010. Altogether, non-agricultural jobs by this later date accounted for 87% of the 86 million workers in Brazil, up from 82% in 2000.[6]

The emergence of an autonomous labor movement is another important development which occurred in the late military period. From the first days of the authoritarian regime, the military had maintained the urban and rural unions under tight government control, intervening in most unions and expelling most of their active leadership. In the urban area, the trade unions' structure set up in the Vargas period remained rather stable, giving the state great power to manipulate the unions through the use of the *"pelegos"* (professional trade union leaders linked to the government). In the rural areas, the very active peasant leagues which existed prior to the military regimes were destroyed and new unions controlled by the government were created. But in the Geisel period there was an emergence of new union leadership in both the rural and urban areas. In the rural areas, new peasant groups were formed free of government intervention and closely associated with the Roman Catholic Church. In the urban area, new independent leadership emerged within trade unions. Ten years after the violent repression of the Osasco and Contagem strikes, the first major strikes initiated in the military era, the automobile workers from São Paulo's ABC industrial region went on strike again. This time the head of the strike movement was Luiz Inácio Lula da Silva (known as "Lula"), at that time a trade union leader and future president of Brazil, who had broad popular support.[7] To avoid violent confrontations, the workers negotiated directly with employers. The employees accepted the negotiations and settled the strike before the government could intervene.[8]

In 1978, the military leadership accepted General João Baptista Figueiredo to be the president. Figueiredo was determined to transfer his mandate to a civilian successor, but within a complex process of political negotiations and in the context of a period of economic crisis. From the first oil crisis in 1973, the military regimes had chosen a heterodox (or non-recessionary) economic adjustment, promoting a strong investment program with foreign funding that

---

[6] IBGE, Sidra, Tables 1985 and 3591.

[7] The strikes of the metalurgical workers at Osasco, São Paulo, and at Contagem in Minas Gerais, both in 1968, were the last ones after the military coup of 1964. Ten years later, in 1978, the strike movements began again in the industrial areas of the metropolitan region of São Paulo.

[8] The archdioceses of São Paulo became an important center of opposition to the military regime, defending human rights, condemning political persecutions and torture. It also played a key part in the organization of new union movements which developed in the region.

completed the industrialization process and made the country less dependent on foreign resources. The price to be paid was the public sector's financial exhaustion and an expansion of foreign indebtedness. The second oil crisis in 1979 and the widespread debt crisis of the emerging countries made such a program no longer viable. Figueiredo's government faced the need of a brutal recessive adjustment, without foreign support. In addition, the deterioration of the economy caused the complete deterioration of the political scene.

The original strategy of the government had been to create two parties, with the idea that the military could maintain its power base both in the military period and even in a democratic period with free elections. But the government party had little popular support. Given this situation, military leaders decided to support a multi-party solution instead, hoping to split the opposition into many smaller parties, and this actually occurred. The government party itself was now called the PDS (*Partido Democrático Social*) or Social Democratic Party. Several opposition parties were formed, but the old unified opposition party also survived and became known as the PMDB (*Partido do Movimento Democrático Brasileiro*) or Brazilian Democratic Movement Party. Among the various parties created was the *Partido dos Trabalhadores* – PT (Workers' Party). It was formed by the new authentic trade union leaderships and included left intellectuals and segments of the urban middle class. The Workers' Party was an unusual Brazilian party in that it had a coherent organization, ideology, and leadership with a strong loyal following. The other parties, including the PMDB, were more like opposition fronts than organically structured parties. In fact, most Brazilian parties to this day are defined as weak parties.

One of the characteristics of the Brazilian party system is its fragility in terms of party loyalty, with frequent party changes, even including politicians with a legislative mandate or in an executive office. Coalitions do not always reflect an ideological coherence, particularly those that give political support to the executive in power. It might be the case that governance is enhanced by this party fragility, given the country's political instability and institutional fragility. But it can also lead to unusual leaders and parties emerging and tends to promote vote buying either through appointments to federal jobs or direct corruption. The executive usually achieves the necessary majority for the government through these incentives. Another characteristic of the Brazilian party system is the creation of new parties or the utilization of small parties to support the emergence of new political leaders that could not find space in the major parties. This feature of the Brazilian political system has only become more entrenched over time due to legislation, which has not promoted the consolidation of strong, representative parties that allow governability with coherent ideological coalitions or based on solid principles and government programs. Today there are thirty-five legally constituted parties, of which thirty have representation in the Chamber of Deputies, but there is an ongoing process involving the formation of dozens of other parties.[9]

The transition to a democratic system had a significant moment in 1982 with the direct elections for state governors where the opposition parties were victorious. The deepening economic crisis further harmed the military government, and popular protest now became the norm as the government permitted mass demonstrations. The most important of these movements was the massive mobilization of civil society and opposition parties in favor of direct elections to choose the next president of the Republic. In spite of that, indirect elections were maintained. But the elections were still a surprise to the military. The government party split when choosing its candidate and thus permitted the victory of the opposition civilian slate. Although the elections were still indirect, the PMDB candidate, the governor of Minas Gerais, Tancredo Neves, a respected politician, and known for his moderation and political abilities, won.

The death of Tancredo Neves before assuming office brought vice president José Sarney to the presidency instead. José Sarney's presidency represents an irony in history, since it installed in office a traditional pro-government politician rather than the leader of the democratic opposition. But Sarney understood his rather unusual position, keeping the ministers that Tancredo Neves had already named and deciding to base his political support on the PMDB's parliamentary majority. His administration undoubtedly represented a major development in the consolidation of the democratic process. One may say that the long transition, started during Geisel's government and continued during Figueiredo's, would be completed in the Sarney period.

The major development under the Sarney government was the approval of a new constitution in 1988 which returned Brazil to a more decentralized

---

[9] On this theme, see Yan de Souza Carreirão, "O sistema partidário brasileiro," *Revista Brasileira de Ciência Política* 14 (2014), pp. 255–295; Cesar Zucco, "Stability Without Roots: Party System Institutionalization in Brazil," SSRN, 4 February 2010. Accessed 25 April 2018, at: https://papers.ssrn.com/sol3/papers.cfm?abstract_id=2002359; Scott Mainwaring, Timothy J. Power, and Fernando Bizzarro, "The Uneven Institutionalization of a Party System: Brazil." In Scott Mainwaring, ed., *Party Systems in Latin America: Institutionalization, Decay, and Collapse* (Cambridge: Cambridge University Press, 2018), pp. 164–200. In 2017, a constitutional amendment was approved that created electoral performance clauses so that only parties with a minimum electoral vote have access to state funds and the right to free time on radio and television. Given the results of the general elections of 2018, some fourteen of the thirty-five officially constituted parties will not reach the established minimum.

democratic federal government. The Constitution of 1988 was seen as one of the most advanced in terms of social and political rights, including those for minorities. Illiterates were give the right to vote and the voting age was lowered to sixteen years. Elections for president were now made by direct voting in a two-stage process if a majority was not obtained on the first vote. Although the main opposition leaders preferred a parliamentary system over a presidential one, this was defeated. For all the positive features of the new decentralization, the fiscal system was initially not well organized. Budgets became more rigid and at the same time it became more difficult to balance government accounts. Several public monopolies were enshrined in the constitution and the document also had a distinctly nationalist tone. The 1988 Constitution nevertheless was considered a powerful document solidifying the democratic state.

The election of 1990 was to be the first direct election since that of 1960 and occurred during a major economic crisis with inflation closing in on the hyper-inflation level of 50% price increases per month. To the surprise of many, a governor from the small and poor Northeastern state of Alagoas won on a platform of a populist, moralistic, and essentially rightist campaign. Fernando Collor de Mello began his government with a highly unusual and quite authoritarian economic shock, which involved the freezing of personal financial assets kept in the banking system. The justification offered for this extraordinary action was the need to reduce the immense liquidity in the market. More significant in the long term was his initiation of the neoliberal discourse in Brazil known as the "Washington Consensus." Collor took the first measures toward the opening of the market to international competition, the promotion of foreign investments, and finally the privatization of the economy and the liquidation of the government monopolies in the production of goods and services.

This neoliberal agenda meant the end of Brazil's traditional state intervention in the economy, both as regulator and producer. Given that a small party had been his base and that he gained the election because of the fear of the supposedly radical Lula, he owed nothing to any major political or economic groups and felt empowered to make fundamental changes in the economy. But his political isolation, his authoritarian governing style, and the economy's continued deterioration, along with clear evidence of massive personal corruption, led to formal impeachment of the president. The anti-Collor campaign called forth mass popular demonstrations; nevertheless, the impeachment took place within constitutional rules and without an institutional crisis, a key indicator of the maturation of the democratic process.

While the new government of Itamar Franco, Collor's vice-president, maintained the neoliberal program, it also succeeded in establishing the most successful post-1950 plan for the stability of the economy and the resolution of the structural inflation which was so fundamental a part of the growth of the Brazilian economy. In December 1993, it adopted the *"Plan Real."* This complex program brought down inflation and had a profound effect on the economy. The success of the *Plan Real*, which was carried out under Fernando Henrique Cardoso as Minister of Finance, enabled him to win the presidential election of 1994. Once elected, Fernando Henrique Cardoso focused on the consolidation of the Stability Plan while implementing a broad program of neoliberal reforms. This dismantling of the interventionist state now became a full-fledged and consistent program of the government, and by the end of his two terms the transformation of the Brazilian state from an active agent in the national productive structure to a regulatory state which left production to the private sector was completed. The Brazilian state would henceforth limit its actions to typical state responsibilities in the areas of security, justice, education, welfare, and health. Tariff reforms were enacted to open up the national market to international competition, and state monopolies in oil, electric power, telecommunications, and coastal shipping were disbanded. Cardoso also tried to implement a broad social security and public administration reform program but much of this program was not enacted due to the high political cost of Cardoso's demand for a second term. The administration wasted much of its energy, political capital, and credibility in an effort to approve a constitutional amendment that allowed the reelection of executive officers at the three levels of government.

Following his two terms in office, Fernando Henrique Cardoso was replaced by the leader of the Workers' Party, Luiz Inácio Lula da Silva. With its coming to power, however, the Workers' Party moved more to the center, thus causing many defections from its ranks as it reduced its radical program in order first to gain the presidential elections and then to maintain Brazil's international economic stability. But in this first administration Lula and the party leaders began to work on many of the social and political reforms which had been discussed but not implemented under the Cardoso governments. Major changes were finally made to the social security system. Against the opposition of the party's traditional supporters among government workers, it forced them to become a paying part of the system. At the same time, all the previous income transfer programs were brought together in the *Bolsa Família* (Family Grant Program), which now included everything for the support for children's education to retirement income for persons not in the social security system. In addition to the expansion of *Bolsa Família*, and continuing support for all the income transfer programs such as the National Family Agriculture Program, the Lula government launched numerous important new programs for popular housing, student fellowships, national electrification, and a host of others. It also increased the real minimum wage (*salário mínimo*), the key base on which all salaries and grants were calculated, which would have a profound impact on the national population.

But for all its initial success and popularity the party virtually collapsed in 2005 due to a massive corruption scandal. Rather than playing the democratic game, the party had paid monthly fees to opposition politicians to support its programs. That systematic and pervasive corruption eventually involved not only the extraction of government funds and private money from special interest groups to support electoral campaigns and purchase opposition votes, but, as was inevitable, it involved traditional personal corruption as well. Within the space of a few months, in mid-2005, almost all of the leadership of the party was caught up in these corruption scandals and forced from the government, and the party was seriously fractured as a result.

Although Lula was elected for a second term in 2006, the party had lost its seasoned leaders to corruption. This and the slow abandonment of the liberal program he carried through from the Cardoso period to the end of his first term would in turn have a profound impact on the economy and politics. The government did continue some social reforms and obtained major popularity through its increase of conditional cash transfers to the population, above all the *Bolsa Família*, which had a major impact on poverty reduction in Brazil. Lula's great popularity at the end of his term in 2010 allowed him to choose Dilma Rousseff as President of the Republic. But the turn back toward protectionism and defense of national industry would increasingly lead to lower growth and finally to a major recession in 2015–2016. Equally, the Workers' Party corruption schemes only increased in his second term and during the government of Dilma with the national petroleum company *Petrobras* becoming a major source of illicit funds for the party, its leaders, and other private individuals, all leading to the near collapse of this major international company.

All of this corruption revealed in the *Lava Jato* (or "operation car wash") investigation destroyed the legitimacy of the government. This investigation started with a seemingly small-time money-laundering operation in Curitiba that eventually revealed an enormous national corruption scheme which affected all the major parties – initially the Workers' Party and its allies, but later reaching all the other parties. At the same time, the impact of the government's abandonment of fiscal constraint in the name of growth drove the national economy into the worst recession in the nation's history. Popular opposition to the government finally led to calls for Dilma's impeachment, which was carried out on the grounds of her violation of fundamental fiscal laws of the state. The trail and the ultimate conviction were undertaken with the support of Congress as well as the Supreme Court, the majority of whose members were appointed by the Workers' Party.

The weakness of the succeeding Michel Temer government and the dramatic rejection of the Workers' Party by an expressive part of the Brazilian population allowed for the emergence of a conservative current, led by a former military man. With a conservative political, social, and cultural point of view, but defending liberal reforms, Jair Bolsonaro presented himself as exemplifying an anti-Workers' Party. Bolsonaro created a new party which swept through the country and succeeded in electing several state governors and a significant number of members in the National Congress. Although Bolsonaro himself had defended traditional nationalist, protectionist, and corporatist positions when he was in Congress, he appointed classic neoliberals to the economic ministries. At the same time, he appointed a series of retired military personnel to strategic positions in the government. For the moment, the position of the military officers that made up a large part of the presidential administration has been to defend the democratic process. The government itself seems to be based on a rough coalition of evangelicals and ruralists, with strong support from the business community. But, at the same time, it has expressed some rather conservative cultural positions which could create long-term conflict. The new government in all its economic appointments is clearly committed to continuation of the neoliberal program. It has also begun a major effort to control crime and has undertaken a major reform of pensions, one of the costliest programs of the national government. For the moment it is unclear what the final direction of this relatively diffused government will be, and the appointment of several extremely conservative figures in several ministries has created concern in broad segments of Brazilian society and the international community.

Despite two impeachments and serious problems of corruption and vote buying, the country since 1985 has had free elections and a basic commitment to democratic institutions, which do not appear threatened by the strong influence of the military in the current government. While the party structure remains weak and the government has difficulty in carrying out basic reforms, slowly but steadily many reforms have been carried through. The various governments since the 1990s have succeeded in systematically reducing poverty through the stabilization of the economy and the effective creation of multiple social programs, above all its income transfer programs, which led to some 30 million Brazilians moving into the middle class. While the recent economic crisis did increase the poverty rate again and thus caused a pause in the decline in inequality, it is still not a dominant trend and it is hoped that future economic and political developments will lead to a return to declining inequality in Brazil.

Along with these long-term political developments, the twentieth century marked a crucial change in the economic history of Brazil, with the transition of the nation from an agricultural and mining economy to an industrial one. From its colonization by the Portuguese in the sixteenth century until the late twentieth century, Brazil had depended on mineral exports and single crops – sugar until the end of the eighteenth century and coffee in the nineteenth and twentieth centuries. Slave labor was the major component of labor dedicated to export markets and survived until 1888. It was then replaced by subsidized European immigration from the 1880s until the 1920s. But from the 1930s onward each successive government promoted industrialization and eventually the modernization of Brazilian agriculture.

For the first seventy years of the twentieth century, Brazil experienced a long period of growth. Initially, sustained by the exportation of coffee and later by a process of induced industrialization through the substitution of imports, the country was able to create an ample and complex industrial structure without parallel in Latin America. By the late 1970s, Brazil had established an industrial structure which included an important capital goods sector. The continental size of the country created a market of a scale sufficient to sustain not only a consumer durable goods industry, but one which could produce both basic inputs and finished capital goods as well. This long process of growth was broken by a series of external crises which affected Brazil and the majority of the developing countries at the end of the decade of the 1970s. The crisis began to unfold with the first oil shock of 1973, was reinforced by the second one of 1979, and was followed by the External Debt Crisis of the 1980s. These shocks, for both Brazil and the rest of Latin America, broke their long trend of growth in the twentieth century. In the case of Brazil, the average rate of growth, which had been 5.7% per annum by the last years of the 1970s, dropped to 2.1% in the last twenty years of the century. This later rate of growth was insufficient to maintain the well-being of a still poor country, with great social and income inequalities and with a population growing at 1.7% annually. The post-1970s crisis was also accompanied in Brazil by a seemingly uncontrollable inflation and an ever increasing public debt.

This process of accelerated growth for eighty years began under liberal governments and after 1930 continued with a new orientation and economic policy by leaders who brought the government into direct management of the economy. Beginning with the international crisis of the 1930s, the government under Vargas, and later under Kubitschek,[10] and again under the

---

[10] Among the numerous studies on the economy of the period prior to the *golpe militar*, see Draibe, *Rumos e metamorfoses*; Carlos Lessa, *Quinze anos de política econômica* (São Paulo: Brasiliense, 1981); Benevides, *O governo Kubitschek*; Maria da Conceição Tavares, "Auge

nationalist military regimes of 1964–1985, developed an economic policy which stressed the forced growth of the industrial and agricultural sectors as well as the modernization of the financial sector. These massive government expenditures also created an inflationary pressure which lasted for three decades despite sustained growth of the economy.

While industrialization since the 1930s had increased rapidly, it was under the military regime of 1964–1985 when the industrial sector was fully integrated, with a major expansion of whole new sectors such as petrochemicals and capital goods. At the same time, the military heavily subsidized national agriculture with credits and price supports, forcing it to modernize with the massive introduction of machinery, fertilizers, insecticides, and new crops. They also put into practice a program of stabilization and fiscal reforms with little opposition given the authoritarian nature of the state. In response to the increasing inflation due to massive government spending, they implemented a system of monetary correction for inflation known as indexation. This indexation was first put into effect as a correction for taxes collected and it greatly aided the national treasury in an economy suffering high inflation. Indexation was next applied to the Federal Public Deficit, allowing the sale of public bonds of both short and long term maturity for the first time. Indexation explains how Brazil was able to create a relatively sophisticated capital market from the 1970s onward, though inflation never completely disappeared. If this was a positive result of the creation of monetary correction, the experience of the 1980s and 1990s showed that indexation prevented the control of inflation itself. But these fiscal reforms strongly reduced the public deficit and allowed it to be financed by the sale of government bonds rather than by the previous policy of emission of money.[11]

e declínio do processo de substituição," in Maria da Conceição Tavares, ed., *Da substituição de importações ao capitalismo financeiro* (Rio de Janeiro: Zahar, 1972); Albert Hirschman, "The Political Economy of Import Substitution Industrialization in Latin America," *Quartely of Economics* 82 (1968); Albert Fishlow, "Origens e consequências da substituição de importações no Brasil," in Flavio Versiani and José Roberto Mendonça de Barros, eds., *Formação econômica do brasil: a experiência de industrialização* (São Paulo: Anpec/Saraiva, 1976); Annibal Villanova Villela and Wilson Suzigan, *Política do governo e crescimento da economia brasileira, 1889–1945* (Rio de Janeiro: Ipea, 1973); Antonio Barros de Castro, *Sete ensaios sobre a economia brasileira* (São Paulo: Forense, 1969); Marcelo de Paiva Abreu, "Inflação, estagnação e ruptura: 1961–1964," in Marcelo de Paiva Abreu and Dionísio Dias Carneiro Netto, eds., *A ordem do progresso: cem anos de política econômica republicana, 1889–1989* (Rio de Janeiro: Campus, 1990), pp. 197–231; José Serra, "Ciclos e mudanças estruturais na economia brasileira do pós-guerra," in Luiz Gonzaga de Mello Belluzzo and Renata Coutinho, eds., *Desenvolvimento capitalista no brasil: ensaios sobre a crise* (São Paulo: Brasiliense, 1981).

11 André Lara Rezende, "Estabilização e reforma," in Paiva Abreu, Mario Henrique Simonsen, and Roberto Campos, eds., *A nova economia brasileira* (Rio de Janeiro: José Olympio,

At the same time, the government carried out a policy of deliberate reduction of real wages as another factor in promoting industrial growth in a high-cost protected market, by underestimating the impact of inflation on wage adjustments. This policy was called the "wage squeeze" and restrained both aggregate demand and the costs of labor for private enterprise. Given the control over unions and strikes, the military were able to significantly reduce real wages. The average annual minimum wage, for example, went in real terms from 100 in 1964 to 71 in 1967.[12] This had a perverse distributive effect, and clearly transferred to workers part of the adjustment in aggregate demand.[13]

There were also several reforms which both stabilized the financial sector but also began to generate capital for social activity. The government established the basis of a new banking and capital markets system by creating a Central Bank (*Banco Central do Brasil*). In the same period came a new financial system for housing, through the creation of the National Housing Bank (*Banco Nacional da Habitação*). These funds for housing were generated through a national system of forced savings. The government also changed paid dismissals and replaced them with the Guaranteed Fund for Time of Service (*Fundo de Garantia por Tempo de Serviço*). Companies deposited monthly a fixed percentage of a worker's salary in a bank account in the name of the worker. Workers could then withdraw these sums in the case of dismissal by their employers. These deposits could also be used by the employee in special situations, such as the purchase of a home and/or as their retirement income. The Fund became an important instrument of long-term savings for workers, and its resources represented the principal source of capital for housing and sanitation construction, which developed significantly in this period.

In addition to these reforms, the government directed all its efforts at increasing growth by using traditional incentives and subsidies to jump start the economy. It immediately implanted an expansionist policy, but at the

---

1979); Celso Furtado, *Um projeto para o Brasil* (Rio de Janeiro: Saga, 1968); Albert Fishlow, "Algumas reflexões sobre a política brasileira após 1964," *Estudos CEBRAP* 6 (1974); Mario Henrique Simonsen, *Inflação, Gradualismo x Tratamento de Choque* (Rio de Janeiro: Apec, 1970); Fishlow, "A distribuição de renda no Brasil."

[12] Ipeadata, "Série salário mínimo real." Accessed 22 June 2018, at: www.ipeadata.gov.br/D efault.aspx. The fall of the real minimum wage after the military coup inaugurated a process of decline in that wage, which would only begin its reversal in the mid-1990s, with the stabilization of the economy. But while the minimum wage has doubled in real terms over the last twenty years, it has not yet reached the purchasing power of 1964.

[13] Various authors have dealt with this, like Albert Fishlow, who emphasized the negative character of the measures enacted by the military regime. See Albert Fishlow, "A distribuição de renda no Brasil," in R. Tolipan and A. C. Tinelli, eds., *A controvérsia sobre a distribuição de renda e desenvolvimento* (Rio de Janeiro: Zahar, 1975).

same time put in place an ample system of control and administration of prices. It created a major system of subsidies for determined areas of the economy, especially for the export sector and agriculture. To reduce food prices, which had a major impact on inflation, the government created a sophisticated system of abundant and subsidized credit for farmers, which permitted the rapid growth of this sector. Besides abundant credit, subsidies, and fiscal advantages, the export sector now counted, with a realistic exchange rate that was maintained at a relatively stable rate through a system of periodic mini exchange devaluations which accompanied the differentials between the internal and external rates of inflation. The government also created a system of voluntary and forced savings and directed much of these savings into new economic activity. Fiscal incentives for the capital market were granted since this was seen as a fundamental instrument to mobilize savings necessary to promote growth. The federal government also made its public enterprises invest in areas of infrastructure, and by its direct action through these state enterprises it began to exercise immense control over both public and private decisions in the economy. Now few private projects were established in Brazil without the approval of some public institution, either for obtaining credit or authorization to import goods, or some other type of subsidy. Few products escaped formal price controls. Finally, the state was the grand producer of energy, steel, minerals, fuels, fertilizers, and chemical products and it also controlled port services, telecommunications, and railroads.

Despite the persistence of inflation, indexation permitted the government to create a sophisticated system of finance for long-term investments through the mobilization of both voluntary and forced savings. This led to a large public works program by the government and the state enterprises, expanding employment in this sector and incorporating new workers within the formal sector of the economy. In the industrial area there was a strong expansion in the production of durable consumer goods, including automobiles. The economy benefited from the program of public and private investments, which resulted in the expansion of the urban labor market and in the companies that were created or that expanded, as well as in the construction sector, which were the pull factors which influenced the great migrations of workers from the countryside to the cities.

Gross national product grew at an average annual rate of 10% between 1967 and 1973 and the industrial sector showed an ever higher rate of growth.[14] The economy was modernized, and this explosive growth led to

[14] Data obtained at Ipeadata, IBGE/SCN, PIB, "Variação real anual e PIB da indústria de transformação, valor adicionado, valor real anual."

the incorporation of more workers into the formal labor market and the consolidation of a middle class of consumers, substantially altering the Brazilian social structure. Aside from the success of the economic policy adopted internally, the country also benefited from a period of strong international growth which saw most of the countries of Latin America expanding at a very high average rate of growth.

But all this growth was accompanied by a process of income concentration which occurred for a variety of reasons, but most particularly because of the restrictive salary policy adopted by the government which prevented the gains to productivity obtained by the new economy from being transferred to the workers. Most of the gains were appropriated in the form of profits, which furthered the profound unequal distribution of income within Brazilian society. The very system of subsidies reinforced this pattern of concentration.[15] There was growth, which benefited everyone, but those gains were not equitably distributed among all social classes and this would lead to increasing concentrations of wealth.

It is also evident that while indexing kept the economy functioning, high levels of inflation had a direct impact on workers' standards of living. Wages paid weekly, bimonthly, or monthly had to be spent immediately or they would lose their value. The salary correction rules represented one of the main sources of distributive conflict between workers and government authorities. The initially annual rule for correcting salaries was gradually changed to a half-yearly, quarterly, and then monthly adjustment, but even then, it still lagged behind actual inflation. This intense inflationary pressure also led to class and institutional conflict. Since a large percentage of the labor force in this period was unorganized, in part because of the repression of the authoritarian government, the impact of inflation on the poorer classes was profound.[16]

[15] There was in this period an extensive debate over the question of income concentration. The government affirmed that the high levels of inequality of income distribution was a transitory phenomenon caused by the growth process, while other economists held different opinions. Some argued that there were structural reasons for this distorted distribution, and it would not be eliminated with growth. Others blamed the government's repressive salary policy as the cause for this concentration. On this theme see Carlos G. Langoni, *Distribuição da renda e desenvolvimento econômico do Brasil* (Rio de Janeiro: Expressão e Cultura, 1973); Albert Fishlow, "Brazilian Size Distribution of Income." *American Economic Review* 62.1–2 (1972), pp. 391–402; Edmar Bacha and L. Taylor, "Brazilian Income Distribution in the 1960s: 'Facts,' Model Results and the Controversy," in Lance Taylor, Edmar Lisboa Bacha, and Eliana A. Cardoso, eds., *Models of Growth and Distribution for Brasil* (New York: Oxford University Press, 1980); Ramos and Reis, "Distribuição da renda," pp. 21–45.

[16] Francisco H. G. Ferreira, Philippe G. Leite. Julie A. Litchfield, and Gabriel Ulyssea, "Ascensão e queda da desigualdade de renda no Brasil, *Econômica* 8.1 (2006), p. 150.

The process of increasing external debt represented the other negative aspect of the growth policy of the military regime of this period. Brazilian economic crises are traditionally generated by external market conditions. This explains why the military governments greatly stimulated exports and opened the country to foreign capital, in terms of both direct investments and loans. Because of their lower costs and longer repayment schedules compared to the local lending market, there was a great increase in private financing from abroad. This policy of relying on private international credit fundamentally changed the structure of the external Brazilian debt. Until then this debt was based on official sources of credit such as the World Bank or foreign government loans given over long terms and obtained at fixed rates. The new debt modality, which included financing of the state industries, was based on private short- and medium-term international banking loans with fluctuating interest rates and relatively elevated costs compared to those charged by the previously dominant international agencies. The increase of the external debt, its greater costs and its floating interest rates made the country more vulnerable to changes in the international economy. The first petroleum shock in 1973 was a very clear signal of the next crisis, which would manifest itself in the decade of the 1980s.

The petroleum shock of 1973 profoundly affected the country, since 73% of Brazil's fuel consumption was imported. The trade balance went into deficit and inflation reached 30%. The majority of countries affected by the oil crisis adopted recessionary programs, trying to restrain internal demand and adjust their economies to a new situation of costly energy. These importing countries also had to transfer an important part of their income to the petroleum exporting countries. The Brazilian government followed an alternative route, energizing the economy and developing an ambitious program of investments aimed at increasing the internal offer of capital goods and basic consumption items, thus reducing dependency on imports. The military regime needed political support and opted to adopt aggressive investment policies, seeking to complete its industrialization process. The abundance of external capital generated by the recycling of resources created by the petroleum exporting countries permitted Brazil to follow such a trajectory through an ample system of international loans, but at the cost of a growing internal and external debt, an accelerating inflation, and a progressive liquidation of the financial capacity of the state.[17]

[17] On the period of Geisel, see Antonio Barros de Castro and Francisco Eduardo Pires de Souza, *A economia brasileira em marcha forçada* (Rio de Janeiro: Paz e Terra, 1985); Dionísio Dias Carneiro, "Crise e esperança: 1974–1980," in Abreu and Netto, *A ordem do progresso,*

By the end of the military regime, the country had suffered a profound transformation in its economy; but it remained financially vulnerable. Government support effectively completed the process of import substitution, giving the Brazilian industrial core a totally integrated structure, with an important new capital goods sector. The country now contained one of the largest and most integrated and complex industrial sectors of any developing country. But through this period the country had suffered simultaneously the impact of the increase of oil prices, the acceleration of international interest rates, as well as the slow growth of world exports. The Brazilian option of maintaining the level of economic activity, which was defined by an annual growth rate greater than 6% during this period, led to a high deficit in current transactions. By 1981, the interest paid on the external debt represented half of the value of all Brazilian exports. The stage was then set for an external Brazilian crisis in the context of a deteriorating international financial market. At the same time, by 1979, national inflation surpassed 50% per annum.

In 1982 came the Mexican Debt Crisis. This was the beginning of the world "External Debt Crisis" that would extend through the 1980s and would affect virtually every Latin American country, which were then obliged to restructure their external debt. It was a long period of low growth, with very high social and political costs to the majority of these countries. Most countries turned to the International Monetary Fund (IMF) for help in restructuring their debt with private banks which required them to adopt recessionary adjustment plans. These plans were designed to carry out monetary adjustment of the balance of payments through the reduction of internal consumption, especially through reduction in public spending. Debtor countries needed to obtain a surplus in their balance of trade in order to pay the interest on their external loans and, if possible, amortize the principal.

The international banks closed their doors to Brazil. They demanded that Brazil sign a formal agreement with the IMF to monitor its economic performance, which it did in 1983. But the economic situation continued to deteriorate, since the lack of reserves made the country delay its repayments. Initially, the restrictive internal measures and devaluation, along with

pp. 295–322; Rogério Werneck, *Empresas estatais e política macroeconomica* (Rio de Janeiro: Campus, 1987); Rafael Luís Spegler, "Racionalidade política e econômica no governo Geisel (1974–1979): Um estudo sobre o II PND e o projeto de institucionalização do regime militar," MA thesis, Universidade Federal do Rio Grande do Sul, Porto Alegre, 2015; Pedro Cezar Dutra Fonseca and Sérgio Marley Modesto Monteiro, "O Estado e suas razões: o II PND," *Revista de Economia Política* 28.1 (2008), pp. 28–46; Vanessa Boarati, "A defesa da estratégia desenvolvimentista, II PND," *História Econômica & História de Empresas* 8.1 (2005), pp. 163–193.

favorable international conditions, helped Brazil. GNP grew by a very sub-
stantial 5.4% in 1984, but inflation reached a new high, surpassing 200%
a year.[18] At this rate, even the generalized indexation process was incapable
of controlling its impact. In an attempt to contain the inflationary process,
salaries and public tariffs were corrected less frequently, causing serious
problems of financing for companies that supplied these services and the
deterioration of the public accounts. This was the situation when the military
left power.

The other relevant aspect of the crisis of the 1980s was the ongoing
inflation. Usually policies that reduced internal consumption were efficient
in containing inflationary pressures. However, the Brazilian example
appeared to suggest that there was a component of inflationary inertia and
that the conventional methods were not effective in an economy that had
such a high degree of indexation. In the first half of the 1980s appeared the
first suggestions of alternative policies to fight inflation.[19] These studies
formed the background for the "*Plan Cruzado*" of 1986 – the first of several
such plans which were only successful with the *Plan Real* in 1994. The *Plan
Real* took place after the external debt negotiations were concluded, which
allowed greater control over Brazil's international obligations.[20] Brazil had
fallen behind its external obligations in 1983 and declared a moratorium in
1987. But in November 1993 it reached an agreement with more than 800
creditors and with this accord the country could return to the international
credit market for funds.

It is usual to call the 1980s "the lost decade." In fact, from the political
point of view, there were enormous democratic advances. But from the
economic point of view the 1980s broke a long cycle of rapid growth that
the country had experienced in the first seventy years of the century. In the
1980s, the economy presented an accumulated growth of a bit more than

---

[18] On the crisis and process of adjustment, see Dionísio Dias Carneiro and Eduardo Modiano,
"Ajuste externo e desequilíbrio interno: 1980–1894," in Abreu and Netto, *A ordem do
progresso*, pp. 323–346; Mario Henrique Simonsen, "Inflação brasileira: lições
e perspectivas," *Revista Brasileira de Economia* 5.4 (1985), pp. 15–31; Winston Fritsch,
"A crise cambial de 1982–83 no Brasil: origens e respostas," in C. A. Plastino and R. Bouzas,
eds., *A América Latina e a crise Internacional* (Rio de Janeiro: Graal, 1988); Rogério
L. F. Werneck, "Poupança estatal, dívida externa e crise financeira do setor público,"
Pesquisa e Planejamento Econômico 16.3 (1986), pp. 551–574.

[19] See Persio Arida and André Lara Resende, "Inertial Inflation and Monetary Reform in
Brazil," in J. Williamson, ed., *Inflation and Indexation: Argentina Brazil and Israel*
(Cambridge, MA: MIT Press, 1985) and Francisco L. Lopes, *O Choque Heterodoxo:
combate à inflação e reforma monetária* (Rio de Janeiro: Campus, 1986).

[20] The ex-minister João Sayad, one of the implementers of the *Plan Cruzado*, has made an
interesting comparison between this plan and the *Plan Real*. See João Sayad, *Planos cruzado
e real: acertos e desacertos* (Rio de Janeiro: Ipea, 2000).

30%, as against 130% growth overall in the previous decade. Brazil was not the only developing country to experience this mediocre economic performance in the 1980s. In this period few countries in the region where able to balance their external accounts and restore their capacity for growth.

In 1990 came an abrupt change in government policy, with the adoption of the Washington Consensus, which was a series of neoliberal reforms designed to remove the government from market control and participation. This ideology came late to Brazil, even by Latin American standards. The neoliberal ideology dictated the freedom of the market and opposed previous economic policies which promoted the state's role in the economy. It was held that the state should not be an active player in the economy, but rather should defend the currency, stabilize prices, and guarantee contracts and free competition. Its only role was in education, health, and other social services. In just a few years, neoliberal ideology gained political strength in the principal industrialized countries and quickly spread to the rest of the world. Once this neoliberal economic and ideological reform program was established in Brazil, it would slowly come to dominate government policy from the late 1990s onward, thus breaking with the statist tradition of the previous fifty years.

At the same time, there emerged new processes for production, introduced with new technology and forms of administration. Management, production, and the market now transcended traditional national borders, and were part of a process of globalization. The productive restructuring, the liberation from government control, and globalization made competition more fierce, not only in the market of goods, but in the labor market as well, increasing inequality, social exclusion, and job insecurity: weakening the institutions in general, particularly those designed for social protection. Neoliberalism preached the end of any restrictions in the workplace and was hostile both to unions and state intervention.

It is not hard to understand why such ideas came late in the case of Brazil, where the model of development had been based on a major participation of the public sector in the national economy through state-owned industries, and where national industry was quite advanced compared to other emerging countries. This system was based on deep mutual interests between the public sector and the state bureaucracy, private national entrepreneurs, and foreign capital, through a broadly based system of public credit, administered prices, protective tariffs, and subsidies. Some productive sectors even without any form of monopoly were owned almost entirely by the public sector, as in the case of steel. Whole sectors were under the control of combined state–private, national–foreign companies, such as the petrochemical industry. There were public monopolies like that of petroleum. The public sector was practically the only producer of electricity, and there was profound integration between national private and foreign capital, as in the auto industry. From the time of the Geisel government, the Brazilian industrial sector was practically self-sufficient, closed to world markets, imported relatively few inputs, and even produced capital goods on a major scale. The only exception was petroleum imports. Compared to the other Latin American countries, Brazil had a traditional entrepreneurial base, high earnings, and a deep managerial capacity.

In 1991, the Mercosul agreement created a regional multinational market between Argentina, Brazil, Paraguay, and Uruguay, which led to further tariff reductions, and created another reduced tariff system among these countries. The rise of Mercosul has undoubtedly created an important world free-trade zone and has led to major growth of inter-American trade in South America. Although the succession of external crises of member countries required successive renegotiations of trade rules, an important regional market was created for the member countries.

The opening of the national market to international competition was also a basic element of the *Plan Real*.[21] The fast opening of the national economy and its exposure to international competition, at the same time as the overvalued exchange was being used as a base for the *Plan Real*, had a positive effect on the stability of prices. The imported goods had their prices contained or even reduced by competition. The idea was to expose the Brazilian economy to international competition and also represented integration in the process of productive globalization, with repercussions on the productive structure in Brazil and on labor relations.

But the stabilization brought on by the *Plan Real* also stimulated the expansion of credit, both consumer and corporate. The price to pay for all this was the reversal of the commercial balance, which now turned negative. Maintaining a high real interest rate was necessary to attract capital and maintain the balance of payments. The result was the Real increased in value, making exports even less attractive. There was now a growing dependence on international resources to close the deficit in foreign accounts. The various international crises of the 1990s led to the flight of capital causing a serious fall in national reserves. Faced with this crisis, the government took a series of drastic measures. Interest rates were increased still more, reaching more than

---

[21] Maurício Mesquita Moreira and Paulo Guilherme Correa, "Abertura comercial e indústria: o que se pode esperar e o que se vem obtendo," *Revista de Economia Política* 17.2 (1997), pp. 61–91; Abreu and Werneck, "Estabilização, abertura e privatização," in Abreu, ed., *A ordem do progresso: dois séculos de política econômica no Brasil* (2nd edn; Rio de Janeiro: Elsevier, 2014), pp. 263–280; André Averbug, "Abertura e Integração Comercial Brasileira na Década de 90," *A abertura brasileira* 90. 1 (1999), pp. 43–82.

60% per annum. Even more critically, there was a drastic increase in compulsory bank reserves and a reduction in consumer credit. Taxes on a number of consumer imported goods were raised and quotas were imposed on the importation of automobiles. The exchange regime was altered to permit a gradual devaluation of the Real, but the Real still remained over-valued. All these measured dramatically restricted the liquidity of the economy and imposed a severe brake on economic activity.

In this second half of the 1990s, many companies went bankrupt, and these measures even had an impact on some large national banks which were already facing problems due to the adjustment they had to make because of the end of inflation. To avoid further bankruptcies in the financial sector, the government allowed the *Banco Central* to intervene in the troubled financial institutions. But, despite the criticisms about the negative impact of an open economy and an overvalued currency, this strategy was maintained and reinforced. Then came the Asian Crisis, a crisis that quickly swept through all emerging countries.

Despite the abundant funds obtained by the state through its privatization program of state-owned companies, the public accounts soon deteriorated because of the high interest rates maintained to attract foreign resources. Then came the Russian Crisis of 1998, which brought another harsh blow to the country. International instability grew and the reaction of the Brazilian authorities remained the same: interest rates and taxes were raised and there was a reduction of public spending, all in agreement with the IMF. But this package of measures was not enough to calm the market since Brazil was considered too vulnerable. The deepening of the crisis led to emergency aid being given by the IMF and the developed countries, which in turn feared the risk that a Brazilian default could have on the international financial system. The aid agreement of December 1998 provided a major credit to Brazil, but in that year, growth was zero, and unemployment increased again. The crisis was now called the Brazilian crisis and was due to the refusal of the government to change its exchange policy. But in January 1999 it was forced to allow the exchange rate to float freely, and the real immediately declined by over 60% to the dollar.

The 1990s were thus another lost decade in terms of growth. GDP increased by only 30% in the decade, which represented a rate of only 2.2% a year. Better than the 1.3% from the previous decade, but far from the 7.1% per annum growth rates of the 1970s. The accumulated growth of both decades, 50%, was too low for the population increase of 37% in the same period. That represented a gross increase per capita of only 15% for a country whose population lives mainly with poor health care, low living standards and inefficient sanitary conditions, and with educational deficiencies. Although growth of the 1970s could probably not have been sustained at those extraordinarily high levels, this weak growth of the 1980s and 1990s, though positive, was still below what might have occurred given the major transformations taking place in Brazil. Moreover, in this, Brazil was like almost all the other countries of Latin America which suffered low or stagnant growth in these two decades due to international conditions.

The situation in Latin America became even harder after Argentina declared a moratorium in 2001. The financial markets became even more aggressive and capital became scarce for emerging economies. Brazil suffered a massive reduction in foreign credit even on its regular trade lines, usually the ones with the smallest risk and the greatest stability even in time of foreign turbulence.

But the steady increase in international prices for primary goods due to the explosive growth of China now had a major impact on Brazil. While the Brazilian industrial sector of the economy grew less competitive over time, the agricultural sector became one of the most competitive producers in the world. The two first decades of the twenty-first century would see an explosive growth of agricultural production and exports with an increasingly positive balance of trade. This was the period when Brazilian soybeans and corn became major competitors to the previously dominant United States. By 2016, Brazil had become the world's third largest agricultural producer behind the European Union and the United States, and far ahead of Australia and Canada.[22] It also achieved the greatest surplus of any exporter in its agricultural trade, as few agricultural imports arrived at what was now an economy that was almost totally self-sufficient in food production.

Once inflation was under control and foreign debts began to be resolved, the period from the end of the second administration of Fernando Henrique Cardoso (FHC) through the first administration of Lula saw a rapid growth in the economy, reaching 5.7% annual growth in 2004. It was a scenario that would allow for significant growth in the Lula period, due to both the stabilization obtained by the FHC government in an exceptional period in the international market and the maintenance of the fundamentals of neoliberal economic policy. But in the second term of President Lula the government began to shift toward the resumption of the state taking a fundamental role in the economy to accelerate growth. Fiscal policy would be used this time to fund not only public investments but significant private investments as well, all in the form of financing, subsidies, and

---

[22] FAO, *The State of Agricultural Commodity Markets 2018: Agricultural Trade, Climate Change and Food Security* (Rome: Food and Agriculture Organization of the United Nations, 2008), p. 6, Table 1.2.

incentives. The concept of the regulatory state was abandoned to expand the role of the state in promoting development. This change in the direction of economic policy would be reinforced as a result of the international crisis of 2008.

The conduct of economic policy was not just a conjunctural policy to overcome the crisis of 2008 but indicated a profound change in the fundamentals of government policy. Growth became its main objective. In the promotion of investments, the role of the state development bank, BNDES (*Banco Nacional de Desenvolvimento Economico e Social*), was expanded to include the financing of the public and the private sectors. The government and its development bank started aggressively to finance infrastructure, and also to promote the consolidation of national private groups seeking to create competitive national companies in the international market. One of the more spectacular developments supported by the development bank was the assistance it gave in the creation of JBS, the world's largest meatpacking company, which began as a local producer in Goiás.

The government also tried to support new industries. Thus, the national oil company, *Petrobras*, in addition to becoming the sole operator of exploration activity in the newly discovered offshore petroleum fields known as the pre-salt area, was required to make purchases from local suppliers of all its basic needs, including modern sophisticated equipment and ships not then in local production. This development policy was intended to act on the supply side by massive public investments in the energy and infrastructure sectors, along with credit and incentives to the national industry. Production, consumer, and housing loans grew significantly. Public expenditures in general were broadened, particularly in social programs. But it was more effective in boosting demand. There was a strong expansion of credit in general, and, in addition, the policy of systematically increasing the minimum wage also increased the demand of the lower classes of the population. But an exchange policy was practiced that discouraged national production in all segments, particularly in the industrial area.

The Dilma administration reinforced this orientation, focused on growth, moving further away from the basic lines of economic stability and its fundamentals, in terms of inflation targets and the primary surplus. The new government clearly adopted strong state intervention and an active industrial policy supported by a broad system of subsidies and incentives, abundant credit, and protection in public procurement, particularly in the massive investments made by *Petrobras*. It was proposed that growth of demand would be met by local production, which would have a wide system of incentives and subsidies and this demand would be the engine of growth. The required fiscal effort would be offset by increased revenue from growth.

Despite the ideological constraints of the Workers' Party, an ambitious road, harbor, and airport concessions program was launched in the area of infrastructure.

In addition to the widely granted incentives and subsidies, which represented an important loss of revenue, state expenses were increased by the intensification of social programs, and, along with the constantly increasing pension payments, led to the deterioration of public accounts. Despite some earlier adjustments, there was no adequate reform of pensions that made the structure of financing and benefits of social security compatible with the new increase in the life expectancy of the population. Thus, the pension system overburdened public accounts. Thus began a gradual fiscal deterioration, which reached explosive levels at the end of 2014. By the end of her first administration, this new development model showed signs of exhaustion. Growth in the year was practically zero; inflation accelerated. The signs were clearly recessive, and the main economic indicators deteriorated. Throughout 2015 the picture became dramatic. In 2015, inflation surpassed 10%, GDP fell by 3.8%, and then in 2016 there was further decline in the GDP by 3.6%.

If the Fernando Henrique Cardoso government represented an advance from the standpoint of stabilization, controlling chronic inflation, renegotiating foreign debt, and promoting important state reforms, the Lula period consolidated stability, greatly added to the external reserves, and significantly expanded social programs. The Dilma Government, which undertook a development policy with no compatible fiscal base, created a serious crisis with a deterioration of public accounts, leading the country into a deep recession. This recession undermined some of the social gains made since the success of the stabilization program. Perhaps the most obvious symbol is the 12 million unemployed in 2016.

The post-Dilma governments have returned to the classic neoliberal position, though still maintaining the basic social programs. The Temer government was typically a transitional government. It succeeded in its stability program – controlling inflation, stalling the growth of the public deficit, and allowing the country to obtain positive numbers of growth, although close to zero. In addition, it promoted some important reforms and it raised the fundamental question of the necessity of social security reform. President Bolsonaro, who took office in early 2019, defends an ultraliberal program, with a proposed reduction of the state, and fiscal balance. The resumption of a steady growth path will be its great challenge, since it will not be able to rely on the state as an agent that promotes growth.

The country has grown little in the last forty years – just over 2% per annum, compared to about 7% in the forty years before that. This is low even compared to the performance of the main emerging countries. In addition,

Brazilian industry has lost international competitiveness, and although it has gone through phases of openness and competition it is today extremely protected and with low productivity. On the other hand, agriculture has performed exceptionally well, modernizing itself and fully integrating the main international value chains. Brazil is today one of the most important producers and exporters of agricultural products, leading in several products, such as soybeans and orange juice, thanks to the comparable productivity standards of the best and largest agricultural producers in the world. It also is now highly efficient, accounting for only 10% of the EAP and constantly expanding production without a significant increase in land utilization.

The performance of the Brazilian economy in the last two decades was largely stimulated by the spectacular growth of the Chinese economy. While industry was unable to respond fully, Brazilian agriculture benefited from the general rise in commodity prices in the international market. The Brazilian agricultural sector was exposed to external competition, subsidies and price supports were ended, and producers were forced to obtain private credit. There was a total reorganization of production into Value Chains, with agricultural processors, foreign trading companies, supermarkets, and cooperatives now replacing the government with private credit or using contract sales which had private parties offering inputs to farmers in return for their crops. There was also an expansion of the agricultural frontier, particularly in the Center-West region and accelerated production due to major increase in productivity. Brazil at the beginning of the twenty-first century became one of the largest and most competitive suppliers of agribusiness products in the international market.[23] Agribusiness exports amounted to US$25 billion in 2002 and reached over US$ 101 billion in 2018. As the sector's imports are relatively small, much of the positive Brazilian trade balance can be explained by the performance of the agrobusiness sector.[24]

This exceptional performance was obtained by the competitiveness of Brazilian production and by the high prices obtained for all the main products of the Brazilian agribusiness sector. If we consider the six products that account for about two-thirds of agricultural exports, we see that prices from 2008 have remained at 70% to 100% of the prices prevailing in 2004.[25] The positive position of the trade balance was due to the exceptional performance

[23] According to the Centro de Estudos Avançados em Economia Aplicada (EsalQ/USP), agrobusiness contributed 21.6% of GDP in 2017. See www.cepea.esalq.usp.br/.

[24] FIESP, Informativo DEAGRO (January 2018). Accessed 22 June 2018, at: www.fiesp.com.br /indices-pesquisas-e-publicacoes/balanca-comercial/.

[25] Considering the sugar-alcohol, soybean, citrus, chicken, beef, and coffee sectors. Data from the Secretaria de Relações Internacionais do Agronegócio, of the Ministério da Agricultura, Pecuária e Abastecimento.

of agribusiness, as Brazil lost competitiveness in the production of manufactured goods. Thus, in 2010, for example, the country generated a total trade balance of US$ 20 billion and agribusiness produced a balance of US$ 63 billion, which meant that the trade balance excluding agribusiness presented a negative balance of the order of US$ 43 billion.[26] Moreover, this has been the trend in all subsequent years. After the negative year of 2014 and the minimal positive balance of 2015, foreign trade has grown consistently since then and by 2018 the positive balance of trade was US$ 59 billion. But since agriculture in that year had a positive balance of US$ 87 billion it meant that excluding agribusiness trade balance was negative by US$ 28 billion.[27]

The importance of the international economy for Brazilian development is fundamental. External vulnerability has accompanied the country's economic development throughout the twentieth century. External shocks have created acute internal crises, affecting Brazil's international debt, and creating scarcity of reserves, and have generated continued external instability for Brazil, resulting in exchange controls that for decades represented the most relevant aspect of Brazilian economic policy. Thus, traditionally, the external debt service accounted for a significant part of the value of exports. But that changed from the mid-1990s. First, there was the success in negotiating the foreign debt coupled with the successful elimination of chronic inflation; then there was a long period of political stability and the continuity of economic policy for more than fifteen years. To this was added the potential of Brazilian agriculture and the evolution of local industry and its large domestic market, all of which transformed Brazil into one of the preferred destinations of foreign investors. These investors injected capital into the country in the form of Foreign Direct Investments or through short-term capital attracted by differential interest rates.

Thus, the period from 1950 to the present has been a trying time for the political evolution of Brazil. Emerging from the Vargas dictatorship, the democratic process remained fragile and under constant threat until 1964 when the military instituted a regime that lasted until 1985. Since then Brazil has succeeded in removing the Army control over the political system, impeached two presidents, passed an important constitution, and carried out free elections with high participation rates. Unfortunately, a weak party

---

[26] Banco Central do Brasil. Accessed 12 April 2018, at: www.bcb.gov.br/htms/infecon/Seriehist .asp>.

[27] Ministério da Economia, Indústria, Comércio Exterior e Serviços, *Séries históricas*, January 1997–August 2019, monthly and cumulative totals. Accessed 24 February 2019, at: www.mdic.gov.br/index.php/comercio-exterior/estatisticas-de-comercio-exterior/series-historicas; MAPA, Indicadores Gerais Agrostat. Accessed 24 February 2019, at: http://indicadores.agricultura.gov.br/agrostat/index.htm.

structure has led to high levels of corruption which has almost destroyed the federal and state government budgets and led to the collapse of state investments in infrastructure. The presidential system has also shown itself to be less than ideal for the country. At the same time, the ongoing levels of corruption involved in the electoral process have now affected an entire traditional class of political leaders who have been eliminated. But, at the same time, there have yet to appear seasoned political leaders, free of the questions about campaign financing, who could replace them. Fortunately, for all its problems in terms of delayed justice, the judicial system has proven to be a bulwark of the democratic regime. This period also has been one in which major industrialization occurred which created a massive urban labor force, and at the same time it was a period in which agriculture was modernized and became competitive on the world market. For all the periodic crises, most of the labor force has been moved out of the informal market, rural workers have been brought into the social security system and guaranteed all the traditional labor rights, and a social welfare and educational system has been developed which reaches the overwhelming majority of the national population. Finally, the extreme disparities in wealth, health, and education which existed at mid-century have been reduced as Brazil becomes a more coherent nation by the middle decades of the twenty-first century. It was in this context of industrial growth, modernization of agriculture, mass education, the creation of a modern welfare state, and urbanization of the population that social change would occur.

3

Demographic Change

Among the most dramatic changes in Brazil in this period were the industrialization of the country, the modernization of its agriculture, and its rapid urbanization: all of which set the stage for the single most dramatic historical change in the demographic structure of Brazil, which went from a pre-modern pattern of high fertility and high mortality to a post-demographic transition, with fertility and mortality close to the norms of the world's most advanced countries. The introduction of new contraception practices introduced from abroad effected this evolution and there is little question that these changes were quickly adopted by the entire national population, from the most depressed economic states of the North and Northeast to the most modern ones of the Southern regions. Some of that change was due to a significant rethinking of social norms about family size and fertility by the Brazilian population as it faced the demands of a new urban lifestyle. Some changes were due to the availability of contraception pills after 1960. But some of this change was also the result of active government programs which had a major impact on mortality and health.

In 1950, Brazil with its 54 million people was the eighth most populated country in the world, just behind Germany. Fifty years later, its 170 million residents would rank fifth in the world with Germany, still the largest of the European nations, now ranked twelfth largest in the world.[1] The comparative difference in population growth between these two nations is explained by their differing historical experiences with the "demographic transition," which involved both a fertility and mortality revolution in world history. For the first time in known human history there was a systematic long-term

[1] UN population rankings. Accessed at: www.un.org/esa/population/pubsarchive/india/20most .htm.

decline in both death rates and birth rates. Germany's demographic transition began in the early nineteenth century and was completed by the early twentieth century. By the mid-twentieth century, its annual growth rate was 1% per annum and would even begin to turn negative by the 1970s.[2] By contrast, Brazil's demographic transition began at the end of the nineteenth century but was only completed in the last quarter of the twentieth century. This tripling of the population in just fifty years was due to the very late demographic transition which Brazil experienced in this period, with mortality declining far more rapidly than fertility. In fact, fertility remained at noteworthy levels until the late 1960s: levels which were considered high even by world standards. The result was an extraordinary rate of natural growth which reached close to 3% per annum by mid-century.

The census and vital statistics available for 1950 well reflect this late-stage transition of Brazil. In 1950, Brazil had a crude birth rate of 44 births per 1,000 resident population and a total fertility rate of 6.2 children per woman in her fertile years.[3] In Germany, the total fertility rate had already reached 4.2 children by 1880, but by 1950 it was 1.7 children per 1,000 women of fertile age.[4] Brazil had one of the highest fertility rates in the world, even being slightly above the general Latin American rate in 1960.[5] But these rates would begin to decline at an ever increasing rate in the following quinquennial periods and directly affect the growth rate of the population, which quickly dropped from the highs of the 1950s and 1960s (see Graph 3.1).

Infants under 1 year of age and children under 5 years of age were the age groups, or cohorts, which initially experienced the greatest mortality decline. Their mortality rates fell faster than for any other age cohort until the late twentieth century. By the 1950s, infant mortality was down to 135 deaths of children under 1 year of age per 1,000 live births from a rate of over 200 deaths at the end of the nineteenth century. But even this lower rate was around five times higher than that of advanced countries.[6] Over the next few

---

[2] Gerhard Heilig, Thomas Buttner, and Wolfgang Lutz, "Germany's Population: Turbulent Past, Uncertain Future," *Population Bulletin*, 45. 4 (1990), p. 4, and data on German population growth rates at https://fred.stlouisfed.org/series/SPPOPGROWDEU.

[3] CELADE, *Boletín demográfico* 37.73 (2004), Tables 3, 4.

[4] Michael J. Kendzia and Klaus F. Zimmermann, "Celebrating 150 Years of Analyzing Fertility Trends in Germany," IZA Discussion Papers, 6355 (2011), p. 4, and for 1950, see DESTATIS, "Total Fertility Rate of Female Cohorts." Accessed at: www.destatis.de/EN/FactsFigures/So cietyState/Population/Births/Tables/FemaleCohorts.html.

[5] The Latin American rate in 1960 was 5.9 children, the world rate was 5.0 children, and the Brazilian rate was 6.1 children to women 14–49 years of age. See World Bank, World Development Indicators, "Fertility Rate, Total (Births per Woman)." Accessed 14 September 2017, at: https://data.worldbank.org/indicator/SP.DYN.TFRT.IN.

[6] The USA Infant Mortality rate was 29 in 1950. See Susan B. Carter, Scott Sigmund Gartner, Michael R. Haines, Alan L. Olmstead, and Richard Such, eds., *Historical Statistics of the*

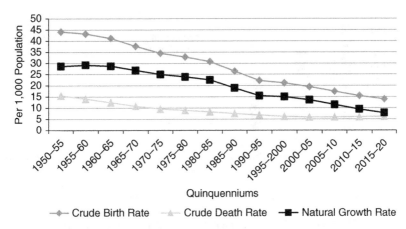

GRAPH 3.1 Crude Birth, Death, and Natural Growth Rates, 1950–2020
(per 1,000 resident population)
Source: CEPALSTAT, "Projections" (2016), Brasil.

decades the infant mortality rate dropped rapidly, reaching 72 deaths per 1,000 live births in 1980–1985 and 34 infant deaths per 1,000 live births by the end of the century.[7] The child mortality rate (that is children dying before 5 years of age per 1,000 live births) also underwent a systematic decline in the modern period, going from 190 deaths in 1980 to just 19 deaths by the 2010s (see Graph 3.2).

So rapid was the decline of both the infant and child mortality rates, Brazil soon reached the average of these rates for Latin America, but well below the levels of the advanced countries of the world. The average rate in 2010 for advanced countries was 7 infant deaths per 1,000 live births, whereas for the countries of the Caribbean and Latin America it was 18, and 19 deaths in Brazil in 2010.[8]

In 1950, the child mortality rate was 190, which was just below the average for Latin America. By 1960, this rate dropped to 155, by 1970 to 122, and by 2010 it reached 24 deaths per 1,000 live births. Thus, for both infant and child rates, the pace of decline in Brazil became ever more rapid toward the end of the century and, finally, in the twenty-first century, reached

United States: Millennial Edition (Cambridge: Cambridge University Press, 2006), Table Ab912-927: "Fetal Death Ratio, Neonatal Mortality Rate, Infant Mortality Rate, and Maternal Mortality Rate, by Race: 1850–1998."

[7] CEPALSTAT, "Infant Mortality Rate, by Sex." Accessed at: http://interwp.cepal.org/sisgen/ConsultaIntegrada.asp?idIndicador=14&idioma=i.

[8] UNICEF, "Levels and Trends in Child Mortality Report 2015" (September 2015), p. 2, Table 1. Accessed at: https://data.unicef.org/resources/levels-and-trends-in-child-mortality-2015/.

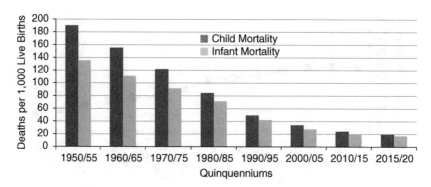

GRAPH 3.2 Infant and Child Mortality Rates in Brazil by Selected Quinquennium, 1950–1955 to 2015–2020
Source: CEPALSTAT. http://interwp.cepal.org/sisgen/ConsultaIntegrada.asp?idIndicador=37&idioma=e.

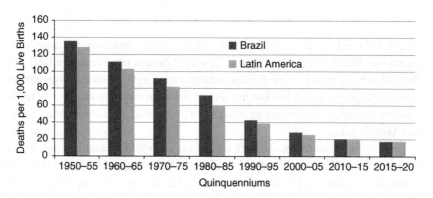

GRAPH 3.3 Infant Mortality Rate in Brazil and Latin America by Selected Quinquennium, 1950–1955 to 2015–2020
Source: CEPALSTAT. http://interwp.cepal.org/sisgen/ConsultaIntegrada.asp?idIndicador=14&idioma=i.

the average rates for all Latin America (see Graph 3.3). However, even with this rapid decline of infant mortality, Brazil's infant mortality rate still remained higher than the average infant mortality rate for the region until the most recent period. Moreover, as late as 2015–2020, Brazil's infant mortality rate of 17.4 deaths per 1,000 live births was still three times the rate now observed in Cuba (5.3 deaths) and two and a half times the 6.7 infant mortality rate registered in Chile in 2016.[9]

[9] CEPAL, *Anuario Estadística de América Latina y el Caribe* (2017), p. 22, Table 1.4.1.

There was also a change in the distribution of infant deaths in this period. Initially, most deaths occurred in the postneonatal period (that is, 28 to 365 days after birth) rather than the neonatal period (up to 27 days after birth), which was a clear indication of the continuing impact of social and economic conditions on infant and child mortality.[10] In the first month of life, the so-called neonatal period, most deaths are due to genetic, congenital, or birth problems related to the mother and child. But those dying in the postneonatal period mostly die from societal diseases and conditions, typically suffering severe dysentery due to contaminated food and water diseases, and from malnutrition. As late as the 1960s, half of all infant deaths occurred in this period and it was not until the 1970s that it dropped to below 40% of all infant deaths. Even as late as 1990, almost a quarter of deaths occurred in the neonatal period, which was above the norm for Latin America and compared to only 9% of such deaths in Chile and Costa Rica and 7% in Cuba, the more advanced countries of Latin American on these indices.[11]

Following a slower pace, maternal mortality also declined in the modern period, though it was still quite high by world standards and subject to occasional spikes. Until the end of the century that was due to these same socio-economic conditions and the lack of health professionals and clinics available for pregnant women.[12] Thus, as late as 1990, maternal mortality in Brazil was 143 maternal deaths per 100,000 live births (see Graph 3.4), a figure that was typical for all Latin America but was quite high by advanced country standards. In the countries of Western Europe and North America in 1990 the rate was 26 deaths per 100,000 live births.[13] But thereafter the decline was more rapid in Brazil than in the rest of Latin America, and at 45 maternal deaths per 100,000 births in 2010 it was half of the average Latin American rate, though still not close to the Western European and North American rates of 16 in the same year.[14]

Adult mortality followed more slowly the changes occurring in infant and child mortality in this period. Especially after the introduction of antibiotics in the late 1940s, adult mortality began a systematic decline, as infectious disease

---

[10] CELADE, *Boletín demográfico* 37.73 (2004), pp. 22, 24, 26, Tables 5, 6, 7.

[11] World Bank, World Development Indicators, "Mortality Rate, Neonatal (per 1,000 Live Births)." Accessed 30 January 2019, at: https://data.worldbank.org/indicator/SH .DYN.NMRT.

[12] Maternal mortality was quite high in the 1950s to 1980s. See Arnaldo Augusto Franco de Siqueira, Ana Cristina d'Andretta Tanaka, Renato Martins Santana, and Pedro Augusto Marcondes de Almeida, "Mortalidade materna no Brasil," 1980, *Revista de Saúde Pública* 18 (1984), pp. 448–465.

[13] WHO, *Trends in Maternal Mortality: 1990 to 2013* (Geneva: WHO, 2014), p. 25, Table 4.

[14] WHO, *Trends in Maternal Mortality: 1990 to 2013*, p. 24, Table 3.

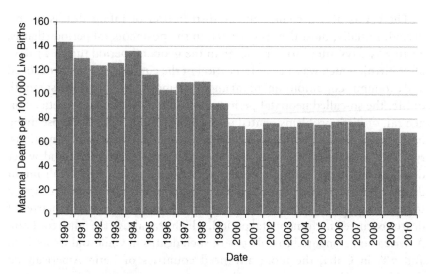

GRAPH 3.4 Maternal Mortality in Brazil, 1990–2010
Source: DATASUS. http://tabnet.datasus.gov.br/cgi/idb2011/C03a.htm.

deaths were progressively eliminated.[15] Much of this decline in adult mortality initially had to do with the improvement in public health and the expansion of welfare institutions. In the 1960s, came a new wave of state, national, and internationally supported programs of infant and child immunization.[16] There was also a major expansion in public health which would significantly affect the health and morbidity of adults. In 1967, a unified National Social Security Institute (*Instituto Nacional de Previdência Social* – INPS) was established and there was a rapid expansion of clinics and hospitals throughout the nation. Between 1970 and 1980, hospital admissions rose from 6 million to 13 million per annum – the latter figure being the norm up to today.[17] All of this growth in public health had a direct impact on infant and more particularly adult mortality. Already the crude annual death rate was 15 deaths per 1,000 residents, which, given the rather steady nature of births and the relatively

[15] For a survey of this epidemiological changes, see Pedro Reginaldo Prata, "A transição epidemiológica no Brasil," *Cadernos de Saúde Pública* 8.2 (1992), pp. 168–175.

[16] The 1970s and early 1980s were also a period of active debate developed among academics and doctors about the nature of the health care system which would have a profound effect on the creation of SUS and the decentralization reforms of health carried out in the post-military period. See Hésio Cordeiro, "Instituto de Medicina Social e a luta pela reforma sanitária: contribuição à história do SUS." *Physis* 14.2 (2004), pp. 343–362.

[17] Jairnilson Paim, Claudia Travassos, Celia Almeida, Ligia Bahia, and James Macinko, "The Brazilian Health System: History, Advances, and Challenges," *The Lancet* 377.9779 (2011), pp. 1778–1797.

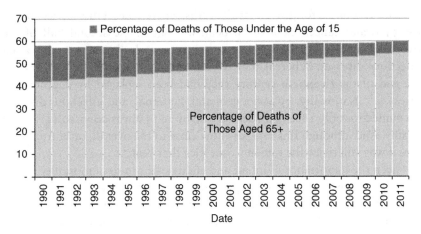

GRAPH 3.5 Changing Share of Total Deaths of Youths and the Elderly, 1990–2011
Source: DATASUS, Table A8.

young age structure of the population, was a low national death rate. While that rate would change little in the next decade, it began to decline at a more rapid pace in the next few years and was down to 8 deaths per 1,000 persons by the early 1980s. This declining crude death rate was accompanied by a basic change in the age component of those dying. There was now a steady increase in the ratio of the elderly in total deaths. But it was not until 2003 that persons 65 years of age and older made up over half the deaths, having been at just 42% as late as 1990. In turn, infant deaths fell to 16% of all deaths in 1990 and had fallen to just 5% in 2011 – the year that deaths of persons 65 years of age and older reached 55% of all deaths (see Graph 3.5).[18]

The causes of deaths as late as 1949–1951 still reflected a traditional society where death from infectious diseases was the major killer for most of the population. In these years the biggest killer was tuberculosis, which accounted for 15% of all deaths of all ages. Next came adult gastroenteritis at 10% of deaths, followed by heart disease at just 9% of all deaths. Well below this were deaths from cancer. Taken together, all the major infectious diseases (TB, gastroenteritis, pneumonia, and syphilis) accounted for 37% of all deaths for all ages, while the two modern generative deadly killers in advanced industrial societies, cancer and heart disease, accounted for only 14% of all deaths.[19] In the United States, by 1950, for example, infectious

[18] DATASUS, Table A.8, "Mortalidade proporcional por idade." Accessed 14 September 2017, at: http://tabnet.datasus.gov.br/cgi/idb2012/matriz.htm#mort.
[19] IBGE, *Estatísticas do Século XX* (2003), Table pop_1956aeb-042. Accessed at: www.ibge.gov.br/seculoxx/arquivos_xls/populacao.shtm.

diseases accounted for just 9% of all deaths, whereas heart disease accounted for 53% and cancer 14% of all deaths.[20] But in the second half of the twentieth century Brazil experienced a systematic decline of mortality from infectious diseases. Whereas they were the prime killers at mid-century, by the end of the twentieth century they had been replaced by degenerative diseases.[21] Nationally, by 2000, neonatal, maternal, and infectious diseases accounted for only 18% of all deaths, and by 2015 it was down to 14% of all deaths. And although this rate was now close to the overall Latin American rate it was still twice the rate in Costa Rica that year.[22]

Given the importance of infant and child deaths in total mortality in this period, life expectancy of the population increased considerably if one survived until one's fifth birthday. Thus, life expectancy went up to 57 years for men and 59 years for women at age 5 in 1950, whereas their life expectancy at birth was only 49 years of age for men and 53 years for women.[23] Until the end of the twentieth century, it was the decline in infant and child mortality which was the primary factor driving up life expectancy. Since the 1950s, the child and infant mortality rate has declined to 54 deaths per 1,000 live births by 1990 and to an estimated 17 deaths per 1,000 live births in the current quinquennium of 2015–2020.[24] This declining infant and child mortality shows in changing life expectancy at birth between 1950–1955 and 2015–2020. In the former period, life expectancy increased by 6 years and 4 months or 7 years and 4 months (for women and men respectively) if one survived to one's fifth birthday compared to what it was at birth, whereas currently there is a difference of just 5 months for men and 1 month for

---

[20] United States Department of Health, Education, and Welfare. *Vital Statistics of the United States, 1950* (Washington, DC, 1954), vol. 1, p. 170, Table 8.26.

[21] For example, infectious diseases accounted for only 5% of the deaths in the state of São Paulo (and 7% of deaths among infants and children) in 2001. By contrast, 30% of the deaths in São Paulo state in 2001 were due to heart disease – the biggest killer, followed by cancers, which accounted for another 15%. SEADE, *Anuário estatístico do estado de São Paulo* (2001), Table 25. Accessed at: www.seade.gov.br.

[22] World Bank, World Development Indicators, "Cause of Death, by Communicable Diseases and Maternal, Prenatal and Nutrition Conditions (% of total)." Accessed 13 September 2017, at: https://data.worldbank.org/indicator/SH.DTH.COMM.ZS?view=chart.

[23] Berquó, "Demographic Evolution of the Brazilian Population in the Twentieth Century," p. 17, Table 4. This 1950 life expectancy figure for Brazil was even a bit low by Latin American standards. See Arriaga and Davis, "The Pattern of Mortality Change in Latin America," p. 226, Table 3. For the standard life table now used by both IBGE and the UN, see CELADE, *Boletín demográfico* 34.74 (2004), p. 62, Table 14.

[24] CELADE, "Brasil, Estimaciones y proyecciones de población a largo plazo, 1950–2100, Revisión 2016. Indicadores de la estructura por sexo y edad de la población estimados y proyectados." Accessed 5 September 2017 at: www.cepal.org/es/temas/proyecciones-demograficas/estimaciones-proyecciones-poblacion-total-urbana-rural-economicamente-activa.

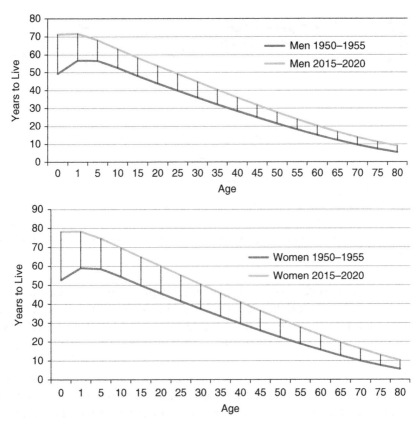

GRAPH 3.6 Life Expectancy by Sex at Different Ages, 1950–1955 and 2015–2020
Source: CELADE, *Boletín demográfico* 34.74 (2004), pp. 62, 74, Table 14.

women between life expectancy at birth and life expectancy for those who reach 5 years of age (see Graph 3.6).

Infant mortality in the second half of the twentieth century declines more rapidly than adult mortality. But the decline in both rates meant that life expectancy was increasing more rapidly than in any previous period of Brazilian history. As was the norm in the rest of the western world, women had higher rates of life expectancy and maintained their advance over men for this entire period. But both men and women experienced this extraordinary increase in life expectancy, with men adding 21.2 years at birth in the 60-year period between 1950 and 2010 and women an even more impressive 25.3 years at birth (see Graph 3.7).

While these patterns of declining mortality were common to most countries of Latin America in this period, what was especially pronounced in Brazil was the variation of these rates between the rich and poor regions of

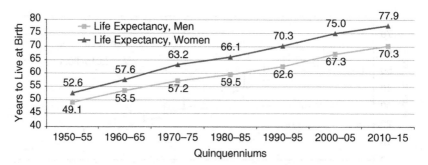

GRAPH 3.7 Life Expectancy at Birth in Brazil, 1950–1955 to 2010–2015
Source: CELADE, "Brasil, Estimaciones y proyecciones de población a largo plazo, 1950–2100, Revisión 2016. Indicadores de la estructura por sexo y edad de la población estimados y proyectados." www.cepal.org/es/temas/proyecciones-demograficas/estimaciones-proyecciones-poblacion-total-urbana-rural-economica mente-activa.

the country. Initially, there was a major difference among regions, with national rates of mortality in Brazil masking sharp regional variations. Although infant mortality declined everywhere, the speed of change differed significantly by region. In Brazil, class and color were well defined by region as well as stratified nationally. The North and Northeast were less white and far poorer than the Southeastern and Southern regions. Thus, it was no surprise that the Northeast had almost one and a half times the rate of infant mortality as the South and Southeast states in 1950. In fact, the regional difference increased in 1960, reflecting the fact that the decline in the more economically advanced regions was faster than in the poorer Northern states. But by 2000 both the regions of the North and Northeast experienced declining infant mortality at faster rates than the South and Southeast regions, with the Northeastern region declining at 6.0% per annum between 2000 and 2011 compared to the South and Southeast, which declined at under 4%, and the North at 4.4%, which meant that the gap between regions was closing at a more rapid pace after 2000 (see Graph 3.8).[25]

There was also a steady decline in regional differences in the rate of postneonatal deaths.[26] But, already by 1990, the North and Northeast were declining somewhat faster than the advanced regions, and this trend

[25] DATASUS, Table A.9, "Mortalidade proporcional por idade, em menores de 1 ano de idade." Accessed 14 September 2017, at: http://tabnet.datasus.gov.br/cgi/idb2012/matriz.htm#mort.
[26] Antônio Prates Caldeira, Elisabeth França, Ignez Helena Oliva Perpétuo, and Eugênio Marcos Andrade Goulart, "Evolução da mortalidade infantil por causas evitáveis, Belo Horizonte, 1984–1998." *Revista de Saúde Pública* 39.1 (2005), p. 68.

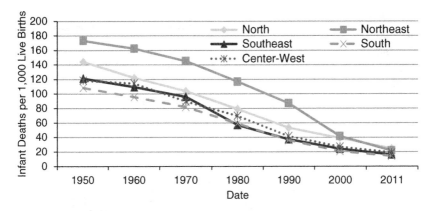

GRAPH 3.8 Infant Mortality Rate by Region, 1950–2011
Source: IBGE, CD 100 to 1980 and Datasus Table C.1 since 1990.

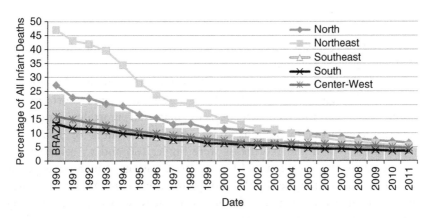

GRAPH 3.9 Post Neonatal Death Rates by Region, 1990–2011
Source: DATASUS, C.1.3 Taxa de mortalidade pós-neonatal.

accelerated in the post-2000 period, with the Northeast declining at double the rate of the most advanced Southeast region (see Graph 3.9).[27]

A pattern equal to infant mortality can be seen in the declining regional differences in child mortality. Thus, in 1990 there was a 52-death difference between the worst (Northeast) and the best (South) regions. By 2011, the difference was just 11 deaths between the worst region (in this case the

---

[27] DATASUS, Table C.1.3, "Taxa de mortalidade pós-neonatal." Accessed 14 September 2017, at: http://tabnet.datasus.gov.br/cgi/idb2012/matriz.htm#mort.

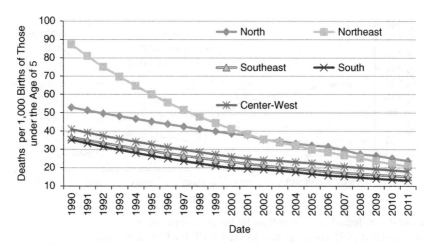

GRAPH 3.10 Under 5 Mortality by Region in Brazil, 1990–2011
Source: http://tabnet.datasus.gov.br/cgi/idb2012/c16b.htm.

North) and the best-case South region, which was now at 13 deaths per 1,000 live births (see Graph 3.10).

But from limited regional studies it appears that maternal mortality has not followed the secular trends in infant and child mortality by region. In a careful reconstruction of maternal mortality rates per 100,000 live births by regions in the first six months of 2002, the rates for the North and Northeast were higher (60 and 73 respectively) than those for the Southern and Center-West regions (which were 45 for the Southeast, 42 for the South, and 49 for the Center-West).[28] A later survey, from 2009 to 2013, found differences as well, but showing a steady narrowing of differences between the regions, with the highest maternal mortality rates in the Northeast and the lowest rates in the South. This was the norm except for 2013, which seems to be an outlier in the general declining trend, mostly due to unusually high rates in the two northern regions of the North and Northeast, since most of the other regions continued their downward trend (see Graph 3.11). The authors of this study found that women aged 20 to 29 years, who were single mothers, brown in color, and with only 4 to 7 years of completed studies, had the highest such mortality rates. The main causes

---

[28] Ruy Laurenti, Maria H. P. Mello Jorge, and Sabina Léa Davidson Gotlieb, "A mortalidade materna nas capitais brasileiras: algumas características e estimativa de um fator de ajuste," *Revista Brasileira de Epidemiologia* 7.4 (2004), p. 455, Table 3.

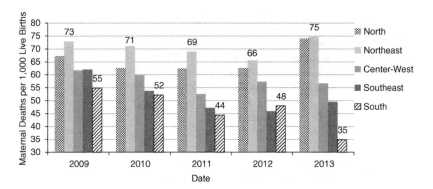

GRAPH 3.11 Rate of Maternal Deaths by Region, 2009–2013
Source: Guimarães, et al., "Mortalidade materna no brasil entre 2009 e 2013"
(2018), p. 82, Table 2.

of deaths were the mother's pre-existing diseases that complicated pregnancy, childbirth and the postpartum period, eclampsia, and gestational hypertension.[29]

While overall rates of life expectancy were changing for all Brazilians, the sharp regional contrasts which reflected class and race differences in access to resources meant that the Northern regions were significantly behind the Southern regions in this crucial variable. The classic pattern of a nation divided between an advanced and retarded region, what one economist called "Belindia," is quite evident in the life expectancy by region even as late as 1980. That is, one area of the country was more like Belgium in its vital statistics while another part was similar to India.[30] Though the increase in life expectancy was faster in the poorer regions after 1950, in 1980 it was still very much in evidence.[31] Thus, the difference in life expectancy from the worst region to the best region was a startling 7.9 years for both men and women. This regional difference reflected class differences, which even within regions clearly marked differential life experiences for Brazilians. In this same year, the difference in life expectancy between those receiving the equivalent of one minimum salary and those who received 5 minimum

---

[29] Thaíse Almeida Guimarães, Andréa de Jesus Sá Costa Rocha, Wanderson Barros Rodrigues, and Amanda Namibia Pereira Pasklan, Thaíse Almeida Guimarães, Andréa de Jesus Sá Costa Rocha, Wanderson Barros Rodrigues, and Amanda Namibia Pereira Pasklan, "Mortalidade materna no brasil entre 2009 e 2013," *Revista de Pesquisa em Saúde* 18. 2 (2018), p. 81.

[30] See Bacha and Klein, *Social Change in Brazil, 1945–1985*, p. 3.

[31] A good survey of the regional differences in this period can be found in Charles H. Wood and José Alberto Magno de Carvalho, *The Demography of Inequality in Brazil* (Cambridge: Cambridge University Press, 1988).

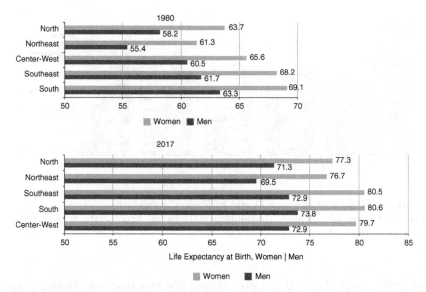

GRAPH 3.12 Life Expectancy at Birth by Sex and Region, 1980 and 2017
Source: Oliveira and Albuquerque, "A mortalidade no Brasil" (2005), pp. 8–9,
Tables 2–3. www.ibge.gov.br/home/presidencia/noticias/imprensa/ppts/0000000243
.pdf.

salaries or more was a startling 14.8 years.[32] But these differences slowly
declined, and by 2017 the difference between the most advanced and most
retarded region was reduced to 4.3 years for men and 3.3 years for women
(see Graph 3.12).

Not only were regional and class differences declining over time, Brazil
also had a major demographic shock in this period, as fertility went into
rapid decline; up until the 1960s it was thought that the population would
continue to expand at extraordinary rates. As Brazil's very high fertility
remained unchanged, declining mortality meant not only an increase in the
survival of children but a population explosion. By mid-century, Brazil
achieved its highest rate of natural population increase, a period in which
there was no significant external migration. This growth affected all regions
as declining mortality was accompanied by declining morbidity. This meant
that far more healthy women were surviving to their fertile years, and in the
1950s the Brazilian population peaked at a natural growth rate of 3% per
annum, one of the highest such rates in the world. At this rate of growth, the

[32] IBGE, *Estatísticas do Século XX* (2003), Table população1981aeb-043.1. Accessed at: www
.ibge.gov.br/seculoxx/arquivos_xls/populacao.shtm.

1950 Brazilian population of 51 million would have doubled in 17.3 years. But the figure of 102 million was not reached until a decade later. By the last decade of the twentieth century the population growth was the lowest recorded for the whole century, falling to 1.6% per annum, and as of 2002 the population had only grown to just 173 million.

The cause for this failure of the population to double by the late 1970s was due to the fact that fertility finally followed mortality and began to decline from the mid-1960s onward. Thus, Brazil, after a very rapid growth spurt of its population in the middle years of the twentieth century, began to experience ever slower growth as it finally entered the classic phase of the "demographic transition" from a high mortality and fertility nation to a modern post-transition low fertility and low mortality society. The single most important factor in this transition was the sharp and systematic decline in fertility.

The causes for this extraordinarily rapid fall in fertility were the introduction of the contraceptive pill, government sterilization programs, the decline in illiteracy, and finally the very rapid shift of the population from rural to urban residence, with women now making up an ever higher proportion of the urban population and an increasing share of the labor force. Given these factors, it was not long before Brazilian women in this period profoundly changed their attitude toward fertility for the first time in the nation's history. The decline of fertility, which began in the 1940s and 1950s in the more advanced urban centers of the country with traditional contraceptive methods, now quickly spread far and wide, even into the most rural areas with the introduction of the birth control pill and other contraceptive methods in the 1960s. In fact, the pill was freely available commercially in Brazil in 1962 two years before it was approved by the US Food and Drug Administration for use in the United States.[33] Family planning was also supported at various levels of intensity both by international organizations and eventually by the government. The *Sociedade Civil de Bem-Estar Familiar no Brasil* (Bemfam) was established primarily by doctors in 1965 and was declared a public utility in 1971. It promoted family planning and contraceptive information to all groups and set up centers throughout the country as well as developing major training programs for doctors.[34] While government policy was pronatalist in the 1960s and 1970s, it shifted to promoting family planning in the 1980s and especially with the establishment of the government's *Programa de Assistência Integral à Saúde da Mulher* (PAISM) in 1983 and the active

---

[33] Joana Maria Pedro, "A experiência com contraceptivos no Brasil: uma questão de geração," *Revista Brasileira de História* 23.45 (2003), p. 242.

[34] On the history and early work of Bemfam, see Walter Rodrigues, "Progress and Problems of Family Planning in Brazil," *Demography* 5.2 (1968), pp. 800–810.

support of contraception by the National Health and Social Security System (*Instituto Nacional de Assistência Médica da Previdência Social* – INAMPS) in 1986.[35]

This rapid decline in fertility can be seen in the fall of the total fertility rate (a period measure of the average number of children born to women in the age group 14–49 at a given point in time) for all of Brazil. Whereas Brazilian women were still on average giving birth to more than six children in their fertile years from the 1940s to the 1960s, by the end of the 1970s women were having almost four fewer children than just twenty years previously. This total fertility rate consistently declined in the following years, reaching just under three children per woman 14–49 years of age in 1991 and 1.8 children by the late 2010s, a figure which indicated that national fertility was below replacement levels (of which a total fertility rate of 2.1 children is considered the basic number for reproduction of the previous generation). Thus, by the end of the first decade of the twenty-first century, Brazilian fertility was already below the level needed for replacing the current population.[36]

This decline in births was directly related to increasing use of some form of contraception by Brazilian women. By the decade of the 1980s, approximately 70% of women married or living in "consensual unions" (*uniões consensuais*), i.e., cohabiting, used some form of birth control.[37] Of those women using contraception, 44% carried out sterilization, a figure slightly below the norm for a less developed country like Brazil, and 41% were using the birth control pill, with a mixture of other contraceptive practices accounting for the rest.[38] Although illegal abortions were relatively high in Brazil by world standards, they were normal for Latin America. Moreover, their trend differed from that of fertility. Initially, the abortion rate remained steady and increased somewhat at the end of the decade of the 1990s, but these abortion rates have since slowly declined as more women and men use modern contraceptive methods.[39] Both the rate and trend of abortions show

---

[35] Augusta Thereza de Alvarenga and Néia Scho, "Contracepção feminina e política pública no brasil: pontos e contrapontos da proposta oficial," *Saúde e Sociedade* 7.1 (1998), pp. 93–94 and Susana Maria Veleda da Silva, "Inovações nas políticas populacionais: o planejamento familiar no Brasil," *Scripta Nova, Revista Electrónica de Geografía y Ciencias Sociales* 69.25 (2000). Accessed at: www.ub.edu/geocrit/sn-69-25.htm.

[36] Data on total fertility rate comes from "Structural Indicators" table of Brazil: CELADE, "Brasil, Estimaciones y proyecciones de población a largo plazo, 1950–2100, Revisión 2016."

[37] Elza Berquó, "Brasil, um Caso Exemplar – anticoncepção e parto cirúrgicos – à espera de uma ação exemplar." *Estudos feministas* 1:2 (2008), p. 368. The figure was 43% for all women, when non-partnered women are included.

[38] Berquó, "Brasil, um Caso Exemplar," pp. 369, 371, Tables 1 and 3.

[39] Greice Menezes and Estela M. L. Aquino, "Pesquisa sobre o aborto no Brasil: avanços e desafios para o campo da saúde coletiva," *Cadernos de Saúde Pública* 25 Supl. 2 (2009), pp. 193–204; Susheela Singh and Gilda Sedgh, "The Relationship of Abortion to Trends in

that it had little impact on the decline in fertility. It was thus the use of contraception methods of all types which drove the decline in fertility.

Nor was this fertility decline due to any change in the initiation of marriage, the percentage of women marrying, or the withdrawal of fertile women from reproduction. The age of women marrying for the first time did not change until long after the fertility transition. Nor did the number of women ever marrying decline or those remaining childless increase; nor did the ratio of births out of wedlock alter or was there any massive increase in abortions. Many of these factors, including the dissolution of unions, did change over time, but these transformations came well after the fall in fertility. The only change which did occur was the mass adoption of contraception, along with sterilizations, in the second half of the decade of the 1960s.[40] It was older women who most enthusiastically adopted the new contraceptive procedures. But no group of women was exempt, and every age group experienced fertility decline from the high in 1965 to a low in the second decade of the twenty-first century. The biggest drop in fertility first occurred among older women, and the relationship between age and decline in age-specific fertility was almost perfectly inverted, with the rate of decline highest in the older age group and slowing through those younger. The age-specific birth rate among women aged 45–49, for example, declined by 95% from 1960 to 2000, by 89% for women aged 40–44, dropping to 80% and 71% in the next two age groups (35–39 and 30–34 respectively), then to 61% in the 25–29 age group and to just 13% in those aged 15–19.

This fertility transition was different from the slower transitions which the advanced industrial nations experienced. There as well it was older women

Contraception and Fertility in Brazil, Colombia and Mexico," *International Family Planning Perspectives* 23.1 (1997), Tables 1 and 3; and for the latest data on world and regional rates, see Gilda Sedgh, Stanley Henshaw, Susheela Singh, Elisabeth Åhman, and Iqbal H. Shah, "Induced Abortion: Estimated Rates and Trends Worldwide," *The Lancet* 370 (2007), pp. 1338–1345. The first complete national survey on abortions carried out in Brazil was done in 2010 and found that 15% of women aged 18–39 had had an abortion, a relatively low rate compared to other Latin American countries. Like all other studies it found that abortions were higher for the poorer, less-educated, and non-whites than for other groups, and thus there were marked differences in these rates between the Northeast and Southern regions. Interestingly, there were no differences in mortality rates by religion of the mother. Debora Diniz and Marcelo Medeiros, "Aborto no Brasil: uma pesquisa domiciliar com técnica de urna," *Ciência & Saúde Coletiva* 15.1 (2010), pp. 959–966. On regional variations in abortion rates, see Leila Adesse and Mário F. G. Monteiro "Magnitude do aborto no Brasil: aspectos epidemiológicos e sócio-culturais." Accessed at: https://jornalggn.com.br/si tes/default/files/documentos/factsh_mag.pdf.

[40] José Miguel Guzmán, "Introduction: Social Change and Fertility Decline in Latin America," in Jose Miguel Guzmán, Susheela Singh, German Rodriguez, and Edith A. Pantelides, eds., *The Fertility Transition in Latin America* (Oxford: Clarendon Press, 1996), p. xxiii.

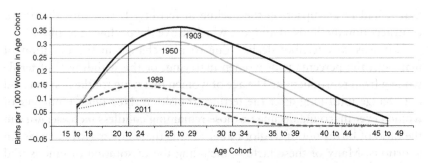

GRAPH 3.13 Age Specific Fertility in Brazil, 1903, 1953, 1988, and 2011
Source: Horta, Carvalho, and Frias, "Recomposição da fecundidade por geração
para Brasil e regiões."

who first adopted contraception in order to reduce their total family size. But
in a later phase the decline was due to delayed marriage and ever later childbearing ages caused by women entering education and the labor market in
large numbers. In Brazil, the decline also first occurred because of the significant fall in births to mothers at older ages. This change among older women
effectively brought down the number of births quickly and was initially not
directly linked to any changing role of women participating in education or the
labor market, though these changing roles were beginning to occur. The
impact of this declining fertility was to move the largest number of births to
ever younger women. Although total births in each age group declined, the
faster decline at older ages meant that mothers aged 20–24, who were
the second most important group in 1903 behind women 25–29, moved to
first place in fertility by 1988. This was the dominant pattern until 2011 when
the distribution of births finally began to look more like Europe and North
America, with the 25- to 29-year-olds again becoming almost as important as
the 20- to 24-year-olds (see Graph 3.13). What is extraordinary is that this
sudden drop in fertility occurred within roughly the same five-year period both
in Brazil and in most of the rest of Latin America, in sharp contrast to the
decades-long decline in Europe. Also differing from the demographic transition
in Europe, the transition in Latin America and Brazil began when birth rates
were very much higher than they were in Europe when its transition began. In
fact, these rates were the highest in the world at mid-century.[41]

---

[41] Juan Chackiel and Susana Schkolnik, "Latin America: Overview of the Fertility Transition,
1950–1990," in Jose Miguel Guzmán, Susheela Singh, German Rodriguez, and Edith
A. Pantelides, eds., *The Fertility Transition in Latin America* (Oxford: Clarendon Press,
1996), p. 4.

As the birth rate declined by the twenty-first century, major societal and attitudinal changes for women would influence even younger women to cut their fertility and slowly move toward a European and North American norm in which increasing education and labor force participation for women finally led to delayed marriage and delayed childbearing. This can be seen in the changes noted in the age-specific fertility rates in 2011. As in the advanced economies, women were finally delaying giving birth as more women sought advanced education or entered the labor force. In 1988, there was a massive decline of births to older women, which was the first stage in the fertility transition in Brazil, whereas by 2011 there was a major shift to older women giving birth and the 25–29 cohort equaling the previously dominant 20–24 year old maternal cohort. But this second phase occurred long after the initiation of the fertility transition. Slowly, as more women have significantly increased their years of schooling, which now exceeds men for the first time ever, there are more births to older women as women delay marriage and/or motherhood.

The fact that increasing education leads to the increasing average age of mothers of first births is evident from a study from a health survey of 2013. The average age of the mother at first birth with no education was 19, compared to 25 years of age for a woman with a university education (see Table 3.1). Interestingly, the same health survey indicates that there was no difference between women in the labor force or out of the labor force in terms of median age at first birth,[42] although there was a slight difference by color (see Table 3.2). Also, in most cases, rural women gave birth at earlier ages than urban women.

Not only were women having children later, but they were also beginning to marry much later by the twenty-first century. Thus, for example, the

Table 3.1 *Median Age of Mothers at First Pregnancy by Residence and Level of Education, Brazil, 2013*

Residence	Total	Level of Education Completed			
		No education	Primary	Secondary Only	University
Urban	21	19	20	22	25
Rural	20	19	20	21	22
Total	21	19	20	22	25

Source: IBGE, Sidra, Tables 5512 and 5516, for color.

[42] See IBGE, Sidra, Table 5518.

Table 3.2 *Median Age of Mothers at First Pregnancy by Color and Residence, Brazil, 2013*

	Total	Urban	Rural
White	22	22	21
Black	21	21	20
Brown	20	21	19
Total	21	21	20

Source: IBGE, Sidra, Table 5516.

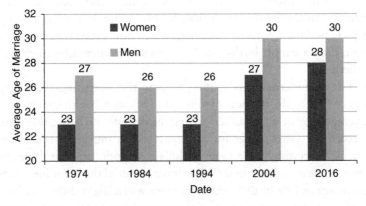

GRAPH 3.14 Average Age of Single Persons Marrying, by Sex, 1974–2014
Source: IBGE, Estatísticas do Registro Civil (2014), vol. 41, Table 8, and, for 2016, Estatísticas do Registro Civil (2016), vol. 43, p. 4.

average age for unmarried single persons (*solteiras* and *solteiros*) getting married in 1974 was 23 years of age for women and 27 years of age for men. By 2016, the average age for women had increased to 28 years of age and for single men it had reached 30 years of age (see Graph 3.14).

These average ages reflected a major shift in the age cohorts of women in terms of their share of total marriages. Between 1984 and 2016, for example, the percentage of single women marrying before the age of 25 dropped from 72% of all such marriages to just 37% of all marriages. In turn, for the older age cohorts, those marrying at age 30 and above went in the same period from just 12% of all marriages to 37% of all marriages (see Graph 3.15). Also, the very institution of marriage was changing, as a lower share of the population married. Thus, the ratio of marriages to total population steadily declined from

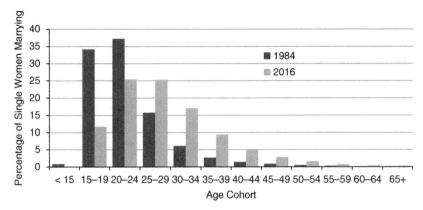

GRAPH 3.15 Percentage Distribution by Age Cohort of Single Women Marrying, 1984 and 2016
Source: IBGE, Sidra, Tables 351 and 3375.

13 marriages per 1,000 population in 1974 to just 7 marriages per 1,000 resident population in 2016.[43]

As could be expected, fertility control began in the richer Southeast and South states. But here as well, toward the end of the fertility transition, fertility rates declined at a much faster pace among the poorest and least-educated women, and between the richest and poorest regions.[44] Given the differing timing of fertility transition by state and region, the actual spread between high and low regions increased until the 1970s. It was only in the late 1980s that Northern women began to enter more systematically into fertility control. Thus, by 2017, there was less than one half a child difference between the highest fertility region (North) and the region with the lowest total fertility rate (Southeast). By then even the North at 2.02 children was practically below replacement like all the other regions and was close to the national average of 1.9 children (Graph 3.16).

Clearly, until the 1980s, fertility rates in the richest states and regions declined more rapidly, but by the census of 1991 the highest fertility regions began to decline faster than the advanced regions, thus reducing their differences from 2.82 children at their maximum difference to just 0.47 children by 2017 (see Graph 3.17). This can be seen in the spread between the lowest and

---

[43] IBGE, Estatísticas do Registro Civil (2014), vol. 41, "Registros de casamentos no País," and, for 2016, Estatísticas do Registro Civil (2016), vol. 43, p. 5.
[44] Elza Berquó and Suzana Cavenagh, "Mapeamento sócio-econômico e demográfico dos regimes de fecundidade no Brasil e sua variação entre 1991 e 2000," Paper presented at the XIV Encontro Nacional de Estudos Populacionais, ABEP, Caxambu, MG, Brazil, 20–24 September 2004.

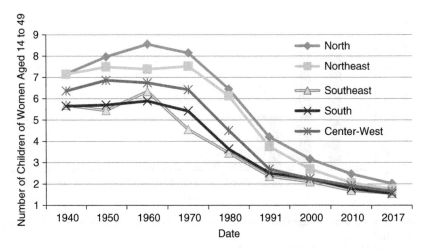

GRAPH 3.16 Total Fertility Rate by Region, 1940–2017
Source: www.ibge.gov.br/home/presidencia/noticias/20122002censo.shtm; for 2017,
www.ibge.gov.br/home/estatistica/populacao/projecao_da_populacao/2013/default_
tab.shtm.

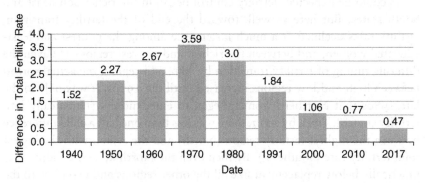

GRAPH 3.17 The Difference in the Total Fertility Rate between the Highest and
Lowest Fertility Regions, 1940–2017
Source: www.ibge.gov.br/home/presidencia/noticias/20122002censo.shtm; for 2017,
www.ibge.gov.br/home/estatistica/populacao/projecao_da_populacao/2013/default_
tab.shtm.

highest states in 1991 and 2011. Amapá in the first year had 2.7 children
more than the women in the state of São Paulo. By 2011, the state of Acre had
the highest rate, but differed by only 1.1 children from São Paulo, still the
lowest state in terms of fertility.[45]

---

[45] DATASUS. Accessed at: http://tabnet.datasus.gov.br/cgi/idb2012/a05b.htm.

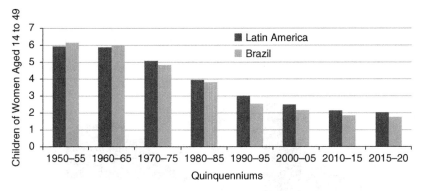

GRAPH 3.18 Total Fertility Rate of Brazil and Latin America in Selected Quinquennium, 1950–1955 to 2015–2020
Source: CEPALDATA. http://interwp.cepal.org/sisgen/ConsultaIntegrada.asp? idIndicador=37&idioma=i.

Although mortality in Brazil was somewhat laggard compared to the changes in the rest of Latin America, in terms of declining fertility it was a leader. Brazil was an early entrant into fertility decline by the standards of the rest of the late-transitioning American nations. Ranked among the high fertility countries at mid-century, as were the majority of the nations of the hemisphere, Brazil was one of the first of these high fertility nations to experience declining fertility. Whereas it was 4% above the region's total fertility rate from 1950 to 1960, and 2% above in the next quinquennium, by 1965–70 it dropped to 1% below the regional rate and by the 1990s it was 10% or more below the Latin American rates. By the period 2015–2020, Brazil's total fertility rate of 1.71 children was 12% below the average for Latin American countries (see Graph 3.18). Brazil's decline was so rapid that it quickly moved to a rate that placed it among the lowest fertility countries in the region, including such previously generally low fertility nations as Cuba, Costa Rica, Uruguay, and Argentina. By the last five years of this period, only Cuba had a lower total fertility rate.[46]

The fact that fewer children were being born after the late 1960s began to show in the change in the age composition of the population. Compared to the age distribution in 1950, the age pyramid by 1975 began to narrow considerably at the base as the share of children in the total population declined. By 2000, there were more adults than children as the classic jar-shaped distribution emerged, and by 2020 Brazil is expected to look like any advanced industrial industry in terms of its age distribution (see Graph 3.19).

---

[46] CEPAL, *Boletín demográfico* 68 (2001), Table 2, "América Latina: Tasas Globales de Fecundidad Estimadas y Proyectadas ... "

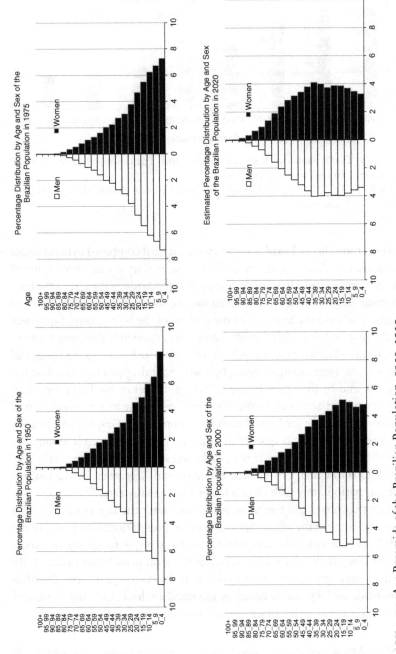

GRAPH 3.19 Age Pyramids of the Brazilian Population, 1950–2020

Source: CEPALDATA. http://estadisticas.cepal.org/cepalstat/WEB_CEPALSTAT/estadisticasIndicadores.asp?idioma=e.

This sudden drop in the total fertility rate finally expressed itself in terms of the median age of the population. Due to the earlier high levels of fertility and decreasing child mortality the median age of the population was actually declining at the beginning of this period. It went from a median age of 19.2 years in 1950 to 18.5 years in 1960 and remained at that level ten years later. But, as the severely declining fertility increased its impact, the median age began to rise in 1980 and reached 20.2 years. By 2000, it was up to 25.4 years and by 2010 it finally passed 30 years of age. By 2017, it reached 32.2 years and by 2020 it is expected to reach 33.5 years – not that different from the median age in most European and North American countries.[47]

This also meant that the ratio of the elderly was increasing constantly. The decline in adult mortality, which followed the earlier decline in infant mortality, now began to have an effect on the ratio of the elderly in the population, and, combined with the fall in fertility, was changing the relationship between the two groups. In 1950, the "aged" (those 65 years of age and older) comprised just 3% of the Brazilian population, and those under 15 comprised 42% of that same population. There were an estimated 7 elderly persons per 100 youths. By 1980, youths under 15 years of age declined to 39% of the total population and the aged increased to 4% of the population. By 2000, youths were now down to 29% and the aged up to 6% – and there were now 17 elderly persons to 100 youths. By 2020, it is estimated that there will be 45 aged per 100 youths and they will represent 10% of the population compared to just 21% for those under 15 years of age (see Graph 3.20).

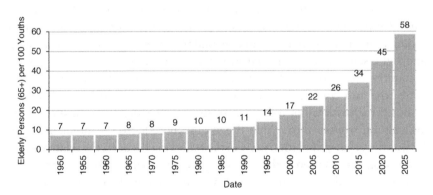

GRAPH 3.20 Number of Elderly Persons (65+) per 100 Youths (0–14), 1950–2025
Source: CEPALSTAT. http://interwp.cepal.org/sisgen/ConsultaIntegrada.asp?idIndicador=31&idioma=e.

---

[47] Data on median age comes from "Structural Indicators" table of Brazil: CELADE, "Brasil, Estimaciones y proyecciones de población a largo plazo, 1950–2100, Revisión 2016."

Fortunately for Brazil, the very high earlier birth rates mean that the working-age population (15–64) has now peaked at 69% of the population and is projected not to fall below 50% until the mid-twenty-first century. Thus, while the population is aging, the ratio of economically active population to dependent population is still increasing as of the second decade of the current century.[48]

This long-term decline in fertility is assumed to continue in the decades to come. Without significant foreign immigration, the latest projections by the national census bureau assume that the Brazilian population will stop growing in 2039 at 219 million persons and will then decline to 215 million persons by 2050 (see Graph 3.21). All this change now makes Brazil a typically post-transition society with fertility systematically falling below replacement for all regions.

If foreign immigration is no longer considered a major source of growth, internal migration has become a major factor in the changing distribution of the population within Brazil. In 1950, Brazil was still primarily a rural society. Even with the generous definition of urban used by the Brazilian census bureau, only 36% of the population was listed as living in an urban center. Of this urban population, almost half lived in cities of fewer than 20,000 persons. There were really only two major metropolitan cities at this time: Rio de Janeiro – the federal capital – and São Paulo, both with just over 2 million persons, which together accounted for almost a quarter of the urban population. The next city in size was Salvador de Bahia, with just half a million persons. At the time it appeared that these two cities and a few of the major capital cities of the states would remain as the only significant urban centers. In fact, for many years secondary cities were slow to develop and some scholars thought that Brazil might become a Uruguay – that is, a country where one or two metropolitan regions dominated the urban landscape and contained a significant share of the national population.

But the growth of an industrial sector and the steady expansion of the agricultural frontier throughout Brazil quickly reduced this domination. In fact, as the urban population grew in the following decades, the relative share of the urban population in these two major cities declined. By 2010, the cities of São Paulo and Rio de Janeiro, with a combined population of 17.6 million people, only accounted for 11% of the urban population. Many regional capitals were now over a million, and there were non-capital urban centers of

---

[48] CELADE, "Brasil, Estimaciones y proyecciones de población a largo plazo, 1950–2100, Revisión 2016."

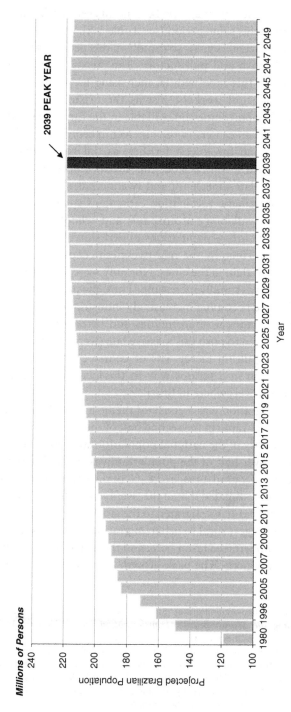

GRAPH 3.21 Projected Growth of the Brazilian Population, 1980–2050 (Based on 2008 IBGE Projections)
Source: IBGE, Projeção da população do Brasil . . . 1980–2050, Revisão 2008 (Rio de Janeiro, 2008), Table 8.

this size as well. Cities of less than 20,000 became an ever smaller share of the urban population over this same period (see Table 3.3).

Why did these urban centers grow so rapidly in this period? The answer is to be found in both push and pull factors. The steady modernization of Brazilian agriculture at this time with its increasing use of machinery was reducing the need for rural workers, just as the urban centers began to provide facilities and opportunities unavailable in the rural areas. Although Brazilian towns and urban centers in the nineteenth century tended to have the highest mortality and the lowest fertility, as did most urban centers everywhere in the world in this period, this urban mortality penalty was slowly changing in the late nineteenth and twentieth centuries. Sanitation, potable water, and systematic vaccination campaigns were all having their effect. Moreover, the availability of hospitals and schools and the higher educational level of the urban populations all led slowly to the decline of mortality in the cities. Thus, by the mid-twentieth century, mortality was higher in the rural areas than in the cities. Not only were the cities healthier, but their stock of jobs was rapidly increasing. Thus, the pull of jobs available in the cities which were becoming increasingly industrial centers, as well as the availability of educational opportunities and better social services, all were factors which helped to push this massive late twentieth-century migration in Brazil. The expulsion factor was of course the mechanization of agriculture which began in a serious way in this period and reduced the need for rural workers everywhere in Brazil.[49]

Although urban migration was a constant theme in Brazilian history, the process became far more rapid in the second half of the twentieth century. As late as 1960, the majority of the national population still resided in the rural areas. But, by 1970, over half of the population was finally listed as urban and this ratio rose steadily until it reached 84% of the national population by the census of 2010. It is estimated that in the twenty years from 1960 to 1980 some 27 million rural Brazilians migrated to the cities.[50] Up to the 1990s, the states which had the biggest rural to urban migration were the south central ones, as agriculture modernized faster here, and the urban centers grew more rapidly than in most regions. The peak growth of most of the state capital

[49] On the changes in Brazilian Agriculture at this time, see Herbert S. Klein and Francisco Vidal Luna, *Feeding the World: Brazil's Transformation into a Modern Agricultural Economy* (Cambridge: Cambridge University Press, 2019).

[50] Ana Amélia Camarano and Ricardo Abramovay, "Êxodo rural, envelhecimento e masculinização no Brasil: panorama dos últimos 50 anos," Texto para discussão 621, Rio de Janeiro, Ipea, 1998, p. 1. The authors point out that Brazil, like several other countries in Latin America, describes urban centers by administrative definition rather than size, which thus tends to underestimate the rural population (p. 6).

Table 3.3 *Distribution of the Urban Population by Size of the City, 1950–2010*

City Size	1950	1960	1970	1980	1991	2000	2010
To 20,000	39	34	27	21	19	19	17
20,000–50,000	13	12	12	11	12	11	12
50,000–100,000	9	10	8	11	10	11	10
100,000–500,000	13	16	20	22	24	26	27
>500,000	26	29	34	35	34	34	34
Total	100	100	100	100	100	100	100
[>100,000]	39	45	54	57	58	60	61]
Total N	18,775,779	31,867,324	52,097,260	80,437,327	110,990,990	137,953,959	160,925,792
Percentage of Total Population	36%	45%	55%	66%	76%	81%	84%

Source: Fausto A. de Brito and Breno A. T. D. de Pinho, *A dinâmica do processo de urbanização no Brasil, 1940–2010* (2012).

cities was in the twenty-year period from 1950 through 1970 when growth often reached well over 5% per annum. Thus, in the decade of the 1950s, Belo Horizonte was growing at 6.8% per annum, and was still increasing its population at over 6% per annum in the next decade. São Paulo was growing at or above 5% per annum in these two decades, and even Curitiba hit 7% growth per annum in the first decade and almost 6% in the 1960s. Only Rio de Janeiro had a slower growth, which was at or above 3% per annum in these three decades.[51] Brasília, of course, had the most sensational growth, increasing its population by 14% per annum in the 1960s.

The result was that all these cities – except Rio de Janeiro – more than doubled their populations in this twenty-year period. By the end of the century there were 20 state capitals with over 1 million population in their metropolitan districts alone. But by then all were growing at much more reduced rates, as the movement from rural to urban had slowed down considerably in all states, and the norm – except for Manaus – was 2% per annum growth rates or less.[52] But, by 2010, some 114 million Brazilians – or 60% of the national population – lived in cities with a population of 50,000 persons or above. Although the growth of the population of the core cities slowed considerably after 1980, and sometimes even stagnated, there was new growth in their greater metropolitan areas, a phenomenon occurring in most countries of Latin America at the end of the century.[53] Thus, by 2000, there were now registered 10 metropolitan areas in Brazil each with a total population greater than 2 million persons, with the leaders being São Paulo with 18 million persons, Rio with some 11 million, Belo Horizonte with 5 million, and Porto Alegre with 3.5 million persons. In all cases the growth was now in the surrounding towns rather than in the core cities, which often represented just half of the total greater metropolitan populations.[54] From 1950 to 2010, the towns over half a million went from accounting for 26% of the urban population to 34%, while the percentage of urban population living in cities greater than 100,000 went from 39% to 61%. Thus, not only did the large centers grow, but so did the middle-size cities, with a consequent decline of the small towns of fewer than 20,000 residents.

---

[51] The transfer of the capital to Brasília in 1960 significantly affected the economic and population of Rio de Janeiro.

[52] IBGE, *Estatísticas do Século XX* (2003),Table pop_S2T04.

[53] Thus, for example, between 1991 and 2002, the municipality of Belo Horizonte grew at only 1.1% per annum, while the towns surrounding the city and now making up the greater metropolitan area grew at 1960s and 1970s rates of 4.4% per annum. In 1991, these towns made up just 41% of the metropolitan regional population, and eleven years later they made up half of the metropolitan population. Fundação João Pinheiro, *Perfil demográfico do estado de Minas Gerais 2000* (Belo Horizonte: FJP, 2003), p. 24, Table 15.

[54] IBGE, *Censo demográfico 2000: Resultados do universo*, Table 411, "População residente, por grupos de idade, segundo as Regiões Metropolitanas, a RIDE e os Municípios."

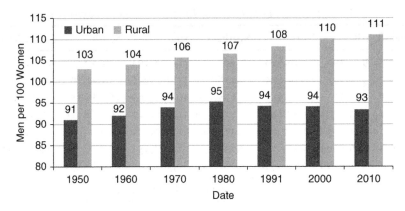

GRAPH 3.22 Sex Ratio of the Urban and Rural Population, 1950–2010
Source: IBGE, Sidra, Table 202; CELADE, Population Projections 2016.

The growth of the cities was through the migration of working-age persons from the rural area, with a significant over-representation of women in the migration stream.[55] The increasing market for domestic services in general and factory work drew these women to the rapidly expanding cities. The result of this migration was that by 2010 the sex ratio in the urban areas was 94 men per 100 women, whereas the ratio was 111 men per 100 women in the rural areas (see Graph 3.22). Nor will this pattern change in the future. The latest estimation of CEPAL for Brazil in 2050 indicates that the sex ratio for the urban area will still be biased toward women, with 92 men per 100 women, and the rural area remains biased toward men at 116 males per 100 females.[56]

Urban growth was not evenly spread across the nation. As might be expected, given its dominance of the expanding manufacturing jobs and its large cities, the leading region in urbanization was the Southeast, which by 1960 had over half the population urban. The Northeastern region, for example, only reached over 50% urban twenty years later. By 2010, however, the differences between regions had declined considerably. This decrease in the rural population and increase in the urban population reached all Brazilian regions, but with different levels of intensities. In the

---

[55] In the census of 2000, the peak age for migrants to the state of São Paulo was 30–34 years. In the state of Rio de Janeiro, which has fewer migrants, most were in their 40s. IBGE, *Censo demográfico 2000, Migração e Deslocamento: Resultados da amostra* (Rio de Janeiro, 2003), Graph 10.

[56] Data on total urban rural rates comes from CELADE, "Brasil, Estimaciones y proyecciones de población a largo plazo, 1950–2100, Revisión 2016."

Table 3.4 *Urban Population of Brazil by Region, 1950–2010*

Year	Brazil	North	Northeast	Southeast	South	Center-West
1950	51,944,397	2,048,696	17,973,413	22,548,494	7,840,870	1,532,924
1960	70,992,343	2,930,005	22,428,873	31,062,978	11,892,107	2,678,380
1970	94,508,583	4,188,313	28,675,110	40,331,969	16,683,551	4,629,640
1980	121,150,573	6,767,249	35,419,156	52,580,527	19,380,126	7,003,515
1991	146,917,459	10,257,266	42,470,225	62,660,700	22,117,026	9,412,242
2000	169,590,693	12,893,561	47,693,253	72,297,351	25,089,783	11,616,745
2010	190,755,799	15,864,454	53,081,950	80,364,410	27,386,891	14,058,094

			Percentage Urban Population			
1950	36%	30%	26%	48%	29%	26%
1960	45%	36%	34%	57%	38%	37%
1970	56%	43%	42%	73%	45%	51%
1980	68%	50%	51%	83%	63%	71%
1991	75%	58%	61%	88%	74%	81%
2000	81%	70%	69%	91%	81%	87%
2010	84%	74%	73%	93%	85%	89%

Source: IBGE, Sidra, Table 1288.

North and Northeast, the urban population reached about 75% of total population in this period. This percentage was 85% in the South region, 89% in the Center-West, and an extraordinarily high percentage of 93% in the Southeast. That is, in the areas of higher agricultural production such as the South, Southeast, and the Center-West, the rural population fell below the national average (see Table 3.4). If we consider the states, São Paulo had 96% of the population living in urban areas, which is surpassed by Rio de Janeiro and the Federal District, both with 97% urban. By contrast, the states with the lowest rate of urbanization have been the least developed agriculture states, with Maranhão (at 63%) and Piauí (at 66%) being the least urbanized ones.[57]

---

[57] There is a recent discussion in Brazil about the extent of urbanization. Some authors, in particular, José Eli da Veiga, claim that there is an overestimation of the degree of urbanization, since there are in Brazil an infinity of small municipalities, whose population is considered urban but living in agglomerates typically rural. About this topic, see: José Eli da Veiga, *Cidades imaginárias: o Brasil é menos urbano do que se calcula* (Campinas: Autores Associados, 2002).

Not only did the rural population migrate in massive numbers to the cities to better their lives, making Brazil by the end of the century an overwhelmingly urban society, but they also migrated to new regions for the same reasons. Initially, to the late twentieth century, migration was primarily to the cities, but by the new century the migration would involve significant movements to the northern and western frontiers as these agricultural frontiers were opened to new farming families.

As of 1930, the international migrations which had brought some 4.4 million European and Asian workers mostly to Southeastern Brazil was slowing down considerably.[58] Most of that migration came in the period from the 1880s to the 1920s and had gone first to the coffee fields of São Paulo and Paraná and then to the expanding cities of the region, above all São Paulo. The continued economic growth of these central and Southern states and the end of significant foreign immigration made these South central regions zones of attraction for the poor of Northeastern Brazil who satisfied the expanding need for workers. Already in the late 1920s migration began on a steady basis from the Northeast and this continued unabated for the next sixty years. By the period 1920–1940, São Paulo received more internal immigrants than foreign-born ones.[59] With each decade the pace increased. Whereas a quarter of the growth of the state of São Paulo in the 1940s was accounted for by migrants coming from other states, this reached 30% of total growth in the next two decades and peaked in the 1970–80 period when 42% of the growth of the state population was accounted for by these internal migrants. But this was the peak period for São Paulo. Thereafter, the importance of migrants in local *paulista* growth dropped to around 10% of the growth rate.[60] Whereas net migration was close to 2 million in the 1970s, and still was over 1 million in the next two decades, it dropped to only 667,000 in the first decade of the new century.[61]

---

[58] Data for 1872–1972 are taken from Maria Stella Ferreira Levy, "O Papel da Migração Internacional na evolução da população brasileira (1872 a 1972)," *Revista de Saúde Pública* 8 (Supl.) (1974), pp. 71–73, Table 1 [São Paulo]. Data for 1820 to 1871 are taken from Directoria Geral de Estatística, *Boletim commemorativo da exposição nacional de 1908* (Rio de Janeiro: Directoria Geral de Estatística, 1908), pp. 82–85.

[59] Merrick and Graham, *Population and Economic Development*, p. 125, Table VI-4.

[60] Carlos Américo Pacheco et al., "Análise demográfica do Estado de São Paulo," in Carlos Américo Pacheco and Neide Patarra, eds., *Dinâmica demográfica regional e as novas questões populacionais no Brasil* (Campinas: Instituto de Economia/UNICAMP, 2000), p. 372, Table 4.

[61] José Marcos Pinto da Cunha and Rosanna Baeninger, "Cenários da migração no brasil nos anos 90," *Caderno CRH* (Bahia) 18.43 (2005), pp. 87–101, and Rosana Baeninger, "Migrações internas no Brasil século 21: evidências empíricas e desafios conceituais." *Revista NECAT* 4.7 (2015), pp. 9–22.

Table 3.5 *Net Migratory Changes by Regions and Selected States, 1965–2010*

Region/State	1965/1970	1975/1980	1986/1991	1995/2000	2005/2010
North	30,160	314,741	122,855	91,071	52,941
NE Northern (1)	−54,128	−186,660	−200,760	−263,347	−315,108
NE Central (1)	−625,638	−571,785	−395,424	−313,028	−334,620
NE Southern (1)	−280,191	−174,334	−258,729	−314,373	−301,737
Northeast Total	−959,956	−932,778	−854,913	−890,747	−951,465
Minas Gerais	−746,853	−237,032	−86,994	57,770	−9,812
Espirito Santo	−104,033	17,114	40,174	40,329	68,001
Rio de Janeiro	504,323	140,756	−36,018	62,092	50,902
São Paulo	592,385	1,066,976	693,524	416,102	382,407
Paraná	582,335	−590,405	−167,195	−68,634	−30,073
South	−325,488	−58,543	19,736	46,485	123,366
Center-West	427,128	279,170	268,832	245,532	313,733

Source: Fausto A. de Brito, José Irineu Rigotil, and Jarvis Campos, *A mobilidade interestadual da população no Brasil no início do século X: mudança no padrão migratório?* (Belo Horizonte: UFMG/Cedeplar, 2012), p. 15.
Note (1): NE Northern (Maranhão e Piauí); NE Central (Ceará, RGN. Paraíba, Pernambuco e Alagoas); NE Southern (Sergipe e Bahia)

Up to the 1970 census, we can see that practically all Northeastern states, particularly Bahia, were net losers of population. So was Minas Gerais. While São Paulo, Paraná, Rio de Janeiro/Guanabara,[62] and Goiás and Mato Grosso were the main recipients of the migration process. The migrations slowed after 1980. São Paulo began to receive a smaller flow of national immigrants, Paraná became a net donor, but the Center-West maintained a position of attraction of immigrants, and Minas Gerais, before a large donor in migratory terms, maintained a relative stability in terms of migratory net flow. The decline of the migration toward São Paulo explains the drastic reduction of the previous patterns of population growth of this state. The long economic crisis of the 1980s and 1990s would have been the main cause of the reduction of migratory flow and the inversion of flows in some cases, as in the state of Minas Gerais (Table 3.5).

Although São Paulo continued to have a positive net immigration balance up to 2010, which in turn influenced the high net migration of the Southeast

---

[62] With the change of capital to Brasília, the former Federal District, constituted by the present city of Rio de Janeiro, was transformed into Guanabara State. Subsequently, in 1975, the former State of Rio de Janeiro merged with Guanabara forming the present State of Rio de Janeiro.

region, the zones of the North and Center-West, the new commercial agricultural frontier, began to attract a steady flow of immigrants, not only from the poor Northeast region, but also modern commercial farmers from the South – the so-called "gaucho migration." While initially the North did very well, the big winner was the Center-West region, all of whose states had positive net inflows in this entire period. Only Goiás lost population in the 1970s, but by the 1990s it was the biggest regional recipient of net migrants, a position which it maintained into the first decade of the new century. From the 1970s to the twenty-first century, there was a steady net outflow of migrants from Paraná in every decade, and in Rio Grande do Sul for every decade except the 1990s. Only Santa Catarina had a steady and growing net immigration, which finally gave the Southern region its positive net migration figures from 1990 to 2010. The Northeast never stopped its outflow of emigrants in this period. All the states of the Northeast except Sergipe and Rio Grande de Norte lost population in every decade. The biggest net outflows were from Bahia, Pernambuco, Maranhão, and Paraiba. It was only in the 1990s that the flow of emigrants slowed somewhat, and the South finally began to have a positive net flow of immigrants.

The impact of this out-migration can be seen in the progressive decline of the Northeastern region in its importance within the national population. In the first national census of 1872 the Northeast was the single most populated region of Brazil and accounted for just under half of the national population (or 47%), with the Southeastern states (Minas Gerais, Espírito Santo, Rio de Janeiro, and São Paulo) just behind it. By 1920, the Southeastern region was now absorbing 47% of the population and the Northeast was down to 37% and would continue its steady decline to just 28% of the total national population by 2017. In the decade of the 1960s, the Northeast lost 1.8 million persons to migration, and in the next decade 2.4 million more left than entered the region.[63] Although the flow of migrants out of the Northeast continued without interruption after 1980, the pattern was for a more dispersed migration, with migrants now heading west and north from the 1990s until today. This explains why the Center-Western region increased its share of population from just 3% in 1950 to 8% in 2017, and the North went from 4% to 9% in the same period (see Map 3.1). In 2014, for example, of the eight states which had 20% or

[63] Neide Patarra, Rosana Baeninger, and José Marcos Pinto da Cunha, "Dinâmica demográfica recente e a configuração de novas questões populacionais," in Carlos Américo Pacheco and Neide Patarra, eds., *Dinâmica demográfica regional e as novas questões populacionais no Brasil* (Campinas: Instituto de Economia/UNICAMP, 2000), p. 30, Table 12.

MAP 3.1 Regional Distribution of the Brazilian Population in 2017
(n = 207.6 million)

more of their native Brazilian population who were born in another state, seven of them were in the North or Center-West regions, and only the state of São Paulo from the Southeastern region came from outside these two expanding regions – and even then São Paulo had the lowest rate of this non-native group, with only 24% of its residents born in other states.[64]

There have also been basic structural changes within the labor force which have had a demographic impact. While total participation rates of the EAP have remained steady in the past 60 years or so, and even slightly declined as the population urbanized (since rates in the rural areas are traditionally higher than the urban rates), the distribution and sex of that labor force have changed. Thus, female rates of participation in the labor force have been constantly increasing in the past twenty years, from an estimated ratio of

[64] IBGE, *Síntese de Indicadores Sociais 2015* (Rio de Janeiro, 2015), n.p., Graph 1.8. I have excluded the federal capital of Brasília, which had 44% of its resident non-native-born.

34% women of working age women who participated in the labor force in 1980 to an EAP rate of 57% in 2014.[65]

Not only did women increase their participation in the labor market, but the majority of women in their fertile years were working. Thus, the PNAD national household survey of 2015 showed that over half of the total of women 18–19 years of age were working, and this rate rose to 61% of all women aged 20–24, and to 71% in the group of women aged 25–29 – the peak reproduction ages in this period.[66] Also, as might be expected, there was a negative correlation between education and level of employment. In 2015, some 15% of all women had a university education compared to 12% of men.[67] In the household survey of 2014, those men and women nationally with university training had an employment figure of 84%, with a progressive fall in participation rates through high school and primary school completions to a rate of just 56% for those with no education.[68]

All these changes in labor force participation and the increasing education of women had a further an impact on fertility as Brazilian mothers began to have first births at ever later ages. In contrast to the first phase of declining fertility, women are now reducing births at their earlier ages, and increasingly delaying births because of educational and occupational opportunities. By 2017, for example, the median age of all mothers giving birth was the 25–29 cohort, and while the 20–24 cohort was still the largest group of mothers nationally, accounting for a quarter of births, the next largest cohorts were 25–29 (24% of all births) and 30–34 (20% of all births). Moreover, as might be expected, the Southeast was different from the nation as a whole, with 25–29 years of age being the median as well as the modal cohort.[69] Given that this was the richest and most advanced region which often led trends in fertility it would appear that the tendency was for ever increasing delay in fertility and the increasing aging of mothers at first births.

---

[65] Calculated from IBGE, *Síntese de Indicadores Sociais 2015*, n.p., Table 1, "Indicadores estruturais do mercado de trabalho para a população de16 anos ou mais de idade, por sexo, com indicação da variação percentual Brasil – 2004/2014."

[66] IBGE, Sidra, PNAD, Table 1864, "Pessoas de 10 anos ou mais de idade, por condição de atividade na semana de referência, sexo, situação e grupos de idade."

[67] IBGE, Sidra, PNAD, Table 272, "Pessoas de 10 anos ou mais de idade, por situação, sexo e anos de estudo."

[68] IBGE, *Síntese de Indicadores Sociais 2015*, n.p., Table 3, "Indicadores estruturais do mercado de trabalho para a população de16 anos ou mais de idade, 16 anos ou mais de idade, total e variação percentual, por nível de instrução Brasil – 2004/2014."

[69] Unfortunately, DATASUS does not provide age-specific birth rates, and these figures are the total births per age of mother. Accessed at: http://tabnet.datasus.gov.br/cgi/tabcgi.exe?sina sc/cnv/nvuf.def.

Thus, by the end of the second decade, Brazilian women have begun to have a pattern of births by age similar to the advanced industrial countries.[70]

As this survey has demonstrated, the social and demographic changes which occurred in Brazil from 1950 to 2017 have been profound. A traditional, highly unequal society with stark indices of poverty and illiteracy even by the standards of Latin America in mid-twentieth century, Brazil has moved to relative equality to the other leading nations of the region in terms of its basic demographic indices. Even more impressively, it has reduced the extreme disparities between regions. It began as a "Belindia," with sharp regional differences in every conceivable metric, and has now become a far more national and uniform society with only moderate regional differences in health, education, and welfare. It has also changed from being a predominantly rural nation to a highly urbanized one. A great deal of this change has to do with systematic government intervention, from vaccination to schools and from modernization of agriculture to the creation of a broad industrial sector. It has also undergone a profound demographic revolution which has led to changes in marriage, smaller families, fewer births, and basic changes in labor markets and rural and urban residence.

[70] The median age of mothers at first births in the USA in 2017 (the latest year for which data exist) was 26.8 years. See *Births: Final Data for 2017*. CDC, NCHS, *National Vital Statistics Reports* 67.8 (2018), p. 5

4

Women, Family, and Work

The massive shift to urban living and the demographic transition which Brazil has experienced since the late 1960s have had a profound impact on the size and nature of the household and family. To these societal developments have been added significant changes in law in the second half of the twentieth century, which have included the extension of legal rights to children born outside of marriage, the legal recognition of consensual unions (cohabiting), and the legalization of divorce, which have had also a major impact on family organization. The consequence of all these developments has meant changes in attitudes concerning what constitutes a traditional family and what the role of women should be in the labor force.

The first obvious impact of declining fertility was the slow but steady decline in family size, from over 5.1 persons per household in 1950 to 2.9 in 2015.[1] Until the end of the 1950s, there was little change, but the decline increased steadily in subsequent years, especially in 1980 and 2015 which saw double the usual rate of decline in family size (see Graph 4.1).

[1] The data for household and family size are found in IBGE, *Censo demográfico 1950*, Série Nacional, vol. 1, p. 286; IBGE, *Censo demográfico 1960*, Série Nacional, vol. 1, p. 112; IBGE, *Censo demográfico 1970*, Série Nacional, vol. 1, p. 206; IBGE, *Censo demográfico 2000: Resultados do universo*, Table 1.3.6; IBGE, *Censo demográfico 2010: Caracteristicas da população e dos domicílios, Resultado do universo*, Table 1.6.1; IBGE, *Censo demográfico 2010: Famílias e domicílios resultados da amostra*, Table 1.1.3. The PNAD data for 1990, 2005, and 2015 is found in IBGE, Sidra, PNAD, Tables 1940, 1948. See also José Eustáquio Diniz Alves and Suzana Cavenaghi, "Tendências demográficas, dos domicílios e das famílias no Brasil," *Aparte: Inclusão Social em Debate* 24 (2012), Table 6 and Suzana Cavenaghi and José Eustáquio Diniz Alves, "Domicilios y familias en la experiencia censal del Brasil: cambios y propuesta para identificar arreglos familiares." *Notas de población* 92 CEPAL (2011), p. 33, Table 1; Arlindo Mello do Nascimento, "População e família brasileira: ontem e hoje," Paper presented at the XV Encontro Nacional de Estudos Populacionais, ABEP, 2006, p. 15, Table 1.

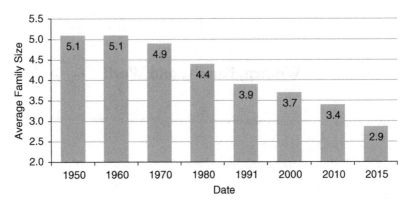

GRAPH 4.1 Average Family Size in Selected Years, 1950–2015
Source: See n. 1.

Household size also declined at the same pace and reached 3.0 persons per household by 2015.[2]

As might be expected, given the different rates of fertility decline by residence, there was a significant difference between the urban and rural rates. Thus, for example, the rural household size in 1950 was 5.3 persons per family and 4.9 persons per family in the urban centers, when the national average was 5.1 persons per family.[3] This pattern could still be seen as late as the census of 2010, when the average urban family was just 2.9 persons per family, compared to the 3.3 average size of the rural family.[4]

Although rapid changes were occurring in fertility and family size, change was much slower to occur in family organization or in Church-sponsored marriages. As would be the case in all subsequent censuses, households still were predominantly formed by families in 1950. In the census of that year, only 12% of households were headed by a person who had never married. At the same time, only 12% of households were headed by a woman alone, and two-thirds of the women who headed households were widows. For both sexes, less than 1% of the heads of households were either divorced or separated (0.1% of male-headed households and 0.8% of female-headed households).[5] Clearly, this was still a very traditional society in terms of stability of marriage, the low incidence of female-headed households, of persons living alone, and of persons divorced or separated.

[2] IBGE, Sidra, Tables 1941 and 1948.
[3] For the urban rate in 1950 we have combined the urban and suburban populations. IBGE, *Censo demográfico 1950*, Série Nacional, vol. 1, p. 280.
[4] IBGE, Sidra, Censo 2010, Tables 3495 and 3521.
[5] IBGE, *Censo demográfico 1950*, Série Nacional, vol. 1, p. 280.

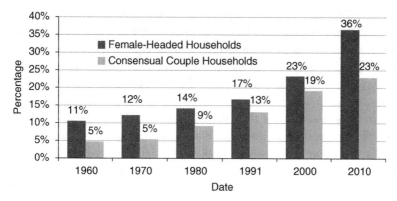

GRAPH 4.2 Ratio of Female-Headed Households and *Uniões Consensuais* by Census, 1960–2015
Source: Ipums, 5% Sample of Brazilian Censuses, 1960–2010.

This relatively stable situation slowly began to change in years that followed. Both consensual unions and female-headed households have increased their share of all households in each subsequent national census. In 1960, only 4.8% of households were maintained by a consensual union and only 10.5% of the households of any type were headed by a woman. By the census of 2010, consensual unions made up 22.9% of all households and women headed 36.5% of households (see Graph 4.2). By the PNAD survey of 2015, such consensual unions were up to 35.2% of all households and were approaching the level of female-headed households, which reached 40.5% of households in that year.[6]

Consensual unions were always part of the Latin American familial organization from colonial times. But changes in the law relating to consensual unions, divorce, and the recognition of the rights of natural children in the twentieth century in Brazil, as in all Latin American countries, has seen consensual unions expand. Initially confined to the lowest economic classes from colonial times, these unions now emerged in the middle and upper classes.[7] Consensual unions only received legal recognition in the Constitution of 1988 and in the so-called Stable Union law of 1996.[8] This

---

[6] IBGE, Sidra, Table 1942.

[7] Jorge A. Rodríguez Vignoli, "Cohabitación en América Latina: ¿modernidad, exclusión o diversidad?" *Papeles de Población* 10.40 (2004), pp. 97–145.

[8] The Constitution of 1988 was the act which finally recognized the legality of consensual unions. Article 226, paragraph 3 stated: "For the protection of the State, the stable union [*união estável*] between the man and the woman as a family entity is recognized, and the law should facilitate their conversion into marriage." Article 4: "It is also understood as a family

guaranteed to these "stable couples" all the traditional rights of inheritance and legal separation held by legally married couples, which also included all property arrangements. As important was the equating of the legal rights of natural children with all legitimate children, which only occurred in 1977 and was amplified in the Constitution of 1988.[9] This guaranteed the rights of all children to their parents' patrimony no matter what the legal standing of their parents, including if they were legally married to other partners. So ingrained has become the acceptance of consensual unions within Brazil that social convention now uses spousal referential terms whether married or consensual in origin. Moreover, given these patterns of seemingly settled domestic life, it is often unknown if a couple has been legally married (*casamento de papel passado*) or not. Given these changes, there has been a steady decline in the ratio of persons officially married. In 1990, for example, there were 7.5 marriages per 1,000 resident population aged 15 years and older and this declined to 5.7 marriages per 1,000 adults in 2002. Moreover, it has been suggested that this decline would have been even more dramatic were it not for the Church campaigns of the mid- to late 1990s to encourage mass marriages for persons living in free unions.[10]

Along with the rise of consensual unions, another major change in Brazilian family structure has been the decline in marriages which were only consecrated in a church and the consequent rise of civil-only marriages. Thus, from 1960 to the census of 2010, civil-only marriages have increased at the cost of both church-only weddings, and church and civil ceremonies (see

entity the community formed by any of the parents and their descendants." Accessed at: www.planalto.gov.br/ccivil_03/constituicao/constituicaocompilado.htm. This was further amplified in 1996 in the so-called "união estável" law (Law 9.278), which stated in Article 1, that the State "recognized as a family entity the lasting, public and continuous coexistence of a man and a woman, established for the purpose of family formation"; and in Article 5 that "The movable and immovable property acquired by one or both of the coexisting persons, in the constancy of the stable union and for pecuniary interest, are considered as the fruit of the work and of the common collaboration, to belong to both, in joint ownership and in equal parts, unless otherwise stipulated by written agreement." www.planalto.gov.br/ccivil_03/leis/L9278 .htm. See also Jamil Salim Amin, "A união estável no Brasil a partir da constituição federal de 1988 e leis posteriores," MA thesis, Universidade Federal de Santa Catarina, 2001.

[9] On the rights of children born outside of a formal marriage, the big change came in 1977 with the recognition and inheritance rights of such children, further reinforced by the Constitution of 1988, which declared that children, "whether or not there is a marriage relationship, or by adoption, shall have the same rights and qualifications, prohibiting any discriminatory designations relating to membership" (Art. 227, § 6). See Mafalda Lucchese, "Filhos – evolução até a plena igualdade jurídica." Accessed 26 November 2017, at: www.emerj.tjrj.jus.br/serieaperfei coamentodemagistrados/paginas/series/13/volumeI/10anosdocodigocivil_231.pdf.

[10] IBGE, Estatísticas do Registro Civil (2002) vol. 29, Graph 10, "Taxa de nupcialidade geral – Brasil – 1991–2002," and IBGE, *Síntese de Indicadores Sociais 2002* (Rio de Janeiro, 2003), pp. 269–270.

Table 4.1 *Percentage of Married Couples Who Had Civil or Religious Wedding or Both, 1960–2010*

Year	Civil-Only	Religious-Only	Civil and Religious
1960	13%	22%	66%
1970	15%	16%	69%
1980	18%	9%	72%
1991	21%	7%	72%
2000	23%	7%	70%
2010	25%	7%	68%

Source: Ipums, 5% Sample of Brazilian Censuses, 1960–2010.

Table 4.1). In the PNAD survey of 2015, these trends continued, with civil-only marriages now at 30% and church-only marriages down to 5% of all married couples listed in the household survey.[11] Thus, from 1960 to 2015, the percentage of people married in a church (church alone or combined with a civil ceremony) has declined from 88% of all married couples to just 70% currently.

What is impressive is that this change in attitude toward the Church and consensual unions can be found in both rural and urban households by the census of 2010. In that census year, women living with spouses in rural areas had quite similar rates of types of marriage bonds as did the urban married couples. They married almost as much in civil marriages and were as likely to be in consensual unions as their urban peers. Moreover, selecting just women who had children (34.9 million women) from all women living with spouses (40.5 million) shows that this pattern has been going on for some time. Older married women showed the same patterns as all married women, again with similar rates for both rural and urban women (see Table 4.2). Yet at the same time this subset of rural married women 10 years of age and older who had children tended more to be Catholic (77%) as opposed to Protestant (17%) than the urban women.[12] Yet their distribution of marriages was still not that different from their younger peers without children. Evidently, the social revolution that this represents is, like fertility control, as much in the rural as in the urban area of Brazil, and even affects traditional Catholics.

Although married and consensual couples are still the predominant form of family and household organization, their ratio is slowly declining and there is a difference by sex. Among male heads of household, the rate of single (around 5%) and of widowed (around 3%) remains relatively constant from 1960 to

[11] Calculated from PNAD 2015.   [12] IBGE, Sidra, Table 97.

Table 4.2 *Percentage of Married Women 10 Years of Age and Older Who Live with a Spouse, by Type of Marriage Arrangement, 2010*

Categories	Urban	Rural
All		
Civil and Religious	43.3	41.2
Only Civil	17.8	14.1
Only Religious	2.5	8.0
Consensual Unions	36.4	36.7
Those with Children		
Civil and Religious	44.7	42.6
Only Civil	18.0	14.1
Only Religious	2.7	8.3
Consensual Unions	34.6	35.0

Source: IBGE, Sidra, Table 102.

2010. But there has been a significant increase in separated and divorced males: from 1% in 1960 to over 9% by 2010. The ratio of "single never married" for women has always been double or more the rate for men. Also, "ever married" by 1980 – the first census that gives complete data – shows that this defined 93% of the male heads of households and only 78% of the female heads; the others were either still married, divorced, separated, or widows. In major contrast to men, women were seven times more likely to be widowed than men in 2010, probably due to two key factors: the longer life expectancy of women compared to men (now at over 7 years' difference) and the higher remarriage rate of widowed men compared to widowed women (see Table 4.3).

The most dramatic change among families and households in the past half century has been in the steady rise of households led by a woman. Such female-headed households (which here include never-married and ever-married women) went from 10.5% of the households in the census of 1960 to 27.3% of all households in the PNAD survey of 2001. Their increase has been especially rapid in the last decade, reaching 41% of all households by the household survey of 2015 (see Graph 4.3). This, of course, was accompanied by a decline in male-headed households, from 89% of all households in the census of 1960 to just 59.5% of all households by the PNAD survey of 2015.

In this growth of female-headed households, there has also been a major change in structure. There has been a decline of those women who were single, and even a major increase of these female-headed households with a spouse present. These changes in family organization can be seen in more detail in the household surveys. In a pattern, not that unusual by Latin

Table 4.3 *Marital Status of Heads of Household by Sex, Censuses 1960–2010*

	Single or Never Married	Married or in Consensual Union	Separated/Divorced or Spouse Absent	Widowed
		Men		
1960	5%	92%	1%	3%
1970	5%	92%	1%	2%
1980	5%	92%	1%	2%
1991	4%	92%	2%	2%
2000	4%	90%	5%	2%
2010	6%	83%	9%	3%
		Women		
1960	17%	n.g.	20%	63%
1970	19%	n.g.	23%	58%
1980	22%	2%	22%	55%
1991	20%	5%	30%	46%
2000	12%	15%	41%	33%
2010	10%	40%	29%	21%

Source: Ipums, 5% Sample of Brazilian Censuses, 1960–2010.

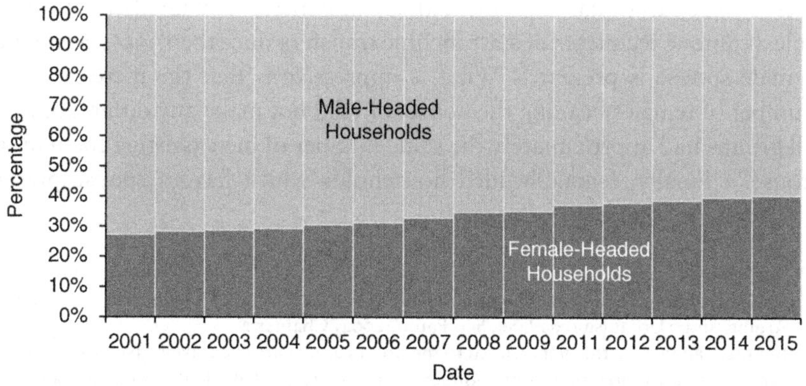

GRAPH 4.3 Ratio of Male- and Female-Headed Households, 2001–2015
Source: IBGE, Sidra, PNAD, Table 1942.

American standards, the increasing importance of female heads of households did not in and of itself mean that males were not present. In fact, the very rapid increase of female-headed households in Brazil has been accompanied by an increasing number of such households having a male spouse as

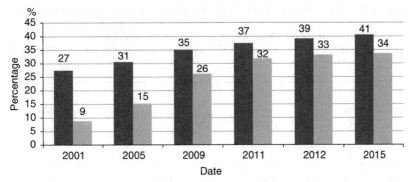

GRAPH 4.4 Importance of Female-Headed Households, and Percentage of Which Had a Male Spouse Present, 2001–2015
Source: IBGE, Sidra, PNAD, Table 1947.

a member. In 2011, some 27% of the households were led by women and 9% contained male spouses. By 2015, the figures were 41% and 34% respectively (see Graph 4.4). This seems to be a result of several factors, including the increasing decline of economically active men within the working age cohorts, the increasing participation of women in the labor force, their increasing educational attainment ahead of males,[13] and finally their crucial role as unique recipients of state income transfers since the 1990s, even when a male spouse is present.[14] What is impressive is that the increase in the number of females heading the household did not make any difference since all groups had approximately the same number of men assisting them in the house.[15] Finally, female-headed households which have a spouse present

[13] See Luiz Guilherme Dacar da Silva Scorzafave, "Caracterização da inserção feminina no mercado de trabalho e seus efeitos sobre a distribuição de renda," PhD thesis, Faculdade de Arquitetura e Urbanismo da USP, São Paulo, 2004, Chapter 2.

[14] In Brazil, all income transfers related to the Bolsa Família are exclusively given to the mother even if a spouse is present. Priscilla Albuquerque Tavares, "Efeito do Programa Bolsa Família sobre a oferta de trabalho das mães," Paper presented at the XVI Encontro Nacional de Estudos Populacionais, ABEP, 2008, pp. 4–5.

[15] IBGE, Sidra, Table 1134. The numbers of males accompanying female heads of households in this census year is below that of the PNAD surveys of the years before and after, giving a ratio of 26% to 29% of female-headed households depending on the color or ethnicity of the women. The lower census figure may be due to the question which asked if there was a *"compartilhamento da responsabilidade pelo domicílio com a pessoa responsável"* – if you had a spouse helping run the household with you. The higher PNAD figure may be due to the existence of male spouses who were not providing any significant support to the female head of household.

have gone from 9% to more than a third of such houses between 2001 and 2015. Thus, even some traditional dual spousal family households are now headed by a woman as they become the primary breadwinners of the family and males become less important in this crucial role.

The other basic change among female-headed households is that they are being led by more ever-married woman than previously. This change is due to legal reforms which have opened up the possibility for easier separation and divorce. Although civil marriage was established in Brazil in 1891 and divorce was made legally possible, the conditions for such a divorce were quite limited. The Civil Code of 1916, however, did permit legal separation, or *"desquite,"* for many of the same reasons, but again with many restrictions and limits. Only in 1977 was full divorce granted, but remarriage was only permitted one more time for the now officially "separated" partners. Finally, in the Constitution of 1988 (article 226), full rights to divorce and remarriage were established which were then incorporated into the Civil Code of 2002. In 2007, divorce could be undertaken by arbitration, without courts, if no small children involved.[16]

That this legal history had an impact on family organization can be seen in the fact that divorce was insignificant in the national population of persons 10 years of age and older until 1980, and then experienced a major growth in that decade. Between 1984 and 2001, the number of divorces granted by the state has grown by 9% per annum.[17] There was also a growth in the number of persons legally separated – made a requirement of the 1988 Constitution which forced a one- to two-year separation before final divorce could be granted. But the ratio of divorces to separations has been steadily climbing and by 2002 final divorces make up 70% of the marriages being dissolved in that year.[18] Despite the increase of persons of all ages getting divorce, the median age of divorced persons in 2015 was high, being 35–39 for women and 40–44 for men, both of which ages have held steady over time.[19] Nor has the number of children affected by divorce changed dramatically, as consistently half of those filing for divorce over time have had only one child or

---

[16] "A trajetória do divórcio no Brasil: a consolidação do Estado Democrático de Direito." Accessed at: https://ibdfam.jusbrasil.com.br/noticias/2273698/a-trajetoria-do-divorcio-no-brasil-a-consolidacao-do-estado-democratico-de-direito.

[17] IBGE, Estatísticas do Registro Civil, Table 426, "Número de divórcios concedidos em primeira instância por grupos de idade da mulher e do marido na data da sentença."

[18] As might be expected, the mean age of persons separating, for both sexes, was three years less than those getting a final divorce. IBGE, Estatísticas do Registro Civil (2002), vol. 29, Graph 14, "Idade média da população de 20 a 64 anos de idade, na data da separação judicial e divórcio – Brasil – 2002."

[19] IBGE, Sidra, Table 1695 for 2015, and for earlier periods, IBGE, Estatísticas do Registro Civil, Table 426.

Table 4.4 *Percentage of Population over 10 Years of Age Separated, Divorced, or Widowed, by Sex, 1960–2010*

Year	Separated	Divorced	Widowed
		Males	
1960	1.3		2
1970	1.3		1.7
1980	1.3		1.6
2000	3.0	2.5	3
2010	2.7	4.5	3.3
		Females	
1960	2.6		7
1970	2.8		6.9
1980	2.9		7.1
2000	4.2	2.5	13.9
2010	3.6	4.5	14.9

Source: Ipums, 5% Sample of Brazilian Censuses, 1960–1980; IBGE, Sidra, Table 1624.
Notes: In the period 1960 to 1980, the number of legal divorces was less than 1% – the maximum was in 1980 when divorced women were 0.07% of the population. Given the unusual results for the census of 1991, which does not fit the trend, these data are excluded.

none.[20] Finally, it appears that after dramatic rises, divorce and separation rates have become fairly stable in the past decade. In 2001, the rates for legal separations among adults 20 years of age and over was 0.9 per 1,000 persons in this age category, a rate that had remained steady since 1994. In turn, the rate of divorce for this same age group slowly rose through the decade of the 1990s and reached 1.2 per 1,000 adults in 1999.[21] As might be expected, these rates were much higher than the national norms in the Southeastern and Southern states, where both separation and divorce rates were 1.3 per 1,000 adults (Southeastern states) and 1.2 per 1,000 adults (Southern states) in 2001.[22] As divorce became easier to obtain, legal separations slowly declined, especially after 2000 (see Table 4.4).

All these changes meant that single-headed households could now be found in the middle and upper classes as well as among the working classes.

[20] IBGE, Estatísticas do Registro Civil, Table 723, "Número de divórcios concedidos em primeira instância por número de filhos do casal." The figure for 2013 was 59%. See IBGE, Sidra, Table 2995.
[21] IBGE, *Síntese de Indicadores Sociais 2002*, p. 271.
[22] IBGE, *Síntese de Indicadores Sociais 2002*, pp. 275, 277, Tables 10.3 and 10.5.

Thus, female-headed households in Brazil are far more diverse in terms of origin, income, and even color than such female-headed homes in North America. In the case of Brazil, as female-headed households increased over time their levels of education and literacy actually passed those of male-headed households by 2015. The annual Brazilian household surveys showed that while initially women household heads had o.6 years less of schooling then men household heads as late as 1992, by the time of the PNAD survey of 2016, female heads of households passed male heads of households in years of education (8.6 for female and 8.5 years for male heads of households).[23] Females in such households thus followed the norms of women in general, since women have since the late twentieth century become more literate and have more years of schooling than men.

Initially, there was a ten-year difference in mean age of male- and female-headed households. This in fact was the norm until 1980. But the increasing arrival of educated divorced and separated women has progressively reduced the age difference – to eight years by 1991 and just a two-year difference between male- and female-headed households by 2010. Clearly, before modern divorce, the existence of widows and never marrieds significantly influenced the higher average and median ages of women heads of households, while the legal changes since 1980 have reduced this difference considerably (see Graph 4.5). The median age for male heads of households

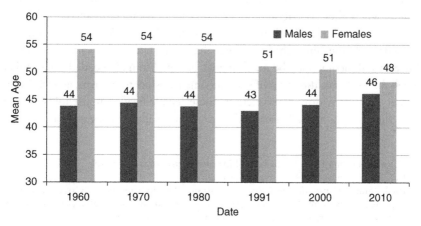

GRAPH 4.5 Mean Age of Head of Household by Sex, 1960–2010
Source: Ipums, 5% Sample of Brazilian Censuses, 1960–2010.

[23] Calculated from the PNAD 2015. For data from 1992 to 2008, see IETS Análises dos Indicadores do PNAD. Accessed at: www.iets.org.br/spip.php?rubrique2.

was 40 to 42 years of age from the 1960 to the 1991 census and for women it was 50 to 52 years of age in the same period. By the census of 2010, the mean ages of male heads of household had risen to 46 years of age for men and had declined to 48 years of age for women (see Graph 4.6).[24] Although the ages of male heads of households has continued to rise to a median of 47 years by the time of the PNAD survey of 2015, the median age of women seems to have stabilized and in fact rose to a median of 50 years.[25] Widows are a declining share of female-headed households, which explains the declining age of women heading such households.

While in 1992 there were slightly more white males than white females as heads of families (57% among male heads vs 53% among women heads), by 2009 there was no difference whatsoever; both were at 49.5% white. There was, however, sharp difference in salary earned by sex of householder, with female-headed households earning on average a third less than male house-holders. While the median monthly salary of women employed in the formal sector was 75% of the value of male workers in the census of 2010, the median monthly salaries of all working women (in both the formal and informal markets) in this census year was 67% of all male workers – approximately the same as in the PNAD survey of 2015, where female-headed households earned just 68% of their male counterparts.[26] Clearly, in female-headed family households, women were the primary breadwinners and accounted for 88% of the income for a family which had no spouse and contained children, compared to the more minor role of female income in dual-spouse families headed by a man, where they contributed under a quarter of total family income.[27] At the same time, female-headed households were also less employed and less unemployed in relationship to the labor force than men. Thus, while salaries are much lower, total income may be much higher or equal to male-headed households, given the exclusive direction of state income transfers to women, as well as the higher ratio of widow pensioners in these female-headed households.[28] This idea that female-headed households were more likely to be pensioners and

[24] Calculated from Ipums, 5% Sample of Brazilian Censuses, 1960–2010.
[25] Calculated from the PNAD survey of 2015.
[26] IBGE, Sidra, *Censo demográfico 2010*, Resultados do Universo – Características da População e dos Domicílios Table 3170 for all workers; IBGE, Sidra, Table 3577 for workers in the formal sector; and calculations from the PNAD survey of 2015.
[27] IBGE, "Estatísticas de Gênero: uma análise dos resultados do censo demográfico 2010," *Estudos & Pesquisas* 33 (2014), p. 66, Graph 5.
[28] For example, Carvalho shows that the third largest source of income in families in the Southeast metropolitan regions were widows' pensions (65%) – following salaries and retirement pensions (18%) in 2011. Cleuseni Hermelina de Carvalho, "Bolsa Família e desigualdade da renda domiciliar entre 2006 e 2011," MA thesis, Pontifícia Universidade Católica de São Paulo – PUC-SP, 2013, p. 127, Table 29.

Table 4.5 *Mean Number of Children by Sex of Household Head, 1960–2010*

Year	Men	Women	Total
1960	2.9	1.8	2.8
1970	2.8	1.8	2.7
1980	2.4	1.6	2.2
1991	2.2	1.6	2.1
2000	1.8	1.4	1.7
2010	1.3	1.3	1.3

Source: Ipums, 5% Sample of Brazilian Censuses, 1970–2010.

people who have retired from the labor force is reflected in the fact that female heads of households on average were much more likely to be widows and were consistently older than male household heads.

Initially, female-headed households had fewer children, but as fertility declined everywhere, by 2010 there was little difference between male- and female-headed households (see Table 4.4.) There was, however, a major difference in the age of the children in households headed by a married couple and those headed by a single mother. Single mothers had a much lower ratio of young children then married couples and a higher ratio of children over 14 years of age resident in the home. In 2015, for example, some 61% of these female-headed households contained children over 14 years of age, and less than a quarter had children younger than 14. Among males the ratios were reversed (see Table 4.5 and Table 4.6).

All these factors have led scholars to note that the rise of female-headed households has not created a major social problem, as most of these households are created by divorce or widowhood and a very significant percentage of the resident children are much older than among married couples.[29] They also help to respond to the debate about the so-called feminization of poverty – that is whether the increasing ratio of female-headed households automatically leads to increased poverty. Are such households more likely to be poor than dual-spousal ones? Recent analysis of Latin American household surveys suggests that the increase in such households is not in fact linked to increased poverty levels.[30] This seems to be the case in Brazil

[29] Medeiros and Costa, "Poverty among Women in Latin America: Feminization or Overrepresentation?" Working Paper 20, International Poverty Centre, Brasília, 2006.
[30] See Medeiros and Costa, "Poverty among Women in Latin America."

Table 4.6 *Type of Households, with Age of Children, in Selected Years, 1992, 2002, and 2015*

Category	1992	2002	2015
Married couple with children under 14 years of age	50.0	46.5	41.0
Married couple with children 14 years of age and older	18.0	27.8	37.5
Married couple with children both under and over 14 years of age	32.0	25.7	21.5
	100.0	100.0	100.0
Single mothers with children under 14 years of age	34.3	33.9	23.5
Single mothers with children 14 years of age and older	40.8	48.0	61.1
Single mothers with children both under and over 14 years of age	24.8	18.1	15.4
	100.0	100.0	100.0

Source: Generated from PNAD 1992, 2002, and 2015 (v4723).

as well. However, some have argued that there may be other consequences aside from poverty which are negative for such households. Given their lower wages in general, some have argued that children in such homes suffer more negative effects in terms of schooling and ultimate income than do children in male-headed households.[31]

Another new aspect to changing demographic and cultural norms is the rise of so-called "unipersonal households" – that is, households in which just one adult lives. Although growing steadily, unipersonal households are still a small minority of households. Nevertheless, these households have more than doubled their share of all households, going from 5% to 12% from 1960 to the census of 2010. But it is interesting to note that in all censuses women were on average five times more likely to be resident in unipersonal households than men (see Table 4.7)

Over time the age of the householder of these unipersonal homes has steadily increased. This growth has occurred for both sexes. Single householders of 50 years of age and older have gone steadily from 44% of all such households to 64% of all households by 2015 (see Graph 4.6). But while men have concentrated in the middle range of ages, women have consistently been older than men. Thus, in the census of 2010, some 69% of the women

---

[31] Ricardo Paes de Barros, Louise Fox, and Rosane Mendonça, "Female-Headed Households, Poverty, and the Welfare of Children in Urban Brazil," *Economic Development and Cultural Change* 45.2 (1997), pp. 231–257. Their data is based on the PNAD survey of 1984.

Table 4.7 *Percentage of Single-Person Households by Sex, Censuses 1960–2010*

	Male	Female
1960	3.3%	17.2%
1970	3.5%	17.1%
1980	4.2%	20.8%
1991	3.9%	18.9%
2000	5.8%	17.9%
2010	9.9%	14.9%

Source: Ipums, 5% Sample of Brazilian Censuses, 1960–2010.

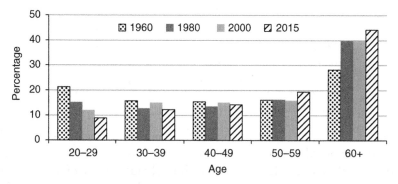

GRAPH 4.6 Distribution of Unipersonal Households by Age, 1960–2015
Source: Ipums, 5% Sample of Brazilian Censuses, 1960–2010; PNAD 2015.

heading such a unipersonal household were over 50 years of age compared to just 45% of the males who were in this age group. Over half the men were in the 20–49 age group, compared to just 29% of the women (see Table 4.8). In terms of color, 60% of the female single-person households were white compared to just 47% that were white among the men. Finally, the census of 2010 shows there was relatively little difference between urban and rural areas, with the urban areas having a slightly higher ratio of such households (12.5% of all households, compared to 10.5% in the rural areas, with little difference by sex).[32] What is probably not surprising is that these unipersonal households were richer than regular family units. In the census of 2010 of all households which had an income, only 18% of the total of households

---

[32] IBGE, Sidra, Table 1134.

Table 4.8 *Age and Sex of Persons Residing Alone in the*
Census of 2010

Age	Men	Women
< = 19	1.3%	0.8%
20 to 24	5.4%	3.4%
25 to 29	8.6%	5.0%
30 to 34	9.7%	4.9%
35 to 39	9.5%	4.4%
40 to 44	10.1%	5.0%
45 to 49	10.4%	6.6%
50 to 54	10.0%	8.5%
55 to 59	8.8%	9.9%
60 to 64	7.6%	11.0%
65 to 69	6.3%	10.8%
70+	12.3%	29.7%
Total	100.0%	100.0%
N	3,571,291	3,409,087

Source: IBGE, Sidra, Table 1134.

earned 2 minimum wages or over. This compared to 32% of all single-headed households having this income – and here there was no difference between male and female single-headed households (32.7% of the males and 32.0% of the females). Moreover, among such households, women had fewer homes which had no income coming in then the men (8.7% of female unipersonal households had no income compared to 10.4% of the men).[33] In fact, a recent study of elderly women living alone aged 60 and above based on the same census of 2010 showed a surprisingly high percentage of these women were quite comfortable economically. Some 92% of them were classified as having an income of the middle/middle class or above, and fully a third were defined as being part of the upper class.[34]

---

[33] IBGE, Sidra, Table 1161. Though strangely these households had a higher percentage of homes without income – 9.6% of all unipersonal households compared to just 4.3% of all households.

[34] On the surprisingly high income and status of elderly women living alone, see Fabio Roberto Bárbolo Alonso, "As mulheres idosas que residem em domicílios unipessoais: uma caracterização regional a partir do Censo 2010," *Revista Kairós: Gerontologia* 18.19 (2015), p. 106, Table 3. This pattern of wealth of women living alone compared to similarly aged women living in families, can be seen in local studies as well. See, for example, Mirela Castro Santos Camargos, Carla Jorge Machado, and Roberto Nascimento Rodrigues, "A relação entre renda e morar sozinha para idosas mineiras, 2003," in João Antonio de Paula et al., eds., *Anais do XII Seminário sobre a Economia Mineira* (Belo Horizonte: Cedeplar, Universidade Federal de Minas Gerais, 2006), pp. 6–7 and Table 1.

It is evident that divorce was causing more working-age men to live alone, but widowhood still was an important factor for women, which may account for the fact of their having more households with income and being comparable in the level of income to men living alone. It has also been suggested that the decline of the multigenerational households and the higher life expectancy and better quality of life of the elderly experienced by the Brazilian population has led to an increasing number of elderly persons living alone even if they have family. In fact, a study of the elderly women (60 years and older) living alone showed that 80% of these women running unipersonal households had one or more children, none of whom was living with them.[35]

Along with changes in the family and in housing arrangements, there has been a massive change in women's level of educational attainment. In 1960, women were more illiterate and less educated then men at all levels. This deficit can be clearly seen in the illiteracy rates by age and sex for the census of 2010, where women were less illiterate than men in every age group except over 60, where the rates were reversed (27.4% for women and 24.9% for men).[36] They had only caught up to men in 1970, and by 1980 they were ahead of males in completing secondary school. By 1991, they were ahead of males at all levels up to university. But by 2000 they even passed the ratio of males at university completion. By 2010, they had not only passed men at every level, but were increasing their distance (see Table 4.9). Thus, women in that year made up 54% of the total of persons 15 years of age who graduated secondary school and 59% of the total graduates of universities

Table 4.9 *Level of Education Completed by Persons 15 Years of Age and Older, by Sex, 1960–2010*

Year	Less than primary completed		Primary Completed		Secondary Completed		University Completed		Total	
	Males	Females	Males	Females	Males	Females	Males	Females	Males	Females
1960	92.2	93.7	4.9	5.5	1.93	0.15	1.0	0.2	100	100
1970	86.2	87.4	8.9	8.0	3.36	3.93	1.6	0.5	100	100
1980	72.7	73.1	17.3	16.7	7.11	8.16	2.8	1.9	100	100
1991	66.3	64.5	19.8	20.0	10.1	12.0	3.8	3.5	100	100
2000	55.1	51.9	26.1	25.8	14.8	17.9	4.0	4.4	100	100
2010	37.0	33.4	33.2	31.0	23.4	26.3	6.4	9.3	100	100

Source: Ipums, 5% Sample of Brazilian Censuses, 1960–2010.

[35] Alonso, "As mulheres idosas," p. 111, Table 6.
[36] IBGE, "Estatísticas de Gênero" (2014), p. 96, Graph 22.

and other tertiary educational institutions. By contrast, they made up only 48% of all those who did not complete their primary education and 49% of those who had just completed their primary school.

But women have been slower to match men in the labor force and in fact were fewer in number than men until the census of 1950. Thus, the sex ratio was a high 107 men to 100 women in the census of 1872 and only slowly dropped down to 99 men per 100 women by 1950. This was the first national census in which women finally surpassed men in the total population and with each subsequent census the number of women grew more rapidly than the number of men so that by the census of 2010 the sex ratio was just 95 men per 100 women.[37] This secular change was due to two factors. The first was the decline of the foreign-born population, since both the Atlantic slave trade and the European and Asian migrations had been predominantly male. By 1950, the foreign born had declined to just 2.4% of the population.[38] The second was the steady decline of maternal mortality, which led to longer life expectancy of women. By the middle of the twentieth century, women lived on average 3.5 years more than men, and were more numerous than men in all ages above 25 years – the peak working ages.

Nevertheless, women until recently were excluded from major areas of the economy and had been concentrated in domestic service and lower-skilled jobs, with incomes lower than their male counterparts. They had very low labor participation rates and were primarily found in the informal economy. But the increasing decline of children per household after 1960 along with the increasing longevity of women (who now lived 7.3 more years then men by the 2010s) and their increasing numbers offered a potential demographic bonus for Brazil, if they could be incorporated into the labor force. That meant that their increasing participation in the labor force made up for the increasing decline of males in the labor force, and thus kept the dependency ratio (the ratio of workers to non-workers – that is children and elderly persons to working persons) quite low.[39] At the same time, cultural and political attitudes toward educating women changed and this led by the last quarter of the century to women finally becoming more literate and having more years of education on average than men. It was their delaying of fertility which allowed them both to enter the labor market and also to obtain more education.

---

[37] IBGE, Sidra, Censo, Table 616.

[38] IBGE, *Censo demográfico 1950*, Série Nacional, vol. 1, p. 8, Table 9.

[39] For a discussion of the demographic bonus in the Brazilian context, see José Eustáquio Diniz Alves, "Crise no mercado de trabalho, bônus demográfico e desempoderamento feminino," in Nathalie Reis Itaboraí and Arlene Martinez Ricoldi, eds., *Até onde caminhou a revolução de gênero no Brasil?* Implicações demográficas e questões sociais (Belo Horizonte: Associação Brasileira de Estudos Populacionais, 2016), p. 23.

All of these factors have led to an extraordinary growth in female labor participation rates. As one economist noted, the growth "of the female demographic bonus was one of the forces responsible for advancing the quality of life of the Brazilian population between 1970 and 2010."[40] In the census of 1950, the female participation rate, that is, women working as a percentage of all women of working age, was only 13.6% at a time when the male participation rate was 80.8% of working-age men. This female participation rate was virtually the same as in the census of 1920 (14%) and even in 1970 it had only risen to 18%. But, by the census of 1991, the female participation rate increased to 33% and the male rate declined to 72% for men in the working-age years.[41] By 2010, women had increased their participation rate to 49%.[42] In the PNAD survey of 2015, at the height of a depression, women's rate reached 55%. These female participation rates were not that different from those in the United States, which had reached 56.8% of women aged 16 and above in the same period.[43] How high these rates might go in Brazil is indicated in the northern European nations, with their systematic state support for working mothers and families. Typical of these is Denmark, where the female participation rate was 77% in 2016, over 20% higher than in Brazil.[44]

But Brazil is far more typical of the rest of the Americas (except for Canada, which has rates comparable to Denmark). In most of the major Latin American countries, compared to the male EAP rate in the late twentieth century, female labor rates have been increasing to a certain basic level. This level is still far from what can be achieved with direct state intervention and the expansion of the welfare state. What is impressive is that, once employed, women have the same ratio of workers with formal work permits as men. Thus, in 2015, some 59% of the EAP males had legal formal employment, while the figure for EAP women was 58%. Of course, the last hired meant that the first fired would be women. This is in fact the case, with the unemployment rate for women going from 41% in the boom year of 2001 to

[40] Alves, "Crise no mercado de trabalho," p. 29.

[41] Adriana Strasburg de Camargo Andrade, "Mulher e trabalho no Brasil dos anos 90," PhD thesis, Universidade de Campinas, 2004, p. 61, Table 01.

[42] IBGE, Sidra, Censo, Table 616 and Alves, "Crise no mercado de trabalho," p. 27 for pre 1991 rates.

[43] US Bureau of Labor Statistics, Table 3.3, "Civilian labor force participation rate, by age, sex, race, and ethnicity, 1996, 2006, 2016, and projected 2026 (in percent)." Accessed at: www .bls.gov/emp/ep_table_303.htm. The Bureau estimates for 2050 are accessible at: www .bls.gov/opub/ted/2007/jan/wk2/art03.htm.

[44] The OECD data are available for 2000–2016 at: https://stats.oecd.org/Index.aspx? DataSetCode=LFS_SEXAGE_I_R.

45% in that of the depression year of 2015. While the male unemployment rate increased, it went to only 23%.[45]

Although numerous datasets for Brazil have been generated from the census and PNAD surveys on male and female participation rates, the basic indices vary from using all persons 10 years of age and older, or those 16 years of age and older, typically used by the Brazilian Census Bureau (IBGE), to the UN standard of using those 15 years of age and older. Using the ILO/World Bank statistics, which uses the 15+ norm worldwide, it is evident that national estimates swing rather dramatically from extremely high and low rates in the 1960s to 1980s to more normal rates by the twenty-first century. From this data it can be seen that initially there was a negative correlation between female and male economically active participation rates – that is as one rose the other declined – and this was due to the increasing rate of female participation and the declining rate of males who were moving out of high participation rural areas to work in lower participation rate cities. Thus, for example, in 2006 the urban rate of the EAP was 72% for men and 52% for women, while the rural rate was 82% for men and 58% for women.[46]

But, since the 1990s, these rates by sex are positively correlated and have moved in harmony with each other, as both have settled into a rather basic range and change together in response to periods of economic growth and decline (see Graph 4.7). Although the growth in labor-force participation for

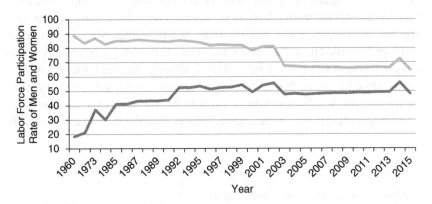

GRAPH 4.7 Labor Force Participation Rate of Men and Women 15 Years of Age and Older in Selected Years, 1960–2015
Source: World Bank data: https://data.worldbank.org/indicator/SL.TLF.CACT.FE.ZS.

[45] IBGE, *Síntese de Indicadores Sociais 2016*, Table 1, "Indicadores estruturais do mercado de trabalho para a população de 16 anos ou mais de idade, por sexo, com indicação da variação percentual – Brasil – 2005/2015."

[46] IBGE, *Síntese de Indicadores Sociais 2006*, Table 3.2–Table 3.2c. Accessed at: www.ibge.gov .br/estatisticas-novoportal/multidominio/genero/9221-sintese-de-indicadores-sociais.html? edicao=10739&t=downloads.

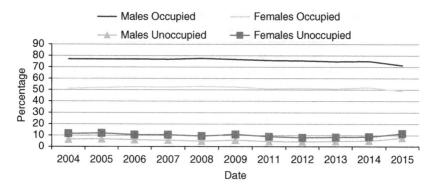

GRAPH 4.8 Percentage of the Population 16 Years of Age and Older Employed and Unemployed, by Sex, 2004–2015
Source: Tables 5.1. www.ibge.gov.br/estatisticas-novoportal/multidominio/genero/9221-sintese-de-indicadores-sociais.html?&t=resultados.

women has slowed considerably since the early 1990s, it has still been consistently faster than that of men, even in the twenty-first century.[47]

Using the more limited definition of the subset of persons 16 years of age and older who were "occupied" (defined as a percentage of these men and women in the total population of those 16 years and older who are currently employed compared to all persons in this age group) in the week of the PNAD survey shows similar patterns of high correlations between the rates for men and women, with women seeming to have reached a plateau of participation far lower than males. This percentage "occupied" has been calculated for the PNAD surveys since 2004 (see Graph 4.8). Conversely, there are far more women "unoccupied" or unemployed (calculated as a percentage of the EAP aged 16 years and older – that is the total of persons employed and unemployed who are working or are looking for work).[48]

---

[47] Simone Wajnman, "'Quantidade' e 'qualidade' da participação das mulheres na força de trabalho brasileira," in Nathalie Reis Itaboraí and Arlene Martinez Ricoldi, eds., *Até onde caminhou a revolução de gênero no Brasil? Implicações demográficas e questões sociais* (Belo Horizonte: Associação Brasileira de Estudos Populacionais, 2016), pp. 46–47.

[48] The IBGE defines EAP as the total number of workers who are employed or unemployed (but looking for work) as a ratio of all persons in their age group. It calls this EAP, the *"Taxa de Participação na força de trabalho,"* as the *"percentual de pessoas na força de trabalho, na semana de referência, em relação às pessoas em idade de trabalhar."* IBGE, *Pesquisa Nacional por Amostra do Domicílios Contínua, Notas Metodológicas* (Rio de Janeiro, 2014), vol. 1, p. 18. The series for employed and unemployed are only available from 2004 for persons 16 years of age and older. Prior to that the only breakdowns by sex and labor market participation are for *"Taxa de Atividade,"* which is the EAP ratio of those over 10 years of age eligible for work in the entire population of persons 10 years of age and older. Finally, the IBGE in its new continuous PNAD surveys carried out every month now defines the economically active population as the population 14 years of age and older for this survey (p. 29, Table 1).

Table 4.10 *Percentage of Economically Active Persons by Sex and Age, 1991–2010*

Age	1991 women	2000 women	2010 women	1991 men	2000 men	2010 men
10–14	6.6	6.7	6.2	14.3	11.9	8.5
15–19	31.8	40.6	35.0	61.9	58.4	45.8
20–24	45.7	60.9	63.3	89.3	86.9	79.9
25–29	46.1	62.4	68.9	95.3	92.3	87.3
30–34	46.6	63.1	70.1	96.4	93.4	89.3
35–39	47.2	63.6	69.7	96.3	93.1	89.7
40–44	45.0	61.2	67.9	95.1	91.8	88.8
45–49	38.8	54.6	63.9	92.1	88.2	87.0
50–54	31.5	n.g.	55.7	84.5	n.g.	82.0
55–59	24.2	n.g.	43.6	75.0	n.g.	73.3
Total	32.9	44.1	48.9	71.5	69.6	67.1

Source: IBGE, Sidra, Table 616.

Nevertheless, in both cases, the ratios for men and women in both categories are highly correlated over time.

Not only are more women entering the labor market, but they are now increasing their activity rates at all ages. This is in sharp contrast with the experience of men in the labor force. Between the census of 1991 and that of 2010 one can clearly see an increase of women working in almost every age category in these three census years. By contrast, men declined in every age group in this same period. The only exception to this was the relative decline or stability of participation in youths under 20 years of age, which was being affected by higher school attendance rates in this same period (see Table 4.10).

Although both men and women are rapidly increasing their participation in school, as seen by the crude participation rates (defined as persons attending school as a percentage of their age cohort), it is clear that women are still outdistancing men in post-secondary education – that is in persons 18 years and above (see Table 4.11). More men than women worked and studied (20% to 14%), but both had the same ratio of those who only worked or neither worked nor studied. Equally, men did poorly compared to women in high school and university drop-out or registration rates. Some 41% of the males and 32% of the females in the age group 18–24 years of age dropped out of school in 2010 – a rather high rate by European standards. At the same time, 15% of the women and only 11% of the men of this age group were attending

Table 4.11 *Ratio of Children in Each Age Group Attending School by Sex, 2000 and 2010*

Age	2000			2010		
	Total	Men	Women	Total	Men	Women
4–5	51.4	50.7	52.1	80.1	79.8	80.4
6–14	93.1	92.7	93.5	96.7	96.5	96.9
15–17	77.7	77.6	77.8	83.3	83.2	83.4
18–24	32.7	32.4	32.9	30.6	29.4	31.9
25+	5.1	4.3	5.7	7.4	6.6	8.0

Source IBGE, "Estatísticas de Gênero: uma análise dos resultados do censo demográfico 2010," *Estudos & Pesquisas* 33 (2014), Graph 23 for data up to 17 years; and Table generated from IBGE www.ibge.gov.br/apps/snig/v1/?loc=0.

universities or other schools of high learning.[49] Although men and women even as late as 2010 are far from parity, recent projections suggest that if women continued to increase their level of education at past rates their labor participation will reach 80% in the high participation ages by the 2040s.[50]

As might be expected, the rates of activity for urban women were higher in all age categories except 50 years and older compared to rural women in the census of 2010. In total, some 44.7% of urban women were economically active, compared to 35.8% of rural women who were in the labor force. In the peak age groups, the difference was even more extreme, reaching a 19% difference for the cohort 20–24 years of age and a 20% difference in the next cohort, 25–29 (see Graph 4.9). Much of this difference can probably be explained by urban women having a much higher rate of education than rural women.

The increasing level of education among women has been a significant influence in the type of work available to them. From the extremely low rates in the twentieth century, when women primarily worked as agricultural laborers or domestic servants, women have slowly and steadily increased their participation in industry as well as the professions. This rate has even increased in the industrial sector, from 22.5% of all workers in 1995 to 25.8% of all workers by 2015. They are also several industries in which women are even better represented than this average. Thus, women currently make up over a third of workers in the fields of electricity and

---

[49] IBGE, "Estatísticas de Gênero" (2014), p. 103, Table 15; p. 104, Graph 28; and p. 106, Graph 30.
[50] Wajnman, "'Quantidade' e 'qualidade,'" pp. 48–49.

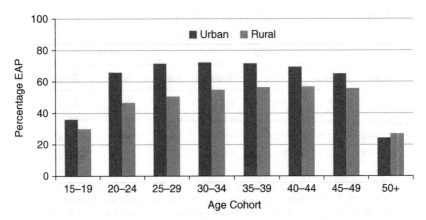

GRAPH 4.9 Rates of Labor Activity of Urban and Rural Women by Age Cohort in 2010
Source: IBGE, Sidra, Table 616.

communications, the paper and publishing industries, and in the food and drinks industries.[51] The ratio of domestic workers among women has also significantly declined as they shifted into all the other sectors of the economy. At current trends, all indicators suggest that in the future many prestigious fields will be dominated by women, much as has been occurring in advanced industrial societies. Women have slowly emerged as the majority of students in professional fields, some of which are considered high status ones in Brazil. Although 44% of the doctors who graduated in 2010 were women, women now make up 54% of all current medical students. While 46% of lawyers who had graduated by 2010 were women, women now make up 52% of all current law students. Women dominate in education and nursing, currently and in the past, and these are not considered prestigious occupations. But they have also begun to take up engineering in Brazil. Thus, only 20% of engineers who have graduated have been women, but in 2010 women made up 28% of those studying engineering.[52]

However, this positive development is qualified by data on levels of employment. At this stage of the evolution of women entering the labor

---

[51] On current industrial participation rates of women, see www.portaldaindustria.com.br/age nciacni/noticias/2016/11/participacao-de-mulheres-no-mercado-de-trabalho-industrial-cres ce-143-em-20-anos/.

[52] Amélia Artes and Arlene Martinez Ricoldi, "Mulheres e as carreiras de prestígio no ensino superior brasileiro: o não lugar feminino," in Nathalie Reis Itaboraí and Arlene Martinez Ricoldi, eds., *Até onde caminhou a revolução de gênero no Brasil? Implicações demográficas e questões sociais* (Belo Horizonte: Associação Brasileira de Estudos Populacionais, 2016), p. 89, Table 1.

Table 4.12 *Percentage of Economically Active Population Employed by Sex and Level of Education in 2015*

Educational Attainment	Men	Women
Total	71.5	48.8
No education or incomplete primary	64.7	34.5
Primary complete or middle school incomplete	67.4	41.6
Middle complete or tertiary incomplete	78.4	58.0
Tertiary education completed	84.7	74.4

Source: IBGE, *Síntese de Indicadores Sociais*, 2016, Table 5.2. www.ibge.gov.br/estatisticas-novoportal/multidominio/genero/9221-sintese-de-indicadores-sociais.html?&t=resultados.

market, women have still not converted their educational advantages into employment as well as have men. Thus, more men who had completed high school and or university were likely to be employed then were women with the same educational level, though again in both groups the most highly educated had the highest ratio of employment as of 2015 (see Table 4.12).

But the industries in which the better-educated workers participated were approximately the same for both sexes by 2015. The public sector and service industries, which included health, education, and social services, were major occupations for women, with high participation rates. Those who completed primary education and a high school degree tended to be more evenly distributed. But those without education were concentrated in agriculture in the case of both sexes. Overall, the patterns of industrial concentration were relatively similar for men and women, suggesting that education was the key variable determining in which industry one was employed (see Table 4.13). Moreover, for persons employed who were 25 years of age or older, 6.2% of the males were in administration or directed companies compared to 4.7% of the women in these same positions – which was just a quarter less than the male rate.[53]

Along with increased penetration in the market in all sectors, there has also been a profound change in the formal and informal market participation of women. Women are now equal to men in terms of being part of the formal labor force. Since the beginning of the century, the ratio of working women who held a signed work card was roughly equal to men. This work booklet (*Carteira de Trabalho Assinada*) is a fundamental instrument which indicates

[53] IBGE, *Síntese de Indicadores Sociais*, 2016, Table 5.15. www.ibge.gov.br/estatisticas-novoportal/sociais/trabalho/9221-sintese-de-indicadores-sociais.html?edicao=9222&t=downloads.

Table 4.13 *Percentage of Employed Population by Industry, Sex, and Level of Education, 2015*

Sector of the Economy	No Education or Primary Incomplete		Primary School Complete and High School Incomplete		High School Complete or University Incomplete		University Completed		Total	
	Men	Women	Men	Women	Men	Women	Men	Women	Men	Women
Total	36	26	18	14	35	40	12	20	100	100
Agriculture	73	72	14	13	12	12	2	2	100	100
Industry	25	28	19	18	46	42	10	12	100	100
Construction	51	16	23	14	23	40	3	29	100	100
Commerce	28	17	22	17	43	56	8	10	100	100
Housing and food	32	31	24	23	38	40	5	5	100	100
Transport and warehousing	30	7	21	13	42	57	7	23	100	100
Public administration	14	8	10	7	48	43	29	42	100	100
Education, health, and social services	6	6	5	5	38	40	51	50	100	100
Other services	18	31	13	18	42	37	27	14	100	100
Poorly defined occupations	57	19	20	34	19	21	3	25	100	100

Source: IBGE, *Síntese de Indicadores Sociais*, 2016, Table 5.9. www.ibge.gov.br/estatisticas-novoportal/multidominio/genero/9221-sintese-de-indicadores-sociais.html?edicao=10739&t=downloads.

that a person is contributing to social security and had standard worker rights and benefits.[54] These workers were under the codified labor code (*Consolidação das Leis do Trabalho* – CLT).[55] Public officials, however, fall under two separate regimes. The statutory regime (*Estatutário*) and the labor regime (CLT). In this statutory scheme there is no signed work permit and retirement is through the civil service pension schemes, which may be from the federal, state, or municipal government, depending on where they are employed. In 2001, 55% of male and 54% of female employees were in the formal sector and had such working papers. By 2015, this had increased to 65% for employed men and 62% for employed women.[56]

This equal participation of men and women in the formal labor market holds across all ethnic and racial groups as well. Although women earn less than men at all levels of education and occupation and are often less numerous then men in given occupations, in this one area there is surprising equality between men and women in the labor market. That is, both are identical in their participation in the formal economy, which in 2010 involved 109,000 Amerindians, 0.5 million Asians, some 21 million browns, and 4 million blacks, along with 24 million whites (see Graph 4.10).

Even the wage differential between women and men has narrowed over time as women's wages have increased faster than those of male workers, thus reducing the distance between the two. Thus, in 2004, women's average salary was 70% of male salaries and by 2015 it was 76% of the value of average male salaries (see Graph 4.11). But, at the same time, the number of hours per week worked by women was just 34.9 hours in 2015, which compared to an average of 40.8 hours for men. By contrast, women spent 20.5 hours per week on domestic chores compared to half that rate for

---

[54] A useful definition of the "*Carteira de Trabalho*" or Labor Booklet is defined by Noronha as "a sort of a 'labor ID' in which employers are obliged to write down information about their wages, social security, hiring and firing dates and conditions, among others details. Therefore, the Labor Booklet tells the history of all formal jobs the worker has had, and it is frequently used to show that the worker is a reliable citizen when he is hired for a new job or needs to get a loan, and that he deserves to be respected by the society" (translation of original article: Eduardo G. Noronha, "Informal, Illegal and Unfair: Perceptions of Labor Markets in Brazil," *Revista Brasileira de Ciências Sociais* 18.53 (2003), pp. 111–129). The aticle was revised and republished in 2005 at: http://socialsciences.scielo.org/scielo.php?pid=S0102-69092005000100009&script=sci_arttext&tlng=en.

[55] This was first issued by the Vargas government in 1943 (Decree Law 5.452 of 1 May 1943), and has been amended constantly through the years, with the latest occurring in 2017 to include part-time workers' rights. See Marcelo Moura, Marcelo. *Consolidação das leis do trabalho* (7th edn; Salvador: JusPodivm, 2017). Accessed 12 July 2017 at: www.editorajuspodivm.com.br/cdn/arquivos/ca61542oc19a66758beaf108395feo1b.pdf.

[56] IBGE, Sidra, Table 1916.

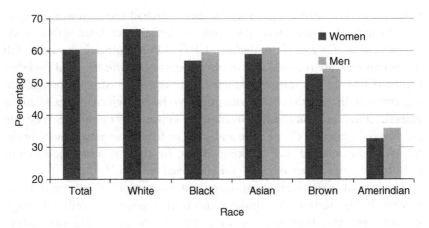

GRAPH 4.10 Percentage of Workers Contributing to Social Security by Sex and Color, 2010
Source: IBGE, Sidra, Censo 2010, Table 3581.

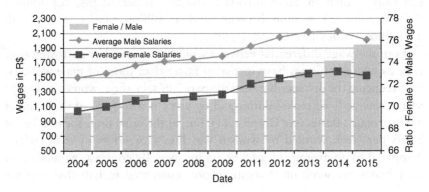

GRAPH 4.11 Average Wage by Sex of Persons 16 Years of Age and Older, 2004–2015
Source: IBGE, *Síntese de Indicadores Sociais*, 2016, Table 5.10. www.ibge.gov.br/estatisticas-novoportal/multidominio/genero/9221-sintese-de-indicadores-sociais.html?&t=resultados.

men.[57] Even in high-status professions, average male salaries are always higher than female salaries even though many of these professions have at least half or more employees who are women (see Table 4.14).

---

[57] IBGE, *Síntese de Indicadores Sociais 2016* (Rio de Janeiro, 2016), Table 5.13. Accessed at: www.ibge.gov.br/estatisticas-novoportal/multidominio/genero/9221-sintese-de-indicadores-sociais.html?edicao=10739&t=downloads.

Table 4.14 *Comparative Salaries of Men and Women and Ratio of Women in Liberal Professions, 2010*

Fields	Women's Salaries as Ratio of Male Salaries (%)	Percentage of Women Workers
Education	72	83
Humanities and Arts	79	74
Social Sciences, Business, and Law	66	49
Sciences, Math, and Computing	65	47
Engineering, Production, and Construction	66	22
Agriculture and Veterinarians	63	27
Health and Social Welfare	56	68
Services	53	55

Source: IBGE, "Estatísticas de Gênero" (2014), p. 107, Table 17.

Finally, in terms of their structural position within the labor market, the ratios of women in most categories are quite close to those of men. Women do better in public administration, largely on account of their domination of primary and secondary teaching, though they are well represented in the universities. Women are equal to men in participating in the legally recognized labor market and paying into social security. But they are double the male rate in non-paid labor (see Table 4.15).

But the wage differential, though narrowing, still shows up in almost all occupations. Thus, in the same census of 2010, women's wages, even when working for the government or the military, are usually a quarter less than male monthly wages (see Graph 4.12).

But, when broken down by age group, it is evident that the younger the female workers are, the more likely their salary is closer to their male cohorts. Thus, for the employed age cohort 16–24 in the year 2010, women make 88% of the wages of men, for 25–39 it drops to 78%, for 40–59 it declined further to 69%, and then drops to 60% for women who are 60 years of age and older.[58] This would suggest that the increasing educational level of women is finally having an impact on wages and that if this trend continues wages should begin to reach parity in the future, especially if the trends in education keep pace with the advances women have made in the last few decades.

[58] IBGE, "Estatísticas de Gênero" (2014), p. 137, Table 37.

Table 4.15 *Ratio of Workers in Various Categories of Work by Sex, Census of 2010*

Type of Work	Men	Women
Employed	68.1	74.5
Employed with signed work booklet	46.1	48.0
Employed in military or public administration	4.1	7.8
Employed without signed work booklet	17.9	18.8
Non-remunerated work	1.1	2.4
Work for their own consumption	3.9	2.7
Employer	2.3	2.2
On own account	24.5	18.2
Total	100.0	100.0

Source: IBGE, Sidra, Table 3461.

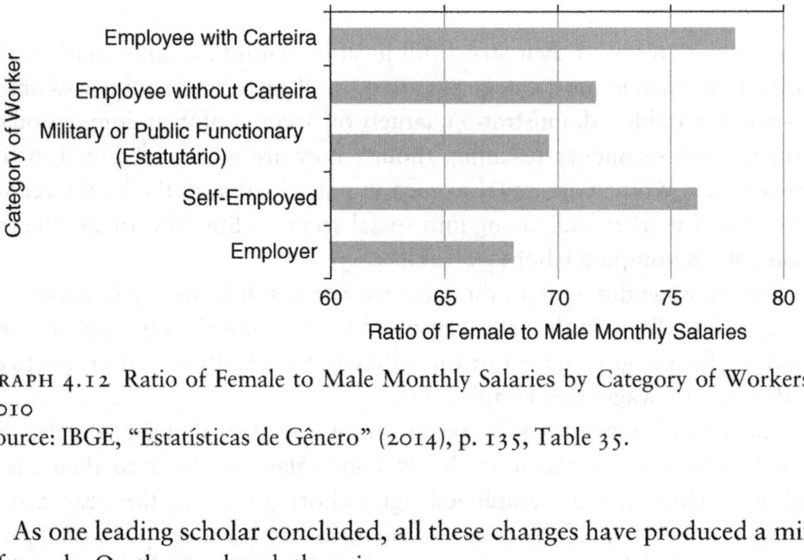

GRAPH 4.12 Ratio of Female to Male Monthly Salaries by Category of Workers, 2010
Source: IBGE, "Estatísticas de Gênero" (2014), p. 135, Table 35.

As one leading scholar concluded, all these changes have produced a mix of trends. On the one hand, there is

the massive and steady increase of female participation in the labor market ... and on the other hand, the prevalence of high unemployment rates among women and the lower quality of female jobs; on the one hand, there is access to prestige careers and jobs, and to management and board positions, and on the other hand, the prevalence of female presence in precarious and informal activities.[59]

[59] Maria Cristina Aranha Bruschini, "Trabalho e gênero no Brasil nos últimos dez anos," *Cadernos de Pesquisa*, 37.132 (2007), p. 537.

But even in these precarious positions there have been some very important recent changes. One such occupation which still absorbs 14% of economically active women in 2016 is the traditional occupation of domestic service. The post-1988 constitutional civil and labor codes have given domestic workers far more rights and have incorporated many more such workers into the formal sector. Thus, domestic servants with signed working papers went from 25% of all such women domestics in 2001 to 30% in 2016. Moreover, given these changes, live-in workers are now the exception rather than the norm, and modern apartment construction in Brazil no longer provides a living space for domestic servants. All these changes began in 1972 with the first law which recognized basic rights for domestic workers (vacations, contributions to social security, etc.).[60] Then came a far more detailed law in 2015 which more precisely defined formal domestic service as being more than two days per week (2 days or less was a "day worker"), requiring a legal formal labor contract between workers and their employers, as well as providing the usual vacations, right to organize, and very specific regulation about daily hours and payment for overtime.[61] This law took on even more significance with the anti-slavery laws which defined very specific working conditions for all workers, and was put into practice in the 1990s.[62] Finally, the existence of a complete set of autonomous Labor Courts guarantees that cases against employers can easily be undertaken by domestic workers.

At the same time, the ratio of female domestic service workers in the female labor force has been systematically declining. In the census of 1950, some 27% of the women employed worked as domestic servants and they were the second largest category of workers after agricultural laborers.[63] By 2001, such workers absorbed only 22% of all women employed in the labor force, and by 2015 the ratio was down to 16% of all economically active women. By contrast, 63% of working women now are employed in industry and commerce and very few in primary activities (see Table 4.16). But for all the changes this still remains an overwhelmingly female occupation, with women making up 92% of all domestic servants by 2016, a ratio that had changed little since 2001.[64] Moreover, domestic servants in 2015 were the lowest paid category of women workers, earning half of the average monthly salary of all

---

[60] For this law 5859/72, see www.normaslegais.com.br/legislacao/trabalhista/lei5859_1972.htm.

[61] Law 150/2015. Accessed at: www.planalto.gov.br/ccivil_03/leis/LCP/Lcp150.htm.

[62] The first of these anti-slavery laws was passed in the penal code of 1940 (article 149), but it really became effective in the 1990s and was only recently revised in 2017. See www.jusbrasil.com.br/topicos/10621211/artigo-149-do-decreto-lei-n-2848-de-07-de-dezembro-de-1940.

[63] Andrade, "Mulher e trabalho no Brasil," p. 62, Table 03.   [64] IBGE, Sidra, Table 1906.

Table 4.16 *Percentage Share of Women Workers in Sectors of the Labor Force for Women 10 Years of Age and Older, 2001–2015*

Year	Salaried Employee	Domestic Servant	Employer	Self-Employed
2001	56.4	21.6	2.8	19.2
2002	56.6	21.0	3.1	19.3
2003	56.9	20.8	2.9	19.3
2004	57.5	20.4	2.9	19.2
2005	57.3	20.3	3.1	19.3
2006	58.1	19.7	3.2	18.9
2007	59.1	19.3	2.7	18.9
2008	60.4	18.3	3.2	18.0
2009	59.4	19.5	2.9	18.1
2011	62.9	17.6	2.4	17.1
2012	63.9	16.4	2.7	16.9
2013	64.4	16.3	2.7	16.6
2014	64.2	15.6	2.6	17.6
2015	63.0	15.7	2.6	18.8

Source: IBGE, Sidra, Table 1907.

working women, less than half of what salaried employed women make, and even 37% less than the next worst paid workers, self-employed women.[65]

One last question worth examining in terms of women and work is whether all female workers are treated equally. Given the racial divides that still define much of Brazilian society it is no accident that not all women are treated equally in the labor market. White employed women in the formal labor market had a much higher ratio of university graduates and a much lower ratio of uneducated among its members (see Table 4.17).

In turn, this made for different median salaries of women by color. But even when women of color had the same education as white women they were earning consistently less median salaries at every level of completed education (see Table 4.18). This later finding may be more complex to explain than just racism, since the university degrees are probably not equivalent. In Brazil, non-white students tend to go to public secondary schools and private universities, while white female students tend to do just the opposite and go to better-performing private secondary schools and public universities. In Brazil, entrance to public universities is by

[65] IBGE, Sidra, Table 1908.

Table 4.17 *Educational Level of Women Working in the Formal Market by Color, Census of 2010*

Level of Education	All Women	White	Brown + Black
No education or primary incomplete	32.2	25.8	39.3
Primary complete and secondary incomplete	17.0	15.9	18.3
Secondary complete and some university	34.1	35.3	32.8
University complete	16.8	23.0	9.6
Total known	100.0	100.0	100.0
Number whose education is known	36,356,345	18,957,289	16,815,643

Source: IBGE, Sidra, Table 3577.

examination and the schools are of international quality, while the private universities are essentially unregulated, and, with only a few exceptions, offer inferior degrees. Thus, a university title is not equal across all schools in what is one of the biggest blockages to social mobility in Brazil.

Along with changes in family, education, and labor participation, various NGOs and women's defense organizations have also actively promoted better protection for women within families against male violence. Traditionally, domestic violence was considered a minor offense and efforts were made to reconcile the conflicting partners. Even under a special law on the subject in 1995, there was no real effort to protect victims. But, after a particularly vicious attempt by a husband to murder his wife, the so-called *Lei Maria da Penha*, in honor of the victim, was enacted in 2006. This anti-domestic violence law (Law 11.340/06) put in place some of the most advanced legislation protecting women, treating cases of violence as serious crimes, and providing a coherent structure for women to obtain support and legal help. This led to a combination of changed and new institutions. The Special Police Units for Women (*Delegacias de defesa da mulher* – DDM), which had been created in 1985, and were the first such special units created in Latin America, were given more autonomy and power after 2006.[66] The new law also created special courts specifically to deal with these domestic violence issues (*Juizados de violência*

[66] There are currently more than 400 of these DDMs or Women's Police Stations in Brazil. See Nadine Jubb et al., *Regional Mapping Study of Women's Police Stations in Latin America* (Quito: Centro de Planificación y Estudios Sociales, 2008), pp. 1, 9.

Table 4.18 *Median Income of Workers in the Formal Labor Market by Sex and Color, Census of 2010*

Level of Education	Total		Women				
	Men	Women	White	Black	Asian	Brown	Amerindian
No education or primary incomplete	510	500	500	500	480	400	45
Primary complete and secondary incomplete	750	510	510	510	510	510	500
Secondary complete and some university	1000	650	650	600	650	590	569
University complete	3000	1800	2000	1500	2000	1500	1485
Total known	800	600	600	510	600	510	300
Number of workers	49,618,496	36,356,345	18,957,289	2,757,690	463,107	14,057,953	120,149

Source: IBGE, Sidra, Table 3577.

doméstica e familiar contra a mulher – JVD). More-significant punishments were imposed for aggression and more protection was offered to women. Equally, the state proposed creating multi-professional groups to provide support and counseling for these women through the DDM.[67] With all the problems related to the availability of very limited resources and the need to confront still dominant traditional attitudes,[68] it appears that these Police Units have had some impact on protecting vulnerable women and in dealing with domestic violence.[69]

There are now more data than ever collected on this matter, which has become a public health issue. The Ministry of Health published data from twenty-four hospitals and clinics in state capitals, and the Federal District issued a report on domestic violence between 2009 and 2010. There were almost 76,000 women who contributed to this data. What is impressive is that only 47% were non-white, and some 46% had nine or more years of schooling. There were probably more single women than the average for the population, but otherwise they seemed to be better educated and more solidly middle class than one might have expected. Some 48% had been married (divorced, separated, and married), which is probably a relatively low rate, but the number of children involved was quite high, and even the elderly were not exempt from this violence (see Graphs 4.13a and 4.13b).

Women's defense groups have also put pressure on the government to protect women against violence in all situations. After much agitation, in 2009 was passed the *Lei de Dignidade Sexual* – a fundamental change in the law which expanded greatly the definition of sexual aggression, including rape or attempted rape (*Estupro e tentativa de estupro*). Rape and attempted rape were now more broadly defined as unwilling acts of a libidinous nature practiced by one person against another (gender left open). If the other

---

[67] Beatriz Accioly Lins, "A lei nas entrelinhas: a Lei Maria da Penha e o trabalho policial em duas Delegacias de Defesa da Mulher de São Paulo," MA thesis, Universidade de São Paulo – USP, 2014, Chapter 1.

[68] How traditional these can be is seen in the survey on attitudes toward rape and their victims carried out by the Brazilian government. See Ipea, Sistema de Indicadores de Percepção Social (SIPS), "Tolerância social à violência contra as mulheres, 04 de abril de 2014." Accessed at: www.ipea.gov.br/portal/images/stories/PDFs/SIPS/140327_sips_violencia_mulheres.pdf.

[69] For detailed studies of the functioning of local DDMs, aside from the excellent study of Lins cited above, see the ethnographies of Fabiana de Andrade, "Fios para trançar, jogos para armar: o fazer policial nos crimes de violência doméstica e familiar contra a mulher," MA thesis, Universidad de Campinas, 2012 on Campinas; Ana Pereira dos Santos, "Entre embaraços, performances e resistências: a construção da queixa de violência doméstica de mulheres em uma delegacia," MA thesis, Universidade Federal de Viçosa, 2014 for the local one in Viçosa in Minas Gerais; and Ana Lúcia dos Santos, "Delegacia de defesa da mulher: um lugar de queixas – queixas de um lugar," MA thesis, Assis, Universidade Estadual Paulista – Unesp, 2007, undertaken in a *Delegacia* in the interior of São Paulo.

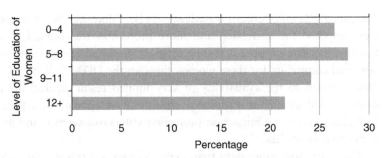

GRAPH 4.13A Level of Education of Women Victims of Domestic Violence (%)

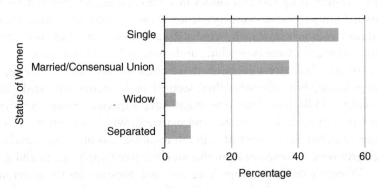

GRAPH 4.13B Civil Status of Women Victims of Domestic Violence (%)
Source: Ministério da Saúde, *Viva: Vigilância de Violências e Acidentes, 2009, 2010
e 2011* (Brasília: Ministério da Saúde, 2013), p. 122, Table 40.

person was a minor, prison terms increased, and the state was required to prosecute even if the family rejected prosecution.[70]

As part of this new movement to protect women as essentially a health issue as well as a police concern, various government and private agencies have begun to collect systematic data on homicide and sexual aggression against women. Some general patterns have emerged from these data. As might have been expected, fewer women were murdered than men, but incidents of rape and attempted rape were far more numerous than previously thought and are almost as great as the number of murders of men. Although most of the data gathered are quite recent, certain clear patterns are emerging. The female murder rate remains relatively stable at 4–5 deaths per

[70] Law 12015 of August 2009. For a commentary on the law, see Gleick Meira Oliveira and Thaís Maia Rodrigues, "A nova lei de combate aos crimes contra a liberdade sexual: uma análise acerca das modificações trazidas ao crime de estupro," *Âmbito Jurídico* (2011). Accessed at: www.ambito-juridico.com.br/site/index.php?n_link=revista_artigos_leitur a&artigo_id=9553. The law itself is available at: www.planalto.gov.br/ccivil_03/_ato2007-2010/2009/lei/l12015.htm.

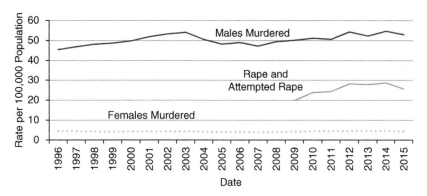

GRAPH 4.14 Incidence of Murder by Sex and Rape and Attempted Rape, 1996–2015
Source: www.ipea.gov.br/atlasviolencia/dados-series; and www.forumseguranca.or
g.br/estatisticas/tableau-dignidade/.

100,000 population, whereas male murder rates are 10 times higher.[71] The younger the age cohort the higher the ratio of homicides. Thus, 15% of the deaths of women age 15–19 are caused by violence.[72] Even in peak years 20–29, violence accounts for 10% to 13% of all deaths in this age group. On the other hand, numbers of reported rapes and attempted rapes (data available only from 2009) are 5 to 6 times higher than the homicide rate for women, being between 24 and 29 per 100,000 population, and fluctuate far more than do murders (see Graph 4.14).[73]

The Ministry of Health has also reported on the incidence of violence against women from victims who appeared in the emergency rooms of twenty-six capital cities and Federal District hospitals and clinics in a two-month period in 2011. There were some 1,070 cases reported, and 73% of the women were non-white – a quite different ratio than was found for

[71] The overall murder rate of 25–30 homicides per 100,000 population is a relatively high rate by world standards. It is double that rate in most of the Central American republics and some of the Caribbean islands, but in South America only Colombia, at 32–35 in the period since 2004, exceeds that rate. The rate in the United States in the period 2000–2012 is around 5 deaths per 100,000 population. United Nations Office on Drugs and Crime (UNODC). *Global Study on Homicide 2013: Trends, Contexts, Data* (Vienna: UNODC, 2013), pp. 126–127, Table 8.1.

[72] Daniel Cerqueira et al., *Atlas de Violência 2017* (Rio de Janeiro: Ipea/FBSP, 2017), p. 8, Table 1.1.

[73] The leading experts on this subject estimate that "a cada ano, no mínimo 527 mil pessoas são estupradas no Brasil. Desses casos, apenas 10% chegam ao conhecimento da polícia." Daniel Cerqueira and Danilo Santa Cruz Coelho, *Estupro no Brasil: uma radiografia segundo os dados da saúde* (preliminary version), Nota Técnica 11 (Brasília: Ipea, 2014), p. 26.

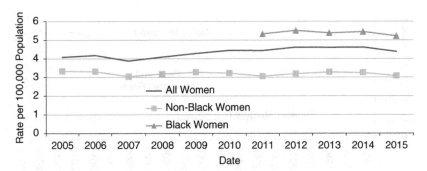

GRAPH 4.15 Incidence of Murders of Women by Color, 2005–2015
Source: www.ipea.gov.br/atlasviolencia/dados-series; www.forumseguranca.org.br/
estatisticas/tableau-dignidade/.

female victims of domestic violence. But the age spread was about the same, with the largest cohort being women aged 20–39 (55% of the cases). Educational level was only slightly below that of the domestic violence victims, with 43% of the women having nine or more years of education.[74] These data and other reports show that in violence, as in work and education, there is a difference by color in Brazil. Violence against women of color is seen not only in these victim studies but also in the higher homicide rates they have compared to non-black or brown women. These data are available only for homicide victims and for a generic black group which also includes browns. But these same differences by color probably also occur for victims of rape and sexual aggression as well (see Graph 4.15).

The national mortality figures for 2016 well reflect these patterns. Fewer women than men in 2016 died from accidents and other external causes of violence, and a much lower percentage died from infectious diseases (women made up only 38% of all infectious deaths and 43.7% of all deaths in that year). However, in terms of the major killers within Brazilian society, there was surprisingly little difference between the sexes (see Table 4.19) and this has been the pattern since 1990.[75] Nevertheless, women still lived longer than men. It is estimated that the life expectancy for women in 2018 was still 7.1 years longer than for men (79.8 years for women and 72.7 years for men).[76]

[74] Ministério da Saúde, *Viva: Vigilância de Violências e Acidentes, 2009, 2010 e 2011* (Brasília: Ministério da Saúde, 2013), p. 56, Table 5.
[75] Ministério da Saúde, DATASUS, Table C4. Accessed at: http://tabnet.datasus.gov.br/cgi/ta bcgi.exe?idb2012/c04.def.
[76] IBGE, "BRASIL, Projeção da população por sexo e idade: 2000/2060." Accessed at: www .ibge.gov.br/home/estatistica/populacao/projecao_da_populacao/2013/default.shtm.

Table 4.19 *Causes of Death, by Sex, in Brazil, 2016*

Cause of Death	Men	Women
Heart	25.8	30.0
Cancer	15.5	17.6
Pulmonary diseases	11.1	13.4
Diabetes	4.8	7.4
Accidents	17.4	4.8
Gastrointestinal diseases	5.5	4.4
Infectious diseases	4.4	4.4
Genito-urinary diseases	2.6	3.6
Neurological	2.3	3.5
Congenital	1.6	1.6
Other	9.0	9.3
Total	100.0	100.0

Source: Ministério da Saúde, DATSUS. http://tabnet
.datasus.gov.br/cgi/deftohtm.exe?sim/cnv/obt10uf.def.

The revolution that began with the equalization of education, the introduction of the contraceptive pill, and the subsequent massive decline of
fertility all have had a liberating effect on women in Brazilian society. The
past half-century has been one of profound changes for both families in
general and for women in particular. Families over the course of this period
have become far more diverse. Consensual unions, once confined to the
poorer classes, can now be found among all economic groups in Brazil. Male-
headed households have steadily declined, with a consequent increase in
female-headed households. In turn, these female-headed households have
not only increased their share of all households, but also changed in terms of
their composition, now holding more children, more educated women, and
younger ones – a result in the increase of divorce and separation.

Women as a whole have also experienced profound changes in this period
in relation to education and their participation in the labor force. The
traditional deficit that women had in years of education and school attendance at all education levels prior to 1950 has been replaced by an increasingly male deficit as women have entered high schools and universities in ever
larger numbers and now are more numerous than males at all educational
levels, including at the most elite professional schools.

Women have also massively entered the labor market as never before.
Although still not at the male level of participation, they have dramatically
increased their participation at all ages. They have now entered the elite

professions and have become managers and administrators in impressive numbers. Although their pay is still less than men's, the gap has been slowly closing over time. Within the labor market they are now as much in the formal labor market as men. Although they are still more likely to be unemployed than men – last hired being the first fired – their indices of employment and unemployed closely correlate with male rates and both are highly correlated with changes in the economy. All of these profound labor market changes for women have been made possible by the revolution in fertility which occurred in this period, giving women more time to enter and remain in the labor force.

Also, the rise of women's support groups, NGOs dedicated to women's issues, and a more sympathetic government, have profoundly changed the national laws in favor of women since the 1980s. They have raised consciousness about the rights of women within Brazilian society, made it easier for women to control their own lives, and have brought them into the labor market as never before in Brazilian history. But, as the latest statistics on crime show, there is still a great deal of violence against women, and domestic violence is still a significant and troubling issue for all women. Finally, for all the gains for women in general, not all women have experienced the same rates of participation and success. Here, as in so many other areas of Brazilian life, there are differences based on race and class.

5

The Welfare State and Income Transfers

If economic growth provided the impetus for major social change, and if the demographic transition finally enabled the nation to control its growth and women to enter the labor force on a major scale, it was the transformed state which finally distributed the resources needed to educate and provide for the health and income support for the entire population. For it was in this period that Brazil finally established a welfare state comparable to such welfare regimes in the advanced industrial world. And, for all its limitations as a welfare state in a developing economy, the reforms nevertheless succeeded in reducing many regional and income disparities and in effectively lessening both indigence and poverty in the nation.[1]

The beginnings of the modern welfare state in Brazil started with the government of Getúlio Vargas from 1930 to 1945. Although some European nations had initiated a few state welfare institutions as early as the 1880s, the major developments in most countries began just before World War II and came to full development in the decades after it ended. Thus, the timing of Brazilian developments was not that different from those in Europe and America. In most cases these reforms were enacted slowly

---

[1] These are two distinct categories. Indigence is defined as a family or person that cannot "purchase the lowest cost food basket that meets the estimated nutritional needs." Poor persons can purchase such basic calorific needs, but do not have adequate income to pay for decent housing or have access to basic services. See Sonia Rocha, "opções metodológicas para a estimação de linhas de indigência e de pobreza no Brasil," Paper presented at the IBGE, ECLA, INE-Portugal sponsored Third Meeting of the Expert Group on Poverty Statistics (Rio Group), Lisbon, 22–24 November 1999. Accessed at: https://ww2.ibge.gov.br/poverty/pdf/s onia_rocha_brazil.pdf.

under democratic regimes after arduous negotiations between different factions and classes, but in the case of Brazil it was created by series of authoritarian regimes and was imposed from above.[2] Almost all of the basic structure of the welfare state was developed under two authoritarian regimes, that of Vargas and the governments of the Brazilian military from 1964 to 1985. Though that structure would be modified, universalized, and reformed in the post-1985 period of democratic rule, the structure itself and many of its basic features are still operative today when the state spends 42% of its budget on social welfare.[3]

Thus, Brazil stands as a deviant case in contrast to the usual history of democratic politics and welfare legislation.[4] Instead of the government responding to worker demands and negotiating with employers, in the Brazilian case it was governments which anticipated demands and imposed conditions on both workers and employers. It was a top-down approach with the consumers and payers having little voice in the development of these institutions.

Initially, it appeared that the Brazilian path would be the usual one, with rising worker demand slowly leading to complex negotiations between employers, workers, the government, and the middle and upper classes in response to those demands. Although labor conflict was relatively late in Brazil due to the survival of slavery until the end the 1880s, thereafter there was major growth of organized labor, especially after the arrival of immigrant Italian and Spanish workers. The decades from the 1890s to the 1920s were filled with an ever-increasing confrontation between workers and management and between the elite and the working classes. Initially, the major centers of strike activity were the cities with the largest industries, that is Rio de Janeiro and São Paulo, and the key port of Santos. From the beginning, anarcho-syndicalist, socialist, and "bread and butter" unionism (variously referred to as *trabalhismo* or *sindicalismo reformista*) competed for control of the embryonic labor movement. The evolution of the Brazilian labor movement moved in

---

[2] Peter H. Lindert, *Growing Public: Social Spending and Economic Growth since the Eighteenth Century* (New York: Cambridge University Press, 2004) and Gøsta Esping-Andersen, *The Three Worlds of Welfare Capitalism* (Cambridge: Polity Press, 1990).

[3] This is the estimated average for central government expenditures in Brazil on social security programs, health, and education for the period 1973–2000. This compares to 45% and 46% in the United States and Canada but is below the 50–60% range of the Nordic countries. In turn, this represents 13.5% of GDP. See Alex Segura-Ubiergo, *The Political Economy of the Welfare State in Latin America: Globalization, Democracy, and Development* (Cambridge: Cambridge University Press, 2007), pp. 14–15.

[4] Along with Esping-Andersen, *The Three Worlds of Welfare Capitalism* and Lindert, *Growing Public*, see Peter Baldwin, *The Politics of Social Solidarity: Class Bases of the European Welfare State, 1875–1975* (Cambridge: Cambridge University Press, 1990); and Isabela Mares, *The Politics of Social Risk: Business and Welfare State Development* (Cambridge: Cambridge University Press, 2003).

the traditional trajectory from mutual aid societies and multi-occupational and district associations, to craft and then industrial unions and eventually to labor confederations, though the formation of a Brazilian confederation was slow compared to other labor movements in the Americas. Because of their higher ratio of native workers, the labor movement in the Federal Capital (Rio de Janeiro) tended to be more ameliorative, while the more foreign-immigrant-dominant labor force in São Paulo tended toward more radical solutions. The demand for an eight-hour day was the basic issue from 1900 onward, along with wages, working conditions, and the right to strike, as these local unions became ever more powerful and allied themselves with middle-class intellectuals in the socialist, anarchist, social-Catholic, and eventually with the new communist movement after World War I.

The first wave of significant strikes throughout the country came in the period 1905–1913. The response of the government was a series of repressive laws in 1907 and 1913 which gave the government unrestrained power to expel foreign-born workers, and some 556 immigrants were expelled from 1907 to 1922. The leaders of these early strikes were workers in the skilled trades, and especially typographic workers, along with railway and port workers – the elite of the labor movement or those who worked in key transport infrastructures. After limited attempts in 1910 to control the labor movement, the government resorted to repression. The first general strike occurred in São Paulo in May of 1917, which began a period when the first major industrial unions were formed, with a consequent increase in ever-larger strikes. These strikes now involved the textile and metallurgical workers – the largest industrial labor force in the country. This was followed by a general strike in Rio de Janeiro in 1920, which led the government to incarcerate 2,000 strikers and take over many of the unions. The last decade of the Old Republic was a period of violent repression as the government desperately attempted to destroy the labor movement. During most of the decade the government in fact operated in a state of siege, and the "social question" (meaning labor conflict) and the "dangerous classes" became a major theme among the political elite.[5]

The fall of the Old Republic in 1930 and the implantation of a new regime commanded by Getúlio Vargas would change this government position dramatically and would lead to the initiation of the social welfare state in Brazil. The old liberal oligarchic federalist system based on the cooperation of the regional oligarchies and the control of the central government by the coffee

---

[5] For a chronology of this period, see Vito Giannotti, *Historia das lutas dos trabalhadores no Brasil* (Rio de Janeiro: Mauad X, 2007). The standard analyses of these movements is that of Boris Fausto, *Trabalho urbano e conflito social* (São Paulo: DIFEL, 1997) and Claudio Batalha, *O movimento operário na Primeira República* (Rio de Janeiro: Zahar, 2000).

barons was now replaced by a new authoritarianism centralist government which would include new political actors. But at the outset none of these new groups had the power to dominate the government: the middle class, because it had no political autonomy in relation to traditional interests; the coffee elite, because they had been cut off from political power; and the working class, because they were not incorporated into the political system. Given the initially hostility of the elite to Vargas, he decided to seek the support of the urban masses, which would become the main basis of legitimacy for the new government.[6] The style of government inaugurated by Vargas, classified by some as populism and by others as a regime of mass politics, sought to lead by responding to popular aspirations of the middle and working classes.[7] For this reason the government initiated the first serious labor legislation in Brazil and began to develop pension and health programs for the popular classes. The nationalists of the 1930s believed that only a paternalistic authoritarian regime under a charismatic leader could promote industrialization in an underdeveloped country. At the same time, Vargas and his supporters believed that they could defuse the growing radicalism of the working class by incorporating them within the state under direct government control.[8]

On assuming government, Vargas dissolved the National Congress and the state and municipal assemblies and appointed "interventors" to replace the governors of the states. After approval of a new constitution in 1934, Vargas was elected by indirect elections for four years. In 1935, he justified further authoritarian repression of political movements with a new law of state security which gave the government unlimited power.[9]

---

[6] Francisco Weffort, *O populismo na política brasileira* (Rio de Janeiro: Paz e Terra, 1980), pp. 49–50.

[7] Weffort, *O populismo*, p. 61. Populism in Brazil is the subject of numerous studies since the 1960s. Recent works include: Jorge Ferreira, "O nome e as coisas: o populismo na política brasileira" and Angela de Castro Gomes, "O populismo e as ciências sociais no Brasil: notas sobre a trajetória de um conceito," in Jorge Ferreira, ed., *O populismo e sua história* (Rio de Janeiro: Civilização Brasileira, 2000); Angela de Castro Gomes, *A invenção do trabalhismo* (São Paulo: Vértice, 1988); and Boris Fausto, "Populismo in the Past and Its Resurgence," Paper presented at the Conference in Honor of Boris Fausto, Stanford, California, 21 May 2010. See also the major three-volume study of Vargas by Lira Neto: Lira Neto, *Getúlio: dos anos de formação à conquista do poder (1882–1930)* (São Paulo: Cia. Das Letras, 2012), *Getúlio: do governo provisório à ditadura do Estado Novo (1930–1943)* (São Paulo: Cia das Letras, 2013), and *Getúlio: da volta pela consagração popular ao suicídio* (São Paulo: Cia das Letras, 2014).

[8] For their ideas, see Boris Fausto, *O pensamento nacionalista autoritário:(1920–1940)* (Rio de Janeiro: Zahar, 2001). See also Boris Fausto, *Getúlio Vargas* (São Paulo: Cia das Letras, 2006).

[9] See Robert M. Levine, *Father of the Poor? Vargas and His Era* (New York: Cambridge University Press, 1998); Thomas E. Skidmore, *Politics in Brazil, 1930–1964: An Experiment in Democracy* (New York: Oxford University Press, 1967); and John D. Wirth, *The Politics of Brazilian Development, 1930–1954* (Stanford, Calif.: Stanford University Press, 1970).

In November 1937, he abandoned any pretense of democratic rule and carried out a coup and imposed a new constitution which created the *Estado Novo* on the fascist model. Until being ousted from power in 1945, Vargas ruled by decree, without a national legislature. If, in its initial period, the Vargas government was already centralizing and authoritarian, with the creation of the *Estado Novo* the regime moved toward a repressive state with suspension of civil liberties, arbitrary arrests, and total censorship.[10]

Although it violently repressed left-wing and even incipient fascist movements, the government implemented a new policy of co-opting urban workers through modern labor legislation, which involved the basic right to strike and support for collective bargaining, and also established major institutions related to social welfare. But this top-down reform was intended to control the unions and make them dependent on government support. Many of the reforms were initiated by the government rather than being responses to labor's demands. They reflected the government's perception that urban workers and their organizations, especially in the industrial sector, had become a potentially important new political power. Although such a policy resulted in government-controlled unions and co-optation of union leaders, these reforms brought real benefits to workers in terms of the right to strike, minimum wages, guaranteed holidays, etc.[11] Vargas's subsequent political power was largely derived from the control he exercised over the labor movement.

[10] See José Maria Bello, *História da República* (São Paulo: Companhia Editora Nacional, 1976), pp. 315–317, and Karl Loewenstein, *Brazil under Vargas* (New York: Macmillian, 1942), Chapter 2. Although the regime resembled fascism, and had the sympathy of many of the Integralismo movement, this fascist group was also outlawed in 1938 after the attempted coup to overthrow the President. After closing the Congress, dissolving the political parties, the government eliminated the fascist integralists, the last organized political force. On this, see Eli Diniz, "O Estado Novo: estrutura de poder e relações de clase," in Boris Fausto, ed., *História geral da civilização brasileira* (São Paulo: Difel, 1981), vol. 3, *Sociedade e Política* (1930–1964), pp. 77–119 and Lourde Sola, "O Golpe de 37 e o Estado Novo," in Carlos Gilherme Motta, ed., *Brasil em Perspectiva* (São Paulo: Difusão Europeia do Livro, 1969), pp. 257–284. On this theme, see Beatriz M. de Souza Wahrlich, *Reforma administrativa da Era Vargas* (Rio de Janeiro: Fundação Getúlio Vargas, 1983); Sonia Miriam, *Rumos e metamorfoses, estado e industrialização no Brasil, 1930–1960* (Rio de Janeiro: Paz e Terra, 1985), Chapter 1. On the government of Vargas, see also Pedro Paulo Z. Bastos and Pedro Cezar Dutra Fonseca, eds., *A era Vargas: desenvolvimentismo, economia e sociedade* (São Paulo: Editora Unesp, 2012); Pedro Cezar Dutra Fonseca, *Vargas: o capitalismo em construção, 1906–1953* (São Paulo: Brasiliense, 1999).

[11] According to Fausto, the state that emerged from the Revolution of 1930 maintained the fundamental policy of politically weakening the working classes, violently repressing its vanguard and its party organizations, but at the same time sought to establish a new relationship with the working class. Boris Fausto, *A revolução de 1930* (São Paulo: Brasiliense, 1975), pp. 107–108.

Labor legislation promulgated by Vargas was comprehensive. With the creation of the Ministry of Labor in 1930, numerous legal norms were established which controlled relations between unions and companies intermediated by the state. In addition, the government adopted the so-called "union unity" policy, which established a single union for each industrial sector and/or municipality.[12] It also limited the number of foreign workers per company (requiring that two-thirds of workers be nationals), limited the hours of the workday, guaranteed holidays, and determined conditions for the work of women and children. To deal with contracts and disputes there were also collective labor contracts and Labor Conciliation Boards, composed of representatives of the workers and the administration.[13] Labor Day (May 1) was made a national holiday, and Vargas signed the first minimum-wage decree in Brazilian history. In 1940, he established the union tax (compulsorily paid by the workers but distributed by the government to the unions), which provided income to the unions and represented a fundamental instrument of co-optation between the state and the unions.[14] These mandatory contributions to the unions and the single union model by industrial sector were used to solidify labor support for the government.[15] In 1941, a separate system of Labor Courts was created to adjudicate labor disputes, and in 1943 all labor laws were consolidated into a unified code that guaranteed workers' rights, the CLT, which still forms the basis of labor relations in Brazil today.

Another important part of Vargas's social policy was the establishment of social welfare institutions. As was the norm in most western nations, the first formal retirement plans (the "pension funds") began with small groups of

---

[12] In 1939, "uniqueness" or monopoly of the labor union by a territorial unit was established, which prohibited more than one union from representing the same labor category. This rule, combined with the union tax, represents the linkage of union power to the state, and has remained a basic part of labor legislation until recently, although the Constitution of 1988 now guarantees freedom of association for workers.

[13] Convenções Coletivas de Trabalho e Juntas de Conciliação e Julgamento.

[14] The union tax was a contribution paid by all workers, whether or not they were unionized, and corresponded to the value of a day's work, and was collected and controlled by the government. The funds raised were then distributed to the unions, which lived on this discretionary contribution. Therefore, the unions depended on the state and not on the contributions of their unionized workers. This tax was maintained unchanged until 2017. Due to the recent changes in labor legislation, the contribution was no longer compulsory.

[15] The issues of union unity and the compulsory union tax were opposed by the trade union movement that emerged under Lula during the military period. Although the Workers' Party ruled the country for more than a decade with Lula and Dilma as presidents, they did not make any changes to these norms. Only in the Temer government was there a change in the union tax (Law 13.467 of 13 July 2017), which was maintained, but requires express authorization of the worker, which had not occurred previously. This change was strongly opposed by trade unions.

workers in well-defined sectors of the economy in the 1920s and 1930s. As in most of Latin America, it was elite public servants who were the first and usually the only beneficiaries of retirement plans. In the colonial period these plans were called *"montepios."* But modern plans going beyond the army and the civil service only began in Brazil in the 1920s. The first of these plans was created in 1923, when the *Elói Chaves* law gave railroad workers the right to create retirement plans and widows' pensions along with medical care. In 1926, these rights were extended to port workers, and, in the following decades, to more and more groups of workers. In 1931, these retirement and pension funds (*Caixas de Aposentadoria e Pensões* – CAPs) were extended to all public employees and, in 1932, to the miners. A retirement institute for seamen was created in 1934, followed by organizations for workers in commerce and banks in 1936 and workers in transportation in 1938. Each sector had its own CAP, organized with funding from three sources – workers, employers, and government – through mandatory contributions. The government then rationalized the system by integrating the local CAPs into Retirement and Pension Institutes (*Institutos de Aposentadorias e Pensões* – IAPs), which guaranteed pensions for entire sectors of the economy. By 1939, there were 98 CAPs and five Institutes, which covered approximately 1.8 million workers, all under the control of the Ministry of Labor. As many have noted, the move to the IAPs represented a significant shift in the social insurance system, which went from private management to the public sphere, and from caring for individual enterprise workers to benefiting entire classes of workers.[16] Beginning in 1936, surplus funds collected by these CAPs and new IAPs were now invested in various types of public securities in order to create capital equity for these pension programs.[17] Most of these securities involved investments in companies developed by the government. In this practice, Brazil was like many other countries, applying these financial surpluses to national industrial activities.[18]

---

[16] Amélia Cohn, *Previdência social e processo político no Brasil* (São Paulo: Editora Moderna, 1981), p. 8.

[17] E. I. G. Andrade, "Estado e previdência no Brasil: uma breve história," in R. M. Marques, Einar Braathen, and Laura Tavares Soares, eds., *A previdência social no Brasil* (São Paulo: Fundação Perseu Abramo, 2003), pp. 71–74.

[18] Francisco Eduardo Barreto de Oliveira, Kaizô Iwakami Beltrão, and Antonio Carlos de Albuquerque David, "Dívida da união com a previdência social: uma perspectiva histórica," Texto para discussão 638, Rio de Janeiro, Ipea, 1999. Such use of pension reserves to finance public projects or even private industries was not an atypical behavior, as can be seen in Mexico's experience in establishing a welfare state under President Aleman in the 1940s and in the fascist state under Mussolini during the 1930s. See Rose J. Spalding, "Welfare Policymaking: Theoretical Implications of a Mexican Case Study," *Comparative Politics* 12.4 (1980), pp. 419–438 and Maria Sophia Quine, *Italy's Social Revolution: Charity and Welfare from Liberalism to Fascism* (New York: Palgrave, 2002), p. 115.

Finally, the government carried out its main initiative in relation to health policies as early as 1930, when an independent Ministry of Education and Health was organized, with a Health Department attached to it. By 1934, it was reorganized as a larger National Health and Social Medicine Department, which brought together under its aegis several departments and services that dealt with hospitals, ports, the Federal District, and numerous formal campaigns against specific diseases in certain areas. These campaigns, which seemed dormant in the period from 1930 to 1934, gained new life after 1935, in most cases with the help of the Rockefeller Foundation. In 1937, the federal public health department assumed the role of coordinator of all state health departments, and a special fund for public health was created in all municipalities under the direction of the federal government. Also, at that time, the first systematic attempts to finance and develop health clinics in rural areas occurred. The federal government maintained an active role as the protagonist in national public health in the 1930s and 1940s, and finally in 1953 an independent Ministry of Health was created, which took control of all actions undertaken by the federal government, from health statistics and education of workers in health care to the creation of nursing schools and the financing of research institutes to evaluate the quality of medicines produced in the country.[19]

Despite the intense discussion about education reform in this period, the primary and secondary student population grew relatively slowly in the Vargas era. But a new and very important beginning of state-supported industrial education was implemented by the regional industrial associations that emerged in the 1930s. In 1939, when decreeing that large companies with 500 or more workers had to provide commissary facilities, the government also required that such companies maintain "courses of professional development" for their workers.[20] This idea of a privately organized industrial educational system was being pushed by both the new Ministry of Labor and the São Paulo Industrial Federation (*Federação das Indústrias do Estado de São Paulo* – FIESP) under the leadership of Roberto Simonsen, largely against the wishes of the Education Ministry.[21] Influenced by the German

---

[19] On the reforms and initiatives related to health in this period, see Cristina M. Oliveira Fonseca, *Saúde no Governo Vargas (1930–1945): dualidade institucional de um bem público* (Rio de Janeiro: Editora Fiocruz, 2007); André Luiz Vieira de Campos, *Políticas internacionais de saúde na era Vargas: O Serviço Especial de Saúde Pública, 1942–1960* (Rio de Janeiro: Editora Fiocruz, 2006); and Lina Faria, *Saúde e política: a Fundação Rockefeller e seus parceiros em São Paulo* (Rio de Janeiro: Editora Fiocruz, 2007).

[20] Simon Schwartzman, Helena M. B. Bomeny, and Vanda M. R. Costa, *Nos tempo de Capanema* (São Paulo, Editora USP and Paz e Terra, 1984).

[21] Simonson had also been one of the key persons, along with Júlio de Mesquita Filho, owner of *O Estado de São Paulo*, and the political leader Armando de Sales Oliveira, behind the

ideas of a modern industrial apprenticeship, the industrialists pushed for control over an area totally neglected by the state until that time. The result was the creations of what would become one of the world's largest modern privately run industrial education systems, with first the creation in 1942 of SENAI (*Serviço Nacional de Aprendizagem Industrial*) for industry and in 1946 of SENAC (*Serviço Nacional de Aprendizagem Comercial*) for commerce.[22] The industrialists convinced the federal government to create a payroll tax to develop a school system administered by the private industrial associations in each state. SENAI quickly established training courses and would enroll many hundreds of thousands of students in short- and long-term programs and would even educate a future president of the republic.[23] By 2015, SENAC and its affiliates had 1.9 million students matriculating in its courses,[24] while SENAI had over 600 schools and programs throughout Brazil operating in 22,000 municipalities.[25]

These state-supported institutions and initiatives were rapidly creating a well-trained group of administrators who could support and extend the government initiative.[26] At the same time, the pressure for expansion was constant and the number of people receiving pensions, benefits, and health care through the new IAPs was growing steadily. These numerous social and economic initiatives undertaken throughout the Vargas period created the basis for a modern welfare state, though still relatively restricted to covering a limited portion of the modern urban sector. The ideas and institutions created at that time profoundly influenced the post-1950 development of a modern welfare state. It is therefore not surprising that all the governments that followed the Vargas era, authoritarian or democratic, would be profoundly influenced by the changes made in this period. Post-1950 governments, whether democratic or authoritarian, never questioned the right of the state to intervene in the economy, nor the responsibility of the state for the welfare of its citizens. All post-Vargas regimes recognized the growing

establishment of the University of São Paulo. Simon Schwartzman, *A Space for Science: The Development of the Scientific Community in Brazil* (College Station: Pennsylvania State University Press, 1991), Chapter 5.

[22] Federação das Indústrias do Estado de São Paulo (FIESP), Serviço Nacional da Aprendizagem Industrial (SNAI), and the Serviço Nacional da Aprendizagem Comercial (SNAC) were founded in 1946.

[23] On the origins of SENAI, see Barbara Weinstein, "The Industrialists, the State, and the Issues of Worker Training and Social Services in Brazil, 1930–50," *Hispanic American Historical Review* 70.3 (1990), pp. 379–404 and her book-length study: *For Social Peace in Brazil: Industrialists and the Remaking of the Working Class in São Paulo, 1920–1964* (Chapel Hill: University of North Carolina Press, 1996).

[24] SESI, SENAI, IEL, *Relatório Anual 2015*: 16. [25] See www.senac.br/.

[26] See James Malloy, *The Politics of Social Security in Brazil* (Pittsburgh, Pa.: University of Pittsburgh Press, 1979).

power of the working classes and the importance of the new middle class in creating stability and in supporting any effective government. Although little committed to resolving the inequalities of income and wealth distribution, all the regimes that followed the Vargas period committed themselves to the expansion of the welfare state and its goal of universal access to health, education, and social insurance.

The fragile democratic governments from 1945 to 1964 tried to advance the earlier programs of Vargas. The most important effort in this period was the first national social security act called the *Lei Orgânica da Previdência Social*, or LOAS, which was enacted in 1960. It put in one comprehensive piece of legislation all the basic institutions and rights related to social welfare. This law also extended basic rights to include support for pregnancy, funeral expenses, and nursing homes.[27] This would become the foundational act which would be revised several times in later years, but which remained the basic code. Also, by this time, coverage had been extended to all urban workers except domestics, although rural workers were still excluded. This later situation was resolved in 1963 with the enactment of the first law to insure rural workers, with the creation of the FUNRURAL (*Fundo de Assistência ao Trabalhador Rural*).

The coming to power of the military government in 1964 was in many ways a continuation of the Vargas authoritarian model in social legislation. However destructive these governments were of democratic rule, and however much they violated basic human rights, they continued and deepened the welfare policies begun under Vargas, also with the same aims of winning popular support and repressing popular mobilization for reform, with a top-down program of expanding social welfare programs.

The governments that followed the Vargas period expanded the policies initiated during his rule, but the military were able successfully to fund these programs even though they were especially hostile to labor and popular mobilizations. The rise of a strong labor movement allied with radical political leaders was one of the main factors that led the military to seize power. But instead of abolishing the unions, it used the Vargas legislation to control and neutralize them. With the need to reduce labor conflict and win support of the growing middle class, it also committed itself to expanding the welfare system and modernizing its administration. Equally, the military remained true to Vargas's vision of creating a modern industrial state, but one which was centralized, conservative, and with little popular mobilization.

---

[27] See, for example, the supplementary Law 6.887 of 10 December 1980. Accessed at: www .planalto.gov.br/ccivil_03/LEIS/L6887.htm#art1. Added into the 1960 LOAS code (Law 3.807 of 26 August 1960). Accessed at: www.planalto.gov.br/ccivil_03/LEIS/1950–1969/L3807.htm.

The military period was thus an era of major social changes, many of which were due to processes that preceded the military regime but were intensified in that period. This period of what would be rapid industrialization was probably the period of greatest and most rapid social mobility in Brazilian history, as a new industrial and bureaucratic elite emerged from more humble backgrounds than was the norm in more developed industrial societies. It was also a period of intense internal migration from poor to rich areas of the country, accompanied by rapid and massive growth of metropolitan areas. This chaotic urban growth also resulted in expanding illegal migrant settlements known as favelas in all major cities.

In a successful effort to win popular support from the emerging urban middle classes, the military carried out a massive expansion of free primary and secondary education, as well as an expansion of university and technical education. The government also compensated for its repressive wage and salary policies with social welfare policies, which led to important advances in health and the expansion of the national pension system, implementing a massive housing and sanitation program. In this respect, the military period was a time when Brazil finally laid the foundations of a modern welfare state. Although it was based on authoritarian and technocratic models, the democratic regimes after 1985 kept the basic structure even as they continued to modify it.[28]

As a result of their complete reorganization of Brazil's financial system, the military were able to create a market for medium- and long-term credit and also laid the foundation for the marketing of public debt. One part of this reorganization was a new scheme for financing mortgages, with the creation of the National Housing Bank (*Banco Nacional da Habitação* – BNH) and its agents in the financial sector. The funds for housing were generated through a national system of forced savings. Until 1963, dismissed employees were compensated by payment of one month's salary for each year of service. After ten years of employment the employer was required to double this compensation. This tended to limit the mobility of labor. This system was abolished in 1966 and replaced by the Guarantee Fund for Length of Service (*Fundo de Garantia do Tempo de Serviço* – FGTS), with funding by a payroll tax of 8% paid by employers. The fund was to be used as a type of unemployment insurance for any workers fired – under the now much looser forms of labor

---

[28] Sonia Draibe, "O welfare state in Brazil: caracteristicas e perspectivas," *Caderno de Pesquisa* 8 (1993), pp. 19–21, defined this period as one establishing a welfare state in Brazil because of the universalization of services and the creation of active governmental institutions in all areas defined by a welfare state. Although this model was profoundly reformed in the post-military period, the basic structure was elaborated in the 1960s and 1970s.

tenure being enacted – or could be used as a reserve fund for the worker for retirement or housing purchases. In fact, most of the monies collected went to the national housing bank BNH to promote a major expansion of home construction.[29] These funds became crucial in developing urban housing as the cities of Brazil massively expanded in this period and represented the main source of funding for the construction of housing and sanitation projects for the middle and working classes.[30]

In the twenty-one years of the military period, Brazil become a predominantly urban and industrial society, and for the first time the rural population began to experience negative growth rates. This, coupled with the onset of modernization in agriculture, resulted in massive internal migration, toward both cities and the country's open frontiers. However, Brazil was marked by sharp inequality in terms of social class and skin color of its population, which was reflected initially in increasing regional disparities. Although all regions witnessed significant advances in wealth, health, and education, the Northeast changed more slowly and was falling behind the other regions. By the 1980s, Brazil's more-advanced regions were reaching the standard of living of the world's developed countries, while the Northeast still remained at levels of the underdeveloped countries in Africa and Asia. It can even be said that this was a time when regional differences were the most notable in the nation's history because of the explosive economic growth and its initial concentration in the Southern regions.

Policies aimed at creating an industrial base were at the heart of military rule. By controlling wages, closing the market for foreign products, and investing in basic infrastructure, the government encouraged the investment of domestic capital in industrial activities, resulting in extraordinarily rapid economic growth, which was already high before the military took power.[31] There was also major structural change in the labor market, with a massive increase in the number of jobs in the service and manufacturing sectors. From 1960 to 1980, the number of workers in the primary sector remained

[29] Malloy, The Politics of Social Security in Brazil, pp. 125–126.
[30] Francisco Vidal Luna and Herbert S. Klein, *Brazil since 1980* (Cambridge: Cambridge University Press, 2006), Chapter 3.
[31] Measured in money of 2006, the per capita income doubled from 2,110 reais in 1940 to 4,490 reais in 1960, then grew at an even faster rate to 11,040 reais in 1980. By 1960, agriculture was still responsible for 18% of GDP, which in 1980 fell to 11%, while industry's share of GDP rose from 33% to 44%, its highest level in the twentieth century. Adalberto Cardoso, "Transições da escola para o trabalho no Brasil: persistências da desigualdade e frustação de expactativas," *Dados: Revista de Ciências Sociais* 51.3 (2008), p. 573.

constant at 11 million while the secondary sector went from 2.4 million to 9 million workers and the tertiary sector from 5.2 million to 11.4 million.[32]

In response to this growth of both urban workers and the middle class, the military government made a major effort to modernize and stabilize the post-Vargas pension system.[33] In 1966, individual and pensions associations, the IAPS and the CAPS, were replaced by a National Social Security Institute (*Instituto Nacional de Previdência Social* – INPS), which put the whole system on a more solid financial footing and expanded coverage to a larger proportion of the national population. In 1968, two years after its foundation, the INPS had 7.8 million participants in its pension plans.[34] In the 1970s, the INPS systematically expanded coverage of national workers and in 1971 it was extended to rural workers, transforming FUNRURAL into an effective institution for the first time. Finally, in 1972, domestic service workers were incorporated into this system.

The enrollment of insured workers thereafter grew rapidly: in 1980, the INPS had tripled the number of insured participants to 24 million people.[35] Together with pensions and insurance of various types, INPS and FUNRURAL also began to provide health benefits through INAMPS. In 1974, an independent Ministry of Social Security was established, which incorporated all insurance plans, pensions, and health services under one ministry.

The growth of welfare and health services was fundamental in leading to the rapid decline in infant mortality in this period. When the Ministry of Social Security was established in 1974 there was a clear demarcation between pensions and health, with the latter now under the National Social Security Healthcare Institute (*Instituto Nacional de Assistência Médica e Previdência Social* – INAMPS).[36] A host of other institutional changes led to a major expansion of a public health system. Between 1970 and 1980, hospital admissions went from 6 million to 13 million – the latter figure being the norm up to today.[37] Finally, in the 1960s, came state national and internationally supported programs of infant and child immunization.[38]

---

[32] Carlos Antonio Costa Ribeiro, *Estrutura de classe e mobilidade social no Brasil* (Bauru: EDUSC, 2007), p. 310, Table 6.

[33] Malloy, *The Politics of Social Security in Brazil*, pp. 124–125. The first Minister of Labor in the military regime, Arnaldo Lopes Süssekind, was a specialist in social security.

[34] IBGE, *Estatísticas do Século XX* (2003).   [35] IBGE, *Estatísticas do Século XX* (2003).

[36] Mauricio C. Coutinho and Cláudio Salm, "Social Welfare," in Bacha and Klein, *Social Change in Brazil, 1945–1985*, pp. 233–262.

[37] Paim et al., "The Brazilian Health System."

[38] The 1970s and early 1980s were also a period of active debate developed among academics and doctors about the nature of the health care system which would have a profound effect on the creation of the SUS and the decentralization reforms of health carried out in the post-military period. See Cordeiro, "Instituto de Medicina Social e a luta pela reforma sanitária."

All of this growth in public health had a direct impact on mortality. Already the crude death rate was at 15 deaths per 1,000 residents. While that rate would change little in the next decade, it began to decline at a more rapid pace in the next few years and was down to 8 deaths per 1,000 population by the early 1980s.

This decline was driven mostly by the steady decline in infant mortality, which fell by half, from 135 deaths of infants to 1,000 live births in 1950–1955 to just 63 deaths per 1,000 live births in 1980–1985. The impact of this decline is also seen in the steady decline in the importance of the deaths of young persons (0–14 years of age) as a share of total Brazilian deaths, which went from over half of all deaths recorded to just a third of such deaths by the early 1980s. At the same time there was a rapid increase in the share of total deaths accounted by the aged (those over 65 years of age), which went from 14% of all persons dying in the 1950s to a third of deaths in the early 1980s.[39]

For all its hostility to free speech, the military programs in education and scientific research were impressive. Although there had been slow but steady progress in the development of primary and secondary education before 1964, it was the military regime which gave a great impulse to these two areas of activity. In 1960, only 73% of children aged 5 to 9 attended primary school, but this figure rose to 89% by 1968. Though comparable figures are not available for later years, by 1985, some 79% of children 5–14 years of age were in primary school.[40] Moreover, both secondary and university education enrollments were growing faster than the national population in the period from 1960 to 1980.[41]

It was in the secondary school system that the most dramatic changes occurred. While the primary school system had been on a long trajectory of growth, which was simply stimulated by continuing investments by the military governments, there was a major initiative begun in the expansion and change in secondary education. Between 1963 and 1984, the number of secondary school teachers doubled, from approximately 121,000 to 215,000, and enrollments increased from 1.7 million to 3 million students. But the big change was the role the government now played in this secondary market. In 1963, some 60% of secondary students were enrolled in private secondary schools, but by 1984 this was reversed and 65% of the students were enrolled in public schools.[42] These approximately 3 million secondary

[39] CELADE, "Brasil Indices de Crescimento Demográfico." Accessed at: www.eclac.org/celade/proyecciones/basedatos_BD.htm.
[40] Ribeiro, *Estrutura de classe e mobilidade social*, p. 309, Table 4.
[41] Schwartzman, *A Space for Science*, Table 10.
[42] These numbers come from IBGE, *Anuário Estatístico do Brasil*, 1964, pp. 341–342, and *Anuário Estatístico do Brasil*, 1986, pp. 174–175.

school students now made up 22% of all children aged 15–19, up from just 12% of this age group enrolled in 1972.[43]

This was also a period when the government invested heavily in science and technology for the first time in its history, so much so that the leading scholar of the history of science in Brazil has declared this period "The Great Leap Forward."[44] The government's National Development Bank (BNDES) in 1964 established a ten-year fund for technology, with US$ 100 million. Then, in 1974, the small national research council was expanded and more adequately funded and became the *Conselho Nacional de Desenvolvimento Científico e Tecnológico* – CNPq (National Council for Scientific and Technical Development). Soon the military government was investing heavily in advanced research as well as in basic infrastructure and industrial development, all in the name of a nationalist program. But, at the same time, scientists at the University of São Paulo, and a growing number of newer centers, pushed for the creation of an institution modeled on the US National Science Foundation (NSF). It was the NSF which played such a crucial role in post-World War II America in turning the United States into a premier world center for science and technology. Starting as early as 1953, the Brazilian government had established a fund for scholarships for students training primarily in the sciences. This program was run by *Coordenação de Aperfeicoamento de Pessoal de Nível Superior* – CAPES, which had been founded in 1951.[45] By the 1960s, several hundred Brazilian scientists had been trained abroad, especially in the United States and England, and on their return they formed a powerful interest group pressing for the creation of modern laboratories and other crucial research tools to allow Brazil to compete in this new post-war world. In 1968, came a new University Reform law, which essentially established the North American system of Departments, and three levels of degrees, from undergraduate titles to masters and doctorates. Recently founded federal universities in Minas Gerais and in Brasília were developed along this model and new publicly supported federal ones were soon established in all the states. The state of São Paulo had founded a new state university in the city of Campinas, with a significant representation of foreign scholars, two years earlier, which became known as UNICAMP and quickly competed with the University of São Paulo as the nation's premier university. UNICAMP was designed from the beginning to be an advanced research center, especially in physics, and

---

[43] Ribeiro, *Estrutura de classe e mobilidade social*, p. 309, Table 4.
[44] Schwartzman, *A Space for Science*, Chapter 9.
[45] Campanha Nacional de Aperfeiçoamento de Pessoal de Nível Superior. On the history of this institution, see www.capes.gov.br/sobre-a-capes/historia-e-missao.

several Brazilian scientists working at Bell Labs in the United States and US universities returned to work at the new university.[46] The government also created an aeronautical, computer, and nuclear research program both inside and outside the university. All this effort led to Brazil becoming a significant player in world science, and along with India and China was one of the few from the less-developed world which could now begin to compete internationally.

It was the expansion of the secondary schools especially which began to lead to a slow growth in the number of university students. By 1984, there were 68 universities in Brazil, 35 federal ones, 10 state universities, 2 municipal ones, and 20 private institutions. The university student population expanded from 142,000 in 1964 to 1.3 million in 1984, with women slightly outnumbering men.[47] Within this group, graduate programs doubled their student enrollments to the 40,000 level by the mid-1980s.[48] The percentage of youths 20–24 years of age who were in tertiary educational institutions – universities and technical schools – rose from just 2% of this age cohort in 1965 to 12% in 1985.[49]

All of this increase in schooling was rapidly reducing national illiteracy rates. By 1970, two-thirds of the population were literate and by 1980 they represented 74% of the nation.[50] It was only in the census of 1960 that for the first time literate men and women represented the majority of the population. In 1950, men 10 years of age and older had become a majority literate for the first time, but in that year women were still at only 44% literate. In 1960, the key transition year, literate women now accounted for 57% of the female population 10 years of age and older and literate men had risen to 64% of that male age group.[51] But it would take until the early 1980s for women to become as literate as men, following a major increase in women attending school.

One lasting and very expensive reform which was established in this period was the guaranteed-income program for disabled (handicapped) and other persons of whatever age incapable of working in the labor market, as well as those over 70 who had no pension benefits or other means of

---

[46] Schwartman, *A Space for Science*, Chapter 9.

[47] Carlos Benedito Martins, "O ensino superior brasileiro nos anos 90," *São Paulo em Perspectiva* 14.1 (2000), pp. 42, 43, 48, Tables 1 and 4. And for the breakdown by sex, see IBGE, *Anuário Estatístico do Brasil*, 1984, p. 251, Table 2.6.

[48] Schartzman, *A Space for Science*, Table 10.

[49] Ribeiro, *Estrutura de classe e mobilidade social*, p. 309, Tables 4 and 5.

[50] IBGE, *Estatísticas do Século XX* (2003), Table "População1981aeb-002." Accessed at: www .ibge.gov.br/seculoxx/arquivos_xls/populacao.shtm.

[51] IBGE, *Estatísticas do Século XX* (2003), Table pop_1965aeb-06.2. Accessed at: www .ibge.gov.br/seculoxx/arquivos_xls/populacao.shtm.

support. This Monthly Life Income (*Renda Mensal Vitalícia* – RMV) was established in 1974 for these two sectors of the population and initially it was stipulated that they would get a stated percentage of a minimum wage for life so long as they were not receiving any income, or were being sustained by their family.[52] In the Federal Constitution of 1988 this was defined as a constitutional right and the amount was now raised to be a full minimum wage for life, independent of their contribution or lack thereof into social security, and the age for the elderly without pensions was lowered to 65 years. This program in 1996 became known as the Continuing Social Assistance Program (*Benefício de Prestação Continuada da Assistência Social* – BPC) and would eventually become the most expensive of the income transfer or social welfare programs.

The return to democracy in 1985 opened the nation to new movements and ideas. In relation to the welfare state, the most significant reform was a move toward a decentralized and more democratic political structure. Most of these reformist ideas found expression in the new Constitution of 1988. The new Constitution was highly advanced in terms of political and social rights, extending the right to vote to the illiterate and reducing the minimum voting age. It also pledged the government to support the health, education, and economic livelihood of its citizens. But it was less successful in organizing state financial and institutional arrangements.[53] The charter reflected the clash of many segments of society now free from the shackles of dictatorship, but without a dominant group or vision. The consequence of accommodating multiple pressure groups created difficulties for the new democratic governments, which were required to make more than 100 post-charter changes to the constitution to allow for greater economic flexibility, federal equity, and fiscal balance. The universalization of rights was imposed without the corresponding fiscal base for their implementation. Many public monopolies were consecrated under the pressure of nationalist groups or as reflections of corporate interests, which later proved to be inadequate, particularly when there was a need for greater openness and globalization of the Brazilian economy.

Having expanded and reinforced most of the basic structures of the welfare state, the new post-1985 democratic governments faced a continuing crisis of

---

[52] See www.planalto.gov.br/ccivil_03/leis/L6179.htm.

[53] The Partido dos Trabalhadores did not approve the new Constitution. In an interview in the *Folha de São Paulo* (5 October 2008), the then Presidente Lula accepted that this was a mistake, saying, "The PT came to Congress with a draft constitution ready and finished which, if approved, would certainly have made it much more difficult to govern than today. As an opposition party that had never reached power, we had magical solutions to all the ills of the country. Perhaps we had not realized that in such a short time we could come to power. And then we would have the responsibility to put into practice everything we proposed."

inflation and slow growth and were forced to adopt severely recessionary orthodox policies. The end of the military regime and the beginning of democracy hindered the continuation of such recessive measures. However, the overall situation was critical because of high external debt, a crisis in the public accounts, and high monthly inflation.[54] In order to deal with the crisis, a number of unorthodox plans were tried but which were unsuccessful in combating inflation, which reached dramatic levels of around 50% a month. These inflationary price levels hindered growth, which remained low for a decade, and lowered the income of wage earners and the poorer segments of the population. Only in 1994 was it possible to implement a successful stabilization plan, which definitively controlled the high inflation that had persisted for half a century.

From the political point of view, the 1980s and 1990s was a period of significant democratic advances, but from the economic perspective, this period interrupted the long cycle of growth experienced in the first seven decades of the century.[55] This economic crisis compromised the social conditions of the population and made it difficult to implement many of the obligations imposed by the new constitution (See Graph 5.1).

But with the *Plan Real* of 1994 and the subsequent stabilization and growth of the national economy, the governments of Fernando Henrique Cardoso and those that followed were able to make significant advances in the welfare state. The end of inflation and its inflationary tax, which especially affected the poor, is one of the fundamental factors that explain the exceptional performance in the social area that the country has experienced in recent years. Domestic demand exploded under the *Plan Real*, particularly for consumer goods for low-income groups. The process of social mobility that began to affect all classes occurred not only because of the *Plan Real*, but also because of the increase in employment, which grew significantly. Brazil maintained high employment and low levels of unemployment for several years, especially in the period of the first Lula administration.[56] It was also a period when formal employment increased at the expense of the informal

---

[54] In March of 1985, when Sarney assumed the presidency, monthly inflation was as follows: Cost of Living for São Paulo-FIP: 12%; General Index of Prices-FGV: 10%; Índice Nacional de Preços ao Consumidor-FIBGE: 12%. After two years of government, and after the failure of the first heterodox plan to control inflation (*Plan Cruzado*), the country was forced to decree a moratorium on its external debts, which would have serious consequences for Brazil's international standing (February 1987).

[55] Ipeadata, PIB var. real anual (% a.a.) – Instituto Brasileiro de Geografia e Estatística, Sistema de Contas Nacionais Referência 2000 (IBGE/SCN 2000 Anual) – SCN_PIBG.

[56] The rate of unemployment in the metropolitan areas was 13% in 2001 and fell to 7.9% in 2011, a rate still that low in 2014. Ipeadata, Table, Taxa de desemprego (%) DISOC_DESE.

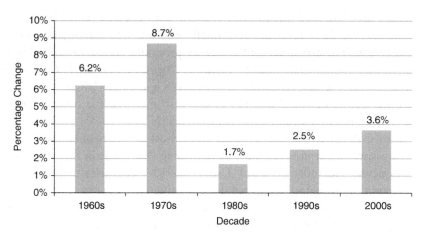

GRAPH 5.1 Average Variation of GDP by Decade, 1960–2000 (in US$ 2004)
Source: Ipeadata, GAG_PIBCAP.

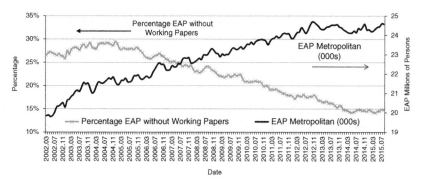

GRAPH 5.2 Population Economically Active and Workers without Signed Labor Cards, All Metropolitan Regions, 2002–2015
Source: IBGE, Pesquisa Mensal Emprego; Seade.

labor market, created a growing contingent of workers with rights to social benefits and social security retirement funding (see Graph 5.2).

Thus, in the late 1990s, the state was finally able to implement successfully many of rights declared in the Constitution of 1988. The integrated system of social insurance and social assistance established in the 1988 Constitution now included all federal government workers, and all private workers were put into one unified social security system. Financing of the system was put on a more solid tax base, and the value of pensions was now pegged to inflation. Finally, pension rights were now made universal for all women and men in the rural areas, whether registered workers or not, and regardless of whether they had paid into any previous pension schemes. At the beginning of the 1990s, these reforms were finally enacted into an organic social security law. The assistance and insurance programs were reorganized into a new National Social Security Institute (*Instituto Nacional do Seguro Social* – INSS), which replaced both the INPS and FUNRURAL and other separate sectors of social assistance, and also involved the transfer of all health activities to a separate Ministry of Health.[57]

In this, Brazil essentially deviated from most of the neoliberal pension reforms carried out in Latin America beginning with Chile in the 1980s and subsequently expanded to many Latin American countries in the 1990s. Unlike many other nations, Brazil did not privatize its pension scheme but instead solidified and rationalized its PAYG (pay as you go) system, though it did open the door for supplementary private insurance plans.[58] By 2004, it was estimated that some 42 million Brazilian workers (aged 16 to 59) were contributing to the INSS and state and municipal pension systems (some 29.7 million through the RGPS, another 7.7 million rural workers covered by RGPS, and 4.8 million through state employee pension plans), and some 22 million persons were beneficiaries. Although approximately 27 million active workers were still not covered,[59] by 2009 it was estimated that a significant 59.3% of the EAP was now included in a pension plan.[60]

This new commitment to universal pensions, especially for rural workers and the elderly who had no previous pension plans, has had a profound impact on reducing indigence and poverty among the older populations and those situated in rural areas.[61] Although these rural pensions were originally quite small – with some 85% of the rural population receiving below the

---

[57] Beltrão et al., "*Population and Social Security in Brazil*," pp. 5–6.

[58] For the comparative differences from other regional reforms, see Florencia Antía and Arnaldo Provasi, "Multi-Pillared Social Insurance Systems: The Post-Reform Picture in Chile, Uruguay and Brazil, *International Social Security Review* 64.1 (2011), pp. 53–71; Fabio M. Betranou and Rafael Rofman, "Providing Social Security in a Context of Change: Experience and Challenges in Latin America," *International Social Security Review* 55.1 (2002), pp. 67–82; and Segura-Ubiergo, *The Political Economy of the Welfare State in Latin America*.

[59] *Informe de Previdência Social* 16.5 (2004), pp. 1, 18. This growth in the number of beneficiaries was quite fast. Beginning in 1995, only 15.7 million people were benefiting from the system, and by 2003 this number had risen 40%, to 21.7 million beneficiaries. *Informe de Previdência Social* 16.2 (2004), p. 1.

[60] This was up from 53.8% in 2002. Ipea, *Políticas Sociais: Acompanhamento e Análise*, 19 (2011), p. 18, Table 1, "Evolução da cobertura previdenciária – 2002–2009."

[61] In 1999, approximately 79% of Brazilians 60 years of age and over were receiving pensions. Helmut Schwarzer and Ana Carolina Querino, "Benefícios sociais e pobreza: programas não contributivos da seguridade social brasileira," Texto para Discussão 929, Brasília, Ipea, 2002, p. 7.

minimum wage in 1985 – they have progressively become ever more important. In the Constitution of 1988, the basic pension for rural retirees was raised to the minimum wage.[62] It is estimated that such pensions for rural workers has not only reduced rural poverty but has also significantly reduced inequality in rural Brazil.[63] Brazil, in fact, is among the most advanced countries in the developing world in reducing levels of poverty among its rural population.[64] Thus, for the first time, being elderly and of rural residence are no longer automatically correlated with poverty in Brazil.

The 1990s also saw the beginnings of the modern income transfer programs which have had a major impact in Brazil as in many other developing countries in the world. The Cardoso government established several such income transfer programs, which were expanded and consolidated into one program by the Lula government and today benefit an important part of the national population. In the first Fernando Henrique Cardoso administration came the establishment of the Program to Eradicate Child Labor (*Programa de Erradicação do Trabalho Infantil* – PETI) – which it eventually expanded in 2001 into a more complete *Bolsa Escola*. This was a national program designed to eliminate child employment and encourage school attendance through a conditional cash payment from the state to poor families with school-age children if they maintained these children in school.[65] The *Bolsa Escola* and *Bolsa Alimentação* (School and Food Grants) of the Cardoso government were focused on poor families with children. The School Grant benefited low-income families with children aged 6 to 15 years and the Food Grant served families with children up to 7 years of age. The structure of the two programs was relatively similar, with direct payments to beneficiaries through ATM cards.[66] In the Lula government, there was a change in income

---

[62] Kaizô Iwakami Beltrão and Sonoe Sugahara Pinheiro, "Brazilian Population and the Social Security System: Reform Alternatives," Texto para discussão 929, Rio de Janeiro, Ipea, 2005, p. 6.

[63] It is estimated that in 2002 the GINI index for income distribution, excluding pensions, would have been 0.56, falling to 0.52 when pensions are included. Beltrão and Pinheiro, *Brazilian Population and the Social Security System*, p. 12.

[64] Approximately 35% of the persons who received a pension in 2003, with residence declared, lived in the rural area, a much higher proportion than the actual total population. *Informe de Previdência Social* 16.2 (2004), p. 1. The unusual form adopted by Brazil in the provision of retirement for the rural elderly, even by Latin American standards, can be seen in CELADE, *Los adultos mayores en América Latina y el Caribe: datos e indicadores*. Boletín informativo. Edición especial (Santiago de Chile: Comisión Económica para América Latina y el Caribe, 2001), Graphs 8, 9, 16, 18.

[65] Schwarzer and Querino, "Benefícios sociais e pobreza."

[66] Sonia Rocha, "Impacto sobre a pobreza dos novos programas federais de transferência de renda." Associação Nacional dos Centros de Pós-Graduação em Economia (n.d.). Accessed at: www.anpec.org.br/encontro2004/artigos/A04A137.pdf.

transfer programs, with the launching of the *Bolsa Família* (Family Grant Program),[67] which unified all income transfer programs and changed the profile of the beneficiaries. This now included average household income as well as the numbers and ages of children. Currently, there are 13.8 million families benefiting from *Bolsa Família*;[68] it was one of the most popular programs enacted by the Lula government.[69] Even more significant has been the growth of the BPC (Continuous Cash Benefit) (the renamed RMV) or monthly life benefits for handicapped persons and those over 65 without pensions. By 2018, this program was almost double the size of the more well-known *Bolsa Família*.[70] Moreover, all these income transfers were based on the same level of the minimum wage, which has increased its value over time (see Graph 5.3).

---

[67] Then, on assuming the government in 2003, Lula launched with great acclaim the Zero Hunger Program (*Programa Fome Zero*), but, given the difficulties in its implementation, it was also incorporated into the *Bolsa Família* program.

[68] Ministério do Desenvolvimento Social www.mds.gov.br/bolsafamilia. In addition to the income criteria, there are conditionalities in the area of education (as a minimum frequency of school attendance) and in health, including taking the children to health clinics for monitoring and participating in vaccination campaigns. Marcelo Medeiros, Tatiana Britto, and Fábio Soares, *Programas focalizados de transferência de renda no Brasil: contribuições para o debate* (Brasília: Ipea, 2007), p. 8.

[69] For an analysis of these programs, see Rocha, "Impacto sobre a pobreza dos novos programas federais." Several scholars argue that the preference of government programs for the *Bolsa Família*, in relation to the other continuous benefits (such as the monthly transfer of income to people of any age with severe disabilities and seniors over 65), is because the political effect is greater with the *Bolsa Família*. Medeiros, Britto, and Soares, *Programas focalizados de transferência de renda no Brasil*, pp. 9–10.

[70] The latest data for BPC recipients is from 2015 and lists the total at 4.2 million persons obtaining such benefits, of which 2.3 million were handicapped and 1.9 million were elderly retirees who had not contributed to social security. *Boletim BPC 2015*, p. 12, Table 2. Accessed at: www.mds.gov.br/webarquivos/arquivo/assistencia_social/boletim_BPC_2015 .pdf.

As of 2017, 13.2 million families were receiving *Bolsa Família*. See http://mds.gov.br/area-de-imprensa/noticias/2017/junho/bolsa-familia-governo-federal-repassara-r-2-4-bilhoes-aos-beneficiarios-em-junho.

In the proposed budget of 2018, BPC and *Bolsa Família* will cost an estimated 83.1 billion reais (or US$ 23.7 billion at the official rate of 3.50 reais per dollar). The breakdown of these programs is 31 billion reais (US$ 8.8 billion) for handicapped (*Benefícios de Prestação Continuada* (BPC) *à Pessoa com Deficiência e da Renda Mensal Vitalícia* (RMV) *por Invalidez*). For the pension part of BPC (*Benefícios de Prestação Continuada* (BPC) *à Pessoa Idosa e da Renda Mensal Vitalícia* (RMV) *por Idade*), the amount is 23.9 billion reais (or US$ 6.8 billion). The amount for Family Transfers (*Transferência de Renda Diretamente às Famílias em Condição de Pobreza e Extrema Pobreza*) is 28.2 billion reais (US$ 8 billion). *Orçamento fiscal e da seguridade social exercício financeiro de 2018*. Accessed at: www.planejamento.gov.br/assuntos/orcamento-1/orcamentos-anuais/2018/orcamento-anual-de-2018#LOA, anexo I.

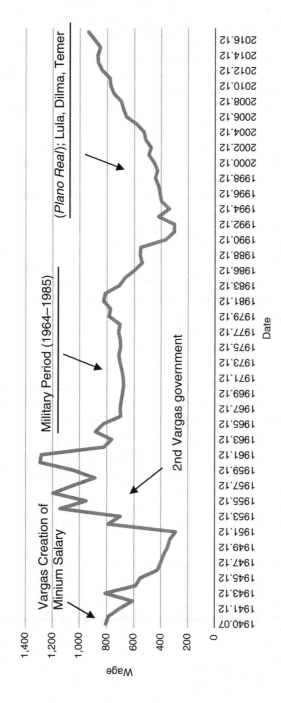

GRAPH 5.3 The Real Minimum Wage, 1940–2017, Expressed in Reais of August 2017
Source: Ipeadata (preços agosto/2017).

163

The results of these income transfer policies can be seen in the social transformations that occurred in Brazil in the last two decades of the twentieth century and in the first decade of the twenty-first century. Many of these trends, evident in the period from 1945 to 1980, have accelerated in the post-military democratic era, and the most significant changes have been those that have affected poverty, population growth, health, and education, all resulting in a significant decline in regional disparities. Over the past thirty years, all the states and regions of the country have reached close to the standards of the more advanced states of the South and Southeast, showing that the pace of development of the poorest regions has generally been at a faster rate than that of the advanced regions. Thus, the Northeastern states have now reached levels of income, education, fecundity, and mortality that are increasingly closer to those in the South and Southeast. Although Brazilian society still remains exceptionally unequal, the more extreme division of the country between the backward and poor North and the industrialized and modern South has been reduced. Class, race, and region still define important inequalities in Brazil, but are no longer so large, geographically speaking, as to define two different societies. Industrialization, urbanization, and modernization of agriculture everywhere also reduced the differences between regions and thus slowed the movements of Brazilians between regions. The late 1980s marked the peak of migration between regions in Brazil, and this migration has declined since then, as factors driving such migrations, such as the regional income gap, have diminished and opportunities for a better life have become more equally distributed.

These post-1985 changes have been due to the impact of the income transfer programs, falling food prices, increasing participation in the legal labor market and general economic growth.[71] In this period, the *Bolsa Família* was but one of several major income transfer programs which included the rural pension program and the BFC for handicapped persons, and guaranteed monthly pensions for all retired persons with incomes below the minimum wage.[72] By 2005, at least half of all families received some type

---

[71] "Between February 1976 and August 2006, the cost of a basic basket of foods in Brazil declined at a significant –3.13% per annum. "The biggest beneficiaries were the poorest consumers. Without this decline, the income transfer programs would not have been successful." José Eustáquio Diniz Alves, "Fatos marcantes da agricultura brasileira," in Roberto de Andrade Alves, Geraldo da Silva, and Souza Eliane Gonçalves, eds., *Contribuição da Embrapa para o desenvolvimento da agricultura no Brasil* (Brasília: Embrapa, 2013), p. 22.

[72] For the evolution of these recent programs, see André Portela Souza, "Políticas de distribuição de renda no Brasil e o Bolsa Família," in Edmar Lisboa Bacha and Simon Schwartzman, eds., *Brasil: A nova agenda social* (Rio de Janeiro: LTC, 2011), pp. 166–186. There have been a large number of studies attempting to explain the fall of both extreme poverty and the GINI index of inequality. Most argue that non-labor income

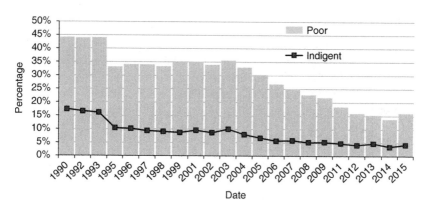

GRAPH 5.4 Percentage of the Brazilian Population Considered Indigent and Poor, 1990–2015
Source: Sonia Rocha, "Poverty Upsurge in 2015 and the Rising Trend in Regional and Age Inequality among the Poor in Brazil," *Nova Economia* 29.1 (2019): 249–275.

of funding from the state.[73] This combination of factors finally broke the long-term pattern of poverty which affected between 40% and 45% of the population in the 1970s and 1980s, and another 20% reduced to indigence in these two decades.[74] These levels of poverty were still evident at the beginning of the 1990s, but by the 2010s both poverty and indigence were half these rates (see Graph 5.4).

through public transfers is as crucial as universal education and the value of the minimum wage (upon which so much of the income and pension schemes are based) in explaining this decline. See, for example, Ricardo Paes de Barros, Mirela de Carvalho, Samuel Franco, and Rosane Mendonça, "Markets, the State and the Dynamics of Inequality: Brazil's Case Study," in Luis Felipe Lopez-Calva, and Nora Lustig, eds., *Declining Inequality in Latin America: A Decade of Progress?* (Washington, DC: Brookings Institution Press, 2010), pp. 134–174; Barros, Carvalho, and Franco, "O papel das Transferências Públicas na queda recente da desigualdade de renda Brasileira," in Bacha and Schwartzman, *Brasil: A nova agenda social*, pp. 41–85; Sergei Soares, "Análise de bem-estar e decomposição por fatores da queda na desigualdade entre 1995 e 2004," *Econômica* 8:1 (2006), pp. 83–115; and Hoffmann, "Transferências de renda e a redução da desigualdade no Brasil," pp. 55–81. Hoffman has stressed that there is an obviously regional variation in this impact, which was far greater in the Northeast and other very poor regions than in the rest of the country. For one of the few opponents to this emphasis on the impact of government income transfers on poverty reduction, see Emerson Marinho and Jair Araujo, "Pobreza e o sistema de seguridade social rural no Brasil," *Revista Brasileira de Economia* 64.2 (2010), pp. 161–174.

[73] Barros, Carvalho, and Franco, "O papel das Transferências Públicas na queda recente da desigualdade de renda Brasileira," p. 41. These authors emphasize the causal importance of both the *Bolsa Família* and the BFC cash transfers.

[74] The data for the 1970s and 1980s comes from Ricardo Henriques, ed., *Desigualdade e pobreza no Brasil* (Rio de Janeiro: Ipea, 2000), p. 24.

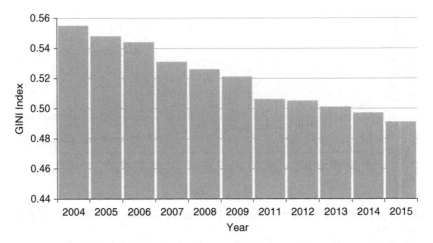

GRAPH 5.5 GINI Index of Monthly Income of Persons 15+ Years Receiving Income, 2004–2015
Source: IBGE, Sidra, Table 5801.

All of these changes have had a major impact in reducing not only rural poverty but the traditional levels of income inequality, especially after the beginning of the new century. Throughout the 1980s and 1990s, the GINI distribution index was in the lower 0.60s,[75] and only began a slow decline at the end of the century, which accelerated in the late 2000s (see Graph 5.5).

This decline in inequality combined with the greater incorporation of workers into the formal market and the consequent impact of the raising of the minimum wage have led to the decline of extreme poverty and the virtual elimination of malnutrition and hunger in Brazil. It is estimated that over 15.9 million families had moved out of poverty (that is those living in extreme poverty, as well as the poor and those earning above the minimum wage but were considered vulnerable) in the period from 2004 to 2009. This resulted in the percentage of non-poor families climbing from 35.8% of all families in 2004 to 51.5% of the 56.8 million families five years later (see Graph 5.6).[76]

A recent study shows that by 2005 a quarter of family income came from non-labor sources, and 90% of this non-labor income came from government pensions and income transfers. Of these government sources, the

[75] The IBGE currently uses the 15 years or older persons earning income as the basic category, but previously used a 10 years or older base, or, as in the censuses of 1991 and 2000, just listed the GINI for heads of households regardless of income. But all these GINIs are rather close and can give only an approximate idea of trends. Thus, the GINI in the census of 1991 was at 0.64 and 0.61 for the census of 2000 for all Brazil. IBGE, Sidra, Table 155.
[76] Osorio, Souza, Soares, and Oliveira, *Perfil da pobreza*, Table 2:17.

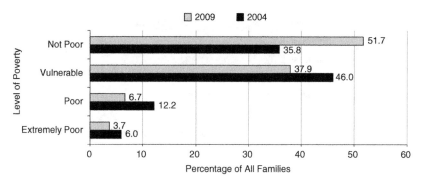

GRAPH 5.6 Reduction of Poverty for Brazilian Families in 2004 and 2009
Source: Osorio, et al., "Perfil da pobreza no Brasil e sua evolução no período 2004–2009," Texto para discussão 1647, Rio de Janeiro, Ipea, 2011, p. 17, Table 2.

largest single program in coverage was the *Bolsa Família*, which grew from 2.6 million persons in 2001 to 6.5 million in 2005. There was also an expansion of the BPC (MIV) program, which increased from 180,000 beneficiaries to 1.2 million in the same period.[77]

While the poverty rate in all regions has declined, in 2014 the North and Northeast were still well above the national average of 13% of the population being poor. Interestingly, the Southeast is almost equal to the Center-West, and only the small farm region of the South has extraordinarily low levels of poverty. Not surprisingly given the efforts of the government to reduce rural poverty, traditionally the worst place for the poor, it is now the metropolitan regions which have the highest levels of poverty (see Graph 5.7).

Along with the reduction in poverty has come a major advance in education. From the middle of the twentieth century there were significant investments in education throughout Brazil. Previously with one of the hemisphere's highest illiteracy rates, the nation has become one of the least illiterate in Latin America over the past seventy years. Regarding the number of schools and school attendance, there has been a secular trend going from the middle of the twentieth century until today. Although the quality of the education delivered has been questioned, there is little debate that the government has succeeded in ending most child labor and placed most children in school, as the net matriculation rates suggest. Currently, primary education enrollment is close to being complete for all children in the relevant age group, and there has been a massive change in participation in secondary and

---

[77] Ricardo Paes de Barros, Mirela de Carvalho, and Samuel Franco, "O papel das Transferências Públicas na queda recente da desigualdade de renda Brasileira." *Desigualdade de renda no Brasil: uma análise da queda recente* (2 vols; Brasília: Ipea, 2007), vol. 2, pp. 46–49.

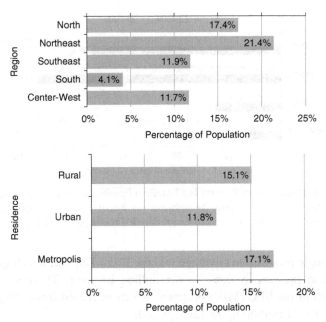

GRAPH 5.7 Percentage of the Population Who Are Poor, by Region and Residence, 2014
Source: Rocha, IETS Tables.

tertiary education in recent years. Much of this rapid growth began in the military era but has continued uninterrupted in the post-1985 democratic period. This can be seen in the net rates of matriculation (that is the percentage of the relevant age cohort in school) of children of primary school age who attended school. This rate went from 81% to 96% between 1992 and 2014. In the same period the net matriculation rate for secondary schools went from 18% to 58%, and for tertiary educational institutions from 5% to 18%. All of this educational advancement has had the expected impact on both average years of schooling and the literacy rates of the population. Thus, from 1992 to 2014, the percentage of illiterates dropped from a still high of 17% to 8% of the adult population 15 years of age and older. In turn, the average number of years of schooling went from 4.9 to 7.7 years for persons 25 years of age or older (see Graph 5.8).

Without question, both sexes have benefited from these changes, but, clearly, growth of education and literacy has changed faster for women than for men. In 1950, there was a very significant educational disadvantage against women. Whereas 43% of men were literate in 1950, only 39% of women could read and write. By 2015, however, more women were literate than men (91.3% of women and 90.3% of men), with some modest variation

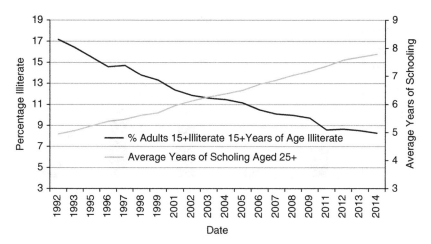

GRAPH 5.8 Average Years of Schooling for Adults Aged 25+ and Percentage Illiterate among Those Aged 15+, 1992–2014
Source: IETS, PNAD data at www.iets.org.br/spip.php?article406.

by region – being considerably higher for women in the least developed areas of the nation. Moreover, for both sexes, regional differences have been steadily declining. Thus, from just 1950 to 2015, the least literate region, the Northeast zone of states, has experienced the fastest growth in the recent period. The region is rapidly closing the gap and within a few decades looks to equal the most advanced regions (see Graph 5.9).

Much of this social change has come about with increasing income and a more diversified market as a result of economic growth. But a major share of change in health, education, and welfare is due to the state and its activities. Although such activity began in the 1930s, the expansion of the welfare state had taken decades to create and Brazil has only slowly and laboriously begun to provide the basic social services that a modern industrial society takes for granted in the twenty-first century. The provision of unemployment insurance, pensions, workmen's compensation, and health care are only now being addressed nationally in the past quarter-century.

But government policies aimed at growth in the second decade of the new century were developed without any concern for fiscal balance, resulting in one of Brazil's most intense economic crisis and a subsequent return to austerity and orthodox shocks. Thus, after a period of extraordinary growth in the past twenty years of so, there has been a sharp drop in GDP and a significant increase in the level of unemployment. But it is still too early to assess the social consequences of the severe recession of 2015–2016, when GDP fell by 7%. Along with this there are severe problems in the current

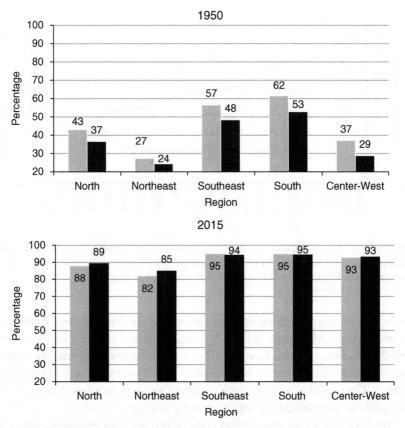

GRAPH 5.9 Literacy by Sex and Region, 1950 and 2015
Source: IBGE, *Censo demográfico 1950*, Série Nacional, vol. 1, p. 90, Table 47, using contemporary regional divisions; IBGE, Sidra, Table 2585.

structure of social security, which still need to be resolved before sustained investments can be made in the system. Too many beneficiaries do not contribute in proportion to their actuarial benefits, thus leaving the system badly underfunded, which requires supplementary and growing support out of the federal budget. The current fiscal situation is not sustainable. Growth of social security expenditure is outpacing income and thus compromises the state's fiscal balance. There is now a total of 32.7 million active beneficiaries of social security, of which 23.3 million are urban and 9.4 are rural, which approximately reflects the distribution of these populations nationally.[78]

---

[78] Research supported by the Ministry of Agrarian Development estimates that 36% of the Brazilian population is rural, unlike the 16% indicated by the last census of the Brazilian

In the urban area, most of the benefits are for pensions, of which about half are for length of contribution and approximately one-third for age. But it is noteworthy that 24% of the pensions are a consequence of disability. Social security benefits in the urban area include pensions for widows and orphans, which accounts for about a quarter of all social security benefits. In the rural area, the most important are the benefits for age and pensions for death (survivor benefits). There are few benefits granted for length of contribution, since rural retirement allows non-contributory participation of retirees, and it suffices to demonstrate that one partook of rural activity and reached the age of 60 for men and 55 for women.

Retirement accounts for 61% of the amount spent on social security benefits, pensions for death 22%, and aid (sickness, confinement, and accident) 5%. There are also important differences by residence and who obtains the most income from the social security program. Thus, only 15% of the urban benefits are due to retirement age, whereas 67% of benefits in the rural areas go to persons retiring due to age (see Table 5.1). By gender, there is a balance in the number of benefits granted to men and women, but men account for 58% in value. By age it is noticeable that almost 20% of the beneficiaries are 54 years old or less, a percentage that rises to 30% when we include those up to the age of 60. Only slightly more than half the beneficiaries (54%) are over the age of 65 (see Table 5.2). Finally, we see that in the urban areas beneficiaries up to 60 years of age represent about 35% of both beneficiaries and in value; in rural areas this percentage declines to around 15% (Table 5.3).

Understanding the reform proposals which have been a major concern in the second decade of this current century requires understanding the structure and scope of social security in Brazil as currently elaborated by the 1988 Constitution and in the revised Organic Social Security Act of 1991. These created two types of pension schemes: allocation and capitalization. In its origin this system was constituted by the capitalization system that is fully funded by workers and employees. But already by the middle of the twentieth century the accumulated reserves were expended, and the system gradually became an underfunded allocation or distribution system. If in the capitalization system the benefits are funded by the capture of resources accumulated throughout the active life of the worker, in the distribution system the

Institute of Geography and Statistics (IBGE). The greater percentage comes from the application of a different concept of rural defended by the researchers. According to the survey, since there is only the concept of urban in legislation, rurality ends up being defined by exclusion. See http://agenciabrasil.ebc.com.br/geral/noticia/2015-03/pesquisa-diz-que-populacao-rural-do-brasil-e-maior-que-apurada-pelo-ibge.

Table 5.1 *Active Beneficiaries of Social Security Income as of December 2015 in R$ 000*

Types of Benefits	Beneficiaries			Value of Benefits (R$)		
	Total	Urban	Rural	Total	Urban	Rural
Total	32,658,862	23,295,036	9,363,826	35,961,514	28,583,105	7,378,408
Beneficiaries of the RGPS (CLT)	28,225,898	18,937,254	9,288,644	32,449,782	25,130,617	7,319,165
Regular beneficiaries	27,392,602	18,136,061	9,256,541	31,597,649	24,304,243	7,296,407
Pensioners	18,331,635	11,617,192	6,714,443	21,861,844	16,555,198	5,306,646
Death benefits	7,429,823	5,101,580	2,328,243	7,941,233	6,114,571	1,826,661
Persons supported	1,576,299	1,368,908	207,391	1,743,974	1,585,969	158,005
Maternal support	54,700	48,236	6,464	50,505	45,411	5,094
Work injuries	833,296	801,193	32,103	852,132	829,374	22,759
Assistance benefits	4,422,134	4,346,952	75,182	3,493,300	3,434,057	59,243
Related assistance	4,251,726	4,251,726		3,350,338	3,350,338	
RMV Monthly Life Incomes	159,273	84,091	75,182	125,507	66,264	59,243
Encargos Previdenciários da União – EPU	10,830	10,830		18,432	18,432	

Source: Table C.2, Ministério Previdência Social. www.previdencia.gov.br/dados-abertos/.

Table 5.2 Active Beneficiaries of Social Security by Sex and Age as of December 2015

Ages	Persons				Value of Benefits in R$ 000			
	Total	Men	Women	Unknown	Total	Men	Women	Unknown
Total	25,091,262	12,738,373	12,319,282	33,607	27,843,895	16,055,524	11,761,026	27,346
To 19	598,200	352,035	246,163	2	473,379	278,594	194,783	2
20–24	242,731	141,929	100,800	2	200,954	118,749	82,205	1
25–29	302,238	175,631	126,600	7	264,314	155,263	109,045	5
30–34	387,559	225,555	161,994	10	354,887	207,901	146,978	8
35–39	479,598	278,283	201,299	16	455,127	269,789	185,326	12
40–44	579,603	335,822	243,741	40	587,936	358,482	229,422	32
45–49	805,474	451,211	354,070	193	909,241	553,887	355,202	153
50–54	1,348,607	727,026	621,072	509	1,760,951	1,047,569	712,975	407
55–59	2,654,054	1,221,548	1,431,671	835	3,488,165	1,972,845	1,514,653	668
60–64	4,077,322	1,966,847	2,109,351	1,124	5,033,298	2,865,246	2,167,072	980
65–69	4,593,051	2,434,806	2,156,757	1,488	5,183,511	3,127,207	2,055,002	1,302
70–74	3,492,958	1,812,659	1,677,997	2,302	3,702,548	2,179,389	1,521,235	1,924
75–79	2,599,166	1,282,265	1,313,523	3,378	2,614,785	1,467,697	1,144,344	2,745
80–84	1,588,192	745,998	839,592	2,602	1,547,086	828,221	716,737	2,128
85–89	859,725	389,855	466,828	3,042	825,673	421,898	401,193	2,582
90+	478,946	194,730	266,309	17,907	438,208	200,497	223,419	14,292
Unknown	3,838	2,173	1,515	150	3,830	2,289	1,436	105

Source: Table C.5 created by Ministério Previdência Social. www.previdencia.gov.br/dados-abertos/.

Table 5.3 *Active Beneficiaries of Social Security by Residence, December 2015*

	Urban		Rural	
Ages	Persons	Vale(R$ 000)	Persons	Vale(R$ 000)
Total	18,059,664	22,295,494	7,031,598	5,548,401
To 19	594,539	470,684	3,661	2,695
20–24	236,745	196,402	5,986	4,552
25–29	289,620	254,798	12,618	9,516
30–34	365,078	337,929	22,481	16,958
35–39	445,557	429,344	34,041	25,783
40–44	531,117	550,895	48,486	37,041
45–49	730,349	851,234	75,125	58,007
50–54	1,237,806	1,674,623	110,801	86,329
55–59	1,937,386	2,923,319	716,668	564,846
60–64	2,708,154	3,950,885	1,369,168	1,082,413
65–69	3,195,724	4,079,053	1,397,327	1,104,458
70–74	2,374,535	2,818,683	1,118,423	883,865
75–79	1,680,693	1,889,578	918,473	725,208
80–84	991,326	1,075,602	596,866	471,485
85–89	518,378	555,883	341,347	269,791
90 +	219,311	233,140	259,635	205,068
Unknown	3,346	3,442	492	388

Source: Ministério Previdência Social. www.previdencia.gov.br/dados-abertos/.

benefits, pensions, and other forms of benefits are borne by the next generation and come out of general state funds. Changes in the structure between
assets and retirees, in the age and dependency ratios, or proportion of formal
and informal jobs, have direct effects on the balance of the system. Although
there are important capitalization regimes in the Brazilian pension system, as
is the case of the pension funds, for the most part the majority of the paid-out
benefits are from distribution on unfunded allocation.[79]

[79] Meiriane Nunes Amaro and Fernando B. Meneguin, "A evolução da previdência Social após
a constituição de 1988." Senado Federal. Accessed 4 January 2018, at: www12.senado.leg.br
/publicacoes/estudos-legislativos/tipos-de-estudos/outras-publicacoes/volume-v-constitui
cao-de-1988-o-brasil-20-anos-depois.-os-cidadaos-na-carta-cidada/seguridade-social-a-evo
lucao-da-previdencia-social-apos-a-constituicao-de-1988; Christiano Ferreira, "Mudança
do Regime Previdenciário de Repartição para o Regime Misto: uma perspectiva para
o Brasil," MA thesis, Pontifícia Universidade Católica do Rio Grande do Sul – PUCRS,
2012; Luciana Caduz da Almeida Costa, "O custo de peso morto do sistema previdenciário
de repartição: analisando o caso brasileiro." FGV, 2007. Accessed 4 January 2018, at: https://
bibliotecadigital.fgv.br/dspace/handle/10438/310.

Another characteristic of the Brazilian social security system is the coexistence of two parallel systems, the general RGPS (*Regime Geral da Previdência Social*) and the special RPPS (*Regime Único da Previdência Social*). Private-sector employees are governed by the General Regime (RGPS), which also incorporates some public employees. The system corresponds to the employees governed by the labor code which is the CLT (Consolidation of Labor Laws). By contrast, the RPPS is unique to civil servants. The general RGPS was created in parallel with the CLT and from the beginning was based on a contribution ceiling, which limited the benefits to the same level, defined by the average contributions paid by the beneficiary. The ceiling and the calculation of the average have undergone variations over time. Currently, the ceiling corresponds to just over 5 minimum wages or about US\$ 1,700. There is a progressive contribution from the worker, which starts from 8% and reaches 11%. The employer pays as a general rule 20% on the payroll, without ceiling limitation.[80] Recently, the legislation defined sectors in which the contribution was based on billing and not the payroll.[81] In addition, most of the social security benefits of the general regime are corrected by the minimum wage, which had an accelerated growth in the last twenty years.

Public servants have a far more generous retirement system and one that was unfunded. The 1988 Constitution declared that public servants could retire voluntarily, with full salaries based on their last remuneration, after 35 years of service, if male, and 30 years of service, if female. Teachers had a requirement of 5 years less. They could also retire with proceeds proportional to their time of service, from 30 years of service for men and 25 years of service for women. In addition, the legislation provided for voluntary retirement at 65 years of age for men, and 60 years of age for women. In this case also, salaries were proportional to the time of service. In the case of proportional retirements, the calculation basis is also the last salary received. There was no cap on the value of retirement and the system was non-contributory. The constitution maintained the principle of isonomy or equality with active state workers. That is, retirement benefits would be revised in the same proportion and on the same date whenever the compensation of active employees was changed, including when they were transformed or reclassified

---

[80] In addition to the 20% contribution on the payroll, entrepreneurs pay from 1% to 3% as a Work Accident Risk, depending on the risk level of the activity. They also contribute 5.8% to other entities such as SENAI, SESC, SESI, and SEBRAE. In this case the INSS functions as a mere collector, since the activities are carried out directly by these entities which are managed by employers.

[81] Some economic sectors, such as construction, public transportation, and newspaper companies, have a contribution linked to the billing.

from the position or function in which the retirement occurred. The constitution also established that the benefit of the widow or widower's death pension should correspond to the total salary or earnings of the deceased public servant. That is, the 1988 Constitution maintained the traditional principles of public service retirement: full retirement salary, non-contributory, and no retirement age requirement.[82] Because the length of service in activities governed by the CLT could be counted, someone who started work with formal working papers at the age of 14 (the minimum age required in the past) could retire at the age of 49, with the full salary of the position he had at the time of retirement, and without having contributed to the system. The Constitution (article 195) also created Rural Social Security, matching the benefits of rural workers to urban workers, reducing the retirement age by five years, and increasing the value of the benefit to a minimum wage.[83]

The unsustainability of the entire system was clear from the beginning, primarily for public employees and rural workers. As early as the mid-1990s, after the implementation of the *Plan Real*, discussions began on the need for social security reform, especially as it affected public employees. The so-called social security factor was created, which adjusts the value of the retirement to be received by the expectation of life after retirement. Another important reform attempted the financial balance of social security, which modified the social security system of public servants, demanding the contribution of retired public servants who receive benefits above the ceiling of the value of the benefits of the General Social Security System.[84] In 2012, Law 2618 made another profound change in the retirement benefits of new public servants. They would no longer be entitled to full retirement but would be subject to the same limits established by the General Regime. This affected only newly appointed functionaries. There is now a ceiling to contributions and a ceiling to benefits. A public servant has the right to participate in a Supplementary Pension Program, contributing to the difference between the actual compensation and the contribution ceiling for the RPPS. This Complementary Pension Plan offered to public servants had already existed in Brazil for many years for those workers who wished to

---

[82] Article 40 of the Constitution of 1988, in its original approved form.

[83] Guimarães notes that with the promulgation of the Federal Constitution of 1988, rural workers became fully integrated into social security, but it required the passage of enabling legislation to give full effect to these constitutional rights, and this only occurred with the publication of Laws 8.212/91 and 8.213/91 and other such regulatory laws. Roberto Élito dos Reis Guimarães, *O trabalhador rural e a previdência social: evolução histórica e aspectos controvertidos*. Accessed 4 January 2018, at: www.agu.gov.br/page/download/index/id/580103.

[84] Emendas Constitucionais no. 41 de 19 de dezembro de 2003 and no. 45 de 23 de fevereiro de 2005.

increase their retirement and were in the private sector and under the CLT rules. Although it is broadly based, most of the contributors to this fund came from public companies such as *Petrobras, Banco do Brasil, Telebrás,* and *Eletrobrás,* as well as privatized public companies, which sponsored complementary retirement plans.[85]

But these reforms were insufficient to slow the growing deficits of the social security system which jeopardized the system's sustainability and the federal government's own budget balance, given the amount of the current deficit and future forecasts. For this reason, in 2017, another major overhaul of the system was proposed which involved two key points. The first is the imposition of an age limit versus years of service to obtain the benefits of retirement, a practice common to most social security regimes in the West.[86] The second is the reduction of the differences that still exist between the retirement of the beneficiaries of the public servants, and those in the private sector. These reforms are necessary to maintain the system designed to provide a reasonable pension for all workers, and their aim is to make all participants, especially in the previously protected public sector, into active contributors to the pension scheme.

How serious is the economic situation in relation to pensions can be seen in the latest available figures. The General Social Security System currently has a deficit of R\$ 149 billion (US\$ 46 billion). Two-thirds of this deficit is due to rural pensions and pensions for non-contributory public servants. The increase in benefits between 2015 and 2016 was in the order of 17% (for urban recipients) and 13% (for rural ones), compared with a 6.29% infraction occurring in the year (Table 5.4). The deficit of the General Regime should be added to the financial deficit identified in pension system of the government, which totaled R\$ 77 billion in 2016 (US\$ 23 billion). When we consider the aggregate of the three levels of government – the Federal government (Union), the states, and the municipalities – the deficit reaches double that rate, or approximately R\$ 156 billion (US\$ 47 billion).

Another aspect of this pension crisis is the high ratio of retirees and pensioners to active contributors, which is currently 1.2 contributors to 1 pensioner in the federal union and 1.3 active contributors to 1 pensioner in the states. That is, in a few years, the number of beneficiaries will exceed the

---

[85] See José Cláudio Rodarte, "A evolução da previdência complementar fechada no Brasil, da década de 70 aos dias atuais: expectativas, tendências e desafios," MA thesis, UFMG – Universidade Federal de Minas Gerais, 2011.

[86] A study of Ipea presents an interesting comparison of social security in several countries, putting Brazil's institutions in an international context. Marcelo Abia-Ramia Caetano and Rogério Boueri Miranda, "Comparativo internacional para a previdência social," Texto para discussão 1302, Brasília, Ipea, 2007.

Table 5.4 *Cash Flow of INSS in Millions of Nominal R$, 2015–2106*

	2015	2016	Change
Total net income	350,272	358,137	2%
Total net income – urban	317,742	332,622	5%
Total net income – rural	7,081	7,920	12%
Other	25,449	17,595	
Social security waivers	40,832	43,421	6%
Expenses with benefits	436,090	507,871	
Urban benefits	328,961	385,277	17%
Rural benefits	95,754	108,659	13%
Legal cases	9,622	11,597	
Social security income and waiver	−44,986.60	−106,313.30	136%
Social security results	−85,818.10	−149,733.90	74%

Source: Marcelo Caetano, "Apresentação do secretário de Previdência, Marcelo Caetano, sobre a proposta de Reforma da Previdência enviada pelo Governo Federal" (8 March 2017). www .fazenda.gov.br/centrais-de-conteudos/apresentacoes/2017/apresentacao-m-caetano.pdf/view.

number of contributors. The current proposed reform of the national government aims to guarantee the present and future sustainability of social security, in view of the demographic transition of the Brazilian population. The reform aims to harmonize pension rights, conform to international practices, and ensure that no retiree receives less than one minimum wage. The growing deficit in social security explains the urgency of the reform movement, although to date the political support for this reform is still lacking.

A recent World Bank study on Brazilian public spending concluded that the most important requirement for long-term fiscal viability of the Brazilian state finances is the reform of social security. It also noted that the current pension system is inequitable in that 35% of pension subsidies benefit the richest 20% of the population, while only 18% of this subsidy benefits the poorest 40% of the population. The study suggested that the deficits of the RPPS pensions systems are projected to increase sharply in the next five to ten years, as many civil servants who entered government before the 2003 reform will retire. This will jeopardize the fiscal solvency of many of the state governments. Therefore, additional measures will be required to align the benefits of the RPGS and RPPS to the level of contributions. Even more importantly, the Bank recommends decoupling the minimum retirement value from the minimum wage and correcting it to living costs instead.

Finally, the government should consider rural retirement and the BPC, or Continuous Pension Benefits as social programs, and not social security ones.[87]

For all the issues related to costs and fiscal imbalances in the pension schemes, there is little question that the development of a modern welfare system has provided enough benefits to enough of the population to have a major impact in reducing income and regional inequalities and in underpinning the almost universal availability to health education and pension support for the entire national population. Clearly, reform will be needed as Brazil rebuilds its capacity to provide funding for all of these important activities. Without a growing economy many of these benefits may not be sustainable. But the picture to date shows that the increasing levels of education and health of the population and the reductions in inequality have created a more uniform society, one in which hunger has been eliminated and indigence has been severely reduced. It has also helped in generating a new and far larger middle class than ever existed before. Brazil today is overwhelmingly urban and a very different society from the society that existed in the middle of the twentieth century.

---

[87] Grupo Banco Mundial, *A Fair Adjustment: Efficiency and Equity of Public Spending in Brazil*, vol. 1, *Síntese* (Washington, DC: World Bank, 2017), pp. 9–17. In addition to social security expenditure, the study analyzes other important components of public spending in Brazil.

6

Urban Life in the Twentieth and Twenty-First Centuries

Despite the dominance of rural life in Brazil until the mid-twentieth century, Brazil is today one of the most urbanized countries in the world. In 1960, less than half of the Brazilian population lived in urban areas, which was below the average even in Latin America, well below the European and Central Asian average (of 55%), and only higher than the level of urbanization in East Asian and Pacific nations. But in the last fifty years the movement from countryside to city in Brazil was superior to these other regions and even to most developed countries, reaching in 2016 a position comparable to the majority of American and European countries. This year, Brazil's ratio of 86% urban population exceeded Canada and the United States and such European countries as Spain, France, Germany, and Italy. Its level of urbanization was surpassed only by Australia and Chile (both at 90% urban), Argentina (92% urban), and Japan (94% urban).[1]

The great migration of the rural population was driven by the attraction of the newly industrializing sector which was growing at 3% per annum between 1949 and 2017. At the same time, the increasing mechanization of national agriculture after 1960 was to prove the major push factor which drove this migration. It began as early as the 1920s with the end of significant international migrations but gained massive proportions in the second half of the twentieth century. This migration involved not only movements between rural and urban areas within the states and regions, but also the migration of millions of persons across regions, and especially from the poorer Northeast to the Southeast.

---

[1] UN, Population division, Table WUP2018-F02-Proportion_Urban.xls. Accessed at: https://esa.un.org/unpd/wup/Download/.

A result of this urbanization was the constant reduction in the share of the population employed in agriculture and eventually even the size of this labor force. Starting from accounting for two-thirds of the EAP in 1940,[2] rural workers were down to only 9% of the national labor force by the time of the 2006 agricultural census. Although the size of this rural labor force continued to grow in absolute numbers and peaked at 23.4 million in 1985, after that date their actual numbers were in decline. By the time of the agricultural census of 2006, there were just 16.6 million persons working in agriculture and their numbers declined to just an estimated 15.7 million by 2015.[3]

By contrast, the size and relative importance of the urban labor force grew dramatically. By the time of the census of 1991, the population of economically active persons 10 years of age and older in the urban area had reached 45.6 million persons, or 78% of the EAP nationally, and by 2010 there were 84.5 million urban workers who now represented 86% of the EAP of this age group.[4] By 2015, the economically active urban population reached 89.8 million persons.[5] Women in the urban areas also had a higher participation in the labor force than women in the rural areas. By the census of 2010, for example, some 45% of the urban women 10 years of age were in the labor force, while in the rural area only 36% were employed, a figure that urban women had reached by 1991.[6]

Unlike the mass immigration of African slaves and European immigrants, which was dominated by men, this new rural to urban migration was thus dominated by women. With a large domestic service sector in the urban centers women found work more easily than men, given the low levels of literacy and skills of the majority of these migrants. This, in fact, was the pattern for most European and North American cities in the nineteenth and early twentieth centuries. Thus the sex ratio in the cities, being the number of men for every 100 women, remained in the range from 91 to 95 males per 100 females from 1940 to 2010, whereas the rural rate never fell below 104 and hit 111 males per 100 females by the census of 2010 (see Table 6.1).

This massive rural–urban migration, while often positive for the migrant, had serious consequences for the urban centers in which they arrived, which

[2] IBGE, Brasil no Século XX (2003), Table pop_1971aeb-002.
[3] IBGE, Sidra, Tables 265 and 2859.   [4] IBGE, Sidra, Table 616.
[5] IBGE, Sidra, Table 2859 gives the most recent estimate. An earlier government estimate was for 94.5 million in 2015. See IBGE, Series Historicas, Table PD374, Situação rural ou urbana. Período de referência de 365 dias. Accessed at: https://seriesestatisticas.ibge.gov.br/series.as px?no=7&op=o&vcodigo=PD374&t=situacao-rural-urbana-periodo-referencia-365.
[6] IBGE, Sidra, Table 616.

Table 6.1 *Urban and Rural Population of Brazil
in the Censuses, 1940–2010*

Census	Urban	Rural	Total
1940	12,880,182	28,356,133	41,236,315
1950	18,782,891	33,161,506	51,944,397
1960	31,303,034	38,767,423	70,070,457
1970	52,097,260	41,037,586	93,134,846
1980	80,437,327	38,573,725	119,011,052
1991	110,990,990	35,834,485	146,825,475
2000	137,953,959	31,845,211	169,799,170
2010	160,925,804	29,829,995	190,755,799

Source: IBGE, *Estatísticas do Século XX*, Table
"População1992aeb-003" to 1960 and IBGE, Sidra, Table
202 from 1980 to present.

were often unprepared for or incapable of providing the housing and services needed to integrate these migrants. At first, this massive migration went to the capital cities of the states, since they usually were the largest city in each unit of the federation. Rio de Janeiro and São Paulo increased dramatically in the second half of the twentieth century, while other state capitals increased at a slower pace. But by the end of the twentieth century, middle-sized non-capital cities grew more quickly everywhere. This explains why the share of the capital cities has remained the same percentage of total population since 1970 (see Table 6.2).

In the late twentieth century, it was the city of São Paulo which would show the greatest absolute growth. Starting from a modest position in 1872 when it was far smaller than most of the capital cities of Brazil, it would reach the size of Rio de Janeiro by the middle of the twentieth century. With a major share of Brazilian industry consolidated in the city and its surrounding districts, the city until the 1990s grew at an accelerated pace. Between 1940 and 1980, while the national population grew at about 2.7% per year and the state population expanded by approximately 3.2% per year, the city of São Paulo and its metropolitan region grew at more than 5% per annum. By 2010, the city of São Paulo, with more than 11 million inhabitants, represented a quarter of the population of all Brazilian capitals, 27% of the population of the state of São Paulo, and 6% of the Brazilian population. The metropolitan region of São Paulo, with its 39 municipalities and 19.7 million inhabitants, represented almost half the population of the state and one-tenth of the Brazilian population. By then, the city of São Paulo had

Table 6.2 *Population of Brazil, the Federal Capital, and Capital Cities of the States, 1972–2010*

Census Year	Population, Total Capitals	Percentage of Total Population	São Paulo	Rio de Janeiro	Salvador	Brasília	Fortaleza	Belo Horizonte	Manaus	Recife	Porto Alegre	Belém
1872	956,092	10%	31,385	274,972	129,109	–	42,458	–	29,334	116,671	43,998	61,997
1890	1,286,637	9%	64,934	522,651	174,412	–	40,902	–	38,720	111,556	52,421	50,064
1900	1,965,306	11%	239,820	811,443	205,813	–	48,369	13,472	50,300	113,106	73,674	96,560
1920	3,386,158	11%	579,033	1,157,873	283,422	–	78,536	55,563	75,704	238,843	179,263	236,402
1940	5,558,336	13%	1,326,261	1,764,141	290,443	–	180,185	211,377	106,399	348,424	272,232	206,331
1950	8,120,554	16%	2,198,096	2,377,451	417,235	–	270,169	352,724	139,620	524,682	394,151	254,949
1960	13,064,674	18%	3,825,351	3,307,163	655,735	141,742	514,818	693,328	175,343	797,234	641,173	402,170
1970	20,235,126	21%	5,978,977	4,315,746	1,027,142	546,015	872,702	1,255,415	314,197	1,084,459	903,175	642,514
1980	29,175,524	24%	8,587,665	5,183,992	1,531,242	1,203,333	1,338,793	1,822,221	642,492	1,240,937	1,158,709	949,545
1991	35,300,818	24%	9,626,894	5,473,909	2,072,058	1,598,415	1,765,794	2,017,127	1,010,544	1,296,995	1,263,239	1,244,688
2000	40,388,490	24%	10,405,867	5,851,914	2,440,828	2,043,169	2,138,234	2,232,747	1,403,796	1,421,993	1,360,033	1,279,861
2010	45,466,045	24%	11,253,503	6,320,446	2,675,656	2,570,160	2,452,185	2,375,151	1,802,014	1,537,704	1,409,351	1,393,399

Source: IBGE, Sidra, Table 1287.

become one of the world's largest cities and the economic and financial capital of the nation.[7]

This urban growth initially was predominantly though not exclusively confined to the capital cities. While the Brazilian population as a whole grew at 2.5% in the 1970s, the metropolitan regions of most cities were growing at a rate of 4.5%. The fastest growing metropolitan regions, those growing at above 6% per annum in this decade, included not only such capital cities as the Federal District, Manaus, and Vitória, but also the non-capital city of Campinas, which also grew at the same fast pace. The slowest-growing metropolitan area in this period of the 1970s was the metropolitan region of Rio de Janeiro, which grew at only 2.4%.[8] This was due to the loss of industries and finance to São Paulo,[9] as well as the impact of the transfer of the capital to Brasília, which occurred gradually during the 1950s to the 1970s. In addition, there were profound changes with the political-administrative reorganization of the region, which ceased to be a Federal District, and eventually became the capital of the state of Rio de Janeiro.[10]

---

[7] On this theme, see Manuel Castells, *The Urban Question* (London: Arnold, 1977); J. V. Beaverstock, R. G. Smith, and P. J. Taylor, "A Roster of World Cities." *Cities* 16.6 (1999), pp. 445–458. Accessed at: www.lboro.ac.uk/gawc/rb/rb5.html; P. J. Taylor, "Worlds of Large Cities: Pondeering Castells' Space of Flows." Globalization and World Cities Study Group and Network, Research Bulletin 14. Accessed at: www.lboro.ac.uk/gawc/rb/rb14.html. Several recent national studies apply this methodology for the study of São Paulo. See Stamatia Koulioumba, "São Paulo: cidade mundial?" PhD thesis, Faculdade de Arquitetura e Urbanismo da USP, São Paulo, 2002, and João Sette Whitaker Ferreira, "São Paulo: o mito da cidade-global," PhD thesis, Faculdade de Arquitetura e Urbanismo da USP, São Paulo, 2003; and Tamás Szmrecsányi, ed., *História Econômica da cidade de São Paulo* (São Paulo: Editora Globo, 2005).

[8] Fausto A. de Brito and Breno A. T. D. de Pinho, *A dinâmica do processo de urbanização no Brasil, 1940–2010* (Belo Horizonte: UFMG/CEDEPLAR, 2012), p. 14, Table 5.

[9] On the concentration of activities in São Paulo, see Francisco Vidal Luna, "São Paulo: a capital financeira do país," in Szmrecsányi, *História Econômica da cidade de São Paulo*, pp. 328–355; Lucia Maria Machado Bógus and Maura Pardini Bicudo Véras, "A reorganização metropolitana de São Paulo: espaços sociais no contexto da globalização," *Cadernos Metrópole* 3. Accessed 20 November 2017, at: https://revistas.pucsp.br/index.php/metro pole/article/view/9329; and Ana Fani Alessandri Carlos, "A metrópole de São Paulo no contexto da urbanização contemporânea," *Estudos Avançados* 23.66 (2009), pp. 304–314.

[10] Marly Silva da Motta, "O lugar da cidade do Rio de Janeiro na Federação Brasileira: uma questão em três momentos," Rio de Janeiro, Centro de Pesquisa e Documentação de História Contemporânea do Brasil (CPDOC), 2001. Accessed 20 November 2017, at: https://biblio tecadigital.fgv.br/dspace/bitstream/handle/10438/6799/1232.pdf; Ana Cláudia Nonato da Silva Loureiro, "Rio de Janeiro: uma análise da perda recente de centralidade," MA thesis, Universidade Federal de Minas Gerais, 2006; Mauro Osório da Silva, "A crise do Rio de suas especificidades." Accessed 20 November 2017, at: www.ie.ufrj.br/intranet/ie/userintranet/h pp/arquivos/especificidades_crise.pdf; Marly Silva da Motta, "A fusão da Guanabara com o Estado do Rio: desafios e desencantos," in Américo Freire, Carlos Eduardo Sarmento, and Marly Silva da Motta, eds., *Um Estado em questão: os 25 anos do Rio de Janeiro Rio de Janeiro* (Rio de Janeiro: Editora Fundação Getulio Vargas, 2001), pp. 19–56.

This migration process accelerated the formation of the great urban conglomerates and the beginnings of the metropolitan regions with their satellite towns and cities. The lack of an adequate urban infrastructure and housing to accommodate the massive arrival of poorly educated migrants stimulated the peripheral occupation of major cities, forming poverty belts around the city centers in town and cities, which usually grew in a disorderly, precarious, and irregular way. This explains an essential characteristic of all the major Brazilian metropolitan regions. They are formed with an active, organic center where employment is concentrated, and poor peripheries with inadequate urban infrastructure, which are often dormitory cities far from the center and requiring long daily commutes for workers to reach their jobs.[11]

Thus the growth of these metropolitan areas, that now represented more than half of all the urban population, saw more rapid growth in the periphery than in the central city (see Table 6.3). In the metropolitan region of São Paulo, for example, the central city grew in the 1970s at an annual 3.6%, against 4.1% of the peripheral areas. The same occurred in the 1980s: the center core fell to a rate of growth of 1.6% while the periphery was still growing at 3.3%. The most explosive period of this growth for these metropolitan areas was in the 1970s and 1980s. From the 1990s on, growth slowed considerably so that by 2010 these metropolitan areas now accounted for only 43% of the national urban population, down from the high of 52% in 1970.[12]

Table 6.3 *Metropolitan Regions, Rates of Growth, and Annual Average Increase in Population, 1970–2010*

Rate of Increate	1970/1980	1980/1991	1999/2000	2000/2010
Rate of Growth				
Nucleus	3.57	1.60	1.33	1.03
Periphery	4.98	3.27	2.94	1.51
Total	4.05	2.23	2.00	1.24
Annual population Growth				
Nucleus	770,753	450,813	434,629	375,201
Periphery	558,644	560,705	684,850	435,212
Total	1,329,397	1,011,518	1,119,478	810,413

Source: Fausto A. de Brito and Breno A. T. D. de Pinho, *A dinâmica do processo de urbanização no Brasil, 1940–2010* (2012), pp. 13–14.

---

[11] Brito and Pinho, *A dinâmica do processo de urbanização no Brasil*, pp. 13–14.
[12] Brito and Pinho, *A dinâmica do processo de urbanização no Brasil*, p. 13, Table 4.

This relative decline of the metropolitan areas is due to the rise of medium-sized cities throughout Brazil. Especially in the last thirty years there has been major growth in such cities. In the 2010 census, for example, cities between 100,000 and 500,000 inhabitants represented 27% of the total urban population, up from 15% of that population, and now close to the share held by cities of over half a million in population.[13] These new medium-sized cities could be found in all the states. An estimate of population in 2017 shows that Brazil had 17 cities with more than 1 million inhabitants, 42 with more than 500,000 inhabitants, and more than 300 cities with more than 100,000 inhabitants. If we consider only the state of São Paulo, there are 3 cities with more than 1 million inhabitants, 9 with more than 500,000 and 78 with more than 100,000 inhabitants.[14]

By 2016, the population of all the major metropolitan regions amounted to 94 million people and represented 46% of the total population of Brazil in that year. There were two metropolitan regions with more than 10 million inhabitants: São Paulo (21.2 million) and Rio de Janeiro (12.3 million), and another six state capitals had a population of 4 to 6 million (Belo Horizonte, Federal District, Porto Alegre, Fortaleza, Salvador, and Recife). There were also large metropolitan regions with over a million persons which were not state capitals. The state of São Paulo, for example, had five such large metropolitan areas, including most notably the Campinas Metropolitan Region, with 3.1 million inhabitants (see Table 6.4).[15]

This rapid urban growth throughout Brazil had serious consequences for living conditions in large cities and their metropolitan regions. It exacerbated existing social problems such as housing, sanitation, and transportation. But for all the difficulties this created for the migrants, their relocation improved their lives. The overall improvement of almost all social indicators in Brazil was influenced by urbanization, which provided more educational and health services of the government than was available in the rural areas as well as far more jobs. Thus this urban and regional migration transferred population from

[13] Thomaz Almeida Andrade and Rodrigo Valente Serra, *O recente desempenho das cidades médias no crescimento populacional Brasileiro* (Brasília: Ipea, 1998); Tompson Almeida Serra and Rodrigo Valente Serra, eds., *Cidades médias brasileiras* (Rio de Janeiro: Ipea, 2001); Diva Maria Ferlin Lopes and Wendel Henrique, eds., *Cidades médias e pequenas: teorias, conceitos e estudos de caso* (Salvador: SEI, 2010), p. 250.

[14] IBGE. Accessed 3 November 2017, at: www.ibge.gov.br/estatisticas-novoportal/sociais/po pulacao/9103-estimativas-de-populacao.html?&t=downloads.

[15] Besides the Metropolitan Region (RM) of Campinas, there is an RM of the Paraíba Valley and North Coast (2.5 million inhabitants), an RM of Sorocaba (1.9 million), an RM of the Baixada Santista (1.8 million), and the Urban Megalopolis of Piracicaba (1.5 million). IBGE: https://agenciadenoticias.ibge.gov.br/agencia-sala-de-imprensa/2013-agencia-de-noticias/re leases/9497-ibge-divulga-as-estimativas-populacionais-dos-municipios-em-2016.html.

Table 6.4 *Population of Metropolitan Regions and Their Rates of Growth, 1970–2016*

Metropolitan Region	Population 1970	Population 2010	Annual Growth Rate 1970/1980	Annual Growth Rate 2000/2010	Population Increase 1970/1980	Estimate of Population in 2016*
São Paulo	8,139,705	19,683,975	4.46	0.97	444,904	21,242,939
Rio de Janeiro	6,879,183	11,835,708	2.44	0.86	187,925	12,330,186
Belo Horizonte	1,724,820	4,883,970	4.51	1.15	95,696	5,873,841
Porto Alegre	1,751,889	3,958,985	3.49	0.63	71,614	4,276,475
Distrito Federal	761,961	3,717,728	7.15	2.33	75,807	4,284,676
Recife	1,827,173	3,690,547	2.71	1.01	55,928	3,940,456
Fortaleza	1,130,145	3,615,767	4.16	1.69	56,928	4,019,213
Salvador	1,211,950	3,573,973	4.31	1.37	63,586	3,984,583
Curitiba	907,391	3,174,201	5.38	1.38	62,499	3,537,894
Campinas	680,826	2,797,137	6.49	1.81	59,598	3,131,528
Goiânia	509,570	2,173,141	5.82	2.23	38,781	2,458,504
Manaus	404,514	2,106,322	6.38	2.5	34,644	2,568,817
Belém	685,616	2,101,883	4.31	1.35	35,990	2,422,481
Florianópolis	418,273	1,687,704	4.05	2.14	11,929	1,152,115
Vitória	245,043	877,116	6.07	1.61	33,569	1,935,483
Total of metropolitan regions	27,278,059	69,878,157	4.05	1.24	1,329,397	77,159,191
Total urban population	52,097,260	160,925,792	4.44	1.55	2,834,007	
Total national population	93,134,846	190,755,799	2.48	1.17	2,587,621	206,081,432
Metropolitan regions/Total urban population	52.36	43.42				
Metropolitan regions/Total population	29.29	36.63				

Source: Fausto A. de Brito and Breno A. T. D. de Pinho, *A dinâmica do processo de urbanização no Brasil, 1940–2010* (2012), pp. 13–14; and for s016, see IBGE https://agenciadenoticias.ibge.gov.br/agencia-sala-de-imprensa/2013-agencia-de-noticias/releases/9497-ibge-divulga-as-estimativas-populacionais-dos-munici pios-em-2016.html.

* When IBGE considers all Metropolitan Regions and Urban Agglomerations with more than 1 million inhabitants, the population totals 94,183,623, or 45.7% of the total population.

areas of lower economic productivity to the main dynamic poles of the country, where industry was concentrated and a broad labor market developed in manufacturing and services, capable of absorbing workers with extremely diverse levels of skills and education.[16] In the most intense phase of this migratory process workers were not only absorbed in the expanding industrial labor market but also in the growing construction industry. The rapid growth of these cities required housing and all kinds of infrastructure, expanding the labor market even for low-skilled workers in housing, road construction, and in the large electrification and sanitation projects.

But the cities themselves were unprepared. Fiscal limitations prevented the major investments that would be needed to provide adequate infrastructure to the population that reached the main metropolitan centers. Public sources were inadequate to finance these developments; there was a lack of a long-term credit market to finance housing, coupled with laws that prevented the correction of rents for inflation. This lack of capital made it difficult to adequately supply the urban infrastructure and reduce the chronic housing shortage.[17] There were also serious legal issues concerning which institutions were to deal with these developments. Despite the importance of metropolitan regions there was a relative void in their regulation and management. Key metropolitan issues in the areas of transportation, sanitation, the environment, waste management, and security, for example, still do not have the legal and institutional frameworks that allowed for the coherent management of these issues. This led to conflicts of interest between municipal and state authorities and hindered the creation of institutions and systems to deal with these issues.[18]

---

[16] Paul Singer, *Economia Política de la Urbanización* (Mexico: Siglo Ventiuno Editores, 1978), p. 44.

[17] According to Santos, the Brazilian housing sector is in crisis. There is explosive growth in demand for urban housing (due to the intensification of the country's urbanization). But capital is in short supply due to inflationary pressure, fixed nominal interest rates, and populist laws in the rental market. He estimates a deficit of 8 million housing units. Cláudio Hamilton M. Santos, *Políticas federais de habitação no Brasil, 1964–1980* (Brasília: Ipea, 1999), p. 10. See also Sérgio de Azevedo and Luís Aureliano Gama de Andrade, *Habitação e poder: da Fundação da Casa Popular ao Banco Nacional de Habitação* (Rio de Janeiro: Centro Edelstien de Pesquisas Sociais, 1982); Sérgio Azevedo, "Vinte e dois anos de política de habitação popular (1946–86): criação, trajetória e extinção do BNH." *Revista de Administração Pública* 22.4 (1988), pp. 107–119; José Maria Aragão, *Sistema Financeiro da Habitação: uma análise jurídica da gênese, desenvolvimento e crise do sistema* (Curitiba: Juruá Editora, 2000).

[18] Lucia Camargos Melchiors and Heleniza Ávila Campo, "As regiões metropolitanas brasileiras no contexto do Estatuto da Metrópole: desafios a serem superados em direção à governança colaborativa," *Revista Política e Planejamento Regional* 3.2 (2016), pp. 181–203; Joroen Johannes Klink, "Novas governanças para as áreas metropolitanas: o panorama internacional e as perspectivas para o caso brasileiro," *Cadernos Metrópole* 11.22 (2009), pp. 415–433; Sol Garson Braule Pinto, "Regiões metropolitanas: obstáculos institucionais à cooperação em políticas urbanas," PhD thesis, Universidade Federal do Rio de Janeiro – UFRJ, 2007.

Housing was the first fundamental issue to be faced by the immigrants. But it was also a major issue for long-term urban residents. Inflation had become a major part of the national economy since the 1950s, with annual rates that remained between 20% and 40% per year. The traditional Usury Law remained in effect preventing the issuance of any type of medium- and long-term financial instrument in Brazil, including public debt. The financing of the public deficit was made either by obtaining external loans or by issuing more currency. Immediately after the implementation of the military regime, a monetary correction instrument was created, initially to correct public debt, but gradually implemented in all medium- and long-term financial assets and liabilities.[19] The implementation of a monetary correction mechanism allowed for the creation of a medium- and long-term credit market in Brazil, which was crucial for the housing market and for sanitation infrastructure.

The resources for housing were generated through a national system of forced savings. Until 1963, dismissed employees were compensated with the payment of a month of salary for each year of service. Ten years after hiring, it was even more difficult to dismiss workers, since the employer was required to pay double the rate. This tended to limit the mobility of labor. This system was abolished, replaced by the Guarantee Fund for Length of Service (FGTS). The new system was an important long-term savings instrument, and its resources became the main source of financing for housing and sanitation works. In order to use these resources, the so-called Housing Finance System was set up, led by the National Housing Bank (BNH), a public financial entity that used the resources of the FGTS, along with those available from other public (the *Caixas Econômicas* or Government Savings Banks) and private sources such as the Housing Credit Cooperatives.[20] In addition to the compulsory resources of the FGTS, financial agents could freely raise funds in the market through savings accounts, a traditional credit instrument in Brazil, and through the issuance of real estate letters. Both the active and passive operations of the system were indexed by the monthly

---

[19] Law no. 4.357 of 17 July 1964 authorized the emission of National Treasury bonds (*Obrigações do Tesouro Nacional*) adjusted for variations in the purchasing power of the national currency. Francisco Vidal Luna and Thomaz de Aquino Nogueira Neto, *Correção monetária e mercado de capitais: a experiência brasileira* (São Paulo: Bolsa de Valores de São Paulo (BOVESPA), 1978).

[20] Law 4.380 of 21 August 1964 established the Housing Finance System (*Sistema Financeiro da Habitação*), composed of the National Housing Bank with participation by federal, state, and municipal agencies that financed housing and related works; by the real estate credit companies; by foundations, cooperatives, mutual aid societies, and other non-profit groups dedicated to home construction. On the history of the formation of the BNH, including legal aspects, see Aragão, *Sistema Financeiro da Habitação*, Parts 1 and 2.

monetary correction.[21] Given its autonomy, this system required the remuneration of depositors, and so the financing was directed mainly to the middle-class market and to workers with the capacity to pay for housing, not directly targeting housing for the poor who were dependent on subsidies to own their own apartments or houses.[22]

This funding system boosted the real estate market and allowed ample financing for sanitation works built and operated by state sanitation companies.[23] The creation of the system met two objectives simultaneously. It helped remedy the serious housing shortage and it stimulated the economy by expanding construction and labor-intensive economic activities and strengthening the industries providing the inputs for the sector.[24] The resulting increase in housing, the increased level of construction activity, and the expansion of employment of workers in the home construction sector were important in giving political legitimization to the military regime.

The financial system for housing that was created undoubtedly had an important role in the major expansion of middle-class housing and in publicly funding some working-class residences. It successfully merged compulsory private resources (Guaranteed Fund for Time of Service) with funds raised in a wide network of private and public financial agents. It operated

---

[21] Claudia Magalhães Eloy, "O papel do Sistema Financeiro da Habitação diante do desafio de universalizar o acesso à moradia digna no Brasil," PhD thesis, Faculdade de Arquitetura e Urbanismo da USP, São Paulo, 2013.

[22] Although fiscal resources were not used directly, the system operated with interest rate differences for different segments of the real estate market, favoring the low-income segments. In addition, there were cross-subsidies between borrowers and the holders of the forced savings that funded the system, as the system did not always fully pay back the accumulated savings. Azevedo, "Vinte e dois anos de política de habitação popular," p. 109. There was also a partial correction of the debts of the borrowers, which created immense liabilities in the system and that helps explain the crisis and eventual demise of the program.

[23] From the 1930s onwards, popular housing programs emerged developed by the Retirement and Pension Institutes. According to Azevedo, these entities operated in a fragmented way, reaching only a small number of their associates. The official experience with the creation of the 1946 Casa Popular Foundation (*Fundação da Casa Popular*) would have little practical result. According to the author, after the arrival of the military government in 1964, the foundation of popular housing was abandoned because of its close connection with the Goulart regime. And twenty-two years later, with the redemocratization of the country, the new authorities would use some similar arguments to justify the removal of the National Housing Bank. Azevedo, "Vinte e dois anos de política de habitação popular," pp. 107–108. See also the chapter "Habitação e populismo: a fundação da Casa Popular," in Azevedo and Andrade, *Habitação e poder*.

[24] According to Azevedo, the main motivation for the creation of the National Housing Bank was political. According to BNH mentors, the production of popular houses would allow the emerging military regime to obtain the sympathy of broad sectors of the classes that constituted the main support of the previous populist government overthrown in 1964. Azevedo, "Vinte e dois anos de política de habitação popular," p. 109, and Aragão, *Sistema Financeiro da Habitação*.

with market logic, accepting the need for profits to all investors, public and private. In the two decades of its operation, BNH constructed approximately 4.5 million homes, with just under half in the so-called average or middle-class market. The remainder consisted of traditional COHAB [Metropolitan Housing Company of São Paulo] programs (housing cooperatives), favela eradication programs, self-construction programs, cooperatives, and programs developed by trade union associations. But only one-third of households were targeted in the poorest segment. Thus, this market-driven system was less successful for supplying the low-income market, which constituted and still constitutes the sector with the greatest housing needs. Given the costs and lack of return on capital, this sector could only be supplied by direct government financing.[25]

The other major problem was the lack of coherent planning. The BNH was little concerned with the social and urbanistic impacts of the large housing estates that it financed. Construction for these large projects was carried out in peripheral areas where land was cheaper but little infrastructure existed, creating large housing complexes without adequate transportation, and distant from job-generating centers. This was the norm in the main Brazilian cities, particularly in Rio de Janeiro and São Paulo. The *"Cidade Tiradentes,"* a major housing complex created in the eastern part of the city of São Paulo in the 1970s, is an illustrative case. The housing blocks were built by both the public and private sectors. In this satellite city there live some 200,000 people, part inhabiting the houses built by the housing system and part residing in favelas and informal settlements that have formed around the large housing complex. But lack of an infrastructure, of transportation, and jobs led to the creation of a major population center with serious social problems, which still persist to this day.[26]

---

[25] On the organization of the system, see Aragão, *Sistema Financeiro da Habitação*.

[26] As the local district notes, "The District of Cidade Tiradentes houses the largest housing complex in Latin America, with about 40,000 units, most of them built in the 1980s by COHAB (Metropolitan Housing Company of São Paulo), CDHU (Housing Development Company and Urban of the State of São Paulo) and by large contractors, who even took advantage of the last important financing from BNH (National Bank of Housing), before its closure. The neighborhood was planned as a large peripheral and monofunctional 'dormitory neighborhood' type for the displacement of populations affected by public works, as was the case with Cidade de Deus, in Rio de Janeiro. At the end of the decade of the 1970s, the government began the process of acquiring farmland located in the region, which was known as Fazenda Santa Etelvina, then formed by eucalyptus and stretches of the Atlantic Forest. Residential buildings began to be built, modifying the landscape and locality began to be inhabited by huge contingents of families, who waited in the 'queue' at the offices of the housing companies. In addition to the vastness of housing complexes that make up the so-called Formal City, there is also the 'Informal City,' made up of favelas and clandestine and irregular housing developments housed in private areas. Tiradentes City therefore has a population of 211,501 inhabitants (2010 census)

Despite the importance of the National Housing Bank, it had an ephemeral life. Created in 1964, it was liquidated in 1986.[27] With the resumption of inflation in the late military era, attempts were made to reduce the impact of full indexation on benefits and or the debt balance of borrowers who had taken out inflation-linked real estate loans.[28] This happened even in the National Bank of Economic Development, whose loans from 1975 onward were only partly corrected for the actual inflation. The monetary correction would have a ceiling of 20%, when inflation was above 30%, and increasing.[29]

in a single district. The high population concentration – 14,100 inhab./km² – is added to one of the highest growth rates of the city and serious social problems. This population counts a total of 52,875 families residing in the territory covered by the respective Regional City Hall. Of this total, 8,064 families are in situations of high or very high economic vulnerability. The areas occupied by the 'Informal City' population are gaps left in the construction of the COHAB buildings; occupations at the edges of the groups of housing, and also expansion of the urban district. The identity of the residents of *Cidade Tiradentes* is directly linked to the process of constitution of the neighborhood, which occurred without a pre-established plan which took into account the basic needs of the population. Many people came to Tiradentes City in search of the dream of home ownership, although many moved reluctantly in the absence of alternative housing options. The fact that they did not find in place an infrastructure adequate to their needs and of the failure of the region to offer work opportunities, made the City Tiradentes, like dormitory district and one of temporary residence rather than a permanent destination." Prefeitura de São Paulo, Prefeitura Regional Cidade Tiradentes, histórico. Accessed 27 November 2017, at: www.prefeitura.sp.gov.br/cidade/secretarias/regionais/cidade_tiradentes/hi storico/index.php?p=94; For a review of social and racial tensions in this and similar projects, see Reinaldo José de Oliveira, "Segregação urbana e racial na cidade de São Paulo: as periferias de Brasilândia, Cidade Tiradentes e Jardim Ângela," PhD thesis, PUC-SP, 2008).

[27] Although there were objective economic reasons that could explain the closure of the BNH, which experienced a serious financial crisis, there were political factors that contributed to this decision, without any planning as to the future of the operations which had been carried out by the bank. Azevedo states that "the extinction of the BNH, without any attempt to address its concrete problems, seemed to be a government strategy to garner political support at a time when the Economic Stabilization Plan was failing and when it proposed extremely unpopular corrective economic measures. In this sense, the end of the BNH, an institution seen by much of the public as expensive, with debatable efficiency and identified with the previous regime, would be the government's counterpart to the sacrifices required of the population. It would serve as an example of the willingness to contain public spending." Azevedo, "Vinte e dois anos de política de habitação popular," p. 118. See also José Maria Aragão, *Sistema Financeiro da Habitação* and Fundação Getúio Vargas, *O Crédito imobiliário no Brasil, caracterização e desafios* (São Paulo: FGV, 2007), pp. 529–534; Santos. *Políticas Federais de Habitação no Brasil: 1964/1998*, pp. 10–17.

[28] On the impact of accelerating inflation on indexed liabilities, see João Sayad and Francisco Vidal Luna, "Política anti-inflacionaria y el Plan Cruzado," in *Neoliberalismo y políticas economicas alternativas* (Quito: Corporacion de Estudios para el Desarrolo, 1987), pp. 189–204.

[29] That is: 34% (1974), 30% (1975), and 46% (1976). See Sheila Najberg, "Privatização dos recursos públicos: os empréstimos do sistema BNDES ao setor privado nacional com correção monetária parcial," MA thesis, Pontifícia Universidade Católica do Rio de Janeiro – PUC-Rio, 1989. See also Aragão, *Sistema Financeiro da Habitação*, Chapter 10.

The economic instability which began in the mid-1970s and continued through the mid-1990s, as well as the acceleration of inflation, reduced the population's purchasing power. This significantly increased the system's default rate and affected the very solvency of the financial entities involved in the system, including BNH. The Federal Government granted successive and cumulative subsidies to home owners to meet their mortgage obligations and in 1983 the government even passed on these payment obligations to the *Fundo de Compensações Salariais* – FCVS.[30] The FCVS was a fund originally created to compensate for expected system imbalances, such as housing insurance, to cover the balance due in the event of the death of the debtor, etc. But it became responsible for all imbalances caused by subsidies to the system, including the monetary correction differential. The costs became unsustainable, due to the various heterodox anti-inflation plans.[31] After 1986, with the closing of the BNH, many of its functions were gradually accumulated by the *Caixa Econômica Federal*, which now became the principal source for housing loans. There was undoubtedly a loss of operational quality in this change, since there was a loss of experience accumulated in BNH.[32] Despite the various attempts to develop social housing programs fully paid by the government, the economic turbulence of the 1980s and 1990s hampered the implementation of more consistent measures. Housing construction declined dramatically in this period, exacerbating the living standards of the population in the main metropolitan centers (Graph 6.1).

---

[30] Ministério da Fazenda, Fundo de Compensações Salariais. Accessed 27 November 2017, at: www.tesouro.fazenda.gov.br/documents/10180/380517/PFI_texto+fcvs+na+internet+p%C3%A1gina+tesouro+abr+2016.pdf/dedafcb2-d8f0-4adb-8a2f-c962682a063d. See also Aragão, *Sistema Financeiro da Habitação*, Chapter 20 and FGV, *O Crédito imobiliário no Brasil*, Chapter 2.

[31] Interestingly, the existence of monetary restatement allowed the financial system to operate even at high inflationary levels. The major problems arose when there were sharp declines in inflation, as in the *Plan Cruzado* (1986) and the *Plan Real* (1994). This represented the stabilization plan that effectively contained the inflationary process in Brazil. When implemented, the crisis of the financial system was significant and to avoid a systemic crisis of the system, the government implemented a plan to help the financial system (Proer), which was successful. See Luna and Klein, *Brazil since 1980*, Chapter 3.

[32] Santos affirms that, "In fact, what followed the extinction of the BNH was an immense institutional confusion provoked by constant reformulations in the institutions responsible for the urban question in general and the housing sector in particular … The housing area was placed under various government agencies … such as the Central Bank (which became the regulatory and oversight body of SBPE), *Caixa Econômica Federal* (FGTS manager and SFH financial agent), the urban ministry of the moment (formally responsible for housing policy) and the so-called Special Secretariat for Community Action, which was responsible for managing alternative housing programs." Santos. *Políticas Federais de Habitação no Brasil*, p. 19.

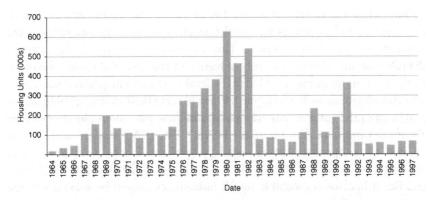

GRAPH 6.1 Number of Housing Units Financed by SBPE and FGTS, 1964–1997
Source: José Maria Aragão, *Sistema Financeiro da Habitação: uma análise jurídica da gênese, desenvolvimento e crise do sistema* (Curitiba: Juruá Editora, 2000), p. 162; Cherkezian and Bofatti (1998): 131.

Finally, with inflation controlled with the *Plan Real*, two new government housing programs were created in 1997. The first was the System of Real Estate Financing (*Sistema de Financiamento Imobiliário*), which provided for the securitization of real estate loans. The new system operates with Real Estate Credit Certificates (CRI), Real Estate Credit Letters (LCI), and Real Estate Credit Notes (CCI). They are instruments of the capital market which operate at market rates. This system was primarily used to create commercial properties.[33] The second was initiated by the new Ministry of Cities in 2005, with the creation of the National Social Interest System (*Sistema Nacional de Interesse Social* – SNHIS) and the National Social Interest Fund. There was also now a new National Plan for Housing (*Plano Nacional de Habitação* – PlanHab), which represented an advance in the identification of housing needs, with officials working with local municipalities to develop public policies on housing, sanitation, and urban transport.[34] While this program was still in its implementation phase, it was emerged into the My House My Life (*Minha Casa Minha Vida* – MCMV) program, undergoing a complete transformation in housing policy.[35]

---

[33] In Brazil there are still legal and institutional issues related to property rights and the ability to execute guarantees. Several legal instruments have been approved to give greater equity guarantees to help develop a mortgage market. See Law 10.931 of 2 August 2004 and FGV, *O Crédito imobiliário no Brasil*, Chapter 2. In 2003, the Ministry of Cities was also created, giving the system greater coordination; and in 2004 a new National Housing Policy was approved.

[34] Law 11.124 of 16 June 2005.   [35] Law 11.977 of 7 July 2009.

The second Lula and the Dilma governments decided to use the MCMV program as a counter-cyclical policy in response to the world economic crisis which began in 2008. It proposed to build 1 million houses, with funds coming from the budget of the Union, FGTS, and the BNDES, the national development bank. The program aimed to serve the various segments of the housing sector and to reduce the estimated deficit of 7.2 million dwellings. The program was intended to meet the needs of the poorest segments by producing 400,000 units for families earning up to three minimum wages, which would be developed with a massive contribution of fiscal resources from the federal government, which proposed to provide 70% of the investment in housing for poor families.[36]

But there were criticisms of the MCMV program for allocating only 40% of its resources to this poorest segment of the market, where 90% of the housing deficit was concentrated.[37] But the biggest problem of the program was the resumption of a model of producing large housing complexes located on the outskirts of large cities, areas without jobs and without provision of basic infrastructure such as transport, or of social institutions such as schools and health clinics. It essentially reproduced the old BNH projects.[38] Despite these criticisms, it is undeniable that public housing construction resumed, reaching all segments of the real estate market, financed by resources from the SBPS, FGTS, and from consumers (Tables 6.5 and 6.6). Between 2009 and 2016, some 4.5 million dwellings were contracted and 3.2 million of them were finished and delivered. Of the units which were built and delivered, around 40% were given to the poorest families (Level 1) with the

---

[36] Caio Santo Amore, "'Minha Casa Minha Vida' para iniciantes," in Caio Santo Amore, Lúcia Zainin Shimbo and Maria Beatriz Cruz Rufino, eds., *Minha Casa ... e a cidade? Avaliação do programa Minha Casa Minha Vida em seis estados brasileiros* (Rio de Janeiro: Letra Capital, 2015), pp. 11–28.

[37] According to Maricato, the Lula administration resumed investments in housing (2005) and sanitation (2003) after twenty-three years of the erratic course of these public policies at the federal level. However, the main challenge of housing policy remains the low-income population, and in order to face it, deeper and more persistent changes are needed. Ermínia Maricato, "O 'Minha Casa' é um avanço, mas segregação urbana fica intocada," *Carta Maior*, 27 May 2009. Accessed 27 November 2017, at: www.cartamaior.com.br/?/Editoria/Politica/O-Minha-Casa-e-um-avanco-mas-segregacao-urbana-fica-intocada/4/15160.

[38] According to Rolnik and Nakano, "The way of producing popular housing beyond the city limits has serious consequences that end up harming everyone. In addition to increasing the extent of urban infrastructures, which need to reach increasingly distant locations, the distance between workplaces, urban facilities and housing areas deepen socio-spatial segregation and increase the costs of urban mobility. The long daily journeys between the residence and the work or educational places congests the roads and collective transports, damaging the quality of collective life." Raquel Rolnik and Kazuo Nakano, "As armadilhas do pacote habitacional," *Le Monde diplomatique, Brasil* (5 March 2009). Accessed 27 November 2017, at: https://diplomatique.org.br/as-armadilhas-do-pacote-habitacional/.

Table 6.5 *Real Estate Financing Granted with Funds from SBPE (Brazilian Savings and Loan System)*

Year	Construction		Purchases		Total	
	Value R$	Units	Value R$	Units	Value R$	Units
1994	1,123,664,153	39,767	611,431,475	21,617	1,735,095,628	61,384
1995	825,710,383	22,128	1,050,673,234	24,466	1,876,383,617	46,594
1996	698,696,098	21,439	763,980,180	16,847	1,462,676,278	38,286
1997	856,501,397	19,556	868,104,951	15,931	1,724,606,348	35,487
1998	1,161,499,530	22,234	984,109,638	18,081	2,145,609,168	40,315
1999	757,675,347	17,110	915,651,660	18,390	1,673,327,007	35,500
2000	1,047,597,302	19,899	887,901,293	17,853	1,935,498,595	37,752
2001	665,818,386	15,498	1,216,170,368	20,636	1,881,988,754	36,134
2002	594,682,885	10,317	1,174,703,843	18,615	1,769,386,728	28,932
2003	965,283,031	16,797	1,252,388,376	19,683	2,217,671,407	36,480
2004	1,394,392,606	24,961	1,607,863,590	28,866	3,002,256,196	53,827
2005	2,855,228,721	34,762	1,996,854,935	26,461	4,852,083,656	61,223
2006	4,483,511,118	45,433	4,856,775,892	68,440	9,340,287,010	113,873
2007	9,400,686,375	89,011	9,008,997,801	107,122	18,409,684,176	196,133
2008	16,220,846,923	162,299	13,811,491,211	137,386	30,032,338,134	299,685
2009	13,853,857,571	138,721	20,163,406,837	163,970	34,017,264,408	302,691
2010	24,412,172,265	201,758	31,785,406,148	219,627	56,197,578,413	421,385

(continued)

196

2011	35,193,181,820	226,733	44,723,573,547	265,756	79,916,755,367	492,489
2012	28,086,332,539	168,170	54,690,647,923	285,154	82,776,980,462	453,324
2013	35,157,456,147	183,763	83,755,599,365	398,215	118,913,055,512	581,978
2014	32,787,469,412	169,912	84,238,616,133	387,008	117,026,085,545	556,920
2015	21,430,599,031	109,063	56,943,199,771	246,801	78,373,798,802	355,864
2016	11,133,373,732	53,346	38,649,155,029	161,613	49,782,528,761	214,959
2017	4,462,186,735	17,299	16,520,836,997	67,184	20,983,023,732	84,483

Source: CBCI, Table_04-A.96_28. www.cbicdados.com.br/menu/financiamento-habitacional/sbpe,
Arquivo: Valores (em R$) e Unidades Financiados: Construção e Aquisição de- Total Brasil.

Table 6.6 *Housing and Sanitation Projects Undertaken with Funds from FGTS, 2000–2016*

| | Housing | | Value (R$) | | | |
Year	Units	Value (R$)	Sanitation	Urban Infrustructure	Others	Total Value (R$)
2000	316,398	3,872,463,808	16,656,400	144,228	–	3,889,264,435
2001	264,021	3,072,801,097	–	35,214	–	3,072,836,310
2002	253,190	3,730,846,454	220,240,504	–	–	3,951,086,959
2003	246,107	3,818,289,389	1,499,952,646	–	–	5,318,242,035
2004	267,362	3,879,398,166	1,735,194,597	–	–	5,614,592,764
2005	337,846	5,532,466,903	17,067,990	–	–	5,549,534,893
2006	407,901	6,982,900,389	1,396,107,423	57,055,924	–	8,436,063,736
2007	333,237	6,899,141,256	3,247,489,568	717,120	–	10,147,347,944
2008	285,446	10,559,372,788	3,740,513,594	–	–	14,299,886,381
2009	396,367	15,836,350,930	1,668,770,083	–	–	17,505,121,013
2010	665,885	27,688,850,670	3,959,037,114	4,877,542,575	–	36,525,430,359
2011	549,661	34,224,193,737	1,049,341,646	2,101,373,929	–	37,374,909,312
2012	515,342	35,990,547,687	3,098,094,435	2,234,698,158	2,427,284,996	43,750,625,276
2013	491,861	40,133,317,658	5,813,684,881	5,577,145,445	2,401,093,888	53,925,241,873
2014	486,229	43,960,920,802	7,228,688,819	9,707,934,014	1,707,219,778	62,604,763,413
2015	632,729	54,249,675,631	2,421,567,038	1,141,309,672	600,000,000	58,412,552,342
2016	617,851	52,239,972,637	356,898,555	1,811,275,597	16,688,362,052	71,096,508,841

Source: CBIC, Table.04_B.01_04. www.cbicdados.com.br/menu/financiamento-habitacional/fgts.

government providing 90% of the cost of the housing (Table 6.7).[39] The greatest intensity of housing construction and completion occurred during the first years of the MCMV program, similar to what occurred with the BNH housing program in the 1970s.[40]

But in 2013 the home construction industry entered into crisis, due both to sector problems and to a recession of the national economy. Between the third quarter of 2013 and the third quarter of 2017, GDP declined by 6% and the GDP of the construction industry fell by 23%, which badly affected the housing sector.[41] The number of units financed decreased from 581,000 to 214,000. There was a decrease in both house and apartment construction and a significant drop in the average real estate price. In turn, the social housing market, meaning that directed toward the poorest population, suffered the most severe retrenchment due to the crisis in government finance on which it depended so heavily. It will only be possible to resume significant construction in this sector of the market when the public finances of the various levels of government recover to pre-recession levels.

Despite all these home construction programs in the past fifty or so years, there is still a massive lack of adequate housing in Brazil. The João Pinheiro Foundation of Minas Gerais has developed a methodology for estimating the

[39] According to the analysis of the Budget Consultancy of the National Congress, with the rules defined in the MCID Ordinance 267/2017 and the Interministerial Administrative Rule 99/2016, the PMCMV beneficiary can purchase property and receive a budget subsidy of up to 90% of the value of the property purchased. In addition, in more specific situations, such as those relating to resettlement, emergency, or disaster, the financial participation of the beneficiaries in the form of monthly installments is exempted, in which case the grant may correspond to 100% of the value of the property. *Avaliação de Políticas Públicas, Programa Minha Casa Minha Vida*, Brasília, Congresso Nacional, Consultoria de Orçamentos, Fiscalização e Controle, October 2007. Accessed 7 December 2007, at: www2.camara.leg .br/orcamento-da-uniao/estudos/2017/InformativoAvaliacaoPoliticasPublicasPMCMV_ WEB.pdf.

[40] There is a lot of literature on the Minha Casa Minha Vida program, which represented the most visible program of the Lula and Dilma governments. See Amore, Shimbo, and Rufino, eds., *Minha Casa ... e a cidade?*; Renato Balbim, Cleandro Krause, and Vicente Correia Lima Neto, *Para além do Minha Casa Minha Vida: uma política de Habitação de Interesse Social?* (Brasília: Ipea, 2015); Adauto Lucio Cardoso, ed., *Programa Minha Casa Minha Vida e seus Efeitos Territoriais* (Rio de Janeiro: Letra Capital, 2013); Viviane Fernanda de Oliveira, "Do BNH ao Minha Casa Minha Vida: mudanças e permanências na política habitacional," *Caminhos de Geografia* 15.50 (2014), pp. 36–53. Accessed 7 December 2017 at: www.seer .ufu.br/index.php/caminhosdegeografia/article/view/22937; Marlon Lima da Silva and Helena Lúcia Zagury Tourinho, "O Banco Nacional de Habitação e o Programa Minha Casa Minha Vida, duas políticas habitacionais e uma mesma lógica locacional," *Cadernos Metrópolis* 17.34 (2015), pp. 401–417.

[41] On the housing construction sector, see Bradesco, *Mercado Imobiliário* (São Paulo: DEPEC, 2017). Accessed 7 December 2017, at: www.economiaemdia.com.br/EconomiaEmDia/pdf/ infset_imobiliario.pdf.

Table 6.7 *Program* Minha Casa Minha Vida, *Units Contracted and Units Delivered as of December 2016*

Year	Units Contracted				Units Delivered			
	Level 1*	Level 2	Level 3	Total	Level 1	Level 2	Level 3	Total
2009	143,894	98,593	43,818	286,305	67	66,367	10,499	76,933
2010	338,847	277,174	102,805	718,826	9,340	233,736	35,551	278,627
2011	104,310	296,707	77,935	478,952	113,060	177,108	16,856	307,024
2012	384,821	307,018	97,711	789,550	174,572	200,530	24,939	400,041
2013	537,185	281,744	93,961	912,890	162,920	272,021	46,703	481,644
2014	200,289	331,002	37,447	568,738	217,076	314,712	45,692	577,480
2015	16,890	349,486	40,557	406,933	202,330	163,880	24,579	390,789
2016	35,008	277,193	68,204	380,405	258,182	392,573	85,079	735,834
Total	1,761,244	2,218,917	562,438	4,542,599	1,137,547	1,820,927	290,198	3,248,672

Source: Avaliação de Políticas Públicas, Programa Minha Casa Minha Vida. Brasília, Congresso Nacional, Consultoria de Orçamentos, Fiscalização e Controle, October 2007.

* Levels indicate income and go from the poorest class (level 1) to the richest (level 3).

housing deficit, which is considered the most reliable index.[42] It estimates that the deficit figure reached 7.2 million units in 2000, and stood at 6.1 million in 2015, of which 5.3 million correspond to housing in urban areas. The areas with the highest concentration of housing need are the Southeast and Northeast, which together need a total of 3.7 million houses in the urban area, and account for about 70% of the existing shortage (See Table 6.8). Looked at regionally, the absolute prevalence of the class of band of up to 3 minimum wages (more than 80%) is evident, being the predominant segment throughout Brazil, with little regional variation (Table 6.9).[43]

The failure to fulfill housing needs has led to illegal occupations of undeveloped urban areas or empty buildings in the central areas of cities and has created a major alternative housing arrangement. Broadly, these settlements are known as favelas and have been both spontaneously developed and established with the help of outside organizations. Urban social movements were organized during the period of the military dictatorship around the struggles for housing, land regularization, health, and sanitation, with the then progressive Catholic Church playing a major role in this process. In the period of redemocratization, housing movements were allied with other organizations (unions, universities, non-governmental organizations), constituting a network of urban reform grouped in the National Forum of Urban Reform (*Fórum Nacional da Reforma Urbana* – FNRU). Their program emphasizes universal access to urban services through urban redistributive policies.[44]

---

[42] The studies of the Fundação João Pinheiro of the government of the State of Minas Gerais can be accessed at: www.fjp.mg.gov.br/index.php/produtos-e-servicos1/2742-deficit-habitacional-no-brasil-3.

[43] At the same time that there exists this housing deficit, there exists significant unused real estate throughout the country. The 2010 census lists a total of 56.7 registered households. Of these, 7.3 million were vacant, and another 2.6 million having occasional use and 4.7 million classified as a "private, unoccupied, vacant" domicile. The major Brazilian cities today present a problem of underutilization of old real estate, particularly in the central areas with their greater urban infrastructure. Despite official efforts, little has been recovered for reuse as housing.

[44] There is an enormous literature on the establishment and organization of the favelas and life within these centers, mostly for those in Rio de Janeiro. See the classic studies of Janice E. Perlman, *The Myth of Marginality: Urban Poverty and Politics in Rio de Janeiro* (Berkeley: University of California Press, 1979) and *Favela: Four Decades of Living on the Edge in Rio de Janeiro* (New York: Oxford University Press, 2010). On the early evolution of the Rio favelas, see Brodwyn Fischer, *A Poverty of Rights: Citizenship and Inequality in Twentieth-Century Rio De Janeiro* (Stanford, Calif.: Stanford University Press, 2008). Recent studies on these Rio favelas include Bryan McCann, *Hard Times in the Marvelous City: From Dictatorship to Democracy in the Favelas of Rio de Janeiro* (Durham, NC: Duke University Press, 2013); Robert Gay, *Popular Organization and Democracy in Rio De Janeiro: A Tale of Two Favelas* (Philadelphia: Temple University Press, 2010). More specific studies include Enríque Desmond Arias, "Faith in Our Neighbors: Networks and Social Order in Three Brazilian Favelas," *Latin American Politics and Society* 46.1 (2004), pp. 1–38. On the role of crime in the favelas and how this relates to the wider society, see Enrique Desmond Arias, *Drugs and Democracy in Rio De Janeiro: Trafficking, Social Networks, and Public Security* (Chapel Hill: University of North Carolina Press, 2009).

Table 6.8 *Estimated Housing Deficit in Brazil by Region, 2007–2015*

Region/Year	Urban	Rural	Total	Precarious	Cohabitated	Costs	Density
Housing Deficit by Regions in 2015							
North	488,729	138,647	627,376	156,875	253,814	179,586	37,101
Northeast	1,401,625	522,708	1,924,333	492,789	619,768	754,200	57,576
Southeast	2,383,963	46,373	2,430,336	109,292	599,895	1,540,013	181,136
South	649,051	48,585	697,636	117,610	157,854	410,451	11,721
Center-West	491,432	15,390	506,822	48,246	126,485	304,809	27,282
Brazil	5,414,800	771,703	6,186,503	924,812	1,757,816	3,189,059	314,816
Housing Deficit in Brazil 2000–2015							
2000	5,469,851	1,752,794	7,222,645				
2007	5,003,418	985,646	5,989,064	1,240,922	2,450,029	1,950,087	348,026
2008	4,629,832	916,478	5,546,310	1,138,890	2,182,002	1,888,203	337,215
2009	5,089,160	909,750	5,998,909	1,064,457	2,480,465	2,088,458	365,529
2010	5,885,528	1,055,163	6,940,691	1,343,435	2,991,313	2,124,404	481,539
2011	4,689,405	892,563	5,581,968	1,187,903	1,916,716	2,091,392	385,957
2012	4,664,113	766,449	5,430,562	883,777	1,865,457	2,310,642	370,686
2013	5,010,839	835,201	5,846,040	977,264	1,905,085	2,553,436	390,255
2014	5,315,251	752,810	6,068,061	863,030	1,911,598	2,926,543	366,890
2015	5,414,800	771,703	6,186,503	924,812	1,757,816	3,189,059	314,816

Source: Fundação João Pinheiros, Governo de Minas Gerais, Belo Horizonte, annual for various years.
The data for 2015 are preliminary. The methodology of the identification of the deficit was different from the current one. Density is the excessive crowding of residents in rented dwellings.

Table 6.9 *Percentage of Housing Deficit by Level of Income by Region in 2014* As Defined by Multiples of Minimum Wage

Region	Up to 3	More than 3 and Less than 5	More than 5 and Less than 10	More than 10	Total
North	79.5%	11.8%	6.5%	2.2%	100%
Northeast	88.2%	7.0%	3.5%	1.2%	100%
Southeast	83.7%	10.0%	5.2%	1.0%	100%
South	78.2%	13.1%	6.4%	2.3%	100%
Center-West	83.9%	8.8%	5.0%	2.4%	100%
Brazil	84.4%	9.5%	4.7%	1.4%	100%

Source: Fundação João Pinheiro, *Déficit Habitacional no Brasil* (2016), p. 31.

The election of Lula generated a great expectation for advancing these struggles. In fact, in 2003, a process of public conferences began at the three levels of government (municipal, state, and federal) to discuss the different policies. The reforms promoted popular self-management in urban policies, which the government finally accepted for its social interest housing (HIS) program.[45] Some of these demands have been addressed over the last twenty years, particularly with the approval of the Statute of Cities (Law 10,257, dated 10 July 2001), of the National Social Interest Housing Fund (Law 11,124 of 10 June 2005), and the National Housing Plan (PLANHAB) of 2009.

There has also been a profound change in policies dealing with the growth of substandard housing, particularly the urban favelas that spread through most of Brazil's metropolitan areas. In the past, the tendency was to adopt favela eradication programs, displacing their inhabitants and relocating them to the peripheral regions of the cities and building new housing agglomerations without infrastructure and distant from the places that generate employment and income, and where the best public transport, education and health services are concentrated. But in the last twenty years local governments have decided to regularize and incorporate the favelas into city life through intensified programs of urbanization of favelas and

---

[45] In the 1980s, the two main housing movements were organized nationally: The National Union for Popular Housing (UNMP) and the National Movement for Housing (MNLM). Regina Fátima Cordeiro Fonseca Ferreira, "Movimentos de moradia, autogestão e política habitacional no Brasil: do acesso à moradia ao direito à cidade," Paper presented at the 2nd Sociology Forum, "Social Justice and Democratization," Buenos Aires, 1–4 August 2012. Accessed 12 December 2017, at: www.observatoriodasmetropoles.net/download/artigo_re ginaferreira_isa.pdf (pp. 2–3).

regularization of land titles. Since 1967, there has been the so-called Real Use Law, which permits the use of public and private land for specific purposes of urbanization, industrialization, cultivation, or other use with a social interest.[46] The Law of 2007 also included the possibility of the right to regularize land tenure for social interest.[47] The legal framework for all these developments was the Statute of Cities, which defined general principles and instruments of urban management,[48] later clarified in the land regularization section of Law 11,977/2009, which created the *Minha Casa Minha Vida* program, establishing that land regularization included a set of legal, urban, environmental, and social measures aimed at normalizing irregular settlements and giving land titles to its occupants, in order to guarantee their social right to housing, the full development of the social functions of urban property, and the right to an ecologically balanced environment.[49]

It is important to emphasize that this legalization of favela land and housing keeps the tenants in the same place where they have settled, in opposition to the earlier resettlement process which was based on eradication and displacement of the population to areas without infrastructure, transportation, and, more important, without employment.[50] Many favelas, however, are relatively well located in relation to these services and centers of employment. This was one of the important reasons for the strong opposition to the old eradication and resettlement program by the residents and popular movements. The favela regularization processes that were already taking place intensified with this new urban legislation. In the case of the State of São Paulo, for example, a "Legal City" program was created in 2007 which sought to provide technical support to municipalities for the regularization of land parceling and the construction of public or private housing estates for residential purposes, to be located in urban or urban expansion area. By 2017, the program had issued 1,469 certificates of land

---

[46] Decree Law 217 of 28 February 1967.   [47] Law 11.481 of 31 May 2007.

[48] Law 10.257 of July 2001.

[49] Article 46 of Law 11.977, 7 July 2009. For studies of this reform, see, for example, Paulo Bastos, "Urbanização de favelas," *Estudos avançados* 17.47 (2003), pp. 212–221; Adauto Lúcio Cardoso, "Avanços e desafios na experiência brasileira de urbanização de favelas," *Cadernos Metrópole* 17 (2007), pp. 219–240.

[50] Vitor da Cunha Miranda, "A concessão de direito real de uso (CDRU) e a concessão de uso especial para fins de moradia (CUEM) como instrumentos de regularização fundiárias públicas no Brasil." Accessed 28 May 2018, at: https://jus.com.br/artigos/48642/a-conces sao-de-direito-real-de-uso-cdru-e-a-concessao-de-uso-especial-para-fins-de-moradia-cuem-c omo-instrumentos-de-regularizacao-fundiaria-em-areas-publicas-no-brasil. Also on this theme, see IBAM, "Estudo de avaliação da experiência brasileira sobre urbanização de favelas e regularização fundiária," Rio de Janeiro, 2002, and Patrícia Cezario Silva Spinazzola, "Impactos da regularização fundiária no espaço urbano," MA thesis, Faculdade de Arquitetura e Urbanismo da USP, São Paulo, 2008.

regularization that benefited 2.5 million families living in irregular housing.[51] This type of program was repeated in many states.

Another major change in the urban landscape has been the significant increase in apartment construction. Since the implementation of the BNH, there has been a process of housing verticalization in urban centers, which particularly served the middle and upper classes. Despite this major change, the house is still dominant in Brazil, representing 88% of the dwellings and housing 90% of the residents. Even where apartment construction is highest, houses still predominate. In the city of São Paulo, for example, houses represent two-thirds of households; in the ten largest Brazilian cities, the average is similar: 69%.[52] This means that the large Brazilian cities are sparsely populated and their inhabitants spread over large areas.[53] This creates the paradox of unused infrastructure usually in the central older urban areas, and a dramatic lack of infrastructure in the outlying regions of cities. In several cities, such as the city of São Paulo, there are efforts and incentives to promote greater concentration of the population in the areas with infrastructure. This has been a feature of the city's latest master plan, which guides urbanization policy and infrastructure investments.[54]

Nevertheless, such careful planning is still not the norm in many cities. The disorganized occupation of the cities and the persistent housing deficit identified by the João Pinheiro Foundation have resulted in the proliferation of substandard clusters in most large and medium-sized cities in Brazil. In Brazil, 11.4 million people live in 3.2 million such substandard homes, corresponding to 7% of the urban population. The Southeast, with 5.6 million people and 1.6 million households, represents the numerically larger area, followed by the Northeast, with 3.2 million people and 926,000 households. But, proportionally, the North has the worst indicators, since about 15% of the households and the residents are in substandard households. Even the large cities have a significant portion of their population residing in substandard clusters. In São Paulo, there are 1.3 million people (11% of the population) living in such housing; in Rio de Janeiro there are 1.4 million (22% of the population); in Salvador there are 882,000 people (or 33% of the population). The most dramatic situation among the state capital cities is Belém, which has 758,000 people living in these units, representing 54% of the population (Graph 6.2).[55]

[51] Secretaria da Habitação do Estado de São Paulo. Accessed 28 May 2018, at: www.habitacao .sp.gov.br/noticias/viewer.aspx?Id=8270.
[52] IBGE, Sidra, Table 3152.   [53] IBGE, Sidra, Table 1952.
[54] In the 2010 census, of the four largest cities, São Paulo was the densest with 7,298.3 inhabitants/km², followed by Belo Horizonte (7,167.0 inhabitants/km²), Rio de Janeiro (5,265.3 inhabitants/km²), and Salvador (3,858.4 inhabitants/km²).
[55] IBGE, Sidra, Table 3770 and Eduardo Cesar Leão Marques, ed., *Assentamentos precários no Brasil urbano* (Brasília/São Paulo: Ministério das Cidades/CEM, 2007); Caio Santo Amore,

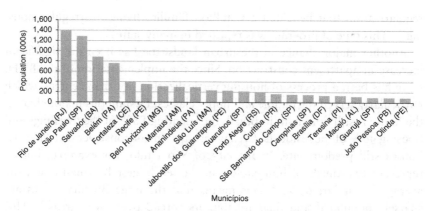

GRAPH 6.2 Municípios with Largest Population in Subnormal Clusters (Census 2010)
Source: IBGE, Censo 2010, Subnormais.

In examining where the substandard housing is located within the metropolitan areas, it is evident that they are not confined to the peripheral districts. In most cases, both in the central cities and the suburbs, there exist zones which often are quite precarious in terms of housing, with large irregular subdivisions, illegal occupations, or even old housing estates, built without the necessary basic infrastructure. The national census of 2010 provides the data to examine the distribution of substandard housing tracts within these metropolitan districts.[56] The largest metropolitan region is that of São Paulo followed by Rio de Janeiro. In general, these substandard houses are found in both the central city and in the peripheral municipalities. For example, in the

"Entre o nó e o fato consumado, o lugar dos pobres na cidade: um estudo sobre as ZEIS e os impasses da reforma urbana na atualidade," PhD thesis, FAU-PSP – Faculdade de Arquitetura e Urbanismo da Universidade de São Paulo, 2013; Rosana Denaldi, "Políticas de urbanização de favelas: evolução e impasses," PhD thesis, Faculdade de Arquitetura e Urbanismo – USP, 2003; Suzana Pasternak, "Favelas no Brasil e em São Paulo: avanços nas análises a partir da Leitura Territorial do Censo de 2010," *Cadernos Metropolítanos* 18.35 (2016), pp. 75–99; Nadalin, Krause, and Neto, "Distribuição de aglomerados subnormais na rede urbana"; Izabel Cristina Reis Mendes, "O uso contemporâneo da favela na cidade do Rio de Janeiro," PhD thesis, Faculdade de Arquitetura e Urbanismo da USP, São Paulo, 2014; Mayara Silva de Noronha, "Multiplicidades da Favela," PhD thesis, FGV/SP, São Paulo, 2017; Gary A. Dymski, "Ten Ways to See a Favela: Notes on the Political Economy of the New City," *Revista Econômica* 13.1 (2011), pp. 7–36; Marcos Roberto Cotrim Brito and Alexandre Nicolas Rennó, *"A favela da Geografia: análise e uso do termo favela,"* *Observatorio Geográfico*. Accessed 8 December 2017, at: http://observatoriogeograficoamer icalatina.org.mx/egal12/Teoriaymetodo/Conceptuales/16.pdf.

[56] IBGE, *Censo demográfico 2010, Aglomerados Subnormais. Informações Territoriais* (Rio de Janeiro: IBGE, 2010); see also IBGE, *Censo demográfico 2010*, Primeiros Resultados (2011). Accessed 12 August 2017, at: https://ww2.ibge.gov.br/home/presidencia/noticias/imprensa/ppts/00000015164811202013480105748802.pdf.

metropolitan region of São Paulo, although it is comprised of 39 municipalities, two-thirds of the homes in substandard settlements are located inside the central city of São Paulo. In the metropolitan region of Rio de Janeiro, this situation is repeated, since 82% of the households belonging to substandard housing clusters are located within the city of Rio de Janeiro.[57] Within these two major two cities, the total of such substandard housing contains around 10% of the city population. But in many of the Northeastern metropolitan regions the ratio is in the 20% range, with Belém being the outlier, with over half of the residents living in substandard housing.[58]

These substandard homes are also defined by the census bureau by the type of materials used in the external walls. In the metropolitan regions about 15% of households have inadequate characteristics, such as uncoated masonry and walls constructed of wood. In the case of Curitiba and Porto Alegre, the use of wood is relatively common, even in houses in good habitable condition; but not in other metropolitan areas, where this type of material is usually found in the worst housing of these clusters of substandard housing. In later evolution, these wooden houses are changed to uncoated masonry, characteristic of the great favelas of São Paulo and Rio de Janeiro.[59]

The availability of public services represents another way of assessing the conditions of people living in urban areas. One of the key services is the supply of drinking water and this is almost universal. In 2010, some 91% of the urban population received potable water through a general distribution network and only 6% still depended on wells or springs on their property. Although the water distribution network was extensive in all regions, it is worth noting the lesser coverage of such networks in the North, where only 66% of the households received such a service. The supply of electricity is almost universal for urban housing.

But the same cannot be said about the availability of sewage treatment. In the 2010 census, only 54% of the urban population was served by a general fluvial sewage network, with 16% of the population served by septic tanks and 21% by rudimentary cesspits. It is noteworthy that 3% of the population, or more than 5 million people, did not have any type of sewage treatment process. As expected, there are significant regional differences. While in the Southeast, 86% of the households in the urban area were served by general networks of sewage collection, this percentage fell to only 18% in the North and 45% in the

[57] IBGE, *Censo demográfico 2010*, pp. 55–69.
[58] IBGE, *Censo demográfico 2010*, Primeiros Resultados (2011). Accessed at: https://ww2.ibge .gov.br/home/presidencia/noticias/imprensa/ppts/00000015164811202013480105748802 .pdf.
[59] IBGE, Sidra, Table 1617.

Northeast. Even in the South region, an area with social and economic conditions higher than the Brazilian average, only 53% of the households were served by the general network, 25% by septic tank, and 19% by cesspits.

But even these numbers do not tell the complete story of sanitation. While the collection of waste is generalized, its treatment is limited. According to data from 2015, a total of 99 million people had access to sanitary sewage systems, through 29 million connections that served 32.8 million residences. Of the volume of 5.2 million cubic meters which this system used, only 3.8 million cubic meters, or 73%, were treated. This is a serious problem of public health and increases contamination of the environment.[60]

Another relevant issue in the identification of the quality of life in the city concerns the destination of garbage. In general, there is a wide range of garbage collection in all regions of Brazil. As with sanitation, the issue is not just the scope of the collection but the fate of the garbage collected. According to the Ministry of the Environment, the collection and transport of solid waste has been the primary focus of solid waste management, especially in urban areas. In 2009, the coverage rate reached almost 90% of total households, and is approaching the totality of urban households. The question still not resolved is the destination of the garbage. In 2008, of 5,565 municipalities, only 1,540 operated a landfill, which was considered the most environmentally sound system. Another 1,074 operated landfills with less environmental security. But there were 2,810 municipalities that operated with "open pits," the so-called "dumps," and they accounted for half the garbage collected in Brazil (see Table 6.10).[61]

This is a serious public health problem involving contamination of the environment. The National Policy on Solid Waste Management was

---

[60] On sanitation, see Ministério das Cidades, Sistema Nacional de Informações sobre Saneamento (SNIS), "Diagnóstico dos serviços de água e esgotos" (2015). Accessed 8 December 2017, at: www.snis.gov.br/diagnostico-agua-e-esgotos/diagnostico-ae-2015; Valdemar F. de Araujo Filho, Maria da Piedade Morais, and Paulo Augusto Rego, "Diagnóstico e desempenho recente da política nacional de saneamento básico," *Brasil em desenvolvimento: Estado, planejamento e políticas públicas*, 3 vols (Brasília: Ipea, 2009), vol. 2, pp. 431–449; Felipe von Atzingen Dantas et al., "Uma análise da situação do saneamento no Brasil," *FACEF Pesquisa, Desenvolvimento e Gestão* 15.3 (2012), pp. 272–284; Victor Toyoji de Nozaki, "Análise do setor de saneamento Básico no Brasil," MA thesis, Faculdade de Economia, Administração e Contabilidade de Ribeirão Preto da Universidade de São Paulo – FEA-USP, Ribeirão Preto, 2007; Aluizio Tadeu Furtado Vidal, "As perspectivas do Saneamento Básico no Brasil," MA thesis, Fundação João Pinheiro, Belo Horizonte, 2002.

[61] Bruno Milanez and Luciana Miyolo Massukado, *Caderno de diagnóstico: resíduos sólidos urbanos* (Brasília: Ipea, 2011). On its impact on health, see Kevan Guillherme Nóbrega Barbosa and Ayla Cristina Nóbrega Barbosa, *"O impacto do lixo na saúde e a problemática da destinação final e coleta seletiva dos resíduos sólidos."* Accessed 8 December 2017, at: www.e-publicacoes.uerj.br/index.php/polemica/article/view/11669/9146

Table 6.10 *Water, Sewage, and Electricity Services and Disposal of Waste in Urban Areas and Subnormal Housing Clusters,*
Census 2010
A: Brazil – Dwellings in Urban Areas

	Residents	Dwellings in All Urban Areas					
	Brazil	Brazil	North	Northeast	Southeast	South	Center-West
Type of water supply							
Total	160,246,510	49,226,751	3,012,377	11,199,960	23,539,756	7,615,138	3,859,520
General distribution network	91%	92%	66%	90%	95%	95%	90%
Well or spring on property	6%	6%	27%	4%	3%	4%	9%
Well or spring not on property	2%	2%	6%	3%	1%	1%	1%
Others	1%	1%	1%	2%	1%	0%	0%
General sewage or rainwater network							
Total	137,015,685	49,226,751	3,012,377	11,199,960	23,539,756	7,615,138	3,859,520
General sewage or rainwater network	54%	64%	18%	45%	86%	53%	43%
Septic tank	16%	11%	22%	12%	5%	25%	13%
Rudimentary cesspit	21%	20%	48%	36%	5%	19%	43%
Ditch	2%	2%	4%	2%	2%	2%	0%
River, lake, or sea	2%	2%	3%	2%	3%	1%	0%
Other type	1%	1%	3%	1%	0%	0%	0%
Do not have	3%	1%	2%	2%	0%	0%	0%
Disposal of waste							
Total	160,246,510	49,226,751	3,012,377	11,199,960	23,539,756	7,615,138	3,859,520
Collected	97%	97%	94%	94%	99%	99%	98%
Collected by cleaning service	90%	90%	84%	80%	93%	95%	92%
Collected on cleaning service bucket	7%	7%	10%	13%	5%	4%	6%
Other	3%	3%	6%	6%	1%	1%	2%

(continued)

Table 6.10 *(continued)*

	Residents	Dwellings in All Urban Areas					
	Brazil	Brazil	North	Northeast	Southeast	South	Center-West
Existence of electric energy							
Total	160,246,510	49,226,751	3,012,377	11,199,960	23,539,756	7,615,138	3,859,520
They have	100%	100%	99%	99%	100%	100%	100%
They have a distribution company	99%	99%	98%	99%	99%	100%	99%
They have other source	1%	1%	1%	1%	1%	0%	0%
They do not have	0%	0%	1%	1%	0%	0%	0%

B: Dwellings in Subnormal Housing Clusters

	Residents	Dwellings in All Urban Areas					
	Brazil	Brazil	North	Northeast	Southeast	South	Center-West
Type of water supply							
Total	11,425,644	3,220,713	462,834	925,115	1,605,757	169,948	57,059
General distribution network	88%	88%	60%	90%	95%	97%	94%
Well or spring on property	6%	6%	28%	3%	2%	2%	2%
Well or spring not on property	4%	4%	10%	5%	2%	0%	2%
Others	2%	2%	2%	2%	2%	1%	1%
General sewage or rainwater network							
Total	11,425,644	3,220,713	462,834	925,115	1,605,757	169,948	57,059
General sewage or rainwater network	56%	56%	18%	49%	72%	63%	20%
Septic tank	11%	11%	27%	14%	4%	13%	23%
Rudimentary cesspit	16%	16%	38%	24%	4%	7%	54%

(continued)

Ditch	6%	6%	6%	5%	7%	10%	2%
River, lake, or sea	8%	8%	6%	5%	11%	4%	1%
Other type	2%	2%	2%	1%	2%	1%	0%
Do not have	0%	0%	0%	0%	0%	0%	0%
disposal of waste							
Total	11,425,644	3,220,713	462,834	925,115	1,605,757	169,948	57,059
Collected	95%	95%	94%	92%	97%	99%	89%
Collected by cleaning service	76%	76%	85%	73%	74%	93%	67%
Collected on cleaning service bucket	19%	19%	9%	20%	23%	6%	22%
Other	5%	5%	6%	8%	3%	1%	11%
Existence of electric energy							
Total	11,425,644	3,220,713	462,834	925,115	1,605,757	169,948	57,059
They have	100%	100%	99%	100%	100%	100%	100%
They have a distribution company	96%	96%	97%	98%	95%	97%	90%
They have from other source	4%	4%	3%	2%	5%	3%	10%
They do not have	0%	0%	1%	0%	0%	0%	0%

Source: IBGE, Censo 2010, Sidra, Tables 3370, 3217, and 3382.
Note: In the absence of information on residents we used a population estimator for households.

approved in 2010, which proposed great advances in the management and destination of solid waste, including the end of all the municipal dumps by 2014. But, four years after the approval of the law, there has been little progress due to the lack of funding in the municipalities.[62] These sites also represent a serious public health problem, due to the persistence of families who live from collecting recyclable products in organic and inorganic waste in these untreated dumps. In Brasília, 15 km from the Planalto Palace, the seat of the federal government, there is the largest landfill in Latin America, where 2,000 families make their living.[63] Although this is considered an extreme case, illegal garbage dumps continue to exist throughout Brazil, causing environmental contamination problems and placing at risk the poor population that depends on these waste dumps for their livelihood.[64]

The precarious conditions of life in urban areas was shown in the PNAD national household survey of 2016. It found that 34% of Brazilians live in houses without any form of sewage and 30% of those which had access still used a cesspit without connection to the appropriate sewer system. The data are even more alarming when examined regionally. In the South, 89% of families have treated sewage; whereas in the North, only 19% have such access. Moreover, 3.5 million families receive treated water from their taps at most three times a week, and hundreds of thousands spend weeks without receiving a drop of water.[65] Thus, even when the aggregated data look good, this does not present a complete picture. In the case of the water supply, the survey found that persons are sometimes connected to a water supply network but there is no water in the network.

---

[62] Law 12.305 of 2 August 2010. According to the Ministry of Environment, the deadline established in law foreseeing the end of the dumps in the fourth year of PNRS is definitive. But the Ministry is open to discussion on how to improve the law. It also recognizes the difficulty of small, often remote, municipalities, which, in addition to requiring specific treatment of waste, are not always in a position to implement the necessary actions or get federal government funding. Accessed at: www.mma.gov.br/informma/item/10272-pol%C3%ADt ica-de-res%C3%ADduos-s%C3%B3lidos-apresenta-resultados-em-4-anos.

[63] BBC Brasil, 12 March 2016. Accessed 9 December 2017, at: www.bbc.com/portuguese/not icias/2016/03/160310_galeria_lixao_estrutural_pf.

[64] Another large dump located in Duque de Caxias in Rio de Janeiro, and then considered the largest in Brazil, was closed in 2012, but as late as the end of 2017 there was still no recovery program. Along with the closure of the activities of the largest dump in Latin America came a series of promises of recovery of the mangrove area, revitalization of the neighborhood, and professional qualifications for thousands of waste pickers, which were promised for the Olympics and were never carried out. *O Dia* 9 December 2017. Accessed at: http://odia.ig .com.br/rio-de-janeiro/2016-09-11/fechamento-do-aterro-de-jardim-gramacho-deixou-frus tracao-a-milhares-de-pessoas.html.

[65] Alexandre Baldy, "Pela modernização das cidades," *Folha de São Paulo* (5 December 2017), Tendências/Debates, p. A3.

Another major problem facing all urban areas is the steady increase in crime and violence. Brazil has experienced increasing penetration of drug trafficking which greatly affects the urban poor and leads to high and increasing levels of crime, particularly in the Northeast regions. Moreover, the long delays common to the Brazilian judicial system creates both a sense of insecurity for the population as a whole and a sense of impunity for the criminal class. At the same time, the penitentiary system itself is broken. According to the National Penitentiary Department of the Ministry of Justice, the prison situation is in a serious condition, with overcrowding, violence, and control by criminal gangs, and notes the government's relative inability to solve the problems. Brazil today has a prison population of 607,000 people with space for only 377,000 prisoners, representing an occupation rate of 161%. The imprisonment rate is 300 prisoners for every 100,000 inhabitants. Moreover 41% of the prisoners are incarcerated prior to their conviction. These figures put Brazil in a very poor situation compared to other countries in the world. Brazil has the world's fourth largest prison population, although far behind the United States and China, but with numbers similar to Russia. Among the twenty countries in the world with the largest prison population, Brazil is surpassed only by the United States, Russia, and Thailand in terms of the prisoners to total population rate and sixth in terms of the rate of prisoners held without formal conviction, being surpassed by India, the Philippines, Pakistan, Peru, and Morocco. In addition, while the United States, China, and Russia showed a reduction in the imprisonment rates between 2008 and 2014, in Brazil there was a growth of 33% in this indicator.

Prisoners are primarily young men of color with little education. One-third are young people between the ages of 18 and 24 and more than half are under 30. Whites represent only 31% of the incarcerated population. Only about 9% completed high school. Trafficking alone is the largest cause of incarceration, accounting for a quarter of male and 63% of female incarceration.[66] The color and class make-up of this prison population reflects the norms of the favelas and other poor housing zones from which they come. Among the residents of the substandard agglomerations, whites in 2010 account for only 31%, whereas non-whites represent 69% of the people living in these substandard houses and areas.

In terms of violent crime, the situation has become increasingly more serious over time. By 2015, the homicide rate was 28.9 homicides per

---

[66] Ministério da Justiça. Departamento Penitenciário Nacional (DEPEN), "Levantamento Nacional de Informações Penitenciárias. Infopen – junho de 2014." Accessed at: www.justi ca.gov.br/news/mj-divulgara-novo-relatorio-do-infopen-nesta-terca-feira/relatorio-depen-v ersao-web.pdf.

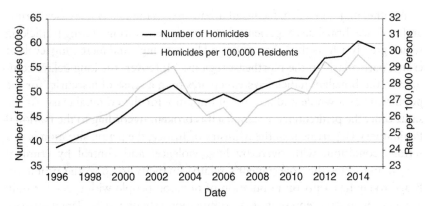

GRAPH 6.3 Number and Rate of Homicides in Brazil, 1996–2015
Source: Cerqueira et al., *Atlas da violência*.

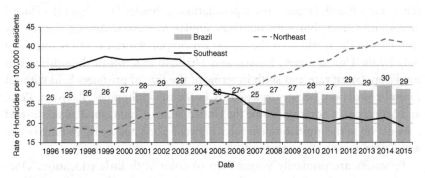

GRAPH 6.4 Rate of Homicides per 100,000 Residents for Brazil, Northeast and Southeast Regions, 1996–3025
Source: Cerqueira et al., *Atlas da violência*.

100,000 inhabitants. After a period of systematic increase between 1996 and 2002, there was a temporary decline in the mid-2000s followed by a strong increase thereafter (Graph 6.3). But the regional distribution of homicide rates shows that most recently there has been an inversion by region. In 1996, the rate in the Northeast was 18.1 per 100,000 inhabitants, while the Southeast had a much higher rate of around 34.0 homicides. Since then, there was a systematic fall in the rate in the Southeast and a rapid increase in the Northeast rate, which currently shows that the rate in the Northeast is 41.1 and the Southeast is now 19.2 per 100,000 (Graph 6.4). The 59,627 homicides which occurred in Brazil in 2017 represent more than 10% of the homicides registered in the world and place Brazil as the country with the highest absolute number of homicides. In a comparison with a list of 154 countries with data available for 2012, Brazil would be placed among the twelfth highest homicide rate per 100,000 inhabitants using the estimates of 2015.[67]

Given the correlation between poverty and crime, it is no surprise that young male non-whites experienced the most homicides. The homicide rate in 2015 was 37.6 among blacks and mulattos and less than half that rate, 15.3 homicides, for Asians and whites and has held steady for a decade. Moreover, it is the young of all groups who most suffer this violence. Thus, half or more of deaths which occur to men 15–24 years of age are due to homicides, and 40% of those 25–29 suffered death by homicide; this when the overall rate due to killings for all ages is only 8% of all deaths.

Most of the violent crime which occurs is in the cities, but with major differences by region. Florianópolis and São Paulo are the capitals with the lowest homicide rates, followed by Campo Grande and Rio de Janeiro. The Rio de Janeiro rate is quite surprising given that it is the scene of a succession of violent clashes between the police forces and the army and organized crime which has entrenched itself in the favelas of the city.[68] Except Recife, all other Northeastern capitals were at the highest levels of homicide (see Table 6.11). The three worst state capitals were São Luiz, Fortaleza, and Belém, in the North (see Table 6.12). Even for secondary non-capital cities with a population of more than 100,000 inhabitants, most of them with the highest rates are located in the North and Northeast regions.[69] All

---

[67] Cerqueira et al., *Atlas da violência 2016* (Brasília: Ipea, 2016), p. 6. The World Bank presents data on violence at: https://datos.bancomundial.org/indicador/VC.IHR.PSRC.P5?order=wbapi_data_value_2012+wbapi_data_value+wbapi_data_value-last&sort=des. Accessed 9 December 2017. Considering the data available from 2012 to 2015, Brazil, with 26.7 homicides per 1,000 inhabitants, would be the eleventh worst country for homicides in the world. Among the countries with worse indicators than Brazil, almost all are from Central America and the Caribbean, with San Salvador, Honduras, Guatemala, and Venezuela in South America (57.1). Colombia has values similar to Brazil (26.5), but Mexico (16.3), Bolivia (12.4), and Paraguay (9.3) have a lower homicide rate compared to Brazil.

[68] By the Constitution of 1988, public safety is constitutionally a function of states. However, given fiscal crises and the high levels of corruption demonstrated by state administrations, in 2018 the federal government carried out an intervention in the public safety of a state for the first time. On the relationship between drugs, crime, and violence in the Rio favelas, see Enrique Desmond Arias, *Drugs and Democracy in Rio De Janeiro: Trafficking, Social Networks, and Public Security* (Chapel Hill: University of North Carolina Press, 2009); Enrique Desmond Arias and Corinne Davis Rodrigues, "The Myth of Personal Security: Criminal Gangs, Dispute Resolution, and Identity in Rio De Janeiro's Favelas," *Latin American Politics and Society* 48.4 (2006), pp. 53–81; Enrique Desmond Arias, "Trouble en route: Drug Trafficking and Clientelism in Rio de Janeiro Shantytowns," *Qualitative Sociology* 29.4 (2006), pp. 427–445.

[69] On the violence in the Northeast, see José Maria Pereira de Nóbrega Júnior, "Os homicídios no Brasil, no nordeste e em Pernambuco: dinâmica, relações de causalidade e políticas públicas," PhD thesis, Universidade Federal de Pernambuco, Recife, 2010 and his essay "Os homicídios no nordeste Brasileiro," *Segurança, Justiça e Cidadania* (undated). Accessed 10 December 2017, at: www.justica.gov.br/sua-seguranca/seguranca-publica/analise-e-pesquisa/download/estudos/sjcvolume6/os_homicidios_ne_brasileiro.pdf.

Table 6.11 *Homicides and Violent Deaths for Unknown Causes in the State Capitals and the Most Violent Cities, 2015*

State Capitals	Population	Number of Homicides	Number of Violent Deaths Cause Unknown	Homicide Rate	Violent Deaths for Causes Unknown Rate	Total Homicide and Violent Deaths Rate*
Florianópolis (SC)	469,690	61	2	13.0	0.4	13.4
São Paulo (SP)	11,967,825	1,584	483	13.2	4.0	17.3
Campo Grande (MS)	853,622	170	30	19.9	3.5	23.4
Rio de Janeiro (RJ)	6,476,631	1,444	422	22.3	6.5	28.8
Belo Horizonte (MG)	2,502,557	610	116	24.4	4.6	29.0
Vitória (ES)	355,875	89	18	25.0	5.1	30.1
Brasília (DF)	2,914,830	742	41	25.5	1.4	26.9
Curitiba (PR)	1,879,355	518	83	27.6	4.4	32.0
Rio Branco (AC)	370,550	126	1	34.0	0.3	34.3
Palmas (TO)	272,726	98	1	35.9	0.4	36.3
Recife (PE)	1,617,183	582	220	36.0	13.6	49.6
Boa Vista (RR)	320,714	120	14	37.4	4.4	41.8
Macapá (AP)	456,171	188	12	41.2	2.6	43.8
Porto Velho (RO)	502,748	208	3	41.4	0.6	42.0
Teresina (PI)	844,245	351	27	41.6	3.2	44.8
Cuiaba (MT)	580,489	256	24	44.1	4.1	48.2
Porto Alegre (RS)	1,476,867	688	28	46.6	1.9	48.5
Goiânia (GO)	1,430,697	698	10	48.8	0.7	49.5
Natal (RN)	869,954	446	92	51.3	10.6	61.8
Salvador (BA)	2,921,087	1,542	191	52.8	6.5	59.3

(continued)

216

Manaus (AM)	2,057,711	1,130	17	54.9	0.8	55.7
Maceió (AL)	1,013,773	573	4	56.5	0.4	56.9
Aracaju (SE)	632,744	371	29	58.6	4.6	63.2
João Pessoa (PB)	791,438	467	9	59.0	1.1	60.1
Belém (PA)	1,439,561	875	15	60.8	1.0	61.8
Fortaleza (CE)	2,591,188	1,729	295	66.7	11.4	78.1
São Luís (MA)	1,073,893	758	36	70.6	3.4	73.9

Cities over 100,000 Inhabitants with highest mortality rates*

Marabá (PA)	262,085	201	15	76.7	5.7	82.4
Cabo de Santo Agostinho (PE)	200,546	147	24	73.3	12.0	85.3
Porto Seguro (BA)	145,431	123	2	84.6	1.4	86.0
Piraquara (PR)	104,481	83	8	79.4	7.7	87.1
Teixeira de Freitas (BA)	157,804	114	25	72.2	15.8	88.1
Maracanaú (CE)	221,504	172	26	77.7	11.7	89.4
Simões Filho (Ba)	133,202	112	11	84.1	8.3	92.3
São José de Ribamar (Ma)	174,267	159	9	91.2	5.2	96.4
Nossa Senhora do Socorro (SE)	177,344	159	12	89.7	6.8	96.4
Lauro de Freitas (BA)	191,436	177	10	92.5	5.2	97.7
Altamira (PA)	108,382	114	2	105.2	1.8	107.0

Source: Cerqueira et al., *Atlas da violência 2017* (2017), pp. 63–74.
* Rate per 100,000 resident population.

this violent crime has implications for health, demography, and economic and social development, and the failure to deal effectively with this issue indicates a lack of commitment on the part of the authorities at the federal, state, and municipal levels to the complex agenda of public security.[70]

The rapid and disorderly growth of cities and their metropolitan areas has created other problems, among which transport has become fundamental. Mobility may be one of the most serious issues faced by urban residents, particularly in their daily commute to work. Cities without planning, without adequate road infrastructure, without the availability of mass transportation, such as subway networks, suburban trains, and BRT, VLT, or monorail systems, create serious problems for its working classes. The majority of the workers in their daily commutes are forced to use tire-based systems, that is cars and urban buses, most of which are polluting and slow. In the metropolitan areas of São Paulo and Rio de Janeiro, for example, about a quarter of commuting takes between one and two hours and 5% of commuting takes more than two hours. And to a lesser extent this situation is generally repeated in several large cities and metropolitan regions (Table 6.12).

In all large and medium-sized cities motorized transport is fundamental, with private cars almost as important as public transport. In 2014, cars made 17.3 billion trips, similar to the number of trips made by public transport, which totaled 18.2 billion in the same year. Moreover, public transport is overwhelmingly dominated by inefficient buses. Of the total trips made by the public transportation system in that same year, 86% were made by urban and intercity buses and only 14% by the far more efficient and less-polluting rail system.[71]

Brazilian cities, regardless of eventual planning provided by municipal administrators and despite laws regulating urban occupation, depend primarily on the private decisions of real estate entrepreneurs or individual landowners who are not always guided by the common good or willing to meet the requirements of urban legislation. Even publicly controlled programs, such as the large housing projects financed by BNH and the *Minha Casa Minha Vida* program, are carried out without

---

[70] Cerqueira et al., *Atlas de Violência 2017*, p. 8. The systematic monitoring of public safety by the Ipea is made available at: http://ipea.gov.br/atlasviolencia/; the Forum Brasileiro de Segurança Pública, also has a website with information on this theme at: www.forumseguranca.org.br/publicacoes/atlas-da-violencia-2017/.

[71] ANTP (Associação Nacional de Transportes Públicos), "Sistema de Informações da Mobilidade Urbana: Relatório Geral 2016," p. 5.

Table 6.12 *Usual Time of Travel to Work in Metropolitan Areas, Census 2010*

Metropolitan Region	Number of Persons Employed	Up to 5 minutes	From 6 to 30 minutes	From 31 to 60 minutes	More than an Hour up to 2 hours	More than 2 hours
São Paulo (SP)	6,877,980	5%	32%	35%	23%	5%
Rio de Janeiro (RJ)	3,856,724	6%	32%	33%	23%	5%
Belo Horizonte (MG)	2,036,937	7%	41%	34%	17%	2%
Porto Alegre (RS)	1,504,973	9%	49%	31%	11%	1%
Curitiba (PR)	1,204,263	8%	46%	32%	13%	1%
Salvador (BA)	1,180,176	7%	38%	36%	17%	2%
Recife (PE)	1,132,393	7%	42%	35%	15%	2%
Fortaleza (CE)	1,123,240	10%	48%	31%	11%	1%
Campinas (SP)	1,055,989	8%	54%	28%	8%	1%
Goiânia (GO)	823,844	10%	50%	28%	11%	1%
Belém (PA)	639,920	9%	47%	31%	13%	1%
Grande Vitória (ES)	630,781	8%	45%	32%	14%	1%
Manaus (AM)	610,128	9%	39%	36%	14%	2%
Baixada Santista (SP)	575,446	7%	50%	31%	10%	1%
Natal (RN)	427,763	10%	51%	31%	8%	1%
Florianópolis (SC)	425,378	12%	56%	24%	7%	1%
Norte/Nordeste Catarinense (SC)	424,409	13%	62%	21%	4%	0%
Grande São Luís (MA)	407,490	7%	41%	37%	14%	2%
João Pessoa (PB)	366,437	10%	56%	27%	7%	1%
Maceió (AL)	341,183	9%	48%	30%	11%	2%

Source: IBGE, Sidra, census 2010, Table 3422.

meeting minimum standards of support for urban infrastructure, and most particularly without any criterion for connecting residents to their centers of work and employment. The price of land is the determining factor. As a result, Brazil's cities have a large share of their populations – mostly the poorest – living in areas far away from their workplaces, requiring long journeys which consume daily hours for millions of people and using a slow and low-quality, polluting transport system. All this represents a significant financial burden for the large, low-income population living in large cities. Moreover, the recent fiscal crisis and low investment capacity of Brazilian cities makes the mobility problem one of the most complex facing Brazil's urban centers.[72]

Fundamental is the total lack of metro-rail infrastructure in Brazil in all but two cities. Of the 2.5 billion passengers per year transported by a metro-rail system in Brazil, 71% use the São Paulo system and 17% use the Rio de Janeiro metro. Moreover, even with its 82 kilometers of subway lines, the city of São Paulo's metro system is small compared to the great metropolises of the world. São Paulo and Mexico City began their metro systems at the same time; however, the metro network in Mexico City is almost three times larger than the São Paulo network and transports almost twice as many passengers.[73] On the other hand, due to the size of the city and its reduced metro network, the São Paulo metro is one of the systems with the highest number of passengers per km of network in the world. Fortunately, it operates with a high degree of efficiency.[74]

The metropolitan area of São Paulo also has an extensive network of metropolitan suburban trains thanks to the legacy of the old railroad system used for the transportation of coffee from the producing regions in the interior of the state to the port of Santos. It has been transformed into a collective transportation system and today accounts for the largest extension of São Paulo's metro-railway lines (260 km), which have been modernized and efficiently integrated into the existing metro system. Despite this unique integration of suburban trains and urban metro lines, the São Paulo system transports only a third of the number of passengers carried by the regional bus system (Table 6.13).[75]

---

[72] On urban transport, see Marcos Kiyoto de Tani e Isola, "Transporte sobre trilhos na Região Metropolitana de São Paulo. Estudo sobre a concepção e a inserção das redes de transporte de alta capacidade," MA thesis, Faculdade de Arquitetura e Urbanismo da USP, São Paulo, 2013; ANTP, "Sistema de Informações da Mobilidade Urbana: Relatório Geral 2014" (May 2018); Carlos Henrique Ribeiro de Carvalho, "Mobilidade urbana: tendências e desafios," Texto para discussão 94, São Paulo, Ipea, 2013; Centro de Estudos e Debates Estratégicos, Consultoria Legislativa. *O desafio da mobilidade urbana* (Brasília: Câmara dos Deputados, 2015); Alexandre de Avila Gomide, *Transporte urbano e inclusão social: elementos para políticas públicas* (Brasília: Ipea, 2003); "Mobilidade urbana: hora de mudar os rumos," *Discussão: revista de audiências públicas do Senado Federal* 4.18 (November 2013); Marilene de Paula and Dawid Danilo Barlet, eds., *Mobilidade urbana no Brasil: desafios e alternativas* (Rio de Janeiro: Fundação Heinrich Boll, 2016).

[73] Luiz Roberto Hupsel Vaz et al., "Transporte sobre trilhos no Brasil: uma perspectiva do material rodante," BNDES, Ferroviário, Setorial 40, 2014: 235–282. Accessed 14 June 2018, at: https://web.bndes.gov.br/bib/jspui/bitstream/1408/3021/2/Transporte%20sobre%20trilhos%20no%20Brasil.pdf.

[74] Silvanilza Machado Teixeira et al., "Qualidade do transporte urbano de passageiros: uma avaliação do nível de serviço do sistema do metropolitano de São Paulo," *Revista Metropolitana de Sustentabilidade* 4.1 (2014), pp. 3–20; Metrô, "Relatório da Administração 2016," www.metro.sp.gov.br/metro/institucional/pdf/rel-administracao.pd f; Janice Caiafa, "O metro de São Paulo e problema da rede," Paper presented at the XXV Encontro Anual da Compós, Universidade Federal de Goiás, June 2016. Accessed 10 December 2017, at: www.compos.org.br/biblioteca/caiafacompo_s2016_3317.pdf.

[75] Isola, "Transporte sobre trilhos na Região Metropolitana de São Paulo."

Table 6.13 Characteristics of the Metro-Suburban Railway System in 2014

Systems	Municípios	Lines	Extension	Wagons	km/year (million)	Passengers/year (million)	Employees	Relation between Income and Expenses*
Metro SP	São Paulo	6	81.9	1,012	145	1,090	10,536	1.05
CPTM	São Paulo	6	260.8	1,294	202	655	8,591	0.64
Opportrans	Rio de Janeiro	2	42.0	296	44	256	2,742	1.31
Supervia	Rio de Janeiro	5	270.0	783	67	164	2,917	1.29
Metrorec	Recife	3	71.4	173	17	110	1,794	0.76
CBTU-BH	Belo Horizonte	1	28.1	96	2	64	999	1.07
Trensurb	Porto alegre	1	44.6	138	16	59	1,120	0.43
Metro DF	Brasília	1	40.4	128	4	43	1,063	0.32
CBTU fortaleza	Fortaleza	2	43.6	84	7	4	1,201	0.14
CBTU JP	João Pessoa	1	30.0	25	0	2	104	0.09
CBTU Terezina	Teresina	1	13.6	9	0	2	91	0.57
CBTU Salvador	Salvador	1	13.7	9	0	4	127	0.06
CBTU Maceio	Maceió	1	32.1	24	1	3	129	0.12
CBTU Natal	Natal	2	56.2	10	0	2	113	0.09
Total		33		4,081	505	2,458	31,527	0.84

Source: ANTP, "Sistema de Informações da Mobilidade Urbana: Relatório Geral 2014."
* Ticket income/operation costs.

The consequence of this system of urban transport in Brazil's large and medium-sized cities is that the average time spent on the daily commute increases with the size of the cities. Thus, people living in large cities with more than 1 million inhabitants spend on average 55 minutes on a daily commute in all types of transport, of which 27 minutes are spent on collective transport.[76] This time is reduced proportionally as the size of the city declines. In medium-sized cities (between 100,000 and 250,000 inhabitants, for example), there is a reduction of the average time to 23 minutes – in this case with the time distributed equally between collective and non-motorized transport (10 minutes each), with little importance for cars.

It is evident from this survey that the population growth of cities in Brazil since the middle of the last century has not been accompanied by the growth of the necessary urban infrastructure nor in adequate urban planning and financing to deal with the housing, sanitation, water supply, education, health, and transport needs of these immigrants. But if Brazil's large and medium-sized cities have serious problems of housing and integrating these immigrants, then the question is why rural migrants flocked to these cities. It is clear that such migrants find enough resources, institutions, and infrastructure to make the move worthwhile, since even basic institutions are unavailable to them in the rural areas. But, even more importantly, these urban centers are main sources of employment, particularly of high-quality jobs, and they can offer better facilities for health, for education, and even for culture. In short, they still are able to offer services that are not available or are of lower quality in the smaller towns or the rural areas from which the migrants come. It is only in cities that the most complex health services and the best education offerings are available. Cities are centers of culture and leisure. Cities represent trade centers, which attract buyers to satisfy their personal or professional needs. The large shopping malls or the traditional popular and wholesale shopping centers such as Rua Vinte de Cinco de Março in the city of São Paulo attract millions annually.

Moreover, it is in the urban centers, due to the economies of scale, that the main transformations in the form and organization of services have developed. Medium and large cities provide the most complete health care available in Brazil. Initially, most of the professional health system was concentrated in the cities, and this was the norm until the 1980s. Thus, access to these facilities was an important draw for people coming to the urban

---

[76] According to the ANPT report, not all people travel, and many people do so only a few times a month. So these average data per inhabitant are smaller than the data that would correspond only to people who travel regularly to work, for example. ANTP, "Sistema de Informações da Mobilidade Urbana: Relatório Geral 2014" (May 2018), p. 12. We have previously presented data on the time spent in travelling to work. Here we have daily travel.

centers. Over time, however, this is one area that Brazil has tried to balance since the 1980s. Especially since the return to democratic rule, there has been a sustained effort to service the rural area and smaller cities, though this has always been a costly and difficult system to maintain.

In 1990, the National Health Service was reorganized and decentralized, with a new focus on local authorities.[77] The resulting national Universal Health System (*Sistema Único de Saúde* – SUS), which now offers universal health care to everyone in Brazil, nevertheless still puts the more complex facilities in urban centers. Cities also have the highest concentration of doctors.[78] In the new hierarchical organization, it was primarily municipalities which provided the services and implemented health policies. A network with different levels of complexity was formed to serve a given region, with municipalities being responsible for basic health management. This local care through the Family Health Program has been extremely successful in reducing child mortality everywhere and providing a group of health professionals that provide basic preventive care for all local communities and rural areas.[79] But more advanced treatment is provided in the medium and larger cities.[80] The basic idea is a network in which services of lower

---

[77] Câmara dos Deputados, Consultoria de orçamento e fiscalização financeira, Nota Técnica no. 10 (2011). Accessed 16 December 2017, at: www2.camara.leg.br/orcamento-da-uniao/estudos/2011/nt10.pdf.

[78] The Constitution of 1988 established (Article 96) that "Health is the right of all and the duty of the State, guaranteed by social and economic policies aimed at reducing the risk of disease" and promotes "universal and equal access to" health services. Article 198 creates the single health system, which will be provided by a decentralized regional-based hierarchical network. Article 199 states that health care is open to private initiatives and private institutions may participate in a complementary form of the single health system, through a contract or agreement – with preference being given to philanthropic and non-profit organizations.

[79] Sarah Escorel, Ligia Giovanella, Maria Helena Magalhães de Mendonça, and Mônica de C. M. Senna, "Programa de Saúde da Família e a construção de um novo modelo para atenção básica no Brasil," *Revista Panamericana de Salud Pública* 21.2 (2007), p. 165 and Deborah Carvalho Malta et al., "A cobertura da Estratégia de Saúde da Família (ESF) no Brasil, segundo a Pesquisa Nacional de Saúde, 2013," *Ciência & Saúde* 21 (2016), p. 331, Table 1. A recent survey of the national population finds access to this service quite good, but costs for medicines still are not fully covered. See Andréa Dâmaso Bertoldi, Aluísio Jardim Dornellas de Barros, Anita Wagner, Dennis Ross-Degnan, and Pedro Curi Hallal, "Medicine Access and Utilization in a Population Covered by Primary Health Care in Brazil." *Health Policy* 89. 3 (2009), pp. 295–302.

[80] Georgia Costa de Araújo Souza, "O SUS nos seus 20 anos: reflexões num contexto de mudanças," *Saúde Social* 19.3 (2010), p. 512. See also Gilson Carvalho, "A saúde Pública no Brasil," *Estudos Avançados*, 27.78 (2013), pp. 7–26; Fátima Aparecida Ribeiro, "Atenção Primária (APS) e o Sistema de Saúde no Brasil: uma perspectiva histórica," MA thesis, Faculdade de Medicina da Universidade de São Paulo – FMUSP, 2007; Telma Maria Gonçalves Menicucci, "Público e privado na política assistência à saúde no Brasil: atores, processos e trajetória," PhD thesis, FFCH/Universidade Federal de Minas Gerais, 2003; Sandra Maria Spedo, "Desafios para implementar a integralidade da assistência à saúde no SUS: estudo de caso no município de São Paulo," PhD thesis, Faculdade de Saúde Pública/USP, 2009.

technological density, such as Basic Health Units, are offered in a dispersed manner and the services with greater technological density that benefit most from economies of scale tend to be concentrated in the largest urban centers.[81] Although there are problem related to the difficulty of coordination between federative levels, integrated management problems, and, particularly, the permanent lack of resources to finance such an essential but expensive program, the SUS can be considered a great advance in equalizing access to health care for rural and urban residents alike.[82] Overall, the system has been quite impressive. SUS has some 6,000 hospitals, more than 2 billion ambulatory procedures per year, 10 million chemotherapy and radiotherapy procedures, and more than 200,000 heart surgeries a year, and its transplant and AIDS programs are internationally recognized.[83]

Also, unlike most of the other government services, sharp regional differences have been eliminated in terms of health care. The system creates an intense flow of people between the less dense, poorer areas to the major regional urban medical centers. They are true caravans run by the city halls themselves, taking their residents to the centers where the necessary services will be provided. We can cite the case of Teresina, capital of Piauí, one of the important medical centers of the Northeast. Unlike other Northeastern capitals, Teresina is located in the interior of the state, at an important road junction, with connections to Belém, São Luís, Fortaleza, Recife, Salvador, and Brasília. It has become an important regional health center serving a public from the interior regions of several Northeastern states.[84] The same is true of the main metropolitan areas, or regional centers of importance, where medical services of medium and high complexity are

---

[81] "Curso de autoaprendizado redes de atenção à saúde no Sistema Único de Saúde," Brasília, Ministério da Saúde, 2012, pp. 12–13. Accessed 17 December 2017, at: https://edisciplinas .usp.br/pluginfile.php/2921879/mod_resource/content/1/Apostila%20MS%20-%20RAS_c urso%20completo-M%C3%B3dulo%202-APS%20nas%20RAS%20-%20Pg%2031-45 .pdf.

[82] On the current financial and staffing problems of the system, see Silvio Fernandes da Silva, "Organização de redes regionalizadas e integradas de atenção à saúde: desafios do Sistema Único de Saúde (Brasil)" *Ciência & Saúde Coletiva* 16 (2011), pp. 2753–2762.

[83] "25 anos do Sistema único de Saúde: resultados e desafios." *Estudos Avançados* 27.78 (2013), p. 28.

[84] Some 30% of the daily services of the Hospital Getúlio Vargas, at the center of the "Health Polo," are for inhabitants of the capital, 50% of the patients come from the interior of Piauí, and 20% from other states. Teresina is a reference center in several specialized areas, developing advanced medicine and procedures of high complexity and with a large number of clinics, doctors, and equipment. Samanta Petersen, "O polo Saúde de Teresina é referência em atendimento." Cidadeverde.com. Accessed 17 December 2017, at: https://cidadeverde .com/vida/68938/especial-polo-saude-de-teresina-e-referencia-em-atendimento.

concentrated, while only the basic health posts are maintained at the local level in small urban agglomerations.

When considering the general network of care, in terms of both health units and hospital beds, there is a very wide coverage in Brazil. In the case of hospital beds, there is not significant difference among the various regions of Brazil. Almost all regions have the same number of beds per 1,000 inhabitants. But, as might be expected from the organization of the system, metropolitan regions have most of the hospitals. Some 46% of the hospital beds are in the twenty-five largest metropolitan regions and 57% in the metropolitan areas as a whole. Of the 437,000 hospital beds, 39% are in the public sphere, mostly municipal, 37% controlled by non-profit entities, and the others owned by private business entities. As might be expected, given its size and economic importance, São Paulo is the area with the greatest coverage of health services, with numerous highly complex medical facilities that attract people from all the states of Brazil to the city. Most of the hospitals of national importance in numerous specialties are also located in the São Paulo.[85]

Even with all this infrastructure, actual delivery of services is still different between the rural areas even during the best periods. Thus, two health surveys, carried out in 2003 and 2008, showed that rural persons were less likely to have visited a dentist, and far less likely to have health insurance.[86] Moreover, there is an evident shortage of doctors and medical personnel in the rural areas, only partially compensated for by the use of Cuban health professionals.[87] The recent economic crisis and the decline of government efficiency in the second half of the 2010s has badly affected this system, especially at the municipal level throughout Brazil.

Education is also an area that is far more developed in the urban centers than in the rural areas and which traditionally brought rural residents to the cities. Like health, it is another major area of government activity designed to

[85] Ministério da Saúde – Cadastro Nacional dos Estabelecimentos de Saúde do Brasil – CNES, *Número de Estabelecimento por tipo*, and *Leitos por tipo de estabelecimento*. Despite this, a report published on 16 February 2017 by the newspaper *Folha de São Paulo* points to surveys which suggest that health is the main problem for Paulistas (29%), followed by safety. Accessed 17 December 2017, at: www1.folha.uol.com.br/cotidiano/2017/02/1859141-mor ador-de-sp-considera-saude-maior-problema-da-cidade-diz-datafolha.shtml.

[86] IBGE, Sidra. PNAD, Suplemento Acesso e Utilização de Serviços de Saúde – 2003/2008, Tables 2526 and 2494.

[87] The program "*Programa Mais Médicos*" was established in 2013 and lasted until the beginning of 2019. Some 14,000 Cuban and foreign medical personnel were employed in Brazilian rural areas to work in local family health clinics. See Felipe Proenço de Oliveira et al., "Mais Médicos: um programa brasileiro em uma perspectiva internacional," *Interface-Comunicação, Saúde, Educação* 19 (2015), pp. 623–634, and Leonor Maria Pacheco Santos, Ana Maria Costa, and Sábado Nicolau Girardi, "Programa Mais Médicos: uma ação efetiva para reduzir iniquidades em saúde," *Ciência & Saúde Coletiva* 20 (2015), pp. 3547–3552.

reduce the inherent inequality in rural access to education. But important differences have existed until today. In 2016, there were 183,000 schools in Brazil, of which 120,000 were in urban areas and 63,000 in rural areas. Of the existing schools, the public sector accounts for 79%, run predominantly by municipal administrations (62% of all existing schools), as they are the primary government body responsible for the provision of elementary education. Since the middle of the last century, the majority of schools have been public schools, with private primary and secondary schools accounting for only 21% of existing schools. Of the 48 million students, 58% are enrolled in elementary education, 17% in high school, and 18% in pre-schools and day care centers. Of the 28 million students enrolled in the nine grades of elementary education, the public sector accounts for 83%, of which more than half are enrolled in the municipal network spread throughout Brazil.

But the differences between rural and urban schooling are important in terms of the composition and structure of the schools. Some 70% of rural students are enrolled in elementary education and only 6% in high schools. In the urban area, elementary education absorbs 56% of enrollments and 18% secondary education. Only in pre-school registration is there no difference between urban and rural areas. But it is clear that rural students primarily stop their education after completing the fundamental level or are dropping out of school or going to urban areas to continue their studies. This differentiated pattern can also be seen within the nine grades of elementary school. In the urban area there is stability in the number of students, in contrast to the rural areas, where there is a 40% dropout in the 5 to 9 series. School buildings are also less supplied with services than urban ones. While 94% of urban schools are served by public water, this occurs only in 29% of schools in rural areas, and while 71% of urban schools have adequate sewage systems, only 5% of the rural schools have them. Some 48% of urban schools have a library, but this is true in only 15% of rural schools. Rural schools are poorly served in terms of laboratories, reading rooms, sports courts, etc. Some 88% of urban schools are connected to the internet, 76% with broadband; in rural areas only 30% of schools have internet, and only 17% have broadband (Table 6.14).

These differences in the availability and quality of the schools can be seen in the quite sharp differences there are for both men and women in the levels of education obtained. Rural persons 25 years of age and older in the census of 2010 systematically had worse completion rates than urban dwellers, for both men and women (see Table 6.15).

Urban opportunities not only include advanced medical services and better education, but they provide a far more abundant market of goods and services for all social and economic classes. Retailing is part of the distribution systems between the producer and the consumer, acting as an intermediary and functioning as a link between the level of consumption and

Table 6.14 *Matriculation, Numbers, and Characteristics of Urban and Rural Schools, 2018*

Total Number of Schools	Total	Urban Schools	Rural Schools
	183,376	66%	34%

Matriculation by Level and Type of Teaching

Matriculation in nurseries	3,238,894	94%	6%
Matriculation in pre-schools	5,040,210	86%	14%
Matriculation in initial years	15,442,039	84%	16%
Matriculation in final years	12,249,439	88%	12%
Matriculation in Middle School	8,133,040	96%	4%
Matriculation of youths and adults (EJA)	3,482,174	89%	11%
Matriculation in Special Education	174,886	99%	1%

Characteristics of the Schools

Services	Percentage Total	Percentage of Urban	Percentage of Rural
Water via public network	72%	94%	29%
Electricity via public network	95%	100%	86%
Sewage via public network	49%	71%	5%
Periodic garbage collection	76%	99%	31%
Dependencies			
Library	37%	48%	15%
Kitchen	92%	92%	90%
Computers labs	42%	52%	23%
Science labs	11%	17%	2%
Sports fields	34%	46%	12%
Reading hall	24%	31%	9%
Room for Director	68%	86%	33%
Rooms for Professors	56%	74%	24%
Room for Special Attention	18%	23%	7%
Sanitation inside the school building	87%	94%	73%
Sanitation outside the school building	16%	13%	22%
Equipment			
DVD machines	77%	89%	54%
Printers	69%	83%	43%
Parabolic antenna	23%	26%	18%
Copying machines	45%	58%	21%
Overhead projector	30%	40%	10%

(continued)

Table 6.14 *(continued)*

Services	Percentage Total	Percentage of Urban	Percentage of Rural
Characteristics of the Schools			
Television	82%	94%	58%
Technology			
Internet	68%	88%	30%
Broadband	56%	76%	17%
Computers per school	7.44	10.07	2.4
Computers per administrator	3.12	4.31	0.84
Food			
Schools furnish food	86%	79%	100%
Schools offer filtered water	87%	92%	78%
Other characteristics			
Officials in all schools	31	41	12
Schools with organization by cycles	24%	24%	24%

Source: Qedu. http://qedu.org.br/brasil/censo-escolar?year=2016&dependence=0&localization=0&education_.

Table 6.15 *Distribution of the Population 25 Years of Age and Older, by Level of Education Completed, by Sex and Residence, 2010*

Level of Education Completed	Women		Men	
	Urban	Rural	Urban	Rural
No education or primary incomplete	43.5	77.3	45.0	81.7
Primary complete and secondary incomplete	15.0	10.1	16.0	9.4
Secondary complete and university incomplete	27.2	10.0	27.2	7.6
University complete	14.0	2.5	11.6	1.2

Source IBGE, "Estatísticas de Gênero" (2014), n.p., Table 16.

the level of production, assuming increasingly a proactive role in the identification of needs and in defining what should be produced to meet market expectations. Among these retailing institutions, the rise of the supermarket and shopping centers throughout major cities in Brazil in the past two decades has profoundly affected urban life.

According to Knoke, when supermarkets appeared in the United States, the typical emporium was small and relatively inefficient. In general, grocers and butchers offered all the required services: personal sale, credit, and delivery. Although there is no precise data on the gross margin with which they operated, it has been estimated that it was approximately 20% to 21%. With unemployment, declining incomes, and reduced purchasing power – factors that accompanied the depression of the early 1930s – the scene was set for the establishment and development of a retail institution that could bring consumer prices down and provide more abundant choice in one location. This was precisely the function of the first North American supermarkets. Savings on food purchases in supermarkets were large enough to serve as a strong stimulus to consumers in order to make them change their buying habits.[88]

In Brazil, as in the United States, the distribution of food products used to be made exclusively through the small specialized store. In the Brazilian case, however, there also existed the traditional open air or farmers' markets (*feiras*), which never disappeared and are still a fundamental part of Brazilian urban life everywhere. These markets are held weekly in public spaces, usually a public road, in most urban neighborhoods. Even in large cities, the multiplicity of fairs that move daily allows virtually all residents to access a fair on foot. This organization allows these markets to be competitive, particularly in horticultural products. In the city of São Paulo alone there are approximately 850 such markets, involving more than 16,000 vendors.[89]

It was only in the mid-twentieth century that the first supermarkets appeared in Brazil.[90] It was the massive increase in urban populations in this period that stimulated the search for more modern mechanisms of production and distribution of food. The transformations that occurred in agricultural policy in the 1970s reflected the need adequately to supply the growing urban population at affordable prices to keep urban wages under control.[91] Also, the military governments supported the supermarket sector, considering them a useful control of inflation; the economies of scale of the

---

[88] William Knoke, "O supermercado no Brasil e nos Estados Unidos: confronto e contrastes." *Revista de Administração de Empresas* 3.9 (1963), p. 93.

[89] A complete list of the fairs of São Paulo, with day of the week, name of the fair, address, and size can be accessed at the city's website: www9.prefeitura.sp.gov.br/secretarias/sdte/pesquisa/feiras/lista_completa.html.

[90] By the middle of the twentieth century there were already some self-service experiences in various parts of the country, such as the Serve Yourself network opened in 1953. But the first supermarket was born from the sweetshop Doceria Pão de Açúcar. In 1959, the first Pão de Açúcar Supermarket store was opened, with 2,500 items on sale. "Few compared to a current supermarket, but self-service itself was new and it was astonishing to the ladies of society that they had to put their own goods in the trolleys, where men, in the rare times when they frequented them, the most they did was push the carts." Armando João Dalla Costa, "A importância da Logística no Varejo Brasileiro: o caso Pão de Açúcar." Accessed 10 December 2017, at: www.empresas.ufpr.br/logistica.pdf (p. 4). On this pioneer period, see Umberto Antonio Sesso Filho, "O setor supermercadista no Brasil nos anos 1990," PhD thesis, Universidade de São Paulo – Escola Superior de Agricultura "Luiz de Queiroz," 2003.

[91] See Klein and Luna, *Feeding the World*.

supermarket chains could reduce prices and thus inflation.[92] In the 1970s, various formats were tested in terms of size and variety of products, including the emergence of "hypermarkets."[93] In the 1980s and 1990s, in the face of the fiscal crisis, which dramatically reduced public funding for agricultural production, a profound transformation took place in Brazilian agriculture, which led to the integration of the processing, distribution, and export process. In this development the relative power of the efficient distribution channels, of which the supermarkets were part, expanded and soon replaced some of the lost government credit made available to farmers.[94]

Throughout the 1980s, supermarkets were consolidated as the most efficient distribution channels. By 1989, for example, the supermarkets totaled 32,950 stores, directly employing 533,000 employees, with 95,677 checkout points.[95] Since then the system has increased exponentially.[96] By the end of 2016, the sector had more than 89,000 stores, with 225,025 checkout points, a total area of 21.7 million square meters, and sales of 338.7 billion *reais*, representing about 5.4% of national GDP. São Paulo, with 31.8%, Rio Grande do Sul, with 11.6%, and Minas Gerais, with 10.8% lead the rankings in terms of participation in the sector's revenues (Table 6.16).[97]

---

[92] Sesso Filho, "O setor supermercadista no Brasil nos anos 1990," p. 12; Denise Cavallini Cyrillo, *O papel do supermercado no varejo de alimentos* (São Paulo: Instituto de Pesquisas Econômicas, 1987).

[93] In 1975 Carrefour inaugurated the first supermarket in the city of São Paulo. On the process of consolidating supermarkets in this early phase, see Cyrillo, *O papel do supermercado no varejo de alimentos*.

[94] Klein and Luna, *Feeding the World*, Chapter 10.

[95] Mariana Pires de Carvalho e Albuquerque, "Análise da Evolução do setor supermercadista brasileiro: uma visão estratégica," MA thesis, IBMEC, Rio de Janeiro, 2007, p. 52.

[96] Jony Lan, "A diversificação dos canais comerciais como fonte de vantagem competitiva da em redes de supermercados no Brasil," MA thesis, Universidade Presbiteriana Mackenzie, São Paulo, 2010; Fernanda Bittencourt Pamplona, "Os investimentos diretos estrangeiros na indústria do varejo nos supermercados no Brasil," MA thesis, Universidade Federal de Pernambuco, Recife, 2007; Ariel Wilder, "Mudanças no setor supermercadista e a formação de associações de pequenos supermercados," PhD thesis, Escola de Superior de Agricultura "Luiz de Queiroz," Universidade de São Paulo, Piracicaba, 2003; PWC, "O setor de varejo e o consumo no Brasil: como enfrentar a crise." January 2016. Accessed 11 December 2017, at: www.pwc.com.br/pt/estudos/setores-atividade/produtos-consumo-var ejo/2016/pwc-setor-varejo-consumo-brasil-como-enfrentar-crise-16.html; Paulo Roberto do Amaral Ferreira, "O processo de globalização do varejo de massa e as lutas competitivas: o caso do setor supermercadista no Brasil," MA thesis, COPPEAD/UFRJ, Rio de Janeiro, 2013. APAS provides research on consumer trends and data from the supermarket sector during fairs and congresses. January 2016. Accessed 11 December 2017, at: www.portala pas.org.br/wp-content/uploads/2016/06/COLETIVA-Pesquisa-APAS-Nielsen-Kantar.pdf.

[97] Information taken from ABRAS – Associação Brasileira de Supermercados. Accessed 11 December 2017, at: www.abras.com.br/economia-e-pesquisa/ranking-abras/os-numeros-d o-setor/.

Table 6.16 *The Supermarket Sector in Brazil, 1994–2012*

Years	Number of Stores	Number of Employees	Sales Area (in millions of square meters)	Share of GDP
1994	37,543	650,000		6.0
1995	41,439	655,200		6.6
1996	43,763	625,000		6.2
1997	47,847	655,000	12.0	6.0
1998	51,502	666,752	12.7	6.1
1999	55,313	670,086	13.1	6.1
2000	61,259	701,622	14.3	6.3
2001	69,396	710,743	15.3	6.2
2002	68,907	718,631	15.9	6.1
2003	71,372	739,846	17.9	5.7
2004	71,951	788,268	18.1	5.5
2005	72,884	800,922	18.4	5.5
2006	73,695	838,047	18.9	5.3
2007	74,602	868,023	18.8	5.2
2008	75,725	876,916	18.8	5.5
2009	78,300	899,700	19.3	5.6
2010	81,100	920,000	19.7	5.5
2011	82,000	967,700	20.6	5.4
2012	83,600	986,100	21.0	5.5
2016	89,009	1,809,852	21.7	5.4

Source: Ferreira, "O processo de globalização do varejo de massa e as lutas competitivas: o caso do setor supermercadista no Brasil," (2013), p. 163, and Santos, Estudo da Estrutura de mercado. www.fee.rs.gov.br/4-encontro-economia ... /estudos-setoriais-sessao3-3.doc, data from 2006: ABRAS. www.abras.com.br/economia-e-pesquisa/ranking-abras/as-500-m aiores/.

The modernization of the retail sector was complemented by the establishment of a network of multi-store shopping centers, following the world trend. In 1966, the first such center, the Shopping Center Iguatemi, in São Paulo, was inaugurated, which would have a great impact in the urban district where it was built. Financed by thousands of investors, Iguatemi opened the 25,000 square meter center of gross leasable area. The early years of Iguatemi were marked by an almost complete rejection of its innovative content and facilities: stores within the center closed and there was no financial return to investors.[98] In 1971, the Shopping Center Conjunto Nacional opened in Brasília, and in the mid-1970s several new enterprises were built, three in São Paulo, one in Salvador, and one in Belo Horizonte. The 1980s represented the phase of strong expansion and consolidation of the shopping center industry in Brazil. The success of these new and older centers depended on a basic change in the rent charged shop tenants. "Percentage of rent" clauses were introduced which provided that the shop tenant would pay a pre-established percentage of their sales as rent, which allowed potential investors to protect themselves from the losses caused by inflation, as well as to participate in the growing success of each mall, thus guaranteeing and increasing their eventual financial return.[99]

The 1990s marked important changes in the configuration of the enterprises, which started to count on extended leisure areas, cinema networks, and large food courts, to serve a varied public. The mall became part of the city's life, particularly for the young, who use the secure space for multiple interests, mostly as leisure. The ease of shopping malls, with ample space, parking facilities, and especially with their high levels of security, is an attraction in Brazilian cities given the increasing problems of crime. Surveys of customers found numerous uses of these centers, from shopping and strolling, to services, restaurants, and simple leisure activities.[100]

By the end of 2016, there were 558 shopping malls in Brazil, with 99,990 stores, making a leasable area of 15,237 million square meters. They employed more than 1 million people and were used by 439 million visitors per month

---

[98] "At the end of the 1960s, Rua Augusta was almost completely commercial, and Iguatemi's new presence was characterized by the absence of consumers/buyers, the regularity with which stores closed and the lack of financial returns, not only for shopkeepers, but also to the legion of investors who had bought – for some reason – the titles of the visionary's hawkers." Alfredo Mathias, "Semma Empresa de Shopping Centers." Accessed 11 December 2017, at: www.semma.com.br/historia-dos-shopping-centers-no-brasil/.

[99] Semma Empresa de Shopping Centers. Accessed 11 December 2017, at: www.semma.com .br/historia-dos-shopping-centers-no-brasil/.

[100] See *Censo Brasileiro de Shopping Centers*, ABRASCE. Accessed 11 December 2017, at: www.portaldoshopping.com.br/uploads/general/general_4b58c194fec5e617b0e01f c71487af24.pdf; Bradesco. *Shopping Center*, DEPEC, June 2017. Accessed 11 December 2017, at: www.economiaemdia.com.br/EconomiaEmDia/pdf/infset_shop pings_centers.pdf. Fernando Garrefa, "Shopping Centers, de centro de abastecimento a produto de consumo," PhD thesis, Faculdade de Arquitetura e Urbanismo da USP, São Paulo, 2007; Madalena Grimaldi de Carvalho, "A difusão e a integração dos shopping centers na cidade: as particularidades do Rio de Janeiro," PhD thesis, Universidade Federal do Rio de Janeiro – UFRJ, 2005; Silvia Catarina Araújo das Virgens, "Shopping Center e a produção do espaço urbano em Salvador-BA," MA thesis, Universidade Federal da Bahia, Salvador, 2016; Charles Albert de Andrade, "Shopping Center também tem memória: uma história esquecida dos shoppings centers nos espaços urbanos do Rio de Janeiro e de São Paulo nos anos 60 e 70," MA thesis, Universidade Federal Fluminense, Niterói, 2009.

Table 6.17 *The Shopping Center Industry in Brazil, 2006–2016*

Year	Number of Shopping Centers	Gross Rental Area (millions of square meters)	Number of Stores	Revenues (billions a year)	Employees	Traffic of Persons (millions a month)
2006	351	7,492	56,487	50	524,090	203
2007	363	8,253	62,086	58	629,700	305
2008	376	8,645	65,500	65	700,650	325
2009	392	9,081	70,500	74	707,166	328
2010	408	9,512	73,775	91	720,641	329
2011	430	10,344	80,192	108	775,383	376
2012	457	11,403	83,631	119	804,683	398
2013	495	12,940	86,271	129	843,254	415
2014	520	13,846	95,242	142	978,963	431
2015	538	14,680	98,201	152	990,126	444
2016	558	15,237	99,990	158	1,016,428	439

Source: Abrasce. www.abrasce.com.br/monitoramento/evolucao-do-setor.

(Table 6.17). The malls represent an industry of great economic importance and have had a marked impact on the social life of the cities. In the regional distribution of shopping malls, 30 are concentrated in the Southeast, 95 in the South, and 88 in the Northeast. The State of São Paulo has 180 malls and the city of São Paulo alone has 54, followed by the city of Rio de Janeiro with 39.[101] Despite the importance of these mall projects in Brazil, the areas offered by shopping centers in the country are modest compared to other countries. If we consider the gross leasable area per inhabitant (in square meters), Brazil's position is very small. In the United States it is 1,872; 1,127 in Canada; 590 in Australia; 303 in Japan; with values of just over 200 in France, South Africa, and Spain; and 81 in Mexico compared to just 40 in Brazil.[102]

The city also represents centers of culture production, from art to music, and from movies to stage plays.[103] Although the culture can be

[101] Information obtained from Abras – Associação Brasileira de Supermercados. Accessed 11 December 2017, at: www.abras.com.br/economia-e-pesquisa/ranking-abras/os-numeros-do-setor/.

[102] Abrasce (Associação Brasileira de Shopping Centers). https://abrasce.com.br/monitoramento/publicacoes-de-pesquisas.

[103] Paula Abreu and Claudino Ferreira, "Apresentação: a cidade, as artes e a cultura." *Revista Crítica de Ciências Sociais* 67 (2003), pp. 3–6.

produced and consumed in any territorial space, cities represent the main centers of production and supply of such services, and today bring an important differential to many cities of the world. Population density provides a scale for the multiplicity of cultural manifestations that characterize some medium and large cities in the world. And part of the prestige of a great metropolis is its ability to offer a wide range of cultural options to its inhabitants – libraries, permanent or temporary exhibitions, music of all categories, along with live theater productions and cinemas – and tourists can be attracted by the offer of cultural activities. There are even outdoor public events such as the Carnival in Rio de Janeiro and Salvador, the religious festival of the Círio de Nazaré in Belém do Pará, the Folklore Festival of Parintins in Amazonas, the washing of the Bonfim staircases in Salvador, the feasts of São João in the Northeast, the Party of the Peon de Boiadeiro of Barretos in the State of São Paulo, and the International Literary Festival of Paraty in Rio de Janeiro. The city of São Paulo attracts thousands of tourists annually through its cultural events, its museums – several of international quality – its plays, its musical spectacles, and even its Gay Pride Parade.[104] In addition, it attracts millions of visitors from the interior for so-called "shopping tourism," which highlights the commercial corridor of Rua Vinte and Cinco de Março. Minas Gerais also attracts national and international tourists to its Baroque architectural ensemble. Rio de Janeiro attracts thousands of tourists to Carnival. They are different cultural manifestations, reflecting a cultural diversity of Brazil.

Even in culinary terms, the cities have the grand restaurants, which support a large number of workers and attract numerous well-to-do patrons from all over the nation. In terms of popular participation, however, it has been sports and popular musical shows which have drawn the most crowds. Brazil has been the scene of an explosion of national and international live music shows, held in large open spaces such as the Rockin in Rio and Lollapalooza and even in football fields, new or refurbished, some of which were built for the world cup held in Brazil in 2012.[105] There are varied musical shows, many of international

---

[104] According to estimates, the gay parade of São Paulo was attended by more than 3 million people in 2018.

[105] The most commonly used football stadium for shows is the Allianz Parque in the city of São Paulo, recently rebuilt for use as both a soccer field and a stage for big shows. According to news reports, Allianz Parque was considered the second largest arena in the world for shows and events in 2016, just behind MetLife in New Jersey. There would be 27 football matches and 14 shows. See *Veja*. Accessed 16 December 2017, at: https://veja.abril.com.br/blog/ra dar/allianz-parque-e-a-segunda-arena-com-mais-shows-e-eventos-do-mundo/

music, as well as Brazilian music of all genres, including country music. Although these shows spread throughout Brazil, São Paulo and Rio de Janeiro have become the main centers of the international shows. The most traditional is the Rock in Rio, begun in 1985, with ten consecutive days of musical events, in an area of 250,000 square meters, attracting an audience of 1.4 million people.[106] São Paulo has several large shows such as the Lollapalooza, created in the United States, and with a São Paulo edition that gathers 190,000 people in two days of presentation at the Autodrome of Interlagos. In 2016, for example, São Paulo received 423 international artists, in 468 shows and 17 international festivals. Among the attractions were the Rolling Stones. There were more than 20 mega-events, with more than 10,000 people and 75 with a public participation of between 2,000 and 10,000 people. Rock, metal, indie, pop, and jazz predominated.[107] In addition to Rio de Janeiro and São Paulo, there are other very active centers, such as Salvador, which hosts the Salvador Summer Festival. In 2014, the festival boasted a total audience of 120,000 people, which included tourists from all over Brazil attracted by the Northeastern summer.[108] In fact, Brazil occupies the second place in Latin America in the live music market, behind Mexico.[109]

But beyond these great gatherings and shows, there is an active, permanent body of cultural services that are offered by cities of greater or smaller size. A survey of culture carried out by the IBGE[110] reveals the strong

---

[106] According to the organizers, the innovations include the biggest stage in the world at the time, and for the first time the audience of a great show was illuminated. The audience was beginning to become part of the show and thus was born the biggest music festival in the world. There have been 17 shows since 1985, featuring 1,588 artists, generating 182,000 jobs, with 11 million fans online. See Rock in Rio. Accessed 16 December 2017, at: http://rockinrio.com/rio/pt-BR/historia

[107] 2016. O mercado de shows internacionais. Accessed 16 December 2107, at: www.rockinchair.com.br/especial/2016/.

[108] Governo do Brasil. Accessed 16 December 2017, at: www.brasil.gov.br/turismo/2014/09/brasil-ocupa-segundo-lugar-no-mercado-de-eventos-musicais. This festival was estimated to have created 21,000 direct and indirect jobs.

[109] During Rock in Rio in 2013, hotel occupancy in the city of Rio de Janeiro was 90%. Of the 7 million people who attended the shows, 46% were from other states. São Paulo, the biggest concert destination in Brazil, also brings the benefits of great music shows. For the second Lollapalooza, in 2013, which attracted 167,000 people, 58% did not live in the city. Governo do Brasil. Accessed at: www.brasil.gov.br/turismo/2014/09/brasil-ocupa-segundo-lugar-no-mercado-de-eventos-musicais.

[110] IBGE, *Perfil dos estados e dos municípios brasileiros: cultura 2014: coordenação de população e indicadores sociais* (Rio de Janeiro: IBGE, 2015), p. 9. Since the 1970s, UNESCO established a new conceptual framework for the production of cultural statistics, based on the original concept of the culture industry, incorporating the dimension of

influence of open TV, present in almost all Brazilian municipalities, and the existence of a public library in almost every one of them as well. The internet is available in almost two-thirds of cities and towns, having grown 44% between 2006 and 2014. Cultural centers are less common than are book-stores, news-stands, and theaters – being present in only the largest cities. Surprisingly, cinemas are relatively rare in most communities, and shopping centers exist in only 7% of the cities. On the other hand, most communities have handicraft groups, cultural organizations, and dance and band activities. There are theater groups in 43% of the municipalities and orchestras in 22% of them.

Clearly, there is a direct relationship between the size of the city and the capacity to maintain culture activities and support the existence of cultural groups. In addition, we can see the high correlation between the size of the municipalities and the existence of all types of festivals and cultural production. Only 20% of municipalities of up to 50,000 inhabitants have councils for heritage preservation; this percentage doubles for municipalities with more than 100,000 inhabitants and triples for those with more than 500,000 inhabitants. Also, it is medium and large municipalities with film and video shows which are able to support audio visual production. Almost half of the municipalities with more than 500,000 inhabitants and capitals fall into this category.[111]

With the expectation of having a better life, migrants have flocked to the cities. They came primarily to find work for themselves and a better education for their children. The rapidly growing cities, with their major building activities and expanding industries, offered them jobs. The more abundant schools provided their children with education, and the easy availability of health professionals gave them a better life. Fairs and shopping centers, then malls, all added to the expanding horizons of these migrants. Although they faced poor housing and long travel times, and an even higher incidence of crime than existed in their rural back-grounds, the costs were worth it. Social mobility was only possible by

---

historical heritage. In the interaction with their member countries, they redefined the field of culture, incorporating the language as an intangible heritage to be preserved as a good of humanity, as well as singular and expressive celebrations and artistic manifestations for a given community. See Leandro Valioti and Ana Letícia do Nascimento Fialho, eds., *Atlas econômico da cultura brasileira: metodologia* (2 vols.; Porto Alegre: UFRGS/CEGO, 2017); Ministério da Cultura, *Cultura em números: anuário de estatísticas culturais* (2nd edn; Brasília: MinC, 2010); Rodrigo Manoel Dias da Silva, "As políticas culturais brasileiras na contemporaneidade: mudanças institucionais e modelos de agenciamento," *Revista Sociedade e Estado* 29.1 (2014), pp. 199–204; Antonio Albino Canelas Rubim, ed., *Políticas Culturais no Governo Lula* (Salvador: Edufba, 2010).

[111] IBGE, Pesquisa de Informações Básicas Estaduais, Cultura, 2014, pp. 18, 22, 81.

moving to the city, which offered the income and educational opportunities to move up in the class structure. For women there was greater participation in the labor force and a more independent life, and the city itself with its restricted housing would also lead to changes in family size and organization. The city was changed by its migrants, just as the migrants were changed by the city.

7

Stratification and Mobility

Brazil is one of the most unequal societies in the world. This statement is even more emphatic when we consider just the industrial countries. None of these countries presents indicators of inequality similar to Brazil. In 2014, the top 10% of the population controlled 44% of salaried income and the bottom 50% accounted for just 16%.[1] How severe this distortion is can be seen from comparable data for Canada in 2014. There the top 10% of the population accounted for only a quarter of the national income and the poorest half for 27%. In a typical Scandinavian country like Sweden in 2014, the richest decile controlled just 20% of the national income and the poorest half accounted for a third.[2] Brazil has an estimated GINI coefficient of inequality calculated from the annual household surveys (PNAD)[3] of 51.4, compared to Sweden, with just half that rate (or a GINI of 25.2). In this, Brazil is like most Latin American countries with GINIs in the 50s, which compare with indexes in the upper 20s to lower 40s for most advanced industrial countries (see Graph 7.1).[4]

---

[1] UNU/WIDER World Income Inequality Database WIID3.4, released in January 2017, Table WID2. Accessed at: www.wider.unu.edu/database/world-income-inequality-database-wiid34.
  For Brazil, the latest 2006 PNAD survey gives 16% for the bottom, and 50% and 45% for the top 10%. IBGE, Sidra, Table 297.

[2] IBGE, Sidra, Table WID2a1. Ipea lists Brazil's top 10% as owning 47% of total income in 1981 and 46% in 2002. Ipeadata, "Renda – parcela apropriada por 10% mais ricos (% renda total)."

[3] Usually inequality studies in Brazil are based on PNAD (*Pesquisa Nacional por Amostra de Domicílios*), which includes in the questionnaire income from work, pensions, retirement income, donations, transfers from social programs, rent, and interest from financial investment and dividends. IBGE, PNAD, *Dicionário de variáveis da PNAD 2015*. Accessed at: https://ww2 .ibge.gov.br/home/estatistica/populacao/trabalhoerendimento/pnad2015/microdados.shtm.

[4] As a recent World Bank study concluded, "According to household surveys, the richest 10% of individuals receive between 40% and 47% of total income in most Latin American societies, while the poorest 20% receive only 2% to 4%. These differences are substantially higher than in OECD countries, Eastern Europe, and most of Asia. Moreover, the most

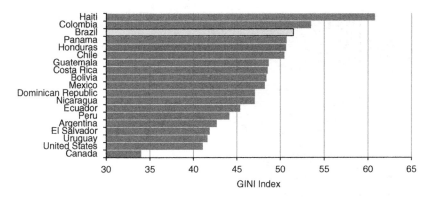

GRAPH 7.1 World Bank Estimates of GINI Index of Inequality for Western Hemisphere Countries *c*.2014
Source: https://data.worldbank.org/indicator/SI.POV.GINI?year_high_desc=false, data updated 30 January 2019. The data for the United States and Canada are for 2013.

Although the GINI for Brazil is not as extreme as in Haiti, or even Colombia, other measures suggest that the inequality is even more pronounced. When data from the income tax returns are used, which more accurately captures income derived from rents, interest, and dividends as well as salaries,[5] Brazil is even more skewed toward the top earners than in almost any other country. When we compare the pre-taxed total income of the top 1% of income earners and the total of national wealth which they gain, it is evident that Brazil, even as late as 2010, stands out as the country with the most extreme inequality in the modern world. In Brazil, the top 1% control 28% of the wealth, compared with Denmark, where the same group holds just 6% (see Graph 7.2).

Even when government income transfers such as pensions and conditional cash transfer programs are included, this finding of stable and extremely high inequality is found. The best data on combined salaries and government

distinctive attribute of Latin American income inequality is the unusually large concentration of income at the very top of the distribution . . . Even the most equal countries in Latin America (Costa Rica and Uruguay) have significantly higher levels of income inequality." David de Ferranti, Guillermo E. Perry, Francisco Ferreira, and Michael Walton, *I Inequality in Latin America: Breaking with History?* (Washington, DC World Bank, 2004), Summary 3. For the lasts GINI indices for Latin America, see Figures 2-3, 2-10.

[5] Traditionally the studies on the distribution of income were made on the basis of the PNAD surveys which have been carried out in Brazil annually since the mid-1970s. To these annual surveys were added the data from the decennial censuses. Recently, several studies were undertaken based on annual Income Tax declarations. These are usually more accurate, particularly for the top of the income scale, and have resulted in studies showing higher ratios of concentration than were found for the PNAD and census-based studies alone.

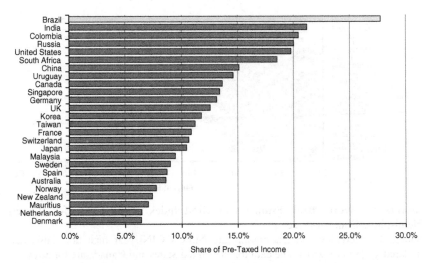

GRAPH 7.2 Share of Pre-Taxed Income for Richest Top 1% for 2010
Source: http://wid.world/data/.

transfers, as well as a host of economic and social indicators, come from the
PNAD national household surveys. These surveys are among the largest such
household surveys undertaken in the world and have been carried out on
a systematic basis for the past forty years. Combining the salary data from
these surveys and income from tax returns (*Declaração Anual de Ajuste do
Imposto de Renda da Pessoa Física* – DIRPF), the GINI for adults between
2006 and 2012 was around 0.70, an extraordinarily high rate and well above
the salary alone rate, which was in the lower 0.50s in the same period.[6]
Equally, the share of total salary and income of Brazil going to the top 1%
remained stable at a quarter of the total income from 2006 to 2013.[7]

It would appear that this high level of inequality is not new. Inequality
levels have been relatively stable for Brazil since at least the 1930s, in contrast
to other countries where reforms or economic crises have led to some
significant fluctuations.[8] This can be seen in a comparison of Brazil with

[6] Marcelo Medeiros and Pedro H. G. F. Souza, "A Estabilidade da desigualdade no Brasil entre
2006 e 2012: resultados adicionais," *Pesquisa e Planejamento Econômico* 46.3 (2016), p. 21,
Table 1.
[7] Medeiros and Souza, "A Estabilidade," p. 20, Graph 2.
[8] While comparisons are difficult due to changing tax collections, taxable rates, and estimates of
gross income and wealth in earlier periods, a recent study suggest relative stability of shares of
total income for the top 1% going back to the 1930s. See Pedro H. G. F. de Souza, "Top
Incomes in Brazil, 1933–2012: A Research Note." SSRN, 11 December 2014. Accessed
10 June 2017, at: http://dx.doi.org/10.2139/ssrn.2537026 and accessed 10/6/2017.

Table 7.1 *Average Fraction of Income and Capital Gains of the*
1% Richest Persons, 1930–2015

Country	Quinquennium		
	1930–1935	1970–1975	2010–2015
Brazil	24.3	24.6	23.2
United States	16.9	9.2	20.7
Sweden	12.3	5.8	8.8

Source: Souza, "A desigualdade vista do topo: a concentração de renda entre os ricos no Brasil, 1926–2013," (2016), p. 249, Table 5.

Sweden and the United States in three quite different time periods. In the 1930s, 1970s, and 2010s, Brazil's top 1% of wealth holders controlled almost an identical quarter of total national income and capital. Sweden and the United States by contrast saw rates change over time, going from high rates in the pre-World War II period to quite low rates post-war due to massive changes in education of their populations and the introduction of the modern welfare state with high taxes and state redistribution of income. As Piketty and others have shown,[9] the most recent period has seen a rise of these shares from their lows in the 1970s, but even the United States has not reached the level of Brazil in the current period (see Table 7.1). While the first two decades of the current century saw the bottom half of the population grow the fastest and increase their share of total wealth to 13.9%, the top 1% also increased their share to 28.3% of wealth from all sources of income.[10]

It is not easy to understand the cause of this extraordinary disparity between Brazil and other countries of its size, type of organization, and even historical evolution. Since the 1970s, there has been an intense debate in the country about the cause for this concentration of wealth, and many have used accepted international models to study the question. But such instruments of analysis only permit us to understand the distribution of current income, and above all of salaries. In this area, of course, education

---

[9] Thomas Piketty, *Capital in the 21st Century* (Cambridge, Mass.: Harvard University Press, 2014). See also Facundo Alvaredo, Anthony B. Atkinson, Thomas Piketty, and Emmanuel Saez, "The Top 1 Percent in International and Historical Perspective," *Journal of Economic Perspectives* 27.3 (2013), pp. 3–20 and Branko Milanovic, "Global Inequality and the Global Inequality Extraction Ratio: The Story of the Past Two Centuries," *Explorations in Economic History* 48 (2011), pp. 494–506.

[10] Marc Morgan, "Extreme and Persistent Inequality: New Evidence for Brazil Combining National Accounts, Surveys and Fiscal Data, 2001–2015," Working Paper 12, World Wealth and Income Database, 2017, p. 47, Table 2.

proves to be the fundamental variable. But if the question of education is so fundamental in explaining current inequality, may we not ask another question, about why the distribution of education remains so unequal despite all the massive changes which have occurred. In fact, until the 1930s, the offer of an education was far more limited than today and yet can we say that inequality was worse in 1930 then now? Why has it been that since then, despite major industrialization and the modernization of the economy, there has been little improvement in the distribution of income and resources among the Brazilian population who now have obtained much higher levels of education?[11]

While it is impossible to provide a definitive answer to such questions, we can offer some considerations which may perhaps help us to understand the characteristics which defined the evolution of this country and contributed to its extraordinary inequality. In the first place, we know that until the beginning of the nineteenth century land was given out in only great extensions and its possession represented a clear indication of power. In these large landholdings there was an enormous disparity between their size and their level of effective economic occupation. Slaves were also the primary workers. At the margin of this universe of great estates was formed a world of small subsistence farmers, many of whom were squatters or held only precarious title to the land. These subsistence farmers represented the majority of the population.

In the middle decades of the nineteenth century, with abolition of slavery and the abandonment of the plantations by the ex-slaves, European immigrants were introduced as their replacements, and this led to an alteration in the rules of access to land. The colonial *sesmaria* forms of extensive land grants would be replaced by a modern land market. But the Land Law of 1850 which regulated this new form of access to land made it difficult for immigrants to purchase property.[12] These free workers were brought to serve as salaried workers in the existing commercial agriculture, especially in coffee, and not to become small independent farmers.

[11] Recent data correlating income groups and years of schooling show that Brazil has consistently improved for all age groups over time in average years of schooling, even for the bottom deciles of income. Moreover, its overall GINI index of years of schooling and income by 1990 finally declined below the Latin American average. Nevertheless, income inequality levels have changed little. For education and income distribution data, see Ferranti, et al., *Inequality in Latin America*, pp. 419–420, 422, Tables A22, A23, and A25. See also the age breakdown in more detail in the supplementary educational/age and GINI tables for this volume Accessed at: www.depeco.econo.unlp.edu.ar/cedlas/wb/.

[12] Warren Dean, "Latifundia and Land Policy in Nineteenth-Century Brazil." *Hispanic American Historical Review* 51.4 (1971), pp. 606–625.

There were colonies of small freehold farmers established in the south of the country, with a well-defined colonization policy based on the granting of small properties. In this Southern region there arose a society with characteristics distinct from the other areas of Brazil. But this small farmer migration was limited, local, and constantly attacked by the large landed elite, who were more concerned with replacing slaves with free landless workers than promoting land sales to small farmers. Given the continental size of the country, the majority of Brazilian territory consisted of empty unclaimed state land, which was settled by poor squatters and then gradually appropriated by the great landowners, often in an illegal manner. There was never in Brazil, except with the southern agricultural colonies, a generalized distribution of land to small landowners who could effectively exploit the land, as would occur in the west of the United States. Nor was there ever a violent or organized form of agrarian reform, or any abrupt break in the power of the elite, which could have altered the structure of land ownership. Even when the occupation of land was extended in the twentieth century and commercial agriculture expanded and became generalized throughout Brazil, the agrarian structure remained one of the most concentrated in the world.

The technological revolution in Brazilian commercial agriculture, which has become one of the most productive in the world in the last twenty years, involved only a minority of some 5 million rural properties in Brazil. What some authors call a "bifurcated" process of agrarian development is occurring. This means that there is a dynamic minority of highly productive, capitalized, and globalized agricultural producers, and a majority of farmers who are engaged in subsistence or minimal agricultural production, who now and in the future depend on public subsidies through income transfers to remain in the rural world.[13]

During the last few decades there has been an intense process of what the government called "agrarian reform," but that could be more appropriately classified as a process of colonization, involving a total area of 88 million hectares, which represents about a quarter of the total land area in agriculture in the country and involved 19% of all the farm families in the 2006 agricultural census. But, despite this "reform," the concentrated agrarian structure persists. As measured by the GINI Index, land distribution remains

---

[13] Antonio Marcio Buiainain, Eliseu Alves, J. M. da Silveira, and Zander Navarro, "Sete teses sobre o mundo rural brasileiro," in Buainain et al., eds., *O mundo rural no Brasil do século 21: a formação de um novo padrão agrário e agrícola* (Brasília: Embrapa, 2014), pp. 1159–1182. On the recent development of Brazilian agriculture, see Klein and Luna, *Feeding the World*.

virtually unchanged since the first agricultural census in 1920. Since then its value has remained in the mid-0.80s. Although over time there was a change in median farm size, there was little change in the distribution of land ownership. From 1920 to 2017, the GINI index of distribution of land remained virtually unchanged, fluctuating between 0.832 and 0.859 (see Table 7.2).[14]

While this is very high by world standards, it is close to the norm for most Latin American countries – the world region with the highest inequality in land distribution.[15] There was variation by crop, with the GINI index for basic food crops being much lower than the average, whereas it was the highest in such commercial export crops as soybeans and above all in sugar (0.88).[16] Despite this great inequality in land ownership, actual production of commercial agricultural products is not confined to the largest estates. There is a significant participation of small and medium-sized farms in commercial agricultural production despite the increasing importance of large farms of 1,000 hectares or more. Thus, of the most wealth-producing farms of Brazil in 2006, some 20% were in the 5–20 hectare range, 37% in the 20–100 hectare size group, and 22% in the 100–500 hectare range. In total, 79% of the wealthiest farms were under 500 hectares.[17] Nevertheless, the majority of farms can be said to be subsistence farms whose owners survive only through retirement pensions and other income transfers from the federal government. In 2006, three-quarters of the farms contained less than 2 hectares and these farms earned just half of a minimum salary and accounted for just 3% of gross value agricultural production (see Table 7.3).

Aside from historical distortions of land ownership, slavery and its substitution by European immigrants is another process of colonization and economic exploitation which has left its traces – difficult to measure, but worth discussing. Brazil was occupied and commercially exploited on the base of slave labor, which existed in all parts of the country, not only in the areas of commercial export agriculture and mining, but also in production dedicated to the internal market. Some small groups of free persons, especially blacks and mulattos, were inserted into the labor market. But free persons under slavery were mostly concentrated in rudimentary agriculture, essentially dedicated to subsistence – selling, if possible, excess production

[14] See Bastiaan Philip Reydon, "Governança de terras e a questão agrária no Brasil," in Buainain et al., eds., *O mundo rural no Brasil do século 21*, p. 736, Table 3.

[15] Dietrich Vollrath, "Land Distribution and International Agricultural Productivity," *American Journal of Agricultural Economics* 89.1 (2007), p. 204, Table 1.

[16] Luiz A. Martinelli, Rosamond Naylor, Peter M. Vitousek, and Paulo Moutinho, "Agriculture in Brazil: Impacts, Costs, and Opportunities for a Sustainable Future," *Current Opinion in Environmental Sustainability* 2.4–5 (2010), p. 433, Table 1.

[17] Steven M. Helfand, Vanessa da Fonseca Pereira and Wagner Lopes Soares, "Pequenos e médios produtores na agricultura brasileira: situação atual e perspectivas," in Buainain et al., *O mundo rural no Brasil do século 21*, p. 543, Table 1.

Table 7.2 *Number of Farms, by Size, in Hectares and GINI Index of Inequality, Censuses 1920–2017*

Number of Farms by Size of Area

Year	Total	GINI Index	Less than 10 ha	10–100 ha	less than 100 ha	100–1,000 ha	1,000+ ha
1920	648,153	0.832	–	–	463,879	157,959	26,045
1940	1,940,589	0.833	654,557	975,441	1,629,995	243,818	27,822
1950	2,064,642	0.844	710,934	1,052,557	1,763,491	268,159	32,628
1960	3,337,769	0.842	1,495,020	1,491,415	2,986,435	314,831	32,480
1970	4,924,019	0.844	2,519,630	1,934,392	4,454,022	414,746	36,874
1975	4,993,252	0.855	2,601,860	1,898,949	4,500,809	446,170	41,468
1980	5,159,851	0.857	2,598,019	2,016,774	4,614,793	488,521	47,841
1985	5,801,809	0.857	3,064,822	2,160,340	5,225,162	517,431	50,411
1995	4,859,865	0.856	2,402,374	1,916,487	4,318,861	469,964	49,358
2006	5,175,636	0.872	2,477,151	1,971,600	4,448,751	424,288	47,578
2017	4,994,694	0.859	2,543,778	1,979,915	4,523,693	420,136	50,865

Area of Farms Grouped by Size Categories, in Hectares

Year	Total	Average Size	Less than 10 ha	10–100 ha	less than 100 ha	100–1,000 ha	1,000+ ha
1920	175,104,675	270	–	–	15,708,314	48,415,737	110,980,624
1940	197,720,247	104	1,993,439	33,112,160	36,005,599	66,184,999	95,529,649
1950	232,211,106	112	3,025,372	35,562,747	38,588,119	75,520,717	118,102,270
1960	249,862,142	75	5,592,381	47,566,290	53,158,671	86,029,455	110,314,016

(continued)

Table 7.2 (continued)

Area of Farms Grouped by Size Categories, in Hectares

Year	Total	Average Size	Less than 10 ha	10–100 ha	less than 100 ha	100–1,000 ha	1,000+ ha
1970	294,145,466	60	9,083,495	60,069,704	69,153,199	108,742,676	116,249,591
1975	323,896,082	65	8,982,646	60,171,637	69,154,283	115,923,043	138,818,756
1980	364,854,421	71	9,004,259	64,494,343	73,498,602	126,799,188	164,556,629
1985	374,924,929	65	9,986,637	69,565,161	79,551,798	131,432,667	163,940,463
1995	353,611,246	73	7,882,194	62,693,585	70,575,779	123,541,517	159,493,949
2006	333,680,037	64	7,798,777	62,893,979	70,692,756	112,844,186	150,143,096
2017	350,253,330	70	63,783,346	112,029,612	175,812,958	166,451,258	350,253,330

Source: Dados Básicos: IBGE – Censo Agropecuário- Sidra Table 263, 6710; GINI: IBGE, Censo Agropecuário, 2006. Brasil, Grandes Regiões e Unidades da Federação, 2009, p. 109; Sczmrecsányi (2007), and Hoffmann and Ney (2010).

Table 7.3 *Distribution of the Annual Gross Value of Agricultural Production, by Classes of Minimum Monthly Salaries, Agricultural Census of 2006*

Minimum Monthly Salary	Farms*	Percentage	Gross Value of Production	Percentage	Gross Value of Production /Farms (Value)	Gross Value of Production / Farms in Minimum Monthly Salaries
0–2	2,904,769	66.0%	5,518,045,129	3.3%	1,900	0.52
2–10	995,750	22.6%	16,688,283,807	10.1%	16,760	4.66
10–200	472,702	10.7%	58,689,461,376	35.5%	124,157	34.49
200+	27,306	0.6%	84,727,015,692	51.2%	3,102,872	861.91
Total	4,400,527	100.0%	165,522,806,004	100.0%	37,614	10.45

Source: Eliseu Alves, Geraldo da Silva Souza, and Daniela de Paula Rocha. "Lucratividade da agricultura." *Revista de Política Agrícola* 21.2 (2012), p. 48.
* Only farms which declared Gross Value of Production are considered.
Source: IBGE Censo 2006 (data updated to 2010). Minimum monthly salary = R$ 300. IBGE (2012).

only on the local markets. There was little economic integration among the various areas of occupied territory, which had only precarious roads.[18]

With the abolition of slavery in 1888, most of the former slaves were incorporated into the labor market as wage workers or turned toward subsistence agriculture. But, initially, the skilled occupations and the major commercial activities, especially in agriculture, went to the European immigrants who arrived in massive numbers in the last two decades of the nineteenth century. The Afro-Brazilians from the slave era remained at the lowest levels of the free labor market in the post-slavery era for most of the first half of the twentieth century. Even the industrial process, which was firmly implanted by the 1930s, depended initially for a greater part of its labor force on European immigrant workers and their descendants, and only later on were native rural workers attracted to the urban centers.[19] Much of this history helps to explain the variations in opportunities by color as well as class within Brazil.

[18] For an overview of slavery in Brazil, see Herbert S. Klein and Francisco Vidal Luna, *Slavery in Brazil* (Cambridge: Cambridge University Press, 2010).

[19] There are few specific studies on the transition of the freed slaves in 1888 and their immediate insertion in the labor market, either in the coffee plantations, in supplementary activities, in subsistence agriculture, or their integration into urban life. On the sociological aspects of this transition, see the seminal work of Florestan Fernandes, *A integração do negro na sociedade de classes* (São Paulo: Ática, 1978). See also Hebe Maria Mattos, *Das cores do silêncio* (Rio de Janeiro: Nova Fronteira, 1998).

It was not until the middle of the twentieth century that the Brazilian government finally committed itself to public education for all its citizens, long after this had become the norm in most other Latin American countries. This policy explains in large part the extraordinarily high levels of illiteracy in the country even today. What little public education was available, however, was of a reasonable quality and the poor as well as the middle classes that had access to public education usually benefited from a higher quality of teaching, especially in what were then elite public secondary schools. They then had a good chance of entering the free public universities and competing for jobs with the rich students who came from private schools.

Paradoxically, the opening up of the public educational system to the entire population would eventually lead to even greater inequalities. From the 1970s on, there was undertaken a policy of universalization of basic education, which finally reached its goal of complete coverage by the last decade of the twentieth century. But this universalization did not signify equality of opportunity, since "massification" of primary and secondary education occurred at the cost of quality. This has created a bifurcated system in which the poor go to public primary and secondary schools and the rich send their children to high-quality private primary and secondary schools. In turn, these better-educated private school graduates gain a disproportionate share of entrance, via difficult entrance exams, into the free public universities, which are the best schools in the country. But the graduates of the public schools in the great majority do not obtain an education sufficient for them to pass the university entrance exams and most often end up paying for an inferior university education in poorly organized for-profit private faculties. Although there are some high-quality private institutes and university faculties, they in turn only take students who can pass the entrance examinations for the public universities. Private university graduates find themselves ill prepared for the labor market, in contrast to those who go to the free public universities and special institutes.

Thus, the Brazilian education system, as it is now constituted, although it undeniably promotes social mobility, has helped little to reduce the process of concentration of wealth. There are now quite distinct trajectories for the rich and the poor: the first receive an education comparable to first world standards; the latter, despite their universal access to primary education, are marginalized by the quality of the teaching they receive. So poor is the quality of primary public education that many students who have attended the primary grades are still defined as functional illiterates.[20] The identification

[20] Helena Sampaio, Fernando Limongi, and Haroldo Torres, "Eqüidade e heterogeneidade no ensino superior brasileiro," Núcleo de Pesquisas sobre Ensino Superior Universidade de São Paulo, Working paper 1/00 (undated); Maria Helena Guimarães de Castro, *Avaliação do*

of inequality in the access to public universities has recently resulted in the implementation of a quota system, giving students with less economic and social advantage an opportunity to enter high-quality public universities.[21]

The process of induced industrialization, which occurred from the 1930s onward, profoundly altered the productive structure of the country, modernizing the economy and provoking a dramatic movement of the population to the urban centers. Today, all parts of the nation are integrated into a market economy, which without doubt was furthered by industrialization and the expansion of the modern labor market. For the population as a whole income has risen dramatically. But, despite all these changes, the structure of wealth concentration which marks the country as one of the most unjust in the world has only modestly changed. The recent growth of the economy and the beginning of government income transfers since the late 1990s has seen the share of income and wealth going to the bottom 50% of the population increase faster than that going to the top 10%. This in turn explains the progressive reduction of the GINI in the two most recent decades. From the 1950s to 2001, the GINI fluctuated around 0.60, with no secular trend evident. But from that date there has been a slow but very steady decline to the low 0.50s by the mid-2010s (see Graph 3.3).[22] Whether this decline will continue is still not clear since we do not yet know the consequences of the profound political and economic crisis that began in the mid-2010 and which caused a sharp drop in GDP and reduced future growth prospects.

sistema educacional brasileiro: tendências e perspectivas (Brasília: INEP, 1998); Nadir Zago, "Do acesso à permanência no ensino superior: percurso de estudantes universitários de camadas populares," *Revista Brasileira de Educação* 11.32 (2006), pp. 226–237; Nilson José Machado, "Qualidade da educação: cinco lembretes e uma lembrança," *Estudos Avançados* 21.61 (2007), pp. 277–294; José Goldemberg, "O repensar da educação no Brasil," *Estudos Avançados* 7.18 (1993), pp. 65–137; Simon Schwartzman, Eunice Ribeiro Durham, and José Goldemberg, "A educação no Brasil em perspectiva de transformação," Trabalho realizado para o Projeto sobre Educação na América Latina do Diálogo Interamericano, São Paulo, June 1993. Accessed 18 November 2017, at: www.schwartzman.org.br/simon/transform.htm

[21] The system was started in 2004 at the University of Brasília, reserving 20% of the vacancies of each course for black students. Subsequently, several public entities followed the same process and the federal government instituted the quota system for all federal universities (Law 12.711 of 29 August 2012). In addition to federal universities, other state and municipal public entities are gradually adopting some quotas, privileging less-favored social groups. On this development, see Lara Vilela, Naercio Menezes-Filho, and Thiago Yudi Tachibana, "As cotas nas universidades públicas diminuem a qualidade dos alunos selecionados?" Simulações com Dados do ENEN, Insper Policy Paper 17, June 2016. The study shows that the new quota system has not had a significant impact on the average grades of those approved for admission. The reason for this result is the existence of a large pool of eligible students with good grades: poor, black, or public school graduates who were admitted under the quota system.

[22] Rodolfo Hoffmann and Régis Oliveira, "The Evolution of Income Distribution in Brazil in the Agricultural and the Non-Agricultural Sectors," *World Journal of Agricultural Research* 2.5 (2014), p. 194, Table 1.

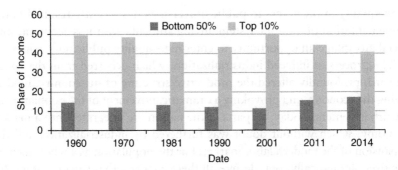

GRAPH 7.3 Changing Shares of Income of Bottom 50% and Top 10% per Capita in
Brazil, 1960–2014
Source: WIID ver. 3.4 – using mostly ECLA numbers.

Besides the historical factors that we have suggested that negatively influenced Brazilian equality, there are other issues which can be seen to have affected distribution of wealth. These are related to political power and government policies. Several studies have shown how some political policies have had perverse effects on income distribution. These include the impact of the tax system,[23] as well as the system of pensions,[24] and the pay differential between the public and private sectors in Brazil.[25] Others have argued that even when the public sector provides services which should have a positive

[23] José Roberto R. Afonso, I"IRPF e desigualdade em debate: o já revelado e o por revelar," Texto para discussão 42, Rio de Janeiro, FGB IBRE, 2014; Sérgio Wulff Gobetti and Rodrigo Octávio Orair, "Tributação e distribuição da renda no Brasil: novas evidências a partir das declarações tributárias das pessoas físicas." Working Paper 136, International Policy Centre for Inclusive Growth, Brasília, February 2016; Fernando Gaiger Silveira, "Equidade fiscal: impactos distributivos da tributação e do gasto social no Brasil," Brasília: ESAF, Tesouro Nacional, 2012; Fernando Gaiger Silveira, "Tributação, previdência e assistência sociais: impactos distributivos," PhD thesis, Universidade de Campinas, 2008; José Adrian Pintos-Payeras, "Análise da progressividade da carga tributária sobre a população brasileira," *Pesquisa e Planejamento Econômico* 40.2 (2010), pp. 153–186; Sonia Rocha, "O impacto distributivo do imposto de renda sobre a desigualdade de renda das famílias," *Pesquisa e Planejamento Econômico* 32.1 (2007), pp. 73–105.

[24] Rodolfo Hoffmann, "Desigualdade da distribuição de renda no Brasil: a contribuição de aposentadorias e pensões e de outras parcelas do rendimento domiciliar per capita," *Economia e Sociedade* 18.1 (2009), pp. 213–231; Brian Nicholson, *A previdência injusta: como o fim dos privilégios pode mudar o Brasil* (São Paulo: Geração Editorial, 2007); Silveira, "Tributação, previdência e assistência sociais."

[25] Walter Belluzzo, Francisco Amatti-Neto, and Elaine T. Pazello, "Distribuição de salários e o diferencial público-privado no Brasil." *Revista Brasileira de Economia* 59.4 (2005), pp. 511–533; Miguel N. Foguel, Indermit Gill, Rosane Mendonça, and Ricardo Paes de Barros, "The Public–Private Wage Gap in Brazil," *Revista Brasileira de Economia* 54.4 (2000), pp. 433–472.

effect on expanding the opportunities of the most vulnerable segments, and positively influencing distributional effects, the quality of these services may influence wealth inequality.[26] They argue that studies on public spending, which usually focus on the volume and composition of spending, pay little attention to expenditure results. Their studies suggest that state spending on levels of social inequality actually contribute to inequality in Brazil, proportionally contributing more than the private sector.[27]

Finally, even the industrialization of the country, which brought about increased wealth for many, did not dilute the inequality inherited from the agrarian past. Although an industrial policy was proposed by the government from the 1930s, it was the reforms made by the Kubitschek regime in the mid-1950s that were fundamental in creating a modern national market. In just a few years a major automotive and durable consumer goods industry was established which quickly supplied the basic needs of the internal market and equally supported the creation of a modern consumer market. This market needed a large sector of the population to have high income and this in turn was developed by these new industries which created a new laboring class with high-paying jobs. Government policy supported both workers and industrialists in creating this modern market, but it tended to reinforce the process of concentration. The reason is that these benefits did not expand to the entire population and the growth of this sector was so rapid that it left behind large segments of the population. Given the size of Brazil in terms of area and population, this non-modern consuming population could still exist and might even expand without affecting the overall efficiency of the industrial sector. Efficiencies of scale could be created on the basis of just the modern consuming sector of the national population. Bountiful subsidies were granted by the government to all segments involved

---

[26] Marcelo Medeiros and Pedro H. G. F. Souza, *Gasto público, tributos e desigualdade de renda no Brasil* (Rio de Janeiro: Ipea, 2013).

[27] "The decomposition of the GINI coefficient of available per capita family income shows that approximately one-third of all inequality in the country can be related to transfers and taxes that flow directly between the state and households. The two main categories of state transfers affecting inequality are wages and pensions. The other two-thirds of the inequality refer to transfers from the private sector, mostly in salaries. This remuneration, however, is less concentrated than the salaries in the public sector." Medeiros and Souza, *Gasto Público*, p. 28. These observations regarding the quality of expenditure and the type of expenditure performed can be confirmed by the recent past in Brazil. In the Lula/Dilma administration, social expenditures, such as numerous new programs or the intensification of existing programs, increased. Although there was undoubtedly an improvement in the living conditions of the most vulnerable population, there is clear evidence that little care was taken with the management and control of these programs, many with ineffective results when we consider the resources spent. Thus, even during President Dilma's second term, several programs were re-evaluated and many lost resources.

in this process, whether producers or consumers. During the military period, especially in the 1970s, this process of creating a modern labor and consumer market was expanded even more as ever more workers were incorporated into the system. Without doubt, everyone benefited from these years of growth. But it was exactly in this period that was initiated the national debate on the issue of the distribution of wealth in the country, questioning the whole Brazilian model which relied on a restriction in salary growth to subsidize this expansion.

Defenders of government policy argued that these policies had promoted major integration of new workers into the market economy and that the high income distortions were only transitory.[28] It was held that the disequilibrium between the growing demand for highly qualified professionals, still scarce in the market, was cause for the high inequalities in the salary structure. This, it was argued, would only be a transitory problem once there was an increase in the supply of more qualified workers. Opponents argued that this was not a transitory concentration provoked by distortions in the labor market but was the consequence of an economic policy implanted by the government especially in relation to the artificial control of wages carried out by the military even in years of extraordinary growth. This deliberate reduction of real wages, the so-called "wage squeeze," restricted both aggregate demand and labor costs to private enterprise. This procedure was introduced under an extremely repressive regime (which included control of union activities) and led to a significant reduction in real wages. Such measures could hardly have been implemented under an open regime and freedom of association.[29]

The crisis of the 1980s, marked by low growth and high inflation, did not reduce these distortions in income. Absolute income per capita grew little in this period and there was no redistributive process. Inflation in fact was a perverse process which caused a deterioration in all incomes, but above all those of workers who had no effective mechanism in place to protect them from this inflation. Other sources of income, particularly those related to the financial market, and even those who received very high salaries, used indexation to protect their earnings. Thus, recession and high inflation

---

[28] Langoni, *Distribuição da renda e desenvolvimento econômico do Brasil.*

[29] Albert Fishlow, "Distribuição de renda no Brasil: um novo exame," *Dados* 11 (1973), pp. 10–80. On this theme, see also Albert Fishlow, "Brazilian Size Distribution of Income." *American Economic Review* 62.1–2 (1972), pp. 391–402; Edmar Bacha and Lance Taylor, "Brazilian Income Distribution in the 1960s: 'Facts,' Model Results and the Controversy," in Lance Taylor, Edmar Lisboa Bacha, and Eliana A. Cardoso, eds., *Models of Growth and Distribution for Brasil* (New York: Oxford University Press, 1980); Lauro R. A. Ramos and José Guilherme Almeida Reis, "Distribuição da renda: aspectos teóricos e o debate no Brasil," in José Marcio Camargo and Fabio Giambiagi, eds., *Distribuição de renda no Brasil* (Rio de Janeiro: Paz e Terra, 2000), pp. 21–45.

were profoundly negative in the evolution of the absolute level of income and its distribution. In 1986, there occurred the first stabilization plan, which was capable of temporarily controlling inflation and promoting strong growth. Since this program lasted hardly one year it was incapable of permanently reversing any distributive indicator, though it did temporarily reduce income inequalities.[30]

In the 1990s, profound changes occurred in the political thinking of the ruling classes in Brazil, first with the election of Fernando Collor de Mello and particularly in the term of President Fernando Henrique Cardoso. Although economic liberalism, represented by the so-called Washington Consensus, was already well entrenched in the western world,[31] it had little affected Brazil up to that time. The short-lived Collor initiated the process of liberalization of the Brazilian economy, and in the successor-government occurred the successful stabilization *Plan Real* in 1994. The *Plan Real* contained the inflationary process that had plagued the country for decades, an inflation that often reached levels that could be considered hyperinflation, and which had a particularly negative influence on worker wages.[32] The

---

[30] There is an extensive literature on the *Plan Cruzado*, which represents a theoretical innovation in the policies of combating inflation inertia. On this experience, see Eduardo Modiano, "A Ópera dos três Cruzados: 1985–1989"; João Sayad, *Planos cruzado e real: acertos e desacertos* (Rio de Janeiro: Ipea, 2000); Maria Silva Bastos Marques, "O plano cruzado: teoria e prática," *Revista de Economia Política* 8.3 (1988), pp. 101–130; Luiz Carlos Bresser Pereira, "Inflação inercial e o plano cruzado," *Revista de Economia Política* 6.3 (1986), pp. 9–24; Edmar Bacha, "Moeda, inércia e conflito: reflexões sobre políticas de estabilização no Brasil." *Pesquisa e Planejamento Econômico* 18.1 (1988), pp. 1–16; J. M. Rego, *Inflação inercial, teoria sobre inflação e o plano cruzado* (Rio de Janeiro: Paz e Terra, 1986).

[31] The Washington Consensus represented a guideline to be followed by developing countries facing serious economic problems, particularly those needing to deal with external debt. A number of internal reforms were suggested in the sense of opening up the economy, generating a fiscal balance, and reducing the size of the state, which would allow for the adjustment of external accounts. US Treasury, the World Bank, and the IMF were the main advocates of these measures.

[32] After years of combating inflation by orthodox and heterodox methods, the *Plan Real* obtained effective results in the combating of inflation, which has remained stable for ten years. Among the extensive literature in this subject are the following: Sayad, *Planos Cruzado e Real*; Luiz Filgueiras, *História do Plano Real* (São Paulo: Boitempo Editorial, 2000); Aloizio Mercadante, ed., *O Brasil pós real: a política econômica em debate* (Campinas: Unicamp, 1997); Fabio Giambiagi and Maurício Mesquita Moreira, *A economia brasileira nos anos 90* (Rio de Janeiro: BNDES, 1990); Maria da Conceição Tavares, *Destruição não criadora* (Rio de Janeiro: Record, 1990); Gustavo Franco, *O plano real e outros ensaios* (Rio de Janeiro: Francisco Alves, 1995). Even the former Minister of Agriculture and Planning in the Military Government, and one of Brazil's most respected economists, said that the *Plan Real* was "a little gem. It was an important, and practical contribution of the Brazilian economists who participated in it. Some of them had the experiences of other stabilization programs, but it was a new concept." Despite these accolades, he would emphatically criticize the appreciation of the national currency that occurred after its implamention.

stability created by the *Plan Real* provided a breathing space for the poorest segments of the population. The end of inflation represented an end to the inflation tax which had consumed their income and it now permitted a major increase in demand in food and goods, particularly for the poorer segments of the societies.

The success of the *Plan Real* made it possible for the Fernando Henrique Government (1995–2002) to fully implement a comprehensive neoliberal program of reforms, which represented a break with the statist model that had begun with Vargas and was further emphasized during the military period. This dismantling of the interventionist state now became a full-fledged and coherent program in the administration of Fernando Henrique Cardoso. The aim was to reduce the role of the state as an active agent in the national productive structure and transform it into the regulator state responsible only for typical state activities, such as security, justice, education, and health. The production of goods now fell to the private sector. Cardoso also sought to implement an ambitious program of state reform.[33] Thus, state monopolies of oil, electricity, telecommunications, and coastal shipping were abolished and had a great impact on the Brazilian economy, one of the most closed of the world until the late 1980s.

This opening up of the Brazilian economy coincided with a succession of external crises: Mexico (1994/95), Asia (1997/98), Russia (1998), and finally a Brazilian crisis. Despite the stability promoted by the *Plan Real*, Brazil experienced yet another external balance of payments crisis. To avoid external collapse, Brazil turned to the International Monetary Fund[34] and was forced to implement harsh adjustment measures, raising interest rates,

---

Ribamar Oliveira, "Delfim Netto: plano real acentuou redução da capacidade exportadora brasileira," *Jornal Valor Econômico* (29 June 2014).

[33] Although ambitious, the plan to reform the state had partial results, even despite strong opposition to changes in the structure of the functioning of the state. Even innovative actions like the regulatory agencies, successfully deployed during the Fernando Henrique Cardoso, were subsequently distorted by the appointment of politicians to purely executive technical positions. On the reform of the state, see Valeriano Mendes Ferreira Costa, "A dinâmica Institucional da Reforma do Estado: um balanço do período FHC," in *O estado numa era de reformas: os anos FHC*. 2 vols (Brasília: Ministério do Planejamento/Pnud/OCDE, 2002), vol. 2, pp. 9–56.

[34] The worsening crisis in Brazil led to emergency aid from the IMF and developed countries. For the size of the country and size of the debt, it was feared that the deterioration of external conditions in Brazil would magnify the crisis in other emerging countries. This explains the rapidity of the agreement made in December 1998, which gave the country a credit of US$ 41.5 billion. The signed document, as always, involved compromises on the behavior of several important indicators, such as the public deficit, the need for a positive balance in current accounts, and the approval of fiscal measures which were then under discussion in Congress.

reducing expenses, and devaluing the national currency.[35] The consequence was a period of low growth (average of 2.5% per year), limiting the positive effects that the end of inflation could have on the social conditions of the country, particularly its perverse distribution structure.

Although Lula and the Workers' Party criticized the government of Fernando Henrique Cardoso, the economic policy of the Lula government followed the general guidelines established at the end of the Fernando Henrique Cardoso period. Nevertheless, it is possible to identify a slightly different general orientation evolving over eight years of the Lula government, and in fact showing some differences between his two terms. At first, there was greater rigor with inflation targets, even compromising growth. In the second term, he preserved the overall direction of economic policy, including inflation targeting, but now there was a greater concern with growth through the so-called "Growth Acceleration Program" and some scattered industrial policy measures. Unfortunately, the Growth Acceleration Program was not a coherent plan of development nor were the specific measures of industrial policy a coherent program to promote national production. All such attempts at encouraging industry would be impaired by the maintenance of an over-valued national currency, which made domestic producers less competitive.

But the Lula government did succeed in expanding social policies already initiated in the previous government, with intensification of conditional cash transfer programs and a significant increase of the minimum wage. The most important of these cash transfer programs would be the *Bolsa Família*, a consolidation of several existing programs. There were also numerous other programs created, some pre-existing, others established in the period, and several re-launched with a new name and configuration. Among the most important are the *Minha Casa Minha Vida* program for state-subsidized housing, the PRONATEC (National Program for Technical Education and Employment), the FIES (Student Financing Fund), PROUNI (University for All Program), and PRONAF (National Program for Strengthening Family Agriculture). In addition to these programs, which absorbed significant amounts of state funds, the gradual increase in the

---

[35] Although the federal government failed to achieve full success in the measures announced, much was achieved. These successes involved the regulation of administrative reform, the reform of social welfare both public and private, the creation of a Fiscal Responsibility Law, tax reform, restructuring of the Federal Tax administration (*Receita Federal*), a Multi-Year Plan and Budget of the Union, and deregulation of the fuel sector. The government also wanted to enact labor reform but faced strong opposition from the Workers' Party. In other areas, such as tax reform, although it was not really a reform, it took advantage of ordinary legislation to expand federal revenue. In the welfare area, despite strong opposition, the government obtained significant results. For detail of the Plan Fiscal Stabilization, see https://web.archive.org/web/20130309151803/www.fazenda.gov.br/portugues/ajuste/respef.asp.

minimum wage was significant, growing over two and a half times in real
terms from July 1994 (the date of the *Plan Real*) until August 2017. Most of
these programs had a positive effect in providing basic services and financial
support for the poor and indigent population. These policies, along with an
expanding economy, brought millions of workers into the formal economy
and thus increased the number of persons participating in social security. It
also succeeded in massively reducing extreme poverty (indigence) in Brazil
and expanding the middle class.

If during his second term in office Lula had already changed the course of
economic policy, becoming gradually more interventionist, less committed to
fiscal balance (particularly after the international crisis of 2008), and more
concerned with the consolidation of the ruling Workers' Party,[36] the succeeding Workers' Party government of Dilma would deepen this trend, and
would totally abandon the fiscal balance previously practiced. At the end of
the two Workers' Party governments, many of the achievements in the area
of economics and social affairs were reversed in one of the worst depressions
Brazil has ever suffered. The fiscal crisis led to a deep economic and social
malaise, resulting in a sharp drop in GDP, an extraordinary increase in
unemployment, and the collapse of the Dilma government.

The succeeding government of Michel Temer, although it achieved
some positive results, faced great difficulties in implementing fundamental reforms, particularly in the fiscal area. GDP declined sharply in 2015
and 2016, reaching a cumulative drop of 7.5% and the unemployment
rate has practically doubled in the last few years, reaching a rate of
12%, which represents more than 12 million unemployed. Fortunately,
the crisis has not led to a return to significant inflation nor has there
been a problem in the balance of payments, thanks to the extraordinary
volume of international reserves, and high interest rates, which represent
a significant cost to the country, but offer comfort for overcoming
internal and external economic crises.[37]

But the recent poor performance of the Brazilian economy compromises
the continuity of improvements in the living conditions of the population and

[36] Ever since Lula's inauguration, the Workers' Party began to develop a long-term power
project, not caring about the means necessary for its purpose, and attacking the republican
principles and creating a corruption network that involved the party itself, its main leaders
and allied parties. The lawsuits in progress have amply demonstrated this program.

[37] Despite the relative stability of its international position, Brazil has been suffering successive
reductions in the rating of the main international agencies. The high fiscal imbalance
generates a progressive increase of the ratio between public debt and GDP, reducing con-
fidence in the country's long-term economic stability. After years of systematic improvement
in these indicators, which achieved Investment Grade by 2010, the country's international
rating has gradually reduced, with now investment in Brazil being considered speculative.

in the reduction of inequalities. This has led to a dramatic retraction of the resources allocated to the main social programs, with an increasingly negative impact on inequality. In addition, the sharp decline in the investment rate, which has fallen dramatically, remaining around 15% of GDP in 2016 and 2017, also jeopardizes the future performance of the Brazilian economy. Given the decline of the GDP and the low estimates for growth in the coming years, the forecast is that the per capita income obtained in 2013 will only be reached in 2023. If predictions are confirmed, it will be a lost decade in terms of per capita income![38] This is a drastic scenario for a middle-income country with high wealth concentration (see Table 7.4).

Thus, despite a very significant recent advance in the reduction of inequalities in the past three decades, this reduction has now slowed or even reversed. Moreover, Brazil still suffers inequality not only by income class but also by residence, gender, and race. Like many countries, Brazil has strong regional disparities, which though common to even advanced industrial societies was especially pronounced in this continental country. It was argued that Brazil in the 1980s was a "Belindia."[39] But today, even as most social and demographic indices indicate a closing of regional differences in Brazil, economic indicators show far less homogeneity.

There have been some significant changes in some of the regions, but for others their growth has not significantly reduced the gap between the poorest and the richest regions. In the middle of the twentieth century, the poorest regions were the Center-West, North, and Northeast, but this changed over the next seventy or so years. The biggest change occurred in the Center-West, which by 2010 had a per capita income which equaled the richest Southeastern and South regions. Although the Northeast and North regional average per capita income increased faster than in the richest zones, the former still enjoyed less than half the income of the Southeast and the North – just 52% of that income in 2010 (see Table 7.5).

The explanation for this rapid growth of Center-West post-1950 is the massive introduction into the region of modern commercial agriculture. The gradual establishment of commercial agriculture into the region of the North suggests that it will slowly follow the Center-West out of poverty in the coming decades. The Northeast, on the other hand, seems to have less potential for

---

[38] Utilizing the estimates of the population given by IBGE (accessed at: www.ibge.gov.br/home/ estatistica/populacao/projecao_da_populacao/2013/default.shtm) as well as the estimates of GDP published by the *Banco Central* (*Focus: Relatório do Mercado*, accessed at: www .bcb.gov.br/pec/GCI/PORT/readout/R20180720.pdf. O Relatório Focus apresentada estimativas de produto apenas até 2021. The *Relatório Focus* present product estimates only until 2021. For the next two years we estimate GDP growth of 3% per year.

[39] See Bacha and Klein, *Social Change in Brazil, 1945–1985*, p. 3.

Table 7.4 Economic Performance Indicators, 2000–2016

Year	Annual GDP Variation	Rate of Inflation (IGPM – annual)	Interest Rate (Rate Year 1–12)	Primary Budget Surplus (Percentage of GDP)	Gross Debt (Percentage of GDP)	Rate of Unemployment (PAD continuous)	Rate of Investment (Percentage of GDP)	Transaction Balance (Percentage of GDP)	International Reserves (Ending Period Balance)
2016	-3.6	7.2	13.8	-2.5	77.5	12.0	15.6	-1.3	365
2015	-3.8	10.5	14.3	-1.9	71.7	9.0	16.7	-3.3	356
2014	0.5	3.7	11.8	-0.6	61.6	6.5	19.2	-4.2	363
2013	3.0	5.5	10.0	1.7	59.6	6.2	20.3	-3.0	359
2012	1.9	7.8	7.3	2.2	61.6	6.9	20.5	-3.0	373
2011	4.0	5.1	11.0	2.9	60.6		20.1	-3.0	352
2010	7.5	11.3	10.8	2.6	62.4		20.0	-3.4	289
2009	-0.1	-1.7	8.8	1.9	64.7		19.8	-1.6	238
2008	5.1	9.8	13.8	3.3	61.4		18.9	-1.8	194
2007	6.1	7.8	11.8	3.2	63.0		18.0	0.0	180
2006	4.0	3.8	13.3	3.2	64.6		16.6	1.3	86
2005	3.2	1.2	18.0	3.7	67.0		16.3	1.6	54
2004	5.8	12.4	15.8	3.7	68.0		16.8	1.8	54
2003	1.1	8.7	16.5	3.2	71.5		16.1	0.8	49
2002	3.1	25.3	25.0	3.2	76.1		17.7	-1.5	38
2001	1.4	10.4	19.0		67.3		16.8	-4.2	36
2000	4.3	10.0	15.8				17.1	-3.8	33

Source: Banco Central, IBGE, Ipeadata.

Table 7.5 *Average Household Income per Capita by Region,*
Censuses 1991, 2000, and 2010

Year	1991	2000	2010
	R$		
North	232	356	494
Northeast	178	305	459
Southeast	470	766	943
South	364	674	920
Center-West	390	679	935
Total	348	586	767
Percentages			
Northeast/Southeast	38%	40%	49%
Center-West/Southeast	83%	89%	99%

Source: DATASUS at http://tabnet.datasus.gov.br/cgi/tabcgi.exe?ibge/censo/
cnv/rendauf.def.

such growth. The expansion of the Center-West can be seen in all the statistics for the Northern and Center-Western regions, which prior to 1950 had been lightly populated and had relatively low standards of living. The Center-West accounted for only 3% of the national population in the census of 1950, but grew to 7% of the national population by 2010.[40] From 1984 to 1995, the per capita GDP of the Center-West climbed from 63% to 82% of that of the Southeastern states – this when the ratio of the Northeast per capita income remained at just over a third of that of the Southeastern region in the same period.[41] Its share of GDP went from 5.6% of the national total in 1985 to 7.1% in 1998.[42] These trends continued well into the twenty-first century. By 2013, the Center-West accounted for 9% of Brazilian GDP, and its population's per capita income was 94% of that of the Southeastern region. Already by 2006 the Center-West had achieved the second highest per capita GDP rate in Brazil ahead of the states of the Southern region.

[40] IBGE, Sidra, Censo 2010, Table 1286, and *Sinopse do Censo demográfico 2010* (Rio de Janeiro, 2011), Table 1.13
[41] Eduardo Henrique Garcia, Marcelo Rubens do Amaral, and Lena Lavinas, "Desigualdades regionais e retomada do crescimento num quadro de integração econômica," Texto para discussão 466, Rio de Janeiro, Ipea, 1997, p. 3.
[42] Antonio Braz de Oliveira e Silva and Mérida Herasme Medina, "Produto interno bruto por unidade da federação, 1985–1998," Texto para discussão 677, Brasília, Ipea, 1999, Tables 3 and 4.

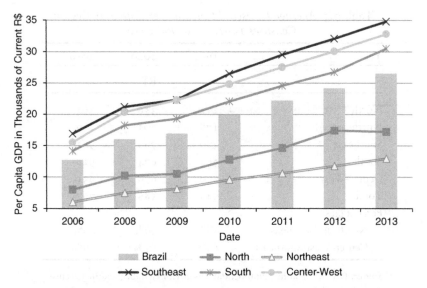

GRAPH 7.4 Per Capita GDP by Region, 2006–2013
Source: IBGE, Sidra, Table 1194.

In this same period, the Northeast lost its share of national population, declining to 28% in the census of 2010 and its share of national GDP remained at 14% in 2013 which was the same as it was in 1985. Its per capita GDP remained at 37% of the Southeastern rate, a rate not that different from the 1980s. The North and Northeast regions have grown far less rapidly in per capita income and have fallen further from the three more advanced regions (see Graph 7.4).

But this regional growth has not been uniform within the Center-West region. Although the per capita GDP of the Center-West is close to that of the Southeast and ahead of the South, the distribution of salaried incomes shows that the Center-West is only moderately more advanced than the poorer North and Northeast areas. These differences can be seen in per capita family income as measured in ratios of the minimum salary. Thus, in 2006, some 73% of the households in the Northeast made less than one minimum salary, and in the North the figure was 69%, but in the Center-West it was still 53% (see Table 7.6). The Center-West, having benefited from recent commercial development on a grand scale, still had pockets of poverty made up of small subsistence farms. By contrast, salary income was better distributed in the South and Southeast and such poor families making less than one minimum salary were just 43% and 44% respectively of the region's households (see Graph 7.6).

Table 7.6 *Cumulative Percentage of Family Income per Capita in Shares of Minimum Salaries by Region in 2006*

Minimum Salary	North	Northeast	Southeast	South	Center-West
To ¼	13%	20%	4%	4%	5%
¼–½	37%	47%	17%	16%	22%
½–1	69%	76%	44%	43%	53%
1–2	88%	91%	73%	73%	78%
2–3	94%	95%	84%	85%	87%
3–5	97%	97%	92%	93%	93%
> 5	100%	100%	100%	100%	100%

Source: IBGE, Sidra, PNAD, Table 405.

Table 7.7 *GINI Index of Household Income per Capita by Region, 1991, 2000, and 2010*

Region	1991	2000	2010
South	0.586	0.589	0.534
Southeast	0.598	0.609	0.585
Center-West	0.624	0.642	0.602
Northeast	0.659	0.668	0.628
North	0.626	0.655	0.632

Source: DATASUS. http://tabnet.datasus.gov.br/cgi/ibge/censo/cnv/gini uf.def.

These regional differences also show up in income of persons as well as families. Thus, an estimate of the GINI coefficient of inequality of income per capita shows a modest long-term decline in inequality since 1991. It also shows that the North and Northeast remain the most unequal regions – with the South and Southeast being the least unequal of Brazil's regions, as expected (see Table 7.7).

The fact that overall inequality has slowly declined over time is due to the expansion of the economy which has led to more persons entering the formal labor market and thus receiving at least one or more minimum wages in monthly salary. If there has been little change in the share going to the elite within Brazil in total wealth, in the past quarter century there has been significant change in the salary income of the poorer half of the country as poverty rates measured by wage income have significantly declined in the twenty-first century. Although there has been little change in the relative share of those living at the lowest income level (less than one minimum wage) since 2001 there has been a big growth in those earning from one to two minimum wages. These have increased their share in the population from 28% to 35%, while those earning significantly above them have lost their share of total population. By contrast, persons earning two minimum wages and above have declined from 41% of the salaried population in 2001 to just 29% in 2015. This has been accompanied by a major shift of the working class from the informal to the formal labor sector (see Table 7.8).

This slow but steady growth of the working poor has led to a long-term trend in the decline of the population below the poverty line. This trend has been recently slowed by the crisis of 2013/2014 and the subsequent depression in Brazil. Nevertheless, the changes so far have been modest, with the poverty estimate currently at 15% and with no return to the earlier 1992 level of 46% (see Graph 7.5). It would appear from the latest estimates taken during the beginning of the economic crisis of 2015–2017 that while there has been a reversal of this trend of declining poverty there has so far been only a modest increase in poverty and no change so far in extreme poverty rates.[43] But, given the unpromising estimates for product growth over the next few years, there may be a dampening of the social inclusion process in the coming decades.

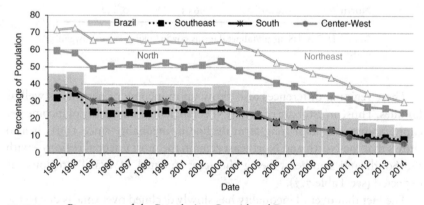

GRAPH 7.5 Percentage of the Population Considered Poor, 1992–2014
Source: IETS Elaboration of the PNAD data. www.iets.org.br/spip.php?article406.

---

[43] Calculations provided 10 September 2017 by Sonia Rocha with data of these two types of poverty from 1985 to 2015.

Table 7.8 *Persons 10 Years of Age and Older and Their Earnings Stated in Minimum Wages by Region, 2001–2015*

Wage Levels (Minimum Wages)	2001	2002	2003	2004	2005	2006	2007	2008	2009	2011	2012	2013	2014	2015
< 1/2 mw	8.2	10.7	12.3	11.8	12.0	12.5	10.9	12.0	11.9	10.4	11.4	10.7	10.5	10.4
1/2–1 mw	23.0	24.2	24.1	24.0	26.4	26.2	25.6	24.9	25.4	24.9	25.8	24.6	25.0	25.8
1–2 mw	27.7	27.6	26.9	29.6	29.6	30.8	31.4	31.7	32.5	33.5	33.6	34.4	33.0	34.6
2–3 mw	13.7	13.1	13.5	11.1	11.1	11.5	12.4	12.4	11.4	13.5	11.4	14.0	14.1	12.2
3–5 mw	12.3	11.1	11.2	11.8	10.4	8.6	9.5	9.8	9.9	8.9	10.2	8.1	9.2	8.8
5–10 mw	9.1	8.3	7.2	7.5	6.8	7.0	6.8	6.1	5.8	6.1	5.2	5.5	5.7	5.6
10–20 mw	4.1	3.4	3.3	3.1	2.6	2.4	2.6	2.4	2.3	2.1	1.8	2.0	1.9	1.9
20+ mw	1.9	1.7	1.5	1.2	1.0	0.9	0.9	0.9	0.8	0.7	0.6	0.7	0.7	0.6
Total	100.0	100.0	100.0	100.0	100.0	100.0	100.0	100.0	100.0	100.0	100.0	100.0	100.0	100.0

Source: IBGE, Sidra, PNAD, Table 1860.

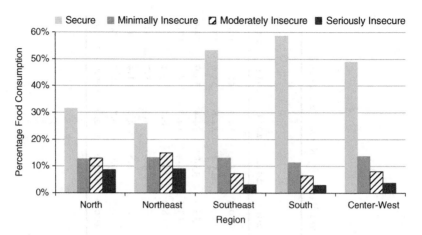

GRAPH 7.6 Household Food Consumption by Region, 2004
Source: IBGE, Sidra, PNAD, Table 2998.

But variation in income and wealth by region is still significant despite these trends. This same variation in wealth can also be seen by regional residence in a survey of food consumption carried out by the government in 2004, which found that only 43% of Brazilian households had food security, that is that they could satisfy all their calorific needs. But there were sharp differences by region, with the North and Northeast well below this rate, and the three regions of the South, Southeast, and Center-West well above the national figures (see Graph 7.6). But, if these scarcities still exist, it is not for lack of national food production, but rather from economic restraints on poor consumers who cannot buy the available products.

With higher than normal indices of poverty, the North and Northeast regions also had until recently a much poorer quality of housing stock. As late as the 2001 household survey, for example, only 67% of the homes in the Northeast had an adequate water supply compared to 97% in the Southern states. Internal plumbing was indicated in just 78% of the Northeastern region's urban and rural homes but accounted for over 90% of the homes in every other region.[44] Only in adequate electrical supply were there close ratios – 89% had adequate electricity in their homes in the former zone and well over 96% to 99% in all other regions.[45]

But these indices have improved everywhere in the recent period. By the time of the household survey of 2015, some 99% of homes in all regions had electricity, with the outlier being the North, where the figure was only 98%. Indoor plumbing was now available for 95% of the homes even in the North

---

[44] IBGE, Sidra, PNAD, Tables 1955, 1956, and 1957.   [45] IBGE, Sidra, PNAD, Table 1959.

and Northeast and 99% of the homes in all other regions.[46] The few differences in regional housing quality now are in sanitation and such advanced items as computers. While 91% of urban homes in the Southeast in 2015 are connected to a municipal waste system, the figure in the Northeast is only 49% of urban homes so connected. Moreover, 19% of urban homes in the Northeast still have primitive outhouses; in the Southeast the figure is just 2%.[47] By contrast, 93% of Brazilian homes in 2015 had telephones, with only modest regional differences. As for computers, over half of the Southeastern homes had computers, while only 30% had them in the Northeast.[48]

Urban living conditions are also considerably worse in the Northeastern capital cities. This we examined in detail in Chapter 6. But it is worth stressing that this is a major problem in all urban areas regardless of region. While some of the metropolitan regions of the Northeast, like Belém, Salvador, and Recife, had a large share of their population living in such substandard houses, the metropolitan regions of Rio de Janeiro and São Paulo had a lower proportion of such housing. Although these latter two metropolitan regions had fewer such clusters of poor housing, they were the largest in absolute terms of people living in substandard households, which numbered more than 2 million people alone in the São Paulo metropolitan area and another 1.7 million in Rio de Janeiro (see Table 6.8).

While there remain significant regional differences in wealth and housing, in most basic indices of health and education the regional gap is closing rapidly, especially in the past two decades. Despite this dramatic improvement in standard of living and the provision of public services in the poorest regions, the continued failure to catch up economically to the rest of the nation made the Northeast a major exporter of population.[49] The Northeast accounted for 44% of the poor persons in the country in the 1985 census and this increased to 56% in 2015.[50] By contrast, the Southern region contained 14% of the national population in 2010 but accounted for only 11% of those listed as being poor in Brazil in 2015.[51] This explains the decline of the Northeast share of national

---

[46] IBGE, Sidra, PNAD, Tables 1955, 1957, and 1959.   [47] IBGE, Sidra, PNAD, Table 1956.
[48] IBGE, Sidra, Table 2387.
[49] On the continued regional economic disparities, see Lena Lavinas, Eduardo Henrique Garcia, and Marcelo Rubens do Amaral, "Desigualdades Regionais e retomada do crescimento num quadro de Integração Econômica," Texto para discussão 466, Rio de Janeiro, Ipea, 1997; Claudio Monteiro Considera and Mérida Herasme Medina, "PIB por unidade da federação: valores correntes e constantes – 1985/96," Texto para discussão 610, Rio de Janeiro, Ipea, 1998; and for 2013, see IBGE, Sidra, Table 1194.
[50] Sonia Rocha, "Desigualdade regional e pobreza no Brasil: A Evolução – 1981/95," Texto para discussão 567, Rio de Janeiro, Ipea, 1998, p. 20 and IBGE, Sidra, PNAD, Table 1860. Here defining poverty as less than half of a minimum wage.
[51] IBGE, Sidra, Censo 2010, Table 1286 and IBGE, Sidra, PNAD, Table 1860.

population which went from 35% of the national population in 1950 to just 28% in the census of 2010.[52]

This regional disparity also appeared in terms of human capital, as can be seen in regional rates of literacy. As late as 1999, the Northeastern region contained a startling 46% of persons fifteen years or older who were functionally illiterate, compared to only some 21% who were functional adult illiterates in the Southern region.[53] These literacy rates have improved over time. By 2001, the illiteracy rate for persons 15 years of age or older was 24% in the Northeast compared to 7% in the South. As of 2015, these rates had declined to 16% and 4% respectively, though the Northeast still remained the region with the most illiterates in Brazil, and even the North by 2015 was down to 9% illiterates among those 15 years and older.[54] Moreover, despite the increase in years of schooling everywhere, persons over the age of 10 in the Northeast in 2015 had 2.3 years less schooling than those in the Southern region.[55]

But the regional gap in educational attainment as in health is continuing to decline. As late as 1990, the Northeastern region registered only 75% of school-age children 7 to 9 years of age matriculated in schools, compared to 91% in the South.[56] Already by 1998 the crude enrollment rate for primary education (the percentage of children attending school compared to the total children in the age group) was 92% in the Northeastern region and 97% in the South.[57] And by the census of 2010 all regions registered an attendance rate in this group of 98% and 99%, with only the North showing 95% attendance.[58] There are still major problems in school completion rates, and the quality of schooling in the poorest and richest regions is still quite different, with the state governments in the South spending more per primary school student than those of the Northeast.[59] But all indicators suggest that

---

[52] Silva and Medina, "Produto interno bruto por unidade da federação, 1985–1998"; and IBGE, Sidra, Censo 2010, Table 1286.

[53] IBGE, *Estatísticas do Século XX* (2003), Table educação 2000s2_aeb-82.

[54] IBGE, Sidra, PNAD, Table 271.

[55] IBGE, *Estatísticas do Século XX* (2003), Table educação 2000s2-aeb-86.

[56] IBGE, *Estatísticas do Século XX* (2003), Table população 1992aeb-055.1.

[57] Maria Helena Guimarães de Castro, *Educação para o Século XXI: o desafio da qualidade e da eqüidade* (Brasília: INEP/MEC, 1999), p. 11.

[58] IBGE, Sidra, Censo 2010, Table 3544.

[59] In 1996, the Fundo de Manutenção e Desenvolvimento do Ensino Fundamental e de Valorização do Magistério (FUNDEF) was created (Law 9424 of 24 December 1996). Later it was transformed into FUNDEB – Fundo de Manutenção e Desenvolvimento da Educação Básica e de Valorização dos Profissionais da Educação (Law 11.494 of 20 June 2007), with the objective of increasing the status of the teaching career and giving greater homogeneity to the remuneration of teachers throughout the national territory.

within a decade or two there will be little regional differences as the nation becomes a more unified society in terms of health and education, if not of income and wealth.

If some regional inequalities are declining, there are still other structural inequalities evident within Brazil besides class and region. Although the rural population has declined dramatically, those who remain in the rural area have less wealth than those living in the urban areas. It is evident that most of the growth of income for the working-class population has come in the urban area, now accounting for a steady 86% of the wage-earning population from 2001 to 2015. By contrast, there has been relatively little change in rural wage distribution over this entire period. Thus, on average, only a third of urban workers earned one minimum salary or less, compared to over 60% of the rural workers who earned this salary. Moreover, the growth of the urban population earning one to two minimum wages has increased steadily in the 2001 to 2014 period at the cost of those earning above two minimum wages, an indication of declining inequality. By contrast, there is little change in shares of population by minimum wages in the rural area (see Table 7.9).

There is also a distinct inequality between men and women. Traditionally, women were less educated and less literate than men for most of the nineteenth and twentieth centuries. In the census of 1950, for example, the literacy rate for those 15 years of age and older for men was 55% and for women it was only 44%. With each subsequent census, women increased their literacy faster than men. In 1960, the rate for 15 years and older was now 65% for men and 56% for women.[60] By the census of 2000, women in this age group finally equaled men at 88% literate,[61] and subsequently passed the literacy rate of the men in later years. According to the household survey of 2016, women over 15 years of age were 92.3% literate, compared to 91.7% of the men.[62] This literacy rate reflected the fact that women were obtaining more years of schooling then men, a trend which would only increase over time.[63] In 1950, men and women attended primary and secondary schools equally, at a rate of 18% among persons 10 years of age and older. For those who obtained a university or post-high school degree, however, the

---

[60] Brazil, *Estatísticas do Século XX* (2003), Table pop_1965aeb-05.1.

[61] IBGE, Sidra, Censo 2000, Table 2097.

[62] IBGE, Censo 1991, Table 141 and IBGE, PNAD, Table 1187.

[63] In the census of that year, 13% of women had 11 or more years of schooling, compared to only 11% of the men. IBGE, Sidra, Censo 1991, Table 142.

Table 7.9 *Persons 10 Years of Age and Older*
According to Their Current Salary by Residence
Expressed in Levels of the Minimum Wage, 2001–2015

Year	< 1	1–2	2+	Total
		Urban		
2001	27.1	27.7	45.1	100.0
2002	30.7	27.9	41.4	100.0
2003	32.4	27.4	40.2	100.0
2004	31.7	30.1	38.2	100.0
2005	34.3	30.3	35.4	100.0
2006	34.5	31.7	33.8	100.0
2007	32.3	32.3	35.5	100.0
2008	32.7	32.7	34.6	100.0
2009	33.1	33.6	33.3	100.0
2011	31.1	34.6	34.3	100.0
2012	32.9	35.0	32.1	100.0
2013	30.9	35.7	33.4	100.0
2014	31.4	34.0	34.6	100.0
2015	31.9	36.0	32.2	100.0
		Rural		
2001	56.1	27.5	16.4	100.0
2002	60.4	25.4	14.2	100.0
2003	60.5	24.1	15.4	100.0
2004	58.3	26.6	15.1	100.0
2005	61.2	25.9	13.0	100.0
2006	62.1	25.6	12.2	100.0
2007	60.4	26.4	13.3	100.0
2008	60.3	26.4	13.2	100.0
2009	61.2	26.3	12.5	100.0
2011	61.3	26.4	12.2	100.0
2012	63.5	25.3	11.2	100.0
2013	61.3	26.5	12.2	100.0
2014	60.7	26.5	12.9	100.0
2015	62.2	26.5	11.3	100.0

Source: IBGE, Sidra, PNAD, Table 1860.

spread was quite large, with 29% of the men and only 3% of the women being tertiary education graduates.[64] It was only in the census year of 1991 that women finally passed men in years of schooling.[65] By the PNAD household survey of 2015, women were listed with 8.0 years of schooling compared to just 7.7 years for men.[66] In this year only 12% of men 25 years and older had completed university (superior) education compared to 15% of the women.[67]

But if education has become a major area of advance for women, income, as we noted previously, has not experienced the same change. Household surveys from 1992 to 2011 showed that women's income has fluctuated at around two-thirds of the average male monthly wage, with no basic change over this long period.[68] Even as late as the first semester of 2018, for persons 14 years of age or older, women earned 78% of the salary of men.[69] But the trends noted for men are also evident for women. By 2015, those earning 1–2 minimum wages went from 27% to 36% for men and 28% to 34% for women, while those earning over 2 minimum wages declined for both sexes from 48% to 36% for women and from 32% to 22% for men (see Table 7.10).

Some of the difference in average salaries is due to the concentration of women in the lower strata of occupations. This can be seen in their distribution among the major occupational groups in 2015. Women dominated the low-paying domestic service sector and were more likely to be employees than to be self-employed or employers (see Table 7.11).

Nevertheless, better-educated women have carved out significant participation in high-status jobs as well. Thus, while women were 45% of the estimated labor force in 2015, they were above that ratio in many health-related fields, the legal profession, teaching, and in administration at the intermediate level. In the PNAD survey of 2015, women were 45% of the doctors, 56% of the dentists, 59% of the pharmacists, and 86% of the nurses (see Table 7.12). In the legal profession they made up 46% of the lawyers, 44% of public defenders, and 41% of the judges. They were only 43% of auditors and accountants but they made up

[64] IBGE, *Estatísticas do Século XX* (2003), Table Educação1955aeb-05.

[65] Kaizô Iwakami Beltrão and José Eustáquio Diniz Alves, "A reversão do hiato de gênero na educação brasileira no Século XX," *Anais* (2016), p. 10, Graph 1.

[66] IBGE, Sidra, PNAD, Table 1189. And for 2016, see IBGE, PNAD, Indicadores Sociais, 2016, Table 4.13. Accessed at: www.ibge.gov.br/estatisticas-novoportal/sociais/populacao/9221-sintese-de-indicadores-sociais.html?edicao=9222&t=downloads.

[67] IBGE, PNAD, Indicadores Socias, 2016, Table 4.14. Accessed at: www.ibge.gov.br/estatisticas-novoportal/sociais/populacao/9221-sintese-de-indicadores-sociais.html?edicao=9222&t=downloads.

[68] IBGE, Sidra, PNAD, Table 1172.   [69] IBGE, Sidra, PNADC/T, Table 5429.

Table 7.10 *Persons 10 Years of Age and Older According to Their Current Salary by Sex, Expressed in Levels of the Minimum Wage, 2001–2015*

Year	< 1	1–2	2+	Total
		Males		
2001	24.3	27.4	48.2	100.0
2002	27.5	28.0	44.4	100.0
2003	28.9	27.4	43.8	100.0
2004	27.7	30.1	42.2	100.0
2005	30.7	30.9	38.4	100.0
2006	30.4	32.4	37.2	100.0
2007	28.2	32.5	39.3	100.0
2008	28.8	32.8	38.4	100.0
2009	29.0	33.8	37.3	100.0
2011	26.7	34.2	39.1	100.0
2012	29.0	34.6	36.4	100.0
2013	27.2	35.1	37.7	100.0
2014	27.5	33.3	39.3	100.0
2015	28.2	35.7	36.1	100.0
		Females		
2001	40.0	28.0	32.0	100.0
2002	43.9	27.0	29.1	100.0
2003	45.4	26.5	28.1	100.0
2004	45.0	29.0	26.0	100.0
2005	47.4	28.2	24.4	100.0
2006	47.9	29.0	23.1	100.0
2007	45.9	30.1	24.0	100.0
2008	45.8	30.5	23.6	100.0
2009	46.4	31.1	22.5	100.0
2011	44.5	32.7	22.8	100.0
2012	45.9	32.6	21.5	100.0
2013	43.8	33.6	22.6	100.0
2014	43.8	32.7	23.5	100.0
2015	44.6	33.5	21.9	100.0

Source: IBGE, Sidra, PNAD, Table 1860.

Table 7.11 *Structure of the Labor Market by Sex, 2015*

Sex	Employee	Domestic Worker	Self-Employed	Employer	Miscellaneous	Total
			Share of Position by Sex			
Men	68.0	1.2	24.8	5.1	0.9	100.0
Women	62.5	15.7	17.3	2.6	1.8	100.0
Total	65.5	7.7	21.5	4.0	1.3	100.0
			Share by Sex within Each Position			
Men	57.2	8.3	63.8	71.0	37.9	55.2
Women	42.8	91.7	36.2	29.0	62.1	44.8
	100.0	100.0	100.0	100.0	100.0	100.0

Source: Elaborated from microdata of PNAD 2015.

95% of bilingual secretaries and 100% of the cartographers. They were well represented in the textile industry but largely absent in other factory labor and very poorly represented in engineering professions, but made up 58% of the architects.[70] From these data it would appear that highly educated women have slowly broken through in a number of liberal professions, though they are still far from achieving equality with men in many of these fields. Also, in the recent crisis, while women have consistently had a higher unemployment rate than men for all levels of education in 2016, like the men, the best-educated women had the lowest unemployment rates.[71]

As in almost all developing countries, Brazil also has shown a major distinction between its rural and urban populations, but one which is slowly but progressively disappearing. Until 1970, in fact, Brazil was primarily a rural society and most of the agricultural population was engaged in subsistence. Here was the most poverty-stricken group in society with the lowest standard of living, the highest mortality and fertility, and the lowest levels of education. Poverty was endemic in the rural area and the contrast between rural and urban society could not have been sharper. But a combination of the growth of a modern urban sector and an agricultural revolution have both reduced the number of rural workers within the entire society, even in absolute terms, and also led to a major decline in the ratio of indigent and poor persons who remained in the rural area.

---

[70] These percentages are generated from the microdata of the PNAD survey of 2015.
[71] IBGE, *Síntese de Indicadores Sociais 2017* (Rio de Janeiro, 2017), Graph 8.

Table 7.12 *Distribution of Workers in the Major Sectors of the Economy by Sex, 2015*

Sex	Agriculture	Transformative Industries	Construction	Commerce	Food and Lodgings	Transport and Communications	Public Administration	Education, Health and Social Services	Domestic Services	Miscellaneous	Total
					Share of Sector by Sex						
Men	17.1	13.2	15.6	18.6	3.8	8.4	5.3	4.4	0.9	12.7	100.0
Women	9.7	10.8	0.8	18.0	6.6	1.7	4.6	18.5	14.4	15.0	100.0
					Share of Sex within Sector						
Men	69.7	61.5	96.3	57.3	43.0	86.4	59.9	23.4	7.7	52.4	56.5
Women	30.3	38.5	3.7	42.7	57.0	13.6	40.1	76.6	92.3	47.6	43.5

Source: Elaborated from microdata of PNAD 2015.

With the tremendous growth of modern commercial agriculture, and the slow penetration of modern communications into the rural areas, the traditionally sharp disparities within the national population due to residence are very slowly declining. To these economic factors must be added the extraordinary late twentieth-century state decision to provide social welfare and services to the previously neglected rural area. Among the many policies which were enacted, the most revolutionary was the government decision in 1991 to provide a basic retirement (of one minimum salary) to all rural workers – a revolutionary concept in Latin American social security and one that virtually eliminated abject poverty in the rural area. Although work accident and partial pensions for rural workers had been developed from the 1950s, it was only in the Constitution of 1988 that the right to a pension was granted to all rural persons of a given age and only in 1991 was this provision finally implemented. This pension was provided to all agricultural workers who reached 60 years of age for men and 55 years of age for women regardless of whether they had contributed to the national pension plans or not.[72] There were also the beginnings of the delivery of education and social services to the rural areas from the mid-twentieth century onward that brought health, education, and other services to many of the previously isolated rural communities.

All these factors have meant that the actual gap between the urban and rural population has been progressively declining in a host of areas. As was the norm in all of Latin America, for example, the birth and mortality rates of the rural population were far higher than those of their urban compatriots. But both rural fertility and mortality rates have followed urban trends and the spread between urban and rural has declined in many areas. But, however much these rates declined over time, there still remained important economic differences between the two populations. Clearly, the urban populations were better educated and had higher-status jobs. The rural populations also turned out to contain more persons of color than the urban populations (some 84% of the whites resided in the urban area in 1999 as opposed to 74% of the persons of color).[73] Average rural family income was just half of what it was in the urban centers. Three-quarters of rural adults 10 years of age and older received less than the minimum salary compared to just 39% of urban workers (see Table 7.13). Clearly the wealthy and better-educated population was not to be found in rural Brazil, as only 1.6% earned 5 minimum salaries or more, compared to 9% of the urban population. But the programs of rural pensions have led to a startling reversal of poverty, with elderly retired persons having fewer poor among their midst than the younger age groups

[72] Betrão et al., "A população rural."
[73] IBGE, *Estatísticas do Século XX* (2003), Table população 2000aeb_s2_021.

Table 7.13 *Salary of Persons 10 Years of Age and Older, by Residence and Color, 2010*

Income Minimum Wage	Residence			Color/Ethnicity				
	Total	Urban	Rural	White	Black	Asian	Brown	Indigenous
¼	4.9	3.4	15.2	2.7	5.7	5.1	7.6	12.3
¼–½	5.1	4.0	12.6	3.2	6.2	4.9	7.4	12.3
½–1	33.6	31.8	45.5	27.6	40.7	30.5	39.8	39.4
1–2	30.0	31.7	19.0	31.3	30.4	25.9	28.4	22.4
2–3	10.0	10.9	3.8	12.1	8.2	10.0	7.7	6.0
3–5	8.0	8.9	2.3	10.6	5.3	9.7	5.2	4.2
5–10	5.7	6.4	1.2	8.3	2.8	9.0	3.0	2.5
10–15	1.1	1.2	0.2	1.6	0.4	1.9	0.4	0.4
15–20	0.9	1.0	0.1	1.4	0.2	1.7	0.3	0.3
20–30	0.4	0.5	0.1	0.7	0.1	0.9	0.1	0.1
30+	0.3	0.3	0.1	0.4	0.1	0.5	0.1	0.1

Source: IBGE, Sidra, Censo 2010, Table 3177.

(or an estimated 23% versus the non-elderly rate of 39%).[74] Also, in every major region of the country, the distribution of income was moderately less concentrated in the rural areas than in the urban area.[75]

If differences by sex, residence, and possibly even race have slowly declined, the general unjust distribution of income by class remains significant despite recent modest changes. This is the single most intractable problem which Brazil faces. Despite the "massification" of school enrollments at both the primary level and to a lesser extent at the secondary level, the creation of a vast network of state, federal, and private universities, and the extraordinary drop in illiteracy, inequality in Brazil has changed only moderately. Poverty and illiteracy are declining through more-intensive state social policies, but wealth distribution has changed only moderately over time.[76] The slow recent decline of inequality has been due to the increasing share of income taken by the bottom half of Brazilian households. From

[74] Ricardo Paes de Barros, Rosane Mendonça, and Daniel Santos, *Incidência e natureza da pobreza entre idosos no Brasil* (Rio de Janeiro: Ipea, 1999), p. 25, Table 4.

[75] On the order of a GINI of 0.59 in the urban areas and 0.55 in the rural zones. IBGE, Sidra, Table 2037, Índice de GINI da distribuição do rendimento nominal mensal dos domicílios particulares permanentes, com rendimento domiciliar, por situação do domicílio.

[76] PNUD, Fundação João Pinheiro, Instituto de Pesquisa Econômica Aplicada, *Atlas do desenvolvimento humano no Brasil* (2003). Accessed at: http://atlasbrasil.org.br/2013/.

1992 to 2012, their share of total household wages rose from 12.5% to 16.7% of total wage income. Though this percentage is low by world standards, it has had a major impact on distribution of income. The top 10% share dropped in this period from 47.7% to 41.5%, that of the top 5% dropped 34% to 29.5%, and even the top 1% saw their share decline in this period by 1.5%. This has led to a progressive decline of the GINI from 0.60 in 1992 to 0.52 in 2012.[77] The cause of this decline is due to both rising employment and better wages as well as government income transfers.

Thus, the picture of stratification in Brazil is both quite startling and yet holds modest possibilities of change if government finances and the general economy can be sustained. The recent depression has evidently led to a pause in long-term trends. Only the resumption of sustainable growth and the maintenance of social programs, preferably under better management, should allow the positive trend observed since the mid-1990s to continue. Literacy has become universal, the formal economy has expanded greatly, and the welfare state has successfully redistributed income in a massive way to the urban and rural poor. This has led to a very significant shift of the population out of extreme indigence and poverty and fortified greatly the working classes.

It has also resulted in Brazil experiencing high levels of mobility in the recent period. As a rapidly industrializing and urbanizing country in the middle decades of the twentieth century, Brazil initially experienced high rates of upward social mobility. It went from a predominantly rural society with low levels of education at mid-century to high levels of urbanization and industrialization with much higher levels of education in the last half of the twentieth century. This led to a major expansion of the EAP and a greater segmentation and diversification of the labor force. Thus, the EAP went from 17 million in 1950 to 30 million in 1970 and 44 million in 1980.[78] Non-manual labor went from 2.5 million persons in 1960 to 8.2 million twenty years later, while the number of workers in the tertiary sector (that is in services) went from 4.5 million to 8.1 million in the period from 1979 to 1989. All of these rapid changes can be seen in the decline of workers in the primary sector, which went from 61% of the labor force in 1950 to 31% by 1980, while the secondary sector (industry) increased its share from 17% to 29% and the tertiary sector went from 22% to 40% in the same period.[79] Clearly, the most rapidly growing sector was services, although not all of

---

[77] Hoffmann and Oliveira, "The Evolution of Income Distribution in Brazil," Table 2.
[78] Brazil, *Estatísticas do Século XX* (2003), Table, trabalho1981aeb_01.
[79] Carlos Antonio Costa Ribeiro and Maria Celi Scalon, "Mobilidade de classe no Brasil em perspectiva comparada, *Dados: Revista de Ciências Sociais* 44.1 (2001), pp. 53–96.

these service occupations were skilled ones. It is estimated that domestic servants went from 680,000 to 1.8 million between 1950 and 1970, and another significant segment were to be found in the informal economy.[80] Nevertheless, overall, there seems to have been a significant expansion of high-skilled jobs in both the secondary as well as the tertiary sectors throughout the last half of the twentieth century and until today. Thus, just in the period from 2002 to 2014 there was an expansion of 19.6 million urban jobs, compared to a loss of 1.6 million rural occupations in the same period. Of these urban jobs, 4.5 million were in occupations defined as upper-class or upper middle-class occupations.[81]

All this early rapid growth led to a major change in mobility as new occupational opportunities opened up for the first time. Thus, instead of the more traditional circular pattern of an advanced industrial society where there is as much upward as downward mobility, Brazil for a short period of time experienced more upward than downward mobility, which has been termed "structural mobility."[82] It has been estimated by one study that by the 1970s Brazilian social mobility was predominantly structural (57% of the change between fathers' and sons' occupations was structural and 47% was circular). This is a common pattern in developing societies due to increasing employment opportunities, to changes in occupational structures, and the consequent decline of rural occupations and the massive increase of urban ones.[83] More-recent studies using more-refined occupational groupings found that structural mobility went from 61% in 1973, to 67% in 1988, and 66% in 1996: these three years being ones when the PNAD survey provided questions on parents' and children's occupations. Immobility – that is the failure to move beyond parents' occupation – declined from 39% to 33% in this period.[84] A more complete analysis by sex, which was added in the PNAD survey of 2008, showed that mobility for men went from 55.3% in 1973 to 67.3% in 2008, and for women it went from 57.5% in 1973 to 75.4% in 2008.[85]

But, for all the mobility, most authors agree that much of this structural mobility came at the bottom shares of the occupational structure, whereas most

[80] José Pastore, *Inequality and Social Mobility in Brazil* (Madison, University of Wisconsin Press, 1981), Chapter 4.

[81] Adalberto Cardoso and Edmond Préteceille, "Classes médias no Brasil: do que se trata? Qual seu tamanho? Como vem mudando?" *Dados: Revista de Ciências Sociais* 60.4 (2017), p. 999, Table 2.

[82] Pastore, *Inequality and Social Mobility in Brazil*, p. 21.

[83] Pastore, *Inequality and Social Mobility in Brazil*, pp. 32–33.

[84] Ribeiro and Scalon, "Mobilidade de classe no Brasil," p. 66, Table 4.

[85] These data are from Carlos Antonio Costa Ribeiro, "Quatro décadas de mobilidade social no Brasil," *Dados: Revista de Ciências Sociais*, 55.3 (2012), p. 656, Table 1.

of the elite occupations still tended to be circular. That is, the bulk of the change was manual rural workers moving to manual urban work. Thus, in these years between 1973 and 1996, some 24% to 25% of rural workers ended in urban unskilled manual labor and another 17% to 19% ended in urban skilled manual labor. Thus, the surveys of mobility to 2008 for men show a steady and increasing decline in sons following their fathers in agricultural labor, going from 36.7% in 1973 to 13.7% in 2008.[86] Of course, this trend would be reversed later on as the rural population stopped bleeding workers into the urban sector and education and job quality increased in the rural area.

All these authors also stress the relative immobility in the upper levels of the occupational categories as the elite uses the educational, tax, and pension system to its advantage to pass on their wealth and prevent downward mobility of their children.[87] But at the same time the increasing level of education for all workers over time has meant that the excessive bonus for education which existed in the earlier period when the average of schooling was 3.4 years (1973) has declined as the average years of schooling rose to 8.4 in 2014, and this has had an important impact in reducing inequality and the GINI index from the low 0.60s to the low 0.50s. In every level of occupation, from the highest to the lowest, there has been an increase in the years of schooling, with the rural workers and skilled and unskilled urban workers doubling their years of schooling in this period from 1973 to 2014.[88]

Given the steady expansion of education in the post-1950 period, the age of entry into the labor market kept getting older. It is estimated from the PNAD surveys that persons entering the labor market in the 1920s and 1930s were 14 years of age, and this age rose steady until it reached 17 years of age by the 1960s, as more and more persons continued to complete their primary education and even their secondary education.[89] Thus, using the 17-year age of entry into the labor market, we can assess the maturing of social mobility in the PNAD survey of 2014, which is the latest to ask questions of occupational and educational differences between children and parents. This survey also broke down the child's occupation by age for some 55 million persons, thus permitting a view of this slowing mobility.

---

[86] Ribeiro and Scalon, "Mobilidade de classe no Brasil," Table A and Ribeiro, "Quatro décadas de mobilidade social no Brasil," Table 1.

[87] For an interesting discussion of these strategies, see Marcelo Medeiros, "O que faz os Ricos ricos: um estudo sobre fatores que determinam a riqueza," PhD thesis, Universidade de Brasília, 2003.

[88] Carlos Antonio Costa Ribeiro, "Tendências da desigualdade de oportunidades no Brasil: mobilidade social e estratificação educacional," *Boletin Mercado de Trabalho: conjuntura e análise* 62 (2017), pp. 49–65, Table 1.

[89] Pastore, *Inequality and Social Mobility in Brazil*, p. 69, Table 5.1.

The group 45 to 65 years of age in 2014 entered the labor market in the late 1960s to the late 1980s, while the younger group aged 25 to 44 years of age entered the labor market from the late 1980s to 2006. What is evident from this PNAD 2014 survey is that the older group had more upward mobility in the highest occupations, that is for stratum A (defined as administrators, executives, and liberal professionals) and stratum B (skilled technical workers) than did the younger age group, even though the total number of positions was smaller in the earlier period (see Table 7.12). There was also a big change in origin, with 50% of the children interviewed among the older group having fathers who were farm workers (stratum F), while among the younger workers only 36% had fathers who came from this rural background. This clearly shows that in the more recent period the slowing of out migration from the rural areas and the increasing number of workers born in urban areas means that ever fewer workers are coming from a rural background. It also shows that for the elite positions immobility is becoming more important in the more recent period with fewer recruits entering from the lowest two occupational strata and a higher ratio remaining in their fathers' high-status positions (see Table 7.13). Looking at the absolute differences between the younger and older cohorts, it is evident that those older cohorts who entered the labor force in the 1960s and 1970s had much higher rates of mobility. They were far more likely to reach the upper strata, were in most cases more likely to be in different strata than their fathers, and a much higher ratio of them moved from the lowest strata of rural and non-manual urban occupations (see Table 7.14). Overall, half of the persons were upwardly mobile, but among the older contingent only 15% were downwardly mobile, compared to 18% among the younger workers (see Table 7.15 and Table 7.16). All of this would seem to suggest that the structural mobility is slowly being replaced by the traditional circular one.[90]

Thus, relative stability of stratification and increased social mobility are the dual patterns which emerge from this study of Brazilian society in the post-1950 period. The elite still retain a very large share of national wealth, but there has been massive socio-economic change at the lowest economic levels leading to the emergence of a large middle class, a pattern which can be

[90] A recent study by Torche and Ribeiro supports this idea of changing patterns of mobility in the pre- and post-1980s period. They also stress the declining bonus given to education as more workers achieve equal levels of education. See Florencia Torche and Carlos Costa Ribeiro, "Pathways of Change in Social Mobility: Industrialization, Education and Growing Fluidity in Brazil," *Research in Social Stratification and Mobility* 28 (2010), pp. 291–307.

Table 7.14 *Percentage Relationship of Occupation Strata of Persons Aged 25–64 by Occupational Strata of Fathers, PNAD 2014*

Children	Fathers						
	A	B	C	D	E	F	Number (000s)
	Persons 25–44 Years of Age						
A	55.7	32.4	38.2	14.5	19.3	8.4	5,906
B	11.9	19.3	12.9	9.3	9.4	4.0	2,666
C	9.4	15.1	14.6	13.8	13.0	4.9	3,333
D	7.9	13.6	15.6	31.4	21.0	25.5	8,040
E	14.2	18.2	18.7	28.9	35.2	28.4	9,005
F	1.0	1.3	0.2	2.2	2.1	28.8	3,771
	100	100	100	100	100	100	32,721
	Persons 45–65 Years of Age						
A	51.5	38.6	36.4	16.7	18.7	7.8	3,540
B	15.6	14.6	10.8	7.5	8.8	3.0	1,394
C	8.1	5.8	10.1	8.2	10.0	2.9	1,276
D	8.9	16.5	17.7	31.7	24.5	22.9	5,432
E	14.1	22.0	23.8	32.6	34.8	27.4	6,408
F	1.7	2.3	1.3	3.3	3.1	35.9	4,393
	100	100	100	100	100	100	22,443

Source: Calculated from Table 3.9 of PNAD 2014 mobility dataset. https://ww2.ibge.gov.br/h ome/xml/suplemento_pnad.shtm.

found in other rapidly growing Latin American countries.[91] The access to a universal education combined with a major increase in non-manual and non-rural occupations have all fostered rapid mobility in the second half of the twentieth century. Yet, despite these significant advances in reducing educational and income gaps among region, classes, genders, and races, and the clear increase in socio-economic mobility for all persons, the rigidity

[91] See the two essays by Florencia Torche, "Unequal but Fluid: Social Mobility in Chile in Comparative Perspective," *American Sociological Review* 70.3 (2005), pp. 422–450, and her study, "Intergenerational Mobility and Inequality: The Latin American Case," *Annual Review of Sociology* 40 (2014), pp. 619–642.

Table 7.15 *Occupation Strata of Persons Aged 25–64 by Occupational Strata of Fathers, PNAD 2014*
(000s)

| Children | Fathers | | | | | | |
	A	B	C	D	E	F	Total
			Persons 25 to 44 Years of Age				
A	27.4	7.1	6.4	28.0	14.4	16.6	100
B	13.0	9.4	4.8	39.5	15.5	17.8	100
C	8.2	5.9	4.4	47.0	17.1	17.4	100
D	2.8	2.2	1.9	44.4	11.4	37.2	100
E	4.6	2.6	2.1	36.6	17.1	37.0	100
F	0.8	0.5	0.1	6.6	2.4	89.7	100
Number	2,909	1,301	995	11,389	4,384	11,744	32,722
			Persons 45 to 65 Years of Age				
A	20.4	7.5	5.6	28.1	13.4	25.0	100
B	15.7	7.2	4.2	31.9	16.1	24.7	100
C	8.9	3.1	4.3	38.0	19.9	25.8	100
D	2.3	2.1	1.8	34.7	11.5	47.7	100
E	3.1	2.4	2.0	30.2	13.8	48.5	100
F	0.5	0.4	0.2	4.5	1.8	92.6	100
Number	1,400	690	547	5,941	2,540	11,325	22,443

Source: Calculated from Table 3.9 of PNAD 2014 mobility dataset. https://ww2.ibge.gov.br/home/xml/suplemento_pnad.shtm.

Table 7.16 *Absolute Percentage Difference between Younger and Older Persons in Relation to Father's Occupation, 2014*

| Children's Occupation | Father's Occupation | | | | | |
	A	B	C	D	E	F
A	−7.1	0.4	−0.8	0.0	−0.9	8.4
B	2.7	−2.2	−0.6	−7.7	0.6	6.9
C	0.7	−2.8	0.0	−9.0	2.8	8.4
D	−0.6	−0.1	−0.1	−9.7	0.0	10.5
E	−1.5	−0.3	0.0	−6.3	−3.3	11.5
F	−0.2	−0.1	0.1	−2.1	−0.6	2.9

Source: Based on Table 7.14.

of such institutions as education and government taxation have become new areas of blockage in terms of mobility and a movement of the working classes into the middle and upper classes. Moreover, while women have advanced more rapidly than men in recent years, the gap between whites and non-whites has not closed as rapidly. But at the same time the universality of access to education and major increase in skilled occupations has led to Brazil becoming a society more like most advanced western societies, and one which has greatly changed from the underdeveloped rural-dominated society of 1950 in which illiteracy was the norm.

8

Race and Stratification

Like class, gender, and residence, color is one of the major factors defining the Brazilian population since the introduction of African slavery in the sixteenth century. For all the mobility of African and Afro-Brazilians which occurred before and after the abolition of slavery in 1888, color still remains an important if not always a precise marker of class and status in Brazil. To confuse things even more, Brazil went from a primarily non-white society in 1872 to a primarily white society in 1900 after the massive immigration of some 5 million European and Asian immigrants. It remained a predominantly white nation until the latest census of 2010 when it once more became a primarily non-white society and will continue to be primarily a non-white society for the foreseeable future. Clearly, the census of 1940 was the peak year for whites and the nadir for the browns. Since that time there has been a steady rise of browns and a relative decline of whites – with no significant differences in fertility accounting for these changes. Of course, increasing racial inter-marriage would have an impact on the growth of the brown population. But it also appears that changing attitudes toward color and the generalized acceptance of brown as the normal color for Brazilians, combined with both a rising Afro-Brazilian consciousness and the recent movement for affirmative action for non-whites, have all led to this profound change of color self-identity. The only group affected by migration are the Asians, which have now risen to 1.1% of the population in 2010 due to the arrival of Korean and other Asian immigrants along with the original Japanese migrants (see Graph 8.1).[1]

---

[1] Amerindians comprised 4% of the population in 1872, but only 0.4% in the census of 2010, and they were not counted in twentieth-century censuses until 1991. Race was not listed in the census of 1920 and was again dropped from the census of 1970.

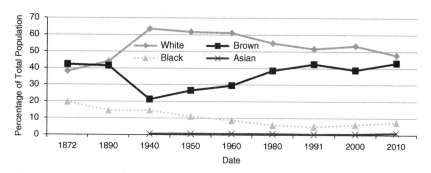

GRAPH 8.1 Percentage of Population by Color and Ethnicity in Brazil, 1872–2010
Source: *Recenseamento geral de 1950*, Série Nacional, Censo demográfico, vol.1,
Table 1 to 1950; 1960–1980, Série Nacional, vol. 1; 1991–2010, IBGE, Sidra,
Table 136.

Does color matter as much as class in Brazil in defining a person's place in
Brazilian society? This is one of the most debated questions in contemporary
social sciences. This is the theme we will explore in this chapter. To begin
with, it is clear that the three color distinctions of white (*branco*), brown
(*pardo* or *mulato*), and black (*preto*) which dominate Brazilian society allows
for a more integrated system then simply black and white and is far more
ambiguous in terms of defining a person's color. While discrimination against
blacks is more clear cut, discrimination against browns – the largest of this
color class in Brazil today – is far less precise. This is because defining who is
brown is not a simple definition of skin color or so-called "African features"
but may also include a host of class and educational characteristics. In fact,
there is even confusion among Brazilians as to their actual color definition.[2]

There is much debate in the literature as to whether racial discrimination
ever existed, or existed only in the slavery period and will disappear in the
modern industrial society, or that it is a reflection of the accumulated inheritance of poverty and earlier racist positions which affects subsequent generations, or is still functioning within Brazilian society today as a form of
guaranteeing white elite positions.[3] It is worth noting that ex-slaves entered
the free market economy with few financial resources and a limited number

[2] Rafael Guerreiro Osorio, "O sistema classificatório de 'cor ou raça' do IBGE," Texto para
discussão 996, Brasília, Ipea, 2003. On these intergenerational boundary-crossings among
families, see Luisa Farah Schwartzman, "Does Money Whiten? Intergenerational Changes in
Racial Classification in Brazil," *American Sociological Review* 72 (2007), pp. 940–963.
[3] For a very good review of the Brazilian sociological literature on this debate about racism, see
Rafael Guerreiro Osorio, "À mobilidade social dos negros brasileiros," Texto para discussão
1033, Brasília, Ipea, 2004.

of skills and thus tended to form the poorest element of post-emancipation society. The usual discrimination against the poor in general, who were mostly rural unskilled illiterate workers, with limited access to government services, also meant that blacks and browns started from a lower economic level than most whites during the early part of the twentieth century. This meant that mobility was slower and took more generations than it did for literate white foreign-born workers, for example.

In analyzing intermarriage, family, education, and income by color, we will try to determine the levels and intensity of this discrimination over time. The earlier quantitative materials available on race show much higher rates of disadvantage in income, education, and health of non-whites (hereafter defined as blacks and browns or *pretos* and *pardos*) due to their greater isolation in rural areas and their concentration in the poorest states of the federation. Given the control over health and education by state governments, this in turn meant that the richer and whiter Southeastern and Southern states provided their citizens with greater benefits than were available in the poorer Northeastern states where the non-white population was concentrated. In 1950, for example, the largest Northeastern state, Bahia, had a non-white population of 70% compared with São Paulo, the largest state in the Southeastern region, which had only 11% listed as non-white residents. The North and Northeast regions as a whole were 69% and 58% non-white and accounted for two-thirds of all the browns in the nation and 44% of all blacks. In the Southeast and South regions, non-whites were 29% and 11% respectively in these two areas. As late as 1991, even despite the mass migration from the Northeast to the Southern regions, the North and Northeast were still 77% and 73% non-white compared to the South and Southeastern regions, which were 37% and 17% respectively non-white.[4]

But this pattern was changing. Whereas in 2001 only 31% of the population of the Southeastern and Southern regions combined were browns and blacks, by 2015, their combined percentage had grown to 40% of the total population of these two predominantly white regions.[5] With the combination of the migrations out of the North and Northeast toward the Southern regions and the creation of an ever more universal system of education and health, things began slowly to change. Blacks and browns had been less literate, had had fewer years of education, and enjoyed lower incomes and health than whites or Asians at mid-century, but this gap between whites and non-whites has slowly begun to decline in the decades following.

---

[4] IBGE, Sidra, Table 136 and *Censo demográfico 1950*, Série Nacional, vol. 1 p. 69, Table 39.
[5] IBGE, Sidra, Table 262.

This change can be seen in terms of health and fertility. Initially, blacks and browns did much worse than whites in terms of health. The first estimates we have on life expectancy by race show that in the census year of 1872 Brazilian slaves, which by then included less than half the black and brown population, had a low life expectancy compared to the total free population (whites and non-whites). In 1872, male slaves lived 3.7 years less than free men, and female slaves had an average life expectancy of 2.3 years less than free women.[6]

In saying that life expectancy for a male slave in Brazil was 23 years in this period (an upper bound estimate) does not mean that the average slave died at that age. It should be remembered that infant mortality was so high in nineteenth-century Brazil that one-third of all male children born died before the age of one, and just under half died before the age of five. For those slave male children who reached the age of one, the expectation of life was 33.6 years; for those who survived the first five years of life, the average number of years of life remaining was 38.4 years (see Graph 8.2). Thus, a male slave who survived the extremely dangerous years of infancy and early childhood stood an excellent chance of reaching his 40s. For women slaves, life expectancy was better. Only 27% died before the age of one and 43% before the

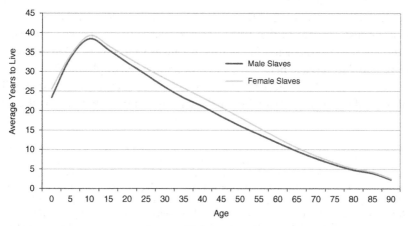

GRAPH 8.2 Estimated Upper Bound Life Expectancy of Slaves (From Birth and by Five-Year Cohorts)
Source: Carvalho de Melo, "The Economics of Labor in Brazilian Coffee Plantations," p. 123.

---

[6] Arriaga, *New Life Tables*, pp. 29–30, Table III.3 and Pedro Carvalho de Mello, "The Economics of Labor in Brazilian Coffee Plantations," PhD thesis, University of Chicago, 1975, p. 123, Table 31.

age of five, which meant that life expectancy for female slaves at birth was 25.5 years, with the corresponding expectations of those who survived to one reaching 34 years and those who survived to five achieving 39 years. Finally, the data available suggest that while slaves had a higher infant mortality rate than the total population, and thus a lower life expectancy at birth (a difference of two years), by the age of five, life expectancy differed by only one year.

The differences in race and infant mortality continued on well into the twentieth century, long after emancipation had occurred. Although vital statistics by race were not systematically collected by the national government until the late 1990s,[7] there are some regional level data and national estimates which do provide some approximate idea of basic differences. In general, the heavily non-white region of the Northeast was systematically worse off in all health indices – from infant mortality to life expectancy and from diseases to health outcomes – than were the population of the mostly white Southern region.[8] But of course this introduces an ecological bias, since it is difficult to separate out poverty from color in these data. From time to time there is some actual data by color. Thus, it has been estimated that blacks (in this case defined as both *pardos* and *pretos*) had a 40% higher rate of infant mortality than whites in the late twentieth century (see Graph 8.3).

Equally, another estimate shows that while whites and non-whites have all experienced rising average life expectancy since the 1950s, there have only been modest changes in the difference between white and non-white rates. Although the difference has fluctuated by census year, it was still a minimum of six years' difference between 1950 and 2000 (see Graph 8.4).[9]

Many of the above statistics are estimates, but even once systematically collected data become available in the current century there are still some

---

[7] "In the 1990s, reflections on the demography of inequalities emerged as a new object of study in the public health field … and leaders from the black movement began to question the relationship between racism and health, urging the public health administration to include the race/color category in the health information systems. This inclusion first took place in São Paulo City (Ordinance n. 696/90 7). In 1996, the color category was included in the Brazilian Ministry of Health's Mortality Information and Live-Births Information Systems (Ordinance n. 3,947/98 8)." Luis Eduardo Batista and Sônia Barros, "Confronting Racism in Health Services." *Cadernos de Saúde Pública* 33 (2017), pp. 65–76; and Rubens de C. F. Adorno, Augusta Thereza de Alvarenga, and Maria da Penha Vasconcellos, "Quesito cor no sistema de informação em saúde," *Estudos Avançados* 18.50 (2004), pp. 119–123.

[8] See Luna and Klein, *The Economic and Social History of Brazil since 1889*, Chapter 4.

[9] It should be noted that the data that appear in Wood, Carvalho, and Horta, "The Color of Child Mortality in Brazil, 1950–2000," and which we have used in Graph 8.4, differ considerably for 1950 from the estimates for 1950 given in Wood and Carvalho, *The Demography of Inequality in Brazil*, p. 145, Table 6.2. Moreover, it would seem that in this and many other aspects the census of 1991 is not very reliable.

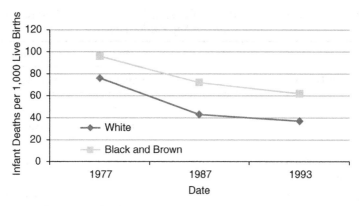

GRAPH 8.3 Infant Mortality by Race in Brazil, 1977–1993
Source: Cunha (2001), p. 78, Table 5.

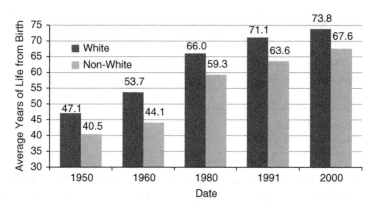

GRAPH 8.4 Estimated Life Expectancy of Whites and Non-Whites, 1950–2000
Source: Wood, Carvalho, and Horta, "The Color of Child Mortality in Brazil,
1950–2000" (2010), p. 126, Table 2.

mortality differences by color. One early study was based on some 169,000
deaths of whites and blacks in the state of São Paulo in 1999. Although
excluding *pardos* and with a relatively small sample of *pretos*, the data
clearly show certain basic patterns. Among women, blacks suffered over
six times the rate of maternal mortality than white women. Men suffered
much higher rates of violent death than women. And black men had twice the
rate of such deaths as white men, though the difference among women was
far less dramatic. For other causes of death, whites had much higher rates
than blacks for both men and women in the case of cancer, but the reverse
was true for cardiovascular and infectious diseases. With other diseases,
there was generally no difference in terms of color, with sex being the more
important determinant of mortality differences (see Table 8.1).

Table 8.1 *Rates of Mortality by Cause of Whites and Blacks (*Pretos*)* in the State of São Paulo, 1999*

	Women		Men	
Cause of Death	Whites	Blacks	Whites	Blacks
Infectious and parasitic diseases	19.3	31.0	36.3	67.3
Cancer	81.7	74.8	108.6	87.0
Lymphoma and leukemia	2.1	1.4	2.3	2.2
Diabetes, thyroid diseases	29.8	39.7	25.9	30.8
Mental and behavioral disorders	1.9	3.3	6.4	19.6
Neurological diseases	7.4	5.4	9.8	11.4
Cardiovascular diseases	174.5	199.6	212.9	244.5
Pulmonary diseases	56.3	43.8	77.4	72.5
Gastrointestinal diseases	20.9	21.9	46.4	44.4
Genitourinary diseases	8.8	9.8	10.7	11.0
Maternal mortality	37.9	245.5		
Congenital malformations	5.5	2.3	7.0	3.5
External causes (accidents and violence)	23.3	30.4	136.2	274.4
Total numbers	64,512	4,085	93,000	6,921

* *Pardos* are not included.
Source: SEADE (2005), p. 988.

This same pattern emerged in a more complete study of deaths in the state of São Paulo from 1999 to 2001. Blacks and browns (now included) suffered much higher rates of infectious diseases, maternal mortality, diabetes, and violent deaths, but it was whites who were more likely than either of the other two to die of cancer, lung disease, and most other major forms of disease.[10] A study of maternal mortality from 2004 to 2007 in the Southern region state of Rio Grande do Sul also found that black and brown women, controlling for age, had consistently higher rates of maternal mortality than white women, with black women having the worst rates.[11] In another Southern state, that of Paraná, the maternal mortality of whites in the period 2000 to

[10] This study, however, did not control for age, so the higher white rates for classic degenerative diseases may be due to differences in life expectancy. See Luís Eduardo Batista, Maria Mercedes Loureiro Escuder, and Julio Cesar Rodrigues Pereira, "A cor da morte: causas de óbito segundo características de raça no Estado de São Paulo, 1999 a 2001," *Revista da Saúde Pública* 38.5 (2004), p. 633, Table 2.
[11] Ioná Carreno, Ana Lúcia de Lourenzi Bonilha, and Juvenal Soares Dias da Costa, "Perfil epidemiológico das mortes maternas ocorridas no Rio Grande do Sul, Brasil 2004–2007," *Revista brasileira de epidemiologia* 15.2 (2012), p. 401, Table 3.

Table 8.2 *Infant Mortality by Region for the Year 2009/2010*
(August–July)

Region	White	Black	Asian	Brown	Total
North	29.9	52.5	28	18.8	21.5
Northeast	26.5	50.1	8.8	17.8	19.7
Southeast	13.3	24.1	8.1	13.6	13.6
South	11.5	11.4	6.8	11.9	11.6
Center-West	16.7	43.2	6.3	14.4	16.2
Brazil	15.2	29.1	9.7	16.6	16.3

Source: Caldas et al., "Mortalidade infantil segundo" (2017), p. 6, Table 3.

2002 was 49 deaths per 100,000 live births, but for black women the figure was 407 and for browns it was 214 maternal deaths per 100,000 live births.[12]

On the other hand, a study of strokes and other cardiovascular disease deaths in Brazil in 2010 found that cerebrovascular mortality rates adjusted for age showed major differences by color which differed from the São Paulo study. Among men, whites had a median 44.4 deaths per 1,000 population for heart disease, for browns it was 48.2 deaths, and for blacks 63.3 deaths per 1,000 population; with women the rates for whites was 29 deaths per 1,000 population; for brown women it was 33.7 deaths, and it was highest for black women at 51 deaths per 1,000 population. As the study concluded, "the burden of stroke mortality is higher among blacks compared to browns and whites."[13] Finally, a study of deaths from the city of Vitoria in Espírito Santo in 2006 showed that blacks were moderately more likely to die from any cause and in any age group both in relation to whites and in relation to the browns, the latter group being at the same level as the whites.[14]

But it should be noted that region plays a major role in influencing racial differences in mortality. Thus, a detailed study of some 34,000 infant deaths shows that, except for the Asians, there is virtually no difference by race for the rate of infant mortality in the three states of the Southern region, in contrast to the sharp black/white differences in the Northeastern regions. Even there, however, browns have lower rates than whites, as they do in the North and Center-West as well (see Table 8.2). Finally, in this same study, postneonatal

[12] Alaerte Leandro Martins, "Mortalidade materna de mulheres negras no Brasil," *Cadernos de Saúde Pública* 22.11 (2006), p. 2477, Table 1.
[13] Paulo Andrade Lotufo and Isabela Judith Martins Bensenor, "Raça e mortalidade cerebro-vascular no Brasil," *Revista de Saúde Pública*, 47.6 (2013), p. 1201.
[14] Nathalia Modenesi Fiorio, "Mortalidade por raça/cor em Vitória/ES: análise da informação e das desigualdes em saúde," MA thesis: Universidade Federal de Espirito Santo, 2009, p. 79, Table 14.

deaths were highest among whites and blacks in the North and Northeast compared to all other groups, but the same for all groups in the other regions. Other data also show contradictory findings. Thus in the 2003 PNAD national household survey of 2003, among persons aged 18 years and older who had chronic diseases, there was virtually no difference between whites and blacks (42% of those questioned saying they had a chronic disease), with browns and Amerindians being the outliers: browns being low at 38% and Amerindians higher at 48%.[15] Another study on persons declaring that their state of health was bad showed only modest and not very significant differences by color groups, though it was significant by sex. Moreover, the "magnitude of the association between race and self-reported health status was much lower than that found in US studies."[16]

Almost all studies find some health differences by race, but not always in a similar pattern by region and sex. All such studies also indicate that the differences between the groups are slowly declining as all states close in on a common national pattern. Much of this decline has occurred since the late 1990s and especially in the twenty-first century with the expansion of the national health system (SUS). As the latest National Health Survey (*Pesquisa Nacional de Saúde*) of 2013 shows, there is relatively little difference between whites and the leading groups of non-whites in basic access to health care, examinations, and utility of health services.[17] Thus, for example, the number of pregnant women who had an ultrasound in that year went from 99% of the whites down to 97% for the browns, and the same ratios were evident for pre-natal visits.[18] But in long-term care there were still some differences among women by race. Thus, 83% of the white women had had a pap smear in the past three years, compared to 77% of the blacks and 76% of the browns. It should be noted that in the United States in the same year of 2013, only 69% of all

[15] Marilisa Berti de Azevedo Barros, Chester Luiz Galvão César, Luana Carandina, and Graciella Dalla Torre, "Desigualdades sociais na prevalência de doenças crônicas no Brasil, PNAD-2003," *Ciência & Saúde Coletiva* 11.4 (2006), p. 915, Table 2.

[16] Ana Luiza Braz Pavão, Guilherme Loureiro Werneck, and Mônica Rodrigues Campos, "Autoavaliação do estado de saúde e a associação com fatores sociodemográficos, hábitos de vida e morbidade na população: um inquérito nacional," *Cadernos de Saúde Pública* 29.4 (2013), p. 731.

[17] All of these indices of access to health care can be accessed at IBGE, Sidra, Pesquisa Nacional de Saúde (https://sidra.ibge.gov.br/pesquisa/pns) and especially Saúde de Mulheres, vols 1 and 4. A more recent study has suggested that there are still some differences in pre-natal care, and hospital birth experiences between blacks, whites, and browns. Maria do Carmo Leal et al., "The Color of Pain: Racial Iniquities in Prenatal Care and Childbirth in Brazil," *Cadernos de Saúde Pública* 33 Supl. 1 (2017), pp. 2–17.

[18] IBGE, Sidra, Table 5835.

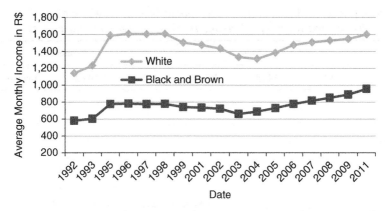

GRAPH 8.5 Average Monthly Income of Persons 10 Years of Age and Older, by Race, 1992–2011
Source: IBGE, Sidra Table 1173.

women had taken a pap smear in the past three years.[19] Only 13% of white Brazilian women 50 to 69 years of age had never had a mammogram, compared to 23% of the blacks and 24% of the browns in this age group.[20] This too was below the rates for the United States, which were 28% for white and black women 50 to 64 years of age.[21] Surprisingly, there was still a difference among younger women in having a doctor attend their latest birth, with 92% of white women attended by a doctor, compared to 85% of the blacks and 84% of the browns.[22]

If things have improved in terms of the narrowing of health disparities by race, the differences in income have changed only modestly over time. Average monthly income has increased for both whites and non-whites (using 2007 deflated numbers), but in the last few years there has been a modest increase in the distance between whites and blacks and browns in terms of average income (see Graph 8.5).

Broken down by region, wages of blacks and browns are consistently 40% to 50% below white wages, with little regional difference. Blacks do best in the South and North regions, and browns do poorest in the Southeastern

---

[19] Using the crude data, found in CDC, NCHS, Health, United States, 2016 (Washington DC, 2017), p. 270, Table 71. The updated version of the data are available at: www.cdc.gov/nchs/hus/contents2016.htm#071. More African American women had the examination than whites – though the figure was only 75%.

[20] IBGE, Sidra, Tables 5473 and 5488.

[21] CDC, NCHS, Health, United States, 2016, Table 70. Accessed at: www.cdc.gov/nchs/hus/contents2016.htm#070.

[22] IBGE, Sidra, Table 5888.

Table 8.3 *Ratio of Black and Brown Median Income to White Median Income by Sex and Region for Persons 10 Years of Age and Older, 2010*

Region	Men			Women		
	White	Black	Brown	White	Black	Brown
North	100	98	59	100	94	
Northeast	100	80	40	100	100	80
Southeast	100	64	64	100	98	35
South	100	73	68	100	100	50
Center-West	100	77	73	100	81	39
Brazil	100	85	85	100	44	18
Persons with income	27,219,066	4,708,870	21,868,690	24,437,053	3,699,098	18,521,944

Source: IBGE, Sidra, Table 1381.

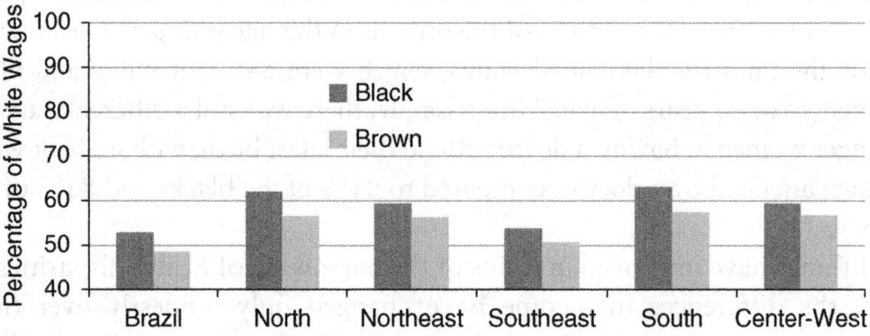

GRAPH 8.6 Average Nominal Monthly Wages of Blacks and Browns as Share of White Income by Region in Census 2010
(Whites = 100)
Source: IBGE, Sidra, Table 1382.

region. What is surprising is the consistent lower level of average brown salaries compared to black wages (see Graph 8.6).

Even more differences emerge in median monthly income when we consider sex and color. Women in general earned 61% less than the median male wage, though for whites the difference was reduced to 15% less than men. For black women it was two-thirds less than men and for browns it was 82% less than white men. When compared within each sex, very significant differences emerged in most regions between whites and non-whites (see Table 8.3).

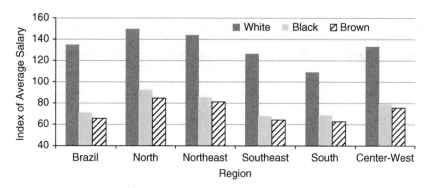

GRAPH 8.7 Index of Average Salary by Color by Region, Census 2010
(All Persons=100)
Source: IBGE, Sidra, Censo 2010, Table 1382.

The PNAD household surveys consistently found the same spread in income between whites, blacks, and browns in all occupations and all regions. In 2003, for example, whites earned twice the income of blacks and mulattos, and this was consistent across all regions, with the only exception being the North, where blacks and mulattos earned two-thirds of an average white salary. Moreover, there was no major difference by sex, with men of color doing only modestly better than women of color. Moreover, years of education made little difference, with blacks and browns earning less than whites with the same years of education.[23] This differential has continued to today, as can be seen in the census of 2010. What is surprising, however, is the fact that in the census blacks did better in average wages than did browns in every region of the country, though both were considerably below whites (see Graph 8.7). This may be due to the fact that blacks are as concentrated as whites in the richest Southeastern zone, whereas browns until recently were concentrated in the poorest region the Northeast. This was evident in the censuses of 1991 and 2000, as it was in the census of 2010.[24]

The population of color of Brazil was also far more likely to be in the lower half of the income deciles than the non-whites. Some 51% of the whites were to be found in the top 30% of income earners, whereas only 27% of black and brown income earners were found in this elite position. This strong inequality was evident in the occupational distribution as well as in wages.[25] In 2015, some

---

[23] IBGE, *Síntese de Indicadores Sociais 2004*, Table 11.11.   [24] PNAD, Sidra, Table 136.

[25] PNAD (*Pesquisa Nacional por Amostra de Domicílios 2001*): microdados (Rio de Janeiro: IBGE, 2002). CD-ROM, Table 9.16.

Table 8.4 *Structure of the Labor Market by Color, 2015*

Color	Employee	Domestic Worker	Self-Employed	Employer	Miscellaneous	Total
			Share of Position by Color			
White	67.3	5.7	20.3	5.5	1.2	100.0
Black	64.8	11.5	20.8	1.9	1.0	100.0
Brown	63.7	9.2	23.0	2.6	1.5	100.0
Total	65.5	7.7	21.5	4.0	1.3	100.0
			Share by Color within each Position			
White	49.4	35.2	45.3	66.4	42.5	47.9
Black	9.8	14.8	9.6	4.6	7.8	9.9
Brown	40.7	49.7	44.6	27.3	48.8	41.7
Total	100.0	100.0	100.0	100.0	100.0	100.0

Source: Elaborated from microdata of PNAD 2015.

6% of the whites were in domestic service, compared to 10% of blacks and browns – and in this occupation blacks and browns made up 75% of the labor force. By contrast, they made up half the ratio of employers than did the whites, and in turn only accounted for a third of these employers (see Table 8.4).[26] Even when the population of color had the same occupation, their average income was consistently lower than that of the whites. Thus, in 2003, black and brown workers in the formal sector earned a third less on average than white workers and those in the informal sector gained just under half of a white informal worker's salary. By 2004, only 54% of the whites and 37% of the black and brown population were in the formal sector, with working papers, and receiving at least a minimum monthly wage. By 2015, the figures were respectively 66% for whites and 52% for the total population of all persons of color.[27] Nevertheless, the gap persisted and in all regions white workers were more to be found in the formal sector than were black and brown workers, though the difference was least in the three richest regions – the South, Southeast, and Center-West – and worst in the poorest of the regions (see Graph 8.8).

[26] IBGE, *Síntese de Indicadores Sociais 2004*, Table 11.13.
[27] IBGE, *Síntese de Indicadores Socias, uma análise das Condições da Vida da População Brasileira, 2015* (Rio de Janeiro, 2016), Table 5.8, found in a separate appendix dataset at: www.ibge.gov.br/estatisticas-novoportal/sociais/populacao/9221-sintese-de-indicadores -sociais.html?edicao=9222&t=downloads.

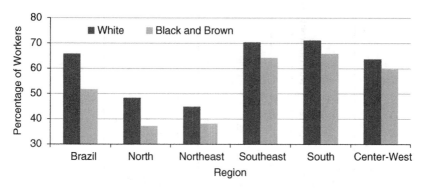

GRAPH 8.8 Percentage of Workers in the Formal Sector by Color by Region, 2015
Source: IBGE, *Síntese de Indicadores Sociais*, 2015, Table 5.8.

Among military and government workers in 2003 the blacks and browns earned a third less than whites, and among employers – the highest income group for both whites and non-whites – blacks and browns gained just under half of the earnings of the whites.[28] All this explains the skewed wealth distribution by color. In 2015, the combined blacks and browns made up 76% of the poorest 10% of the wealth holders and income earners in the country, while they made up only 18% of the richest 1%. This was only a modest improvement from 2004 when they made 12% of the top 1%. In both cases these were far lower ratios than their representation in the population as a whole.[29] It has been estimated that the proportion of non-whites living below the poverty line in Brazil was 50%, while that of the white population was just 25%.[30]

As revealed in the household survey of 2015, blacks and browns were over-represented in domestic service and under-represented as employers in contrast to whites. Blacks were above their ratio in the labor force in terms of self-employed. But among self-employed only 23% of both browns and blacks contributed to the social security system, compared to 40% of the white self-employed. Clearly, they were more to be found in the informal market than were whites. When examining their role within each major sector of the economy, it is evident that browns were over-represented in agriculture and in domestic service. Both blacks and browns were under-represented in public administration and education and health, areas were whites were over-represented. What is impressive is that browns together

[28] IBGE, *Síntese de Indicadores Sociais* 2004, Table 11.14.
[29] IBGE, *Síntese de Indicadores Sociais* 2015 (Rio de Janeiro, 2016), Table 6.7, found in a separate appendix dataset at: www.ibge.gov.br/estatisticas-novoportal/sociais/populacao/9221-sintese-de-indicadores-sociais.html?edicao=9222&t=downloads.
[30] PNUD, CEDELPAR, "Atlas Racial Brasileiro – 2004."

Table 8.5 *Distribution of Workers in the Major Sectors of the Economy by Color, 2015*

Color	Agriculture	Transformative Industries	Construction	Commerce	Food and Lodging	Transport and Communications	Public Administration	Education, Health and Social Services	Domestic Services	Miscellaneous	Total
					Share of Sector by Color						
White	10.4	13.9	7.1	19.0	4.7	5.7	5.5	12.6	5.2	16.1	100.0
Black	12.6	10.2	12.2	16.5	5.5	5.3	4.7	9.2	10.1	13.8	100.0
Brown	17.7	10.9	10.6	18.1	5.2	5.3	4.5	8.7	7.7	11.2	100.0
Total	13.9	12.2	9.1	18.3	5.0	5.5	5.0	10.5	6.8	13.7	100.0
					Share of Color within Sector						
White	34.3	51.9	35.2	47.2	42.7	47.2	50.3	54.6	34.6	34.6	45.6
Black	9.0	8.3	13.3	8.9	10.9	9.6	9.3	8.8	14.8	14.8	10.0
Brown	56.7	39.8	51.5	43.9	46.3	43.2	40.4	36.6	50.6	50.6	44.4
Total	100.0	100.0	100.0	100.0	100.0	100.0	100.0	100.0	100.0	100.0	100.0

Source: Elaborated from microdata of PNAD 2015.

with blacks made up two-thirds of agricultural and domestic workers and half or more in all other fields except education and health and industries (see Table 8.5). Browns were especially well represented at all levels in the police and military organizations and were to be found along with blacks as lab technicians in numerous fields. They also had a significant representation as primary school teachers, in the transport industry, and in the arts, but were under-represented in the liberal professions.

Clearly, then, well over a century after emancipation, the African descendent population of Brazil remains overwhelmingly poor and under-represented in the higher-level occupations and among the wealthiest classes. But, just as there has been a major migration out of indigence and poverty in the last quarter-century, occupation, income, and education have improved for this subsection of the national population. The differences in health between whites and non-whites have narrowed considerably and the gap in average years of education has been slowly narrowing. So quick has this been that it could be expected that the difference between whites and non-whites in educational achievement will disappear in a few years. This can be seen in the school enrollment figures for 2003, which show little difference by color in the enrollment ratios of almost all age groups. Only in the older groups was there a meaningful difference and here the spread was not that extreme. Thus, for 15- to 17-year-olds (that is, among high school students) and for 20- to 24-year-olds (those enrolled in post-secondary schools), there was a 7% spread between black/brown and white enrollments.[31] While years of schooling are now becoming normalized for all groups, the increasing divide between public and private primary and secondary education in terms of quality has become a major blockage as the rich have dominated private primary and secondary education and the poor have been left with a public primary and secondary education of poor quality. The reverse has occurred with tertiary education, with the rich dominating the far more advanced public universities and the poor relegated to mostly unqualified private faculties. Thus, education, which initially became the prime motor for mobility until the 1980s and 1990s, has now created new blockages, just as all whites and non-whites are achieving similar levels of years of schooling,

Almost all the studies of income and race show significant differences up to today, some of which may be due to this new blockage in education. Thus, a much-cited Ipea study shows that differences still exists through discrimination, but suggests that it is far worse regarding gender difference than in terms of race, with average white salaries being around 11% to 12% higher

---

[31] The figures were 86% to 79% for the 15–17 cohort and 30% to 23% for the 20–24 age group. IBGE, *Síntese de Indicadores Sociais 2004*, Table 11.4.

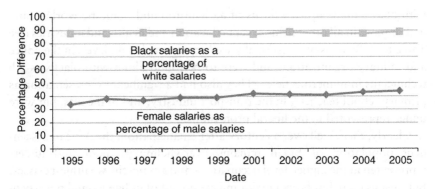

GRAPH 8.9 Average Salary Differences between Men and Women and between Blacks and Whites, 1995–2005
Source: Ricardo Paes de Barros et al., "Discriminação e segmentação" (2007), p. 14.

than black salaries, but male salaries in general being two-thirds to more than half greater than female wages, though the difference is declining fast (see Graph 8.9). Thus, overall, Ipea found discrimination greater for gender than for color in all their studies.[32]

These results for blacks and browns as well as for men and women raise the question of what explains these continuing if declining differences. Is it due to active discrimination by employers, to a segmentation of the market, with women or non-whites concentrated in low-paying jobs? Is the segmentation only by type of industry or is it spatial by region or state? Is it the relative weight of formal and informal markets, or is it due to different individual characteristics for women and blacks compared to white males? As Ricardo Paes de Barros and his coauthors noted:

The market generates inequality both when it remunerates differently men and women or whites and blacks of the same productivity, as when there are differences of remuneration between perfect substitute workers in production occupying positions in different segments of the labor market. In the first case, we say that the differentials result from discrimination in the labor market and, second, from its segmentation.[33]

This is the fundamental question in the literature and has been answered in several different ways. Several studies show that although the percentage of women who are employed is smaller than men, for those who are

---

[32] Ricardo Paes de Barros, Samuel Franco, and Rosane Mendonça, "Discriminação e segmentação no mercado de trabalho e desigualdade de renda no Brasil," Texto para discussão 1288, Rio de Janeiro, Ipea, 2007, p. 14.
[33] Barros, Franco, and Mendonça, "Discriminação e segmentação," 8.

economically active there is little difference in employment and unemployment ratios. In general, a woman's work week is five hours less than that of a man, which can explain some of the wage differences. But several authors have stressed that there is segmentation in the market, with a very high ratio of women working in female-dominated industries (such as teaching or domestic service) which employ fewer men, which explains their wage differences. But even controlling for education and segmentation of the market, women still receive lower salaries than men. Recently it is argued that the big difference is intra-occupational status, with men consistently having higher status and thus more income than women, possibly due to their earlier positioning in the labor market compared to late-arrival women.[34] Nevertheless, all studies suggest that the higher the educational level of the workers the less wage discrimination occurs, all of which suggests a continued decline of discrimination by sex as women continue to increase their levels of education compared with men.[35]

But if this wage discrimination is declining for white women, what is the situation for non-whites versus whites. Even when blacks achieve higher occupational status, they find their income less than whites. In fact, median income was half that of whites for directors and administrators of enterprises in São Paulo in 2002. But moving down the occupational hierarchy, monthly wage workers with registered work permits show only a modest difference between white and blacks and browns of both sexes and between white men and white women. At the bottom of the income scale there is equality by color and sex (see Graph 8.10). Among managers and directors in the state of São Paulo and the state of Bahia, based on average salaries, black men are paid better than white women. Finally, the higher the educational level, the lower the wage differences between all four categories, though white males still do the best. However, in conclusion, the authors of this comparative 2002 study still find that "discrimination [racial and sexual] is to a greater or lesser extent present in the Brazilian labor market," no matter what the structure of the market or the racial composition of the labor force.[36]

---

[34] Sérgio Pinheiro Firpo, "Inserção no mercado de trabalho: diferenças por sexo e conseqüências sobre o bem-estar," Texto para discussão 796, Rio de Janeiro, Ipea, 2001, pp. 4–5.

[35] On the secular decline of differences, which has been faster in Brazil than in the United States, see Ana Carolina Giuberti and Naércio Menezes-Filho, "Discriminação de rendimentos por gênero: uma comparação entre o Brasil e os Estados Unidos," Economia Aplicada 9.3 (2005), pp. 369–383.

[36] Maria Cristina Cacciamali and Guilherme Issamu Hirata, "A influência da raça e do gênero nas oportunidades de obtenção de renda: uma análise da discriminação em mercados de trabalho distintos: Bahia e São Paulo," Estudos Econômicos 35.4 (2005), pp. 767–795.

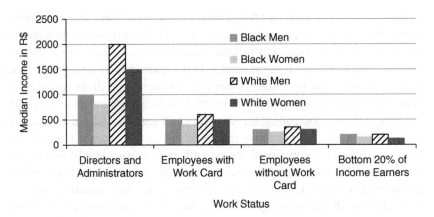

GRAPH 8.10 Median Income by Color and Sex and Status of Work, São Paulo, 2002
Source: Cacciamali and Hirate, "A influência da raça e do gênero" (2005), p. 775,
Table 2.

Because of its crucial role in mobility and in income, the role of discrimination in education has become a major area of recent research. As numerous
studies have emphasized, wages and mobility are intimately linked to levels
of education. So, the question is, how well or poorly do blacks and browns
do compared with whites? In fact, the differences between the sexes in terms
of education have changed more rapidly than changes between whites and
non-whites. Whereas women reached equality of school attendance by the
1980s, it is only now at the end of the second decade of the twenty-first
century that non-whites and whites are approaching equality in school
matriculations. As late as 1991 there was a 9% difference in school attendance, but this fell to less than 1% by 2009 (see Graph 8.11).

This in turn has led to a slow but steady decline in the spread between
white and non-white literacy rates. But, given the late development of equal
educational participation at the primarily level it will take more generations
before the literacy rates will be the same between whites and blacks and
mulattos. In 2004, the literacy rate for the population 15 years of age and
older was 92.8% for whites while for non-whites it was only 83.7%. The gap
has slowly closed as literacy has increased faster for blacks/browns than for
whites, so that the difference between the two groups has declined from 10%
in 2004 to just 6% in 2015 (see Graph 8.12).

These changes can also be seen in the evaluation of functional illiterates:
those who have had some schooling, but still cannot properly read and write.
In the PNAD survey of 2004, for example, some 67% of the non-white adults
were functionally illiterate, while only half of the whites were considered this

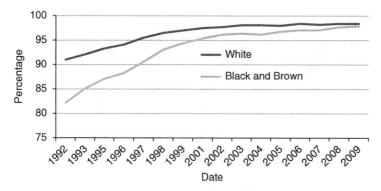

GRAPH 8.11 Percentage of Persons 7–14 Years of Age Attending School, by Race, 1992–2009
Source: IBGE, Sidra, Table 1186.

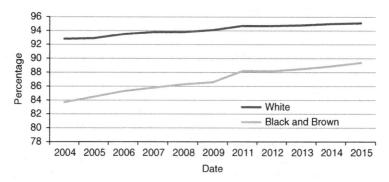

GRAPH 8.12 Percentage of Adults Literate, 15 Years of Age and Older, by Race, 2004–2015
Source: IBGE, Sidra, Table 1188.

disadvantaged. By 2015, some 49% of black and brown adults (those 25 years of age and older) were functionally illiterate compared to some 35% of the whites who could not effectively read and write. Though still disadvantaged, the slowly declining gap between whites and non-whites should continue over time since blacks and browns are increasing their literacy more rapidly than the whites.[37]

---

[37] IBGE, *Síntese de Indicadores Sociais 2016*, Table 4.14, found in a separate appendix dataset at: www.ibge.gov.br/estatisticas-novoportal/sociais/populacao/9221-sintese-de-indicadores -sociais.html?edicao=9222&t=downloads. The functionally illiterate were defined as those with no education, or primary school incomplete (sem instrução e fundamental incompleto).

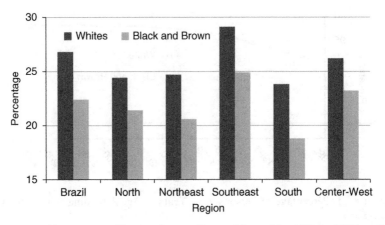

GRAPH 8.13 Percentage of Persons 25–64 Years of Age with 11 Years of Education, by Color, 2009
Source: IBGE, Sidra, Table 3899.

In the same period, the difference in the average years of schooling of blacks and browns has declined from 2.1 years below the white 7.0 years of schooling in 2001 to just 1.8 years less than the 8.8 years of schooling for whites in 2015.[38] This gap between whites and non-whites is the norm for all regions of Brazil. But, as in all other educational indices, the spread in years of schooling between whites and non-whites has declined considerably in the recent period as far more persons obtain an advanced secondary education. High school graduates among whites increased by 0.4% per annum between 2009 and 2015 and accounted for 29.4% of all adult whites in this period, but blacks and browns increased their numbers by 2.9% per annum in the same period which meant that 27.4% of them by 2015 were high school graduates. Thus, the gap was reduced by half, with blacks and browns now at 93% of the white graduation rate. Moreover, the Southeastern region moved from having one of the larger gaps between whites and non-whites (at 86% of the white graduation rate in 2009 to 98% of the white rate in 2005), a change not experienced in the South region, which remained the worst of all the regions in 2015 in terms of the difference between the white and the brown and black rates of graduation (see Graph 8.13).

[38] IBGE, *Síntese de Indicadores Sociais* 2016, Table 4.13, found in a separate appendix dataset at: www.ibge.gov.br/estatisticas-novoportal/sociais/populacao/9221-sintese-de-indicadores -sociais.html?edicao=9222&t=downloads.

Table 8.6 *Average Years of Schooling by Sex and Color,*
1989 and 2015

	White	Black	Brown	Total
1989				
Men	7.4	4.9	5.7	6.6
Women	7.9	5.0	6.0	6.9
Total	7.6	4.9	5.9	6.7
2015				
	White	Black	Brown	Total
Men	8.3	7.5	6.9	7.6
Women	8.7	7.9	7.4	8.1
Total	8.5	7.7	7.1	7.8

Source: Cavalieri and Fernandes, "Diferenciais de salários por
gênero" (1988), p. 161, Table 3; 2015. Elaborated from microdata
of PNAD.

But there are still differences by sex and color. While all women have done
better than men in terms of educational attainment, non-white women are
still well behind the levels achieved by white women and white men. This can
be seen in the evolution of years of schooling. By the late 1980s, in the PNAD
surveys, women were consistently better educated than men of their color
(see Table 8.6) and this has continued. Although all groups of men and
women increased their educational levels by 2015, it is blacks who have
increased the fastest, going from 2.5 years difference from black men compared to white men and a full three years difference between black women
and white women in 1989 to just 0.9 and 0.8 years difference respectively in
2015. By contrast, browns have only moderately changed their position from
1989 (see Table 8.6).

The overall differences between whites and non-whites in educational
attainment has continued to decline systematically in the current century. Between 2004 and 2014 there was a steady increase in years of
schooling among those 25 years of age and older. Men fell further
behind women (from 0.02 years to 0.4 years) and blacks reduced their
difference from whites, but the gap was still 1.8 years. By 2014, Women
had 8.1 years and men 7.7 years of study. White men had 8.8 years of
study while non-white men (blacks and browns) had 7.0, though the
differences which initially seemed to change little have declined

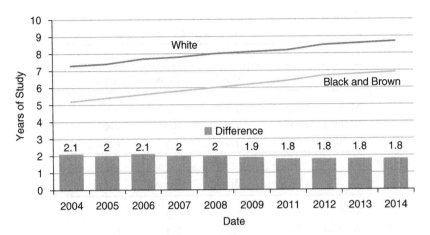

GRAPH 8.14 Average Years of Study of Persons 25 Years of Age and Older, by Color, 2004–2014
IBGE, *Síntese de Indicadores Sociais* 2017, Table 3.12.

moderately since 2006 (from two years of differences between the two groups of color to 1.8 years) (see Graph 8.14).[39]

As all studies show, there has been a massive increase in the educational level of the population in the period between the census of 1960 and the census of 2010. Both sexes and all races have greatly increased their educational levels, especially after the universalization of primary education in Brazil by the 1990s. But it is evident that women have done better than men in schooling and that blacks and browns are still below white educational attainment at all levels. The major change for whites and non-whites for both sexes is that the gap has narrowed considerably among men and women since 1960. The brown–white gap among men went from 10% of the white rate of graduates of secondary school and above to almost two-thirds of that rate by 2010. And this reduction also occurred even more quickly for brown women, who reached 71% of the white female rate by 2010 (see Table 8.7).

A summary of the levels of education attained by persons 25 years of age and older for the PNAD household surveys using the simpler Brazilian educational definitions finds the same patterns as the decennial census data. From 2004, the first when comparable data are available, to 2015

---

[39] IBGE, Síntese de Indicadores Sociais 2016, Table 4.13. Accessed at: https://ww2.ibge.gov.br /home/estatistica/populacao/condicaodevida/indicadoresminimos/sinteseindicsociais2015/d efault_tab_xls.shtm.

Table 8.7 *Years of Schooling for Persons 25 Years of Age and Older, by Sex and Race, 1960 and 2010*

	1960			2010		
Males	**White**	**Black**	**Brown**	**White**	**Black**	**Brown**
No schooling	33.0	65.1	60.5	0.9	2.1	2.2
Some primary completed	33.3	25.2	28.7	22.5	32.8	33.2
Primary (4 years) completed	23.5	8.9	9.2	13.7	13.6	13.8
Primary (6 years) completed	4.8	0.6	1.1	20.7	21.6	21.5
Lower secondary general completed	0.3	0.0	0.1	5.0	5.8	5.5
Secondary, general track completed	2.4	0.1	0.3	20.5	18.0	17.4
Some college completed	0.5	0.0	0.1	4.6	2.6	2.4
University completed	2.2	0.0	0.2	12.0	3.6	3.9
Total	100.0	100.0	100.0	100.0	100.0	100.0
Females	**White**	**Black**	**Brown**	**White**	**Black**	**Brown**
No schooling	43.8	76.8	72.3	0.8	1.9	1.7
Some primary completed	25.9	16.1	19.3	21.4	30.8	30.4
Primary (4 years) completed	22.7	6.7	7.3	13.4	12.8	12.9
Primary (6 years) completed	4.7	0.3	0.7	18.4	20.1	20.2
Lower secondary general completed	0.2	0.0	0.0	4.7	5.8	5.7
Secondary, general track completed	2.3	0.1	0.2	21.3	19.4	19.5
Some college completed	0.1	0.0	0.0	4.5	3.3	3.1
University completed	0.3	0.0	0.0	15.5	6.0	6.5
Total	100.0	100.0	100.0	100.0	100.0	100.0

Source: Ipums, 5% Sample of Brazilian Censuses, 1960–2010.

shows the gap between whites and blacks and browns has continued to decline as the latter group increases its educational level at a faster rate than whites (Table 8.8).

In most of the other educational indices analyzed, such as age of enrolled students by grades and retention rates, the racial gap has also been closing recently. Thus, for enrolled students 15–17 years of age who were older than their respective class age group, a clear sign of dysfunctional education, there was initially a much higher gap between

Table 8.8 *Schooling Completed by Persons 25 Years of Age and Older, by Race, 2004–2015*

Color	None	Primary Incomplete	Primary Complete	High School Incomplete	High School Complete	University Incomplete	University Complete
				2004			
White	10.5	39.5	9.6	3.8	20.7	3.7	11.8
Black and brown	22.1	44.8	8.0	4.0	15.5	1.7	3.3
				2015			
White	7.4	27.8	9.5	3.4	27.4	4.6	19.7
Black and brown	14.4	34.6	9.8	4.7	25.5	3.1	7.7

Source: PNAD 2016, Table 4.14, Nível de ensino das pessoas de 25 anos ou mais de idade.
Notes: primary = *fundamental*; high school = *medio*; university = *superior*.

whites and blacks and browns. As late as 2004, fully half of the brown and black students were over age, compared to just over a quarter of the whites. By 2015, the rate was down to 19% for whites and to 31% for non-white students.[40]

Two distinct patterns emerge when we compare completion rates by level of schooling for color and sex in 2015. Women consistently do better than men for all race groups. At the same time, blacks and browns still are the least educated. Whites who had no education or an incomplete primary education accounted for 35% of all white persons over 25 years of age, for black it was 47% and browns 50% of this age group. By contrast, the impact of increasing educational opportunities is seen in the middle school graduates who are basically equal in all sexes and colors. But this equalization has yet to appear among university graduates. Among these tertiary-level graduates not only do women outpace men but there is still a very significant difference between male and female whites and non-whites (see Table 8.9).

What of marriage and cohabitation and race? Do these reflect discrimination based on skin color? How endogamous are the cohabiting partners in terms of color? To begin with, it is important to recognize that there has been a significant change in cohabitation which now affects all classes and all racial

[40] PNAD 2016, Table 4.8, "roporção de estudantes de 15 a 17 anos de idade com distorção idade-série." Accessed at: www.ibge.gov.br/estatisticas-novoportal/sociais/populacao/9221-sintese-de-indicadores-sociais.html?edicao=9222&t=downloads.

Table 8.9 *Level of Education Completed, by Color and Sex, for Persons 25 Years of Age and Older, 2015*

Race	Male	Female	Total
No Education			
White	7.2	7.6	7.4
Black	14.6	14.3	14.5
Brown	15.1	13.7	14.4
Primary school incomplete			
White	28.7	27.2	27.9
Black	34.3	31.2	32.7
Brown	36.5	33.8	35.1
Primary School Completed			
White	10.1	9.0	9.5
Black	10.3	5.1	6.3
Brown	10.1	9.4	9.7
High School Incomplete			
White	3.6	3.2	3.4
Black	5.3	4.7	5.0
Brown	4.8	4.6	4.7
Secondary School Complete			
White	27.3	27.6	27.4
Black	26.7	27.9	27.4
Brown	24.3	25.9	25.2
University Incomplete			
White	5.0	4.3	4.6
Black	3.0	3.6	3.3
Brown	2.8	3.3	3.0
University complete			
White	18.1	21.2	19.8
Black	5.8	8.5	7.2
Brown	6.4	9.2	7.9

Source: Elaborated from microdata of PNAD 2015.

Table 8.10 *Distribution of Type of Union, by Color of Women 20–29 Years of Age, Censuses of 1980, 1991, 2000, and 2010**

	1980		1990		2000		2010	
Race	In Consensual Union	Married	In Consensual Union	Married	In Consensual Union	Married	In Consensual Union	Married
White	9.7	90.3	18.8	81.2	37.4	62.7	49.4	50.6
Black	19.1	80.9	32.1	67.9	51.0	48.3	55.8	44.2
Brown	27.7	72.3	40.7	59.3	58.1	41.9	60.8	39.2

Source: Luciene Aparecida Ferreira de Barros Longo, "Uniões intra e inter-raciais" (2011), p. 96, Table 7 for 1980–2000; and IBGE, Sidra, Table 3487 for 2010.
* Longo uses samples from the first three censuses and the IBGE, Sidra Table gives the data for women 20–29 years of age.

groups. This of course is the decline of formal marriage and the growth of consensual unions. Although consensual unions were traditionally a lower-class arrangement going back to colonial times, and were thus more prevalent with blacks and browns, the changes in the legal status of women living in free unions and the guarantee of the rights of their children (discussed earlier) have led to consensual unions increasingly appearing among all groups, including whites.

As can be seen in an analysis of the cohort of women in the 20–29 age group (Table 8.10), the ratio of those living with men in consensual unions has been growing steadily from the late twentieth century and has increased steadily for all groups. Among white women in this age group, those living in consensual unions has gone from 10% to 49% of all women living with men. This change has gone farthest and fastest for brown and black women but is now becoming the dominant form of relationship for this key age group of women of all races. According to the latest census (2010), consensual unions accounted for 56% of all couples living together (see Table 8.10).

Equally, there has been a decline in endogamous relationships based on color; that is, whites marrying whites went from over 90% in 1960 to around 80% approximately for both men and women in heterosexual unions in 1991.[41] Overall, for all groups of blacks, browns, and whites, racial endogamy went from 88% of marriages in 1960, to 80% in 1980, and down to 69% in 2000. While there is far from total equality for all groups, the decline in endogamous relationships is coming closer to what would occur if no class or color prejudice existed. One estimate based on shares of population

[41] Edward E. Telles, *Race in Another America: The Significance of Skin Color in Brazil* (Princeton, NJ: Princeton University Press, 2014), pp. 176–177.

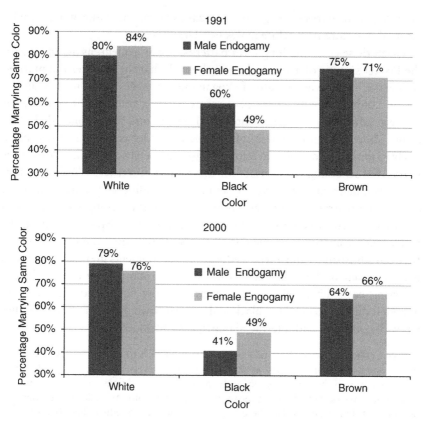

GRAPH 8.15 Racial Endogamy of Couples, Censuses 1991 and 2000
Source: IBGE, Sidra, Tables 273 and 2642.

suggests that endogamous rates would have been 51% in 1960, 48% in 1980, and 45% in 2000 if no preferences by color existed.[42]

Of these self-identified color groups, most whites and browns lived with partners within their racial groups in the census of 1991, while blacks of both sexes were the most who "married out." Of the black women who married out, 32% were living with brown men and 19% with white men. By contrast, 26% of the brown women lived with white men and only 3% had a black male partner, suggesting the traditional "whitening" aims of Brazilian coupling. Initially, women married out of their racial identity more than men, except for white women in the year 1990. But this was reversed in 2000, as

---

[42] Carlos Antonio Costa Ribeiro and Nelson do Valle Silva, "Cor, Educação e Casamento: Tendências da Seletividade Marital no Brasil, 1960 a 2000," *Dados: Revista de Ciências Sociais* 52.1 (2009), p. 25.

far more men married exogenously, again except for white women, who married out more than white males (see Graph 8.15).

Given these changing long-term patterns, it was evident, as an analysis of the PNAD surveys of 1987 and 1998 showed, that the younger the married couple the higher was the rate of exogamous marriages, and this was similar for all color groups.[43] There also seems to be a trade-off at some levels between education and racial intermarriage. As one study concluded, "the results show that an individual of a race/color of lesser social status is more likely to join a partner of a race/color of greater social status when differences in levels of schooling compensate for these racial differences."[44] Thus, whatever advantages of beauty versus status may traditionally have influenced cross-racial marriages, education now is an important component which in some cases seems to compensate for lesser color status. Moreover, given the increasing advantage of women at all levels of education, the overall spread between a husband's and a wife's educational attainments in these exogamous marriages has declined by half from 1960 to 2000. In the case of blacks marrying each other, educational levels are now equal and there is only a modest difference in white–black and white–brown marriages.[45] As another study of education and interracial marriages concluded:

between 1960 and 2000 there was a decrease of barriers to marriage between white, brown and black people, as well as across educational levels. This means that Brazilian society seems to be becoming significantly more open to weddings crossing educational and color barriers. This does not mean, however, that color and educational barriers do not exist, but indicates that there is a strong tendency to reduce these barriers.[46]

Summing up their basic findings, these authors concluded that there is a steady increase in interracial marriages. "In 1960, 1 in every 10 marriages was between persons of different color groups; in 1980 this number increased to 1 in every five marriages; in 2000 to 1 in every 3 marriages."[47]

Another area where discrimination plays a role is in housing and residence. A methodology has been developed in the United States to measure racial segregation in housing. The two most frequently cited indices are those of "dissimilarity" and "isolation." Dissimilarity measures racial concentration by showing what percentage of one racial group would have to leave an

---

[43] José Luis Petruccelli, "Seletividade por cor e escolhas conjugais no Brasil dos 90," *Estudos Afro-Asiáticos* 23.1 (2001), p. 40, Table 9.

[44] Luciene Aparecida Ferreira de Barros Longo, "Uniões intra e inter-raciais, status marital, escolaridade e religião no Brasil: um estudo sobre a seletividade marital feminina, 1980–2000," PhD thesis, Universidade Federal de Minas Gerais – UFMG, 2011, p. 152.

[45] Ribeiro and Silva, "Cor, Educação e Casamento," p. 27, Table 3.

[46] Ribeiro and Silva, "Cor, Educação e Casamento," pp. 45–46.

[47] Ribeiro and Silva, "Cor, Educação e Casamento," p. 8.

area for equality to be achieved with a second group. The index of isolation shows how much exposure one group has to another group: the higher the percentage of isolation indicating the smaller the contact between groups. A recent detailed study of all the major metropolitan centers of Brazil found that the index of dissimilarity was quite low in Brazil compared to the United States. Thus, in 1980, New York City had a dissimilarity index of 75 and São Paulo 37; Washington 79 and Brasília 39; Chicago 92 and Salvador 48. It also found that "white residential exposure to non-whites in Brazil is clearly greater than in US cities of comparable racial composition."[48] Another study did find increasing discrimination in housing at the upper levels of the income bracket in Brazil.[49] But, again, income, like racial segregation in housing, was only mild to moderate in Brazil, especially compared to the United States, with its deliberate policies of creating segregated ghettos in the northern cities in the modern period, which resulted in severe levels of segregation.

Another question to ask is whether race influences chances of social mobility. From the most recent studies of social mobility in Brazil it appears that upward mobility is determined primarily by economic and social conditions and not by color, but that in patterns of downward mobility race begins to have far more of an impact than income.[50] Brazil has undergone a great deal of structural mobility due to rapid urbanization and late industrialization. Brazil in just a few decades in the second half of the twentieth century went from a predominantly rural to a predominantly urban population, which resulted in a great deal of social mobility at the top of the occupational ladder. Some 80%

---

[48] Telles, *Race in Another America*, Chapter 8. The quote is from p. 205.

[49] Overall, the rate of dissimilarity was 30 and went from 18 at the lowest economic strata to 0.36 at the highest (above 20 minimum salaries). See Danilo Sales do Nascimento França, "Raça, classe e segregação residencial no Município de São Paulo," MA thesis, Universidade de São Paulo, 2010, pp. 71–72. For other studies of income segregation, see Elvis Vitoriano da Silva, "Desigualdade de renda no espaço intra-urbano: análise da evolução na cidade de Porto Alegre no período 1991–2000," MA thesis, Universidade Federal do Rio Grande do Sul, 2011, p. 141. For a very detailed analysis of indices of isolation by income class in all the districts of a Southern town of 261,000 population, see Thayse Cristiane Severo do Prado, "Segregação residencial por índices de dissimilaridade, isolamento e exposição, com indicador renda, no espaço urbano de Santa Maria, RS, por geotecnologias," MA thesis, Universidade Federal de Santa Maria, 2012.

[50] For the classic position, see Carlos A. Hasenbalg, Nelson do Valle Silva, and Marcia Lima, *Cor e estratificação social no Brasil* (Rio de Janeiro: Contracapa, 1999) and Ricardo Henriques, "Desigualdade racial no Brasil: evolução das condições de vida na década de 90," Texto para discussão 807, Rio de Janeiro, Ipea, 2001. For alternative arguments stressing non-racial factors influencing the differences, see Pedro Ferreira de Souza, Carlos Antonio Costa Ribeiro, and Flavio Carvalhaes, "Desigualdade de oportunidades no Brasil: considerações sobre classe, educação e raça," *Revista Brasileira de Ciências Sociais* 25.73 (2010), pp. 77–100 and Carlos Antonio Costa Ribeiro, "Classe, Raça e Mobilidade Social no Brasil," *Dados: Revista de Ciências Sociais* 49.4 (2006), pp. 833–873.

of administrators, owners, and professionals come from rural classes.[51] At the bottom of the occupational structure, as late as the 1990s over half of urban manual workers had a rural origin. All this meant that Brazil had an increasing amount of social mobility from the 1970s to the 2000s.[52]

A recent group of studies based on the detailed questions concerning parent and child occupations in the PNAD national household surveys have provided economists and sociologists with a wealth of data to analyze this question of social mobility by race. Do children stay in the same occupational status as their parents or do they move to a higher or lower occupational and income level then their fathers? In the latest such survey, carried out in 2014 and recently made available, the IBGE provided panel data on older and younger persons and their occupational positions compared to their fathers, broken down by race. The census categorizes these occupations from high-status (a), mid-level (b), low-level (c), semi-skilled urban (d), unskilled urban (e), to unskilled agricultural laborer (f), in a declining gradation of skills, income, and status (see Table 8.11).

To understand these differences better we have created a table of absolute differences between whites and non-whites for each occupational grouping which is derived from Table 8.11 by subtracting each percentage for non-whites from the corresponding percentage for whites.[53] This shows the relative likelihood of mobility between each category for the two racial groups. What is striking about the table is that with one exception all the percentages below the diagonal are negative and with two exceptions all the percentages above the diagonal are positive. This suggests that the chances of upward mobility for whites are greater than for blacks and that the chances of downward mobility for blacks are greater than for whites. It is also the case that the children of whites in the highest status group are much more likely to retain their father's status than are blacks, and that whites in the lowest occupational status group (agricultural laborers) are much more likely than blacks to be upwardly mobile (see Table 8.12).

This same survey also broke down the sons and daughters into two age groups: those aged 25–44 and those aged 45–65 years. The older cohort thus includes a generation that came of working age in the late 1970s to early

---

[51] Ribeiro and Scalon, "Mobilidade de classe no Brasil."

[52] For two basic surveys of social mobility in this period, see Ribeiro and Scalon, "Mobilidade de classe no Brasil"; Ribeiro, "Quatro décadas de mobilidade social no Brasil" and his *Estrutura de classe e mobilidade social*; Maria Celi Scalon, *Mobilidade social no brasil: padrões e tendências* (Rio de Janeiro: Revan, 1999). And the classic studies of Pastore, *Inequality and Social Mobility in Brazil* and the updated revisions in José Pastore and Nelson do Valle Silva, *Mobilidade Social no Brasil* (São Paulo: Makron, 2000).

[53] This is the model used by Telles.

Table 8.11 *Percentage Occupational Mobility between Father and Offspring, 25 Years of Age and Older, by Race and Age in Brazil, 2014*

Child's Occupation	Father's Occupation					
	A	B	C	D	E	F
White						
A	58.8	42.3	43.4	20.0	23.8	11.1
B	12.3	16.7	11.0	9.5	11.2	3.9
C	9.5	11.3	12.9	13.3	14.1	4.8
D	6.8	11.1	13.8	28.8	16.9	25.0
E	12.1	17.4	18.4	26.4	32.0	27.3
F	0.6	1.2	0.5	2.0	2.0	27.9
Total	100	100	100	100	100	100
N (ooos)	3,145	1,235	928	8,553	3,481	9,716
Non-White						
A	39.9	22.2	28.5	10.2	13.9	5.9
B	15.4	20.4	13.9	8.0	6.8	3.2
C	7.6	12.2	13.2	10.3	10.0	3.3
D	13.4	20.8	19.9	34.2	27.5	23.3
E	20.3	22.4	23.9	34.1	38.8	28.1
F	3.5	2.0	0.6	3.3	3.0	36.2
Total	100	100	100	100	100	100
N (ooos)	1,060	744	612	8,622	3,356	13,216

Source: IBGE, Síntese (2017), Tables 3.12 and 3.12a. www.ibge.gov.br/estatisticas-novoportal /multidominio/genero/9221-sintese-de-indicadores-sociais.html?&t=resultados.

1990s, that is in the period of major structural change. The results of absolute difference are approximately the same for both age groups of offspring, thus suggesting that little has changed over time in the pattern of social mobility by race. The 2014 survey suggests that there was only modest difference between men and women by race at least among the elite positions of middle (B) and high-status (A) positions. In turn, non-white women, like non-white men, did poorly for all combinations of parent and child status for children who currently were unskilled urban (E) or unskilled rural laborers (F) (see Table 8.13).

But, as several others have suggested, these data do not take into account education, income, share of the population, residence, and other variables

Table 8.12 *Absolute Difference between White and Non-White Mobility, by Father's Occupation*

Child's Occupation	A	B	C	D	E	F
A	18.9	20.1	14.9	9.8	9.9	5.2
B	-3.1	-3.7	-2.9	1.5	4.4	0.7
C	1.9	-0.9	-0.3	3.0	4.1	1.5
D	-6.6	-9.7	-6.1	-5.4	-10.6	1.7
E	-8.2	-5.0	-5.5	-7.7	-6.8	-0.8
F	-2.9	-0.8	-0.1	-1.3	-1.0	-8.3

Source: Calculated from Table 8.11.

Table 8.13 *Absolute Difference between White and Non-White Mobility, by Sex*

Men	Father's Occupation					
Child's Occupation	A	B	C	D	E	F
A	18.0	19.8	16.5	1.5	10.8	4.6
B	0.0	-1.2	-1.6	-0.1	5.7	1.2
C	2.0	-0.3	-0.7	-0.5	5.0	0.5
D	-10.0	-15.9	-12.1	-0.7	-19.1	1.3
E	-6.0	-1.4	-2.3	-0.3	-0.1	-0.3
F	-4.0	-1.0	0.2	0.2	-2.3	-7.3
Women	**Father's Occupation**					
Child's Occupation	A	B	C	D	E	F
A	18.0	20.2	11.4	-0.4	8.9	6.0
B	-6.0	-6.9	-4.2	-0.7	3.0	-0.3
C	0.0	-2.0	-0.9	-3.3	3.1	2.9
D	1.0	-0.9	4.5	1.2	-1.2	2.8
E	-12.0	-9.8	-10.2	2.7	-14.2	-2.0
F	-1.0	-0.8	-0.8	0.4	0.3	-9.5

Source: IBGE, Síntese (2017), Tables 3.13a and 3.14a.

which could mitigate the impact of race. Thus, one study selected just São Paulo, using the 1996 PNAD dataset, and eliminated all migrants. But it too used the model of absolute differences, and the results obtained suggest that race was influential. But this study also showed a much more extreme difference in mobility by race for women compared to men than is evident from the 2014 mobility dataset from the PNAD surveys.[54]

But, to analyze the impact of race fully, it is essential to include all the variables and to assess the relative importance of each color group within each original occupational stratum.[55] Several recent detailed studies based on the same datasets from the household surveys, but using far more causal variables than sex and race, found that upward mobility was the same for whites and non-whites when all the relevant variables were included, but that a racial difference emerged in downward mobility, with fathers of color unable to maintain their children in equal or better positions as much as white fathers were able to do. As the author of one of the key studies noted, "The main conclusion . . . is that racial inequality affects the chances of mobility only for individuals within the highest classes. White, brown, and black men of origin in the lower classes have similar chances of social mobility." For several of these more recent analysts there is some influence of racial prejudice functioning in Brazilian society, but it is not as powerful as other factors, such as income and education, in determining a person's life chances and opportunities.[56] It would thus appear from the latest and more sophisticated surveys that racial prejudice is one of several factors influencing mobility but is less important than income, education, and a host of other factors. It would also appear that color becomes more important at the very elite positions at the same time as it has less of an influence in social mobility for all other classes and groups.

But what of other aspects of Brazilian life? Are differences by color apparent? A major change in modern Brazilian society has been the rise of Pentecostalism and the decline of traditional Catholicism, though Brazil remains even today the largest Catholic country in the world. Examining

[54] Telles, *Race in Another America*, pp. 140–145.

[55] As Ribeiro has noted, "The main problem in the analysis of the intergenerational mobility of whites, browns and blacks is that the first group tends to be over represented in the highest origin classes, and the last two groups in the lowest origin classes. This fact makes opportunities greater for whites than those for blacks and browns. Therefore, when analyzing the chances of mobility using only gross rates (percentages), we cannot separate the effect of the origin class from that of skin color." Ribeiro, "Classe, Raça e Mobilidade Social no Brasil," p. 862.

[56] Ribeiro, "Classe, Raça e Mobilidade Social no Brasil," pp. 862–866. And, as Osorio noted in his detailed study on income distribution, "Social origin is the principal factor explaining the reproduction of inequality, but its persistence is only made possible through the complement of discrimination." Rafael Guerreiro Osorio, "A desigualdade racial de renda no Brasil: 1976–2006," PhD thesis, Universidade de Brasília, 2009, p. 315.

Table 8.14 *Religious Identity by Color, 2000–2010*

	2000			2010		
Religion	White	Black	Brown	White	Black	Brown
Roman Catholic	74.7	69.2	73.2	66.4	58.2	64.1
Traditional Protestants	4.7	3.2	3.4	6.6	6.4	5.8
Pentecostal Evangelicals	9.5	11.7	11.4	11.6	14.9	15.0
Other Christian denominations	3.8	0.0	2.8	6.5	7.5	6.2
Espírita	1.9	1.0	0.6	2.9	1.8	1.1
Umbanda and Candomblé	0.3	0.9	0.2	0.3	0.9	0.2
No religion	6.1	11.0	8.4	6.7	11.8	8.7

Source: IBGE, Sidra, Table 2094.

Table 8.15 *Religious Identity by Sex and Color, 2010*

	White		Black		Brown	
Religion	Male	Female	Male	Female	Male	Female
Roman Catholic	67.2	65.7	59.2	57.1	65.1	63.0
Traditional Protestants	4.1	4.7	3.3	4.2	3.3	4.1
Pentecostal Evangelicals	10.6	12.5	13.3	16.7	13.5	16.5
Other Christian denominations	8.3	9.8	9.4	12.0	8.2	10.1
Espírita	2.5	3.3	1.4	2.1	0.9	1.2
Umbanda and Candomblé	0.3	0.3	0.8	1.0	0.2	0.2
No religion	8.2	5.3	14.1	9.4	10.4	7.0

Source: IBGE, Sidra, Table 1489.

religious identity by color, it is evident that black and brown Brazilians have changed their religious identity more than whites and that there is only a moderate preference for Afro-Brazilian religions among blacks; and yet blacks are among the most non-believers of any group (see Table 8.14).

When religious identity is broken down by sex, some interesting patterns emerge. More men than women are Catholics or non-religious in all racial groups. But more women than men in all color groups are involved in the other churches (see Table 8.15). Given the role of Pentecostalism in supporting family and community, this finding is not surprising. Also, following their male counterparts, black women tend to be the most non-religious – in fact higher than both white men and women and brown women.

What all this suggests is that there is no particular pattern of religious behavior by color, as even among the Afro-Brazilian religions there is a higher white participation than among browns. Even though black men and women are more representative in these religions, they are far more representative among those who express their non-religious positions, and even browns have a higher rate of non-religiousness than whites. As we will see in Chapter 9, residence is more important in determining religious participation than color.

What all the data on health, education, occupational mobility, and religion suggest is that class is more dominant than race, but that race continues to have an impact on social mobility in Brazilian society. The welfare state has leveled the playing field for all Brazilians, and all indices of health, access to services, and participation in non-compensatory income transfer programs now show all color groups moving toward a more universal pattern for all citizens. Though blacks and browns are in many indices of health and education still below whites, the secular trend is for the gap to be closing. Even in intimate relationships, such as cohabitation, the crossing of color boundaries has now become the norm rather than the exception and education and class now weigh more heavily than color.

As for mobility, both the studies of a few basic indices and more sophisticated multiple variable analyses point to the same direction of increasing equality for all groups. As for mobility, Brazil now has a fluid system of mobility in which half the population ends in an occupational class different from their fathers because of the enormous growth of jobs through industrialization and urbanization from the 1950s to the 1970s. Although mobility has tended to slow somewhat since the first PNAD surveys, the structural impact of mass migration from rural to urban centers and ever higher rates of education for all persons has meant the expansion of the lower, middle, and upper middle-class occupations as well as the urban working classes at the expense of the rural unskilled workers. Even in the latest PNAD survey, half the working population was in the upper lower class and the lower middle class combined, and a quarter of the population did not do manual work. All this meant that there was a major shrinking of the weight of the lowest class of workers. As of 1996, some 82% of the upper-class sons came from lower-class positions. Some 86% were either in the class of their fathers or in higher classes and only 13% declined from their fathers' positions, roughly comparable to the 90% and 11% found in 1973. The movement was predominantly to the next social class and much less commonly to two or more classes above their fathers' socio-economic positions.[57] The survey of 2014 shows that

[57] In the famous study by Pastore, some 50% of children in the PNAD survey of mobility of 1973 changed class status compared with their fathers. Some 47% rose at least one class,

mobility has slowed and that now 83% (of both men and women) are in the same class as their fathers and 17% of them had declined from their fathers' class. Thus, downward mobility is increasing, suggesting a return to more circular mobility. Equally, the upper occupational class (stratum A) shows increasing retention of the sons and daughters from that class, a further major indication of increasing immobility in the Brazilian elite.[58]

In terms of mobility, blacks and browns have rapidly increased their ascent from the lowest class and also reduced the gap between themselves and the whites through the massive expansion of their levels of education. But education itself has become increasingly a blockage for further social mobility. Brazil has one of the lowest matriculation rates for tertiary education in the Americas. Moreover, of the 8 million students matriculated in higher education in 2016, three-quarters of them were attending private universities, of which half were for-profit institutions as of 2005.[59] These institutions have been poorly governed by the state even as the government has promoted the expansion of private systems and given students federal scholarships to attend them. The majority of these for-profit schools offer second-rate degrees from a part-time faculty who have relatively few advanced degrees, which thus results in the students having poor occupational outcomes.[60] Federal public

42% remained in the same class, and only 11% moved down in class status compared with their fathers – all of which indicated major structural mobility. See José Pastore and Nelson do Valle Silva, "Análise dos Processos de Mobilidade Social no Brasil no Último Século," Paper presented at the XXV Encontro Anual da Anpocs, Caxambu, 16–20 October 2001. Accessed at: www.josepastore.com.br/artigos/td/td_015.htm. A more recent study also agrees with these findings from 1973 and 1996 concerning increased mobility and a relative decline in the weight of education as more people are better educated. See Torche and Ribeiro, "Pathways of Change in Social Mobility."

[58] Calculated from PNAD 2014, Table 3.9, Pessoas de 25 a 65 anos de idade, ocupadas na semana de referência, cujo pai, com quem moravam, estava ocupado quando tinham 15 anos de idade .... Accessed at: www.ibge.gov.br/estatisticas-novoportal/multidominio/genero/9 221-sintese-de-indicadores-sociais.html?&t=resultados.

[59] Some 69% of graduates of higher education came from private schools and 93% of all new course openings occurred in these private institution. See INEP, Instituto Nacional de Estudos e Pesquisas Educacionais, "Sinopse Estatística da Educação Superior 2016," Table 1.3. Available at http://portal.inep.gov.br/basica-censo-escolar-sinopse-sinopse. Brazil has the world's largest private for-profit education system. These private schools have become big business, listed on the stock exchange, and have resulted in the establishment of significant oligopolies controlling large numbers of such institutions. See Romualdo Portela de Oliveira, "A transformação da educação em mercadoria no Brasil," *Revista Educação e Sociedade* 30.108 (2009), pp. 739–760 and especially José Marcelino de Rezende Pinto, "O acesso à educação superior no Brasil," *Revista Educação e Sociedade* 25.88 (2004), pp. 727–756.

[60] Some 63% of the professors in the public Federal Universities have doctorates, compared to just 22% in the private universities. Moreover, an extraordinary 88% of the professors are part time in the private universities compared to only 9% in the federal ones. INEP, "Sinopse Estatística da Educação Superior 2016," Tables 2.1 and 2.3.

universities, the elite of the system, and among the best in Latin America, which do have roughly the same ratio of blacks, browns, and whites as private institutions, nevertheless account for only 31% of university students.[61] But the majority of lower- and middle-class students cannot pass the exams for public universities if they are graduates of public schools, and are thus forced to attend private universities, which have expanded rapidly, and have more places than they can fill. Through the PROUNI program, the government has offered hundreds of thousands of fellowships to poor students, the majority for study at private universities, which are for-profit institutions subsidized through tax rebates.[62] Thus, there is a question about how far this mobility based on education will go, with the total years of schooling not resulting in equal value as the poorer element is denied access to public universities because of their inferior-quality public education. The government has recently made efforts to compensate for this growing problem though affirmative action programs at state universities.[63] But there is a need to reform private tertiary education before this blockage can be fully eliminated.

From this survey it is evident that the recent massive government provision of education and public health has reduced the traditional extreme disparities by class, region, and by race. Increase in the size of the brown population, which is now 42% of the Brazil population, the increasing interracial rate of marriage and cohabitation, and the relative decline of residential segregation, all seem to suggest a declining influence of race as a factor in social stratification. Increasing equality of education has also led to common patterns of mobility. That residence, income, and color still function as markers of status is accepted, but an increasing uniformity across regions and groups have reduced their impact over time.

---

[61] INEP, "Sinopse Estatística da Educação Superior 2016," Tables 1.2 and 1.10.

[62] In the second semester of 2018, for example, some 174,289 full fellowships were offered at 1,460 universities and faculties of high education. Candidates had to come from families with a low income (up to 1.5 minimum salaries) and another several thousand 50% fellowships were offered to students whose families earned up to 3 minimum salaries. There were also student loans made available through the FIES. *O Globo*. Accessed at: https://g1.globo.com /educacao/noticia/prouni-2018-resultado-da-primeira-chamada-do-20-semestre-e-divul gado.ghtml. On the tax relief arrangement, see Pinto, "O acesso à educação superior no Brasil, p. 750.

[63] For a useful survey of the evolution of affirmative action in Brazil, which now stresses class as well as race, see Edward E. Telles and Marcelo Paixão, "Affirmative Action in Brazil," *Lasa Forum* 44.2 (2013), pp. 10–12; Luisa Farah Schwartzman and Graziella Moraes Dias da Silva, "Unexpected Narratives from Multicultural Policies: Translations of Affirmative Action in Brazil," *Latin American and Caribbean Ethnic Studies* 7.1 (2012), pp. 31–48; and Luisa Farah Schwartzman and Angela Randolpho Paiva, "Not Just Racial Quotas: Affirmative Action in Brazilian Higher Education 10 Years Later," *British Journal of Sociology of Education* 37.4 (2016), pp. 548–566.

9

Organization of Civil Society

Brazil, like most Latin American countries, is thought to have a limited civil society compared to countries such as the United States. Some scholars have argued that this supposed lack of voluntary institutions is somehow detrimental to the evolution of democratic institutions in the region.[1] But in this Brazil is more like the majority of nations in the world in that the government often provides many of the social and cultural needs of its citizens, which is far less common in the United States. Like most democratic societies, however, Brazil does have a vibrant civic culture made up of a complex mix of voluntary associations, which range from private non-profits to semi-autonomous public–private organizations. It also has a tradition of mass popular protest movements.

These voluntary organizations can be found in everything from religious associations to musical societies, from samba schools to football fan clubs, and to relatively well-organized protest movements of all kinds. The country has innumerable non-profit non-governmental organizations defending, teaching, promoting, or analyzing everything from the poor to industrialists, from children to the aged, from Indians to homosexuals, from animals to rain forests. There are probably as many associations defending women, children, or sexual minorities as there are pressure groups defending the interests of cooperatives, producers, consumers, or industrialists. In addition, it has strong and powerful corporate advocacy groups, representing segments of the civil service, such as teachers, tax officials, or judges. Even neighborhood associations are now to be found everywhere. Although many scholars date

---

[1] See the survey of these opinions in Leonardo Avritzer, "Democratization and Changes in the Pattern of Association in Brazil." *Journal of Interamerican Studies and World Affairs* 42.3 (2000), pp. 59–76.

the rise of these non-profit organizations and social movements to civil opposition to the military era (1964–1985), some of these foundations and entities were created long before. At the same time, in the post-military era there has been an ever-increasing number of these organizations established every decade, with such organizations today numbering in the several hundred thousands, with volunteers and employees reaching over 2 million persons.[2]

In sketching out these associations we will try to show how these voluntary organizations have developed and what role they play in the social evolution of Brazil. These autonomous and semi-autonomous institutions prove a counterbalance to the state and offer citizens alternative ways to express their political, social, and economic needs beyond their direct relation to the state. For this analysis we use the model proposed by Ernest Gellner, who defined civil society as "that set of diverse non-governmental institutions which is strong enough to counterbalance the state, and, whilst not preventing the state from fulfilling its role of keeper of the peace and arbitrator between major interests, can nevertheless prevent the state from dominating and atomizing the rest of society."[3]

What is obvious from examining the Brazilian case is that the line between voluntary organizations and the state is not an either/or situation. That is, some voluntary associations receive funds or legal support from the state and others have no connection to the state – and still others perform services for the government but are autonomous. There are even some which represent the private interests of segments of public employees.

It is useful to separate the various categories of institutions found in Brazilian society in terms of their independence from the public sector. First, there is an important set of civil society entities with total or broad independence of the public sector, organized in the form of non-governmental organizations or Foundations. These are called in Brazil *Fundações Privadas e Associações sem Fins Lucrativos* (FASFILs), or simply NGOs (ONGs in Portuguese). They usually are non-profit organizations that defend or support various issues or minorities, the environment, or human rights. They sometimes have a little government support, but in general they are independent in their ideas, actions, claims, and funding. Although they may lobby for their causes, they do not represent specific economic groups or sectors of activity.

---

[2] For a survey of the major areas in which these private non-profit entities operate (officially called "*Fundações Privadas e Associações sem Fins Lucrativos*"), see Aldino Graef and Valéria Salgado, *Relações de parceria entre poder público e entes de cooperação e colaboração no Brasil* (Brasília: Editora IABS, 2012).

[3] Ernest Gellner, "The Importance of Being Modular," in John A. Hall, ed., *Civil Society: Theory, History, Comparison* (Cambridge: Polity Press, 1995), p. 32.

Next there are independent non-profit organizations with their own administrations, which are paid directly by the government or through tax arrangements and have governmental power over their members. These include the unions, professional associations such as the Law and Medical Orders and Councils, and the enormous private educational systems known as the "System S" schools (that is, the technical training schools of Senai, Sesi, Senac, Sesc, and Sebrae). The trade unions were until recently supported by a syndical tax and the S system relies on a payroll tax. The professional entities have legal regulatory power over their professions, but do not have public resources.[4] The Brazilian Bar Association (*Ordem de Advogados do Brasil* – OAB), for example, is an especially effective and powerful organization of this type with complete independence of the government.[5]

The third category of voluntary organizations are the so-called "Social Organizations" created in 1998, which represent entities under private law and provide services to the public sector and manage public resources through a management contract. Today they play an important role in health and culture. There are also the cooperatives, legally recognized as early as 1907,[6] which in general are private entities, organized by civil society, usually not for profit, which economically support producers (for example, agricultural cooperatives) or consumers (consumer cooperatives, housing cooperatives). They aim to obtain a profit to be distributed to members as well as seeking cost reduction or the executing of a project, as in the case of housing cooperatives, with the entities themselves having the collective interest of the group they represent.

But even these categories do not completely define all these groups at all times. Sometimes these independent private non-profit foundations and associations run special schools or cultural activities with international

---

[4] There is much controversy as to the legal categorization of entities that regulate professional activities. Ferraz, for example, believe that "alongside the Direct Administration and Indirect Administration (Decree Law 200/67), there is, like Portugal, an Autonomous Public Administration, formed precisely by professional orders and councils, whose legal regime is different from that applicable to the Indirect Administration, also formed by other entities with a similar profile, commonly known as parastatals (entities of the 'Sistema S')." Luciano Ferraz, "Regime jurídico aplicável aos conselhos profissionais está nas mão do Supremo," *Consultor Jurídico* (2017). Accessed 4 August 2018, at: www.conjur.com.br/20 17-mar-02/interesse-publico-regime-juridico-conselhos-profissionais-maos-stf.

[5] It exercises state functions, and regulates the professional activities of lawyers, yet is highly independent. On their major autonomous role in the military era, see Denise Rollemberg, "Memória, opinião e cultura política: a ordem dos advogados do brasil sob a ditadura (1964–1974)," in Daniel Aarão Reis and Denis Rolland, eds., *Modernidades Alternativas* (Rio de Janeiro: Fundação GetúlioVargas, 2008), pp. 57–96.

[6] Law 1.637 of 5 January 1907. Accessed at: www2.camara.leg.br/legin/fed/decret/1900–1909/ decreto-1637–5-janeiro-1907–582195-publicacaooriginal-104950-pl.html.

funding. Some are exclusively membership supported and are apolitical, and others, such as the landless rural workers movement (*Movimento dos Trabalhadores Rurais SemTerra* – MST), are aligned with the government during the administrations of the Workers' Party, and often mobilize popular demonstrations and protests. At the same time, many NGOs with government support can voice opposition and influence government policies, while others are completely independent but play only a minor role in providing an alternative voice to the government. Lobbying groups often have legal status and still can oppose government actions or support group interests which are distinct from those of the government. Churches have also played a significant role in influencing state policies or even organizing their own political alliances, and elect officials even though they are completely independent of the state. NGOs born of social movements often have difficult relations with these popular movements as they become more technically and administratively autonomous by creating separate power structures.[7] Finally, many popular mobilizations which may seem chaotic and disorganized turn out to have coherent patterns and well-known features that make such mobilizations a normal part of civil society.

As is obvious from this discussion and from the varying definitions of civil society provided by differing social scientists, Brazil can be found to have numerous institutions and voluntary associations which give individuals a voice beyond the family and kin group. Moreover, as Bernardo Sorj has noted, their power changes over time. Under authoritarian military rule some associations and groups gain unusual power, as was the case with the synod of Catholic Bishops and the OAB.[8] But the return of democratic rule reduces their importance as more groups, associations, and institutions fill the void created during the military era. Thus, the return of independent and uncensored newspapers and journalists, the revival of independent unions, and the return to independence of various economic and political institutions all permitted the expansion of the public space and multiple voices for the autonomous expression of protest or accommodation. New groups have constantly emerged dealing with new issues or redefining old ones (this has

---

[7] A well-balanced analysis of these complex relationship is found in Ana Claudia Chaves Teixeira, "A atuação das organizações não-governamentais: entre o Estado e o conjunto da sociedade," in Evelina Dagnino, ed., *Sociedade civil e espaços públicos no Brasil* (São Paulo: Paz e Terra, 2002), pp. 26–78. Also dealing with these issues of government and the private non-profit entities is Graef and Salgado, *Relações de parceria entre poder público e entes de cooperação e colaboração no Brasil*, Chapter 1.

[8] Bernardo Sorj, "Sociedade civil e política no Brasil," Paper presented at the Seminário sociedade civil e democracia na América Latina: crise e reinvenção da política. Anais do Instituto Fernando Henrique Cardoso e Centro Edelstein de Pesquisas Sociais, São Paulo. 2006.

been the norm in the various health-related associations). Even in a formally Roman Catholic-dominated country, new religious movements have turned Brazil into one the world's largest Protestant countries since the 1970s.

The hundreds of thousands of voluntary non-profit private associations, institutions, and research centers which have filled the public space between citizens and the state have represented given classes and also crossed class boundaries. Though many of these associations existed long before 1964, most scholars date the military era as the basic period of incubation of these associations. It was then that major social movements protesting the military regimes developed, when there were no political parties available to express their opposition.[9] Following the end of military rule, these social movements expanded and evolved into a whole world of associations, organizations, and institutions which have been labeled as the so-called Third Sector – that is the world of autonomous organizations dealing with policy and socio-economic issues that are neither government controlled nor directly market related. These have included everything from research groups studying crime to NGOs protecting the environment.[10] Much of the available literature has concentrated on just these NGOs that have been involved in popular mobilizations and administering to the poorest elements in the society. As one scholar explained, these NGOs are "legally sanctioned civil organizations providing services and support to local grassroots groups in disadvantaged communities and/or engaging in research and advocacy activities."[11] But this definition is really too limited even for NGOs which deal with education or national policies or a whole range of activities, and obviously does not include private producer associations, professional organizations, and of course the churches, which also have outreach programs.[12] Along with these national private non-profit foundations and associations there are also international NGOs which have become embedded in the Brazilian

---

[9] "Prior to that, these social movements were viewed in a certain way as illegitimate, since they occupied the space of the political parties. But the military regimes prevented the parties from functioning and thus opened the space for these new actors. Often cited as typical of these new movements were the CEBs – or comunidades esclesias de base." Céli Regina Jardim Pinto, "As ONGs e a política no Brasil: presença de novos atores," *Dados: Revista de Ciências Sociais* 49.3 (2006), pp. 650–651.

[10] It has been suggested that the ONG designation only came into common use in Brazil in the 1990s as these organizations experienced a major spurt of growth. See Ana Claudio Chaves Teixeira, *Identidade em construção: as organizações não-governamentais no processo brasileiro de democratização* (São Paulo: AnnaBlume, 2003), p. 17.

[11] Nathalie Lebon, "Professionalization of Women's Health Groups in Sao Paulo: The Troublesome Road towards Organizational Diversity," *Organization* 3.4 (1996), p. 589.

[12] For a useful breakdown of the major areas where these entities operate and their activity see Maria da Glória Gohn, *Movimentos sociais e redes de mobilizações civis no Brasil contemporâneo* (Petrópolis: Editora Vozes, 2010).

scene that support local groups and have a great deal of local and international influence.[13]

How many of these organizations are there? In 2002, the UN established a broad set of definitions as to what these NGOs or FASFILs should look like, and this definition has been adopted by Brazil in all its recent censuses of these entities. They were defined as "private non-profit, non-state entities, legally recognized, self-administered, and voluntary and self-governing."[14] By this definition there has been an enormous outpouring of such international and local organizations all over Brazil, working in health, education, human and gender rights, and the environment, as well as protecting the rights of different classes, groups, professions, and occupations. There are even centers studying such social and government issues as crime and government fiscal policies. In sum, they are a diverse and complex a set of organizations as is found in North America. In the most recent IBGE census of 2010, there were 290,692 of these organizations registered employing 2.1 million salaried workers and volunteers, of whom 63% were women and 37% men, and with the median salary being 3.3 the minimum salary.[15]

Just over half (59%) of these FASFILs had been founded before 2000, but in the period 2001–2010 another 119,000 were added, making the decade of the 2000s the period with the largest increase in FASFILs, with the decade of the 1990s the second most important period, when 90,000 were established.[16] Overall, some 80% of these organizations were founded in the post-military era. Clearly, the argument made in the 1980s that these institutions would decline after the military era was wrong, and they have instead become a fundamental part of the public space of Brazil.[17] These organizations can be found in all fields of endeavor, but are especially important in education, religion, professional associations and development, and culture. Though quite well known and of great influence, only 2,000 are in the areas of the environment and animal protection. If we

---

[13] It is estimated that there are currently 40,000 of these international NGOs. Ringo Ossewaarde, Andre Nijhof, and Liesbet Heyse, "Dynamics of NGO Legitimacy: How Organising Betrays Core Missions of INGOs," *Public Administration and Development* 28 (2008), p. 42.

[14] IBGE, *As Fundações Privadas e Associações sem Fins Lucrativos no Brasil, 2010* (Estudos & Estudos 20; Rio de Janeiro, 2012), n.p., "Conceituação" section.

[15] IBGE, Sidra, Table 3608.

[16] IBGE, *As Fundações Privadas e Associações sem Fins Lucrativos no Brasil, 2010*: n.p., Table 9.

[17] As Evelina Dagnino noted, the "re-establishment of formal democratic rule and the relative opening up of most political regimes in Latin America did not remove the importance of civil society as some 'transitologists' had assumed." Evelina Dagnino, "Civil Society in Latin America," in *The Oxford Handbook of Civil Society* (New York: Oxford University Press, 2011), p. 122.

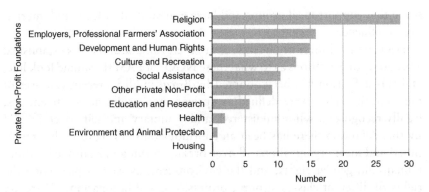

GRAPH 9.1 Private Non-Profit Foundations and Associations in Brazil by Activity, 2010 (percentages)
Source: IBGE (2012), Table 11.

exclude religious associations, the number of lay organizations is still an impressive 202,000 legally recognized associations (see Graph 9.1).

Of these 290,000 or so entities, 44% are in the Southeast, 23% in the Northeast, and 22% in the South – with all the other regions with under 10%. If we divide the types of entities by their main activities by region, some interesting patterns emerge. The Southeast and South, followed by the Center West, have the densest concentration of these entities. The South and Southeast lead in cultural institutions (as could be expected given their wealth), while organizations devoted to development and human rights are significantly above national levels of representation in the Northeast, but, surprisingly, also in the richer Southern region. All regions have about the same ratio of professional associations. The distribution of religious associations most probably reflects the importance of the Pentecostal churches and are most important in the economically more advanced regions (see Table 9.1).

A more-detailed census was carried out in 2002 of just the members of the Brazilian Association of Non-Governmental Organizations (_Associação Brasileira Organizações Não Governamentais_ – ABONG), which also assisted in the IBGE 2010 census. This surveyed only the 271 NGOs in Brazil that were then associated with ABONG. Of these associations, 106 were headquartered in the Southeast (as might be expected, given the middle-class origins of many of them), but 103 were established in the Northeast – the two regions thus accounting for over three-quarters of these organizations. Whatever their location, however, some 38% of these organizations worked in the Northeast, which is the country's poorest region. Some 37% of these NGOs work at the national level, 34% at the state level, and the rest at the local level. The organizations often have multiple areas of interest. Their funding comes from

Table 9.1 *Number of Non-Profit Associations and Foundations per 100,000 Inhabitants, by Region, 2010*

Region	Total	Culture and Social Recreation	Assistance	Religion	Professional and Trade Associations	Development and Human Rights	Other
North	97.5	8.2	6.2	26.2	26.2	10.6	20.1
Northeast	129.5	10.1	8.5	23.4	32.2	31.9	23.4
Southeast	165.7	20.6	18.7	61.3	16.7	17.8	30.6
South	235.8	47.4	33.1	48.2	32.3	34.7	39.9
Center West	146.2	15.1	14.5	51.7	23.4	11.9	29.7
Brazil	148.7	18.9	15.6	42.4	23.0	21.7	27.2

Source: IBGE, Sidra, Table 3846.

all types of sources – from international organizations, local or federal government, or private donors. Initially, the principal source of financing for many of these organizations was international agencies. But over time there has been a shift to local government sources – usually funding specific projects — their own sales of products, and individual contributions.[18] The census shows that the major themes are education, popular participation, and human and gender rights. Many of these national NGOs also support more-local NGOs and their efforts, especially in the area of popular participation (see Graph 9.2)

PNAD surveys for 2014–2015 found that there were 13,659 non-profit NGOs working directly in social assistance. This involves everything from directly helping the disabled, children, adolescents, and the elderly to working with homeless street people. They are well distributed in terms of urban size, with slightly over half working in large cities of 100,000 or more and the other half in small towns and cities. But, regionally, more than three-quarters are found in the South and Southeast regions.[19]

Finally, in its new continuous household survey (*Pesquisa Nacional por Amostra de Domicílios Contínua*), the government asks detailed question about who participates in voluntary organizations. The survey has found that

[18] Vanusa Maria Queiroz da Silva, "O raio-X do terceiro setor," MA thesis, FGV CPDOC, Rio de Janeiro, 2008. See also Victor Cláudio Paradela Ferreira, "ONGs no Brasil: um estudo sobre suas características e fatores que têm induzido seu crescimento," PhD thesis, FGV, Rio de Janeiro, 2005.

[19] IBGE, *As Entidades de Assistência Social Privadas sem Fins Lucrativos no Brasil, 2014–2015*, Tables 1 and 2. Accessed at: www.ibge.gov.br/estatisticas-novoportal/sociais/protecao-social /9021-as-entidades-de-assistencia-social-privadas-sem-fins-lucrativos-no-brasil.html? =&t=resultados.

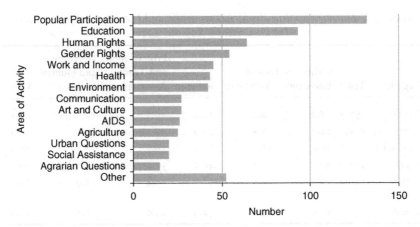

GRAPH 9.2 Areas of Activity of the 685 NGOs in Brazil in 2002
Source: Vanusa Maria Queiroz da Silva, "O raio-X do terceiro setor" (2008), p. 38.

6.5 million people undertook voluntary work in 2016, which corresponds to 3.9% of the population 14 years of age and older; and by 2017 the figure had increased to 7.4 million persons, or 4.4% of the total population over the age of 14 years.[20] The two regions with the highest rate of volunteer activity were the North (5.8%) and the South (5.2%), while the Northeast had the lowest rate (3.2%), with the Southeast at 4.5% and the Center-West at 5.0%. Women were more likely to engage in voluntary labor than men, and the rate of voluntary work increased with age and education. It was higher among women (whites and blacks), in general, than men or browns (see Table 9.2). But the 2016 survey showed that there was little difference by sex in the average number of hours per week dedicated to voluntary work: 6.9 hours for men and 6.6 hours for women. The majority of the voluntary work was done in churches, unions, condominiums, political parties, schools, hospitals, and asylums. Many volunteers worked in more than one organization, and many also gave free time to specific causes, such as animal rights or protecting the environment.[21]

The Brazilian government under Fernando Henrique Cardoso recognized the importance of these voluntary organizations and responded to their demands. This was evident in the field of human rights, which the government eventually accepted as an important issue after the end of military rule.

---

[20] Taken from PNADct (continuous). Accessed 8 February 2108, at: https://agenciadenoticias .ibge.gov.br/agencia-noticias/2012-agencia-de-noticias/noticias/20913-voluntariado-aumen tou-em-840-mil-pessoas-em-2017. On the volunteers, see also Luisa de Azevedo Senra Soares, "A oferta de trabalho voluntário no Brasil," MA thesis, FEA USP, 2014.

[21] Data accessed 12 July 2017, at: https://agenciadenoticias.ibge.gov.br/agencia-detalhe-de-midia.html?view=mediaibge&catid=2103&id=1603.

Table 9.2 *Percentage of Volunteers in Total Population 14 Years of Age and Older, by Level of Education, Sex, and Age, 2017*

Level of Education	Men	Women	Total
No education or primary incomplete	2.2	3.6	2.9
Primary complete and secondary incomplete	3.1	4.3	3.7
Secondary complete and some university	4.1	5.6	4.9
University complete	7.3	8.7	8.1
Total	3.5	5.1	4.4
Color	**Men**	**Women**	**Total**
White	4.0	5.5	4.8
Black	3.3	5.5	4.4
Brown	3.2	4.7	3.9
Total	3.5	5.1	4.4
Age	**Men**	**Women**	**Total**
14–24	2.5	3.3	2.9
25–49	3.7	5.3	4.6
50+	4.0	5.9	5.1
Total	3.5	5.1	4.4

Source: PNADct, "2017 Outras formas de Trabalho, Tabalho voluntário": accessed 8/2/2018 and found at www.ibge.gov.br/estatisticas-novoportal/soc iais/trabalho/ 17270-pnad-continua.html?edicao=20636&t=resultados.

Both local Brazilian NGOs and international organizations such as Amnesty International and Human Rights Watch worked together effectively in these campaigns. Amnesty International worked extensively for some fifty Brazilian prisoners during the military era, and in 1978 many local groups established amnesty committees (*Comitês Brasileiros de Anistia*) in major cities of the country and in the next year came the Human Rights Defense Centers (*Centros de Defesa de Direitos Humanos*). In 1985, a Brazilian section of Amnesty International was established. All these organization put great pressure on the state and federal governments and influenced legislation on torture and basic human rights, which were also incorporated in the Constitution of 1988.[22]

---

[22] Luciana Maria de Aragão Ballestrin, "Estado e ONG's no Brasil: acordos e controversias a propósito de Direitos Humanos (1994–2002)," MA thesis, Universidade Federal do Rio Grande do Sul, 2006, Chapters 2 and 3.

Health was another issue of major campaigns by NGOs. In 1980, the first
notices about AIDS emerged in Brazil and there quickly appeared patient
groups called PVHAs (*Pessoas Vivendo com HIV/AIDS*). By 1985, the first
of the so-called ONG/AIDS groups was established in São Paulo (*Grupo de
Apoio a Prevenção da Aids de São Paulo* – GAPA/SP) and in Rio de Janeiro
(*Associação Brasileira Interdisciplinar de Aids* – ABIA/RJ) by the activists
Herbert Daniel and Herbert de Sousa.[23] The immediate object was to pressure the national health service (SUS) to better respond to the epidemic and
also to control its spread among vulnerable populations. Soon many other
cities had their GAPA organizations.[24] By 1989, these local groups organized
the first national meeting of the ENONG, which brought together all the
ONG/AIDS and other related organizations in the nation.[25] This pressure
resulted in the very effective and world famous government programs treating AIDS victims, but the success has not stopped the work of these
organizations.[26] New NGOs continue to work to educate homosexual men
about sexually transmitted diseases as well as AIDS throughout Brazil.[27]
Allied with this movement are organizations of prostitutes. In 1987, came the
First National Meeting of Prostitutes (*Encontro Nacional de Prostitutas*),
attracting representatives from eight capital cities with demands for

[23] A useful survey of this whole campaign to fight AIDS from all sectors of society is Adriana
Jimenez Pereira and Lúcia Yasuko Izumi Nichiata, "A sociedade civil contra a Aids: demandas coletivas e políticas públicas," *Ciência & Saúde Coletiva* 16.7 (2011), pp. 3249–3257.

[24] On the survivial of GAPA-BA, see Tacilla da Costa and Sá Siqueira Santos, "As diferentes
dimensões da sustentabilidade em uma organização da sociedade civil: uma análise da prática
social do grupo de apoio à prevenção à aids da Bahia," *Sociedade, Contabilidade e Gestão*
2.2 (2007), pp. 61–76.

[25] Átila Andrade de Carvalho, "O campo das ONG/AIDS: Etnografando o ativismo em João
Pessoa," MA thesis, Univerisdade Federal da Paraíba, João Pessoa, 2012, chapter 1. There
are numerous studies of local ONG/AIDS. One of the more interesting, since it stresses the
long-term evolution, from the support of persons with the disease to education and multiple
other social assistance and educational activities as the disease became endemic, is the CAF or
ONG/Casa de Assistência Filadelía. This was founded in São Paulo in 1980 in the home of
a mother with a son who had AIDS. It became a legal ONG in the 1990s and remains active
today in numerous fields, with a major body of volunteers. Ieda Maria Siebra Bochio and
Paulo Antonio de Carvalho Fortes, "A influência da AIDS no processo de desenvolvimento
organizacional das organizações não-governamentais: um estudo de caso sobre a Casa de
Assistência Filadélfia," *Cadernos de Saúde Pública* 24.11 (2008), pp. 2541–2550.

[26] On the world-recognized AIDS programs of the Brazilian government, see Susan Okie,
"Fighting HIV: Lessons from Brazil," *New England Journal of Medicine* 354 (2006),
pp. 1977–1981 and Jane Galvão, "Access to Antiretroviral Drugs in Brazil," *The Lancet*
360.9348 (December 2002), pp. 1862–1865.

[27] This describes the work of GRAB (*Grupo de Resistência Asa Branca*), for example, in
Fortaleza. See Adriano Henrique Caetano Costa, "Homens que fazem sexo com homens
(HSH): políticas públicas de prevenção às dst/aids para uma população anónima," MA
thesis, Universidade Federal do Ceará, 2011.

legalization, protection from police violence, and control of AIDS. Eventually, these groups formed a network, and some of them became legal NGOs. In 2002, they succeeded in having the government legally recognize their profession and in 2005 forced the government to reject USAID funds because of the US decision to block these groups from participating in AIDS work. They also fought Catholic Church groups that wanted to abolish prostitution altogether. One of the biggest NGOs in the network is the OGN-Davila, which works in the metropolitan region of Rio de Janeiro as well as fifteen cities in the interior of the state, with offices providing health, contraceptives, and information on sexually transmitted diseases.[28]

Themes and issues large and small became the basis of policies and activities of these NGOs. Thus, there are the ONG/JARS for Junior Achievement groups modeled along those founded in the United States, the first of which was established in Rio Grande do Sul in 1994 to teach entrepreneurial spirit and promote mini enterprises.[29] At the other extreme is the *Federação de Órgãos para Assistência Social e Educacional* – FASE, founded in 1961, with headquarters in Rio de Janeiro and now operating as an NGO in six states. It is allied with the national trade unions, *Central Única dos Trabalhadores* – CUT, and participated in the founding of the Labor Party. It has worked on adult education, promoting the end of child labor, and arranging food distribution to the poor and indigent. It has received funding from the World Bank, the European Union, ILO, and UNESCO.[30] Among the thousands of other NGOs there is one organized by architects to create viable housing for the poor in Porto Alegre.[31] There is even an NGO founded to provide technical and administrative help to other NGOs called the *Parceiros Voluntários* (Voluntary Partners), which was founded in 1997 in Rio Grande do Sul and which by 2012 had 400,000

---

[28] This rather active organization even sponsors a "*bloco*" in the capital during carnival and runs a clothing workshop, *Daspu*, whose work T-shirts appeared in the Bienal de Arte de São Paulo in 2006 and were publicized internationally. Andreia Skackauskas Vaz de Mello, "Burocratização e institucionalização das organizações de movimentos sociais: O caso da organização de prostitutas Davida," MA thesis, Universidade Federal de Minas Gerais – UFMG, 2007, pp. 64–68, 76–77.

[29] Catia Eli Gemelli, "Motivações para o trabalho voluntário sob a perpectiva do indivíduo: Um estudo de caso no ONG Junior Achievement," MA thesis; Universidade do Valle do Rio dos Sinos – UNSINOS, São Leopardo, 2015, p. 60.

[30] Dilena Dustan Lucas da Silva, "Organizações não governamentais: um estudo de caso da Federação de Órgãos para Assistência Social e Educacional (FASE)," PhD thesis; Universidade Federal do Rio Grande do Sul, 2005, Chapters 1 and 2.

[31] Bibiana Volkmer Martins, "A presença da ONG Cidade para a Construção de um planejamento urbano democrático em Porto Alegre," MA thesis, Universidade Federal do Rio Grande do Sul, Porto Alegre, 2011.

volunteers whose job was to advise and support other NGOs with their professional skills.[32]

Without question, the NGO with the most political power, and one closely tied to the Labor Party, is the landless rural workers movement (MST), which was founded in 1979. This was but one of a long line of syndical efforts, the most important of which were the peasant leagues (*Ligas Camponesas*) founded in 1945 and ruthlessly destroyed by the military regimes in 1964. But these peasant leagues and the subsequent rural unions were based on workers who mostly owned their own land. In the 1950s, a movement of rural workers without land (*Movimento dos Agricultores Sem-Terra* – MASTER) was created in Rio Grande do Sul, which engaged in seizures of unoccupied *fazendas* and which would eventually become the most radical of the groups. These peasant unions and pro-land associations were supported by both the Catholic Church and the Communist Party (PCB), and all these leagues, unions, and associations pushed for agrarian reform. All this activity stopped when the military came to power. But the agrarian question remained a fundamental issue throughout this period even among the docile rural unions organized by the regime. The military governments responded with a massive land colonization scheme which left traditional landholdings untouched. But the pressure continued. In 1975, the Catholic Church created the *Comissão Pastoral da Terra*, which gave cover to new peasant groupings. Again in Rio Grande do Sul a group of landless rural workers in 1979 occupied a farm and from that date more such land invasions developed which grew into the MST being formed in 1985, with Church support.[33] The state often fought these takeovers, but the movement grew constantly in the post-military era and became a powerful force in national politics and in rural education. But its close ties with the Workers' Party have weakened the organization. Moreover, the extraordinarily successful modernization of Brazilian agriculture along with a continuing government colonization program have reduced their power and questioned the need for agrarian

---

[32] Talita Raquel de Oliveira, "Dependência e criação de trajetória no terceiro setor: Um estudo de caso na ONG Parceiros Voluntários," MA thesis, Universidade do Valle do Rio dos Sinos – UNSINOS, São Leopardo, 2013, p. 19.

[33] Useful surveys of the historical origins of MST are found in Bernardo Mançano Fernandes, "Contribuição ao estudo do campesinato brasileiro formação e territorialização do Movimento dos Trabalhadores Rurais Sem Terra – MST (1979–1999)," PhD thesis, University of São Paulo, São Paulo, 1999, Chapters 1 and 2, and Arnaldo José Zangelmi, Fabrício Roberto Costa Oliveira, and Izabella Fátima Oliveira de Sales, "Movimentos, mediações e Estado: apontamentos sobre a luta pela terra no Brasil na segunda metade do século XX," *Sociedade e Cultura* 19.1 (2016), pp. 133–141.

reform; in turn, they have concentrated more of their activities in education.[34]

Of all the issues which have dominated the NGOs in Brazil, probably the ones that have attracted the most international interest and major local activity are the ones dealing with the environment in one form or another. Brazil is of course the center of worldwide concern for the preservation of its extraordinary ecology. But it has also developed its own mass movement concerned with what has become known as the *"meio ambiente,"* or the environment. In the 1970s and 1980s, a major environmental movement emerged in Brazil, the first in Latin America.[35] Given the importance of the Amazon and Atlantic forests and rivers to the world climate there was also a corresponding growth of international concern to the ever greater expansion of farming, ranching, and lumbering in Brazil. Extensive deforestation and unrestrained investment in road and dam construction were supported by international lending agencies. The combination of a grass roots movement in Brazil, the emergence of international NGOs concerned with the environment, and the rise of a new middle class in Brazil now aware of the increasing degradation of urban life due to pollution all combined in the last three decades of the twentieth century to create a powerful green movement in Brazil. All of this came to fruition in the UN-sponsored world conference on environment and development known as Rio 92, which all scholars mark as the coming of age of the NGO movement in Brazil.[36]

The first formal ecological defense group in Brazil was founded in June 1971 in Rio Grande do Sul.[37] It was in fact the first ecological association founded anywhere in Latin America. Other regional groups soon followed, and education campaigns began to raise awareness of conservation issues. The first indication of the impact of national and international

---

[34] On the relation of MST with the PT governments, see Marcos Paulo Campos, "Movimentos sociais e conjuntura política: uma reflexão a partir das relações entre o MST e o governo Dilma," *Revista Cadernos de Estudos Sociais e Políticos* 4.7 (2015), pp. 79–100. This has led the MST to concentrate more of its efforts on rural education. See Anita Helena Helena Schlesener and Donizete Aparecido Fernandes, "Os conflitos sociais no campo e a educação: a questão agrária no Brasil," *Cadernos de Pesquisa: Pensamento Educacional* 10.24 (2017), pp. 131–148.

[35] On the impact of these recent and earlier policies, see Warren Dean, *With Broadaxe and Firebrand: The Destruction of the Brazilian Atlantic Forest* (Berkeley: University of California Press, 1995). For a good survey of this question in Latin America, see Shawn W. Miller, *An Environmental History of Latin America* (Cambridge: Cambridge University Press, 2007) and his earlier study on colonial deforestation, *Fruitless Trees: Portuguese Conservation and Brazil's Colonial Timber* (Stanford, Calif.: Stanford University Press, 2000).

[36] Teixeira, "A atuação das organizações não-governamentais," p. 107.

[37] This was the Gaúcho Association for the Protection of the Natural Environment (*Associação Gaúcha de Proteção ao Ambiente Natural* – AGAPAN).

concern about deforestation and degradation of soil and water resources of the country occurred during the presidency of General Ernesto Geisel. In 1974, he established the Special Secretariat of the Environment (*Secretaria Especial de Meio Ambiente* – SEMA) because of the insistence of international aid organizations on the need for a formal government agency which could produce environmental impact studies before international loans could be approved.

Between the oil crisis of 1974–1978 and the slow return toward democracy, the ecological movement began to expand from an advocacy driven largely by scientists to become a more political and militant movement in Brazil. One of the more impressive such movements was led by the rubber-collection workers of the Northeastern state of Pará, under Chico Mendes, who organized systematic opposition to deforestation in the mid- to late 1970s and became a symbol to the ecological movement internationally.[38] By the late 1970s and early 1980s, state ecological associations had been founded everywhere, the first of many national ecological journals was produced, and a major national discussion had emerged on the need to protect the Amazon. The increasing strength of this movement was shown with the creation in 1985 of a new pressure group intent on influencing the assembly writing the new democratic constitution, the so-called Inter-State Organization of Ecologists for the Constituent Assembly. This highly political organization promoted green candidates for the constitutional assembly and demanded a say on ecology for the new constitution.[39] Its success was evident in the Constitution of 1988, where the environment appeared in numerous sections and the government for the first time systematically committed itself to the defense of the environment.[40] Not only did the movement slowly influence the major opposition parties and push for

[38] Margaret E. Keck, "Social Equity and Environmental Politics in Brazil: Lessons from the Rubber Tappers of Acre," *Comparative Politics* 27.4 (1995), pp. 409–424.

[39] For the early history of this movement, see Eduardo J. Viola, "The Ecologist Movement in Brazil (1974–1986): From Environmentalism to Ecopolitics," *International Journal of Urban and Regional Research* 12.2 (1988), pp. 211–228; Onil Banerjee, Alexander J. Macpherson, and Janaki Alavalapati, "Toward a Policy of Sustainable Forest Management in Brazil: A Historical Analysis," *Journal of Environment & Development* 18.:2 (2009), pp. 130–153; and Wilson José Ferreira de Oliveira, "Gênese e redefinições do militantismo ambientalista no Brasil," *Dados: Revista de Ciências Sociais* 51.3 (2008), pp. 751–777. On the evolution of policies and institutions at the state level, see Barry Ames and Margaret E. Keck, "The Politics of Sustainable Development: Environmental Policy Making in Four Brazilian States," *Journal of Interamerican Studies and World Affairs* 39.4 (1997–1998), pp. 1–40.

[40] Vladimir Passos de Freitas, "A constituição federal e a efetividade das normas ambientais," PhD thesis, Faculdade de Direito da Universidade Federal do Paraná, 1999 and Antonio Herman de Vasconcellos e Benjamin, "O Meio Ambiente na Constituição Federal de 1988." *Informativo Jurídico da Biblioteca Ministro Oscar Saraiva* 19.1 (2008). On regular law changes related to conservation issues, see Carlos José Saldanha Machado, "Mudanças conceituais na administração pública do meio ambiente," *Ciência e Cultura* 55.4 (2003), pp. 24–26.

"green" candidates, but it also led to the foundation of a formal *Partido Verde* (Green Party) in early 1986. By 2010, the party, led by Marina Silva, obtained 20% of the national vote in the presidential election of that year, coming in third after the Workers' Party and the PMDB.

Aside from its formal political involvement and educational campaigns, the ecology movement has had an impact on state and federal laws designed to protect the environment. One of its earliest achievements was the establishment in 1985 of a new Ministry of the Environment and Urban Development in the first democratic government. In 1989, the Brazilian Institute for the Environment and Renewable Natural Resources (IBAMA) was created, which by the Constitution of 1988 was given control over all national forests. Slowly, these government agencies have begun to have an impact on preserving forest and wetlands and establishing systematic legislation to protect the environment. But enforcement has varied from government to government in the past twenty-five years, and in 2012 there was even an attempt to emasculate the important and well-regarded 1965 forestry law – which was eventually opposed by the Dilma administration.[41]

Both Brazilian and international environment groups have also systematically pressured the big international lending agencies to change their lending policies to the Brazilian government. This became evident in the late 1970s when the Word Bank began to give its first loans for work in the Amazon region. The most controversial of these was a major investment in colonization in the Northwest Amazon called the POLONOROESTE project. Although some attempt to control ecological conditions was written into the grant, this was largely unsuccessful and the Bank was roundly criticized for its investment by national and international NGOs, forcing the Bank temporarily to suspend its support in the mid-1980s and change its environmental guidelines.[42] Meanwhile, the Bank itself published two critical reports in the late 1980s showing how Brazilian tax laws fostered ecological degradation and Amazonian deforestation.[43] At the same time, the Bank itself was becoming increasingly more green. By 1987, it had established a central environment

---

[41] Under pressure from the green movement President Dilma was forced to veto twelve items of the code and modify another thirty-two provisions. See the reports in *O Estado de São Paulo* and *O Globo*: www.estadao.com.br/noticias/vidae,dilma-veta-12-pontos-e-faz-32-modificacoes-no-codigo-florestal,877923,0.htm and http://veja.abril.com.br/noticia/brasil/dilma-veta-12-itens-do-codigo-florestal.

[42] On the problems related to ecology on all these joint World Bank and Brazilian government Amazonian projects, see Sérgio Margulis, *O Desempenho ambiental do Governo Brasileiro e do Banco Mundial em Projetos Co-financiados pelo Banco*. Texto para discussão 94 (Brasília: Ipea, 1999).

[43] See the papers: Hans Binswanger, "Brazilian Policies that Encourage Deforestation." Environment Department Paper No. 16, World Bank: Washington, DC, 1988 and Dennis

department, as well as environment divisions for areas of the world which were raised to the level of a vice presidency in 1992.[44]

As a response to the two world oil shocks, the Brazilian government also began to actively concern itself with alternative fuel sources, especially as Brazil was then still a major importer of foreign oil. In 1975, as a result of the oil shock of the previous year, the government established PROACOOL to use sugar as an alternative fuel. It subsidized the production of sugar and ruled that 24% of all gasoline must contain ethanol. It required *Petrobras*, the government oil agency, to distribute ethanol products throughout the country. The government expanded the program after the second oil crisis in 1976, and by 2005 Brazil was producing 4 million gallons of ethanol – about the same as was being produced from corn in the United States. All told, ethanol now accounts for 40% of fuel consumption in Brazil compared to only 3% in the US fuels market. The more-efficient Brazilian program allowed it to produce the same amount of bio-fuel as the US on half the amount of land. By the crop year of 2004/2005, Brazil was not only the world's largest sugar cane producer, by far, but also its leading ethanol producer, accounting for 37% of world production.[45] However, even this ethanol development has led to much debate among ecologists as to its positive and negative environmental impacts.[46]

Despite the developing power of the green movement and increasing government action, there is still a continuation of illegal logging and ranching in the Amazon and other natural habitats, with a decrease in biodiversity and native fauna and flora.[47] Moreover, the rate of deforestation has not

   J. Mahar, Government Policies and Deforestation in the Brazilian Amazon (Washington, DC: World Bank, 1989.

[44] John Redwood II, "World Bank Approaches to the Brazilian Amazon: The Bumpy Road toward Sustainable Development. LCR Sustainable Development." World Bank Working Paper 13, Washington, DC, November 2002.

[45] Marcus Renato S. Xavier, "The Brazilian Sugarcane Ethanol Experience," Issue Analysis, Competitive Enterprise Institute, Washington, DC, 15 February 2007 and Joao Martines-Filho, Heloisa L. Burnquist, and Carlos E. F. Vian, "Bioenergy and the Rise of Sugarcane-Based Ethanol in Brazil," *Choices* 21.2 (2006), pp. 91–96.

[46] Luiz A. Martinelli and Solange Filoso, "Expansion of Sugarcane Ethanol Production in Brazil: Environmental and Social Challenges," *Atmospheric Environment* 18.4 (2008), pp. 885–898.

[47] On the difficulties of controlling deforestation, see Sérgio Margulis, "Causes of Deforestation of the Brazilian Amazon," World Bank Working Papers 22; Washington, DC, 2004. See also Stephen G Bunker, *Underdeveloping the Amazon: Extraction, Unequal Exchange, and the Failure of the Modern State* (Urbana: University of Illinois Press, 1985); Michael Goulding, Nigel J. H. Smith, and Dennis J Mahar, *Floods of Fortune: Ecology and Economy along the Amazon* (New York: Columbia University Press, 1996). On the subtropical Atlantic coast forests of Brazil known as the Mata Atlântica and their precarious survival, see Milton Cezar Ribeiro et al., "The Brazilian Atlantic Forest: How Much Is Left, and How Is the Remaining Forest Distributed? Implications for Conservation," *Biological Conservation* 142

decreased in recent decades and Brazil's environmental efforts have produced far smaller results than in other areas of the world. In its 2011 survey of world forests, the United Nations estimated that Brazil contained 520 million hectares of forests, which represented 13% of the world's forests. In the decade 1990–2000, Brazil lost on average 2.9 million hectares of forest per annum, which represented 35% of the total world forest loss in that decade. But in the decade from 2000 to 2010, Brazil lost another 2.6 million hectares every year, which now accounted for 51% of total world forest destruction.[48] There are also serious and long-term problems of sanitation, air quality, potable water, and substandard housing in many urban centers, which Brazil is only slowly resolving. Nevertheless, there is a powerful green movement, which continues to undertake systematic campaigns to improve conditions in the country, especially from Labor Party governments, which stressed growth over environmental protection. All these national and international movements have led to a massive amount of scientific research on sustainable resources, reforestation, and the protection of the fragile Amazon, which has made the Brazilian environment one of the most studied in the world.[49]

One of the more effective organizations and lobbies in terms of education has been the state industrial confederations. The national CNI Confederation of Industries (founded in the 1930s) has been crucial in developing modern technical education in Brazil. Since the late 1940s, the government has funded these state industrial organizations to set up schools, first for industrial skills (SENAI) and eventually for commercial ones

---

(2009), pp. 1141–1153. To date, most of the native bird loss in Brazil has occurred in the Mata Atlântica zone. See Miguel Angelo Marini and Federico Innecco Garcia, "Bird Conservation in Brazil," *Conservation Biology* 19.3 (2005), pp. 665–671. But it is evident that mammals are being seriously affected by increasing deforestation in the Amazon. See William F. Laurance, Heraldo L. Vasconcelos, and Thomas E. Lovejoy, "Forest Loss and Fragmentation in the Amazon: Implications for Wildlife Conservation," *Oryx* 34.1 (2000), pp. 39–45 and William F. Laurance et al., "The Fate of Amazonian Forest Fragments: A 32-Year Investigation," *Biological Conservation* 144 (2011), pp. 56–67.

[48] FAO, *State of the World's Forests 2011* (Rome: Food and Agriculture Organization of the United Nations, 2011), pp. 110–118, Table 2.

[49] On the relation between deforestation and global warming, see the latest essay by P. M. Fearnside and W. F. Laurance, "Tropical Deforestation and Greenhouse Gas Emissions," *Ecological Applications* 14.4 (2004), pp. 982–986. On sustainable activities, among the more general studies, see Daniel C. Nepstad, Claudia M. Stickler, Britaldo Soares-Filho, and Frank Merry, "Interactions among Amazon Land Use, Forests and Climate: Prospects for a Near-Term Forest Tipping Point," *Philosophical Transactions of the Royal Society B* 363 (2008), pp. 1737–1746; Daniel C. Nepstad et al., "The End of Deforestation in the Brazilian Amazon," *Science* 326 (2009), pp. 1350–1351; Britaldo Silveira Soares-Filho et al., "Modelling Conservation in the Amazon Basin," *Nature* 440.23 (2006), pp. 520–523; Martinelli, Naylor, Vitousek, and Moutinho, "Agriculture in Brazil," pp. 431–438.

(SENAC), and these schools are among the largest such technical education school systems in the world. By 2017, they contained over 900,000 students.[50] But in terms of influencing government policies, these state and national industry associations have been less effective in the more modern period in terms of representing an autonomous power structure independent of the state, especially compared to Europe and North America.[51] Thus, the Confederation of Industries' actual power is quite diluted by national federations which give equal weight to small state associations as well as to the powerful São Paulo association, FIESP. While such associations were strong in the Vargas period and through the 1940s, they have declined since the post-military era. Much of this is probably due to a convergence of interests between the state and these associations, but it can also reflect the declining power of national industry and the growth of multinationals as major factors in the Brazilian industrial market after the 1990s.[52]

But if industrial lobbies and organizations are no longer politically powerful, there have emerged a whole set of new actors in the previously less well represented agricultural sector. As agriculture has modernized and developed into an international powerhouse since the 1960s, so too have these new agricultural sectors begun to organize to protect their interests and promote their policies. At first, most of the rural associations were organized to defend themselves against the MST land invasions.[53] But as commercial agriculture expanded and became vertically and internationally organized, modern producer groups appeared for all the major crops. Much of this reorganization came with deregulation of the market in the late 1990s and the abolition of all the state Crop Institutes which had controlled national

---

[50] Rita Almeida, Nicole Amaral, and Fabiana de Felicio, *Assessing Advances and Challenges in Technical Education in Brazil* (Washington, DC: The World Bank, 2015), p. 11, Figure 1.2. We assume that all private vocational education is carried out in this system.

[51] See Ben Ross Schneider, "From Corporatism to Organized Disarticulation in Brazil," in Ben Ross Schneider, ed., *Business Politics and the State in Twentieth Century Latin America* (Cambridge: Cambridge University Press, 2004), pp. 93–127.

[52] The industrial lobbies had little impact on the democratic Constitution of 1988, and they were completely split on the opening of the national market to foreign industries in the 1990s, with the losing industries unable to stop the process and the passive confederations going along with the government policy which negatively affected many of its members. See Eli Diniz, "Empresariado industrial, representação de interesses e ação política: trajetória histórica e novas configurações," *Politica & Sociedade* 9.17 (2010), pp. 106–109 and Mariele Troiano, "Os empresários no congresso: a legitimação de interesses via audiências públicas," MA thesis; Universidade Federal de São Carlos, 2016.

[53] This was the origin of the first major lobby, the União Democrática Ruralista (UDR), in 1985. See Celso Donizete Locatel and Fernanda Laize Silva de Lima, "Agronegócio e poder político: políticas agrícolas e o exercício do poder no Brasil," *Sociedade e Território* 28.2 (2016), pp. 66–67.

production.[54] Both producer associations and cooperatives have now become major players in commercial agriculture. In the agricultural census of 2006, some 41% of the farms which owned 40% of agricultural land were associated with either a cooperative, a class entity such as a union (*sindicato*), a producers' association or a community organization, and/or both a class entity and a cooperative. The most intensely organized state was Rio Grande do Sul, where 68% of the farms and 72% of the land were associated with these groups.[55] Although the producer associations have largely remained non-profit organizations defending the interest of their members, some of the cooperatives which began as non-profit associations have become major commercial producers as well, or have failed and been purchased by private individuals.[56] Although some commercial sectors such as milk are less dominated by cooperatives than in the United States or Europe, in soybeans, wheat, oats, sugar, and cotton, cooperatives are major independent players with some becoming major industrial and research firms.[57] In a census of agricultural cooperatives in a 2016 government survey, 1,440 agricultural cooperatives were listed.[58] Recently, there have emerged distinct credit cooperatives closely tied to the rural economy. The first were established in 1971, but they are still quite limited, and only accounted for 5% of all rural loans given in 2006.[59] By contrast, in Europe and North America, these

---

[54] On the effects of coffee deregulation, see Fernando Tadeu Pongelupe Nogueira and Danilo R. D. Aguiar, "Efeitos da desregulamentação na extensão e no grau de integração do mercado brasileiro de café," *Revista de Economia* 37.3 (2011), pp. 21–46.

[55] IBGE, Sidra, Censo Agricola, Table 840.

[56] One classic example is the *Cooperativa Central Gaúcha de Leite* (CCGL) which at one point controlled almost half the state production in Rio Grande do Sul, which had to give up most of its control after the collapse of a wheat cooperative, and then several years later returned to purchase the companies it had sold to private entrepreneurs. See Maria Domingues Benetti, "Endividamento e crise no cooperativismo empresarial do Rio Grande do Sul: análise do caso FECOTRIGO/CENTRALSUL – 1975–83," *Ensaios FEE* 6.2 (1985), pp. 23–55, and Guilherme Gadonski de Lima, Emerson Juliano Lucca, and Dilson Trennepohl, "Expansão da cadeia produtiva do leite e seu potencial de impacto no desenvolvimento da região noroeste rio-grandense," Paper presented at the Congresso da Sociedade Brasileira de Economia, Administração e Sociologia e Rural (SOBER), João Pessoa (2015).

[57] Thus was the case of a sugar cooperative in São Paulo. In 1959, the producers cooperative, *Copersucar* [Cooperativa de Produtores de Cana-de-Açúcar, Açúcar e Álcool do Estado de São Paulo], was established by the amalgamation of two local sugar producer cooperatives. It began as a producers' association concentrating on marketing the sugar and alcohol of its members. By the end of the decade, *Copersucar* represented 86% of the São Paulo millers and marketed over 90% of the state's sugar and alcohol production. It quickly evolved into a conglomerate providing everything from credit to owning distilleries and was active in all aspects of the production process including expanding exports overseas. See Marcos Fava Nevesa, Allan W. Grayb, and Brian A. Bourquard, "Copersucar: A World Leader in Sugar and Ethanol," *International Food and Agribusiness Management Review* 19.2 (2016).

[58] IBGE, Sidra, Table 254. [59] IBGE, Sidra Censo Agrário 2006, Table 829.

credit cooperatives account for a quarter to well over half of available rural credit.[60]

Given their importance in the economy, agricultural interests eventually organized a voting bloc in Congress in 1995 known as the *Frente Parlamentar da Agropecuária* (FPA). This caucus, popularly known as the *bancada ruralista*, currently contains 120 federal deputies and 13 senators – or 23% of the lower house and 16% of the Senate.[61] The problem is that the caucus supports both traditional agriculturalists as well as the most modern, and therefore tends to oppose more progressive land, labor, and environmental policies and is considered a very conservative force in the national legislature.[62] Nor is this the only pressure group to emerge in the political arena.

Cooperatives also exist to produce and distribute electricity, to build housing, or to organize producers or consumers of various products. There is even a very significant minority of Brazilian doctors who are organized in medical cooperatives called UNIMEDS, which employ 42% of all Brazilian health professionals and are to be found throughout the country.[63] In all, the cooperative movement is very well established in Brazil and is a powerful alternative force in the public sphere, autonomous from the government though clearly deeply integrated into the market. As can be seen from a 2017 listing of these organizations, they are most important in terms of membership in credit associations, consumer groups, agriculture, and electricity (see Table 9.3).

[60] Marcos Antonio Henriques Pinheiro, *Cooperativas de Crédito: História da evolução normativa no Brasil* (6th edn; Brasília: Banco Central do Brasil, 2008), pp. 7–8, and Fábio Luiz Búrigo, "Finanças e solidariedade: o cooperativismo de crédito rural solidário no Brasil," *Estudos Sociedade e Agricultura* 1 (2013), pp. 312–349.

[61] On the early history of this groups, see Instituto de Estudos Socioeconômicos, "Bancada Ruralista: o maior grupo de interesse no congresso nacional." Accessed 11 March 2017, at: www.terra.com.br/noticias/maior-lobby-no-congresso-ruralistas-controlam-14-da-camara, 4668a418851ca310VgnCLD200000bbcceboaRCRD.html. On its size in the current legislature, see www.terra.com.br/noticias/maior-lobby-no-congresso-ruralistas-controlam-14-da-camara,4668a418851ca310VgnCLD200000bbcceboaRCRD.html.

[62] Ranon Bento Pereira and Glauber Lopes Xavier, "A propriedade da terra e a política brasileira durante a nova república (1985–2014): a bancada ruralista e a questão agrária contemporânea (52ª, 53ª e 54ª legislaturas)." *Anais do Seminário de Pesquisa, Pós-Graduação, Ensino e Extensão do Câmpus Anápolis de CSEH (SEPE)*, vol. 2, *O cenário econômico nacional e os desafios profissionais* (2016).

[63] Evandro Scheidt Ninaut and Marcos Antonio Matos, "Panorama do cooperativismo no Brasil:censo, exportações e faturamento," *Informações Econômicas*, SP 38.8 (2008), p. 44. UNIMEDS which had over 100,000 patients included: Belo Horizonte (MG), the state UNIMED in Paraná (PR) and in the city of Porto Alegre (RS). Those with 20,000–100,000 patients included Unimed Vale dos Sinos (RS), Unimed Sul Capixaba (ES), and Unimed Santa Barbara D'Oeste e Americana (SP). Data from OCB. Accessed 11 January 2017, at: www.ocb.org.br/noticia/20916/unimeds-fazem-bonito-em-ranking-da-ans.

Table 9.3 *Number of Cooperatives by Area of Interest, with Number of Members and Employees, 2017*

Area*	Number of Cooperatives	Members	Employees
Credit	976	7,476,308	50,268
Consumer	147	2,990,020	14,056
Agriculture	1,555	1,016,606	188,777
Electricity and infrastructure	125	955,387	6,154
Health	813	225,191	96,230
Transport	1,205	136,425	11,209
Housing	293	114,567	886
Mining	79	57,204	187
Education	279	50,847	3,966
Industrial production	257	12,494	3,458

* Minor areas of activity have been excluded.
Source: Organização das Cooperativas Brasileiras. www.ocb.org.br/ramos.

Of all the major associations and movements in Brazil, the ones that are less autonomous in most periods of time have been the labor unions, which since the 1930s have tended to be controlled by the government, at least until the 1980s. As in all western capitalist societies, the relation between capital and labor has resulted in conflicts that have led to the organization of workers in various forms of voluntary representative entities. Ultimately, these have become entrenched in the trade union movement which is now the prevalent form of workers' organization. In Europe, these labor movements emerged parallel to the consolidation of the industrial process. In Brazil, due to the persistence of slavery until 1888 and the low level of industrial activity, there was a relative delay in the formation of workers' organizations. It was only with the intense influx of European immigrants from Italy and Spain, who came to replace the slaves in coffee and then constituted the main labor force of the nascent industries, that unions finally emerged in the early years of the twentieth century. In 1903 and 1907, the government recognized the right to unionize, but only for mediation purposes, and was hostile to normal confrontation between capital and labor.[64] Though legal and illegal unions

---

[64] Law 1.637 of 5 January 1907, like the Decree of 1903, proposed that workers should be free to organize a union. See www2.camara.leg.br/legin/fed/decret/1900-1909/decreto-1637-5-j aneiro-1907-582195-publicacaooriginal-104950-pl.html.

appeared in this period, it was only after 1930 that a positive government policy was established.[65]

The Vargas revolution had as its core value the adjustment of the state to the new social realities of a more complex society. Vargas created a series of basic institutions to deal with labor relations, with public health, with pensions, and with the economy, all designed to move the traditional oligarchic rural-based society into the modern era. This was done by non-democratic government which could forge new alliances with the growing industrial sector and harness the evolving labor movement into a permanent support of the regime in exchange for worker protections. The government granted the right to unionize, and basic worker rights to bargaining and social security. This creation of modern labor legislation left ultimate control over the unions with the state. This cooptation diminished the autonomy of labor organization, leading to government-controlled unions, but gave the Vargas government an important political base.[66]

The government adopted the policy of what is called *unicidade sindical* which established one single union for each industry and or municipality.[67] Such legislation limited the number of foreign workers per enterprise (the law of two-thirds national workers), regularized the workday, guaranteed holidays, and provided for controls and protection of women and child labor. There were also collective work contracts and Boards of Labor Conciliation (*Convenções Coletivas de Trabalho* and *Juntas de Conciliação e Julgamento*) composed of representatives of workers and management to deal with labor contracts and disputes. May 1 was declared a major holiday and the government established Brazil's first minimum wage. In 1940, Vargas created the union tax, which provided income to the unions, collected and dispersed by

---

[65] On the creation of the welfare state in Brazil, see Klein and Luna, *Brazil, 1964–1985: The Military Regimes of Latin America in the Cold War*.

[66] On this theme, see Boris Fausto, *A revolução de 1930* (São Paulo: Editora Brasiliense, 1972). On the labor legislation, which was much influenced by the corporatist Italian labor code, see Leôncio Martins Rodrigues, "Sindicalismo corporativo no Brasil," in *Partidos e sindicatos: escritos de sociologia política* (Rio de Janeiro: Centro Edelstein de Pesquisas Sociais, 2009), pp. 38–65 online at: http://books.scielo.org/id/cghr3/pdf/rodrigues-9788579820267-04.pdf and Fabio Gentile, "O fascismo como modelo: incorporação da 'carta del lavoro' na via brasileira para o corporativismo autoritário da década de 1930," *Mediações - Revista de Ciências Sociais* 19.1 (2014), pp. 84–101. Accessed 11 January 2017 at: www.uel.br/revistas/uel/index.php/mediacoes/article/view/19857.

[67] In 1939, the "uniqueness" or monopoly of labor association by territorial unit was established, which represents a ban on more than one union to represent the same job category. This rule, which in combination with the union tax represents the harnessing of the power of unions to the state, continues today, although the constitution set the freedom of association for workers. Even the PT, which in opposition attacked the trade union unity rule and the union tax, did not bother to amend the legislation when it took office.

the Ministry of Labor, and became a fundamental instrument of cooptation between the state and the unions.[68] The legal framework for all this was the codified labor code, the CLT, written during the period of the *Estado Novo* (1937–1945) and definitively established in 1943.[69]

Under this labor code, the unions were to be organized in a pyramidal structure to avoid the horizontal organization of the different occupational categories, and the formation of coordinating bodies between the unions at the local level was forbidden. They can meet only through federations of the same sector of the economy.[70] It provided that all union elections would be controlled by the Ministry of Labor and that elected union officials could be removed by the Minister. Strikes were made virtually illegal by forcing all labor disputes to be resolved by a government Labor Court, and thus in effect prohibiting collective bargaining between unions and employers.[71]

The formal structure implemented by this code remained relatively stable in its fundamental form until 2016. The governments that succeeded the Vargas period fully supported it because it served the interests of the state. Even the military left the legislation virtually intact.[72] However, using the formal instruments existing in the CLT, they intervened in trade unions and dismissed their leaders.[73] They took over 383 unions and the various local, regional, and national confederations and forced out their leadership and replaced them with more traditional leaders who concentrated on bread-and-

---

[68] The union tax represented a contribution equivalent to one workday for all workers, unionized or not. The funds raised were distributed to the unions, which lived on this discretionary contribution. The government receives the resources and distributes them according to the rules of the district. For example, in 2008, 5% was for the corresponding confederation, 10% for the central syndical, 15% for the federation, 60% for the respective union, and 10% for the Special Account for Employment and Wages. The last account today is part of the Workers' Assistance Fund. Union resources depended on this tax, and thus the unions were dependent on the state and not on the contributions from their union workers.

[69] Título V, of the Decree Law 5.452 of 1 May 1943.

[70] Maria Helena Moreira Alves, *Estado e oposição no Brasil (1964–1984)* (Petrópolis: Vozes, 1989), pp. 236–237.

[71] Skidmore, *The Politics of Military Rule in Brazil, 1964–85*, pp. 33–34. On the labor movement in the period 1930–1964, see Leôncio Martins Rodrigues, "Sindicalismo e classe operaria (1930–1964)," in Boris Fausto, ed., *História geral da civilização brasileira* (São Paulo: Difusao Europeia de Livro, 1986), vol. 3/10, pp. 509–555.

[72] Alves, *Estado e oposição no Brasil*, pp. 236–237.

[73] Section VIII of Title V of Decree Law 5.452, in the item dealing with penalties to trade unions, allows the dismissal of directors and members of the board, annulment of the union's legal recognition, closure of the union, Federation or Confederation for a term not exceeding six months. The decree foresaw that once the union administration was dismissed, the Minister of Labor, Trade & Industry would appoint a delegate to direct the association and proceed with electing a new directorate. In addition to these formal possibilities of the original decree, in 1969, during the military period, there was the addition of § 2 that allowed the Minister of Labor to determine the preventive dismissal of a Labor leader based on a formal complaint.

butter union issues and gave up their strike activities.[74] But while not abolishing the unions, the military regimes of 1964–1985 suspended the right to strike, implemented strict wage control, abolished employment stability,[75] and radically altered the system of retirement and pensions.[76]

The impact on unions was severe and it took more than a decade before the effective resumption of labor mobilizations and strike movements could occur.[77] At the end of the 1970s, at the same time as the system began to open toward a democratic resolution, workers' protests were revived and the so-called "new syndicalism" emerged.[78] The strike of the metallurgical workers of the ABC region in greater São Paulo in 1978 represents a milestone in this process of resurgence.[79] Luiz Inácio Lula da Silva, who would later become President of the Republic, emerged as the great leader of this new trade unionism. Strikes followed in 1979 that involved several professional categories and were repressed with violence by the police authorities. The biggest demonstration would be in São Bernardo do Campo and Diadema, where

[74] According to Mattos, this first phase could not completely shut down the most combative activists, which would happen following the victory of oppositionist candidates when new union elections are called. Marcelo Badaró Mattos, *Trabalhadores e sindicatos no Brasil* (São Paulo: Editora Expressão Popular, 2009), pp. 101–105.

[75] Labor legislation stipulated stability after ten years of work in a job. This norm, while on the one hand conferring greater stability on employment, made the labor relationship rigid, hampering the progress of capitalist relations in urban areas. The stability mechanism was replaced by the FGTS (*Fundo de Garantia por Tempo de Serviço*), which had a monthly allowance deposited in the name of the worker and which constituted an important institutional fund for financing housing and sanitation.

[76] See Klein and Luna, *Brazil, 1964–1985: The Military Regimes of Latin America in the Cold War*, Chapters 3 and 4.

[77] Mattos, *Trabalhadores e sindicatos no Brasil*, pp. 101–102. Even in this period of violent repression two historical strikes occurred, one in Contagem (Minas Gerais) and the other in Osasco (São Paulo), both in 1968 and strongly repressed with violence by the police. An overview of the trade union movement in São Paulo can be found in Alessandro Moura, "Movimento Operário e sindicalismo em Osasco, São Paulo e ABC Paulista: Rupturas e descontinuidades," PhD thesis, Universidade Virtual do Estado de São Paulo – UNIVESP, Marília, 2015.

[78] The resurgence of this new syndicalism has strong repercussions on the ABC region and in the so-called "opposition movement." The Sindicato dos Metalurgicos of São Paulo had strong support from segments of the Catholic Church. See Iram Jácome Rodrigues, "Igreja e Movimento Operário nas origens do Novo Sindicalismo no Brasil (1964–1978)," *História, Questões & Debates* 29 (1998), pp. 25–58. Because of its more combative origins, the new syndicalism was also known as "authentic syndicalists."

[79] Under the direction of the São Bernardo and Diadema Metalworkers' Union, headed by Luiz Inácio Lula da Silva, the workers decided not to participate in the annual wage negotiations, denouncing such negotiations as a farce, since wage law limited readjustments. After determining the rate of adjustment, the workers of some companies, starting with Scania, decided to stop the machines and remain in the factory. This form of protest spread to other factories in the ABC region and other cities in São Paulo, representing a milestone in the new trade unionism. Accessed 31 October 2017 at: www.abcdeluta.org.br/materia.asp?id_CON=34.

there was an extended strike sponsored by the local Metalworkers' Union, led by Lula. The Regional Electoral Court considered the strike illegal and there was federal intervention in the union. There were protests on May 1 in São Bernardo, which brought together thousands of people. This strike and the demonstration was another of the milestones in the struggle for the democratization of the country.[80]

The new syndicalism openly criticized the authoritarian and corporative state legislation on unions. The leadership opposed the *unicidade sindical* model and the union tax, two features of the labor code that limited free union organizing and reinforced state interference. The new syndicalism acquired expressive political force. This new syndical force, with the incorporation of intellectuals, representatives of popular movements, and the support of sectors of the Catholic Church,[81] founded the Workers' Party in 1980. Although the so-called new syndicalism consolidated its position in the union movement and was well represented in the struggle for redemocratization, its leadership was not entirely committed to the new political movement and there were strong internal disputes between the new syndicalism concentrated in the region of São Paulo and the more traditional groups in the system-wide unions which were less radical and politically committed. These two groups would be represented in the two main trade union "centrals" that would be created in the early 1980s.[82] In 1983, during the National Congress of the Working Class (*Conclat*), the CUT (*Central Única dos Trabalhadores*) was formed, which would represent essentially the new unionism, and was

---

[80] This act was a defining moment in the struggle for redemocratization, with the participation of representatives of civil society and consolidating Lula's position as one of the main national leaderships.

[81] On the influence of the Catholic Church on the formation of the PT, see Adriano Henriques Machado, "A influência dos setores católicos na formação do Partido dos Trabalhadores: da relação com os movimentos sociais à ideia de formar um novo partido," Paper presented at the ANPUH – XXV Simpósio Nacional de História, Fortaleza, 2009. Accessed 1 November 2017, at: http://anais.anpuh.org/wp-ontent/uploads/mp/pdf/ANPUH .S25.0956.pdf.

[82] The fundamental dispute between the two sectors for the hegemony of the Brazilian trade union movement occurred at the First National Conference of Working Classes (I Conclat) in August 1981. At the time, a Coordinating Committee of the *Central Única* was elected, the Pro-CUT Commission, which added members of both blocs and was charged not only with directing the general struggle of the Brazilian working class, but also with preparing the organization of the II Conclat, in which the CUT should be founded. However, the bloc identified with the *Unidade Sindical*, claiming that 1982 was an election year and that a congress at that time could split the workers committed to postponing the meeting. The issue was over expanding membership or anchoring the new Confederation in the current trade union structure. FGV-CPDOC, Confederação Geral dos Trabalhadores (CGT). Accessed 2 November 2017, at: www.fgv.br/cpdoc/acervo/dicionarios/verbete-biografico/c entral-geral-dos-trabalhadores-cgt.

directly related to the Workers' Party. In 1986, the *Central Geral dos Trabalhadores* – CGT, was formed, in opposition to the CUT.[83] Later internal conflicts provoked successive divisions in the CGT which led to the creation of the General Union of Workers (*União Geral dos Trabalhadores* – UGT). Then, in 1991, the *Força Sindical* was formed, which was an important political force based on the Metalworkers' Union of São Paulo, and it represented another force in opposition to CUT.

The redemocratization in 1985 and the democratic Constitution of 1988 abolished part of the restrictions on free expression and the right to strike. However, the new syndicalism, represented in the CUT, which arose in defense of a radical transformation of the syndical structure, eventually took a more moderate position to the union tax and the single industry norms. Even the Workers' Party when it came to power and held a large majority in Congress did little to alter this traditional syndical legislation. This legal basis also explains the characteristics of the structure of unions in Brazil today, their sources of revenue, the great number of unions that exist, and the relatively high rate of unionization.[84]

In addition, since the Constitution of 1988 allowed for the unionization of civil servants, the process of unionization among these civil servants and employees in state-owned enterprises, particularly those related to public services in general, have progressed rapidly. Today, the main strikes of the workers' movements occur in the public sphere, against both the government itself and state-owned enterprises. The paralysis of the public services administered by the public sector or by public companies has become the main weapon of the syndical struggle in Brazil. Currently, these corporate entities, which represent different segments of the public administration, such as professors, judges, prosecutors, or tax authorities, have enormous power, either directly by their capacity to influence crucial government activities or their power to disrupt the very activity they carry out. In the recent attempts

---

[83] On the Union Conferations, see Edson Gramuglia Araujo, "As Centrais no sistema de representação sindical no Brasil," MA thesis, Faculdade de Direito da USP, 2012, and Leôncio Martins Rodrigues, "As tendência políticas na formação das centrais sindicais," in Armando Boito, ed., *O sindicalismo brasileiro nos anos 80* (Rio de Janeiro: Paz e Terra, 1991), pp. 11–42.

[84] Daniel Pestana Mota, "CUT, Sindicato orgânico e reforma da estrutura sindical," MA thesis, Universidade Estadual Paulista em Marília, 2006; Carlos Alberto Matos, "A Fenajufe e seus sindicatos: a CUT no poder judiciário federal e no ministério público da União," MA thesis, UNICAMP – Universidade Estadual de Campinas, 2002; Alexandre Pinto Loureiro, "O direito de greve do servidor público no Brasil diante do princípio do interesse público," MA thesis, Faculdade de Direito da USP, 2009; and Fábio Túlio Barroso, "Servidores públicos da esfera civil e militar: sindicalização e greve." Accessed 2 November 2017, at: www.ambito-juridico.com.br/site/?n_link=revista_artigos_leitura&artigo_id=11514.

at pension reform, for example, the main opposition forces to reform, and perhaps the decisive ones, were such government employee entities that did not accept changes in the current legislation that reduced their rights and privileges. It is estimated that about a quarter of the federal deputies come directly from government service, which explains their strength in the National Congress.[85]

In 2016, important changes were made in labor legislation, responding to the demands of entrepreneurs who asked for greater flexibility in the procedure of hiring workers, including part-time work and outsourced work, and in the work regime in general. From the point of view of labor relations, one of the most important aspects is the strength of collective agreements between workers and employers. In previous legislation, these agreements were tightly controlled. Any aspect of a collective agreement that contradicted any item of the CLT laws, even if it had the support of the respective union, would have no value. Thus, the new law provided for far more flexibility in the negotiations between workers and management.[86] Under the new law, agreements will have value, as long as they do not contradict the constitution. This was one of the most important points of the new law, as well as the greater flexibility in hiring outsourced workers, in temporary work and in the workday. Another fundamental aspect was the abolition of the syndical tax, one of the main landmarks of the Brazilian syndical structure. There was opposition from the unions, who sought to create some alternative form of levying compulsory contributions from workers. Although the law was approved in 2016, it was only in 2018 that the syndical tax was made effective by a decision of the Federal Supreme Court, which considered the law that removed the tax to be constitutional.

There has been a major expansion of unions since the return of democratic rule, including unions of employers and professional groups. In 2015, there were 17,128 unions, of which 69% were unions of the various categories of workers, professionals, public servants, and others, including rural workers. Employers' unions represented 31% of the workers' and employers' unions: 73% were urban and 27% rural. Regionally, a third of the unions were located in the Southeast region; the Northeast and the South represented about a quarter each. About a fifth were located in the Center-West and

[85] As O Globo noted, it is "The most powerful lobby in Congress, with a quarter of the federal deputies being public servants." Accessed 4 August 2018, at: https://epocanegocios.globo.c om/Brasil/noticia/2018/07/bancada-mais-poderosa-do-congresso-um-quarto-dos-deputa dos-federais-e-servidor-publico.html.

[86] Just as an example, the CLT regulates how often vacations can be divided, rest between work periods, maximum number of hours of work per day, etc. These items and countless others were made more flexible.

North. When we consider the trade union centrals, the CUT stood out numerically, with 754 affiliated unions. The *Força Sindical* had 592 unions and the UGT 559. These three national labor federations have been in political and ideological dispute since their founding. In 2001, the CUT had the affiliation of 7.2 million workers through the unions associated with this central. The CUT was important in both the urban and rural areas, with 3.8 million rural workers. Next in importance was the *Força Sindical*, with 1.7 million affiliates, and the UGT, with 1.1 million. Both these latter national confederations had little representation in the rural area (see Table 9.4).

In 2015, trade unions raised R$ 2.7 billion, of which 72% was obtained by labor unions; the rest was obtained by employers' associations. Regionally, the Southeast accounted for 57% of the total collected, followed by the Center-West and South, with about 15% each (see Table 9.5). According to Rodrigues, the most radical factions of the trade union movement, which were previously quite critical of the union structure, lost much of the critical fervor in gaining leadership and positions in official trade unionism under the Workers' Party regimes.[87]

One important issue to consider is the trade union density rate: since all workers, unionized or not, formally pay the union tax, the actual number of union members can be smaller than the entire labor force in a particular unionized workplace. In Brazil, the percentage of workers in unions has remained around 20% between 2004 and 2015 – similar to the percentage in other important Latin American countries like Mexico, Argentina, and Chile, and not much lower than England (25%), but greater than the United States (11%). In general, the international pattern of unionization is between 10% and 30% (Tables 9.6 and 9.7).

Data gathered from the 2015 PNAD allow a better understanding of the relationship between workers and their unions. About 50% of the workers who declared that they were unionized in the survey affirmed that they joined because the union defended the rights of the workers; 20% claimed they

---

[87] According to Rodrigues, "The most radical factions of the trade union movement, which were previously quite critical of the corporate trade union structure, lost much of the critical fervor in gaining leadership and positions in official trade unionism. In that sense, the 1988 Constitution, by drastically limiting the intervention power of the Ministry of Labor in the internal affairs of the unions, eliminated one of the aspects that the union leaders considered more negative in the corporate model. Consequently, it cooled down the momentum of change and increased the importance of official unions as an instrument of worker pressure, social and political ascendancy of union and employment directors for federation and confederation bureaucrats. Paradoxically, the Constitution strengthened corporate structures by granting them autonomy vis-à-vis the state." Leôncio Martins Rodrigues, "Sindicalismo corporativo no Brasil," p. 64.

Table 9.4 *Number of Union Members by Affiliation to a Syndical Confederation, 2001*

	Total	Not Affiliated to a Confederation	Affiliated	CUT	Força Sindical	UGT (CT + CGT + SDS)	Other Federations
All Brazil	19,528,311	9,317,126	10,211,185	7,251,583	734,733	1,171,214	53,655
Urban	10,391,687	3,958,334	6,433,353	3,860,961	1,596,099	926,615	49,678
Employees	9,216,544	3,088,138	6,128,406	3,697,990	1,522,814	859,644	47,958
Self-employed	522,729	405,108	117,621	15,969	63,742	36,190	1,720
Liberal professionals	567,606	389,403	178,203	143,742	4,562	29,899	
Independent workers	84,808	75,685	9,123	3,260	4,981	882	
Rural	9,136,624	5,358,792	3,777,832	3,390,622	138,634	244,599	
Workers	9,136,624	5,358,792	3,777,832	3,390,622	138,634	244,599	

Source: IBGE, *Sidicatos: Indicadores Sociais, 2001.* https://biblioteca.ibge.gov.br/visualizacao/livros/liv1416.pdf.

Table 9.5 *Number of Union Organizations Existing and the Funds They Generated in 2015*

Characteristics	Number	Income Generated (R$)
Categories		
Total *sindicatos trabalhadores urbanos*	9,069	2,022,422,390
Urban employees in general	5,121	1,473,432,917
Public servants	2,181	138,428,956
Differentiated categories*	667	92,677,241
Liberal professionals	532	131,406,313
Autonomous and independent workers	568	186,476,963
Rural unions	4,601	12,145,899
Employers	3,458	539,132,817
Total	17,128	2,573,701,106
Residence		
Urban unions	12,670	2,727,304,556
Rural unions	4,601	12,145,899
Type		
Worker unions	11,867	1,959,306,734
Employer unions/Associations	5,408	780,143,721
Region		
Center-West	1,850	475,304,975
Southeast	5,853	1,689,203,940
Northeast	4,206	261,852,695
North	1,252	78,629,868
South	4,127	436,775,400
Federations		
No affiliation	980	1,037,487,279
CUT – *Central Única dos Trabalhadores*	754	481,994,729
Força Sindical	592	379,955,836
UGT – *União Geral dos Trabalhadores*	559	341,847,879
NCST – *Nova Central Sindical de Trabalhadores*	361	246,419,313
CBT – *Central Trabalhadores Brasil*	320	104,329,001
Central dos Sindicatos Brasileiros	305	99,533,367

Source: Ministério do Trabalho. http://relacoesdotrabalho.mte.gov.br/pentaho/api/repos/:pub lic:SRT:srt_principal1.xaction/generatedContent.

* Categories with special legislation such as professors and journalists.

Table 9.6 *Increase in the Number of Unionized Workers and Percentage of All Workers Unionized, 2004–2015*

	Workers Unionized			Percentage Change	All Workers Unionized (percentage)		
	2004	2009	2015	2015/2004	2004	2009	2015
Total	15,317	16,651	18,414	20%	19%	18%	20%
Agriculture	4,055	3,994	3,738	–8%	24%	26%	29%
Manufacturing industry	2,572	2,633	2,600	1%	22%	21%	23%
Other industrial activities	251	290	262	4%	37%	37%	37%
Construction	387	581	789	104%	7%	8%	9%
Trade and repair	1,620	1,875	2,274	40%	11%	12%	13%
Accommodation and food	277	331	513	85%	9%	9%	11%
Transport, storage, and communication	969	1,073	1,306	35%	25%	24%	25%
Public administration	1,113	1,282	1,350	21%	26%	27%	27%
Education, health, and social services	2,232	2,506	3,117	40%	30%	29%	30%
Domestic services	98	155	248	153%	2%	2%	4%
Other collective, social, and personal services	354	389	383	8%	10%	10%	9%
Other activities	1,379	1,537	1,831	33%	24%	21%	22%
Not-well-defined activities	10	6	3	–70%	5%	3%	4%

Unionized Workers by Region 2015	Number	Regional Workers (percentage)
Brazil	18,414	20%
North	1,168	16%
Northeast	5,318	22%
Southeast	7,496	18%
South	3,121	21%
Center-West	1,313	17%

Source: IBGE, PNAD, Pesquisa das Relações de Trabalho e Sindicalização, 2015 (2017), pp. 50–63.

joined because of the services offered by the unions; and 27% felt it was mandatory. On the other hand, among the non-unionized there was a general belief that the union did not represent their interest or offer services that they wanted; some had little idea about which union represented them. The

Table 9.7 *Percentage of Workers Unionized in Diverse Countries*

Country	Year	Percentage Unionized
Brazil	2013	16.6
Argentina	2008	37.7
Mexico	2013	13.6
United States	2013	10.8
Chile	2013	15.0
Canada	2012	27.5
United Kingdom	2013	25.4
Italy	2013	36.9
Russia	2013	27.8
Turkey	2013	6.3
Australia	2013	17.0
South Africa	2012	29.6
Japan	2013	17.8
South Korea	2012	10.1

Source: Internacional Labor Organization. www.ilo.org/ilostat/f aces/oracle/webcenter/portalapp/pagehierarchy/Page3.jspx? MBI_ID=9.

reasons given for belonging to a union or not joining one show some confusion about trade unions and their effective roles (see Table 9.8).

Aside from their political and representative roles in economic relations, unions also provide important legal support to its members. In Brazil, the termination of an employment contract signed by an employee with more than one year of work only has value if signed with the assistance of the correct union or a public authority. This union authorization was only abolished in the new labor law of 2016. Brazil is also unusual in having an independent judicial structure of labor law with a separate system of Labor Courts, parallel and similar to the structure of the judiciary. Thus, there are Labor Courts in the first instance, Regional Labor Courts (second instance), and Superior Labor Court (extraordinary instance). In fact, the structure of labor legislation in Brazil, still based on the Vargas labor code, contributes to prodigious litigation. In 2016, there were 4.2 million cases in the Labor Courts, with 5.3 million pending.[88] But this has declined under the impact

[88] "Justiça em Números 2017, ano-base 2016"; Conselho Nacional de Justiça, Brasília, CNJ, 2017, p. 36.

Table 9.8 *Motive for Union Membership by Type of Union, 2015*

	Number	Percentage
Unionized Workers	19,586	
Type of Union		
Urban employees	11,309	58%
Rural employees	4,770	24%
Self-employed workers	273	1%
Independent workers	38	0%
Liberal professional	494	3%
Other type of union	2,702	14%
Motive for Belonging to Union		
Union defends the rights of workers	9,948	51%
Union offers services to members	3,956	20%
Believes that it is obligatory	5,265	27%
Other reasons	418	2%
Do Utilize the Activities Provided by the Union	4,103	21%
Non-Unionized Workers – Reasons Why	83,135	
Unemployed or temporarily laid off	5,499	7%
The fees are expensive	5,798	7%
Does not represent their interests and does not believe in unions	13,833	17%
Union has no services of interest to me	19,617	24%
I did not know about the union which represented my class of work	21,917	26%
Did not know how to join	9,819	12%
Company was hostile to the union	258	0%
Other reasons	6,394	8%

Source: IBGE, PNAD, Pesquisa das Relações de Trabalho e Sindicalização, 2015 (2017), pp. 50–63.

of the new labor code. Six months after the reform of the labor codes, there was a decrease of approximately 50% in the number of new lawsuits; and for the first time in five years there was a reduction in the number of pending cases.[89]

---

[89] "Estoque de Ações cai na Justiça do Trabalho," *Folha de São Paulo* (17 April 2018). Accessed at: www1.folha.uol.com.br/mercado/2018/04/estoque-de-acoes-cai-na-justica-do-trabalho .shtml. See also "after the reform, number of new labor lawsuits fell by half." Accessed at: www.cartacapital.com.br/politica/Apos-reforma-numero-de-novos-processos-trabalhistas-caiu-pela-metade.

Unions also provide sports, education, activities for retired persons, and above all health services. After legal services, health is probably the most important non-work-related service provided by unions. A survey of 2015 found that union members in both rural and urban areas used dental, medical, and legal services of the union most, with sports and education being another significant group of services popular with members.[90]

One aspect of voluntary associations which occupies a major cultural space is athletics. Brazil is known for its passion for football (soccer), which has social and cultural importance in the country. It has even been said that without understanding football one cannot fully understand Brazil.[91] Although Brazil is important in other sports, such as volleyball, for example, no sport resembles soccer in terms of its social and cultural representativeness. Some data serve to demonstrate this importance. According to survey data of IBOP, 63% of sports broadcasts on TV are devoted to football; other sports had less than 5% of the time dedicated to them.[92] Recent research shows that more than 140 million people claim to identify with a football club. Some clubs, like Flamengo (RJ) and Corinthians (SP) have around 30 million fans.[93] Most are loyal fans that daily follow their club news, watch regular club matches,[94] and often are consumers of

[90] IBGE, PNAD, Pesquisa das Relações de Trabalho e Sindicalização, 2015 (2017), pp. 50–63

[91] According to the author, football practiced, lived, discussed, and theorized in Brazil would be a specific way, by which society speaks, presents itself, and reveals itself. Roberto DaMatta, "Esporte na sociedade: um ensaio sobre o futebol brasileiro," in Roberto DaMatta, *Universo do futebol: esporte e sociedade brasileira* (Rio de Janeiro: Pinakotheke, 1982), pp. 21–22. Witter on the other hand stated that contrary to what is believed, football is not related to the great problems of Brazilian society. On the contrary, it involves economic interests, and deals with ideologies in which national and international politics are manifested. José Sebastião Witter, *Breve história do futebol brasileiro* (São Paulo: FTD, 1995), p. 5.

[92] Portal imprensa. Accessed at: www.portalimprensa.com.br/brasil/66895/pesquisa+do+ibope+aponta+que+tempo+dedicado+ao+esporte+na+tv+cresceu+53. The most representative of the other sports had a participation lower than 5%.

[93] Lance. Futebol Nacional, "Última pesquisa LANCE/Ibope mostrou Flamengo na frente, mas vantagem menor para o Timão." Accessed 6 November 2017, at: www.lance.com.br/futebol-nacional/flamengo-segue-com-maior-torcida-mas-vantagem-para-timao-cai.html.

[94] As in other countries, most of the games are on television. But, aside from this convenience and economy, a part of the public interested in soccer has stopped going to the stadiums for security reasons, this being one of the symptoms of the bad administration of football in Brazil. According to IBOPE, 35% of the population states that security is an impediment to attending football matches. Accessed 11 June 2017, at: www.ibopeinteligencia.com/noticias-e-pesquisas/falta-de-seguranca-e-o-principal-motivo-para-torcedor-nao-ir-ao-estadio/. Thus, for reasons of income, organization, or safety, the reality is that Brazil occupies only eighteenth place in the ranking of national soccer championships in terms of attendance at the stadiums. In Brazil, the average game reaches 13,000 spectators (2013), compared with 44,000 for Germany's Bundesliga, 36,000 for the English Premier League, 29,000 for the Spanish League, and 24,000 even for the Mexican League. See Fut Pop Club. Accessed 11 June 2017, at: https://futpopclube.com/tag/ranking-mundial-de-publico-nos-estadios/.

products sold by their club.[95] There is a category of supportive members who regularly pay a club support fee. Some clubs such as Grêmio (RGS), Corinthians (SP), Palmeiras (SP), São Paulo (SP), Internacional (RGS), and Atlético Mineiro (MG) have more than 100,000 fans each in this category.[96]

Although Brazil does not have a prominent role in the Olympics (it occupies the 35th position),[97] it has a significant role in soccer, being the largest country with the largest number of world championships, and often leads the ranking of the International Soccer Federation. This reflects the passion for football and its outstanding role compared to any other sport in Brazil. The passion for soccer is also reflected in the practice of sports in Brazil. According to a sports question in the PNAD national household survey of 2015, 24% of the Brazilian population 15 years of age and older engaged in some type of sport. The percentage was 32% of men and 17% of women, with no difference by color. As expected, the figures were higher by age, with 44% of youths 15 to 17 years of age engaging in sports, compared to only 28% of persons aged 25 to 39 years of age. There is also a correlation between income and sport. Only 23% of those who earn up to 2 minimum salaries engage in sports, 30% of those from 2 to 5 minimum salaries, and 40% of those who earn 5 or more minimum salaries (see Table 9.9).

[95] It should be noted that the level of emotional involvement with the club is high among football fans in Brazil, who follow the news of their club and watch the games with assiduity, in the stadiums or on television. Research shows that 93% of fans, no matter what happens to the club, even if the team is not winning, are always loyal to the team (96% among men). At the same time, 80% said they had good times with the team, especially men (83%). For 63.8% of the interviewees, the team is part of their lives and they identify with the achievements of the team. The survey shows that 62% are uncomfortable when they speak badly about the team – mainly women (73%), those belonging to classes A/B (73%), and fans who declare themselves supporters (75%). On the day of play, 54% said they have a commitment to the favored team, with the highest percentage found in classes A/B (64%) and amateur fans (77%). The frequency with which the interviewees watch a team's games on television or at a stadium is significant: from once or twice a week for 73% of the sample. By contrast, 10% say they rarely watch games (increasing to 20% among women). As the study notes, "It's all a psychological projection, as if the football team were someone the fans cherish immensely, to the point of devoting virtually unlimited time and emotional investment." *Mercado de Consumo do Futebol Brasileiro*, CNDL/SPC Brasil, September 2016. Accessed 11 June 2017, at: www.google.com.br/search?q=Mercado+de+Consumo+do+Futebol+Brasileiro.+CNDL%2FSPC+Brasil%2C+Setembro+de+2016&rlz=1C1SQJL_pt-BRBR778BR778&oq=Merc ado+de+Consumo+do+Futebol+Brasileiro.+CNDL%2FSPC+Brasil%2C+Setembro+de+20 16&aqs=chrome..69i57.446joj8&sourceid=chrome&ie=UTF-8. On this theme, see Roberto Romeiro Hryniewicz, "Torcida de Futebol: adesão, alienação e violência," MA thesis, Instituto de Psicologia da Universidade de São Paulo, 2008.

[96] Accessed 4 August 2018, at: www.90min.com/pt-BR/posts/6076274-atualizado-os-10-clubes-que-lideram-o-ranking-de-socio-torcedor-no-brasil.

[97] Brazil won only 30 gold medals compared with 1,022 for the United States. This compares poorly with other counties: Italy (206), France (212), and Great Britain (263). Brazil had a similar number of medals to Kenya (31) and Greece (33) but was superior to Argentina (21).

Table 9.9 *Percentage of Persons 15 Years of Age and Older Who Participated in Some Sport, 2015*

Characteristics	Percentage
Total	24%
Men	32%
Women	17%
Color	
Whites	25%
Blacks or browns	23%
Age	
15–17 years	44%
18–24 years	34%
25–39 years	28%
40–59 years	18%
60+	13%
Income by Minimum Salary	
No income	21%
½–1	21%
1–2	23%
2–3	30%
3–5	35%
> 5	40%

Source: IBGE, "Práticas de esporte e atividade física, 2015" (2017), pp. 26–50.

What is interesting in the Brazilian case is the great concentration of soccer practice in relation to other sports. Of those who declare that they play a sport, 39% cited soccer against other sports such as cycling, boxing, gymnastics, volleyball, basketball, and handball, which were engaged in by percentages of the order of 3%.[98] There are even some regional differences. The North and Northeast present a higher percentage of soccer players than the South, Southeast, and Center-West. Football is predominantly played by men (95%) and by younger people. Although 39% of the national population practice soccer, among 15- to 17-years-olds this percentage rises to 65%, and is still high in the range of 18 to 24 years (see Table 9.10).

Despite the importance of professional soccer clubs in Brazil, their management is run in an inefficient, amateurish way. All the important sports

---

[98] There were 24% who cited walking as their activity, but this was not considered a sport.

Table 9.10 *Type of Sport Engaged in by Population 15 Years and Over Who Practice a Sport, 2015*

Sport	Percentage Practicing
Football	39.3%
Walking	24.6%
Volleyball, handball, and racket ball	2.9%
Fitness training	9.0%
Cycling	3.2%
Martial arts	3.1%
Rhythmic and artistic gymnastics	3.2%
Other sports	14.7%
Total	100.0%
Regional Distribution of Persons Playing Football	
Brazil	39.3%
North	55.9%
Northeast	48.8%
Southeast	33.3%
South	35.1%
Center-West	32.9%
Percentage Playing Football, by Age	
15–17 years	64.5%
18–24 years	57.6%
25–39 years	41.4%
40–59 years	24.1%
60+	4.9%
Percentage Playing Football by Sex	
Men	94.5%
Women	5.5%
Total	100.0%

Source: IBGE, "Práticas de esporte e atividade física, 2015" (2017), pp. 26–50.

clubs in Brazil are organized as non-profit societies that mix sports and leisure. These same entities represent both amateur and professional sport in Brazil, including the soccer teams that are significant internationally. Thus, it is easy to understand the disparity between the quality of Brazilian football, either in terms of the quality of the selection or in terms of the training of professional players who then go on to play in major football clubs around the world, with the amateur structure that manages Brazilian football clubs. This explains the relatively poor economic position of the main Brazilian clubs compared to major international clubs. A list of the 20 richest football clubs in the world published by *Forbes Magazine* does not include any Brazilian clubs.[99] Revenues collected by the top 20 European clubs are almost 10 times higher than those of the 20 richest Brazilian teams. Flamengo, the top club on the list in Brazil, earns annually about 77 million euros compared with 577 million euros earned by Real Madrid.[100]

There have been attempts recently to privatize these sports clubs. But, in fact, very little has occurred. The first law, dated 1993, called the Zico Law, allowed clubs and sports confederations to be transformed into commercial companies for this purpose. In 1998, a new law was introduced which made it necessary to transform clubs into companies. But this obligation, which had few practical effects, would soon be abolished.[101] Thus, today such a transformation is permitted but not mandatory, as there is open opposition from the sports community. The issue is really not so much about transforming sports entities into profit-making societies. The fundamental aspect is the governance of such entities. Professional management, involving transparency and well-defined responsibilities is fundamental. Unfortunately, the management of sport, even in the more professional segments, is still quite amateurish. The main problem today is the legal nature of these institutions and the permissive relationship they have maintained over time with the football fans. Clubs are private, associative, highly politicized institutions in which positions of power most often are occupied on a voluntary basis, decided through internal elections that do not necessarily take the criterion of meritocracy into account. This produces a deep political bias in the day-to-day administration, decisively affecting the quality of managerial and business decision-making.[102]

Another major group of voluntary associations with unusual activities are the NGOs which take on active roles in support of state activities. It was during the late 1990s under the government of Fernando Henrique Cardoso

[99] Exame. Accessed 11 June 2017, at: https://exame.abril.com.br/negocios/os-20-times-de-futebol-mais-valiosos-do-mundo-em-2016/#

[100] Meio&Mensagem, "Europeus goleiam brasileiros em receita." Accessed 6 November 2017, at: www.meioemensagem.com.br/home/marketing/2016/01/21/europeus-goleiam-brasileiros-em-receita.html

[101] The Zico Law (8.672), was approved in 1993. The second, called the Pelé Law (9.615) of 1998, made such a transformation to an enterprise obligatory.

[102] Michel Mattar, postgraduate coordinator at "Excelência em Gestão do Futebol da Fundação Instituto de Administração." Interview, "Movimento por um Futebol Melhor." Accessed 11 July 2017, at: www.lance.com.br/futebol-melhor/coordenador-fia-analisa-gestao-profissional-nos-clubes-brasileiros.html.

that Social Organizations were legally classified as private non-profit entities and allowed to work with the government.[103] The executive branch could transfer to these Social Organizations the execution of public services and asset management in the areas of education, scientific research, technological development, and the protection and preservation of the environment, culture, and health. The law regulated the structure of these Social Organizations (known as OSs in Portuguese) and the management contracts between the public power and the OSs with a view to forming partnerships between the two parties for the promotion and execution of agreed activities. Based on such a federal standard, a broad field of public–private partnerships was opened, particularly in the areas of health and culture. The public sector defined the areas in which this could occur then signed a management agreement with the OS, which clearly stipulated the goals to be fulfilled and provided the necessary resources for the execution of those activities.

Resources are provided globally for all OS activities. The contracts usually run for 4 to 5 years, with targets and corresponding budgets established. There is quarterly monitoring of the results obtained and annual renegotiation of goals and budgets. In order to carry out the appointed work program, the OSs have freedom of action in the hiring of professionals without competitive appointments but are governed by the standard labor laws (CLT) and they have to meet certain parameters in terms of salary or personnel structure. They have greater flexibility in contracting services in general but must have defined policies for contracting materials and services, preserving competition and for transparency.[104] The OS has to be controlled by an

---

[103] Law 9.637 of 15 May 1998 provides for the qualification of entities as "Social Organizations" and creates the National Publicity Program to establish guidelines and criteria for the qualification of Social Organizations in order to ensure the absorption of activities carried out by entities or public bodies of the Union. On the formal aspects of this legislation on Social Organizations, see Cadernos MARE da Reforma do Estado, *Organizações Sociais* (2 vols; Brasília, 1998). On legislation of the third sector, see the *dispositivos constitucionais, decretos-leis, leis, medidas provisórias*, and the *decretos federais* on public utility and civil society organizations of public interest. *(Oscip)/Câmara dos Deputados* (Brasília, Câmara dos Deputados: Edições Câmara, 2016). Ana C. N. M. Fernandes da Cunha, "As organizações Sociais de Saúde na cidade de São Paulo e a efetivação do Direito Fundamental à Saúde," MA thesis, Faculdade de Direito – Universidade de São Paulo, 2016; Luis Carlos Cancellier de Olivo, *As Organizações Sociais e o novo espaço público* (Florianópolis: Editorial Studium, 2005); Rubens Naves, *Organizações Sociais: a construção do modelo* (São Paulo: Editora Quartier Latin, 2014); Laila Federico Asfora, "Terceiro Setor: Organizações Sociais," MA thesis, Pontifícia Universidade Católica do Rio de Janeiro – PUC-Rio, 2012.

[104] Law 6170/2017 established that the acquisition of products and the contracting of services with resources of the Union transferred to private non-profit entities should observe the principles of impersonality, morality, and economics, and at least a prior quotation of prices on the market before conclusion of the contract. Thus, although with greater flexibility, entities must comply with fundamental principles of public administration.

unpaid board composed of members elected from among the members or associates of the Social Organization, as well as persons of well-known professional capacity and recognized moral repute. There is also a proportion of members elected by OS officials.[105]

Although they are considered private entities, as they execute public policies on behalf of the public sector and receive public resources for this purpose, they need to be fully transparent, and their accounts, after being audited by independent auditors, are controlled by the executive power and by the respective Audit Courts. A fundamental issue, and one provided for by law, is the need to establish boards and other institutions to monitor policies implemented – setting goals and evaluating parameters. This is perhaps the most complex aspect of these contracts, and such supervisory boards have little experience even in the public sector in such activities. This is probably the greatest challenge for public administrations when they sign management contracts with Social Organizations.

The first and most solid experience was developed by the State of Paulo, in the areas of both health and culture,[106] and because of their pioneering and successful work there are several studies on health and culture OSs in São Paulo.[107] The opportunity for the experiment occurred when the State of São

[105] On the basis of the Federal Law that regulated the Social Organizations, states and municipalities approved their own laws based on the legal framework of federal legislation, but with their own peculiarities. The Federal Law, for example, establishes that the Board of Directors must contain representatives from the public sector. Complementary Law no. 846 of 9 June 1998, which addressed Social Organizations' qualification in the State of São Paulo, does not provide for the participation of representatives from the public sector. In each case there are adaptations to meet specific state or municipal situations but keeping within the legal framework established by Federal Law. Vanice M. da Silva, Sheyla L. Lima, and Marcia Teixeira, "Organizações e fundações estatais de direito privado no sistema único de saúde: relação entre o público e o privado e mecanismos de controle social," *Saúde Debate* 39 (2015), pp. 145–159.

[106] In 2007, out of 70 Social Organizations created in the country, health was the largest sector – with 24 organizations: 16 in São Paulo, 1 in Espírito Santo, 3 in Bahia, 3 in Pará, and 1 in Goiás. Hironobu Sano and Fernando Luiz Abrucio, "Promessas e resultados da nova gestão pública no brasil: o caso das organizações sociais em São Paulo." *Revista de Administração de Empresas* 48.3 (2008), p. 69.

[107] On health, see Nilson do Rosário Costa and José Mendes Ribeiro, "Estudo comparativo do desempenho de hospitais em regime de organização social." Programa de pesquisas – Em busca da excelência: fortalecendo o desempenho hospitalar no Brasil. Relatório final. Ministério da Saúde (Rio de Janeiro: World Bank, 2005); André Medici and Robert Murray, "Desempenho de hospitais e melhorias na qualidade de saúde em São Paulo (Brasil) e Maryland (EUA)" (Washington, DC: World Bank. 2013); Clarissa Battistella Guerra, "Gestão Privada na Saúde Pública: um estudo empírico com Hospitais sob contrato de gestão no Estado de São Paulo," MA thesis, Instituição Insper São Paulo, 2015. On culture, see Lúcio Nagib Bittencourt, "As organizações sociais e as ações governamentais em cultura: ação e política pública no caso do Estado de São Paulo," PhD thesis, FGV/SP, São Paulo, 2014; Naila López Cabaleiro Suárez, *O modelo de gestão das organizações sociais de*

Paulo was in the process of completing seventeen new hospitals. Taking advantage of the recently approved federal law on OSs and seeking greater agility and administrative autonomy of the new hospitals which were spread throughout the territory of the state, it was decided to implement the OS management model. As the state wanted to use the new management model for only new equipment and there was a large supply of potential entities already operating in the state that could obtain certification as Social Organizations, state law declared that these new health OSs would need to have prior experience in the administration of health services. Moreover, they could only work with new equipment and could not replace existing public administration equipment. In addition, in order to ensure an efficient follow-up of the state's objectives and established goals, a management committee was created, composed of representatives of the State Health Council, the Health and Hygiene Commission of the Legislative Assembly, and well-known professionals appointed by the state. In addition, the contracts defined that only 90% of remuneration was fixed and 10% variable, which depended on the evaluation of the quality and efficiency of the services provided.[108]

With this new state law numerous contracts were signed in the health field.[109] In 2015, the health network of the State of São Paulo was using these Social Organizations in 40 hospitals, with 42,000 employees, 7,628 doctors, and 6,892 operational beds, with an average patient satisfaction of more than 90%. The network under OS administration also counted on 52 out-patient clinics (*Ambulatório Médico de Especialidade* – AMEs), with 11,000 employees, of which 3,328 are doctors. Almost 4 million medical consultations were carried out in this network of AMEs in the year. There are 28 partner entities, composed of some of the most traditional institutions in the area of Health in the state, several composed by Foundations linked to universities, including the Faculty of Medicine in the University of São

---

cultura em São Paulo (São Paulo: FGV, 2011); Ivan Roberto Ferraz, "Indicadores de desempenho das organizações sociais de cultura do Estado de São Paulo," MA thesis, Pontifícia Universidade Católica de São Paulo – PUC-SP, 2008.

[108] Secretaria de Estado da Saúde, "As organizações Sociais de Saúde no Estado de São Paulo. A experiência da Secretaria da Saúde: planejamento e mecanismos de acompanhamento, controle e avaliação." Accessed 12 January 2018, at: www.saude.sp.gov.br/resources/ses/perfil/gestor/homepage/auditoria/reunioes/organizacoes_sociais_de_saude_no_estado_de_sao_paulo.pdf.

[109] Luiz Roberto Barradas Barata and José Dinio Vaz Mendes, *Organizações Sociais de Saúde: a experiência exitosa de gestão pública de saúde do Estado de São Paulo* (São Paulo: Secretaria de Saúde, 2007).

Paulo and the public/private hospital system known as the *Santas Casas de Misericórdia*.[110] There is a great deal of evidence to show that management by these OS entities is more efficient than the direct administration by the state. This was the conclusion of a World Bank study carried out in 2006.[111] Based on data from 2003, it compared 12 OS hospitals and 10 publicly administered hospitals in the state of São Paulo with similar profiles, demonstrating the greater technical efficiency (capacity to produce the maximum results with a given amount of inputs) of these OS hospitals. The researchers also asserted that OS hospitals had slightly better overall mortality indicators than those under direct administration.[112] Several other studies made by the state Health Ministry, the most recent being one in 2016, showed similar results, as do numerous local studies carried out throughout the state.[113]

In the case of culture, the state of São Paulo took an even more radical position, since it transferred practically all cultural activities to these OSs. A Monitoring Board was created in 2013 with the objective of elaborating guidelines and procedures for overseeing and evaluating state partnerships with OS. In 2014, some twenty-seven management contracts were signed with twenty different Social Organizations, involving cultural training, cultural diffusion, museums, and libraries. The Symphony Orchestra of the State of São Paulo, the Pinacoteca (Art Museum) of the State of São Paulo, the Museum of the Portuguese Language, the Soccer Museum, and the Afro Brazil Museum are some of the institutions that are under contract with OSs.

---

[110] Eduardo Ribeiro Adriano, "Organizações Sociais de Saúde – OSS." Governo do Estado de São Paulo, São Paulo (October 2016). PowerPoint presentation. Accessed 18 June 2018, at http://ses.sp.bvs.br/wp-content/uploads/2017/05/CGCSS-CCTIES_apresentado-na-reuni%C3%A30-Holanda-201016_Dr.-Eduardo.pdf.

[111] Costa and Ribeiro, "Estudo comparativo do desempenho de hospitais." This study was carried out for the World Bank by Luiz Roberto Barradas Barata and José Dinio Vaz Mendes along with the Ministry of Health and researchers from the Fundação Oswaldo Cruz. Barata was secretary and held various positions in the public health area, having been Secretary of Health for the state government of São Paulo from 2003 to 2010, the phase of consolidation of the model of Social Organizations in the state.

[112] Barata and Mendes, *Organizações Sociais de Saúde.*

[113] Aside from the studies of Barata and Mendes, *Organizações Sociais de Saúde* and Adriano, "Organizações Sociais de Saúde – OSS," see also Guerra, "Gestão Privada na Saúde Pública," p. 58; Cunha, "As organizações sociais de saúde na cidade de São Paulo"; Leonardo Ferreira de Santana, "Análise do desempenho dos serviços prestados através das organizações sociais de saúde no Estado do Rio de Janeiro," MA thesis FGV/RJ, Rio de Janeiro, 2015; Assuero Fonseca Ximenes, "Apropriação do fundo público da saúde pela organizações sociais em Pernambuco," PhD thesis, Federal University of Pernambuco – UFPE, Recife, 2015; Tania Regina Kruger, Simone Bihain Hagemann, and Aline Ayres Hollanda, "Organizações sociais e os serviços públicos de saúde em Santa Catarina," Paper presented at the Seminário Nacional de Serviço Social, Trabalho e Política Social, Florianópolis, UFSC, October 2015.

Although there are some private box office receipts for some of these institutions, and often some form of private and public sponsorship, resources from management contracts represent more than 80% of the OSs' total expenses for culture in the state of São Paulo. In 2014, more than 5,000 people worked in cultural organizations managed by an OS and during the year more than 18,000 cultural events occurred in which a population of over 10 million people participated. About 60% of the culture secretariat's budget was spent with these OS.[114]

Aside from all these associations and entities which relate to the daily lives of Brazilians and their interest in making life better for their country through a whole range of activities, there exists a whole other area of life in which voluntary organizations are profoundly important in Brazil. This is of course the popular churches. Non-profit private associations showing spectacular growth include Pentecostal churches. And for a time even the Catholic Church was a major player in organizing popular associations, aside from its usual charity bodies. These were the famous small Christian communities (*Comunidades Eclesiales de base*) that the Catholic Church organized in the 1960s and 1970s, which were priest-led community organizations of all kinds, from Bible study groups to social activist organizations.[115]

But since the end of the military era there has been a relative decline of the Roman Church in such activities. By contrast, there has been an extraordinary expansion of Pentecostal religious associations in this formerly

---

[114] Secretaria da Cultura do São Paulo. Boletim UM, "Cultura em Números, 10 anos de parceria com OSs de Cultura, 2004 a 2014." Accessed at: www.transparenciacultura.sp.gov.br/wp-content/uploads/2016/03/2017.02.01-boletim-UM-n.-2-Balan%C3%A7o-10-anos-atualizado-1.pdf. About partnerships in the field of culture, see Ferraz, "Indicadores de desempenho das organizações sociais de cultura do Estado de São Paulo; José V. R. Netto, Lucio Bittencourt, and Pedro Malafaia, "Políticas culturais por meio de organizações sociais em São Paulo: expandindo a qualidade da democracia?" Seminário Internacional de Políticas Culturais, Rio de Janeiro, 2012. Accessed 12 January 2018, at: http://culturadigital.br/politicaculturalcasaderuibarbosa/files/2012/09/Jose-Verissimo-Rom%C3%A3o-Netto-et-alii.pdf; Suárez, *O modelo de gestão das organizações sociais de cultura em São Paulo*; Bittencourt, "As organizações sociais e as ações governamentais"; Elizabeth Ponte de Freitas, "Por uma cultura pública: organizações sociais, oscips e gestão pública não estatal na área da cultura," MA thesis, Universidade Federal da Bahia, 2010; S. B. Duarte, "Organizações sociais de cultura em São Paulo: desafios e perspectivas," Paper presented at the IV Congresso Consad de Gestão Pública, Brasília, May 2012.

[115] These base communities or CEBS (*comunidades eclesiais de base*) were established in the 1970s and were of great importance during the military era, with many adopting the ideas of liberation theology. But following the end of dictatorship and the move toward the Right, the Catholic church reduced its social activism considerably and their relative importance in the urban centers of Brazil after 1990 was reduced. See Ana Jacira dos Santos, "As comunidades eclesiais de base no período de 1970 a 2000," PhD thesis, Universidade Federal do Rio Grande do Norte, 2002.

overwhelmingly Roman Catholic country. In 1950, some 93% of Brazilians identified themselves as members of the Roman Catholic Church.[116] Sixty years later, in the census of 2010, only 65% identified themselves in this way. Although Brazil remains the largest Roman Catholic country in the world in the twenty-first century, it is now the world's fourth largest Protestant country and has the largest Pentecostal population of any nation.[117] This makes it the world's second largest Christian country – second only to the United States.[118] The major change was not the increase in traditional non-Catholic Christian denominations which took place in the nineteenth century, but the rise of evangelical Protestantism in the twentieth century.[119] In 1930, for example, Baptists comprised 30% of Brazilian Protestants and Presbyterians 24%, while Pentecostals accounted for just 10%. But, by 1964, Pentecostals alone represented 65% of all Protestants, and Baptists just 9%.[120] Only in the past three censuses has the government begun to provide detailed information on all the different Protestant denominations. From 1991 to 2010, the percentage of the population identifying as Protestant went from 9% to 24%, with traditional Protestant denominations only

---

[116] IBGE, *Recenseamento Geral de 1950*, Série Nacional, vol. 1, p. 30, Table 8.

[117] Paul Freston, "'Neo-Pentecostalism' in Brazil: Problems of Definition and the Struggle for Hegemony." *Archives de Sciences Sociales des Religions* 44.105 (1999), p. 145.

[118] These are estimates for all the world's countries from the Pew Religious Census of 2010. Accessed 22 October 2017, at: www.pewforum.org/2011/12/19/table-christian-population-in-numbers-by-country/.

[119] Historians of Protestantism in Brazil usually divide the movement into two groups: those religions introduced by immigrants (*protestantismo de imigração*), who brought their religion with them, and those which were introduced by missionaries from Europe or North America (*protestatismo de missão*). The first is primarily the German Lutherans, but almost all the other traditional Protestant religions were introduced either by immigrants or missionaries coming from their home countries to minister to their nationals as well as seeking Brazilian converts. IBGE has defined all of these traditional churches as Missionary Evangelicals (*Evangélicas de Missão*). Those introduced in the nineteenth century include the Lutherans (founded in 1823), the largest of these traditional churches, followed by the Presbyterians (1859), the Methodists (1867), and the Baptists (1882). Coming after 1900 are the Pentecostals (called by IBGE *Evangélicas de origem Pentecostal*), which have both missionary and indigenous origins. The first missionary-founded Pentecostal churches were the *Congregação Cristã no Brasil* (1910) and the *Assembleia de Deus* (1911) – still the largest of the Pentecostal churches and both founded just a few years after the birth of the Pentecostal movement in Los Angeles in 1906. This first wave of Pentecostal churches was followed by numerous immigrant, missionary, and finally native-founded Pentecostal churches throughout the twentieth and into the twenty-first centuries. See Carl Joseph Hahn, *História do Culto Protestante no* Brasil (São Paulo: Aste, 1981), Antonio Gouvêa Mendonça and Prócoro Velasques Filho, *Introdução ao Protestantismo no Brasil* (São Paulo: Edições Loyola, 1990); and Paul Freston, "Protestantes e politica no Brasil: da constituente ao impeachment," PhD thesis, UNICAMP – Universidade Estadual de Campinas, 1993, p. 41.

[120] Candido Procópio Ferreira de Camargo, ed., *Católicos, Protestantes, Espíritas* (Petropolis: Ediora Vozes, 1973), p. 121, Table 2.

Table 9.11 *Religious Identity of Brazilians in the Censuses of 1991, 2000, and 2010*

Religion	1991	2000	2010
	12,181,2771	124,980,132	123,280,172
Protestants*	4,942,230	6,939,765	7,686,827
Pentecostals†	8,179,706	17,975,249	25,370,484
Other evangelicals unspecified or simply Christians	621,298	1,269,928	10,906,133
Mormons			226,509
Jehovah's Witnesses	–	1,104,886	1,393,208
Umbanda e Candomblé	648,489	525,013	588,797
Spiritists	1,644,355	2,262,401	3,848,876
Jewish		86,825	107,329
All others	2,020,748	2,236,254	2,011,954
No religion	6,946,221	12,492,403	15,335,510
Total	146,815,818	169,872,856	190,755,799

Source: IBGE, Sidra, Table 137.
* This includes Lutherans, Presbyterians, Methodists, Baptists, Congregationalists, Adventists, and 7th Day Adventists.
† Includes mostly local Brazilian evangelical churches.

increasing their share from 3% to 4%. The big change came with the Pentecostal churches, which increased their share from 6% of the population in 1991 to 20% in 2010 (see Table 9.11).

What is impressive about all these developments is that these churches are essentially based in Brazil, and although many have their origin from foreign missionaries or have some international connections, they are now fully staffed by Brazilian ministers. The two largest, the Assembly of God and the Congregation Church of Christ, were both born at the beginning of the twentieth century in the United States and immediately implanted in Brazil in 1910 and 1911 respectively, just a few years after their original foundation.[121] The fourth largest is the Evangelical Quadrangular Church – founded in the United States in 1922 and brought by missionaries to Brazil only in 1951. But the third largest group is the Universal Church of the Kingdom of God (*Igreja Universal do Reino de Deus* – IURD), which was only founded in 1977 in São Paulo by a Brazilian pastor, and is a uniquely

---

[121] Ricardo Mariano, "Expansão pentecostal no Brasil: o caso da Igreja Universal," *Estudos Avançados* 18.52 (2004), p. 123.

Table 9.12 *Membership of Pentecostal Protestant Churches in the Census of 2010*

Total evangelical churches of Pentecostal origin	25,370,484
Igreja Assembléia de Deus	12,314,410
Igreja Congregação Cristã do Brasil	2,289,634
Igreja Universal do Reino de Deus	1,873,243
Igreja Evangelho Quadrangular	1,808,389
Igreja Deus é Amor	845,383
Igreja Maranata	356,021
Igreja o Brasil para Cristo	196,665
Comunidade Evangélica	180,130
Igreja Casa da Benção	125,550
Igreja Nova Vida	90,568
Evangélica renovada não determinada	23,461
Evangélicas de origem pentecostal – outras	5,267,029

Source: IBGE, Sidra, Table 137.

Brazilian national church (see Table 9.12). It has been a leader among the Pentecostal churches in sending missionaries overseas and promoting "televangelism."[122] Other Pentecostal churches founded by Brazilians are the *Igreja Pentecostal O Brasil para Cristo*, established in 1955, and the *Igreja Pentecostal Deus é Amor*, established in 1962.[123] There then followed

[122] Cecília Loreto Mariz, "Missão religiosa e migração: 'novas comunidades' e igrejas pentecostais brasileiras no exterior," *Análise Social* 44.1 (2009), p. 163. The *Assembleias de Deus* (AD) and the Pentecostal *Deus é Amor* (IPDA) have also begun to send missionaries. By 2015, it is estimated that Pentecostal churches of Brazil – most them of native origin – had missionaries in 180 countries in the World. Carmen Rial, "Neo-Pentecostals on the Pitch Brazilian Football Players as Missionaries Abroad," in Jeffrey D. Needell, ed., *Emergent Brazil: Key Perspectives on a New Global Power* (Gainesville: University of Florida Press, 2015), pp. 150–151. In 1990, the IURD church bought the TV Record channel and started a new age of television evangelism. See Patricia Birman and David Lehmann, "Religion and the Media in a Battle for Ideological Hegemony: The Universal Church of the Kingdom of God and TV Globo in Brazil," *Bulletin of Latin American Research* 18.2 (1999), pp. 145–164. The IURD owns the enormous Tempo de Salomão in São Paulo – a building of some 100,000 square meters.

[123] Irineu José Rabuske, Paola Lucena dos Santos, Hosana Alves Gonçalves, and Laura Traub, "Evangélicos brasileiros: quem são, de onde vieram e no que acreditam? *Revista Brasileira de História das Religiões* 4.12 (2012), p. 263. For a detailed history of the founding of the principal pentecostal churches, see Ingo Wulfhorst, "O Pentecostalismo no Brasil," *Estudos Teológicos* 35.1 (1995), pp. 7–20.

a host of so-called charismatic or neo-Pentecostalist churches in the 1970s and 1980s, such as *A Universal do Reino de Deus* (1977), the *Internacional da Graça de Deus* (1980), the *Comunidade Evangélica Sara Nossa Terra* (1976), and the *Renascer em Cristo* (1986), all founded by Brazilian pastors.[124]

These churches differ in terms of the sex, color, and the residence of their congregations. Pentecostals are clearly more an urban than a rural phenomenon: rural areas remained more consistently Roman Catholic than the cities. At the same time, there was an increasing imbalance in the sexes, with men remaining more loyal to Roman Catholicism and women being more committed to these new Protestant movements, in both urban and rural areas. From the census of 2010 it appears that for every 98 women who were Catholic, there were 100 men, while for every 100 women who were Pentecostals, there were 80 men (see Table 9.13).[125] This can probably be

Table 9.13 *Change in Ratio of Roman Catholics by Sex and Residence, Censuses 1980–2010*

	Total			Urban			Rural		
Census	Total	Men	Women	Total	Men	Women	Total	Men	Women
	Roman Catholics								
1980	89.0	89.2	88.7	87.1	87.3	87.0	92.7	92.8	92.6
2000	73.6	74.0	73.1	71.4	71.7	71.1	83.0	83.2	82.7
2010	64.6	65.5	63.8	62.2	62.9	61.5	77.9	78.4	77.3
	Pentecostals, Other Christians, Jehovah's Witnesses, and Mormons								
1980	3.2	3.0	3.5	3.5	3.3	3.7	2.7	2.6	2.9
2000	11.2	9.9	12.5	12.1	10.7	13.3	7.7	6.8	8.6
2010	19.7	17.9	21.5	21.1	19.2	22.8	12.5	11.3	13.9
	Traditional Protestant								
1980	3.4	3.2	3.6	3.7	3.4	3.9	2.8	2.7	2.9
2000	4.1	3.7	4.5	4.4	3.9	4.8	2.9	2.7	3.1
2010	4.0	3.6	4.4	4.2	3.8	4.6	3.0	2.7	3.3

Source: IBGE, Sidra, Tables 1969, 2103; *Censo demográfico 1980*, Série Nacional, vol. 1, pp. 6–7, Table 1.2.

[124] Mariano, "Expansão pentecostal no Brasil," p. 123.
[125] The 1991 census does not provide religious identity by sex, but it does give rural and urban breakdowns, and here the patterns are similar to all censuses after 1980, that is, Catholics more rural than urban (90% in rural areas compared with 81% in urban centers). Protestants, in contrast, were more urban (6%) than rural (4%). IBGE, Sidra, Table 139.

Table 9.14 *Distribution of Pentecostal and Other Church Members by Sex, 2010*

	Percentage Total		Percentage Total		
Churches	Men	Women	White	Black	Brown
All Pentecostal churches	44	56	41.3	8.5	48.9
Igreja Assembléia de Deus	45	55	37.2	8.5	52.8
Igreja Congregação Cristã do Brasil	46	54	54.9	5.7	38.4
Igreja o Brasil para Cristo	44	56	48.3	7.3	43.3
Igreja Evangelho Quadrangular	43	57	48.5	7.9	42.5
Igreja Universal do Reino de Deus	40	60	37.4	11.0	50.4
Igreja Casa da Benção	42	58	34.5	11.1	53.1
Igreja Deus é Amor	43	57	35.1	9.7	53.4
Igreja Maranata	44	56	43.0	7.3	48.4
Igreja Nova Vida	41	59	45.1	10.4	43.1
Evangélica renovada não determinada	44	56	48.4	7.9	42.6
Comunidade Evangélica	43	57	49.8	7.8	41.1
Protestant churches	44	56	51.6	6.9	39.8
Roman Catholics	50	50	48.8	6.8	43.0
Total Brazil	49	51	47.5	7.5	43.4

Source: IBGE, Sidra, Tables 2103 and 2094.

explained by the role of the new churches in tackling alcoholism and promoting family stability: arguably, a theme of direct interest to women.[126]

No matter the size or origin of the Pentecostal church, it was overwhelmingly an urban phenomenon, involving more women than men. In this, the Church differs from the Roman Catholics, who were less urban and more male (see Table 9.14).

But what does this urban identity mean. It has been argued by most scholars that Pentecostals are more marginal then other groups in the population, less-educated, living more in free unions, and, in general,

---

[126] Maria Bernadete Pita Guimarães, "Alcoolismo, Pentecostalismo e Família," PhD thesis, Universidade Federal Juiz de Fora, 2008. This is a theme found in many studies of Pentecostalism. See Ricardo Mariano, "Sociologia do crescimento pentecostal no Brasil: um balanço," *Perspectiva Teológica* 43.119 (2011), p. 15. And for the detailed activities in relation to incorporation, women, and the family in the IURD church, see Patricia Birman, "Conexões políticas e bricolagens religiosas: questões sobre o pentecostalism a partir de alguns contrapontos," in Pierre Sanchis, ed., *Fiéis & cidadãos: Percursos de sincretismo no Brasil* (Rio de Janeiro: EDUERJ, 2001), pp. 59–86.

poorer than the average Brazilian.[127] The censuses of 2000 and 2010 do not support all of these assumptions. Reflecting their higher urban residence, a population which has much higher educational and literacy rates than the rural populations where Catholics predominate means that Pentecostals tend to have more schooling and are more literate than the Roman Catholics. Thus, only 17% of Roman Catholic adherents in the census of 2000 have 8 to 10 years of schooling (equal for both men and women). By contrast, Pentecostals have 19% of its adherents reaching this level (19% of men and 18% of women), and 21% of traditional Protestants have this level of schooling.[128] This same pattern is seen in the census of 2010. In that year, of persons 25 years of age who had completed high school and had some years of university, only 23% were Catholic (23% of the men and 24% of the women), 24% Pentecostal (25% of the men and 24% of the women), and 32% traditional Protestant churchgoers.[129] Even in terms of marriage, Pentecostals did better than traditional Catholics in the census of 2010. Thus, 38% of Catholics over the age of 10 lived in consensual unions versus 28% of the Pentecostals and 21% of the traditional Protestants. Looking specifically at women and their marital status by religion, 38% of Catholic women lived in free unions compared with just 30% of Pentecostal women, and 23% of traditional Protestant women lived in this more precarious arrangement.[130]

But, in terms of income and color, Pentecostals were clearly poorer. In the census of 2000, which provides income data by sex and religion, it is evident that Pentecostals were at the lowest end of the income scale compared with Catholics, traditional Protestants, and followers of *Umbanda* and *Candomblé*. The traditional Spiritist groups were clearly the richest (see Table 9.15).

Catholic congregations are more likely to be white than Pentecostal congregations, but traditional Protestants have the greatest proportion of white adherents. In the census of 2000, traditional Protestant congregations were 61% white, Catholics 54%, and Pentecostals 49%; this at a time when 54% of the entire population was white. The same pattern emerged in the census of 2010, when 52% of traditional Protestants were white, 49% of the Catholics, and 41% of the Pentecostals.[131] These figures were similar for both women and men for each of the religious groups.[132] But in other demographic areas

---

[127] This is the argument of most scholars discussed in the survey by Mariano, "Sociologia do crescimento pentecostal no Brasil," pp. 11–36.
[128] IBGE, Sidra, Table 2106.
[129] IBGE, Sidra, Table 3457. In this same census Catholics had a higher illiteracy rate than Pentecostals. See IBGE, Sidra, Table 2104.
[130] IBGE, Sidra, Table 3487.   [131] IBGE, Sidra, Table 2094   [132] IBGE, Sidra, Table 3487.

Table 9.15 *Distribution of Salaries by Sex and Religion, Census 2000*

Religion	Total		Males		Females	
	10 or More Minimum Salaries	1 or Less Minimum Salaries	10 or More Minimum Salaries	1 or Less Minimum Salaries	10 or More Minimum Salaries	1 or Less Minimum Salaries
Total	7.1	23.3	8.4	20.2	5.0	28.5
Roman Catholic	7.0	24.1	8.3	21.1	4.9	29.0
Traditional Protestants	8.4	18.3	11.4	14.0	5.0	23.2
Pentecostals	3.4	24.3	4.4	17.9	2.0	32.8
Other Pentecostals	7.2	19.3	9.3	14.2	4.7	25.3
Spiritist	23.2	7.7	30.4	5.6	16.9	9.5
Umbanda and Candomblé	9.5	16.5	11.9	12.3	6.7	21.1
Other faiths	10.7	18.3	13.7	13.2	7.0	24.3
Not religious	7.2	23.4	7.6	21.0	6.2	30.5

Source: IBGE, Sidra, Table 2109.

there was an important difference. Evangelicals not only have a much higher ratio of women, but they have a higher proportion of children and youths compared with Catholics and traditional Protestant religions. Moreover, evangelicals recorded a higher birth rate than Catholics (with a total fertility rate in 2010 of 2.1 versus 1.9 for Catholics).[133]

At the pace they are growing, demographers estimate that Catholics will fall below 50% of the Brazilian population by 2030 and a decade later Pentecostals will be equal in number to Catholics.[134] This growth is also based on its theology and church structure. In theological terms, Pentecostalism's concern with this life rather than the afterlife, its acceptance of individual salvation, and its sense of equality and community make it a perfect fit to the migrants to the city in need of structure, community, and identity. Of the Pentecostal churches founded in the second half of the twentieth century, some have even adopted Afro-Brazilian church practices such as

[133] José Eustáquio Diniz Alves, Luiz Felipe Walter Barros, and Suzana Cavenaghi, "A dinâmica das filiações religiosas no brasil entre 2000 e 2010: diversificação e processo de mudança de hegemonia," *REVER – Revista de Estudos da Religião* 12.2 (2012), pp. 161 and 165.

[134] Alves, Barros, and Cavenagh, "A dinâmica das filiações religiosas no brasil entre 2000 e 2010," p. 160.

exorcism, and some have become more secular and more hierarchical in what has been called a neo-Pentecostal movement.[135] However, the overwhelming majority of Pentecostal churches have little hierarchical structure and are the most open of the major religions in Brazil. All are admitted and evangelism is encouraged. The clergy are all Brazilians and whatever hierarchy exists is local or at most regional, and their priesthood is open to all. New pastors need feel only the call of God without the need for formal religious training and thus many of the Pentecostal pastors come from the popular classes.[136] As one of the leading scholars in this field stressed, Brazilian Pentecostalism remains extremely segmented. "If, in the Catholic world, all roads lead to Rome, in the world of Pentecostalism many roads end where they begin: on a hillside in Rio or the periphery of São Paulo. This segmentation is functional for expansion, stimulating social flexibility, competition and localized supply."[137] Their funding is local as is their language and even their music. Thus, the proliferation of pastors and new churches is a constant. All urban favelas in all the major cities are filled with Pentecostal churches, and they are also to be found in large numbers in Brazil's other centers of poverty, the state prisons, where they are the dominant group among the prisoners.[138]

---

[135] The poorly defined "neo-Pentecostalism" movement refers to the Brazilian churches founded in the last quarter of the twentieth century. They supposedly stress exorcism (*libertação*) that includes elements of African Brazilian religions even though they reject these religions. See R. Andrew Chesnut, "Exorcising the Demons of Deprivation: Divine Healing and Conversion in Brazilian Pentecostalism," in Candy Gunther Brown, ed., *Global Pentecostal and Charismatic Healing* (New York: Oxford University Press, 2011), pp. 12,18. These neo-Pentecostal churches seem to be more secular in their teachings than the older Pentecostal churches and more hierarchical. See the studies of Ricardo Mariano, "Expansão pentecostal no Brasil: o caso da Igreja Universal," *Estudos Avançados* 18.52 (2004), pp. 123–124; his "Efeitos da secularização do Estado, do pluralismo e do mercado religiosos sobre as igrejas pentecostais," *Civitas* 3.1 (2003), pp. 111–125; and Patricia Birman, "Mediação feminina e dentidades Pentecostais," *Cadernos Pagu* 6–7 (1996), pp. 201–226. However, given the fluidity of the movement, there is some debate about whether such a sub-group is as coherent as some propose. See Freston, "'Neo-Pentecostalism' in Brazil," pp. 154–162.

[136] As Freston has noted, "Founders of major pentecostal groups [in Latin America] include proletarians, independent artisans and lower middle-class white collar workers. Rare are the founders of higher social origin. Most Pentecostal churches (unlike their historical counterparts) were founded either by Latin Americans who broke with an existing protestant denomination or by independent missionaries, and only rarely by a foreign pentecostal denomination." Paul Freston, "Evangelicals and Politics in Latin America," *Transformation* 19.4 (2002), p. 272. As part of this process, the preachers of the largest of these movements, the *Assemblea de Deus*, opposed the creation of formal seminaries for most of its early history. See Bertone de Oliveira Sousa, "Entre a espera pelo céu e a busca por bem-estar," in Jérri Roberto Marin and André Dioney Fonseca, eds., *Olhares sobre a Igreja Assembleia De Deus* (Campo Grande, MS: Editora UFMS, 2015), p. 51.

[137] Freston, "'Neo-Pentecostalism' in Brazil," p. 147.

[138] On the theology of the Pentecostals and their appeal to the poor, see Cecília Loreto Mariz, *Coping with Poverty: Pentecostals and Christian Base Communities in Brazil* (Philadelphia:

What is also impressive about the Pentecostals is not only the rapidity of their growth, but their extraordinarily high levels of participation. A survey in the Rio de Janeiro metropolitan region in the mid-1990s found that five evangelical churches were founded every week. Even more extraordinary was that 85% of Pentecostal church members participated in weekly services and that 94% went at least every month.[139] By contrast, only 20% of Catholics attend Mass, and the Roman Church has a very low ratio of priests: 1 for every 10,000 or so parishioners.[140]

The power and importance of the Pentecostal churches is felt not only at the level of the favela or the prison, but also more and more in politics. Evangelicals, of both the traditional churches and the Pentecostal movement, have become an enormous force in national politics. The leading church behind this was the Brazilian-originated and Brazilian-based Pentecostal IURD church, which was soon followed by the *Assembleia de Deus* churches in formally promoting their own candidates.[141] This running of their own candidates began in the post-military elections of the late 1980s, and today the so-called evangelical caucus (*Bancada evangélica*) of both individual church members and candidates formally supported by their churches have increased their share of deputies to eighty-five, with two senators in the elections of 2014 whose results stand until 2018.[142] Like the *Ruralistas*, the *Bancada evangélica* have emerged alongside both new and traditional parties and are a response to Brazil's weak party system, which seems unable to represent major group interests. In fact, all these deputies have official

Temple University Press, 1994) and André Corten, *Pentecostalism in Brazil: Emotion of the Poor and Theological Romanticism* (New York: St Martin's Press, 1999). On their role in the favelas and prisons, see Andrew Johnson, *If I Give My Soul: Faith Behind Bars in Rio de Janeiro* (New York: Oxford University Press, 2017), Chapter 3.

[139] Pierre Sanchis, "As religiões dos brasileiros," *Horizonte* 1.2 (2009), p. 30.

[140] Mariz, *Coping with Poverty*, pp. 12–13.

[141] On the evolution of this participation, see Taylor C. Boas, "Serving God and Man: Evangelical Christianity and Electoral Politics in Latin America," Paper presented at the American Political Science Association Annual Meeting, Chicago, 29 August to 1 September 2013). Accessed 28 October 2017, at: http://people.bu.edu/tboas/serving_god_man.pdf and Ari Pedro Oro, "A política da Igreja Universal e seus reflexos nos campos religioso e político brasileiros," *Revista Brasileira de Ciências Sociais* 18.53 (2003), pp. 53–69. Reich and Santos argue that there are two basic forms of political participation by Pentecostals: as individuals and those formally sponsored and promoted by their churches. The latter group has been the less successful and has become involved in some of the major parliamentary scandals. See Gary Reich and Pedro dos Santos, "The Rise (and Frequent Fall) of Evangelical Politicians: Organization, Theology, and Church Politics," *Latin American Politics and Society* 55.4 (2013), pp. 1–22. Finally, on their electoral success or lack thereof, see Fabio Lacerda, "Pentecostalism, eleições e reprentação política no Brasil contemporâneo," PhD thesis, Universidade de São Paulo – USP, 2017.

[142] See www.metodista.br/midiareligiaopolitica/index.php/composicao-bancada-evangelica/.

party identities, but operate as coherent lobbies that cross party lines to support their own causes.

As this survey has suggested, Brazil's voluntary associations are numerous and extensive. They involve a significant portion of the national population and they cross color, class, and regional lines. They range from minority groups to clubs that incorporate thousands of participants and members. These non-profit associations have a long history, but, since 1985, their impact on society has been profound and has continued to grow with each successive decade. Clearly, there is now really a "third sector" in Brazil and social movements and voluntary associations have become a basic part of national life.

Conclusion

As our study has shown, Brazil in 1950 was a very different country from what it is today. Brazil then was a traditional underdeveloped agrarian society with a pre-modern demographic structure. In 1950, Brazil was only a third urbanized and almost three-quarters of its labor force was involved in an agriculture which only partially fulfilled the nation's food needs. Poverty and hunger affected a significant share of the population. The majority of its population was illiterate and life expectancy was low, with correspondingly high rates of fertility and mortality. It thus fit the pattern of a typical third world country of the period.

Today Brazil is a different country. It is overwhelmingly urban and only a tenth of its labor force remains in agriculture. It now has a very large middle class and has experienced very high rates of mobility and a massive change in the level of education of its citizens. In this second decade of the twenty-first century, it educates all of its primary grade students, and an increasing share of the population is finishing high school and even entering university. Its citizens enjoy close to universal access to health care and Brazilian citizens now have a life expectancy close to first world standards. It now stands as one of the more important industrial economies in the world and is second only to the United States as an agricultural producer and exporter to the world.

Despite all the current questions about the political incoherence of the Brazilian party system and government, the welfare state has been successfully implanted. As significant as industrialization, agricultural modernization, and the demographic transition has been the role of the national government in influencing Brazilian societal change in this period. It was the post-1950 welfare state which profoundly altered the lives and incomes of the entire national population. The provision of education and health services and the massive program of redistribution of income to the poor through non-compensatory cash transfers have reduced the extreme inequality in the distribution of income that had characterized the nation in the middle of the twentieth century. The correlation between poverty and old age was broken with the universal expansion of the pension system. Along with over 90% rates of matriculation in primary school, there has even been a massive expansion of secondary education, and in each decade since 1950 the average years of schooling have increased. Although still relatively behind the leading Latin American countries in secondary education, Brazil has succeeded in transforming itself into a literate society. Health has improved dramatically through almost universal vaccination and access to basic health care for all ages. Infant mortality has declined from its catastrophically high levels, and though still relatively high by first world standards has succeeded in greatly increasing life expectancy to close to North American and Western European rates.

All of these changes have occurred as millions of Brazilians have migrated to the rapidly expanding cities as the majority of the population has shifted from rural to urban residence. This urban growth has bettered the lives of all Brazilians, but the costs of this rapid urbanization have been high. Cities have expanded in an often chaotic manner; urban housing has not kept pace with needs, thus giving rise to urban slums which have become common in most cities. Crime is unfortunately increasing and affecting all parts of the country. Nor, for all the federal and state expenditures, has the government been able to satisfy all the basic needs of this new urban population.

In a society undergoing such rapid change, social mobility has been a major preoccupation. There has been a massive expansion of the service sector with a consequent enormous growth of a middle class, all of which has opened up new possibilities of social ascent. Initially, in the middle decades of the century, there was a relatively open period of mobility when large numbers of previously poor persons achieved higher status and income than their parents. But recently this mobility has slowed as Brazil becomes a more mature industrial society. But blockages to social mobility have emerged in recent years which have made it ever more difficult to rise out of the middle class even as working class mobility has increased. One such blockage is higher education. With the government unable to expand the public universities fast enough to satisfy demand, it permitted private for-profit corporations to provide tertiary education. It is these poorly equipped and badly staffed faculties which now provide poor-quality education to the majority of students at university level. Nor has the quality of education at the public primary and secondary level increased fast enough to provide an education competitive with the private primary and secondary schools. Thus, the relation between increased education and social mobility has not followed the path of most industrial countries even as more people are obtaining advanced graduate degrees. Although inequality has declined, Brazil still looks like a typical Latin American country, and it is still an outlier by world standards.

Along with regional convergence in health and education, which has been a fundamental change in this period, there also have been basic changes in the social situation of traditional groups which had suffered discrimination and faced disadvantages in the pre-1950 society. Clearly, women have experienced the most changes, not only in reversing their negative position in education, but also in relation to marriage and the family and in access to the labor market. In the post-1950 period women have massively increased their participation in the workplace at all levels and have now come to be better educated than the men in Brazilian society, in a complete reversal of pre-1950 patterns. Changes in fertility have led to a reduction in family size, and the introduction of civil divorce and the decline of the Roman Catholic Church have led to the rise of female-headed households, the rise of consensual unions, and the consequent decline of traditional marriages.

One of the ongoing historical issues still facing Brazil, as in all the American societies with histories of African slave labor, is the question of race. This is an issue that is constantly being discussed and debated in Brazil. Although all basic indices show blacks and browns behind whites and Asians, this may still be an inheritance of slavery and may be more to do with class than race. Recent studies have suggested greater equality of opportunity by race when controlling for income and education, but differences in downward mobility do seem to indicate that race is still an important factor in Brazilian stratification.

Alongside government investments in welfare policies, which have profoundly affected the national population, Brazil has also experienced the rise of a new and powerful "third sector," which is the rise of voluntary organizations. Although such voluntary organizations have existed among religious groups since 1889, when the state withdrew its support for the Church, and numerous corporations and associations were founded in the following decades, it is only since the massive civil opposition to military rule in the 1970s and 1980s that Brazil has finally developed a vast array of non-state voluntary (social) organizations. These organizations now play an increasingly important role in society. They exist in such diverse areas as environmental protection, education, health, work, and religion. Although traditionally it has been assumed that civil society in Latin America is weak, we find that this thesis does not hold for the Brazilian case, and this so-called third state is now a fundamental part of national society involving several millions of Brazilians.

Finally, it is worth stressing that not only has Brazil changed radically in terms of its massive urbanization, its creation of a large middle class, and its profound demographic transition, but it has also become a more homogeneous society as the sharp differences between regions have declined. Brazil is no longer a "Belindia." In this period, the Center-West has emerged as a new wealthy zone comparable to the South and Southeastern regions. The North is now slowly closing the economic gap with the other regions, and even the Northeast is slowly approaching the levels of income of the richer areas. But if regional differences in income, wealth, and poverty are still apparent, they are not as extreme as in 1950. Moreover, almost all the social indices indicate that regional differences are no longer significant. The years of schooling, the indices of health and well-being and life expectancy are now the same in all parts of the nation.

Bibliography

PRIMARY SOURCES

90min.com. "Atualizado: os 10 clubes que lideram o ranking de sócio-torcedor no Brasil." Accessed 4 August 2018, at: www.90min.com/pt-BR/posts/6076274-atualizado-os-10-clubes-que-lideram-o-ranking-de-socio-torcedor-no-brasil.

ABRAS (Associação Brasileira de Supermercados). "O autosserviço alimentar brasileiro." Accessed 11 December 2017, at: www.abras.com.br/economia-e-pesquisa/ranking-abras/os-numeros-do-setor/.

ABRASCE (Associação Brasileira de Shopping Centers). "Censo brasileiro de shopping centers." Accessed 11 December 2017, at: www.portaldoshopping.com.br/uploads/general/general_4 b58c194fec5e617b0e01fc71487af24.pdf.

Anti-slavery law of 2017. www.jusbrasil.com.br/topicos/10621211/artigo-149-do-decreto-lei-n-2848-de-07-de-dezembro-de-1940.

ANTP (Associação Nacional de Transportes Públicos). "Sistema de Informações da Mobilidade Urbana: Relatório Geral 2014" (May 2018). Accessed at: www.antp.org.br/relatorios-a-p artir-de-2014-nova-metodologia.html.

APAS (Associação Paulista de Supermercados). "APAS revela pesquisa inédita sobre tendências do consumidor e dados do setor supermercadista durante Feira e Congresso" (May 2016). Accessed at: https://web.archive.org/web/20161222053405/www.portalapas.org.br/wp-content/uploads/2016/06/COLETIVA-Pesquisa-APAS-Nielsen-Kantar.pdf.

Banco Central do Brasil. "Focus: relatório do mercado." (20 July 2018). Accessed at: www .bcb.gov.br/pec/GCI/PORT/readout/R20180720.pdf.

"A 15 km do Planalto, a vida no maior lixão ativo da América Latina." (12 March 2016). Accessed 9 December 2017, at: www.bbc.com/portuguese/noticias/2016/03/160310_galeria_lixao_estrutural_pf.

Bradesco. Shopping center, Departamento de Pesquisas e Estudos Econômicos (DEPEC) (June 2017). Accessed 11 December 2017, at: www.economiaemdia.com.br/EconomiaEmDia/pdf/infset_shoppings_centers.pdf.

Mercado Imobiliário, São Paulo, Departamento de Pesquisas e Estudos Econômicos (DEPEC) (November 2017). Accessed 7 December 2017, at: www.economiaemdia.com.br/Econom iaEmDia/pdf/infset_imobiliario.pdf.

Câmara dos Deputados. "Legislação Informatizada – Decreto No. 1.637, de 5 de Janeiro de 1907 – Publicação Original." Accessed at: www2.camara.leg.br/legin/fed/decret/1900-19 09/decreto-1637-5-janeiro-1907-582195-publicacaooriginal-104950-pl.html.

"Consultoria de orçamento e fiscalização financeira," Nota técnica no. 10 (2011). Accessed 16 December 2017, at: www2.camara.leg.br/orcamento-da-uniao/estudos/2011/nt10.pdf.

Campanha Nacional de Aperfeiçoamento de Pessoal de Nível Superior. Accessed at: www .capes.gov.br/sobre-a-capes/historia-e-missao.

Cadernos MARE da Reforma do Estado. *Organizações Sociais* (vol. 2; Brasília: Ministério da AdministraçãoFederal e Reforma do Estado, 1998). Accessed at: www.bresserpereira.org .br/Documents/MARE/OS/caderno2.pdf.

CBIC (Camâra Brasileira de Indústria de Construção). SBPE. Accessed at: www .cbicdados.com.br/menu/financiamento-habitacional/sbpe.

FGTS. Accessed at: www.cbicdados.com.br/menu/financiamento-habitacional/fgts.

CELADE (Latin American and Caribbean Demographic Centre). *Boletín demográfico*. Various years.

"Brasil, Estimaciones y proyecciones de población a largo plazo, 1950–2100, Revisión 2016. Indicadores de la estructura por sexo y edad de la población estimados y proyectados." Accessed 5 September 2017 at: www.cepal.org/es/temas/proyecciones-demograficas/estima ciones-proyecciones-poblacion-total-urbana-rural-economicamente-activa.

"Brasil indices de crecimento demográfico." Accessed 22 November 2017 at: www.eclac.org /celade/proyecciones/basedatos_BD.htm.

"Long-Term Population Estimates and Projections, 1950–2100." Revision 2013. Accessed at: www.cepal.org/celade/proyecciones/basedatos_bd.htm.

Los adultos mayores en América Latina y el Caribe: datos e indicadores. Boletín informativo. Edición especial (Santiago de Chile: Comisión Económica para América Latina y el Caribe, 2001).

Observatorio demográfico. Various years

CEPAL. *Anuario Estadística de América Latina y el Caribe*. Various years.

Panorama Social de América Latina, 2013 (Santiago de Chile: CEPAL, 2013).

CNC (Confederação Nacional do Comércio de Bens, Serviços e Turismo). "Percentual de famílias com contas em atraso recua em janeiro de 2015." Accessed 12 April 2018, at: www .cnc.org.br/sites/default/files/arquivos/analise_peic_janeiro_2015.pdf.

CNI (Confederação Nacional da Indústria). "Nota Econômica." Accessed 12 April 2018, at: http://arquivos.portaldaindustria.com.br/app/conteudo_24/2015/02/20/526/Notaeconom ica01-Competitividade.pdf.

Congresso Nacional. Consultoria de orçamentos, fiscalização e controle. "Avaliação de politicas públicas, Programa Minha Casa Minha Vida," Brasília (October 2007). Accessed 7 December 2007, at: www12.senado.leg.br/orcamento/documentos/estudos/tipos-de-estudos/notas-tecnicas-e-informativos/avaliacao-de-politicas-publicas-programa-minha-casa-minha-vida-feff.

Constitution of 1988. Accessed 26 November 2017, at: www.planalto.gov.br/ccivil_03/consti tuicao/constituicaocompilado.htm.

DATASUS. (Departamento de Informática do SUS). Various tables. Accessed at: http://tabnet .datasus.gov.br/.

DESTATIS. (Federal Statistical Office). "Total Fertility Rate of Female Cohorts." Accessed at: www.destatis.de/EN/FactsFigures/SocietyState/Population/Births/Tables/FemaleCohorts .html.

Directoria Geral de Estatística. *Sexo, raça e estado civil, nacionalidade, filiação culto e analfabetismo da população recenseada em 31 em Dezembro de 1890* (Rio de Janeiro: Officina da Estatística, 1898). Accessed at: https://servicodados.ibge.gov.br/Download/ Download.ashx?http=1&u=biblioteca.ibge.gov.br/visualizacao/livros/liv25487.pdf.

Boletim commemorativo da exposição nacional de 1908 (Rio de Janeiro: Directoria Geral de Estatística, 1908). Accessed at: https://biblioteca.ibge.gov.br/visualizacao/livros/liv25380 .pdf.

FGV-CPDOC. (Fundação Getulio Vargas/Centro de Pesquisa e Documentação de História Contemporânea do Brasil). Confederação Geral dos Trabalhadores (CGT). Accessed

2 November 2017, at: www.fgv.br/cpdoc/acervo/dicionarios/verbete-biografico/central-geral-dos-trabalhadores-cgt.

"A educação no segundo governo Vargas" (2017). Accessed at: http://cpdoc.fgv.br/producao/dossies/AEraVargas2/artigos/EleVoltou/Educacao.

FIESP. (Federação das Indústrias do Estado de São Paulo). Informativo DEAGRO (Departamento do Agronegócio) (January 2018). Accessed 22 June 2018, at: www.fiesp.com.br/indices-pesquisas-e-publicacoes/balanca-comercial/.

Food and Agriculture Organization (FAO). *The State of Agricultural Commodity Markets 2018: Agricultural Trade, Climate Change and Food Security* (Rome: Food and Agriculture Organization of the United Nations, 2008).

State of the World's Forests 2011. (Rome: Food and Agriculture Organization of the United Nations, 2011).

Fundação Getulio Vargas. *O Crédito imobiliário no Brasil, caracterização e desafios* (São Paulo: FGV, 2007).

Fundação Joâo Pinheiro. *Perfil demográfico do estado de Minas Gerais 2000* (Belo Horizonte: FJP, 2003).

"Déficit habitacional no Brasil" (2016). Accessed at: www.fjp.mg.gov.br/index.php/produtos-e-servicos1/2742-deficit-habitacional-no-brasil-3.

Fundo de Financiamento Estudantil (FIES). *O Globo.* Accessed at: https://g1.globo.com/educacao/noticia/prouni-2018-resultado-da-primeira-chamada-do-20-semestre-e-divulgado.ghtml.

Fut Pop Clube. Accessed 6 November 2017, at: https://futpopclube.com/tag/ranking-mundial-de-publico-nos-estadios/.

IBAM (Instituto Brasileiro de Administração Municipal). "Estudo de avaliação da experiência brasileira sobre urbanização de favelas e regularização fundiária." Rio de Janeiro (October 2002).

IBGE (Instituto Brasileiro de Geografia e Estatística). *Anuário Estatístico do Brasil.* Various years.

"Média de moradores em domicílios particulares permanentes." Accessed at: www.sidra.ibge.gov.br/bda/popul/.

"Pessoas responsáveis pelos domicílios particulares permanentes." Accessed at: www.sidra.ibge.gov.br/bda/popul/.

"Séries históricas e estatísticas." Accessed at: https://seriesestatisticas.ibge.gov.br/series.aspx?t=taxa-mortalidade-infantil&vcodigo=CD100.

Sidra (Sistema IBGE de Recuperação Automática).

Síntese de Indicadores Sociais. Various years.

Recenseamento geral de 1950, Série Nacional, Censo demográfico, vol. 1 (Rio de Janeiro, 1956), vol. 1.

Censo industrial, 1950, Série Nacional, vol. 3.1.

Brasil, Censo demográfico, 1960, Série Nacional, vol. 1.

Censo industrial, 1960.

Brasil, Censo demográfico, 1970, Série Nacional, vol. 1.

Estatísticas históricas do Brasil, vol. 3, *Séries econômicas, demográficas e sociais de 1550 a 1988* (2nd edn).

Censo 1991.

"BRASIL, Projeção da população por sexo e idade: 2000/2060." Accessed at: www.ibge.gov.br/home/estatistica/populacao/projecao_da_populacao/2013/default.shtm.

Censo demográfico 2000: Resultados do universo.

Sistema de Contas Nacionais Referência 2000 (IBGE/SCN 2000 Anual).

Censo demográfico 2010, Caracteristicas de la população e dos domicilios, Resultado do Universo (Rio de Janeiro, 2001).

PNAD (*Pesquisa Nacional Por Amostra de Domicílios 2001.* microdados (Rio de Janeiro: IBGE, 2002). CD-ROM.

Brasil, Estatísticas do Século XX (2003).
Brasil no Século XX (Rio de Janeiro, 2003).
Censo demográfico 2000: Migração e deslocamento, resultados da amostra (Rio de Janeiro, 2003).
Tendências demográficas, uma análise dos resultados da amostra do Censo demográfico 2000 (Estudos e Pesquisas no. 13; Rio de Janeiro, 2004).
Censo Agrícola de 2006.
Censo demográfico 2010, Aglomerados Subnormais. Informações Territoriais (Rio de Janeiro, 2010).
Sinopse do Censo demográfico 2010 (Rio de Janeiro, 2011).
As Fundações Privadas e Associações sem Fins Lucrativos no Brasil, 2010, Estudos & Estudos 20 (Rio de Janeiro, 2012).
Censo demográfico 2010: famílias e domicilios resultados da amostra (Rio de Janeiro, 2012).
PEAS (Pesquisa de Entidades de Assistência Social Privadas sem Fins Lucrativos). 2014–2015, tables 1–2. Accessed at: www.ibge.gov.br/estatisticas-novoportal/sociais/protecao-social/9021-as-entidades-de-assistencia-social-privadas-sem-fins-lucrativos-no-brasil.html?=&t=resultados.
"Estatísticas de Gênero: uma análise dos resultados do censo demográfico 2010," *Estudos & Pesquisas* 33 (2014).
Pesquisa Nacional Por Amostra de Domicílios Contínua, Notas Metodológicas (Rio de Janeiro, 2014).
PNAD (*Pesquisa Nacional por Amostra de Domicílios*). Dicionário de variáveis da PNAD 2015. Accessed at: https://ww2.ibge.gov.br/home/estatistica/populacao/trabalhoerendimento/pnad2015/microdados.shtm.
Perfil dos estados e dos municípios brasileiros: cultura 2014: coordenação de população e indicadores sociais (Rio de Janeiro: IBGE, 2015).
Notícias, "IBGE divulga as estimativas populacionais dos municípios em 2016." Accessed at: https://agenciadenoticias.ibge.gov.br/agencia-sala-de-imprensa/2013-agencia-de-noticias/releases/9497-ibge-divulga-as-estimativas-populacionais-dos-municipios-em-2016.html.
IBOPE. "Falta de segurança é o principal motivo para torcedor não ir ao estádio." Accessed 6 November 2017, at: www.ibopeinteligencia.com/noticias-e-pesquisas/falta-de-seguranca-e-o-principal-motivo-para-torcedor-nao-ir-ao-estadio/.
IETS (Instituto de Estudos do Trabalho e Sociedade). "Parâmetros e resultados da PNAD 2014." Accessed at: www.iets.org.br/spip.php?rubrique2.
"Parâmetros e resultados da PNAD 2014." Accessed at: www.iets.org.br/spip.php?article406.
INEP (Instituto Nacional de Estudos e Pesquisas Educacionais). "Sinopse estatística da educação superior 2016." Available at: http://inep.gov.br/sinopses-estatisticas-da-educacao-superior.
INESC (Instituto de Estudos Socioeconômicos). "Bancada Ruralista: O maior grupo de interesse no congresso nacional." Accessed 11 March 2017, at: www.terra.com.br/noticias/maior-lobby-no-congresso-ruralistas-controlam-14-da-camara,4668a4188 51ca310VgnCLD200000bbcceboaRCRD.html.
Informe de Previdência Social, 16.2 (2004). Available at: http://sa.previdencia.gov.br/site/arquivos/office/3_081014-104508-174.pdf.
Informe de Previdência Social 16.5 (2004). Available at: http://sa.previdencia.gov.br/site/arquivos/office/3_081014-104624-246.pdf.
Ipea (Instituto de Pesquisa Econômica Aplicada) *Políticas Sociais: Acompanhamento e Análise*, 19 (2011). Accessed at: www.ipea.gov.br/portal/images/stories/PDFs/politicas_sociais/bps_19_completo.pdf.
"Economia Mundial" (June 2013). Accessed 12 April 2018, at: www.en.ipea.gov.br/agencia/images/stories/PDFs/conjuntura/cc19_economiamundial.pdf.

Sistema de Indicadores de Percepção Social (SIPS). "Tolerância social à violência contra as mulheres, 04 de abril de 2014." Accessed at: www.ipea.gov.br/portal/images/stories/PDFs/ SIPS/140327_sips_violencia_mulheres.pdf.

Ipeadata. www.ipeadata.gov.br/Default.aspx.

IPUMS Internacional. "Census/survey characteristics, 1960–2010." https://international.ipum s.org/international-action/sample_details/country/br#tab_br2010a.

Lance. Futebol Nacional. "Última pesquisa LANCE/Ibope mostrou Flamengo na frente, mas vantagem menor para o Timão." Accessed 6 November 2017, at: www.lance.com.br/futebol-nacional/flamengo-segue-com-maior-torcida-mas-vantagem-para-timao-cai.html.

Lei da União Estável – Lei 9.278, de 10 de maio de 1996. Accessed 26 November 2017, at: www .planalto.gov.br/ccivil_03/leis/L9278.htm.

Moura, Marcelo. *Consolidação das leis do trabalho* (7th edn; Salvador: JusPodivm, 2017). Accessed 12 July 2017 at: www.editorajuspodivm.com.br/cdn/arquivos/ca615420c19 a66758beaf108395fe01b.pdf.

Meio&Mensagem. "Europeus goleiam brasileiros em receita." Accessed 6 November 2017, at: www.meioemensagem.com.br/home/marketing/2016/01/21/europeus-goleiam-brasileiros -em-receita.html.

Mercado de consumo do futebol brasileiro. CNDL/SPC Brasil (September 2016). Accessed 6 November 2017, at: www.scribd.com/document/367275136/Analise-Consumo-Futebol-pdf.

Ministério da Cidadania. Secretaria Especial do Desenvolvimento Social, Benefício assistencial ao idoso e à pessoa com deficiência (BPC), Boletim 2015. Accessed at: www.mds.gov.br/webar quivos/arquivo/assistencia_social/boletim_BPC_2015.pdf.

Ministério da Cultura. *Cultura em números: anuário de estatísticas culturais* (2nd edn; Brasília: MinC, 2010). Accessed at: https://issuu.com/sbpdf/docs/cultura-em-n__meros-web.

Ministério da Fazenda. Fundo de Compensação de Variações Salariais (FCVS). Accessed 27 November 2017, at: www.tesouro.fazenda.gov.br/pt_PT/fundo-de-compensacao-de-variacoes-salariais-fcvs.

Nota técnica: Estimativa da trajetória da Dívida Bruta do Governo Geral do Brasil (29 July 2015). Accessed 12 April 2018, at: www.fazenda.gov.br/centrais-de-conteudos/n otas-tecnicas/2015/29-07-2015-nota-tecnica-do-tesouro.pdf/view.

Ministério da Justiça. Departamento Penitenciário Nacional (DEPEN). "Levantamento Nacional de Informações Penitenciárias. Infopen – junho de 2014." Accessed at: www.justica.gov.br/ news/mj-divulgara-novo-relatorio-do-infopen-nesta-terca-feira/relatorio-depen-versao-web.pdf.

Ministério da Saúde. Cadastro Nacional de Estabelecimentos de Saúde (CNES), Notas Técnicas. "Descrição das variáveis disponíveis para tabulação." Accessed at: http://tabnet.datasus.gov.br /cgi/cnes/NT_RecursosF%C3%ADsicos.htm.

Coordenação Geral de Alimentação e Nutrição (CGAN), Organização Panamericana da Saúde (OPAS), Observatório de Políticas de Segurança Alimentar e Nutrição (OPSAN), and Universidade de Brasília (UnB). *Redes de Atenção à Saúde no Sistema Único de Saúde* (Brasília, Ministério da Saúde, 2012). Accessed at: https://edisciplinas.usp.br/pluginfile.php /4512089/mod_resource/content/1/Apostila%20MS%20-%20RAS_curso%20completo-M %C3%B3dulo%202-APS%20nas%20RAS%20-%20Pg%2031-45.pdf.

Viva: Vigilância de Violências e Acidentes, 2009, 2010 e 2011 (Brasília: Ministério da Saúde, 2013). Accessed at: http://bvsms.saude.gov.br/bvs/publicacoes/sistema_vigilancia_violen cia_acidentes.pdf.

Ministério das Cidades. Sistema Nacional de Informações sobre Saneamento (SNIS). "Diagnóstico dos serviços de água e esgotos" (2015). Accessed 8 December 2017, at: www .snis.gov.br/diagnostico-agua-e-esgotos/diagnostico-ae-2015.

Ministério do Desenvolvimento Social. "Aqui você encontra todas as informações necessárias para fazer a gestão do Programa *Bolsa Família* e do Cadastro Único no seu município." Accessed at: www.mds.gov.br/bolsafamilia.

Miranda, Vitor da Cunha. "A concessão de direito real de uso (CDRU) e a concessão de uso especial para fins de moradia (CUEM) como instrumentos de regularização fundiárias públicas no Brasil." Accessed 28 May 2018 at: https://jus.com.br/artigos/48642/a-concessao-de-direito-real-de-uso-cdru-e-a-concessao-de-uso-especial-para-fins-de-moradia-cuem-como-instrumentos-de-regularizacao-fundiaria-em-areas-publicas-no-brasil.

NEPO (Nucleo de Estudos de População). CENSO 1872: Quadros do Império. Accessed at: www.nepo.unicamp.br/publicacoes/censos/1872.pdf.

O Dia. "Fechamento do Aterro de Jardim Gramacho deixou frustração a milhares de pessoas." (11 September 2016). Accessed 9 December 2017, at: http://odia.ig.com.br/rio-de-janeiro/2016-09-11/fechamento-do-aterro-de-jardim-gramacho-deixou-frustracao-a-milhares-de-pessoas.html.

OECD (Organisation for Economic Co-operation and Development). "Labor Force Survey data by sex and age, 2000–2016." Accessed 12 May 2017, at: https://stats.oecd.org/Index.aspx?DataSetCode=LFS_SEXAGE_I_R.

OSCIP (Organização da sociedade civil de interesse público). Câmara dos Deputados. "Legislação sobre o terceiro setor." Centro de Documentação e Informação Edições Câmara (Brasília 2016). Accessed at: http://bd.camara.leg.br/bd/bitstream/handle/bdcamara/30119/legislacao_terceiro_setor.pdf?sequence=1.

Pew Research Center. Religion and Public Life Census of 2010. Accessed 22 November 2017, at: www.pewforum.org/2011/12/19/table-christian-population-in-numbers-by-country/.

PNUD (United Nations Development Programme). Fundação João Pinheiro, Instituto de Pesquisa Econômica Aplicada, *Atlas do desenvolvimento humano no Brasil* (2003). Accessed at: http://atlasbrasil.org.br/2013/.

Prefeitura de São Paulo, Prefeitura Regional Cidade Tiradentes. "Histórico." Accessed 27 November 2017, at: www.prefeitura.sp.gov.br/cidade/secretarias/regionais/cidade_tiradentes/historico/index.php?p=94.

PwC (PricewaterhouseCoopers). "O setor de varejo e o consumo no Brasil: Como enfrentar a crise." (January 2016). Accessed 11 December 2017, at: www.pwc.com.br/pt/estudos/setores-atividade/produtos-consumo-varejo/2016/pwc-setor-varejo-consumo-brasil-como-enfrentar-crise-16.html.

Rock in Rio. "História." Accessed 16 December 2017, at: http://rockinrio.com/rio/pt-BR/historia.

SEADE (Fundação Sistema Estadual de Análise de Dados). *Anuário estatístico do estado de São Paulo* (2001). Accessed at: http://produtos.seade.gov.br/produtos/anuario/index.php?anos=2001&tip=apreo1.

Secretaria da Cultura do São Paulo. Boletim UM, "Cultura em Números, 10 anos de parceria com OSs de Cultura, 2004 a 2014." Accessed at: www.transparenciacultura.sp.gov.br/wp-content/uploads/2016/03/2017.02.01-boletim-UM-n.-2-Balan%C3%A7o-10-anos-atualizado-1.pdf.

Secretaria da Habitação do Estado de São Paulo. "Programa cidade legal comemora 10 anos." Accessed 28 May 2018, at: www.habitacao.sp.gov.br/noticias/viewer.aspx?Id=8270.

Secretaria de Estado da Saúde. "As organizações Sociais de Saúde no Estado de São Paulo. A experiência da Secretaria da Saúde: planejamento e mecanismos de acompanhamento, controle e avaliação." Accessed 12 January 2018, at: www.saude.sp.gov.br/resources/ses/perfil/gestor/homepage/auditoria/reunioes/organizacoes_sociais_de_saude_no_estado_de_sao_paulo.pdf.

Secretaria do Tesouro Nacional. "Resultado do tesouro nacional." Accessed 12 April 2014, at: www.tesouro.fazenda.gov.br/resultado-do-tesouro-nacional.

SEMMA. "História dos Shopping Centers no Brasil." Accessed 11 December 2017, at: www.semma.com.br/historia-dos-shopping-centers-no-brasil/.

SESI, SENAI, and IEL. *Relatório Anual 2015* (Brasília: SESI, SENAI, IEL, 2016). Accessed at: https://bucket-gw-cni-static-cms-si.s3.amazonaws.com/media/filer_public/30/b5/30b5d040-21cc-4f1c-9640-dcd071e39bf6/relatorio-anual-do-sesi-senai-iel-2015.pdf.

Trans-Atlantic and Intra-American slave trade databases. Emory University. Accessed 4 January 2018, at: www.slavevoyages.org/assessment/estimates.

UNICEF. "Levels and Trends in Child Mortality Report 2015" (September 2015). Accessed at: https://data.unicef.org/resources/levels-and-trends-in-child-mortality-2015/.

United Nations Office on Drugs and Crime (UNODC). *Global Study on Homicide 2013: Trends, Contexts, Data* (Vienna: UNODC, 2013). Accessed at: www.unodc.org/documents/data-and-analysis/statistics/GSH2013/2014_GLOBAL_HOMICIDE_BOOK_web.pdf.

United Nations University. World Institute for Development Economics Research (UNU/WIDER). "World Income Inequality Database WIID3.4." (January 2017). Accessed at: www.wider.unu.edu/database/world-income-inequality-database-wiid34.

United States. *Vital Statistics of the United States, 1950* (Washington, DC, 1954).

United States Census Bureau. "Statistical Abstract of the United States: 2002." Accessed at: www.census.gov/library/publications/2002/compendia/statab/122ed.html.

United States Department of Health and Human Service, CDC, NCHS. *Health, United States, 2016: With Chartbook on Long-term Trends in Health* (Washington, DC: National Center for Health Statistics, 2017). Accessed at: www.cdc.gov/nchs/data/hus/hus16.pdf.

United States Department of Health, Education, and Welfare. *Vital Statistics of the United States, 1950* (Washington, DC, 1954), vol. 1. Accessed at www.cdc.gov/nchs/data/vsus/vsus_1950_1.pdf.

United States Department of Labor. "Bureau of Labor Statistics Estimates for 2050." Accessed at: www.bls.gov/opub/ted/2007/jan/wk2/art03.htm.

Veja. "Allianz Parque é a segunda arena com mais shows e eventos do mundo." Accessed 16 December 2017, at: https://veja.abril.com.br/blog/radar/allianz-parque-e-a-segunda-arena-com-mais-shows-e-eventos-do-mundo/.

World Bank. "Age Dependency Ratio (% of Working-Age Population)." https://data.worldbank.org/indicator/SP.POP.DPND.

"Cause of Death, by Communicable Diseases and Maternal, Prenatal and Nutrition Conditions (% of total)." Accessed 13 September 2017, at: https://data.worldbank.org/indicator/SH.DTH.COMM.ZS?view=chart.

"Fertility Rate, Total (Births per Woman)." Accessed 14 September 2017, at: https://data.worldbank.org/indicator/SP.DYN.TFRT.IN.

"Homicidios intencionales (por cada 100.000 habitantes)." Accessed at: https://datos.bancomundial.org/indicador/VC.IHR.PSRC.P5?order=wbapi_data_value_2012+wbapi_data_value+wbapi_data_value-last&sort=des.

"Labor Force Participation Rate, Female (% of Female Population Ages 15+) (modeled ILO estimate)." Accessed at: https://data.worldbank.org/indicator/SL.TLF.CACT.FE.ZS

"Mortality Rate, Neonatal (per 1,000 Live Births)." Accessed 14 September 2017, at: https://data.worldbank.org/indicator/SH.DYN.NMRT.

A Fair Adjustment: Efficiency and Equity of Public Spending in Brazil, vol. 1, *Síntese* (Washington, DC: World Bank, 2017).

World Health Organization (WHO), UNICEF, UNFPA, The World Bank and the United Nations Population Division. *Trends in Maternal Mortality: 1990 to 2013* (Geneva: WHO, 2014). Accessed at: https://apps.who.int/iris/bitstream/handle/10665/112682/9789241507226_eng.pdf;jsessionid=5201FF4279363E6145801867AB1FA1E8?sequence=2.

SECONDARY SOURCES

Aarão, Daniel, Marcelo Ridenti, and Rodrigo Patto Sá Motta, eds., *A ditadura que mudou o Brasil: 50 anos do golpe de 1964* (Rio de Janeiro: Zahar Editora, 2014).

Abreu, Marcelo de Paiva. "Inflação, estagnação e ruptura: 1961–1964," in Marcelo de Paiva Abreu and Dionísio Dias Carneiro Netto, eds., *A ordem do progresso: cem anos de política econômica republicana, 1889–1989* (Rio de Janeiro: Campus, 1990).

Abreu, Marcelo de Paiva and Rogério L. F. Werneck. "Estabilização, abertura e privatização, 1990–1994," in Marcelo de Paiva Abreu, ed., *A ordem do progresso: dois séculos de política econômica no Brasil* (2nd edn; Rio de Janeiro: Elsevier, 2014): 263–280.

Abreu, Paula and Claudino Ferreira. "Apresentação: a cidade, as artes e a cultura." *Revista Crítica de Ciências Sociais* 67 (2003): 3–6.

Adesse, Leila and Mário F. G. Monteiro. "Magnitude do aborto no Brasil: aspectos epidemiológicos e sócio-culturais." Accessed at: https://jornalggn.com.br/sites/default/file s/documentos/factsh_mag.pdf.

Adorno, Rubens de C. F., Augusta Thereza de Alvarenga, and Maria da Penha Vasconcellos. "Quesito cor no sistema de informação em saúde," *Estudos Avançados* 18.50 (2004): 119–123.

Adriano, Eduardo Ribeiro. "Organizações Sociais de Saúde – OSS." Governo do Estado de São Paulo, São Paulo (October 2016). PowerPoint presentation. Accessed 18 June 2018, at http://ses.sp.bvs.br/wp-content/uploads/2017/05/CGCSS-CCTIES_apresentado-na-reuni%C3%A3 o-Holanda-201016_Dr.-Eduardo.pdf.

Afonso, José Roberto R. "IRPF e desigualdade em debate: o já revelado e o por revelar," Texto para discussão 42, Rio de Janeiro, FGB IBRE, 2014.

Albuquerque, Mariana Pires de Carvalho e. "Análise da Evolução do setor supermercadista brasileiro: uma visão estratégica," MA thesis, IBMEC, Rio de Janeiro, 2007.

Almeida, Monsueto, Renato Lima de Oliveira, and Ben Ross Schneider. "Política industrial e empresas estatais no Brasil: BNDES e Petrobras," in Alexandre de Ávila Gomide and Roberto Rocha C. Pires, eds., *Capacidades estatais e democracia: arranjos institucionais de políticas públicas* (Brasília: Ipea, 2014): 323–327.

Almeida, Rita Nicole Amaral and Fabiana de Felicio. *Assessing Advances and Challenges in Technical Education in Brazil* (Washington, DC:World Bank, 2015).

Alonso, Fabio Roberto Bárbolo. "As mulheres idosas que residem em domicílios unipessoais: uma caracterização regional a partir do Censo 2010," *Revista Kairós: Gerontologia* 18.19 (2015): 99–122.

Alvaredo, Facundo, Anthony B. Atkinson, Thomas Piketty, and Emmanuel Saez. "The Top 1 Percent in International and Historical Perspective," *Journal of Economic Perspectives* 27.3 (2013): 3–20.

Alvarenga, Augusta Thereza de and Néia Scho. "Contracepção feminina e política pública no brasil: pontos e contrapontos da proposta oficial," *Saúde e Sociedade* 7.1 (1998): 87–110.

Alves, Eliseu, Geraldo da Silva Souza, and Daniela de Paula Rocha. "Lucratividade da agricultura." *Revista de Política Agrícola* 21.2 (2012): 45-63.

Alves, José Eustáquio Diniz. "Fatos marcantes da agricultura brasileira," in Roberto de Andrade Alves, Geraldo da Silva, and Souza Eliane Gonçalves, eds., *Contribuição da Embrapa para o desenvolvimento da agricultura no Brasil* (Brasília: Embrapa, 2013).

"Crise no mercado de trabalho, bônus demográfico e desempoderamento feminino," in Nathalie Reis Itaboraí and Arlene Martinez Ricoldi, eds., *Até onde caminhou a revolução de gênero no Brasil?* Implicações demográficas e questões sociais (Belo Horizonte: Associação Brasileira de Estudos Populacionais, 2016).

Alves, José Eustáquio Diniz and Suzana Cavenaghi. "Tendências demográficas, dos domicílios e das famílias no Brasil," *Aparte: Inclusão Social em Debate* 24 (2012).

Alves, José Eustáquio Diniz, Luiz Felipe Walter Barros, and Suzana Cavenaghi. "A dinâmica das filiações religiosas no brasil entre 2000 e 2010: diversificação e processo de mudança de hegemonia," *REVER – Revista de Estudos da Religião* 12.2 (2012): 145–174.

Alves, Maria Helena Moreira. *Estado e oposição no Brasil (1964–1984)* (Petrópolis: Vozes, 1989).

Amaro, Meiriane Nunes and Fernando B. Meneguin. "A evolução da previdência Social após a constituição de 1988." Senado Federal. Accessed 4 January 2018, at: www12 .senado.leg.br/publicacoes/estudos-legislativos/tipos-de-estudos/outras-publicacoes/v olume-v-constituicao-de-1988-o-brasil-20-anos-depois.-os-cidadaos-na-carta-cidada/seg uridade-social-a-evolucao-da-previdencia-social-apos-a-constituicao-de-1988.

Ames, Barry and Margaret E. Keck. "The Politics of Sustainable Development: Environmental Policy Making in Four Brazilian States," *Journal of Interamerican Studies and World Affairs* 39.4 (1997–1998): 1–40.

Amin, Jamil Salim. "A união estável no Brasil a partir da constituição federal de 1988 e leis posteriores," MA thesis, Universidade Federal de Santa Catarina, 2001.

Amore, Caio Santo. "Entre o nó e o fato consumado, o lugar dos pobres na cidade: um estudo sobre as ZEIS e os impasses da reforma urbana na atualidade," PhD thesis, FAU-PSP – Faculdade de Arquitetura e Urbanismo da Universidade de São Paulo, 2013.

"'Minha Casa Minha Vida' para iniciantes," in Caio Santo Amore, Lúcia Zainin Shimbo and Maria Beatriz Cruz Rufino, eds., *Minha Casa ... e a cidade? Avaliação do programa Minha Casa Minha Vida em seis estados brasileiros* (Rio de Janeiro: Letra Capital, 2015): 11–28.

Andrade, Adriana Strasburg de Camargo. "Mulher e trabalho no Brasil dos anos 90," PhD thesis, Universidade de Campinas, 2004.

Andrade, Charles Albert de. "Shopping Center também tem memória: uma história esquecida dos shoppings centers nos espaços urbanos do Rio de Janeiro e de São Paulo nos anos 60 e 70," MA thesis, Universidade Federal Fluminense, Niterói, 2009.

Andrade, E. I. G. "Estado e previdência no Brasil: uma breve história," in R. M. Marques, Einar Braathen, and Laura Tavares Soares, eds., *A previdência social no Brasil* (São Paulo: Fundação Perseu Abramo, 2003): 69–84.

Andrade, Fabiana de. "Fios para trançar, jogos para armar: o fazer policial nos crimes de violência doméstica e familiar contra a mulher," MA thesis, Universidad de Campinas, 2012.

Andrade, Thomaz Almeida and Rodrigo Valente Serra. *O recente desempenho das cidades médias no crescimento populacional Brasileiro* (Brasília: Ipea, 1998).

Antía, Florencia and Arnaldo Provasi. Multi-Pillared Social Insurance Systems: The Post-Reform Picture in Chile, Uruguay and Brazil. *International Social Security Review* 64:1 (2011): 53–71.

Aragão, José Maria. *Sistema Financeiro da Habitação: uma análise jurídica da gênese, desenvolvimento e crise do sistema* (Curitiba: Juruá Editora, 2000).

Araujo Filho, Valdemar F. de, Maria da Piedade Morais, and Paulo Augusto Rego. "Diagnóstico e desempenho recente da política nacional de saneamento básico." *Brasil em desenvolvimento: Estado, planejamento e políticas públicas.* 3 vols (Brasília: Ipea, 2009): vol. 2, pp. 431–449.

Araujo, Edson Gramuglia. "As Centrais no sistema de representação sindical no Brasil," MA thesis, Faculdade de Direito da USP, 2012.

Arias, Enrique Desmond. "Faith in Our Neighbors: Networks and Social Order in Three Brazilian Favelas." *Latin American Politics and Society* 46.1 (2004): 1–38.

"Trouble en route: Drug Trafficking and Clientelism in Rio de Janeiro Shantytowns." *Qualitative Sociology* 29.4 (2006): 427–445.

Drugs and Democracy in Rio de Janeiro: Trafficking, Social Networks, and Public Security. Chapel Hill: University of North Carolina Press, 2009.

Arias, Enrique Desmond and Corinne Davis Rodrigues. "The Myth of Personal Security: Criminal Gangs, Dispute Resolution, and Identity in Rio De Janeiro's Favelas." *Latin American Politics and Society* 48.4 (2006): 53–81.

Arida, Persio and André Lara Resende. "Inertial Inflation and Monetary Reform in Brazil," in J. Williamson, ed., *Inflation and Indexation: Argentina Brazil and Israel* (Cambridge, MA: MIT Press, 1985).

Arriaga, Eduardo E. *New Life Tables for Latin American Populations in the Nineteenth and Twentieth Centuries* (Berkeley: Institute of International Studies, University of California, 1968).

Arriaga, Eduardo E. and Kingsley Davis. "The Pattern of Mortality Change in Latin America." *Demography* 6.3 (1969): 226.

Artes, Amélia and Arlene Martinez Ricoldi. "Mulheres e as carreiras de prestigio no ensino superior brasileiro: o não lugar feminino," in Nathalie Reis Itaboraí and Arlene Martinez Ricoldi, eds., *Até onde caminhou a revolução de gênero no Brasil? Implicações demográficas e questões sociais* (Belo Horizonte: Associação Brasileira de Estudos Populacionais, 2016).

Asfora, Laila Federico. "Terceiro Setor: Organizações Sociais," MA thesis, Pontifícia Universidade Católica do Rio de Janeiro – PUC-Rio, 2012.

Averbug, André. "Abertura e Integração Comercial Brasileira na Década de 90." *A abertura brasileira* 90.1 (1999): 43–82.

Avritzer, Leonardo. "Democratization and Changes in the Pattern of Association in Brazil." *Journal of Interamerican Studies and World Affairs* 42.3 (2000): 59–76.

Azevedo, Sérgio de. "Vinte e dois anos de política de habitação popular (1946–86): criação, trajetória e extinção do BNH." *Revista de Administração Pública* 22.4 (1988):107–119.

Azevedo, Sérgio de and Luís Aureliano Gama de Andrade. *Habitação e poder: da Fundação da Casa Popular ao Banco Nacional de Habitação* (Rio de Janeiro: Centro Edelstien de Pesquisas Sociais, 1982).

Azzoni, Carlos Roberto. "Concentração regional e dispersão das rendas per capita estaduais: analise a partir de séries históricas estaduais de PIB, 1939–1995." *Estudos Economics* 27.3 (1997).

Bacha, Edmar. "Moeda, inércia e conflito: reflexões sobre políticas de estabilização no Brasil." *Pesquisa e Planejamento Econômico* 18.1 (1988): 1–16.

Bacha, Edmar L. and Herbert S. Klein, eds., *Social Change in Brazil, 1945–1985: The Incomplete Transformation* (Albuquerque: University of New Mexico Press, 1989).

Bacha, Edmar and Lance Taylor. "Brazilian Income Distribution in the 1960s: 'Facts,' Model Results and the Controversy," in Lance Taylor, Edmar Lisboa Bacha, and Eliana A. Cardoso, eds., *Models of Growth and Distribution for Brasil* (New York: Oxford University Press, 1980).

Baeninger, Rosana. "Migrações internas no Brasil século 21: evidências empíricas e desafios conceituais." *Revista NECAT* 4.7 (2015): 9–22.

Balbim, Renato, Cleandro Krause, and Vicente Correia Lima Neto. *Para além do Minha Casa Minha Vida: uma política de Habitação de Interesse Social?* (Brasília: Ipea, 2015).

Baldwin, Peter. *The Politics of Social Solidarity: Class Bases of the European Welfare State, 1875–1975* (Cambridge: Cambridge University Press, 1990).

Baldy, Alexandre. "Pela modernização das cidades." *Folha de São Paulo* (5 December 2017), Tendências/Debates.

Ballestrin, Luciana Maria de Aragão. "Estado e ONG's no Brasil: acordos e controversias a propósito de Direitors Humanos (1994–2002)," MA thesis, Universidade Federal do Rio Grande do Sul, 2006.

Banerjee, Onil, Alexander J. Macpherson, and Janaki Alavalapati. "Toward a Policy of Sustainable Forest Management in Brazil: A Historical Analysis," *Journal of Environment & Development* 18.2 (2009): 130–153.

Barata, Luiz Roberto Barradas and José Dinio Vaz Mendes. *Organizações Sociais de Saúde: a experiência exitosa de gestão pública de saúde do Estado de São Paulo* (São Paulo: Secretaria de Saúde, 2007).

Barbosa, Kevan Guilherme Nóbrega and Ayla Cristina Nóbrega Barbosa. "O impacto do lixo na saúde e a problemática da destinação final e coleta seletiva dos resíduos sólidos." Accessed 8 December 2017, at: www.e-publicacoes.uerj.br/index.php/polemica/article/vie w/11669/9146.

Barros, Marilisa Berti de Azevedo, Chester Luiz Galvão César, Luana Carandina, and Graciella Dalla Torre. "Desigualdades sociais na prevalência de doenças crônicas no Brasil, PNAD-2003," *Ciência & Saúde Coletiva* 11.4 (2006): 911–926.

Barros, Ricardo Paes de, Louise Fox and Rosane Mendonça. "Female-Headed Households, Poverty, and the Welfare of Children in Urban Brazil," *Economic Development and Cultural Change* 45.2 (1997): 231–257.

Barros, Ricardo Paes de, Mirela de Carvalho, and Samuel Franco. "O papel das Transferências Públicas na queda recenteda desigualdade de renda Brasileira," in Edmar Lisboa Bacha and Simon Schwartzman, eds., *Brasil: A nova agenda social* (Rio de Janeiro: LTC, 2011): 41–85.

"O papel das Transferências Públicas na queda recente da desigualdade de renda Brasileira." *Desigualdade de renda no Brasil: uma análise da queda recente* (2 vols; Brasília: Ipea, 2007).

Barros, Ricardo Paes de, Mirela de Carvalho, Samuel Franco, and Rosane Mendonça. "Markets, the State and the Dynamics of Inequality: Brazil's Case Study," in Luis Felipe Lopez-Calva, and Nora Lustig, eds., *Declining Inequality in Latin America: A Decade of Progress?* (Washington, DC: Brookings Institution Press, 2010): 134–174.

Barros, Ricardo Paes de, Rosane Mendonça, and Daniel Santos. *Incidência e natureza da pobreza entre idosos no Brasil* (Rio de Janeiro: Ipea, 1999).

Barros, Ricardo Paes de, Samuel Franco and Rosane Mendonça. "Discriminação e segmentação no mercado de trabalho e desigualdade de renda no Brasil." Texto para discussão 1288, Rio de Janeiro, Ipea, 2017.

Barroso, Fábio Túlio. "Servidores públicos da esfera civil e militar: sindicalização e greve." Accessed 2 November 2017, at: www.ambito-juridico.com.br/site/?n_link=revista_artigos_leitura&artigo_id=11514.

Bastos, Paulo. "Urbanização de favelas." *Estudos avançados* 17.47 (2003): 212–221.

Bastos, Pedro Paulo Z. and Pedro Cezar Dutra Fonseca, eds., *A era Vargas: desenvolvimentismo, economia e sociedade* (São Paulo: Editora Unesp, 2012).

Batalha, Claudio. *O movimento operário na Primeira República* (Rio de Janeiro: Zahar, 2000).

Batista, Luis Eduardo and Sônia Barros. "Confronting Racism in Health Services." *Cadernos de Saúde Pública* 33 (2017): 65–76.

Batista, Luis Eduardo, Maria Mercedes Loureiro Escuder, and Julio Cesar Rodrigues Pereira. "A cor da morte: causas de óbito segundo características de raça no Estado de São Paulo, 1999 a 2001." *Revista da Saúde Pública*, 38.5 (2004): 630–636.

Beaverstock, J. V., R. G. Smith, and P. J. Taylor. "A Roster of World Cities." *Cities* 16.6 (1999): 445–458. Accessed at: www.lboro.ac.uk/gawc/rb/rb5.html.

Bell, Felicitie C. and Michael L. Miller. *Life Tables for the United States Social Security Area, 1900–2100*, Actuarial Study No. 120 (Washington, DC: Social Security Administration Office of the Chief Actuary, 2005).

Bello, José Maria. *História da República* (São Paulo: Companhia Editora Nacional, 1976).

Belluzzo, Walter, Francisco Amatti-Neto, and Elaine T. Pazello. "Distribuição de salários e o diferencial público-privado no Brasil." *Revista Brasileira de Economia* 59.4 (2005): 511–533.

Beltrão, Kaizô Iwakami and José Eustáquio Diniz Alves. "A reversão do hiato de gênero na educação brasileira no Século XX." *Anais* (2016): 1–24.

Beltrão, Kaizô Iwakami and Sonoe Sugahara Pinheiro. "Brazilian Population and the Social Security System: Reform Alternatives." Texto para discussão 929, Rio de Janeiro, Ipea, 2005.

Benetti, Maria Domingues. "Endividamento e crise no cooperativismo empresarial do Rio Grande do Sul: análise do caso FECOTRIGO/CENTRALSUL – 1975–83." *Ensaios FEE* 6.2 (1985): 23–55.

Benevides, Maria Victoria de Mesquita. *O governo Kubitschek* (Rio de Janeiro: Paz e Terra, 1976).

Benjamin, Antonio Herman de Vasconcellos e. "O Meio Ambiente na Constituição Federal de 1988." *Informativo Jurídico da Biblioteca Ministro Oscar Saraiva* 19.1 (2008).

Berquó, Elza. "Brasil, um Caso Exemplar – anticoncepção e parto cirúrgicos – à espera de uma ação exemplar." *Estudos feministas* 1:2 (2008):366–381.

"Demographic Evolution of the Brazilian Population in the Twentieth Century," in Daniel Joseph Hogan, ed., *Population Change in Brazil: Contemporary Perspectives* (Campinas: NEPO/UNICAMP, 2001).

Berquó, Elza and Suzana Cavenagh. "Mapeamento sócio-econômico e demográfico dos regimes de fecundidade no Brasil e sua variação entre 1991 e 2000." Paper presented at the XIV Encontro Nacional de Estudos Populacionais, ABEP, Caxambu, MG, Brazil, 20–24 September 2004.

Bertoldi, Andréa Dâmaso, Aluísio Jardim Dornellas de Barros, Anita Wagner, Dennis Ross-Degnan, and Pedro Curi Hallal. "Medicine Access and Utilization in a Population Covered by Primary Health Care in Brazil." *Health Policy* 89.3 (2009): 295–302.

Betranou, Fabio M. and Rafael Rofman. "Providing Social Security in a Context of Change: Experience and Challenges in Latin America," *International Social Security Review* 55.1 (2002): 67–82.

Binswanger, Hans. "Brazilian Policies that Encourage Deforestation." Environment Department Paper No. 16, World Bank: Washington, DC, 1988.

Birman, Patricia. "Mediação feminina e dentidades Pentecostais," *Cadernos Pagu* 6–7 (1996): 201–226.

"Conexões políticas e bricolagens religiosas: questões sobre o pentecostalism a partir de alguns contrapontos," in Pierre Sanchis, ed., *Fiéis & cidadãos: Percursos de sincretismo no Brasil* (Rio de Janeiro: EDUERJ, 2001): 59–86.

Birman, Patricia and David Lehmann. "Religion and the Media in a Battle for Ideological Hegemony: The Universal Church of the Kingdom of God and TV Globo in Brazil," *Bulletin of Latin American Research* 18.2 (1999): 145–164.

Bittencourt, Lúcio Nagib. "As organizações sociais e as ações governamentais em cultura: ação e política pública no caso do Estado de São Paulo," PhD thesis, FGV/SP, São Paulo, 2014.

Boarati, Vanessa. "A defesa da estratégia desenvolvimentista, II PND," *História Econômica & História de Empresas* 8.1 (2005): 163–193.

Boas, Taylor C. "Serving God and Man: Evangelical Christianity and Electoral Politics in Latin America." Paper presented at the American Political Science Association Annual Meeting, Chicago, 29 August to 1 September 2013). Accessed 28 October 2017, at: http://people.bu.edu/tboas/serving_god_man.pdf.

Bochio, Ieda Maria Siebra and Paulo Antonio de Carvalho Fortes. "A influência da AIDS no processo de desenvolvimento organizacional das organizações não-governamentais: um estudo de caso sobre a Casa de Assistência Filadélfia," *Cadernos de Saúde Pública* 24.11 (2008): 2541–2550.

Bógus, Lucia Maria Machado and Maura Pardini Bicudo Véras. "A reorganização metropolitana de São Paulo: espaços sociais no contexto da globalização." *Cadernos Metrópole* 3. Accessed 20 November 2017, at: https://revistas.pucsp.br/metropole/article/view/9329/6924.

Brito, Fausto A. de and Breno A. T. D. de Pinho. *A dinâmica do processo de urbanização no Brasil, 1940–2010* (Belo Horizonte: UFMG/CEDEPLAR, 2012).

Brito, Fausto A. de, José Irineu Rigotil, and Jarvis Campos. *A mobilidade interestadual da população no Brasil no início do século X: mudança no padrão migratório?* (Belo Horizonte: UFMG/Cedeplar, 2012).

Brito, Marcos Roberto Cotrim and Alexandre Nicolas Rennó. "A favela da Geografia: análise e uso do termo favela," *Observatorio Geográfico.* Accessed 8 December 2017, at: http://observatoriogeograficoamericalatina.org.mx/egal12/Teoriaymetodo/Conceptuales/16.pdf.

Bruschini, Maria Cristina Aranha. "Trabalho e gênero no Brasil nos últimos dez anos," *Cadernos de Pesquisa,* 37.132 (2007): 537–572.

Bueno, Miguel and Marcelo Dias Carcalholo. "Inserção externa e vulnerabilidade da economia brasileira no governo Luna," in J. P. A. Magalhães, ed., *Os anos Lula: constribuições para um Balanço Crítico, 2002–2010* (Rio de Janeiro: Editora Garamond, 2010): 109–132.

Buiainain, Antônio Marcio, Eliseu Alves, J. M. da Silveira, and Zander Navarro, eds., *O mundo rural no Brasil do século 21: a formação de um novo padrão agrário e agrícola* (Brasília: Embrapa, 2014).

Bunker, Stephen G. *Underdeveloping the Amazon: Extraction, Unequal Exchange, and the Failure of the Modern State* (Urbana: University of Illinois Press, 1985).

Búrigo, Fábio Luiz. "Finanças e solidariedade: o cooperativismo de crédito rural solidário no Brasil," *Estudos Sociedade e Agricultura* 1 (2013): 312–349.

Cacciamali, Maria Cristina and Guilherme Issamu Hirata. "A influência da raça e do gênero nas oportunidades de obtenção de renda: uma análise da discriminação em mercados de trabalho distintos: Bahia e São Paulo," *Estudos Econômicos* 35.4 (2005): 767–795.

Caetano, Marcelo. "Apresentação do secretário de Previdência, Marcelo Caetano, sobre a proposta de Reforma da Previdência enviada pelo Governo Federal" (8 March 2017). Accessed at: www.fazenda.gov.br/centrais-de-conteudos/apresentacoes/2017/apresenta cao-m-caetano.pdf/view.

Caetano, Marcelo Abia-Ramia and Rogério Boueri Miranda. "Comparativo internacional para a previdência social." Texto para discussão 1302, Brasília, Ipea, 2007.

Caiafa, Janice. "O metro de São Paulo e problema da rede." Paper presented at the XXV Encontro Anual da Compós, Universidade Federal de Goiás, June 2016. Accessed 10 December 2017, at: www.compos.org.br/biblioteca/caiafacompo_s2016_3317.pdf.

Caldas, Aline Diniz Rodrigues, Ricardo Ventura Santos, Gabriel Mendes Borges, Joaquim Gonçalves Valente, Margareth Crisóstomo Portela, and Gerson Luiz Marinho. "Mortalidade infantil segundo cor ou raça com base no censo demográfico de 2010 e nos sistemas nacionais de informação em saúde no Brasil." *Cadernos de Saúde Pública* 33 (2017): 1–12.

Caldeira, Antônio Prates, Elisabeth França, Ignez Helena Oliva Perpétuo, and Eugênio Marcos Andrade Goulart. "Evolução da mortalidade infantil por causas evitáveis, Belo Horizonte, 1984–1998." *Revista de Saúde Pública* 39.1 (2005): 67–74.

Camarano, Ana Amélia and Ricardo Abramovay. "Êxodo rural, envelhecimento e masculinização no Brasil: panorama dos últimos 50 anos." Texto para discussão 621, Rio de Janeiro, Ipea, 1998.

Camargo, Candido Procópio Ferreira de, ed., *Católicos, Protestantes, Espíritas* (Petropolis: Ediora Vozes, 1973).

Camargos, Mirela Castro Santos, Carla Jorge Machado, and Roberto Nascimento Rodrigues. "A relação entre renda e morar sozinha para idosas mineiras, 2003," in João Antonio de Paula et al., eds., *Anais do XII Seminário sobre a Economia Mineira* (Belo Horizonte: Cedeplar, Universidade Federal de Minas Gerais, 2006).

Campos, André Luiz Vieira de. *Políticas internacionais de saúde na era Vargas: o Serviço Especial de Saúde Pública, 1942–1960* (Rio de Janeiro: Editora Fiocruz; 2006).

Campos, Marcos Paulo. "Movimentos sociais e conjuntura política: uma reflexão a partir das relações entre o MST e o governo Dilma," *Revista Cadernos de Estudos Sociais e Políticos* 4.7 (2015): 79–100.

Cardoso, Adalberto. "Transições da escola para o trabalho no Brasil: persistências da desigualdade e frustação de expactativas," *Dados: Revista de Ciências Sociais* 51.3 (2008): 569–616.

Cardoso, Adalberto and Edmond Préteceille. "Classes médias no Brasil: do que se trata? Qual seu tamanho? Como vem mudando?" *Dados: Revista de Ciências Sociais* 60.4 (2017): 977–1023.

Cardoso, Adauto Lucio, ed., *Programa Minha Casa Minha Vida e seus Efeitos Territoriais* (Rio de Janeiro: Letra Capital, 2013).

Cardoso, Adauto Lúcio. "Avanços e desafios na experiência brasileira de urbanização de favelas," *Cadernos Metrópole* 17 (2007): 219–240.

Cardoso, José Celso, Jr. *Brasil em desenvolvimento: estado, planejamento e políticas públicas*, vol. 1 (Brasília: Ipea, 2009). Accessed at: www.ipea.gov.br/portal/images/stories/Livro_Br asilDesenvEN_Vol01.pdf.

Carlos, Ana Fani Alessandri. "A metrópole de São Paulo no contexto da urbanização contemporânea," *Estudos Avançados* 23.66 (2009): 304–314.

Carneiro, Dionísio Dias. "Crise e esperança: 1974–1980," in in Marcelo de Paiva Abreu and Dionísio Dias Carneiro Netto, eds., *A ordem do progresso: cem anos de política econômica republicana, 1889–1989* (Rio de Janeiro: Campus, 1990): 295–322.

Carneiro, Dionísio Dias and Eduardo Modiano. "Ajuste externo e desequilíbrio interno: 1980–1894," in Marcelo de Paiva Abreu and Dionísio Dias Carneiro Netto, eds., *A ordem do progresso: cem anos de política econômica republicana, 1889–1989* (Rio de Janeiro: Campus, 1990), pp. 323–346.

Carreirão, Yan de Souza. "O sistema partidário brasileiro," *Revista Brasileira de Ciência Política* 14 (2014): 255–295.

Carreno, Ioná, Ana Lúcia de Lourenzi Bonilha, and Juvenal Soares Dias da Costa. "Perfil epidemiológico das mortes maternas ocorridas no Rio Grande do Sul, Brasil 2004–2007," *Revista brasileira de epidemiologia* 15.2 (2012): 396–406.

Carter, Susan B., Scott Sigmund Gartner, Michael R. Haines, Alan L. Olmstead, and Richard Such, eds., *Historical Statistics of the United States: Millennial Edition* (Cambridge: Cambridge University Press, 2006).

Carvalho, Átila Andrade de. "O campo das ONG/AIDS: Etnografando o ativismo em João Pessoa," MA thesis, Univerisdade Federal da Paraíba, João Pessoa, 2012.

Carvalho, Carlos Henrique Ribeiro de. "Mobilidade urbana: tendências e desafios." Texto para discussão 94, São Paulo, Ipea, 2013.

Carvalho, Cleurení Hermelina de. "Bolsa Família e desigualdade da renda domiciliar entre 2006 e 2011," MA thesis, Pontifícia Universidade Católica de São Paulo – PUC-SP, 2013.

Carvalho, Gilson. "A saúde Pública no Brasil," *Estudos Avançados*, 27.78 (2013): 7–26.

Carvalho, Madalena Grimaldi de. "A difusão e a integração dos shopping centers na cidade: as particularidades do Rio de Janeiro," PhD thesis, Universidade Federal do Rio de Janeiro – UFRJ, 2005.

Castells, Manuel. *The Urban Question* (London: Arnold, 1977).

Castro, Antonio Barros de. *Sete ensaios sobre a economia brasileira* (São Paulo: Forense, 1969).

Castro, Antonio Barros de and Francisco Eduardo Pires de Souza. *A economia brasileira em marcha forçada* (Rio de Janeiro: Paz e Terra, 1985).

Castro, Maria Helena Guimarães de. *Avaliação do sistema educacional brasileiro: tendências e perspectivas* (Brasília: INEP, 1998).

Castro, Maria Helena Guimarães de. *Educação para o Século XXI: o desafio da qualidade e da eqüidade* (Brasília: INEP/MEC, 1999).

Cavalieri, Claudia and Reynaldo Fernandes. "Diferenciais de salários por gênero e cor: uma comparação entre as regiões metropolitanas brasileiras." *Revista de economia política* 18.1 (1998): 158–175.

Cavenaghi, Suzana and José Eustáquio Diniz Alves. "Domicilios y familias en la experiencia censal del Brasil: cambios y propuesta para identificar arreglos familiares." *Notas de población* 92 CEPAL (2011).

Centro de Estudos e Debates Estratégicos, Consultoria Legislativa. *O desafio da mobilidade urbana* (Brasília: Câmara dos Deputados, 2015).

Cerqueira, Daniel and Danilo Santa Cruz Coelho. *Estupro no Brasil: uma radiografia segundo os dados da saúde* (preliminary version), Nota Técnica 11 (Brasília: Ipea, 2014).

Cerqueira, Daniel, H. Ferreira, R. S. de Lima, S. Bueno, O. Hanashiro, F. Batista, and P. Nicolato. *Atlas da violência 2016* (Brasília: Ipea, 2016).

Chackiel, Juan and Susana Schkolnik. "Latin America: Overview of the Fertility Transition, 1950–1990," in Jose Miguel Guzmán, Susheela Singh, German Rodriguez, and Edith A. Pantelides, eds., *The Fertility Transition in Latin America* (Oxford: Clarendon Press, 1996).

Cherkezian, Henry and Gabriel Bolaffi. "Os caminhos do mal-estar social: habitação e urbanismo no Brasil." *Novos Estudos CEBRAP* 50 (1998): 125–147.

Chesnut, R. Andrew. "Exorcising the Demons of Deprivation: Divine Healing and Conversion in Brazilian Pentecostalism," in Candy Gunther Brown, ed., *Global Pentecostal and Charismatic Healing* (New York: Oxford University Press, 2011).

Cohn, Amélia. *Previdência social e processo político no Brasil* (São Paulo: Editora Moderna, 1981).

Considera, Claudio Monteiro and Mérida Herasme Medina. "PIB por unidade da federação: valores correntes e constantes – 1985/96." Texto para discussão 610, Rio de Janeiro, Ipea, 1998.

Cordeiro, Hésio. "Instituto de Medicina Social e a luta pela reforma sanitária: contribuição à história do SUS." *Physis* 14.2 (2004): 343–362.

Corten, André. *Pentecostalism in Brazil: Emotion of the Poor and Theological Romanticism* (New York: St. Martin's Press, 1999).

Costa, Adriano Henrique Caetano. "Homens que fazem sexo com homens (HSH): políticas públicas de prevenção às dst/aids para uma população anónima," MA thesis, Universidade Federal do Ceará, 2011.

Costa, Armando João Dalla. "A importância da Logística no Varejo Brasileiro: o caso Pão de Açúcar." Accessed 10 December 2017, at: www.empresas.ufpr.br/logistica.pdf.

Costa, Luciana Caduz da Almeida. "O custo de peso morto do sistema previdenciário de repartição: analisando o caso brasileiro." FGV, 2007. Accessed 4 January 2018, at: https://bibliotecadigi tal.fgv.br/dspace/handle/10438/310.

Costa, Nilson do Rosário and José Mendes Ribeiro. "Estudo comparativo do desempenho de hospitais em regime de organização social." Programa de pesquisas – Em busca da excelência: fortalecendo o desempenho hospitalar no Brasil. Relatório final. Ministério da Saúde (Rio de Janeiro: World Bank, 2005).

Costa, Tacilla da and Sá Siqueira Santos. "As diferentes dimensões da sustentabilidade em uma organização da sociedade civil: uma análise da prática social do grupo de apoio à prevenção à aids da Bahia," *Sociedade, Contabilidade e Gestão* 2.2 (2007): 61–76.

Costa, Valeriano Mendes Ferreira. "A dinâmica Institucional da Reforma do Estado: um balanço do período FHC," in *O estado numa era de reformas: os anos FHC*. 2 vols (Brasília: Ministério do Planejamento/Pnud/OCDE, 2002): vol. 2, pp. 9–56.

Coutinho, Mauricio C. and Cláudio Salm. "Social Welfare," in Edmar L. Bacha and Herbert S. Klein, eds., *Social Change in Brazil 1945–1985: The Incomplete Transformation* (Albuquerque: University of New Mexico Press, 1989): 233–262.

Cunha, Ana C. N. M. Fernandes da. "As organizações Sociais de Saúde na cidade de São Paulo e a efetivação do Direito Fundamental à Saúde," MA thesis, Faculdade de Direito – Universidade de São Paulo, 2016.

Cunha, Estela Maria Garcia de Pinto da. "Condicionantes da mortalidade infantil segundo raça/cor no estado de São Paulo, 1997–1998," PhD thesis, Faculdade de Ciências Médicas – Universidade Estadual de Campinas, 2001.

"Mortalidade infantil segundo cor: os resultados da PNAD 84 para o Nordeste." Paper presented at the IX Encontro Nacional de Estudos Populacionais, ABEP, 2006.

Cunha, José Marcos Pinto da and Rosanna Baeninger. "Cenários da migração no brasil nos anos 90," *Caderno CRH* (Bahia) 18.43 (2005): 87–101.

Cyrillo, Denise Cavallini. "O papel do supermercado no varejo de alimentos" (São Paulo: Instituto de Pesquisas Econômicas, 1987).

Dagnino, Evelina. "Civil Society in Latin America," in *The Oxford Handbook of Civil Society* (New York: Oxford University Press, 2011): 122.

Dantas, Felipe von Atzingen, Alexandre Bevilacqua Leoneti, Sonia Valle Walter Borges de Oliveira, and Marcio Mattos Borges de Oliveira. "Uma análise da situação do saneamento no Brasil," *FACEF Pesquisa, Desenvolvimento e Gestão* 15.3 (2012): 272–284.

Dean, Warren. "Latifundia and Land Policy in Nineteenth-Century Brazil." *Hispanic American Historical Review* 51.4 (1971): 606–625.

With Broadaxe and Firebrand: The Destruction of the Brazilian Atlantic Forest (Berkeley: University of California Press, 1995).

Denaldi, Rosana. "Políticas de urbanização de favelas: evolução e impasses," PhD thesis, Faculdade de Arquitetura e Urbanismo – USP, 2003.

Diniz, Debora and Marcelo Medeiros. "Aborto no Brasil: uma pesquisa domiciliar com técnica de urna," *Ciência & Saúde Coletiva* 15.1 (2010): 959–966.

Diniz, Eli. "O Estado Novo: estrutura de poder e relações de clase," in Boris Fausto, ed., *História geral da civilização brasileira* (São Paulo: Difel, 1981), vol. 3, *Sociedade e Política (1930–1964)*: 77–119.

"Empresariado industrial, representação de interesses e ação política: trajetória histórica e novas configurações," *Politica & Sociedade* 9.17 (2010): 106–109.

Draibe, Sonia. *Rumos e metamorfoses: estado e industrialização no Brasil, 1930/1960* (Rio de Janeiro: Paz e Terra, 1985).

"O welfare state in Brazil: caracteristicas e perspectivas," *Caderno de Pesquisa* 8 (1993):19–21.

Duarte, S. B. "Organizações sociais de cultura em São Paulo: desafios e perspectivas." Paper presented at the IV Congresso Consad de Gestão Pública, Brasília, May 2012.

Dymski, Gary A. "Ten Ways to See a Favela: Notes on the Political Economy of the New City," *Revista Econômica* 13.1 (2011):7–36.

Eloy, Claudia Magalhães. "O papel do Sistema Financeiro da Habitação diante do desafio de universalizar o acesso à moradia digna no Brasil," PhD thesis, Faculdade de Arquitetura e Urbanismo da USP, São Paulo, 2013.

Escorel, Sarah, Ligia Giovanella, Maria Helena Magalhães de Mendonça and Mônica de C. M. Senna. "Programa de Saúde da Família e a construção de um novo modelo para atenção básica no Brasil," *Revista Panamericana de Salud Pública* 21.2 (2007): 164–176.

Esping-Andersen, Gøsta. *The Three Worlds of Welfare Capitalism* (Cambridge: Polity Press, 1990).

Faria, Lina. *Saúde e política: a Fundação Rockefeller e seus parceiros em São Paulo* (Rio de Janeiro: Editora Fiocruz, 2007).

Fausto, Boris. *A revolução de 1930* (São Paulo: Editora Brasiliense, 1972).

Trabalho urbano e conflito social (São Paulo: DIFEL, 1997).

O pensamento nacionalista autoritário:(1920–1940) (Rio de Janeiro: Zahar, 2001).

Getúlio Vargas (São Paulo: Cia das Letras, 2006).

"Populismo in the Past and Its Resurgence." Paper presented at the Conference in Honor of Boris Fausto, Stanford, California, 21 May 2010.

Fearnside, P. M. and W. F. Laurance. "Tropical Deforestation and Greenhouse Gas Emissions," *Ecological Applications* 14:4 (2004): 982–986.

Fernandes, Bernardo Mançano. "Contribuição ao estudo do campesinato brasileiro formação e territorialização do Movimento dos Trabalhadores Rurais Sem Terra – MST (1979–1999)," PhD thesis, University of São Paulo, São Paulo, 1999.

Fernandes, Florestan. *A integração do negro na sociedade de classes* (São Paulo: Ática, 1978).

Ferranti, David de, Guillermo E. Perry, Francisco Ferreira, and Michael Walton. *Inequality in Latin America: Breaking with History?* (Washington, DC: World Bank, 2004).

Ferraro, Alceu Ravanello. "Analfabetismo e níveis de letramento no Brasil: o que dizem os censos?" *Revista Educação & Sociedade* 23.81 (2002): 21–47.

Ferraz, Ivan Roberto. "Indicadores de desempenho das organizações sociais de cultura do Estado de São Paulo," MA thesis, Pontifícia Universidade Católica de São Paulo – PUC-SP, 2008.

Ferraz, Luciano. "Regime jurídico aplicável aos conselhos profissionais está nas mãos do Supremo," *Consultor Jurídico* (2017). Accessed 4 August 2018, at: www.conjur.com.br/2017-mar-02/interesse-publico-regime-juridico-conselhos-profissionais-maos-stf.

Ferreira, Christiano. "Mudança do Regime Previdenciário de Repartição para o Regime Misto: uma perspectiva para o Brasil," MA thesis, Pontifícia Universidade Católica do Rio Grande do Sul – PUCRS, 2012.

Ferreira, Francisco H. G., Phillippe G. Leite, Julie A. Litchfield, and Gabriel Ulyssea. "Ascensão e queda da desigualdade de renda no Brasil." *Econômica* 8.1 (2006): 147–169.

Ferreira, João Sette Whitaker. "São Paulo: o mito da cidade-global," PhD thesis, Faculdade de Arquitetura e Urbanismo da USP, São Paulo, 2003.

Ferreira, Jorge, ed., *O populismo e sua história* (Rio de Janeiro: Civilização Brasileira, 2000).

Ferreira, Paulo Roberto do Amaral. "O processo de globalização do varejo de massa e as lutas competitivas: o caso do setor supermercadista no Brasil," MA thesis, COPPEAD/UFRJ, Rio de Janeiro, 2013.

Ferreira, Regina Fátima Cordeiro Fonseca. "Movimentos de moradia, autogestão e política habitacional no Brasil: do acesso à moradia ao direito à cidade." Paper presented at the 2nd Sociology Forum, "Social Justice and Democratization," Buenos Aires, 1–4 August 2012. Accessed 12 December 2017, at: https://agburbana.files.wordpress.com/2013/12/texto_i sa_reginaferreira_port.pdf.

Ferreira, Victor Cláudio Paradela. "ONGs no Brasil: um estudo sobre suas características e fatores que têm induzido seu crescimento," PhD thesis, FGV, Rio de Janeiro, 2005.

Filgueiras, Luiz. *História do Plano Real* (São Paulo: Boitempo Editorial, 2000).

Fiorio, Nathalia Modenesi. "Mortalidade por raça/cor em Vitória/ES: análise da informação e das desigualdes em saúde," MA thesis: Universidade Federal de Espirito Santo, 2009.

Firpo, Sérgio Pinheiro. "Inserção no mercado de trabalho: diferenças por sexo e conseqüências sobre o bem-estar." Texto para discussão 796, Rio de Janeiro, Ipea, 2001.

Fischer Brodwyn M. *A Poverty of Rights: Citizenship and Inequality in Twentieth-Century Rio de Janeiro*. Stanford, Calif.: Stanford University Press, 2008.

Fishlow, Albert. "Brazilian Size Distribution of Income." *American Economic Review* 62.1–2 (1972): 391–402.

"Distribuição de renda no Brasil: um novo exame," *Dados* 11 (1973): 10–80.

"Algumas reflexões sobre a política brasileira após 1964," *Estudos CEBRAP* 6 (1974).

"A distribuição de renda no Brasil," in R. Tolipan and A. C. Tinelli, eds., *A controvérsia sobre a distribuição de renda e desenvolvimento* (Rio de Janeiro: Zahar, 1975).

"Origens e consequências da substituição de importações no Brasil," in Flavio Versiani and José Roberto Mendonça de Barros, eds., *Formação econômica do Brasil: a experiência de industrialização* (São Paulo: Anpec/Saraiva, 1976).

Foguel, Miguel N., Indermit Gill, Rosane Mendonça, and Ricardo Paes de Barros. "The Public–Private Wage Gap in Brazil," *Revista Brasileira de Economia* 54.4 (2000): 433–472.

Fonseca, Cristina M. Oliveira. *Saúde no Governo Vargas (1930–1945): dualidade institucional de um bem público* (Rio de Janeiro: Editora Fiocruz, 2007).

Fonseca, Pedro Cezar Dutra. *Vargas: o capitalismo em construção, 1906–1953* (São Paulo: Brasiliense, 1999).

Fonseca, Pedro Cezar Dutra and Sérgio Marley Modesto Monteiro. "O Estado e suas razões: o II PND," *Revista de Economia Política* 28.1 (2008): 28–46.

França, Danilo Sales do Nascimento. "Raça, classe e segregação residencial no Município de São Paulo," MA thesis, Universidade de São Paulo, 2010.

Franco, Gustavo. *O plano real e outros ensaios* (Rio de Janeiro: Francisco Alves, 1995).

Freitas, Elizabeth Ponte de. "Por uma cultura pública: organizações sociais, oscips e gestão pública não estatal na área da cultura," MA thesis, Universidade Federal da Bahia, 2010.

Freitas, Vladimir Passos de. "A constituição federal e a efetividade das normas ambientais," PhD thesis, Faculdade de Direito da Universidade Federal do Paraná, 1999.

Freston, Paul. "Protestantes e politica no Brasil: da constituente ao impeachment," PhD thesis, UNICAMP – Universidade Estadual de Campinas, 1993.

"Evangelicals and Politics in Latin America," *Transformation* 19.4 (2002): 271–274.

"'Neo-Pentecostalism' in Brazil: Problems of Definition and the Struggle for Hegemony." *Archives des Sciences Sociales des Religions* 44.105 (1999): 145–162.

Fritsch, Winston. "A crise cambial de 1982–83 no Brasil: origens e respostas," in C. A. Plastino and R. Bouzas, eds., *A América Latina e a crise internacional* (Rio de Janeiro: Graal, 1988).

Furtado, Celso. *Um projeto para o Brasil* (Rio de Janeiro: Saga, 1968).

Galvão, Jane. "Access to Antiretroviral Drugs in Brazil," *The Lancet* 360.9348 (December 2002): 1862–1865.

Garcia, Eduardo Henrique, Marcelo Rubens do Amaral, and Lena Lavinas. "Desigualdades regionais e retomada do crescimento num quadro de integração econômica." Texto para discussão 466, Rio de Janeiro, Ipea, 1997.

Garrefa, Fernando. "Shopping Centers, de centro de abastecimento a produto de consumo," PhD thesis, Faculdade de Arquitetura e Urbanismo da USP, São Paulo, 2007.

Gaspari, Elio. *A ditadura envergonhada* (São Paulo: Companhia das Letras, 2002).

A ditadura escancarada (São Paulo: Companhia das Letras, 2002).

A ditadura derrotada (São Paulo: Companhia das Letras, 2003).

A ditadura encurralada (São Paulo: Companhia das Letras, 2004).

Gay, Robert. *Popular Organization and Democracy in Rio De Janeiro: A Tale of Two Favelas.* Philadelphia: Temple University Press, 2010.

Gellner, Ernest. "The Importance of Being Modular," in John A. Hall, ed., *Civil Society: Theory, History, Comparison.* Cambridge: Polity Press, 1995.

Gemelli, Catia Eli. "Motivações para o trabalho voluntário sob a perpectiva do indivíduo: Um estudo de caso no ONG Junior Achievement," MA thesis; Universidade do Valle do Rio dos Sinos – UNSINOS, São Leopardo, 2015.

Gentile, Fabio. "O fascismo como modelo: incorporação da 'carta del lavoro' na via brasileira para o corporativismo autoritário da década de 1930," *Mediações - Revista de Ciências Sociais* 19.1 (2014): 84–101. Accessed 11 January 2017 at: www.uel.br/revistas/uel/index.php/mediacoes/article/view/19857.

Giambiagi, Fabio and Maurício Mesquita Moreira. *A economia brasileira nos anos 90* (Rio de Janeiro: BNDES, 1990).

Giannotti, Vito. *Historia das lutas dos trabalhadores no Brasil* (Rio de Janeiro: Mauad X, 2007).

Giuberti, Ana Carolina and Naércio Menezes-Filho. "Discriminação de rendimentos por gênero: uma comparação entre o Brasil e os Estados Unidos," *Economia Aplicada* 9.3 (2005): 369–383.

Gobetti, Sérgio Wulff and Rodrigo Octávio Orair. "Tributação e distribuição da renda no Brasil: novas evidências a partir das declarações tributárias das pessoas físicas." Working Paper 136, International Policy Centre for Inclusive Growth, Brasília, February 2016.

Gohn, Maria da Glória. *Movimentos sociais e redes de mobilizações civis no Brasil contemporâneo* (Petrópolis: Editora Vozes, 2010).

Goldemberg, José. "O repensar da educação no Brasil," *Estudos Avançados* 7.18 (1993): 65–137.

Gomes, Angela de Castro. *A invenção do trabalhismo* (São Paulo: Vértice, 1988).

Gomide, Alexandre de Avila. *Transporte urbano e inclusão social: elementos para políticas públicas* (Brasília: Ipea, 2003).

Goulding, Michael, Nigel J. H. Smith, and Dennis J. Mahar. *Floods of Fortune: Ecology and Economy along the Amazon* (New York: Columbia University Press, 1996).

Graef, Aldino and Valéria Salgado. *Relações de parceria entre poder público e entes de cooperação e colaboração no Brasil* (Brasília: Editora IABS, 2012).

Guerra, Clarissa Battistella. "Gestão Privada na Saúde Pública: um estudo empírico com Hospitais sob contrato de gestão no Estado de São Paulo," MA thesis, Instituição Insper São Paulo, 2015.

Guimarães, Maria Bernadete Pita. "Alcoolismo, Pentecostalismo e Família," PhD thesis, Universidade Federal Juiz de Fora, 2008.

Guimarães, Roberto Élito dos Reis. *O trabalhador rural e a previdência social: evolução histórica e aspectos controvertidos.* Accessed 4 January 2018, at: www.agu.gov.br/page/download/index/id/580103.

Guimarães, Thaíse Almeida, Andréa de Jesus Sá Costa Rocha, Wanderson Barros Rodrigues, and Amanda Namibia Pereira Pasklan. "Mortalidade materna no brasil entre 2009 e 2013," *Revista de Pesquisa em Saúde* 18.2 (2018): 81–85.

Guzmán, Jose Miguel, Susheela Singh, German Rodriguez, and Edith A. Pantelides, eds., *The Fertility Transition in Latin America* (Oxford: Clarendon Press, 1996).

Hahn, Carl Joseph. *História do Culto Protestante no Brasil* (São Paulo: Aste, 1981).

Hasenbalg, Carlos A. and Nelson do Valle Silva. "Raça e oportunidades educacionais no Brasil," *Cadernos de pesquisa* 73 (2013).

Hasenbalg, Carlos A., Nelson do Valle Silva, and Marcia Lima. *Cor e estratificação social no Brasil* (Rio de Janeiro: Contracapa, 1999).

Heilig, Gerhard, Thomas Buttner, and Wolfgang Lutz. "Germany's Population: Turbulent Past, Uncertain Future," *Population Bulletin*, 45.4 (1990): 1–46.

Helfand, Steven M., Vanessa da Fonseca Pereira, and Wagner Lopes Soares. "Pequenos e médios produtores na agricultura brasileira: situação atual e perspectivas," in Antônio Márcio Buainain et al., eds., *O mundo rural no Brasil do século 21: a formação de um novo padrão agrário e agrícola* (Brasília: Embrapa, 2014).

Henriques, Ricardo, ed., *Desigualdade e pobreza no Brasil* (Rio de Janeiro: Ipea, 2000).

"Desigualdade racial no Brasil: evolução das condições de vida na década de 90," Texto para discussão 807, Rio de Janeiro, Ipea, 2001.

Hirschman, Albert. "The Political Economy of Import Substitution Industrialization in Latin America," *Quarterly of Economics* 82 (1968).

Hoffmann, Rodolfo. "Transferências de renda e a redução da desigualdade no Brasil," *Revista Econômica* 8.1 (2006): 55–81.

"Desigualdade da distribuição de renda no Brasil: a contribuição de aposentadorias e pensões e de outras parcelas do rendimento domiciliar per capita," *Economia e Sociedade* 18.1 (2009): 213–231.

Hoffmann, Rodolfo and João Carlos Duarte. "A distribuição da renda no Brasil," *Revista de Administração de Empresas* 12.2 (1972).

Hoffmann, Rodolfo and Marlon Gomes Ney. *Estrutura fundiária e propriedade agrícola no Brasil, grandes regiões e unidades da federação* (Brasília: Ministério do Desenvolvimento Agrário, 2010).

"Evolução recente da estrutura fundiária e propriedade rural no Brasil," in José Garcia Gasques, José Eustáquio Vieira Filho, Zander Navarro, and Antônio Márcio Buainain. *A agricultura brasileira: desempenho, desafios e perspectivas* (Brasília: Ipea, 2010): 45–64.

Hoffmann, Rodolfo and Régis Oliveira. "The Evolution of Income Distribution in Brazil in the Agricultural and the Non-Agricultural Sectors," *World Journal of Agricultural Research* 2.5 (2014): 192–204.

Horta, Cláudia Júlia Guimarães, José Alberto Magno de Carvalho, and Luís Armando de Medeiros Frias. "Recomposição da fecundidade por geração para Brasil e regiões: atualização e revisão." Paper presented at the XII Encontro Nacional de Estudos Populacionais, ABEP, 2016.

Hryniewicz, Roberto Romeiro. "Torcida de Futebol: adesão, alienação e violência," MA thesis, Instituto de Psicologia da Universidade de São Paulo, 2008.

Isola, Marcos Kiyoto de Tani e. "Transporte sobre trilhos na Região Metropolitana de São Paulo. Estudo sobre a concepção e a inserção das redes de transporte de alta capacidade," MA thesis, Faculdade de Arquitetura e Urbanismo da USP, São Paulo, 2013.

Johnson, Andrew. *If I Give My Soul: Faith Behind Bars in Rio de Janeiro* (New York: Oxford University Press, 2017).

Jubb, Nadine, Gloria Camacho, Almachiara D'Angelo, Gina Yáñez De la Borda, Kattya Hernández, Ivonne Macassi León, Cecília MacDowell Santos, Yamileth Molina, and Wânia Pasinato. *Regional Mapping Study of Women's Police Stations in Latin America* (Quito: Centro de Planificación y Estudios Sociales, 2008).

Júnior José Maria Pereira de Nóbrega. "Os homicídios no Brasil, no nordeste e em Pernambuco: dinâmica, relações de causalidade e políticas públicas," PhD thesis, Universidade Federal de Pernambuco, Recife, 2010.

"Os homicídios no nordeste Brasileiro," *Segurança, Justiça e Cidadania* (undated). Accessed 10 December 2017, at: www.justica.gov.br/sua-seguranca/seguranca-publica/analise-e-pesquisa/download/estudos/sjcvolume6/os_homicidios_ne_brasileiro.pdf.

Keck, Margaret E. "Social Equity and Environmental Politics in Brazil: Lessons from the Rubber Tappers of Acre," *Comparative Politics* 27.4 (1995): 409–424.

Kendzia, Michael J. and Klaus F. Zimmermann. "Celebrating 150 Years of Analyzing Fertility Trends in Germany." IZA Discussion Papers, 6355 (2011).

Klein, Herbert S. *A Population History of the United States* (New York: Cambridge University Press, 2004).

The Atlantic Slave Trade (2nd edn; Cambridge: Cambridge University Press, 2010).

Klein, Herbert S. and Francisco Vidal Luna. *Slavery in Brazil* (Cambridge: Cambridge University Press, 2010).

Brazil, 1964–1985: The Military Regimes of Latin America in the Cold War (New Haven, Conn.: Yale University Press, 2017).

Feeding the World: Brazil's Transformation into a Modern Agricultural Economy (Cambridge: Cambridge University Press, 2019).

Klink, Joroen Johannes. "Novas governanças para as áreas metropolitanas. O panorama internacional e as perspectivas para o caso brasileiro." *Cadernos Metrópole* 11.22 (2009): 415–433.

Knoke, William. "O supermercado no Brasil e nos Estados Unidos: confronto e contrastes." *Revista de Administração de Empresas* 3.9 (1963): 91–103.

Koulioumba, Stamatia. "São Paulo: cidade mundial?" PhD thesis, Faculdade de Arquitetura e Urbanismo da USP, São Paulo, 2002.

Kruger, Tania Regina, Simone Bihain Hagemann, and Aline Ayres Hollanda. "Organizações sociais e os serviços públicos de saúde em Santa Catarina." Paper presented at the Seminário Nacional de Serviço Social, Trabalho e Política Social, Florianópolis, UFSC, October 2015.

Lacerda, Fabio. "Pentecostalism, eleições e reprentação política no Brasil contemporâneo," PhD thesis, Universidade de São Paulo – USP, 2017.

Lan, Jony. "A diversificação dos canais comerciais como fonte de vantagem competitiva da em redes de supermercados no Brasil," MA thesis, Universidade Presbiteriana Mackenzie, São Paulo, 2010.

Langoni, Carlos G. *Distribuição da renda e desenvolvimento econômico do Brasil* (Rio de Janeiro: Expressão e Cultura, 1973).

Laurance, William F., Heraldo L. Vasconcelos, and Thomas E. Lovejoy. "Forest Loss and Fragmentation in the Amazon: Implications for Wildlife Conservation," *Oryx* 34.1 (2000): 39–45.

Laurance, William F., José L. C. Camargo, Regina C. C. Luizão, Susan G. Laurance, Stuart L. Pimm, Emilio M. Bruna, Philip C. Stouffer et al. "The Fate of Amazonian Forest Fragments: A 32-Year Investigation," *Biological Conservation* 144.1 (2011): 56–67.

Laurenti, Ruy, Maria H. P. Mello Jorge, and Sabina Léa Davidson Gotlieb. "A mortalidade materna nas capitais brasileiras: algumas características e estimativa de um fator de ajuste," *Revista Brasileira de Epidemiologia* 7.4 (2004): 449–460.

Lavinas, Lena, Eduardo Henrique Garcia, and Marcelo Rubens do Amaral. "Desigualdades Regionais e retomada do crescimento num quadro de Integração Econômica." Texto para discussão 466, Rio de Janeiro, Ipea, 1997.

Leal, Maria do Carmo Silvana Granado Nogueira da Gama, Ana Paula Esteves Pereira, Vanessa Eufrauzino Pacheco,Cleber Nascimento do Carmo, and Ricardo Ventura Santos. "The Color of Pain: Racial Iniquities in Prenatal Care and Childbirth in Brazil," *Cadernos de Saúde Pública* 33 Supl. 1 (2017): 2–17.

Lebon, Nathalie. "Professionalization of Women's Health Groups in Sao Paulo: The Troublesome Road towards Organizational Diversity," *Organization* 3.4 (1996): 588–609.

Lessa, Carlos. *Quinze anos de política econômica* (São Paulo: Brasiliense, 1981).

Levine, Robert M. *Father of the Poor? Vargas and His Era* (New York: Cambridge University Press, 1998).

Levy, Maria Stella Ferreira. "O Papel da Migração Internacional na evolução da população brasileira (1872 a 1972)," *Revista de Saúde Pública* 8 (Supl.) (1974).

Lima, Guilherme Gadonski de, Emerson Juliano Lucca, and Dilson Trennepohl. "Expansão da cadeia produtiva do leite e seu potencial de impacto no desenvolvimento da região noroeste rio-grandense." Paper presented at the Congresso da Sociedade Brasileira de Economia, Administração e Sociologia e Rural (SOBER), João Pessoa (2015).

Lindert, Peter H. *Growing Public: Social Spending and Economic Growth since the Eighteenth Century* (New York: Cambridge University Press, 2004).

Lins, Beatriz Accioly. "A lei nas entrelinhas: a Lei Maria da Penha e o trabalho policial em duas Delegacias de Defesa da Mulher de São Paulo," MA thesis, Universidade de São Paulo – USP, 2014.

Locatel, Donizete and Fernanda Laize Silva de Lima. "Agronegócio e poder político: políticas agrícolas e o exercício do poder no Brasil," *Sociedade e Território* 28.2 (2016): 66–67.

Loewenstein, Karl. *Brazil under Vargas* (New York: Macmillian, 1942).

Longo, Luciene Aparecida Ferreira de Barros. "Uniões intra e inter-raciais, status marital, escolaridade e religião no Brasil: um estudo sobre a seletividade marital feminina, 1980–2000," PhD thesis, Universidade Federal de Minas Gerais – UFMG, 2011.

Lopes, Diva Maria Ferlin and Wendel Henrique, eds., *Cidades médias e pequenas: teorias, conceitos e estudos de caso* (Salvador: SEI, 2010).

Lopes, Francisco L. *O Choque Heterodoxo: combate à inflação e reforma monetária* (Rio de Janeiro: Campus, 1986).

Lotufo, Paulo Andrade and Isabela Judith Martins Bensenor. "Raça e mortalidade cerebrovascular no Brasil," *Revista de Saúde Pública* 47.6 (2013): 1201–1204.

Loureiro, Alexandre Pinto. "O direito de greve do servidor público no Brasil diante do princípio do interesse público," MA thesis, Faculdade de Direito da USP, 2009.

Loureiro, Ana Cláudia Nonato da Silva. "Rio de Janeiro: uma análise da perda recente de centralidade," MA thesis, Universidade Federal de Minas Gerais, 2006.

Lucchese, Mafalda. "Filhos – evolução até a plena igualdade jurídica." Accessed 26 November 2017, at: www.emerj.tjrj.jus.br/serieaperfeicoamentodemagistrados/paginas/series/13/vol umel/10anosdocodigocivil_231.pdf.

Luna, Francisco Vidal. "São Paulo: a capital financeira do país," in Tamás Szmrecsányi, ed., *História Econômica da cidade de São Paulo* (São Paulo: Editora Globo, 2005): 328–355.

Luna, Francisco Vidal and Herbert S. Klein. *Brazil since 1980* (Cambridge: Cambridge University Press, 2006).

The Economic and Social History of Brazil since 1889 (Cambridge: Cambridge University Press, 2014).

Luna, Francisco Vidal and Thomaz de Aquino Nogueira Neto. *Correção monetária e mercado de capitais: a experiência brasileira* (São Paulo: Bolsa de Valores de São Paulo (BOVESPA), 1978).

Luporini, Viviani and Francisco E.P. de Souza. "A política cambial brasileira de facto: 1999–2015," *Estudos Econômicos* 46.4 (2016): 909–936.

McCann, Bryan. *Hard Times in the Marvelous City: From Dictatorship to Democracy in the Favelas of Rio de Janeiro*. Durham, NC: Duke University Press, 2013.

Machado, Adriano Henriques. "A influência dos setores católicos na formação do Partido dos Trabalhadores: da relação com os movimentos sociais à ideia de formar um novo partido." Paper presented at the ANPUH – XXV Simpósio Nacional de História, Fortaleza, 2009.

Machado, Carlos José Saldanha. "Mudanças conceituais na administração pública do meio ambiente," *Ciência e Cultura* 55.4 (2003): 24–26.

Machado, Nilson José. "Qualidade da educação: cinco lembretes e uma lembrança." *Estudos Avançados* 21.61 (2007): 277–294.

Mahar, Dennis J. Government Policies and Deforestation in the Brazilian Amazon (Washington, DC: World Bank, 1989).

Maia, Rosane de Almeida. "Estado e Industrialização no Brasil: Estudo dos Incentivos ao setor privado, nos quadros do Programa de Metas do Governo Kubitschek," MA thesis, FEA-USP, São Paulo, 1986.

Mainwaring, Scott Timothy J. Power, and Fernando Bizzarro. "The Uneven Institutionalization of a Party System: Brazil." In Scott Mainwaring, ed., *Party Systems in Latin America: Institutionalization, Decay, and Collapse* (Cambridge: Cambridge University Press, 2018), pp.164–200.

Malloy, James. *The Politics of Social Security in Brazil* (Pittsburgh, Pa.: University of Pittsburgh Press, 1979).

Malta, Deborah Carvalho, Maria Aline Siqueira Santos, Sheila Rizzato Stopa, José Eudes Barroso Vieira, Eduardo Alves Melo, and Ademar Arthur Chioro dos Reis. "A cobertura da Estratégia de Saúde da Família (ESF) no Brasil, segundo a Pesquisa Nacional de Saúde, 2013." *Ciência & Saúde* 21 (2016): 327–338.

Mares, Isabela. *The Politics of Social Risk: Business and Welfare State Development* (Cambridge: Cambridge University Press, 2003).

Margulis, Sérgio. "Causes of Deforestation of the Brazilian Amazon." World Bank Working Papers 22; Washington, DC, 2004.

O Desempenho ambiental do Governo Brasileiro e do Banco Mundial em Projetos Co-financiados pelo Banco. Texto para discussão 94 (Brasília: Ipea, 1999).

Mariano, Ricardo. "Efeitos da secularização do Estado, do pluralismo e do mercado religiosos sobre as igrejas pentecostais," *Civitas* 3.1 (2003): 111–125.

"Expansão pentecostal no Brasil: o caso da Igreja Universal," *Estudos Avançados* 18.52 (2004): 121–138.

"Sociologia do crescimento pentecostal no Brasil: um balanço," *Perspectiva Teológica* 43.119 (2011): 11–36.

Maricato, Ermínia. "O 'Minha Casa' é um avanço, mas segregação urbana fica intocada," *Carta Maior*, 27 May 2009. Accessed at 27 November 2017, at: www.cartamaior.com.br/?/Edito ria/Politica/O-Minha-Casa-e-um-avanco-mas-segregacao-urbana-fica-intocada/4/15160.

Marinho, Emerson and Jair Araujo. "Pobreza e o sistema de seguridade social rural no Brasil," *Revista Brasileira de Economia* 64.2 (2010): 161–174.

Marini, Miguel Angelo and Federico Innecco Garcia. "Bird Conservation in Brazil," *Conservation Biology*, 19.3 (2005): 665–671.

Mariz, Cecília Loreto. *Coping with Poverty: Pentecostals and Christian Base Communities in Brazil* (Philadelphia: Temple University Press, 1994).

"Missão religiosa e migração: 'novas comunidades' e igrejas pentecostais brasileiras no exterior," *Análise Social* 44.1 (2009): 161–187.

Marques, Eduardo Cesar Leão, ed., *Assentamentos precários no Brasil urbano* (Brasília/São Paulo: Ministério das Cidades/CEM, 2007).

Marques, Maria Silva Bastos. "O plano cruzado: teoria e prática," *Revista de Economia Política* 8.3 (1988): 101–130.

Martinelli, Luiz A. and Solange Filoso. "Expansion of Sugarcane Ethanol Production in Brazil: Environmental and Social Challenges," *Atmospheric Environment* 18.4 (2008): 885–898.

Martinelli, Luiz A., Rosamond Naylor, Peter M. Vitousek, and Paulo Moutinho. "Agriculture in Brazil: Impacts, Costs, and Opportunities for a Sustainable Future," *Current Opinion in Environmental Sustainability* 2.4–5 (2010): 431–438.

Martines-Filho, Joao, Heloisa L. Burnquist, and Carlos E. F. Vian. "Bioenergy and the Rise of Sugarcane-Based Ethanol in Brazil," *Choices* 21.2 (2006): 91–96.

Martínez-Fritscher, André, Aldo Musacchio, and Martina Viarengo. "The Great Leap Forward: The Political Economy of Education in Brazil, 1889–1930," Working Papers 03-2010, Universidade de São Paulo, Faculdade de Economia, Administração e Contabilidade de Ribeirão Preto, 2010.

Martins, Alaerte Leandro. "Mortalidade materna de mulheres negras no Brasil," *Cadernos de Saúde Pública* 22.11 (2006): 2473–2479.

Martins, Bibiana Volkmer. "A presença da ONG Cidade para a Construção de um planejamento urbano democrático em Porto Alegre," MA thesis, Universidade Federal do Rio Grande do Sul, Porto Alegre, 2011.

Martins, Carlos Benedito. "O ensino superior brasileiro nos anos 90," *São Paulo em Perspectiva* 14.1 (2000).

Martone, Celso Luiz. "O plano de ação econômica," in Betty Mindlin Lafer, ed., *Planejamento no Brasil* (São Paulo: Editora Perspectiva, 1973).

Mathias, Alfredo. "Semma Empresa de Shopping Centers." Accessed 11 December 2017, at: www .semma.com.br/historia-dos-shopping-centers-no-brasil/.

Matos, Carlos Alberto. "A Fenajufe e seus sindicatos: a CUT no poder judiciário federal e no ministério público da União," MA thesis, UNICAMP – Universidade Estadual de Campinas, 2002.

Mattar, Michel. "Excelência em Gestão do Futebol da Fundação Instituto de Administração" (Interview, "Movimento por um Futebol Melhor"). Accessed 7 November 2017, at: www .lance.com.br/futebol-melhor/coordenador-fia-analisa-gestao-profissional-nos-clubes-brasileiros.html.

Mattos, Hebe Maria. *Das cores do silêncio* (Rio de Janeiro: Nova Fronteira, 1998).

Mattos, Marcelo Badaró. *Trabalhadores e sindicatos no Brasil* (São Paulo: Editora Expressão Popular, 2009).

Medeiros, Marcelo. "O que faz os Ricos ricos: um estudo sobre fatores que determinam a riqueza," PhD thesis, Universidade de Brasília, 2003.

Medeiros, Marcelo and Joana Simões Costa. "Poverty among Women in Latin America: Feminization or Overrepresentation?" Working Paper 20, International Poverty Centre, Brasília, 2006.

Medeiros, Marcelo and Pedro H. G. F. Souza. *Gasto público, tributos e desigualdade de renda no Brasil* (Rio de Janeiro: Ipea, 2013).

"A Estabilidade da desigualdade no Brasil entre 2006 e 2012: resultados adicionais," *Pesquisa e Planejamento Econômico* 46.3 (2016).

Medeiros, Marcelo, Tatiana Britto, and Fábio Soares. *Programas focalizados de transferência de renda no Brasil: contribuições para o debate* (Brasília: Ipea, 2007).

Medici, André and Robert Murray. "Desempenho de hospitais e melhorias na qualidade de saúde em São Paulo (Brasil) e Maryland (EUA)" (Washington, DC: World Bank. 2013).

Melchiors, Lucia Camargos and Heleniza Ávila Campo. "As regiões metropolitanas brasileiras no contexto do Estatuto da Metrópole: Desafios a serem superados em direção à governança colaborativa." *Revista Política e Planejamento Regional* 3.2 (2016): 181–203.

Mello, Andreia Skackauskas Vaz de. "Burocratização e institucionalização das organizações de movimentos sociais: O caso da organização de prostitutas Davida," MA thesis, Universidade Federal de Minas Gerais – UFMG, 2007.

Mello, Pedro Carvalho de. "The Economics of Labor in Brazilian Coffee Plantations," PhD thesis, University of Chicago, 1975.

Mendes, Eugênio Vilaça. "25 anos do Sistema único de Saúde: resultados e desafios." *Estudos Avançados* 27.78 (2013): 27–34.

Mendes, Izabel Cristina Reis. "O uso contemporâneo da favela na cidade do Rio de Janeiro," PhD thesis, Faculdade de Arquitetura e Urbanismo da USP, São Paulo, 2014.

Menezes, Greice and Estela M. L. Aquino. "Pesquisa sobre o aborto no Brasil: avanços e desafios para o campo da saúde coletiva," *Cadernos de Saúde Pública* 25 Supl. 2 (2009): 193–204.

Mendonça, Antonio Gouvêa and Prócoro Velasques Filho. *Introdução ao Protestantismo no Brasil* (São Paulo: Edições Loyola, 1990).

Menicucci, Telma Maria Gonçalves. "Público e privado na política assistência à saúde no Brasil: atores, processos e trajetória," PhD thesis, FFCH/Universidade Federal de Minas Gerais, 2003.

Mercadante, Aloizio, ed., *O Brasil pós real: a política econômica em debate* (Campinas: Unicamp, 1997).

Merrick, Thomas W. and Douglas H. Graham. *Population and Economic Development in Brazil, 1800 to the Present* (Baltimore, Md.: Johns Hopkins University Press, 1979).

Milanez, Bruno and Luciana Miyolo Massukado. *Caderno de diagnóstico: resíduos sólidos urbanos* (Brasília: Ipea, 2011).

Milanovic, Branko. "Global Inequality and the Global Inequality Extraction Ratio: The Story of the Past Two Centuries," *Explorations in Economic History* 48 (2011): 494–506.

Miller, Shawn W. *Fruitless Trees: Portuguese Conservation and Brazil's Colonial Timber* (Stanford, Calif.: Stanford University Press, 2000).

An *Environmental History of Latin America* (Cambridge: Cambridge University Press, 2007).

Mineiro, Ademar S. "Desenvolvimento e inserção externa: algumas considerações sobre o período 2003–2009 no Brasil," in J. P. A. Magalhães, ed., *Os anos Lula: constribuições para um Balanço Crítico, 2002–2010* (Rio de Janeiro: Editora Garamond, 2010): 133–160.

Miriam, Sonia. *Rumos e metamorfoses, estado e industrialização no Brasil, 1930–1960* (Rio de Janeiro: Paz e Terra, 1985).

"Mobilidade urbana: hora de mudar os rumos." *Discussão: revista de audiências públicas do Senado Federal* 4.18 (November 2013). Accessed at: www2.senado.leg.br/bdsf/bitstream/han dle/id/496713/Em%20Discuss%c3%a30%21_novembro_2013.pdf?sequence =1&isAllowed=y.

Modiano, Eduardo. "A ópera dos três cruzados: 1985–1989," in Marcelo de Paiva Abreu and Dionísio Dias Carneiro Netto, eds., *A ordem do progresso: cem anos de política econômica republicana, 1889–1989* (Rio de Janeiro: Campus, 1990): 347–414.

Moreira, Maurício Mesquita and Paulo Guilherme Correa. "Abertura comercial e indústria: o que se pode esperar e o que se vem obtendo," *Revista de Economia Política* 17.2 (1997): 61–91.

Morgan, Marc. "Extreme and Persistent Inequality: New Evidence for Brazil Combining National Accounts, Surveys and Fiscal Data, 2001–2015," Working Paper 12, World Wealth and Income Database, 2017.

Mortara, Giorgio. "The Development and Structure of Brazil's Population," *Population Studies* 8.2 (1954): 121–139.

Mota, Daniel Pestana. "CUT, Sindicato orgânico e reforma da estrutura sindical," MA thesis, Universidade Estadual Paulista em Marília, 2006.

Motta, Marly Silva da. "A fusão da Guanabara com o Estado do Rio: desafios e desencantos," in Américo Freire, Carlos Eduardo Sarmento, and Marly Silva da Motta, eds., *Um Estado em questão: os 25 anos do Rio de Janeiro Rio de Janeiro* (Rio de Janeiro: Editora Fundação Getulio Vargas, 2001):19–56.

"O lugar da cidade do Rio de Janeiro na Federação Brasileira: uma questão em três momentos." Rio de Janeiro, Centro de Pesquisa e Documentação de História Contemporânea do Brasil (CPDOC), 2001. Accessed 20 November 2017, at: https://bibl iotecadigital.fgv.br/dspace/bitstream/handle/10438/6799/1232.pdf.

Motta, Rodrigo Patto Sá. *As universidades e o regime militar* (Rio de Janeiro: Zahar, 2014).

Moura, Alessandro. "Movimento Operário e sindicalismo em Osasco, São Paulo e ABC Paulista: Rupturas e descontinuidades," PhD thesis, Universidade Virtual do Estado de São Paulo – UNIVESP, Marília, 2015.

Musacchio, Aldo, André Martínez Fritscher, and Martina Viareng. "Colonial Institutions, Trade Shocks, and the Diffusion of Elementary Education in Brazil, 1889–1930." Working Paper 10-075, Harvard Business School, 2010. Accessed at: www.hbs.edu/resea rch/pdf/10-075.pdf.

Nadalin, Vanessa Gapriotti, Cleandro Krause, and Vicente Correia Lima Neto. "Distribuição de aglomerados subnormais na rede urbana e nas grandes regiões brasileiras." Texto para discussão 2012, Rio de Janeiro, Ipea, 2014.

Najberg, Sheila. "Privatização dos recursos públicos: os empréstimos do sistema BNDES ao setor privado nacional com correção monetária parcial," MA thesis, Pontifícia Universidade Católica do Rio de Janeiro – PUC-Rio, 1989.

Nascimento, Arlindo Mello do. "População e família brasileira: ontem e hoje." Paper presented at the XV Encontro Nacional de Estudos Populacionais, ABEP, 2006.

Naves, Rubens. *Organizações Sociais: a construção do modelo* (São Paulo: Editora Quartier Latin, 2014).

Nepstad, Daniel C., Britaldo S. Soares-Filho, Frank Merry, André Lima, Paulo Moutinho, John Carter, Maria Bowman et al. "The End of Deforestation in the Brazilian Amazon," *Science* 326.5958 (2009): 1350–1351.

Nepstad, Daniel C., Claudia M. Stickler, Britaldo Soares-Filho, and Frank Merry, "Interactions among Amazon Land Use, Forests and Climate: Prospects for a Near-Term Forest Tipping Point," *Philosophical Transactions of the Royal Society B*. 363 (2008): 1737–1746.

Neto, Lira. *Getúlio: dos anos de formação à conquista do poder (1882–1930)* (São Paulo: Cia. Das Letras, 2012).

Getúlio: do governo provisório à ditadura do Estado Novo (1930–1943) (São Paulo: Cia das Letras, 2013).

Getúlio: da volta pela consagração popular ao suicídio (São Paulo: Cia das Letras, 2014).

Netto, José V. R., Lucio Bittencourt, and Pedro Malafaia. "Políticas culturais por meio de organizações sociais em São Paulo: expandindo a qualidade da democracia?" Seminário Internacional de Políticas Culturais, Rio de Janeiro, 2012. Accessed 12 January 2018, at: h ttp://culturadigital.br/politicaculturalcasaderuibarbosa/files/2012/09/Jose-Verissimo-Rom% C3%A30-Netto-et-alii.pdf.

Nevesa, Marcos Fava, Allan W. Grayb, and Brian A. Bourquard. "Copersucar: A World Leader in Sugar and Ethanol," *International Food and Agribusiness Management Review* 19.2 (2016): 207–240.

Nicholson, Brian. *A previdência injusta: como o fim dos privilégios pode mudar o Brasil* (São Paulo: Geração Editorial, 2007).

Ninaut, Evandro Scheidt and Marcos Antonio Mato. "Panorama do cooperativismo no Brasil: censo, exportações e faturamento," *Informações Econômicas, SP* 38.8 (2008):43–55.

Nogueira, Fernando Tadeu Pongelupe and Danilo R. D. Aguiar. "Efeitos da desregulamentação na extensão e no grau de integração do mercado brasileiro de café," *Revista de Economia* 37.3 (2011): 21–46.

Noronha, Eduardo G. "Informal, Illegal and Unfair: Perceptions of Labor Markets in Brazil," *Revista Brasileira de Ciências Sociais* 18.53 (2003): 111–129.

Noronha, Mayara Silva de. "Multiplicidades da Favela," PhD thesis, FGV/SP, São Paulo, 2017.

Nozaki, Victor Toyoji de. "Análise do setor de saneamento Básico no Brasil," MA thesis, Faculdade de Economia, Administração e Contabilidade de Ribeirão Preto da Universidade de São Paulo – FEA-USP, Ribeirão Preto, 2007.

Okie, Susan. "Fighting HIV: Lessons from Brazil," *New England Journal of Medicine* 354 (2006): 1977–1981.

Oliveira, Felipe Proenço de, Tazio Vanni, Hêider Aurélio Pinto, Jerzey Timoteo Ribeiro dos Santos, Alexandre Medeiros de Figueiredo, Sidclei Queiroga de Araújo, Mateus Falcão Martins Matos, and Eliana Goldfarb Cyrino. "Mais Médicos: um programa brasileiro em uma perspectiva internacional," *Interface-Comunicação, Saúde, Educação* 19 (2015): 623–634.

Oliveira, Francisco Eduardo Barreto de, Kaizô Iwakami Beltrão, and Antonio Carlos de Albuquerque David. "Dívida da união com a previdência social: uma perspectiva histórica." Texto para discussão 638, Rio de Janeiro, Ipea, 1999.

Oliveira, Gleick Meira and Thaís Maia Rodrigues. "A nova lei de combate aos crimes contra a liberdade sexual: uma análise acerca das modificações trazidas ao crime de estupro," *Âmbito Jurídico* (2011). Accessed at: www.ambito-juridico.com.br/site/index.php? n_link=revista_artigos_leitura&artigo_id=9553.

Oliveira, J. de C. and F. R. Albuquerque. "A mortalidade no Brasil no período 1980–2004: desafios e oportunidades para os próximos anos." (Rio de Janeiro: Instituto Brasileiro de Geografia e Estatística, 2005).

Oliveira, Ribamar. "Delfim Netto: plano real acentuou redução da capacidade exportadora brasileira," *Jornal Valor Econômico* (29 June 2014).

Oliveira, Romualdo Portela de. "A transformação da educação em mercadoria no Brasil," *Revista Educação e Sociedade* 30.108 (2009): 739–760.

Oliveira, Talita Raquel de. "Dependência e criação de trajetória no terceiro setor: Um estudo de caso na ONG Parceiros Voluntários," MA thesis, Universidade do Valle do Rio dos Sinos – UNSINOS, São Leopardo, 2013.

Oliveira, Viviane Fernanda de. "Do BNH ao Minha Casa Minha Vida: mudanças e permanências na política habitacional." *Caminhos de Geografia* 15.50 (2014): 36–53. Accessed 7 December 2017 at: www.seer.ufu.br/index.php/caminhosdegeografia/article/v iew/22937.

Oliveira, Wilson José Ferreira de. "Gênese e redefinições do militantismo ambientalista no Brasil," *Dados: Revista de Ciências Sociais* 51.3 (2008): 751–777.

Olivo, Luis Carlos Cancellier de. *As Organizações Sociais e o novo espaço público* (Florianópolis: Editorial Studium, 2005).

Oro, Ari Pedro. "A política da Igreja Universal e seus reflexos nos campos religioso e político brasileiros," *Revista Brasileira de Ciências Sociais* 18.53 (2003): 53–69.

Osorio, Rafael Guerreiro. "O sistema classificatório de 'cor ou raça' do IBGE." Texto para discussão 996, Brasília, Ipea, 2003.

"À mobilidade social dos negros brasileiros." Texto para discussão 1033, Brasília, Ipea, 2004.

"A desigualdade racial de renda no Brasil: 1976–2006," PhD thesis, Universidade de Brasília, 2009.

Osorio, Rafael Guerreiro, Pedro H. G. F. de Souza,Sergei S. D. Soares, and Luis Felipe Batista de Oliveira. "Perfil da pobreza no Brasil e sua evolução no período 2004–2009." Texto para discussão 1647, Rio de Janeiro, Ipea, 2011.

Ossewaarde, Ringo, Andre Nijhof, and Liesbet Heyse. "Dynamics of NGO Legitimacy: How Organising Betrays Core Missions of INGOs," *Public Administration and Development* 28 (2008): 42–53.

Pacheco, Carlos Américo and Neide Patarra, eds., *Dinâmica demográfica regional e as novas questões populacionais no Brasil* (Campinas: Instituto de Economia/UNICAMP, 2000).

Paim, Jairnilson, Claudia Travassos, Celia Almeida, Ligia Bahia, and James Macinko. "The Brazilian Health System: History, Advances, and Challenges," *The Lancet* 377.9779 (2011): 1778–1797.

Pamplona, Fernanda Bittencourt. "Os investimentos diretos estrangeiros na indústria do varejo nos supermercados no Brasil," MA thesis, Universidade Federal de Pernambuco, Recife, 2007.

Pasternak, Suzana. "Favelas no Brasil e em São Paulo: avanços nas análises a partir da Leitura Territorial do Censo de 2010," *Cadernos Metropolítanos* 18.35 (2016).

Pastore, José. *Inequality and Social Mobility in Brazil* (Madison: University of Wisconsin Press, 1981).

Pastore, José and Nelson do Valle Silva. "Análise dos Processos de Mobilidade Social no Brasil no Último Século." Paper presented at the XXV Encontro Anual da Anpocs, Caxambu, 16–20 October 2001. Accessed at: www.josepastore.com.br/artigos/td/td_015.htm.

Mobilidade Social no Brasil (São Paulo: Makron, 2000).

Patara, Neide, Rosana Baeninger, and José Marcos Pinto da Cunha. "Dinâmica demográfica recente e a configuração de novas questões populacionais," in Carlos Américo Pacheco and Neide Patarra, eds., *Dinâmica demográfica regional e as novas questões populacionais no Brasil* (Campinas: Instituto de Economia/UNICAMP, 2000).

Paula, Marilene de and Dawid Danilo Barlet, eds., *Mobilidade urbana no Brasil: desafios e alternativas* (Rio de Janeiro: Fundação Heinrich Boll, 2016).

Pereira, Adriana Jimenez and Lúcia Yasuko Izumi Nichiata. "A sociedade civil contra a Aids: demandas coletivas e políticas públicas," *Ciência & Saúde Coletiva* 16.7 (2011): 3249–3257.

Pereira, Luiz Carlos Bresser. "Inflação inercial e o plano cruzado," *Revista de Economia Política* 6.3 (1986): 9–24.

Pereira, Ranon Bento and Glauber Lopes Xavier. "A propriedade da terra e a política brasileira durante a nova república (1985–2014): a bancada ruralista e a questão agrária contemporânea (52ª, 53ª e 54ª legislaturas)." *Anais do Seminário de Pesquisa, Pós-Graduação, Ensino e Extensão do Câmpus Anápolis de CSEH (SEPE)*, vol. 2, *O cenário econômico nacional e os desafios profissionais* (2016).

Perlman, Janice E. *The Myth of Marginality: Urban Poverty and Politics in Rio de Janeiro* (Berkeley: University of California Press, 1979).

Favela: Four Decades of Living on the Edge in Rio de Janeiro (New York: Oxford University Press, 2010).

Petersen, Samanta. "Polo Saúde de Teresina é referência em atendimento." *Cidade Verde*. Accessed 17 December 2017, at: https://cidadeverde.com/vida/68938/especial-polo-saude-de-teresina-e-referencia-em-atendimento.

Petruccelli, José Luis. "Seletividade por cor e escolhas conjugais no Brasil dos 90," *Estudos Afro-Asiáticos* 23.1 (2001): 29–51.

Piketty, Thomas. *Capital in the 21st Century* (Cambridge, Mass.: Harvard University Press, 2014).

Pinheiro, Armando Castelar. "A experiência Brasileira de Privatização: O que vem a seguir." Texto para discussão 87, Rio de Janeiro, Ipea, 2002.

Pinheiro, Marcos Antonio Henriques. *Cooperativas de Crédito: História da evolução normativa no Brasil* (6th edn; Brasília: Banco Central do Brasil, 2008).

Pinheiro, Vinícius Carvalho. "Inflação, poder e processo orçamentário no Brasil, 1988 a 1993," *Revista do Serviço Público* 47.1 (1996): 7–40.

Pinto, Céli Regina Jardim. "As ONGs e a política no Brasil: presença de novos atores," *Dados: Revista de Ciências Sociais* 49.3 (2006): 650–651.

Pinto, José Marcelino de Rezende. "O acesso à educação superior no Brasil," *Revista Educação e Sociedade* 25.88 (2004): 727–756.

Pinto, Sol Garson Braule. "Regiões metropolitanas: obstáculos institucionais à cooperação em políticas urbanas," PhD thesis, Universidade Federal do Rio de Janeiro – UFRJ, 2007.

Pintos-Payeras, José Adrian. "Análise da progressividade da carga tributária sobre a população brasileira," *Pesquisa e Planejamento Econômico* 40.2 (2010): 153–186.

Prado, Thayse Cristiane Severo do. "Segregação residencial por índices de dissimilaridade, isolamento e exposição, com indicador renda, no espaço urbano de Santa Maria, RS, por geotecnologias," MA thesis, Universidade Federal de Santa Maria, 2012.

Prata, Pedro Reginaldo. "A transição epidemiológica no Brasil," *Cadernos de Saúde Pública* 8.2 (1992): 168–175.

Prates, Daniela Magalhães. *O regime de câmbio flutuante no Brasil, 1999–2012: especificidades e dilemas* (Brasília: Ipea, 2015).

Quine, Maria Sophia. *Italy's Social Revolution: Charity and Welfare from Liberalism to Fascism* (New York: Palgrave, 2002).

Rabuske, Irineu José, Paola Lucena dos Santos, Hosana Alves Gonçalves, and Laura Traub. "Evangélicos brasileiros: quem são, de onde vieram e no que acreditam?" *Revista Brasileira de História das Religiões* 4.12 (2012): 255–267.

Raiser, Martin, Roland Clarke, Paul Procee, Cecilia Briceno-Garmendia, Edith Kikoni, Joseph Kizito, and Lorena Vinuela. *Back to Planning: How to Close Brazil's Infrastructure Gap in Times of Austerity* (Washington, DC: World Bank, 2017).

Ramos, Lauro R. A. and Ana Lúcia Soares. "Participação da mulher na força de trabalho e pobreza no Brasil." Texto para discussão 350, Rio de Janeiro, Ipea, 1994.

Ramos, Lauro R. A. and José Guilherme Almeida Reis. "Distribuição da renda: aspectos teóricos e o debate no Brasil," in José Marcio Camargo and Fabio Giambiagi, eds., *Distribuição de renda no Brasil* (Rio de Janeiro: Paz e Terra, 2000): 21–45.

Redwood II, John. "World Bank Approaches to the Brazilian Amazon: The Bumpy Road toward Sustainable Development. LCR Sustainable Development." World Bank Working Paper 13, Washington, DC, November 2002.

Rego, J. M. *Inflação inercial, teoria sobre inflação e o plano cruzado* (Rio de Janeiro: Paz e Terra, 1986).

Reich, Gary and Pedro dos Santos. "The Rise (and Frequent Fall) of Evangelical Politicians: Organization, Theology, and Church Politics," *Latin American Politics and Society* 55.4 (2013): 1–22.

Reydon,Bastiaan Philip. "Governança de terras e a questão agrária no Brasil," in Antônio Márcio Buainain, Eliseu Roberto de Andrade Alves, José Maria Ferreira Jardim da Silveira, and Zander Navarro, eds., *O mundo rural no Brasil do século 21: a formação de um novo padrão agrário e agrícola* (Brasília: Embrapa, 2014).

Rezende, André Lara. "Estabilização e reforma," in Paiva Abreu, Mario Henrique Simonsen, and Roberto Campos, eds., *A nova economia brasileira* (Rio de Janeiro: José Olympio, 1979).

Rial, Carmen. "Neo-Pentecostals on the Pitch Brazilian Football Players as Missionaries Abroad," in Jeffrey D. Needell, ed., *Emergent Brazil: Key Perspectives on a New Global Power* (Gainesville: University of Florida Press, 2015).

Ribeiro, Carlos Antonio Costa. "Classe, Raça e Mobilidade Social no Brasil," *Dados: Revista de Ciências Sociais* 49.4 (2006): 833–873.

Estrutura de classe e mobilidade social no Brasil (Bauru: EDUSC, 2007).

"Quatro décadas de mobilidade social no Brasil," *Dados: Revista de Ciências Sociais*, 55.3 (2012): 641–679.

"Tendências da desigualdade de oportunidades no Brasil: mobilidade social e estratificação educacional," *Boletin Mercado de Trabalho: conjuntura e análise* 62 (2017): 49–65.

Ribeiro, Carlos Antonio Costa, and Maria Celi Scalon. "Mobilidade de classe no Brasil em perspectiva comparada, *Dados: Revista de Sciências Sociais* 44.1 (2001): 53–96.

Ribeiro, Carlos Antonio Costa and Nelson do Valle Silva. "Cor, Educação e Casamento: Tendências da Seletividade Marital no Brasil, 1960 a 2000," *Dados: Revista de Ciências Sociais* 52.1 (2009): 7–51.

Ribeiro, Fátima Aparecida. "Atenção Primária (APS) e o Sistema de Saúde no Brasil: uma perspectiva histórica," MA thesis, Faculdade de Medicina da Universidade de São Paulo – FMUSP, 2007.

Ribeiro, Milton Cezar, Jean Paul Metzger, Alexandre Camargo Martensen, Flávio Jorge Ponzoni, and Márcia Makiko Hirota. "The Brazilian Atlantic Forest: How Much Is Left, and How Is the Remaining Forest Distributed? Implications for Conservation," *Biological Conservation* 142 (2009): 1141–1153.

Roberto DaMatta. *Universo do futebol: esporte e sociedade brasileira*. Rio de Janeiro: Pinakotheke, 1982.

Rocha, Sonia. "Impacto sobre a pobreza dos novos programas federais de transferência de renda." Associação Nacional dos Centros de Pós-Graduação em Economia (n.d.). www .anpec.org.br/encontro2004/artigos/A04A137.pdf.

"Desigualdade regional e pobreza no Brasil: A Evolução – 1981/95." Texto para discussão 567, Rio de Janeiro, Ipea, 1998.

Pobreza no Brasil: afinal, de que se trata?: afinal, de que se trata? (Rio de Janeiro: FGV Editora, 2003).

"O impacto distributivo do imposto de renda sobre a desigualdade de renda das famílias," *Pesquisa e Planejamento Econômico* 32.1 (2007): 73–105.

"Poverty Upsurge in 2015 and the Rising Trend in Regional and Age Inequality among the Poor in Brazil," *Nova Economia* 29.1 (2019): 249–275.

Rodarte, José Cláudio. "A evolução da previdência complementar fechada no Brasil, da década de 70 aos dias atuais: expectativas, tendências e desafios," MA thesis, UFMG - Universidade Federal de Minas Gerais, 2011.

Rodrigues, Iram Jácome. "Igreja e Movimento Operário nas origens do Novo Sindicalismo no Brasil (1964–1978)," *História, Questões & Debates* 29 (1998): 25–58.

Rodrigues, Leôncio Martins. "Sindicalismo e classe operaria (1930–1964)," in Boris Fausto, ed., *História geral da civilização brasileira* (São Paulo: Difusao Europeia de Livro, 1986), vol. 3/10: 509–555.

"As tendência políticas na formação das centrais sindicais" in Armando Boito, ed., *O sindicalismo brasileiro nos anos 80* (Rio de Janeiro: Paz e Terra, 1991): 11–42.

"Sindicalismo corporativo no Brasil," in *Partidos e sindicatos: escritos de sociologia política* (Rio de Janeiro: Centro Edelstein de Pesquisas Sociais, 2009): 38–65.

Rodrigues, Walter. "Progress and Problems of Family Planning in Brazil," *Demography* 5.2 (1968): 800–810.

Rollemberg, Denise. "Memória, opinião e cultura política: a ordem dos advogados do brasil sob a ditadura (1964–1974)," in Daniel Aarão Reis and Denis Rolland, eds., *Modernidades Alternativas* (Rio de Janeiro: Fundação GetúlioVargas, 2008): 57–96.

Rolnik, Raquel and Kazuo Nakano. "As armadilhas do pacote habitacional." *Le Monde diplomatique, Brasil* (5 March 2009). Accessed 27 November 2017, at: https://diplomat ique.org.br/as-armadilhas-do-pacote-habitacional/.

Rubim, Antonio Albino Canelas, ed., *Politicas Culturais no Governo Lula* (Salvador: Edufba, 2010).

Salas, Carlos and Marcia Leite. "Segregación sectorial por género: una comparación Brasil-México," *Cadernos PROLAM/USP* 7.2 (2007): 248.

Sampaio, Helena, Fernando Limongi, and Haroldo Torres. "Eqüidade e heterogeneidade no ensino superior brasileiro." Núcleo de Pesquisas sobre Ensino Superior Universidade de São Paulo, Working paper 1/00 (undated). Available at: http://nupps.usp.br/downloads/docs/dt0001.pdf.

Sánchez-Albornoz, Nicolás. *La población de América latina: desde los tiempos precolombinos al año 2025* (Madrid: Alianza, 1994).

Sanchis, Pierre. "As religiões dos brasileiros," *Horizonte* 1.2 (2009): 28–43.

Sano, Hironobu and Fernando Luiz Abrucio. "Promessas e resultados da nova gestão pública no brasil: o caso das organizações sociais em São Paulo." *Revista de Administração de Empresas* 48.3 (2008): 64–80.

Santana, Leonardo Ferreira de. "Análise do desempenho dos serviços prestados através das organizações sociais de saúde no Estado do Rio de Janeiro," MA thesis FGV/RJ, Rio de Janeiro, 2015.

Santos, Ana Jacira dos. "As comunidades eclesiais de base no período de 1970 a 2000," PhD thesis, Universidade Federal do Rio Grande do Norte, 2002.

Santos, Ana Lúcia dos. "Delegacia de defesa da mulher: um lugar de queixas – queixas de um lugar," MA thesis, Assis, Universidade Estadual Paulista – Unesp, 2007.

Santos, Ana Pereira dos. "Entre embaraços, performances e resistências: a construção da queixa de violência doméstica de mulheres em uma delegacia," MA thesis, Universidade Federal de Viçosa, 2014.

Santos, Cláudio Hamilton M. *Políticas federais de habitação no Brasil, 1964–1980* (Brasília: Ipea, 1999).

Santos, Everson Vieira dos. "Estudo da estrutura de mercado do setor supermercadista do Rio Grande do Sul e Identificação do Grau de concentração." Accessed at: https://docs .google.com/viewer?url=https%3A%2F%2Fwww.fee.rs.gov.br%2F4-encontro-economia -gaucha%2Ftrabalhos%2Festudos-setoriais-sessao3-3.doc.

Santos, Leonor Maria Pacheco, Ana Maria Costa, and Sábado Nicolau Girardi. "Programa Mais Médicos: uma ação efetiva para reduzir iniquidades em saúde," *Ciência & Saúde Coletiva* 20 (2015): 3547–3552.

Sayad, João. *Planos cruzado e real: acertos e desacertos* (Rio de Janeiro: Ipea, 2000).

Sayad, João and Francisco Vidal Luna. "Política antiinflacionaria y el plan cruzado," in *Neoliberalismo y políticas económicas alternativas* (Quito: Corporacion de Estudios para el Desarrollo, 1987).

Scalon, Maria Celi. *Mobilidade social no brasil: padrões e tendências* (Rio de Janeiro: Revan, 1999).

Schlesener, Anita Helena Helena and Donizete Aparecido Fernandes. "Os conflitos sociais no campo e a educação: a questão agrária no Brasil," *Cadernos de Pesquisa: Pensamento Educacional* 10.24 (2017): 131–148.

Schwartzman, Luisa Farah. "Does Money Whiten? Intergenerational Changes in Racial Classification in Brazil, *American Sociological Review* 72 (2007): 940–963.

Schwartzman, Luisa Farah and Angela Randolpho Paiva. "Not Just Racial Quotas: Affirmative Action in Brazilian Higher Education 10 Years Later," *British Journal of Sociology of Education* 37.4 (2016): 548–566.

Schwartzman, Luisa Farah and Graziella Moraes Dias da Silva. "Unexpected Narratives from Multicultural Policies: Translations of Affirmative Action in Brazil," *Latin American and Caribbean Ethnic Studies* 7.1 (2012): 31–48.

Schwartzman, Simon. *A Space for Science: The Development of the Scientific Community in Brazil* (College Station: Pennsylvania State University Press, 1991).

Schwartzman, Simon, Eunice Ribeiro Durham, and José Goldemberg. "A educação no Brasil em perspectiva de transformação." Trabalho realizado para o Projeto sobre Educação na América Latina do Diálogo Interamericano, São Paulo, June 1993. Accessed 18 November 2017, at: www.schwartzman.org.br/simon/transform.htm.

Schwartzman, Simon, Helena M. B. Bomeny and Vanda M. R. Costa. *Nos tempo de Capanema* (São Paulo: Paz e Terra, 1984).

Schwarzer, Helmut and Ana Carolina Querino. "Benefícios sociais e pobreza: programas não contributivos da seguridade social brasileira." Texto para Discussão 929, Brasília, Ipea, 2002.

Scorzafave, Luiz Guilherme Dacar da Silva. "Caracterização da inserção feminina no mercado de trabalho e seus efeitos sobre a distribuição de renda," PhD thesis, Faculdade de Arquitetura e Urbanismo da USP, São Paulo, 2004.

Sedgh, Gilda, Stanley Henshaw, Susheela Singh, Elisabeth Åhman, and Iqbal H. Shah. "Induced Abortion: Estimated Rates and Trends Worldwide," *The Lancet* 370 (2007): 1338–1345.

Segura-Ubiergo, Alex. *The Political Economy of the Welfare State in Latin America: Globalization, Democracy, and Development* (Cambridge: Cambridge University Press, 2007).

Serra, José. "Ciclos e mudanças estruturais na economia brasileira do pós-guerra," in Luiz Gonzaga de Mello Belluzzo and Renata Coutinho, eds., *Desenvolvimento capitalista no brasil: ensaios sobre a crise* (São Paulo: Brasiliense, 1981).

Serra, Tompson Almeida and Rodrigo Valente Serra, eds., *Cidades médias brasileiras* (Rio de Janeiro: Ipea, 2001).

Sesso Filho, Umberto Antonio. "O setor supermercadista no Brasil nos anos 1990," PhD thesis, Universidade de São Paulo – Escola Superior de Agricultura "Luiz de Queiroz," 2003.

Silva, Antonio Braz de Oliveira e and Mérida Herasme Medina. "Produto interno bruto por unidade da federação, 1985–1998." Texto para discussão 677, Brasília, Ipea, 1999.

Silva, Dilena Dustan Lucas da. "Organizações não governamentais: um estudo de caso da Federação de Órgãos para Assistência Social e Educacional (FASE)," PhD thesis; Universidade Federal do Rio Grande do Sul, 2005.

Silva, Elvis Vitoriano da. "Desigualdade de renda no espaço intra-urbano: análise da evolução na cidade de Porto Alegre no período 1991–2000," MA thesis, Universidade Federal do Rio Grande do Sul, 2011.

Silva, Luiz Inácio Lula da. Speech at the 22 January 2007 launch of the Programa de Aceleração do Crescimento (PAC). Accessed 12 April 2018, at: http://Congressoemfoco.uol.com.br/n oticias/leia-o-discurso-de-lula-no-lancamento-do-pac/.

Silva, Marlon Lima and Helena Lúcia Zagury Tourinho. "O Banco Nacional de Habitação e o Programa Minha Casa Minha Vida, duas políticas habitacionais e uma mesma lógica locacional." *Cadernos Metrópolis* 17.34 (2015): 401–417.

Silva, Mauro Osório da. "A crise do Rio de suas especificidades." Accessed 20 November 2017, at: www.ie.ufrj.br/intranet/ie/userintranet/hpp/arquivos/especificidades_crise.pdf.

Silva, Rodrigo Manoel Dias da. "As políticas culturais brasileiras na contemporaneidade: mudanças institucionais e modelos de agenciamento," *Revista Sociedade e Estado* 29.1 (2014): 199–204.

Silva, Silvio Fernandes da. "Organização de redes regionalizadas e integradas de atenção à saúde: desafios do Sistema Único de Saúde (Brasil)" *Ciência & Saúde Coletiva* 16 (2011): 2753–2762.

Silva, Susana Maria Veleda da. "Inovações nas políticas populacionais: o planejamento familiar no Brasil," *Scripta Nova, Revista Electrónica de Geografía y Ciencias Sociales* 69.25 (2000). Accessed at: www.ub.edu/geocrit/sn-69-25.htm.

Silva, Vanice M. da, Sheyla L. Lima, and Marcia Teixeira. "Organizações e fundações estatais de direito privado no sistema único de saúde: relação entre o público e o privado e mecanismos de controle social," *Saúde Debate* 39 (2015): 145–159.

Silva, Vanusa Maria Queiroz da. "O raio-X do terceiro setor," MA thesis, FGV CPDOC, Rio de Janeiro, 2008.

Silveira, Fernando Gaiger. "Tributação, previdência e assistência sociais: impactos distributivos," PhD thesis, Universidade de Campinas, 2008.

"Equidade fiscal: impactos distributivos da tributação e do gasto social no Brasil," Brasília: ESAF, Tesouro Nacional, 2012.

Silveira, Marcos A. C. da. "Intervenção da Autoridade Monetária no mercado de câmbio em regime de flutuação administrada," Notas Técnicas do Banco Central do Brasil 34, Brasília, 2003. Available at www.bcb.gov.br/conteudo/depec/NotasTecnicas/2003nt34intervmerca docambp.pdf.

Simonsen, Mario Henrique. *Inflação, Gradualismo x Tratamento de Choque* (Rio de Janeiro: Apec, 1970).

"Inflação brasileira: lições e perspectivas." *Revista Brasileira de Economia* 5.4 (1985): 15–31.

Singer, Paul. *Economia política de la urbanización* (Mexico: Siglo Ventiuno Editores, 1978).

Singh, Susheela and Gilda Sedgh. "The Relationship of Abortion to Trends in Contraception and Fertility in Brazil, Colombia and Mexico," *International Family Planning Perspectives* 23.1 (1997): 4–14.

Siqueira, Arnaldo Augusto Franco de, Ana Cristina d'Andretta Tanaka, Renato Martins Santana, and Pedro Augusto Marcondes de Almeida. "Mortalidade materna no Brasil, 1980," *Revista de Saúde Pública* 18 (1984): 448–465.

Skidmore, Thomas E. *Politics in Brazil, 1930–1964: An Experiment in Democracy* (New York: Oxford University Press, 1967).

The Politics of Military Rule in Brazil, 1964–85 (New York: Oxford University Press, 1988).

Brasil: de Getúlio a Castelo (Rio de Janeiro: Paz e Terra, 2003).

Soares, Luisa de Azevedo Senra. "A oferta de trabalho voluntário no Brasil," MA thesis, FEA USP, 2014.

Soares, Sergei. "Análise de bem-estar e decomposição por fatores da queda na desigualdade entre 1995 e 2004," *Econômica* 8:1 (2006): 83–115.

Soares-Filho, Britaldo Silveira, Daniel Curtis Nepstad, Lisa M. Curran, Gustavo Coutinho Cerqueira, Ricardo Alexandrino Garcia, Claudia Azevedo Ramos, Eliane Voll, Alice McDonald, Paul Lefebvre, and Peter Schlesinger. "Modelling Conservation in the Amazon Basin," *Nature* 440.7083 (2006): 520–523.

Sola, Lourde. "O Golpe de 37 e o Estado Novo," in Carlos Gilherme Motta, ed., *Brasil em Perspectiva* (São Paulo: Difusão Europeia do Livro, 1969): 257–284.

Sorj, Bernardo. "Sociedade civil e política no Brasil." Paper presented at the Seminário sociedade civil e democracia na América Latina: crise e reinvenção da política. Anais do Instituto Fernando Henrique Cardoso e Centro Edelstein de Pesquisas Sociais, São Paulo. 2006.

Sousa, Bertone de Oliveira. "Entre a espera pelo céu e a busca por bem-estar," in Jérri Roberto Marin and André Dioney Fonseca, eds., *Olhares sobre a Igreja Assembleia De Deus* (Campo Grande, MS: Editora UFMS, 2015).

Souza, André Portela. "Politicas de distribuição de renda no Brasil e o Bolsa Família," in Edmar Lisboa Bacha and Simon Schwartzman, eds., *Brasil: A nova agenda social* (Rio de Janeiro: LTC, 2011): 166–186.

Souza, Georgia Costa de Araújo. "O SUS nos seus 20 anos: reflexões num contexto de mudanças," *Saúde Social* 19.3 (2010): 509–517.

Souza, Maria do Carmo Campello de. *Estado e partidos políticos no Brasil 1930 a 1964* (São Paulo: Alfa-Omega, 1990).

Souza, Pedro Ferreira de, Carlos Antonio Costa Ribeiro, and Flavio Carvalhaes. "Desigualdade de oportunidades no Brasil: considerações sobre classe, educação e raça," *Revista Brasileira de Ciências Sociais* 25.73 (2010), 77–100.

Souza, Pedro H. G. F. de. "Top Incomes in Brazil, 1933–2012: A Research Note." SSRN, 11 December 2014. Accessed 10 June 2017, at: http://dx.doi.org/10.2139/ssrn.2537026.

"A desigualdade vista do topo: a concentração de renda entre os ricos no Brasil, 1926–2013," PhD thesis, Universidade de Brasília, 2016.

Spalding, Rose J. "Welfare Policymaking: Theoretical Implications of a Mexican Case Study," *Comparative Politics* 12.4 (1980): 419–438.

Spedo, Sandra Maria. "Desafios para implementar a integralidade da assistência à saúde no SUS: estudo de caso no município de São Paulo," PhD thesis, Faculdade de Saúde Pública/USP, 2009.

Spegler, Rafael Luís. "Racionalidade política e econômica no governo Geisel (1974–1979): Um estudo sobre o II PND e o projeto de institucionalização do regime militar," MA thesis, Universidade Federal do Rio Grande do Sul, Porto Alegre, 2015.

Spinazzola, Patrícia Cezario Silva. "Impactos da regularização fundiária no espaço urbano," MA thesis, Faculdade de Arquitetura e Urbanismo da USP, São Paulo, 2008.

Suárez, Naila López Cabaleiro. *O modelo de gestão das organizações sociais de cultura em São Paulo* (São Paulo: FGV, 2011).

Szmrecsányi, Tamás. "O Desenvolvimento da Produção Agropecuária (1930–1970)," in Boris Fausto et al., eds., *História da civilização brasileira.* vol. 3, O Brasil republicano, 4. *Economia e cultura (1930–1964)* (Rio de Janeiro: Bertrand Brasil, 1995): 107–207.

ed., *História Econômica da cidade de São Paulo* (São Paulo: Editora Globo, 2005).

Tavares, Maria da Conceição. "Auge e declínio do processo de substituição," in Maria da Conceição Tavares, ed., *Da substituição de importações ao capitalismo financeiro* (Rio de Janeiro: Zahar, 1972).

Destruição não criadora (Rio de Janeiro: Record, 1990).

Tavares, Priscilla Albuquerque. "Efeito do Programa Bolsa Família sobre a oferta de trabalho das mães." Paper presented at the XVI Encontro Nacional de Estudos Populacionais, ABEP, 2008.

Taylor, P. J. "Worlds of Large Cities: Pondeering Castells' Space of Flows." Globalization and World Cities Study Group and Network, Research Bulletin 14. www.lboro.ac.uk/gawc/rb/rb14.html.

Teixeira, Ana Claudio Chaves. "A atuação das organizações não-governamentais: entre o Estado e o conjunto da sociedade," in Evelina Dagnino, ed., *Sociedade civil e espaços públicos no Brasil* (São Paulo: Paz e Terra, 2002): 26–78.

Identidade em construção: as organizações não-governamentais no processo brasileiro de democratização (São Paulo: AnnaBlume, 2003).

Teixeira, Sivanilza Machado, João Gilberto Mendes Dos Reis, Rodrigo Couto Santos, Rone Vieira Oliveira, Walter Hernandez Vergara, and Rodrigo Aparecido Jordan. "Qualidade do transporte urbano de passageiros: uma avaliação do nível de serviço do sistema do metropolitano de São Paulo," *Revista Metropolitana de Sustentabilidade* 4.1 (2014): 3–20.

Telles, Edward E. *Race in Another America: The Significance of Skin Color in Brazil* (Princeton, NJ: Princeton University Press, 2014).

Telles, Edward E. and Marcelo Paixão. "Affirmative Action in Brazil," *Lasa Forum*, 44.2 (2013): 10–12.

Tenjo, Jaime, Rocío Ribero, and Bernat D. Luisa Fernanda. *Evolución de las diferencias salariales por sexo en seis países de América Latina: un intento de interpretación* (Bogotá: Centro de Estudios sobre Desarrollo Económico, Facultad de Economía, Universidad de los Andes, 2005).

Torche, Florencia. "Unequal but Fluid: Social Mobility in Chile in Comparative Perspective," *American Sociological Review* 70.3 (2005): 422–450.

"Intergenerational Mobility and Inequality: The Latin American Case," *Annual Review of Sociology* 40 (2014): 619–642.

Torche, Florencia and Carlos Costa Ribeiro. "Pathways of Change in Social Mobility: Industrialization, Education and Growing Fluidity in Brazil," *Research in Social Stratification and Mobility* 28 (2010): 291–307.

Troiano, Mariele. "Os empresários no congresso: a legitimação de interesses via audiências públicas," MA thesis; Universidade Federal de São Carlos, 2016.

Valioti, Leandro and Ana Letícia do Nascimento Fialho, eds., *Atlas econômico da cultura brasileira: metodologia* (2 vols.; Porto Alegre: UFRGS/CEGO, 2017).

Vaz, Luiz Felipe Hupsel, Bernardo Hauch Ribeiro de Castro, Carlos Henrique Reis Malburg, Allan Amaral Paes de Mesentier, and Filipe de Oliveira Souza. "Transporte sobre trilhos no Brasil: uma perspectiva do material rodante." BNDES, Ferroviário, Setorial 40, 2014: 235–282. Accessed 14 June 2018, at: https://web.bndes.gov.br/bib/jspui/bitstream/1408/3021/2/Transporte%20sobre%20trilhos%20no%20Brasil.pdf.

Veiga, José Eli da. *Cidades imaginárias: o Brasil é menos urbano do que se calcula* (Campinas: Autores Associados, 2002).

Velasco Junior, Licínio. "Privatização: mitos e falsas percepções." BNDES, 1999. Available at: http://web.bndes.gov.br/bib/jspui/handle/1408/11334.

Vidal, Aluizio Tadeu Furtado. "As perspectivas do Saneamento Básico no Brasil," MA thesis, Fundação João Pinheiro, Belo Horizonte, 2002.

Vignoli, Jorge A. Rodríguez. "Cohabitación en América Latina: ¿modernidad, exclusión o diversidad?" *Papeles de Población* 10.40 (2004): 97–145.

Vilela, Lara, Naercio Menezes-Filho, and Thiago Yudi Tachibana. "As cotas nas universidades públicas diminuem a qualidade dos alunos selecionados?" Simulações com Dados do ENEN, Insper Policy Paper 17, June 2016. Accessed at: www.insper.edu.br/wp-content/uploads/2018/09/Cotas-universidades-publicas-diminuem-qualidade-alunos-selecionados-ENEM.pdf.

Virgens, Silva Catarina Araújo das. "Shopping Center e a produção do espaço urbano em Salvador-BA," MA thesis, Universidade Federal da Bahia, Salvador, 2016.

Villela, Annibal Villanova and Wilson Suzigan. *Política do governo e crescimento da economia brasileira, 1889–1945* (Rio de Janeiro: Ipea, 1973).

Viola, Eduardo J. "The Ecologist Movement in Brazil (1974–1986): From Environmentalism to Ecopolitics," *International Journal of Urban and Regional Research* 12.2 (1988): 211–228.

Vollrath, Dietrich. "Land Distribution and International Agricultural Productivity," *American Journal of Agricultural Economics* 89.1 (2007): 202–216.

Wahrlich, Beatriz M. de Souza. *Reforma administrativa da Era Vargas* (Rio de Janeiro: Fundação Getúlio Vargas, 1983).

Wajnman, Simone. "'Quantidade' e 'qualidade' da participação das mulheres na força de trabalho brasileira," in Nathalie Reis Itaboraí and Arlene Martinez Ricoldi, eds., *Até onde caminhou a revolução de gênero no Brasil? Implicações demográficas e questões sociais* (Belo Horizonte: Associação Brasileira de Estudos Populacionais, 2016).

Weffort, Francisco. *O populismo na política brasileira* (Rio de Janeiro: Paz e Terra, 1980).

Weinstein, Barbara. "The Industrialists, the State, and the Issues of Worker Training and Social Services in Brazil, 1930–50," *Hispanic American Historical Review* 70.3 (1990): 379–404.

For Social Peace in Brazil: Industrialists and the Remaking of the Working Class in São Paulo, 1920–1964 (Chapel Hill: University of North Carolina Press, 1996).

Werneck, Guilherme Loureiro, Ana Luiza Braz Pavão, and Mônica Rodrigues Campos. "Autoavaliação do estado de saúde e a associação com fatores sociodemográficos, hábitos de vida e morbidade na população: um inquérito nacional," *Cadernos de Saúde Pública* 29.4 (2013): 723–734.

Werneck, Rogério L. F. "Poupanca estatal, dívida externa e crise financeira do setor público," *Pesquisa e Planejamento Econômico* 16.3 (1986): 551–574.

Empresas estatais e política macroeconomica (Rio de Janeiro: Campus, 1987).

"Alternância política, redistribuição e crescimento, 2004–2010," in Marcelo de Paiva Abreu, ed., *A ordem do progresso: dois séculos de política econômica no Brasil* (2nd edn; Rio de Janeiro: Elsevier, 2014): 357–381.

"Consolidação da estabilização e reconstrução institucional, 1995–2002," in Marcelo de Paiva Abreu, ed., *A ordem do progresso: dois séculos de política econômica no Brasil* (2nd edn; Rio de Janeiro: Elsevier, 2014): 331–356.

Wilder, Ariel. "Mudanças no setor supermercadista e a formação de associações de pequenos supermercados," PhD thesis, Escola de Superior de Agricultura "Luiz de Queiroz," Universidade de São Paulo, Piracicaba, 2003.

Wirth, John D. *The Politics of Brazilian Development, 1930–1954* (Stanford, Calif.: Stanford University Press, 1970).

Witter, José Sebastião. *Breve história do futebol brasileiro* (São Paulo: FTD, 1995).

Wood, Charles H. and José Alberto Magno de Carvalho. *The Demography of Inequality in Brazil* (Cambridge: Cambridge University Press, 1988).

Wood, Charles H., José Alberto Magno de Carvalho and Cláudia Júlia Guimarães Horta. "The Color of Child Mortality in Brazil, 1950–2000: Social Progress and Persistent Racial Inequality," *Latin American Research Review* 45.2 (2010): 114–139.

Wulfhorst, Ingo. "O pentecostalismo no Brasil," Estudos Teológicos 35.1 (1995): 7–20.

Xavier, Marcus Renato S. "The Brazilian Sugarcane Ethanol Experience," Issue Analysis, Competitive Enterprise Institute, Washington, DC, 15 February 2007. Available at: htt p://cei.org/sites/default/files/Marcus%20Xavier%20-%20The%20Brazilian%20Sugarcan e%20Ethanol%20Experience.pdf.

Ximenes, Assuero Fonseca. "Apropriação do fundo público da saúde pela organizações sociais em Pernambuco," PhD thesis, Federal University of Pernambuco – UFPE, Recife, 2015.

Zago, Nadir. "Do acesso à permanência no ensino superior: percurso de estudantes universitários de camadas populares," *Revista Brasileira de Educação* 11.32 (2006): 226–237.

Zangelmi, Arnaldo José, Fabrício Roberto Costa Oliveira, and Izabella Fátima Oliveira de Sales. "Movimentos, mediações e Estado: apontamentos sobre a luta pela terra no Brasil na segunda metade do século XX," *Sociedade e Cultura* 19.1 (2016): 133–141.

Zucco, Cesar. "Stability Without Roots: Party System Institutionalization in Brazil," SSRN, 4 February 2010. Accessed 25 April 2018, at: https://papers.ssrn.com/sol3/papers.cfm? abstract_id=2002359.

Index

abortions
  rate and trend of, 78
adult mortality, 67, 87
African slave labor, 3, 376
Afro-Brazilian religions, 316, 317
agrarian reform, 243, 332, 333
Agribusiness exports, 60
agricultural frontier, 95
agricultural modernization, 2, 34, 374
agricultural production, 57, 244
Amazon, The, 336
amnesty committees (*Comitês Brasileiros de Anistia*), 329
Amnesty International, 329
Asian Crisis, 56
Assembly of God, 365
Associação Brasileira Interdisciplinar de Aids – ABIA/RJ, 330
Atlantic forests

Bahia, 21, 22, 88, 96, 97, 284, 299
Bancada evangélica, 372
Banco Central, 56
basic institutions to deal with labor relations, 342
basic retirement (of one minimum salary) to all rural workers, 273
basic rights for domestic workers, 131
basic structures of the welfare state, 157
Belíndia, 31, 257
Belo Horizonte, 92, 96, 183, 186, 187, 202, 216, 219, 221, 232
"bifurcated" process of agrarian development, 243

blacks and browns
  role within each sector of the economy, 295
BNDES (*Banco Nacional de Desenvolvimento Economico e Social*), 58
BNH (*Banco Nacional de Desenvolvimento Economico e Social*), 191, 193, 199, 205, 218
Boards of Labor Conciliation (*Convenções Coletivas de Trabalho and Juntas de Conciliação e Julgamento*), 342
Bolsa Alimentação, 161
Bolsa Escola, 161
Bolsa Família (Family Grant Program), 43, 162
Bolsonaro, Jair, 45
  ultra liberal program, 59
BPC (Continuous Cash Benefit) (the renamed RMV), 162
BPC, or Continuous Pension Benefits, 179
Brasília, 92, 155, 184, 200, 212, 232
Brazil's agrarian structure, 243
Brazil's crude birth rate, 5
Brazil's crude death rate, 8
Brazil's crude mortality rate, 5
Brazil's financial system
  reorganization of, 151
Brazil's GINI coefficient of inequality, 238
Brazil's infant mortality rate, 66
Brazil's total fertility rate, 85
Brazilian Association of Non-Governmental Organizations (*Associação Brasileira Organizações Não Governamentais* – ABONG), 326

412